Cybersecurity Audit Essentials

Tools, Techniques, and Best Practices

Armend Salihu

Cybersecurity Audit Essentials: Tools, Techniques, and Best Practices

Armend Salihu
Kronberg im Taunus, Germany

ISBN-13 (pbk): 979-8-8688-1711-3 ISBN-13 (electronic): 979-8-8688-1712-0
https://doi.org/10.1007/979-8-8688-1712-0

Copyright © 2025 by Armend Salihu

This work is subject to copyright. All rights are reserved by the Publisher, whether the whole or part of the material is concerned, specifically the rights of translation, reprinting, reuse of illustrations, recitation, broadcasting, reproduction on microfilms or in any other physical way, and transmission or information storage and retrieval, electronic adaptation, computer software, or by similar or dissimilar methodology now known or hereafter developed.

Trademarked names, logos, and images may appear in this book. Rather than use a trademark symbol with every occurrence of a trademarked name, logo, or image we use the names, logos, and images only in an editorial fashion and to the benefit of the trademark owner, with no intention of infringement of the trademark.

The use in this publication of trade names, trademarks, service marks, and similar terms, even if they are not identified as such, is not to be taken as an expression of opinion as to whether or not they are subject to proprietary rights.

While the advice and information in this book are believed to be true and accurate at the date of publication, neither the authors nor the editors nor the publisher can accept any legal responsibility for any errors or omissions that may be made. The publisher makes no warranty, express or implied, with respect to the material contained herein.

Managing Director, Apress Media LLC: Welmoed Spahr
Acquisitions Editor: Susan McDermott
Development Editor: Laura Berendson
Project Manager: Jessica Vakili

Distributed to the book trade worldwide by Springer Science+Business Media New York, 1 New York Plaza, New York, NY 10004. Phone 1-800-SPRINGER, fax (201) 348-4505, e-mail orders-ny@springer-sbm.com, or visit www.springeronline.com. Apress Media, LLC is a Delaware LLC and the sole member (owner) is Springer Science + Business Media Finance Inc (SSBM Finance Inc). SSBM Finance Inc is a **Delaware** corporation.

For information on translations, please e-mail booktranslations@springernature.com; for reprint, paperback, or audio rights, please e-mail bookpermissions@springernature.com.

Apress titles may be purchased in bulk for academic, corporate, or promotional use. eBook versions and licenses are also available for most titles. For more information, reference our Print and eBook Bulk Sales web page at http://www.apress.com/bulk-sales.

If disposing of this product, please recycle the paper

To my beloved wife, Ma.Sc. Ing. Fatlinda Salihu,

Your unwavering strength, boundless love, and selfless sacrifice inspire me every day. As a professional engineer, you could have built empires, but instead, you chose to build a world of love, security, and endless possibilities for our daughters. Your dedication, patience, and resilience in shaping their future are beyond measure.

This book is not just a testament to my work but a tribute to you, the true architect of our family's dreams. Thank you for everything you do, both seen and unseen.

With all my love and deepest gratitude,

Armend Salihu

Table of Contents

About the Author xxvii

About the Technical Reviewer xxix

Introduction xxxi

Chapter 1: Introduction to Cybersecurity Audits 1

What Is a Cybersecurity Audit? 1

    The Technical Perspective of Cybersecurity Audits 2

    The Importance of Cybersecurity Audits... 3

    An Example of a Cybersecurity Audit in Practice.. 4

    Key Takeaways 5

Internal vs. External Cybersecurity Audits 6

    Internal Audits 6

    External Audits 8

    Comparing Internal and External Audits 10

    Key Takeaways 12

Types of Cybersecurity Audits 13

    Regular Audits 15

    Compliance Audits 17

    Risk-Based Audits 19

    Specialized Audits 20

    Putting It All Together: Your Complete Health Plan 22

    Key Takeaways 22

Common Cybersecurity Risks Audits Aim to Mitigate 23

    Insider Threats 24

    Weak or Inadequate Access Controls 24

    Insecure Configurations and Misconfigurations 25

TABLE OF CONTENTS

- Lack of Patch Management 26
- Data Privacy Risks 26
- Insufficient Incident Response Planning 27
- Third-Party Risks 28
- Social Engineering and Phishing Attacks 28
- Audit Types for Cybersecurity Risk 29
- Key Takeaways 30

The Importance of a Risk-Based Approach in Cybersecurity Audits 31
- What Is a Risk-Based Approach? 32
- Key Components of a Risk-Based Cybersecurity Audit 32
- Benefits of a Risk-Based Approach 36
- Implementing a Risk-Based Approach 36
- Technologies That Enable Risk-Based Audits 38
- Challenges of a Risk-Based Approach 38
- Practical Example: Risk-Based Audit in Action 38
- Key Takeaways 39

Key Compliance Frameworks in Cybersecurity Audits 40
- Key Compliance Frameworks 40
- Why Compliance Frameworks Are Crucial in Cybersecurity Audits? 46
- How Auditors Utilize Compliance Frameworks 47
- Challenges in Implementing Compliance Frameworks 47
- Best Practices for Cybersecurity Auditors 49
- Key Takeaways 51

Cybersecurity Audit vs. Penetration Testing 52
- Cybersecurity Audit: A Comprehensive Evaluation 52
- Penetration Testing: Simulating Real-World Attacks 53
- Key Differences Between Cybersecurity Audits and Penetration Testing 54
- How Cybersecurity Audits and Penetration Testing Complement Each Other 55
- Challenges and Considerations 57
- Best Practices for Organizations 57
- Key Takeaways 58

TABLE OF CONTENTS

Essential Skills for Cybersecurity Auditors 59
    Technical Expertise in Cybersecurity 60
    Knowledge of Compliance Frameworks and Regulations 61
    Analytical and Problem-Solving Skills 62
    Risk Assessment and Management 62
    Communication Skills 63
    Familiarity with Audit Tools and Technologies 64
    Attention to Detail 64
    Key Takeaways 65

The Audit Lifecycle: From Planning to Reporting 66
    Planning: Defining the Foundation of the Audit 67
    Risk Assessment: Identifying and Prioritizing Threats 68
    Fieldwork and Testing: Gathering Evidence and Testing Controls 69
    Analysis and Evaluation: Identifying Gaps and Assessing Control Effectiveness 70
    Reporting: Communicating Findings and Recommendations 71
    Follow-Up and Continuous Improvement: Ensuring Actionable Outcomes 72
    Key Takeaways 73

Key Tools and Technologies Used in Cybersecurity 74
    Vulnerability Scanners: Detecting and Prioritizing Security Flaws 74
    SIEM Systems: Monitoring and Analyzing Security Events 75
    Compliance Management Tools: Streamlining the Compliance Process 75
    Network Monitoring and Analysis Tools: Detecting Anomalies in Network Traffic 76
    Data Loss Prevention (DLP) Tools: Protecting Sensitive Data 77
    Risk Assessment and Management Tools: Prioritizing Risks 78
    Automated Audit Platforms: Streamlining the Audit Process 78
    Incident Response and Forensic Tools: Responding to Security Incidents 79
    Key Takeaways 80

Conclusions 80

TABLE OF CONTENTS

Chapter 2: Planning the Cybersecurity Audit 83
Setting the Scope for a Cybersecurity Audit 84
- The Importance of Defining Audit Scope 84
- Key Components of an Audit Scope 85
- Steps to Define Audit Scope 87
- Challenges in Defining Audit Scope 88
- Tools for Scoping Audits 89
- Benefits of a Well-Defined Audit Scope 90
- Key Takeaways 90

Stakeholder Engagement in Audit Planning 91
- The Value of Engagement 92
- Key Stakeholders in Cybersecurity Audits 93
- Strategies for Engagement 95
- Overcoming Challenges 97
- Tools for Streamlining Stakeholder Engagement 98
- Best Practices for Stakeholder Engagement 98
- The Impact of Engagement 99
- Key Takeaways 99

Understanding Business Context Before Auditing 100
- Why Business Context Matters 100
- Key Elements of Business Context 101
- Steps to Understand the Business Context 103
- Tools and Technologies for Context Gathering 106
- Challenges in Understanding the Business Context 106
- The Impact of Business Context on Audit Outcomes 108
- Key Takeaways 108

Why Data Flow Diagrams Are Essential for Cybersecurity Audits 109
- The Importance of DFDs in Cybersecurity 110
- Components of a Data Flow Diagram 111
- Creating an Effective Data Flow Diagram 111

TABLE OF CONTENTS

How DFDs Enhance Cybersecurity Audits 114
Challenges and Solutions in Using DFDs 116
Tools Supporting DFD Creation 116
The Strategic Importance of DFDs 116
Key Takeaways 117

Developing an Effective Cybersecurity Audit Checklist 118
Why an Audit Checklist Is Essential 118
Building the Foundation of a Cybersecurity Audit Checklist 119
Key Components of a Cybersecurity Audit Checklist 121
Challenges and Solutions in Checklist Development 123
Tools to Enhance Checklist Development 124
The Strategic Role of an Audit Checklist 126
Key Takeaways 126

Risk Assessment – Identifying High-Risk Areas in Cybersecurity Audits 127
The Importance of Risk Assessment in Cybersecurity 128
Steps in Risk Assessment 129
Risk Assessment Frameworks 130
Technologies for Risk Assessment 131
Overcoming Challenges in Risk Assessment 131
Best Practices for Effective Risk Assessment 132
The Strategic Role of Risk Assessment 133
Key Takeaways 133

Aligning Audit Objectives with Business Goals 134
Why Alignment Matters 135
Steps to Align Audit Objectives with Business Goals 135
Overcoming Challenges 137
Tools to Facilitate Alignment 142
Best Practices for Alignment 143
Cybersecurity as a Strategic Asset 143
Key Takeaways 144

TABLE OF CONTENTS

Defining Audit Metrics for Success 144
- Why Metrics Matter in Cybersecurity Audits 145
- Key Considerations for Defining Metrics 146
- Examples of Metrics 146
- Challenges in Defining Metrics 147
- Best Practices for Audit Metrics 151
- Key Takeaways 152

Common Pitfalls in the Audit Planning Phase 152
- Why Planning Matters 153
- Common Pitfalls in Audit Planning 153
- Best Practices for Audit Planning 155
- Key Takeaways 156

Best Practices for Effective Planning 156
- Why Effective Planning Matters 157
- Best Practices for Cybersecurity Audit Planning 157
- Key Takeaways 161

Conclusions 161

Chapter 3: Assessing Security Controls 163

Understanding and Implementing Security Controls 164
- Defining Security Controls 164
- Types of Security Controls 166
- Categories of Security Controls 167
- Why Security Controls Matter 168
- Auditing Security Controls 168
- Challenges in Implementing Security Controls 171
- A Layered Approach to Security 173
- Key Takeaways 173

Evaluating Physical Security Controls 174
- What Are Physical Security Controls? 174
- Key Types of Physical Security Controls 176
- Technologies in Physical Security 177

  Real-Life Scenarios 178
  Challenges in Physical Security 178
  Auditing Physical Security Controls 180
  Key Takeaways 182
Assessing Network Security Controls 182
  What Are Network Security Controls? 183
  Steps to Assess Network Security Controls 184
  Key Technologies in Network Security 186
  Challenges in Assessing Network Security 187
  Where Network Security Matters 188
  Auditing Network Security Controls 189
  Best Practices 190
  Key Takeaways 191
The Importance of Access Management Controls in Cybersecurity Audits 192
  Understanding Access Management Controls 192
  Why Access Management Controls Are Critical 193
  Key Components of Access Management Controls 194
  Steps to Audit Access Management Controls 195
  Technologies Supporting Access Management 196
  Examples of Audit Insights on Access Management 196
  Challenges in Access Management Audits 197
  Key Takeaways 199
Testing Application Security Controls in Cybersecurity Audits 199
  Why Application Security Controls Matter in Audits 200
  Understanding Application Security Controls 200
  Steps to Audit Application Security Controls 201
  Tools for Testing Application Security 203
  Real-World Audit Examples 204
  Challenges and Best Practices in Application Security Audits 205
  Key Takeaways 208

TABLE OF CONTENTS

Auditing Data Security Controls for Robust Cybersecurity 208
- The Role of Data Security Controls in Cybersecurity 209
- Understanding Data Security Controls 209
- Key Areas to Audit 212
- Challenges and Best Practices in Auditing Data Security 215
- Key Takeaways 217

Evaluating Cloud Security Controls for Enhanced Cybersecurity 218
- The Role of Cloud Security Controls 218
- Key Areas to Evaluate in Cloud Security Audits 219
- Technologies for Cloud Security Audits 220
- Challenges in Evaluating Cloud Security Controls 221
- Key Takeaways 223

Common Control Failures and How to Identify Them 224
- Understanding Control Failures 225
- Common Control Failures and Their Detection 226
- Effective Auditing Techniques 228
- Mitigating Control Failures 228
- Key Takeaways 229

Validation of Security Control Effectiveness 230
- What Does Validating Security Controls Mean? 230
- Steps to Validate Security Control Effectiveness 231
- Validation Challenges 234
- Key Takeaways 237

Documentation Tips for Control Assessment 238
- Why Documentation Is Crucial in Control Assessment 238
- Key Elements of Effective Control Assessment Documentation 239
- Best Practices for Documentation 242
- Key Takeaways 242

Conclusions 243

TABLE OF CONTENTS

Chapter 4: Compliance and Regulations 245
Navigating Key Cybersecurity Regulations 246
The Role of Cybersecurity Regulations 247
Key Cybersecurity Regulations and Their Significance 247
Auditor's Perspective: Ensuring Regulatory Compliance 263
Tools and Techniques for Regulatory Audits 264
Emerging Trends in Cybersecurity Compliance 267
Preparing for the Future of Compliance 268
Regulatory Bodies' Approach to the Future 268
Benefits of Future-Oriented Compliance Strategies 269
Key Takeaways 270
The Role of Compliance in Cybersecurity Audits 273
Why Compliance Matters in Cybersecurity Audits 273
Compliance Audits in Practice 274
Compliance in Action 277
Challenges in Compliance Audits 277
Key Takeaways 278
Conducting a GDPR Compliance Audit 279
Understanding GDPR and Its Importance 280
Steps to Conduct a GDPR Compliance Audit 280
Tools and Technologies for GDPR Compliance Audits 285
Challenges in GDPR Compliance Audits 286
Key Takeaways 290
Navigating PCI-DSS Requirements in Audits 291
Understanding PCI-DSS 291
Steps to Conduct a PCI-DSS Audit 294
Challenges in PCI-DSS Audits 297
Key Takeaways 299
How to Handle Non-compliance Findings in Cybersecurity Audits 300
Understanding Non-compliance Findings 301
Steps to Handle Non-compliance Findings 301

TABLE OF CONTENTS

    Challenges in Addressing Non-compliance Findings 304

    Best Practices for Managing Non-compliance 304

    Key Takeaways 305

Tips for Communicating Compliance Gaps to Stakeholders 305

    Why Communicating Compliance Gaps Matters 306

    Steps for Communicating Compliance Gaps 306

    Tips for Effective Communication 309

    Tools for Communicating Compliance Gaps 311

    Practical Example 312

    Benefits of Effective Communication 312

    Key Takeaways 313

Staying Ahead of Regulatory Changes 314

    Importance of Staying Updated on Regulations 314

    Challenges in Keeping Up with Regulatory Changes 315

    Integrating Regulatory Changes into Cybersecurity Audits 317

    Benefits of Staying Updated 318

    Key Takeaways 318

Building a Robust Compliance Checklist 319

    The Importance of a Compliance Checklist 319

    Steps to Build an Effective Compliance Checklist 320

    Key Elements to Include in a Compliance Checklist 321

    Technologies for Compliance Checklist Management 327

    Benefits of a Well-Designed Compliance Checklist 328

    Key Takeaways 328

Audit Reporting for Regulatory Bodies 329

    Importance of Audit Reporting for Regulatory Bodies 330

    Key Components of a Regulatory Audit Report 330

    Best Practices for Audit Reporting 332

    Example: GDPR Audit Report 333

    Benefits of Effective Audit Reporting 333

    Key Takeaways 334

Conclusions 334

Chapter 5: Introduction to Cyber Risk Management 337

What Is Cyber Risk Management? 337
- Why Cyber Risk Management Matters 339
- Key Components of Cyber Risk Management 340
- Technology in Cyber Risk Management.. 341
- Preparing for Future Cyber Risks 342
- Benefits of Cyber Risk Management 342
- Key Takeaways 345

Identifying Threats and Vulnerabilities 346
- Understanding Threats and Vulnerabilities 346
- The Importance of Identifying Threats and Vulnerabilities 352
- Steps to Identify Threats and Vulnerabilities 353
- Tools and Techniques for Identifying Threats and Vulnerabilities 359
- Challenges in Identifying Threats and Vulnerabilities 359
- Best Practices for Success 360
- Benefits of Identifying Threats and Vulnerabilities 361
- Key Takeaways 362

Risk Scoring and Prioritization 363
- The Fundamentals of Risk Scoring 363
- Key Components of Risk Scoring 363
- The Process of Risk Prioritization 370
- Steps in Risk Scoring and Prioritization 371
- Tools and Technologies for Risk Scoring 373
- Challenges in Risk Scoring and Prioritization 373
- Best Practices for Effective Risk Scoring 374
- Benefits of Risk Scoring and Prioritization 375
- Preparing for the Future of Risk Management 375
- Key Takeaways 376

How to Perform a Risk Assessment 377
- What Is a Risk Assessment?.. 377
- Why Perform a Risk Assessment?... 377

TABLE OF CONTENTS

- The Risk Assessment Process ... 378
- Challenges and Solutions ... 383
- Best Practices for Risk Assessment ... 385
- Key Takeaways ... 390
- Mitigating Identified Risks: Strategies and Best Practices ... 391
  - Understanding Risk Mitigation ... 391
  - Core Risk Mitigation Strategies ... 392
  - Steps to Mitigate Identified Risks ... 394
  - Technologies That Drive Risk Mitigation ... 398
  - Challenges in Risk Mitigation ... 399
  - Best Practices for Risk Mitigation ... 401
  - Examples of Risk Mitigation in Action ... 401
  - Key Takeaways ... 402
- Conducting a Risk-Based Cybersecurity Audit ... 403
  - Why Risk-Based Audits Are Important ... 403
  - Steps to Conduct a Risk-Based Audit ... 404
  - Challenges in Risk-Based Audits ... 408
  - Best Practices for Risk-Based Audits ... 410
  - Examples of Risk-Based Audits in Action ... 410
  - Key Takeaways ... 411
- The Role of Incident Response in Risk Management ... 412
  - Understanding Incident Response in Risk Management ... 413
  - The Incident Response Lifecycle ... 414
  - Integrating Incident Response and Risk Management ... 417
  - Technologies for Incident Response in Risk Management ... 418
  - Challenges and Solutions in Incident Response ... 419
  - Best Practices for Incident Response and Risk Management ... 420
  - Key Takeaways ... 421
- Creating a Risk Management Plan ... 422
  - Steps to Create a Risk Management Plan ... 423
  - Key Components of a Risk Management Plan ... 425

Best Practices for Risk Management Planning	429
Key Takeaways	430
The Link Between Risk Management and Business Continuity	431
Risk Management and Business Continuity Are Interdependent	432
Key Benefits of Integration	432
Practical Integration Steps	436
Emerging Trends in Risk Management and Business Continuity	440
Key Takeaways	440
Risk Management Mistakes in Cybersecurity Audits	441
Common Mistakes in Risk Management in Cybersecurity Audit	442
Best Practices for Effective Risk Management in Cybersecurity Audits	448
Key Takeaways	449
Conclusions	450

Chapter 6: Tools for Network and Cybersecurity Audits 453

Network Security Audits: Tools and Best Practices	454
Importance of Tools in Network Security Audits	454
Network Security Tools	454
Asset Discovery Tools	458
IDS/IPS/EDR Tools	461
Best Practices for Tool Integration in Network Security Audits	464
Key Considerations for Tool Selection	465
Key Takeaways	466
Advanced Cybersecurity Strategies and Audits with SIEM and DLP Tools	466
What Is a SIEM System?	467
SIEM Tools	467
The Role of SIEM in Cybersecurity Audits	476
Steps to Use SIEM in Audits	477
DLP Tools	478
Challenges in Using SIEM Systems	481
Best Practices for Tool Integration in Security Strategies	482
Key Takeaways	483

TABLE OF CONTENTS

Advanced Security Tools for Vulnerability Management, SAST, and DAST 485
- What Are Vulnerability Scanners? 485
- The Importance of Vulnerability Scanners in Audits 485
- Vulnerability Management Tools 486
- Static Application Security Testing (SAST) 492
- Dynamic Application Security Testing (DAST) 497
- How Vulnerability Scanners Work in Auditing 499
- Challenges in Using Vulnerability Scanners 499
- Best Practices for Tool Integration in Security Testing 500
- Emerging Trends in Vulnerability Scanning 501
- Key Takeaways 501

Automation, Compliance, and Threat Intelligence Tools for Effective Cybersecurity Audit Management 503
- The Role of Automation in Cyber Audits 503
- Key Benefits of Automation in Cyber Audits 504
- Automation and Compliance Tools 505
- Threat Intelligence Platforms for Auditing 514
- What Are Threat Intelligence Platforms? 514
- How TIPs Support Cybersecurity Audits 515
- Key Technologies Behind TIPs 517
- Threat Intelligence Tools 518
- Best Practices for Implementing Automation and Using TIPs in Cyber Audits 521
- Future Trends in Automation and TIPs for Cyber Audits 523
- Key Takeaways 524

Penetration Testing Tools for Comprehensive Security Assessments 525
- What Are Penetration Testing Tools? 526
- The Role of Penetration Testing Tools in Cybersecurity Audits 527
- Penetration Testing Tools 528
- Best Practices for Leveraging Penetration Testing Tools 533
- Future Trends in Penetration Testing Tools 534
- Key Takeaways 535

TABLE OF CONTENTS

User Access Management and Encryption Tools for Robust Cybersecurity 536
    Role in Cyber Audits 536
    Key Benefits of User Access Management Tools in Cyber Audits 537
    Identity and Access Management (IAM) 538
    Privileged Access Management (PAM) 541
    Password Management Tools 542
    Encryption and Key Management Tools 543
    Full-Disk Encryption Tools 545
    Best Practices for User Access Management and Encryption Tools 546
    Future Trends in User Access Management Tools 548
    Key Takeaways 550

Risk Management and GRC Tools: Enhancing Decision-Making and Compliance 552
    Role of Risk Management and GRC Tools in Cybersecurity Audits 552
    Key Benefits of Risk Management and GRC Tools in Cybersecurity Audits 553
    Risk Management and GRC Tools 554
    Best Practices for Implementing Risk Management and GRC Tools 559
    Future Trends in Risk Management and GRC Tools 560
    Key Takeaways 561

Visualization and Collaboration Tools 562
    Role of Visualization and Collaboration Tools in Cybersecurity Audits 562
    Key Benefits of Visualization and Collaboration Tools in Cybersecurity Audits 563
    Visualizing Workflows 564
    Collaboration and Survey Tools 567
    Best Practices for Using Visualization and Collaboration Tools in Cybersecurity Audits 572
    Future Trends in Visualization and Collaboration Tools for Cybersecurity Audits 573
    Key Takeaways 574

Other Relevant Tools for Cybersecurity Audits 574
    Configuration Management Tools 575
    Incident Response and Forensic Tools 577
    API Testing Tools 580
    Security Posture Management 581

TABLE OF CONTENTS

- Pseudonymization Tools 582
- Best Practices for Leveraging These Tools 583
- Key Takeaways 585
- How to Choose the Right Audit Tools 586
  - Why Choosing the Right Audit Tools Matters 586
  - Factors to Consider When Choosing Audit Tools 587
  - Key Features to Look for in Audit Tools 588
  - Best Practices for Selecting Audit Tools 590
  - Key Takeaways 591
- Tips for Conducting a Tool-Based Assessment 591
  - The Role of Tools in Cybersecurity Audits 592
  - Tips for Effective Tool-Based Audits 592
  - Common Pitfalls in Tool-Based Audits 594
  - Key Takeaways 595
- Common Tool Misconfigurations in Audits 596
  - The Importance of Proper Tool Configuration 597
  - Common Tool Misconfigurations in Audits 597
  - Strategies to Avoid Tool Misconfigurations 599
  - Key Takeaways 600
- Conclusions 600

Chapter 7: How to Write an Effective Cybersecurity Audit Report 603

- The Purpose of an Audit Report 604
  - Key Components of an Audit Report 604
  - Writing Best Practices 607
  - Tools for Report Creation 608
  - Common Mistakes to Avoid 609
  - Key Takeaways 610
- Tips for Communicating Technical Findings to Non-technical Stakeholders 610
  - Understand Your Audience 611
  - Use Simplified Language 612
  - Focus on Business Impact 613

TABLE OF CONTENTS

- Use Visual Aids 613
- Prioritize Findings 614
- Provide Clear Action Steps 614
- Anticipate Questions and Concerns 615
- Leverage Storytelling 615
- Follow Up with Documentation 616
- Key Takeaways 616

The Role of Visuals in Audit Reporting 617
- Why Visuals Are Crucial in Audit Reporting 617
- Types of Visuals to Include 618
- Tools for Creating Visuals 622
- Best Practices for Using Visuals in Audit Reports 623
- Example Scenario: Visuals in Action 624
- Key Takeaways 624

Creating an Executive Summary for Audit Reports 625
- The Importance of an Executive Summary 625
- Essential Elements of a Strong Executive Summary 626
- Best Practices for Writing an Executive Summary 629
- Example Executive Summary 629
- Key Takeaways 631

Common Cybersecurity Audit Reporting Mistakes and How to Avoid Them 631
- Importance of Reporting in Cybersecurity Audits 632
- Common Reporting Mistakes 632
- Best Practices to Avoid Reporting Mistakes 634
- Impact of Well-Written Reports 638
- Key Takeaways 639

How to Present Cybersecurity Audit Findings to the Board 640
- Understanding the Board's Perspective 640
- Structuring Your Presentation 640
- Communicating Effectively 643
- Leveraging Technology for Presentations 644

xxi

TABLE OF CONTENTS

- Engaging the Board 646
- Impact of Well-Written Reports and Engaging Presentations 647
- Key Takeaways 648

Action Plans Based on Cybersecurity Audit Recommendations 649
- Importance of an Action Plan 649
- Developing an Effective Action Plan 650
- Implementing the Action Plan 652
- Impact of a Well-Executed Action Plan 653
- Key Takeaways 653

Follow-Up Audits: Ensuring Compliance 654
- The Purpose of Follow-Up Audits 654
- The Follow-Up Audit Process 654
- Benefits of Follow-Up Audits 657
- Best Practices for Follow-Up Audits 657
- Key Takeaways 658

How to Handle Disputes Over Cybersecurity Audit Findings 659
- Understanding the Causes of Audit Disputes 659
- Strategies for Addressing Audit Disputes 660
- Best Practices for Resolving Audit Disputes 663
- Benefits of Resolving Disputes Constructively 664
- Turning Disputes into Opportunities 664
- Key Takeaways 666

Best Practices for Continuous Communication in Cybersecurity Audits 667
- Importance of Continuous Communication 667
- Best Practices for Continuous Communication 668
- Challenges in Continuous Communication and Solutions 670
- Long-Term Communication Practices 671
- Benefits of Continuous Communication 672
- Key Takeaways 673

Conclusions 674

TABLE OF CONTENTS

Chapter 8: Real-Life Scenarios and Case Studies 677

Learning from Breaches – A Case Study 677
- Background 677
- Audit Scope and Objectives 678
- Findings from the Audit 678
- Steps Taken to Remediate the Breach 679
- Lessons Learned 680
- How Audits Help Prevent Breaches 681
- Benefits of Post-breach Audits 681
- Key Takeaways 682

Lessons Learned from a Failed Audit 682
- What Constitutes a Failed Audit? 683
- Example Scenario: A Retailer's PCI-DSS Audit Failure 683
- Key Lessons Learned from Failed Audits 684
- How Organizations Can Recover from a Failed Audit 686
- Best Practices to Avoid Future Failures 689
- Turning Failure into Opportunity 690
- Benefits of Learning from Failed Audits 690
- Key Takeaways 691

Case Study: Cloud Security Audit Challenges 692
- The Complex Nature of Cloud Environments 692
- Example: A Financial Institution's Cloud Audit Challenges 693
- Strategies to Address Cloud Security Audit Challenges 694
- Lessons Learned from Cloud Security Audits 697
- Turning Challenges into Opportunities 698
- Key Takeaways 698

The Impact of Human Error on Cybersecurity Audits 699
- Understanding Human Error in Cybersecurity 699
- Impact of Human Error on Cybersecurity Audits 700
- Why Human Error Occurs 701
- Mitigating Human Error in Cybersecurity Audits 701

xxiii

TABLE OF CONTENTS

    The Role of Cybersecurity Audits in Addressing Human Error 704

    Turning Human Error into an Opportunity 705

    Key Takeaways 707

What Auditors Can Learn from Incident Reports 708

    What Are Incident Reports? 708

    Why Are Incident Reports Valuable for Auditors? 709

    Examples of Lessons from Incident Reports 710

    How Auditors Can Use Incident Reports 711

    Practical Integration of Incident Reports into Audits 712

    Turning Incident Reports into Opportunities 713

    Key Takeaways 713

A Successful Audit Story: Key Takeaways 714

    The Organization: A Financial Services Company 714

    The Audit Goals 714

    The Audit Process 716

    Findings and Recommendations 717

    Overall Added Value of Addressing These Vulnerabilities 720

    Implementation and Results 721

    Lessons Learned from Success 721

    Key takeaways 722

Case Study: Auditing for Insider Threats 723

    The Organization: A Software Development Company 723

    Audit Objectives 724

    The Audit Process 725

    Findings and Recommendations 726

    Lessons Learned 729

    Key Takeaways 730

The Role of Forensics in Cybersecurity Audits 731

    What Is Forensics in Cybersecurity? 731

    How Forensics Enhances Cybersecurity Audits 731

    Integrating Forensics into Audit Processes 734

Example of Forensics in Action	736
Lessons Learned	736
Key Takeaways	737
A Day in the Life of a Cybersecurity Auditor	738
Morning: Planning and Prioritization	738
Mid-Morning: Assessing Security Controls	739
Lunch: Staying Updated	740
Afternoon: Data Analysis and Documentation	740
Late Afternoon: Stakeholder Engagement	741
Evening: Reflection and Continuous Learning	742
Challenges Faced by Cybersecurity Auditors	742
Key Takeaways	745
Conclusions	745
Bibliography	**747**
Abbreviations	**761**
Index	**767**

About the Author

Armend Salihu is a highly experienced IT auditor, cybersecurity professional, and university professor with more than 20 years of work in technology, risk, and digital security. He holds a PhD in theoretical computer science and has helped many organizations across different sectors improve their IT governance, manage cyber risks, and comply with international standards and regulations.

Throughout his career, Dr. Salihu has worked closely with both public and private institutions, helping them understand complex IT and security challenges and implement practical solutions. His ability to explain technical concepts in a clear and useful way has made him a trusted advisor for professionals and organizations alike.

In addition to his industry work, Dr. Salihu teaches in a master's degree program, where he mentors and inspires the next generation of technology and data professionals. His approach to teaching is hands-on and focused on real-world challenges, helping students build the skills they need to succeed in today's fast-changing digital world.

Dr. Salihu holds globally recognized credentials, including CGEIT, CRISC, and CISA, and is the author of numerous peer-reviewed publications. His strong mix of academic knowledge and practical experience gives this book a balance of theory and action.

Outside of work, Dr. Salihu enjoys solving Rubik's cubes, playing the guitar, tackling Sudoku puzzles, and spending quality time with his family. His passion for learning, teaching, and sharing knowledge continues to drive his mission to support IT and cybersecurity professionals in making a real impact and succeeding in today's fast-changing digital world.

About the Technical Reviewer

Artan Luma is a professor of computer science with expertise in cybersecurity, cryptography, and digital forensics. He has extensive academic and practical experience in designing advanced courses in these fields, as well as in developing and implementing the Moodle platform for cybersecurity training. Artan has served as a technical reviewer for research projects and professional publications focusing on the technical aspects of information systems auditing and data protection. His work centers on integrating advanced risk analysis methodologies with modern educational technologies. He continues to contribute to the advancement of secure and sustainable practices in digital learning and professional environments.

Introduction

In today's digital landscape, cybersecurity threats are becoming increasingly sophisticated, making it imperative for organizations to adopt proactive security measures. Cybersecurity audits play a critical role in assessing an organization's security posture, identifying vulnerabilities, ensuring regulatory compliance, and mitigating cyber risks. This book serves as a comprehensive guide to conducting effective cybersecurity audits, offering practical insights, methodologies, and real-world case studies to equip auditors, IT professionals, and compliance officers with the knowledge they need to strengthen security frameworks.

We begin with Chapter 1, "Introduction to Cybersecurity Audits," where we establish the fundamental concepts of cybersecurity audits, their significance, and the key principles that guide an effective audit process. This chapter provides an overview of the auditor's role in evaluating security controls and ensuring organizations meet industry's best practices.

Chapter 2, "Planning the Cybersecurity Audit," explores the importance of a well-structured audit plan. It covers essential elements such as defining objectives, setting the audit scope, selecting appropriate frameworks, and preparing audit checklists. A thorough planning phase ensures that audits are focused, efficient, and aligned with organizational security goals.

The core of any cybersecurity audit lies in Chapter 3, "Assessing Security Controls," where we examine the methodologies for evaluating technical security measures. This includes reviewing access controls, authentication mechanisms, network security configurations, encryption standards, and endpoint protection. The chapter also delves into penetration testing and vulnerability scanning to uncover security gaps.

In Chapter 4, "Compliance and Regulations," we navigate the complex landscape of cybersecurity laws and industry standards, such as GDPR, HIPAA, PCI-DSS, ISO 27001, and NIST. Compliance audits ensure that organizations adhere to legal and regulatory requirements, reducing the risk of fines and reputational damage. This chapter also highlights best practices for aligning security controls with regulatory mandates.

INTRODUCTION

Cybersecurity risk assessment is a critical aspect of auditing, covered in Chapter 5, "Introduction to Cyber Risk Management." Here, we explore how auditors identify, analyze, and mitigate cyber risks using frameworks like NIST Risk Management Framework (RMF) and FAIR (Factor Analysis of Information Risk). Risk-based auditing ensures that high-impact threats receive priority attention.

No audit is complete without the right tools. Chapter 6, "Tools for Network and Cybersecurity Audits," provides an in-depth look at essential cybersecurity audit tools. We explore vulnerability scanners like Nessus and Qualys, network monitoring tools like Wireshark, and compliance management solutions that streamline audit processes.

Effective reporting is key to communicating audit findings and driving security improvements. Chapter 7, "How to Write an Effective Cybersecurity Audit Report," guides auditors through structuring clear, actionable reports. This chapter covers best practices for documenting vulnerabilities, recommending remediation strategies, and tailoring reports for technical and executive audiences.

To bridge theory with practice, Chapter 8, "Real-Life Scenarios and Case Studies," presents real-world cybersecurity audit cases. These examples illustrate how organizations have successfully identified security weaknesses, responded to cyber incidents, and strengthened their security posture through auditing. By analyzing these scenarios, readers gain practical insights into handling cybersecurity challenges in diverse industries.

This book is designed to be a practical resource for cybersecurity professionals, internal and external auditors, IT managers, and compliance officers seeking to enhance their cybersecurity audit capabilities. Whether you are new to auditing or an experienced professional looking to refine your approach, the methodologies, tools, and case studies presented here will provide valuable guidance. By mastering the principles outlined in this book, you will be well-equipped to assess, report, and improve cybersecurity practices within any organization.

CHAPTER 1

Introduction to Cybersecurity Audits

Imagine a business is like a house. There are valuable things inside – family photos, jewelry, important documents – just like the business has customer data, financial records, and trade secrets. Now, wouldn't you want to know if the locks are working? If the windows are secure? If the alarm system is doing its job? That is exactly what a cybersecurity audit does for the digital "house."

In an era where digital threats are constantly evolving, cybersecurity has become a critical concern for businesses and organizations of all sizes. One of the most effective ways to safeguard sensitive data, maintain operational integrity, and comply with regulatory requirements is through cybersecurity audits. These audits serve as a comprehensive review of an organization's information technology (IT) infrastructure, policies, and security controls, identifying vulnerabilities and weaknesses before they can be exploited by malicious actors.

What Is a Cybersecurity Audit?

Think of it as a home inspection, but for a company's digital presence. Just like a home inspector checks the foundation, wiring, and plumbing, a cybersecurity audit examines the digital infrastructure to make sure everything is secure and working properly. The auditor looks at everything from the digital "locks" (passwords and access controls) to the "security system" (firewalls and antivirus software).

A cybersecurity audit is a thorough, systematic evaluation of an organization's IT systems, security policies, and procedures to assess their effectiveness in protecting against cyber threats. The goal is to ensure that the organization's data and critical infrastructure are secure and that it is complying with industry-specific regulations, standards, and legal obligations. A cybersecurity audit focuses on both technical

© Armend Salihu 2025
A. Salihu, *Cybersecurity Audit Essentials*, https://doi.org/10.1007/979-8-8688-1712-0_1

CHAPTER 1 INTRODUCTION TO CYBERSECURITY AUDITS

and administrative controls, covering areas such as firewalls, data encryption, access management, log management, and more. The audit process not only helps identify potential security flaws but also provides organizations with a roadmap for improving their security posture.

At its core, a cybersecurity audit involves reviewing an organization's existing policies, procedures, and technologies to verify that they are working as intended. This evaluation is vital for organizations looking to assess their vulnerability to cyberattacks, data breaches, and other security incidents. By identifying gaps in security, a cybersecurity audit enables businesses to take corrective actions to strengthen their defenses, mitigate risk, and improve overall security practices.

The Technical Perspective of Cybersecurity Audits

A successful cybersecurity audit requires a comprehensive understanding of the organization's entire IT infrastructure, from networks and servers to endpoints and cloud environments. The auditor must be able to assess the effectiveness of security measures across a range of systems, platforms, and technologies, including

- *Vulnerability Scanning*: The audit process often involves using specialized tools to scan systems for vulnerabilities. Tools like Nessus and Qualys are commonly used to perform these scans, identifying weaknesses in the organization's security architecture, such as outdated software, misconfigured systems, or unpatched vulnerabilities. Vulnerability scanning helps auditors pinpoint areas where the organization may be exposed to security threats, enabling them to recommend specific actions to mitigate those risks.

- *Security Frameworks*: To ensure that the audit is thorough and comprehensive, auditors often follow established cybersecurity frameworks. Frameworks like the National Institute of Standards and Technology - Cybersecurity Framework (NIST CSF) or International Organization for Standardization/International Electrotechnical Commission (ISO/IEC) 27001 provide a structured approach to assessing an organization's cybersecurity posture. These frameworks offer guidelines and best practices for evaluating a variety of security controls, including access management, data protection, and incident response. Using such frameworks ensures that the audit covers all necessary aspects of an organization's security measures and provides a well-rounded analysis of its security stance.

- *SIEM Tools*: Security Information and Event Management (SIEM) tools like SolarWinds, IBM QRadar, Splunk, and Microsoft Sentinel are integral to the auditing process. These tools gather and analyze data from across the organization's network, detecting unusual activities that may indicate potential security incidents. SIEM systems aggregate logs and provide real-time insights into system performance, allowing auditors to identify patterns that could indicate security breaches or other anomalies. Through log analysis, SIEM tools play a crucial role in assessing the effectiveness of incident response measures and identifying areas where security monitoring and response protocols may need to be enhanced.

The Importance of Cybersecurity Audits

You would not wait until after a break-in to install a security system, right? That is the idea behind cybersecurity audits.

Cybersecurity audits are not just about identifying vulnerabilities and ensuring compliance with regulations; they are about fostering a proactive security culture within the organization. Regular audits enable organizations to

- *Detect Weaknesses Before Exploitation*: Cybercriminals are constantly searching for vulnerabilities they can exploit. Regular audits help identify weaknesses and gaps in security measures that could otherwise go unnoticed. Organizations can prevent costly security incidents and data breaches by addressing these issues before they are exploited.

- *Enhance Compliance*: For organizations operating in regulated industries, such as healthcare, finance, or retail, cybersecurity audits are critical to ensuring compliance with legal and industry-specific regulations. Audits assess whether the organization is meeting the security requirements outlined in regulations like the Health Insurance Portability and Accountability Act (HIPAA), the General Data Protection Regulation (GDPR), the Payment Card Industry Data

Security Standard (PCI DSS), and others. Non-compliance can result in hefty fines, legal consequences, and damage to the organization's reputation.

- *Improve Incident Response*: Cybersecurity audits are also designed to assess an organization's ability to respond to incidents. This includes evaluating the effectiveness of incident response plans, the monitoring and detection capabilities, and the procedures for containing and mitigating attacks. Regular audits help ensure that an organization's incident response strategy is up to date and effective, ensuring a swift recovery in the event of a breach.

- *Promote Continuous Improvement*: The findings from cybersecurity audits provide organizations with actionable recommendations that drive continuous improvement in their security practices. By addressing audit findings and implementing recommended changes, organizations can progressively enhance their security measures and adapt to evolving threats. This ongoing process of assessment and improvement ensures that the organization remains resilient in the face of new and emerging cyber risks.

An Example of a Cybersecurity Audit in Practice

To better understand how cybersecurity audits work, let's look at an example involving a healthcare organization. In this case, the organization undergoes a cybersecurity audit to assess its compliance with HIPAA regulations, which govern the handling of patient data.

During the audit, the audit team uses a combination of manual reviews and automated scanning tools to evaluate the organization's security practices. These tools assess the security of endpoints, servers, and networks, looking for outdated software, unpatched vulnerabilities, and other potential risks. The audit team may discover that several devices within the organization are running outdated versions of software, which may expose sensitive patient data to security threats.

For example, if certain devices are running software versions that no longer receive security updates, these systems could be vulnerable to exploits that have been discovered in more recent versions of the software. If attackers gain access to these devices, they could steal or compromise sensitive health data, leading to severe consequences for both the organization and its patients.

By identifying these vulnerabilities during the audit, the organization can take immediate action to update the affected systems and patch security gaps. This process ensures that patient data remains secure and helps the organization comply with HIPAA regulations, avoiding potential penalties for non-compliance. In this way, the cybersecurity audit provides the organization with valuable insights that enhance its overall security and safeguard sensitive information.

Key Takeaways

Cybersecurity audits are not just a reactive measure; they are a critical tool in maintaining and improving the security and resilience of the organization. By adopting a proactive approach to these audits, organizations can strengthen their defenses, ensure compliance, and reduce risks, ultimately safeguarding the business's future from the ever-present threat of cybercrime.

In this chapter we covered the following points:

- *Cybersecurity Audits as Preventive Check-ups*: Like regular medical check-ups, cybersecurity audits identify vulnerabilities before they become serious issues, helping to build a stronger and safer digital environment for the business.

- *A Proactive Approach*: Cybersecurity audits are essential for protecting data and business assets, functioning as key safeguards in the digital world, and ensuring the future security of the business.

- *The Importance of Cybersecurity Audits*: Audits are critical for identifying vulnerabilities, assessing the effectiveness of security measures, and ensuring compliance with regulatory requirements.

- *Comprehensive Review and Risk Reduction*: Cybersecurity audits provide a holistic review of systems, policies, and controls to improve security, reduce the risk of data breaches, and enhance incident response capabilities.

- *Staying One Step Ahead of Cybercriminals*: Regular audits help organizations stay ahead of evolving cyber threats, making audits an essential part of a proactive cybersecurity strategy to protect data and assets.

CHAPTER 1   INTRODUCTION TO CYBERSECURITY AUDITS

Internal vs. External Cybersecurity Audits

Imagine taking care of the health. Sometimes is done a self-checks at home (like checking the weight or blood pressure), and other times visiting a doctor for a professional medical exam. Cybersecurity works the same way – there is needed both internal check-ups (self-assessments) and external examinations (independent audits) to stay healthy.

In today's complex cybersecurity landscape, audits are a crucial tool for evaluating and strengthening an organization's security posture. Understanding the distinction between internal and external cybersecurity audits is essential for organizations aiming to address vulnerabilities, ensure compliance, and improve their overall security framework. While both types of audits serve distinct but complementary roles, they differ in scope, purpose, and execution.

Internal Audits

Think of internal audits like having a family doctor who knows complete medical history. These are the check-ups done by the own team – the people who know the business inside and out.

Internal audits are conducted by the organization's own audit team or cybersecurity audit professionals. These audits focus on evaluating the effectiveness of security controls from within the organization and are usually designed to foster continuous improvement. The goal is to identify vulnerabilities and gaps in security policies, processes, and technology, with an emphasis on proactively improving security defenses.

What Makes Internal Audits Special?

- *It Is Like Having a Personal Trainer*: The internal team knows the company's "fitness level" and can create a custom workout plan (security strategy) that fits company's needs perfectly.

- *You Can Check Your Vital Signs Anytime*: Just like you might step on a scale whenever you want, internal audits can happen as often as needed. Notice something feels off? Your team can investigate right away.

- *It Is Budget-Friendly*: Like having exercise equipment at home instead of paying for a gym membership, internal audits are typically more cost-effective since you are using your own team.

Key Characteristics of Internal Audits:

- *Conducted by Internal Teams*: These audits are typically performed by employees who are already familiar with the organization's infrastructure, operations, and internal policies. Their deep understanding of the organization's processes allows for a more customized and detailed assessment.

- *Continuous Improvement Focus*: Rather than solely focusing on compliance, internal audits prioritize identifying and rectifying security weaknesses before they escalate. This makes internal audits proactive, with a goal of enhancing security over time.

- *Flexible Scope*: The scope of an internal audit can be adapted based on the organization's needs. For example, an internal audit might focus on a specific area, such as application security, access control mechanisms, network vulnerabilities, or even the performance of internal systems. This flexibility allows the audit to target the most pressing areas of concern.

- *Informal and Advisory Role*: Internal audits often play an advisory role, with findings shared with management to inform decision-making. The audit team collaborates with various departments to suggest improvements and guide the organization towards stronger security practices.

- *Tool Usage*: Internal audit teams typically rely on a variety of network monitoring and security tools to conduct their assessments. Solutions like SolarWinds, Splunk, and Nagios are often employed to monitor system performance and security, while SIEM tools such as IBM QRadar help with log analysis and detecting anomalies.

Advantages of Internal Audits:

- *Proactive Risk Management*: Internal audits help detect issues early, allowing the organization to address vulnerabilities before they lead to significant security breaches.

- *Increased Familiarity*: The internal audit team's deep understanding of the company's internal systems and processes allows for more targeted assessments and effective mitigation strategies.

- *Cost-Effective*: Since internal audits are performed by the organization's staff, they are less costly than hiring external auditors. They also allow for more frequent and ongoing assessments.

External Audits

Now, imagine visiting a specialist for a thorough medical examination. That is what external audits are like – independent experts coming in to give an unbiased assessment.

What Makes External Audits Different?

- *Fresh Eyes, Fresh Perspective*: Just like getting a second opinion from another doctor, external auditors bring a new perspective to the security setup.

- *They Speak "Regulation"*: These are the experts who know all about industry standards and requirements – like a doctor who keeps up with the latest medical research and guidelines.

- *They Give You a "Clean Bill of Health"*: Successfully passing an external audit is like getting official medical clearance – it shows others that you are taking care of business properly.

External audits, in contrast, are conducted by independent third-party audit organizations that specialize in cybersecurity assessments. These audits offer an unbiased evaluation of an organization's security posture and compliance with industry standards. External audits focus on verifying adherence to regulations and frameworks, providing objective validation of the organization's cybersecurity measures.

Key Characteristics of External Audits:

- *Objective Assessment*: Because they are conducted by independent third parties, external audits provide an impartial evaluation of an organization's security practices. This objective can offer a more accurate view of the organization's security posture, free from any internal biases or influences.

- *Compliance-Focused*: External audits are often driven by the need to verify that an organization complies with industry regulations, standards, and frameworks. Common examples include PCI-DSS, HIPAA, ISO/IEC 27001, and GDPR. These audits help organizations meet regulatory requirements and avoid legal or financial penalties.

- *Certification and Assurance*: Successful completion of an external audit can result in certifications or attestations that demonstrate the organization's commitment to cybersecurity standards. These certifications can be vital for building trust with customers, partners, and stakeholders, and they provide assurance that the organization is managing cybersecurity risks in line with industry best practices.

Advantages of External Audits:

- *Compliance Validation*: External audits are essential for validating that an organization is adhering to regulatory requirements, which is especially important in industries with strict compliance demands such as healthcare, finance, and retail. Failing to comply with these regulations can lead to costly penalties and damage to the organization's reputation.

- *Expertise*: External auditors bring specialized knowledge, experience, and skills that can be valuable, particularly in complex regulatory environments or for industries with specific cybersecurity requirements. Their expertise ensures that the audit covers all relevant security controls and regulatory obligations.

- *Credibility*: Having an external audit conducted and obtaining certification from a reputable third party adds credibility to an organization's cybersecurity practices. This can enhance the organization's reputation and foster greater trust among customers, business partners, and stakeholders.

CHAPTER 1 INTRODUCTION TO CYBERSECURITY AUDITS

Comparing Internal and External Audits

While both internal and external audits are critical for a comprehensive cybersecurity strategy, they each offer distinct advantages.

Table 1-1 presents a comparison between internal and external cybersecurity audits.

Table 1-1. Internal vs. external cybersecurity audits

Aspect	Internal Audit	External Audit	Commonalities
Definition	Conducted by the organization's internal team to assess and improve security controls.	Performed by independent third-party experts to evaluate compliance and security posture objectively.	Both evaluate and strengthen cybersecurity measures.
Scope	Flexible and adaptable to specific organizational needs (e.g., network, application security, access controls).	Typically focused on compliance with industry standards, regulations, and frameworks.	Both examine security policies, processes, and technology.
Purpose	Proactive improvement of security defences and identification of vulnerabilities.	Validation of compliance, assurance, and unbiased evaluation of security measures.	Both aim to enhance an organization's security posture.
Frequency	Can be conducted as often as needed based on organizational requirements.	Conducted periodically or as required by regulatory bodies or clients.	Both follow planned processes and schedules.
Team Involvement	Performed by internal employees who are familiar with the organization's systems, policies, and infrastructure.	Conducted by independent auditors with no prior connection to the organization.	Involve cybersecurity professionals for analysis and reporting.
Focus Area	Continuous improvement and proactive risk management.	Compliance, certification, and credibility-building with external stakeholders.	Both identify gaps and recommend remediation strategies.

(continued)

Table 1-1. (*continued*)

Aspect	Internal Audit	External Audit	Commonalities
Cost	Cost-effective since the organization leverages its existing team and resources.	Higher cost due to hiring independent experts and specialized audit services.	Both require investment in tools, time, and expertise.
Objectivity	Can be influenced by internal biases or limitations.	Provides an impartial and unbiased assessment.	Both rely on accurate data and analysis to identify vulnerabilities.
Outcome	Advisory findings to guide internal decision-making and foster continuous improvement.	Certification or attestation demonstrating compliance with industry standards and best practices.	Both produce actionable recommendations to improve cybersecurity.
Tools Used	Internal monitoring and security tools like SolarWinds, Splunk, Nagios, and SIEM solutions (e.g., IBM QRadar).	Specialized tools and frameworks depending on the compliance or industry requirements.	Both utilize advanced tools for system performance and anomaly detection.
Advantages	Proactive risk management, cost-effectiveness, flexibility, and deep familiarity with organizational processes.	Objective validation, compliance assurance, credibility, and access to specialized expertise.	Both contribute to a stronger and more resilient cybersecurity framework.
Key Role	Focuses on day-to-day "health checks" and continuous improvement of internal systems.	Provides a professional "second opinion" and official certification or validation of cybersecurity practices.	Both are integral to a comprehensive cybersecurity strategy.
Examples of Use Cases	Regularly reviewing internal access control mechanisms, testing disaster recovery plans, and addressing internal vulnerabilities.	Assessing compliance with PCI-DSS, ISO 27001, GDPR, HIPAA, or performing a third-party vendor risk assessment.	Both identify, document, and mitigate security risks.

CHAPTER 1   INTRODUCTION TO CYBERSECURITY AUDITS

Why You Need Both: The Perfect Health Plan

Here is the thing: you would not choose between doing self-checks or seeing a doctor – you need both. The same goes for cybersecurity audits. Internal audits help you stay healthy day-to-day, while external audits make sure you are meeting all the official health standards.

Think of it this way:

- *Internal Audits Are Like Your Daily Health Routine*: Eating right, exercising, and monitoring your vitals.

- *External Audits Are Like Your Annual Physical*: Getting an expert opinion and official confirmation that everything is working as it should.

The Dual Approach: Combining Internal and External Audits

For organizations looking to create a robust and comprehensive security posture, a combination of internal and external audits is often the most effective approach. Internal audits provide ongoing, proactive risk management, helping organizations detect and address vulnerabilities before they become critical issues. External audits, on the other hand, ensure compliance with industry standards, provide expert validation of the organization's security practices, and help maintain external trust.

By integrating both types of audits, organizations can benefit from a well-rounded cybersecurity strategy that addresses both internal weaknesses and external compliance requirements. This dual approach ensures that security measures are not only effective in preventing attacks but also in meeting regulatory obligations, enhancing the organization's overall security maturity.

Key Takeaways

Your internal team knows your "body" best, but sometimes you need external experts to spot things you might miss or to certify that your organization's security is as strong as you believe. Together, internal and external audits form a complete health plan for your organization's digital security.

In this section, we covered the following points:

- *Internal and External Audits Working Together*:
  - Just like good health requires both personal vigilance and professional medical check-ups, good cybersecurity needs both internal and external audits.
  - These audits work together to keep your digital business healthy, compliant, and trusted by stakeholders.
- *Distinction Between Internal and External Audits*:
  - Internal Audits offer flexibility, proactivity, and a deep familiarity with the organization's systems, allowing for continuous improvement.
  - External Audits provide objectivity, compliance assurance, and specialized expertise, offering an unbiased review and helping organizations meet industry standards and regulations.
- *Comprehensive Approach to Cybersecurity*:
  - Combining internal and external audits creates a comprehensive approach to cybersecurity.
  - This collaboration helps organizations stay ahead of cyber threats, manage risks, and ensure compliance with relevant standards and regulations.

Types of Cybersecurity Audits

Just like there are different types of medical check-ups – regular physicals, specialized tests, emergency visits, and routine screenings – there are different types of cybersecurity audits.

Cybersecurity audits are an essential part of an organization's security strategy, offering a structured and systematic approach to evaluating the effectiveness of its cybersecurity posture. These audits are designed to identify potential vulnerabilities, verify the functionality of security controls, and ensure compliance with industry regulations and standards. Depending on the needs and goals of an organization, cybersecurity audits can take various forms, each focused on specific aspects of

CHAPTER 1   INTRODUCTION TO CYBERSECURITY AUDITS

the organization's operations and risk management strategies. In the following, we will explore the four primary types of cybersecurity audits, their objectives, and the technical tools used to conduct them, providing organizations with a comprehensive understanding of each audit type and its purpose in the broader cybersecurity landscape.

Table 1-2 presents key types of cybersecurity audits.

Table 1-2. Types of cybersecurity audits

Audit Type	Description	Purpose	Key Components	Tools and Methods
Regular Audits	Periodic evaluations to check basic cybersecurity "health indicators."	Maintain operational security, verify policy effectiveness, and address emerging threats.	- Review of firewalls, antivirus, patch management. - Log analysis with SIEM tools. - IAM audits.	- SIEM tools: Splunk, IBM QRadar, Azure Sentinel. - Configuration management tools: Ansible, Puppet. - IAM tools: Okta, Microsoft Azure AD.
Compliance Audits	Evaluate adherence to industry regulations, legal requirements, and standards.	Ensure regulatory compliance, avoid penalties, and maintain customer trust.	- Alignment with standards like ISO/IEC 27001, HIPAA, GDPR. - Evidence tracking using GRC platforms. - Automated compliance scans.	- GRC platforms: RSA Archer, ServiceNow GRC. - Compliance tools: Tenable, Qualys Compliance.

(continued)

Table 1-2. (*continued*)

Audit Type	Description	Purpose	Key Components	Tools and Methods
Risk-Based Audits	Focus on high-risk areas and critical assets within the organization.	Identify and prioritize critical vulnerabilities and allocate resources efficiently.	- High-risk asset identification. - Threat modelling and vulnerability scanning. - Risk assessment methodologies.	- Risk assessment tools: OCTAVE, FAIR. - Asset discovery: AssetSonar, SolarWinds. - Threat modelling: STRIDE. - Vulnerability scanners: Nessus, Qualys, Rapid7 InsightVM.
Specialized Audits	Target specific domains like cloud security, privacy, third-party risks, or application security.	Address niche security concerns and ensure robust defences in specialized areas.	- Cloud security assessments. - Privacy compliance. - Vendor risk management. - Application vulnerability scans.	- Cloud tools: Encryption analysis, access control evaluation. - Privacy: GDPR/CCPA compliance tools. - Vendor audits: Supply chain risk tools. - Application: Source code analysis.

Regular Audits

Think of regular audits like your annual physical examination. Just as doctor checks vital signs, weight, and overall health, these audits look at organization's basic security "health indicators."

CHAPTER 1 INTRODUCTION TO CYBERSECURITY AUDITS

What's Included in Digital Physical?

- *Vital Signs Check*: Just like checking blood pressure and heart rate, regular audits look at firewalls and antivirus software.

- *Health History Review*: Like reviewing medical history, regular audits analyze security logs and past incidents.

- *Routine Tests*: Like running basic blood work, regular audits run regular scans and configuration checks.

Regular audits, also known as routine or scheduled audits, are conducted periodically to ensure that an organization's cybersecurity controls are consistently maintained, updated, and functioning as intended. The frequency of these audits typically depends on the organization's risk profile, industry standards, and internal policies. These audits are essential in ensuring that the organization's security posture remains strong over time, as they help identify any weaknesses, gaps, or lapses in security measures before they can be exploited by malicious actors. The primary purpose of regular audits is to maintain operational security, verify the effectiveness of existing policies and procedures, and proactively address emerging threats.

Key Components of Regular Audits:

- Periodic reviews of security measures like firewalls, antivirus software, and patch management.

- Use of SIEM tools such as Splunk, IBM QRadar, or Azure Sentinel to analyze security logs.

- Consistent configuration checks with tools like Ansible, Puppet, and Chef.

- Audits of user access management using Okta or Microsoft Azure Active Directory (AD) to ensure least privilege access.

The technical approach for conducting regular audits is based on a systematic review of the organization's core security controls, processes, and policies. This includes assessing fundamental security measures such as firewalls, antivirus software, patch management practices, and incident response protocols. The audit process often involves utilizing SIEM tools like Splunk, IBM QRadar, or Azure Sentinel to analyze security logs for any unusual activity, misconfigurations, or security incidents that might indicate potential vulnerabilities. Configuration management tools like Ansible,

Puppet, or Chef are also employed to ensure that servers and network configurations remain consistent and that unauthorized changes are quickly identified and addressed. Additionally, Identity and Access Management (IAM) solutions such as Okta or Microsoft Azure AD are used to monitor user access and privileges, ensuring that the principle of least privilege is adhered to and that access rights are properly assigned and managed.

Regular audits are a proactive measure for identifying potential security risks before they escalate, ensuring that all security systems are operating as intended and that critical vulnerabilities are addressed in a timely manner. By conducting these audits on a routine basis, organizations can establish a solid foundation for their cybersecurity program and continuously improve their defenses against evolving threats.

Compliance Audits

This is like getting certified for specific activities – think of a pilot's medical exam or a professional athlete's physical. These audits make sure meeting all the official requirements for your industry.

What Makes These Special?

- *Following the Rulebook*: Just like athletes must pass specific medical tests to play professionally, systems need to meet specific industry standards.

- *Official Documentation*: Like getting a doctor's note for work, these audits provide official proofs that are being followed the rules.

- *Specialized Tests*: Like specialized medical tests for different sports, different industries have different compliance requirements.

Think of It This Way: If you are in healthcare, you need to follow HIPAA rules (like special medical requirements for pilots). If you are handling credit cards, you need to follow PCI DSS (like drug testing for athletes).

Compliance audits are focused on evaluating whether an organization is adhering to the specific regulatory, legal, and contractual requirements set forth by industry standards, governing bodies, and regulators. Compliance is critical in industries such as healthcare, finance, and retail, where strict regulations govern the handling, processing, and storage of sensitive data. Organizations that fail to meet compliance standards risk facing severe legal and financial penalties, as well as reputational damage. As a result, compliance audits are necessary not only to ensure regulatory adherence but also to maintain customer trust and secure business relationships.

Key Components of Compliance Audits:

- Ensure alignment with regulatory frameworks like ISO/IEC 27001, HIPAA, Sarbarnes-Oxley Act (SOX), GDPR, Digital Operational Resilience Act (DORA), Network and Information Systems Directive (NIS2), etc.

- Use Governance, Risk, and Compliance (GRC) platforms like RSA Archer or ServiceNow GRC to track compliance and manage evidence.

- Automated compliance scanning tools such as Tenable Compliance Management or Qualys Compliance verify configuration compliance.

The primary purpose of a compliance audit is to ensure that the organization's operations align with relevant laws and regulations, such as ISO/IEC 27001, HIPAA, SOX, GDPR, DORA, NIS2, etc. During the audit, assessors use established checklists and frameworks derived from these standards to evaluate the organization's security practices across critical areas, including access management, data protection, incident response, and overall risk management. By following predefined templates, auditors can ensure that they are assessing all areas of concern and that the organization is maintaining the necessary controls to mitigate risk and comply with regulatory obligations. GRC platforms such as RSA Archer and ServiceNow GRC are commonly employed to help auditors streamline their efforts by offering centralized dashboards for tracking compliance metrics, managing evidence, and facilitating corrective actions. These tools ensure that all evidence required for compliance reporting is properly documented and readily available.

Automated compliance scanning tools, like Tenable Compliance Management or Qualys Compliance, are also frequently utilized in compliance audits to verify that the organization's configurations meet regulatory benchmarks. These tools automate the scanning process, reducing the manual effort involved in assessing configurations and ensuring that they meet established standards. Compliance audits are an indispensable part of an organization's cybersecurity framework, as they provide an objective assessment of the organization's adherence to legal and regulatory requirements, and they offer a roadmap for any necessary corrective actions to mitigate compliance gaps.

Risk-Based Audits

Imagine there is a family history of heart disease. Doctor would pay extra attention to the cardiovascular health, right? That is what risk-based audits do – they focus on the biggest potential problems.

How It Works?

- *Priority Assessment*: Like focusing on high-risk health factors in family history.

- *Custom Testing*: Like getting additional screening if they are at risk for certain conditions.

- *Targeted Protection*: Like taking extra precautions if they are predisposed to certain health issues.

Use special tools to

- Find the most valuable digital assets (like identifying the most critical health concerns).

- Predict possible attacks (like predicting potential health problems).

- Check for specific vulnerabilities (like screening for particular diseases).

Risk-based audits are distinct from regular and compliance audits in that they prioritize and focus on identifying and addressing areas of the organization's infrastructure that present the highest risks to security and operations. Unlike fixed-scope audits, which follow a rigid checklist approach, risk-based audits are dynamic and adaptive, allowing auditors to concentrate their efforts on the most vulnerable parts of the organization. This type of audit is particularly useful for organizations that face rapidly changing threats or have limited resources and need to prioritize mitigating the most critical risks.

Key Components of Risk-Based Audits:

- Focus on high-risk areas and vulnerable assets using Operationally Critical Threat, Asset, and Vulnerability Evaluation (OCTAVE) or Factor Analysis of Information Risk (FAIR) risk assessment methodologies.

- Identify critical assets with AssetSonar or SolarWinds for prioritizing security efforts.

- Use Spoofing, Tampering, Repudiation, Information Disclosure, Denial of Service, and Elevation of Privilege (STRIDE) threat modeling to predict attack vectors and security gaps.

The primary goal of a risk-based audit is to assess the organization's overall cybersecurity posture by identifying and prioritizing high-risk areas within its infrastructure. Risk-based audits rely on risk assessment methodologies, such as OCTAVE or FAIR, which help auditors evaluate the likelihood and potential impact of various security threats. These methodologies offer a structured approach for identifying risks and determining which areas require immediate attention. Risk-based audits are also highly dependent on asset discovery tools, such as AssetSonar or SolarWinds Internet Protocol (IP) Address Manager, which help auditors identify and catalog critical systems, applications, and infrastructure components that need to be prioritized for security assessments.

In addition to asset discovery, auditors employ threat modeling techniques like STRIDE to identify and anticipate possible attack vectors and security gaps in the organization's defense mechanisms. These models help auditors pinpoint areas where an attacker may be able to exploit weaknesses in the organization's security infrastructure. Vulnerability scanning tools, such as Nessus, QualysGuard, and Rapid7 InsightVM, are then used to identify exploitable weaknesses in high-risk assets, ensuring that vulnerabilities are discovered and addressed before they can be exploited by malicious actors. By focusing on high-risk areas, risk-based audits help organizations prioritize their security efforts and allocate resources efficiently, reducing exposure to critical threats.

Risk-based audits are valuable because they enable organizations to focus their security efforts on the most vulnerable and high-risk areas, ensuring that their defenses are tailored to address the most significant threats to the organization's assets and operations.

Specialized Audits

Sometimes it is needed to see a specialist – maybe a cardiologist, dermatologist, or neurologist. In cybersecurity, there are specialized audits for specific aspects of the digital health.

CHAPTER 1   INTRODUCTION TO CYBERSECURITY AUDITS

In addition to regular, compliance, and risk-based audits, organizations may also require specialized audits that address specific security concerns or areas of operation. Specialized audits are typically designed to assess the security posture in particular domains such as cloud security, privacy, third-party vendor risks, and application security. Each of these specialized audits requires unique approaches and tools to address the specific risks associated with that area, providing a deeper level of analysis, and ensuring that the organization's security measures are comprehensive and robust.

Types of Digital Specialists:

- *Cloud Security Specialists*: Like seeing a respiratory specialist to check how well is the breathing in the cloud.

- *Privacy Experts*: Like visiting a specialist who ensures personal health information stays confidential.

- *Vendor Security Specialists*: Think of this as checking the health and safety standards of all medical suppliers.

- *Application Security Specialists*: Like having a specialist check specific organs or body systems.

Key Areas of Specialized Audits:

- *Cloud Security Audits*: Evaluate encryption, access controls, and incident response protocols in cloud environments.

- *Privacy Audits*: Ensure compliance with privacy regulations like GDPR and California Consumer Privacy Act (CCPA) in handling personal data.

- *Third-Party Vendor Audits*: Assess security practices of external vendors to mitigate supply chain risks.

- *Application Security Audits*: Identify vulnerabilities in custom-developed applications, ensuring secure development practices.

For example, cloud security audits focus on assessing the security of cloud-based infrastructures, including both public and private cloud environments. These audits evaluate the security controls provided by cloud service providers and assess the organization's own security measures, such as data encryption, access control mechanisms, and incident response plans. Privacy audits, on the other hand, ensure that the organization is complying with privacy regulations like GDPR and CCPA, which govern the collection, processing, and storage of personal data. Privacy audits typically assess data protection practices, user consent mechanisms, and data retention policies to ensure that the organization is meeting the necessary legal and regulatory requirements.

Third-party vendor audits are increasingly important in today's interconnected business environment. These audits evaluate the security posture of external partners, suppliers, and service providers to ensure that they meet the organization's security requirements and do not pose an additional risk to the organization's overall cybersecurity. Application security audits focus on identifying vulnerabilities in custom-developed applications, reviewing source code for security flaws, and ensuring that secure development practices are followed. These specialized audits provide a deeper level of insight into specific areas of security, helping organizations maintain a strong overall cybersecurity posture while addressing niche security concerns.

Putting It All Together: Your Complete Health Plan

Just as good health requires different types of medical attention, good cybersecurity needs different types of audits.

Here Is How They Work Together:

- Regular audits keep healthy day-to-day.
- Compliance audits make sure of meeting official standards.
- Risk-based audits focus on the biggest concerns.
- Specialized audits dig deep into specific areas.

Key Takeaways

Just as you would not skip your medical check-ups, you should never skip these important cybersecurity audits. They are essential for maintaining a healthy, secure, and resilient digital organization.

In this section, we covered the following points:

- *Cybersecurity Audits as Healthcare for the Organization*:
  - Cybersecurity audits are like a healthcare system for the organization's digital health, with different types of audits serving distinct roles.
  - Knowing when to use each audit type and how they work together provides a complete picture of the organization's security health.
- *The Role of Cybersecurity Audits*:
  - Audits provide insights into the effectiveness of security measures and ensure compliance with legal and regulatory requirements.
  - The four main types of audits are: Regular Audits; Compliance Audits; Risk-Based Audits; Specialized Audits
- *Building a Comprehensive Approach to Cybersecurity*:
  - Understanding the different types of audits and the tools used in each helps organizations develop a comprehensive, proactive approach to protecting infrastructure from cyber threats.

Common Cybersecurity Risks Audits Aim to Mitigate

Cybersecurity audits play a vital role in identifying, assessing, and mitigating the risks that can compromise an organization's information technology systems. The goal of an audit is not only to find weaknesses but also to provide organizations with the necessary insights to fortify their defenses and ensure that regulatory compliance is maintained. By highlighting potential risks and recommending improvements, cybersecurity audits help organizations stay ahead of cyber threats, reduce the chances of a breach, and protect sensitive data. In this section, some of the most common cybersecurity risks that audits seek to mitigate and how these risks are addressed during the auditing process.

Just like there are common health risks we all need to watch out for – heart disease, diabetes, or the flu – there are common cybersecurity risks that every organization faces. Let us look at what these "digital diseases" are and how the security check-ups help prevent them.

CHAPTER 1   INTRODUCTION TO CYBERSECURITY AUDITS

Insider Threats

Imagine you have gotten a perfectly secure house with state-of-the-art locks, but someone inside keeps leaving the back door open. That is what it is called an insider threat. It comes in two flavors:

- *The Accident Prone*: Like someone who forgets to wash their hands and spreads germs unintentionally, some employees accidentally create security risks by clicking suspicious links or sharing passwords.

- *The Deliberate Actor*: Like someone deliberately contaminating the office coffee pot, these are individuals who intentionally misuse their access to cause harm.

Insider threats represent one of the most challenging risks to mitigate, as they involve individuals with authorized access to an organization's systems, such as employees or contractors. Insider threats can be intentional (malicious) or unintentional (negligent), and both types pose significant security risks. Intentional insider threats could involve employees stealing sensitive data or sabotaging systems, while unintentional threats often stem from negligence, such as clicking on phishing links or mishandling sensitive information.

During a cybersecurity audit, insiders' access to systems and sensitive data is closely evaluated. Auditors review access controls, including policies governing user roles and permissions, and assess whether access is appropriately restricted based on job responsibilities. Tools such as activity monitoring software are used to detect unusual or unauthorized behavior, such as data exfiltration or attempts to access restricted systems. Additionally, training programs are evaluated to ensure that employees are properly educated on security policies and best practices to avoid making costly mistakes.

Weak or Inadequate Access Controls

Think of access controls like the locks and keys in the building. Having weak access controls is like

- Using the same key for every door.
- Never changing the locks when someone moves out.
- Giving everyone a master key when they only need access to one room.

Access control is fundamental in securing an organization's IT infrastructure. Access control risks arise when mechanisms to limit user access to systems or data based on their role are weak or improperly configured. This can lead to unauthorized access, data breaches, or misuse of systems. A weak access control system may grant users excessive privileges or fail to implement necessary restrictions on sensitive data, allowing attackers or insiders to exploit these vulnerabilities.

Cybersecurity audits examine access control policies to ensure they follow best practices, such as Role-Based Access Control (RBAC) or Least Privilege Access. Auditors also review the implementation of Multi-Factor Authentication (MFA), a critical security layer that helps prevent unauthorized access even if user credentials are compromised. Regular audits are essential to ensure that user access rights are regularly reviewed and adjusted as necessary to prevent over-privileged access.

Insecure Configurations and Misconfigurations

Imagine buying a new smart home system but never changing the default password from "1234" – that is, what is called a misconfiguration. It is like

- Leaving Wi-Fi network open with no password.
- Never updating home security system.
- Keeping all the doors and windows unlocked.

During audits, it is looked for these "unlocked doors" using special tools that check for common misconfigurations.

Misconfigurations in IT systems, such as default passwords, open ports, or incorrect firewall rules, can create significant vulnerabilities in an organization's network. These misconfigurations are often exploited by attackers to gain unauthorized access to systems or data. Insecure configurations, which can occur across various IT environments, such as servers, routers, or cloud infrastructure are one of the most common causes of security breaches.

Cybersecurity audits focus on identifying and rectifying these misconfigurations. Auditors use tools such as Center for Internet Security Configuration Assessment Tool (CIS-CAT) or OpenSCAP to perform automated checks for common security misconfigurations. These tools help auditors identify weak points in an organization's infrastructure and ensure that configurations align with security best practices, such as disabling unused ports, enforcing strong password policies, and ensuring proper firewall rules are in place.

Lack of Patch Management

Think of patches like vaccines or medicine for the computer systems. Not applying patches is like

- Ignoring doctor's prescribed medication.
- Skipping flu shot.
- Refusing to take antibiotics for an infection.

A lack of timely patching of software vulnerabilities can leave an organization exposed to cyberattacks. Attackers often exploit known vulnerabilities that could have been mitigated by applying security patches and software updates. If an organization's patch management process is inefficient, critical vulnerabilities may remain unpatched for extended periods, creating an open door for cybercriminals.

Cybersecurity audits involve reviewing an organization's patch management process to ensure that patches are applied regularly and in a timely manner. Auditors assess whether the organization has a structured process for monitoring and testing patches before deployment and check whether critical vulnerabilities have been promptly addressed. The audit may also include an assessment of the organization's ability to handle zero-day vulnerabilities, those that have not yet been patched by the software vendor by reviewing alternative mitigation strategies, such as enhanced monitoring or network segmentation.

Data Privacy Risks

This is like maintaining doctor-patient confidentiality, but for digital data. Privacy risks are like

- Leaving medical records out in the open.
- Discussing patient details in public.
- Storing sensitive information without proper protection.

Data privacy is a growing concern, especially for organizations handling sensitive Personally Identifiable Information (PII) or Patient Health Information (PHI). Breaches of personal data can have devastating consequences, both legally and financially. Regulations such as the GDPR, CCPA, and HIPAA require organizations to adopt stringent data privacy practices to protect individuals' personal data.

Audits focused on data privacy assess how well an organization's systems and practices align with privacy regulations. Auditors review how sensitive data is collected, stored, encrypted, and processed to ensure compliance with privacy laws. They also evaluate data minimization strategies to ensure that only the necessary data is collected, reducing the risk of exposure. Additionally, auditors verify that privacy policies are clear and communicated to both employees and customers, and that employees are trained in proper data handling procedures.

Insufficient Incident Response Planning

Not having an incident response plan is like a hospital without an emergency room protocol. You need to know what to do when things go wrong. Cybersecurity audits check if you have

- A clear emergency response plan (like hospital triage procedures).
- Assigned emergency responders (like having doctors on call).
- Regular emergency drills (like fire drills).

Even the most robust cybersecurity defenses can be compromised. When a breach occurs, having a well-defined Incident Response Plan (IRP) is crucial to minimizing damage, reducing downtime, and ensuring a quick recovery. An insufficient or poorly executed incident response plan can lead to extended downtime, increased costs, and more significant damage from the breach.

Cybersecurity audits assess the effectiveness of an organization's incident response plan by reviewing the procedures in place for detecting, responding to, and recovering from security incidents. Auditors evaluate whether the organization has identified key personnel, defined response roles, and established communication protocols for crisis management. Assessing the effectiveness of the plan through tabletop exercises and simulated breaches is a common part of audits to ensure the organization is well-prepared for any security event.

CHAPTER 1   INTRODUCTION TO CYBERSECURITY AUDITS

Third-Party Risks

Collaborating with other companies is like referring patients to specialists – you need to make sure they maintain the same high standards you do. Cybersecurity auditor checks

- If the partners follow good security practices (like checking if specialists are properly certified).
- How data is shared (like ensuring proper transfer of medical records).
- What security agreements are in place (like having proper medical liability coverage).

Organizations increasingly rely on third-party vendors and service providers for various business functions, such as cloud storage, payroll, or software solutions. While this reliance can enhance efficiency, it also introduces significant cybersecurity risks. Third-party vendors can function as a gateway for attackers if their security measures are not up to requirements.

Auditors assess third-party risks by reviewing the vendor management process, ensuring that vendors meet the organization's security standards. This includes evaluating whether third-party providers follow secure protocols for data transfer, whether access controls are in place, and how vendor access is monitored. Cybersecurity audits also ensure that appropriate Service Level Agreements (SLAs) and Data Protection Agreements (DPAs) are in place to hold vendors accountable for their cybersecurity practices.

Social Engineering and Phishing Attacks

This is like falling for snake oil salesmen in the digital age. Social engineering attacks are like

- Someone pretending to be a doctor to get access to records.
- Fake medications being sold as genuine.
- Scam health products being marketed as miracle cures.

Human error is often the weakest link in cybersecurity. Social engineering attacks, such as phishing, exploit human vulnerabilities by tricking individuals into providing sensitive information, clicking on malicious links, or downloading malware. Even the most advanced technical defenses cannot prevent these attacks if employees are not adequately trained.

CHAPTER 1　INTRODUCTION TO CYBERSECURITY AUDITS

Cybersecurity audits focus on assessing an organization's awareness of social engineering risks. Auditors review the effectiveness of employee security awareness training programs and test the organization's vulnerability through phishing simulations. These exercises help assess how well employees can identify suspicious emails and phishing attempts and respond appropriately. Continuous training and simulated attacks help improve employee readiness and reduce the likelihood of successful social engineering attacks.

Audit Types for Cybersecurity Risk

Table 1-3 presents the link between audit types and cybersecurity risk, as well as key area to focus.

Table 1-3. Common cybersecurity risks and the audit type most suitable for mitigating them

Cybersecurity Risk	Most Suitable Audit Type	Key Focus Areas of the Audit
Insider Threats	Access Control Audit	- Review user roles, permissions, and access logs. - Assess monitoring tools for detecting unusual behaviour. - Evaluate employee training programs.
Weak or Inadequate Access Controls	Access Management Audit	- Assess RBAC and Least Privilege Access. - Verify MFA implementation. - Ensure periodic reviews of access rights.
Insecure Configurations	Configuration and Vulnerability Assessment Audit	- Identify misconfigurations using tools like CIS-CAT or OpenSCAP. - Verify compliance with security benchmarks. - Check for unused ports, strong passwords, and proper firewall rules.
Lack of Patch Management	Patch Management Audit	- Review patch deployment processes and timelines.- Assess zero-day vulnerability handling strategies.- Verify monitoring and testing protocols for patches.

(*continued*)

CHAPTER 1   INTRODUCTION TO CYBERSECURITY AUDITS

Table 1-3. (*continued*)

Cybersecurity Risk	Most Suitable Audit Type	Key Focus Areas of the Audit
Data Privacy Risks	Data Privacy and Compliance Audit	- Check adherence to GDPR, CCPA, HIPAA, etc. - Evaluate data collection, storage, encryption, and minimization strategies. - Review privacy policy communication and employee training.
Insufficient Incident Response Planning	Incident Response Audit	- Assess the existence and effectiveness of IRPs. - Verify role assignments and communication protocols. - Evaluate readiness through tabletop exercises and simulations.
Third-Party Risks	Third-Party Risk Management Audit	- Review vendor security standards and data protection agreements (SLAs/DPAs). - Assess data transfer protocols and access control measures. - Evaluate vendor monitoring and accountability practices.
Social Engineering and Phishing Attacks	Security Awareness and Training Audit	- Assess effectiveness of security awareness programs. - Review phishing simulations and training exercises. - Evaluate employee readiness to recognize and respond to threats.

Key Takeaways

Prevention is always better than cure, in both medical and cyber health! Cybersecurity audits are essential for proactively protecting your organization from digital threats.

In this section, we covered the following points:

- *Cybersecurity Audits as Regular Check-Ups*:
  - Just like good health requires awareness of common diseases and their prevention, cybersecurity means understanding and protecting against common digital threats.

- Cybersecurity audits function as regular check-ups, ensuring protection against these digital health risks in an increasingly connected world.

- *Identifying and Mitigating Common Risks*:
  - Cybersecurity audits help identify and mitigate common risks such as: Insider threats; Weak access controls; Misconfigurations; Patch management failures; Data privacy risks.
  - These audits help organizations strengthen defenses, prevent breaches, and maintain compliance with regulations.

- *Continuous Improvement and Vigilance*:
  - Through regular audits and continuous improvement, organizations can ensure they remain vigilant against evolving cyber threats and safeguard valuable assets.

The Importance of a Risk-Based Approach in Cybersecurity Audits

Imagine you are a doctor with limited time and resources. You would not spend the same amount of time checking a patient's stubbed toe as you would their chest pain, right? That is exactly what a risk-based approach to cybersecurity is all about.

Think of it this way: If you had 100 houses to protect but only 10 security guards, you would not spread them evenly – one guard for every 10 houses. Instead, you had put more guards around the houses with valuable art collections and fewer around empty vacation homes. That is risk-based security in action!

Cybersecurity audits are a vital tool for identifying, assessing, and mitigating risks within an organization's IT infrastructure. With the increasingly sophisticated and dynamic nature of cyber threats, organizations must prioritize their cybersecurity efforts to stay ahead. A risk-based approach to cybersecurity audits addresses this challenge by focusing resources on the areas of greatest potential harm. Unlike traditional audits, which treat all systems and processes equally, a risk-based audit evaluates systems based on their vulnerabilities, the likelihood of attacks, and the potential consequences of those attacks. In the following are explored the key components of a risk-based approach, its benefits, how it can be implemented, and the technologies that enable it.

CHAPTER 1 INTRODUCTION TO CYBERSECURITY AUDITS

What Is a Risk-Based Approach?

A risk-based approach to cybersecurity audits involves identifying, evaluating, and prioritizing risks based on their likelihood and potential impact. This strategy ensures that audit resources are directed toward high-priority areas that pose the greatest threat to the organization's security and compliance. Traditional audit methods typically assess systems uniformly, regardless of their risk profile. In contrast, a risk-based audit focuses on addressing the most critical vulnerabilities that could lead to a data breach, financial loss, or reputational damage.

By using a risk-based approach, organizations can better allocate resources to where they are most needed, enhancing the effectiveness of their cybersecurity efforts. Additionally, this approach allows for a more proactive and dynamic strategy, addressing evolving threats and continuously improving security posture.

Key Components of a Risk-Based Cybersecurity Audit

The risk-based cybersecurity audit process involves several key components to effectively identify and mitigate risks.

Risk Identification

Just like a doctor first asks about the symptoms and family history, auditors starts by identifying potential threats. They use special tools (think of them as digital stethoscopes and X-ray machines) to spot where trouble might be brewing.

The first step in a risk-based approach is identifying the threats that could exploit vulnerabilities within the organization. This involves understanding both internal and external risks and how they might affect critical assets and operations. Tools like Threat Intelligence Platforms (TIPs) (e.g., Recorded Future, ThreatConnect) can provide insights into emerging risks by monitoring the threat landscape.

Risk Assessment

Let us play a game of "what if?" Just like doctors assess:

- How likely are you to get heart disease? (family history and lifestyle)
- How bad would it be if you did? (age and overall health)

Audit assesses digital risks the same way:

- How likely is a cyber-attack?
- How bad would it be if it happened?

Once risks have been identified, the next step is assessing their potential impact and likelihood. This assessment allows auditors to determine which risks pose the greatest threat to the organization. Frameworks like OCTAVE or FAIR can be leveraged to quantify risks and create risk profiles for various systems.

Risk Prioritization

Remember how do emergency rooms use triage? They treated the heart attack before the sprained ankle. Auditors do the same thing with security risks:

- *High Priority*: Like chest pain (needs immediate attention).
- *Medium Priority*: Like a broken arm (important but not life-threatening).
- *Low Priority*: Like a paper cut (can wait).

After assessing the likelihood and impact of each risk, the next step is to prioritize them. Tools like risk heat maps are commonly used to visually represent risk levels and guide decision-making. By ranking risks based on their criticality, auditors can focus their efforts on the most significant threats, ensuring that audit resources are allocated efficiently.

Control Effectiveness Evaluation

Auditors look at what protection is already in place:

- Are digital antibiotics working? (firewalls and antivirus)
- Is the security immune system strong? (access controls)
- Are digital vitamins up to date? (software patches)

Auditors must evaluate the current security controls in place to mitigate identified risks. This includes reviewing firewall configurations, access controls, encryption mechanisms, and other technical measures. The effectiveness of these controls is

CHAPTER 1   INTRODUCTION TO CYBERSECURITY AUDITS

assessed to determine if they are sufficient to protect against the identified risks. Vulnerability scanners like Qualys or Nessus can be used to assess the strength of these controls.

Focus on High-Risk Areas

Just like a doctor spends more time with high-risk patients, auditors focus more attention on the most critical systems:

- Extra care for "vital organs" (crucial databases).
- More frequent check-ups for "at-risk" areas.
- Special treatment for sensitive information.

The final component of a risk-based audit is to ensure that the audit focuses on high-risk areas. This involves conducting detailed assessments of systems, processes, or assets that are most vulnerable to attacks. Penetration testing or red team exercises can be used to simulate real-world attacks and assess how well these high-risk areas stand up to potential threats.

Risk Management Process Flow

Figure 1-1 describes the key components of the risk management process on cybersecurity audits.

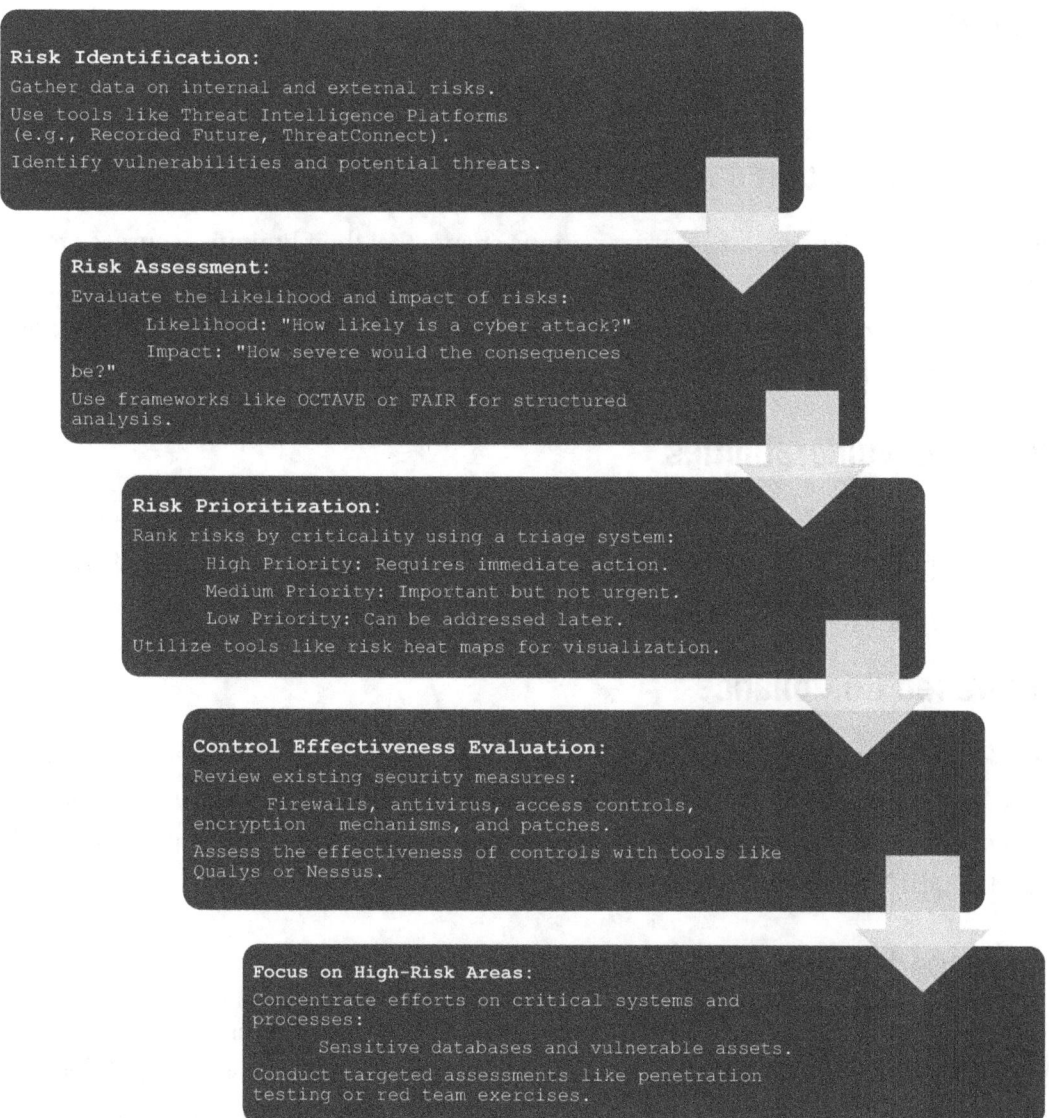

Figure 1-1. *Risk management process flow*

CHAPTER 1   INTRODUCTION TO CYBERSECURITY AUDITS

Benefits of a Risk-Based Approach

Implementing a risk-based approach offers several key benefits for organizations.

Enhanced Resource Allocation

By focusing on high-risk areas, organizations ensure that their limited resources are used effectively to address critical security concerns. Rather than spreading resources thin across all systems, the risk-based approach ensures that efforts are concentrated where they can have the most impact.

Reduced Vulnerabilities

Prioritizing high-risk areas enables organizations to address vulnerabilities before they can be exploited. This proactive approach reduces the likelihood of successful attacks and strengthens the overall security posture of the organization.

Improved Compliance

A risk-based approach aligns with many regulatory frameworks that emphasize risk management as a core principle. By identifying and addressing high-priority risks, organizations can demonstrate their commitment to compliance with regulations such as GDPR, HIPAA, and ISO/IEC 27001.

Increased Stakeholder Confidence

Focusing on the most critical risks assures stakeholders, including customers, partners, and regulators, that the organization is committed to protecting sensitive data and maintaining robust cybersecurity practices. This increased confidence can help build trust and improve the organization's reputation.

Implementing a Risk-Based Approach

Implementing a risk-based approach to cybersecurity audits requires careful planning and execution. The following steps can guide organizations in adopting this strategic approach.

Define the Scope

The first step is to identify the organization's critical assets, including databases, applications, and networks. Understanding how sensitive data moves within the organization is essential for determining which systems and processes require the most attention. Tools like data flow diagrams can be useful for visualizing data movement and identifying areas of vulnerability.

Conduct a Risk Assessment

Once the scope is defined, the next step is to conduct a risk assessment. This involves identifying potential threats to the organization and evaluating the vulnerabilities within its systems. Relevant tools should be used to assess risk levels, and each risk should be assigned a score based on its potential impact and likelihood.

Prioritize High-Risk Areas

Using heat maps or risk matrices, auditors can rank identified risks and determine which ones should be addressed first. This helps ensure that audit resources are focused on systems that handle sensitive information or are particularly vulnerable to attacks.

Audit High-Risk Areas

The audit process should then focus on high-risk areas, where the greatest vulnerabilities are identified. Detailed assessments should be performed on these systems, including penetration testing and other techniques to assess the effectiveness of current security controls.

Report Findings

After completing the audit, auditors should compile their findings into actionable reports. These reports should highlight high-priority risks and provide recommendations for mitigating them. Clear and concise communication of these findings will help stakeholders understand the severity of risks and the steps needed to address them.

Technologies That Enable Risk-Based Audits

Several technologies can facilitate the implementation of a risk-based approach in cybersecurity audits:

- *Vulnerability Scanning Tools*: Tools like Qualys and Nessus help identify vulnerabilities in systems and prioritize them based on severity.

- *Risk Assessment Frameworks*: Standards like ISO 31000 and methodologies like FAIR provide guidance on evaluating and managing risks systematically.

- *TIPs*: Solutions like Recorded Future and ThreatConnect help identify emerging threats, which are essential for guiding risk prioritization.

- *Penetration Testing Tools*: Tools like Burp Suite and Metasploit simulate real-world attacks, allowing auditors to assess vulnerabilities in high-risk systems.

- *SIEM Systems*: SIEM platforms like Splunk and LogRhythm help analyze logs and detect suspicious activities.

Challenges of a Risk-Based Approach

While effective, a risk-based approach presents several challenges:

- *Accurate Risk Identification*: Misidentifying risks can lead to wasted resources or the overlooking of critical vulnerabilities.

- *Evolving Threat Landscape*: As the threat landscape evolves, audits must remain adaptable to account for new and emerging risks.

- *Stakeholder Buy-In*: Convincing management to prioritize specific risks may require detailed explanations supported by data.

Practical Example: Risk-Based Audit in Action

To illustrate the practical application of a risk-based approach, consider a healthcare institution conducting a cybersecurity audit. The audit team identifies an increase in phishing attacks targeting the healthcare sector through a TIP. Given the potential for breaches of sensitive health data, phishing is prioritized as a high-risk area. The team assesses the organization's email filtering system and conducts simulated phishing exercises, revealing that 10% of employees clicked on phishing links. Based on these findings, the audit team recommends implementing advanced phishing filters, conducting mandatory employee training, and increasing the frequency of phishing simulations.

Key Takeaways

Prevention is better than cure, but to be effective, you need to know what to prevent first! A risk-based approach ensures that resources are used wisely to protect against the most critical threats.

In this section, we covered the following points:

- *Risk-Based Approach as a Smart Doctor*:
    - A risk-based approach is like having a smart doctor who knows where to look and what to prioritize. Instead of giving every patient the same check-up, the doctor focuses on what matters most for each individual's health.
    - In cybersecurity, this approach means protecting what's most important first, using resources wisely, and staying ahead of potential problems.
- *Focusing on High-Risk Areas*:
    - A risk-based approach enables organizations to focus on the areas that pose the greatest threat to their security and compliance.
    - By identifying and prioritizing risks based on likelihood and impact, organizations can optimize resources and strengthen defenses against emerging threats.
- *Adapting to an Evolving Threat Landscape*:
    - As the cybersecurity threat landscape evolves, adopting a risk-based approach is key to maintaining a proactive and effective cybersecurity strategy.

CHAPTER 1   INTRODUCTION TO CYBERSECURITY AUDITS

Key Compliance Frameworks in Cybersecurity Audits

Compliance frameworks play a crucial role in cybersecurity audits by providing a structured approach to securing systems, protecting data, and ensuring legal compliance. These frameworks help organizations align their cybersecurity practices with industry standards, regulatory requirements, and best practices, while also enhancing security defenses against evolving threats. By selecting the right framework for their specific industry, data type, and legal obligations, organizations can effectively mitigate risks and improve their overall cybersecurity posture.

Think of compliance frameworks like medical guidelines or health codes. Just as restaurants need to follow food safety rules and hospitals need to follow medical protocols, organizations need to follow security standards. These are not just random rules – they are like tried-and-tested recipes for keeping digital business healthy.

In the following are explored the most widely recognized compliance frameworks, their key components, and the role they play in cybersecurity audits.

Key Compliance Frameworks

There are several compliance frameworks that auditors rely on to assess an organization's cybersecurity practices. These frameworks vary based on industry needs, regional regulations, and specific security objectives.

Some of the most common regulations/frameworks include the following.

NIST Cybersecurity Framework (CSF)

The NIST CSF, developed by the National Institute of Standards and Technology, is not mandatory, but it is designed to help organizations manage and reduce cybersecurity risks. It focuses on a risk-based approach, allowing organizations to identify vulnerabilities and implement effective controls.

Focus: Managing and reducing cybersecurity risks across the entire organization.

Core Functions:

- *Govern*: Establish cybersecurity governance.
- *Identify*: Assess risk, assets, and vulnerabilities.
- *Protect*: Implement safeguards to reduce risks.

- *Detect*: Continuously monitor for anomalies and potential threats.
- *Respond*: Develop and implement a response plan for potential incidents.
- *Recover*: Restore capabilities and services after a cybersecurity event.

ISO/IEC 27001

The ISO/IEC 27001 standard provides a framework for establishing, implementing, operating, and improving an Information Security Management System (ISMS). This internationally recognized standard helps organizations protect their sensitive information through a systematic approach to managing security risks.

Focus: Establishing and improving an ISMS that ensures the confidentiality, integrity, and availability of information.

Core Elements:

- *Risk Assessment*: Identifying and managing security risks.
- *Asset Management*: Ensuring critical assets are properly secured.
- *Access Controls*: Protecting information systems from unauthorized access.
- *Continuous Improvement*: Regularly reviewing and improving security practices.

Payment Card Industry Data Security Standard (PCI DSS)

The PCI DSS framework focuses on securing credit card transactions and protecting cardholder data. This standard is essential for organizations that store, process, or transmit credit card information, ensuring the integrity and security of sensitive financial data.

Focus: Securing credit card transactions and protecting cardholder data.

Key Controls:

- *Data Encryption*: Ensuring the confidentiality of payment data.
- *Access Controls*: Restricting access to cardholder data.
- *Vulnerability Assessments*: Regularly testing for vulnerabilities in systems that handle payment data.

Health Insurance Portability and Accountability Act (HIPAA)

The HIPAA framework is designed to protect patient health information, especially in the healthcare industry. HIPAA compliance is essential for healthcare organizations to ensure the confidentiality, integrity, and security of sensitive health information.

Focus: Protecting PHIs and ensuring compliance with privacy and security regulations.

Key Requirements:

- *Risk Assessments*: Identifying potential threats to PHI.
- *Training*: Providing staff with training on security and privacy best practices.
- *Access Controls*: Restricting access to PHI based on the need-to-know principle.

General Data Protection Regulation (GDPR)

The GDPR framework, enacted by the European Union, sets forth stringent requirements for organizations that handle personal data. It emphasizes the protection of privacy and the rights of individuals in relation to their personal data.

Focus: Safeguarding personal data and ensuring privacy rights.

Key Components:

- *Data Subject Rights*: Providing individuals with control over their personal data.
- *Lawful Processing*: Ensuring data is processed legally and transparently.
- *Breach Notifications*: Notifying individuals and authorities of data breaches in a timely manner.

Digital Operational Resilience Act (DORA)

DORA is a regulation introduced by the European Union to enhance the resilience of financial entities against Information and Communication Technology (ICT)-related disruptions. Effective from January 17, 2025, DORA aims to strengthen the security and operational stability of the European Union (EU) financial ecosystem.

Focus: Incident reporting, ICT risk management, and testing to ensure robust operational resilience.

Core Elements:

- *Incident Reporting*: Establish streamlined processes for reporting major ICT-related incidents to relevant authorities within specified timelines.

- *Risk Management*: Implement comprehensive ICT risk management frameworks to identify, assess, and mitigate potential threats.

- *Testing*: Conduct regular resilience testing to ensure that systems, processes, and tools can withstand cyberattacks and operational disruptions.

- *Impact*: By enforcing these measures, DORA bolsters the overall security and resilience of financial entities, fostering trust and stability across the EU financial ecosystem.

NIS2 Directive

The NIS2 Directive is the updated version of the original NIS Directive, designed to strengthen cybersecurity across critical sectors in the European Union. It has been in effect since October 17, 2024, and targets sectors such as energy, healthcare, and transportation.

Focus: Enhancing risk management, incident reporting, and supply chain security for critical sectors.

Core Elements:

- *Risk Management*: Establish robust frameworks to proactively manage and mitigate cybersecurity risks.

- *Incident Reporting*: Mandate timely reporting of significant incidents to national authorities to ensure rapid response and coordination.

CHAPTER 1   INTRODUCTION TO CYBERSECURITY AUDITS

- *Supply Chain Security*: Require organizations to assess and mitigate cybersecurity risks in their supply chains, ensuring the security of interconnected systems.

- *Impact*: The NIS2 Directive harmonizes cybersecurity practices across EU member states, ensuring a consistent and strengthened approach to protecting critical infrastructure and services.

Regulation (EU) 2024/2847

REGULATION (EU) 2024/2847 introduces updated rules for digital service providers, including cloud platforms and other key digital infrastructure providers. This regulation comes into effect on December 11, 2027, and aims to enhance transparency, security, and compliance within the digital services sector.

Focus: Increasing accountability through transparency, robust security measures, and adherence to regulatory requirements.

Core Elements:

- *Transparency*: Require digital service providers to provide clear information about their security practices, ensuring stakeholders can make informed decisions.

- *Security*: Enforce stricter security measures to protect digital infrastructure from cyber threats.

- *Regulatory Compliance*: Establish oversight mechanisms to ensure that digital service providers comply with EU regulations and standards.

- *Impact*: By fostering greater accountability and trust, this regulation enhances consumer confidence in digital services while ensuring a secure and reliable digital environment.

Comparison of Different Frameworks/Regulations

Table 1-4 presents a comparison of different frameworks and regulations related to cybersecurity.

CHAPTER 1 INTRODUCTION TO CYBERSECURITY AUDITS

Table 1-4. *Comparison of different frameworks/regulations*

Framework/ Regulation	Common Features with Others	Unique Features
NIST Cybersecurity Framework (CSF) 2.0	- Risk-based approach. - Focus on governance, protection, detection, and response. - Incident response planning. - Continuous monitoring.	- Voluntary adoption. - Structured into six core functions: Govern, Identify, Protect, Detect, Respond, Recover.
ISO/IEC 27001	- Risk management focus. - Emphasis on continuous improvement. - Includes access controls.	- Establishes a formal ISMS. - Globally recognized certification.
PCI DSS	- Requires data encryption and access control. - Includes vulnerability assessments.	- Specific to securing payment card transactions. - Mandates encryption for cardholder data.
HIPAA	- Focus on data protection. - Requires risk assessments. - Access control requirements.	- Specifically targets PHI. - Includes mandatory staff training on privacy/security.
GDPR	- Data protection and privacy rights. - Breach notification requirements.	- Strong emphasis on data subject rights. - Legal processing of personal data. - Applies globally to EU-related data.
DORA	- Risk management. - Incident reporting. - Regular testing requirements.	- Focused on financial entities' ICT resilience. - Targets the stability of the EU financial ecosystem.
NIS2 Directive	- Risk management. - Incident reporting. - Focus on supply chain security.	- Specifically enhances cybersecurity for critical sectors like energy, healthcare, and transport.
REGULATION (EU) 2024/2847	- Transparency and accountability. - Security requirements for digital services.	- Focused on digital service providers. - Enhanced consumer trust through mandatory transparency. - Comes into effect in 2027.

CHAPTER 1   INTRODUCTION TO CYBERSECURITY AUDITS

Why Compliance Frameworks Are Crucial in Cybersecurity Audits?

Compliance frameworks are essential tools for cybersecurity audits, offering several benefits.

Regulatory Compliance

Frameworks ensure that organizations adhere to relevant laws, avoiding fines and penalties for non-compliance. By aligning with regulatory standards, organizations can minimize legal risks and avoid costly legal battles.

Risk Mitigation

Auditing against established frameworks helps identify and address vulnerabilities in systems, networks, and processes. Compliance with these frameworks ensures that critical risks are mitigated, reducing the likelihood of data breaches and security incidents.

Enhanced Security

Compliance frameworks promote the consistent implementation of robust security controls, which helps protect against evolving cyber threats. They ensure that organizations follow best practices and continuously improve their security measures.

Trust Building

By adhering to recognized compliance frameworks, organizations can demonstrate their commitment to security, building trust with customers, partners, and other stakeholders. Compliance is a key factor in gaining confidence and fostering long-term relationships with clients.

Industry Standardization

Compliance frameworks provide a common language and set of practices for cybersecurity, making it easier for organizations to collaborate and share information. This standardization simplifies the audit process and ensures that organizations meet the same cybersecurity expectations.

How Auditors Utilize Compliance Frameworks

Cybersecurity auditors rely on compliance frameworks to assess an organization's cybersecurity posture and ensure that it aligns with industry standards. Auditors typically engage in the following activities:

Reviewing Policies and Procedures

Auditors begin by reviewing the organization's policies and procedures to ensure they align with the selected compliance framework. This includes checking for adequate documentation, risk management practices, and security protocols.

Conducting Gap Analyses

Auditors perform gap analyses to identify areas where the organization is not in compliance with the framework. These gaps could relate to technical controls, policies, or operational processes that need improvement.

Testing Technical Controls

Auditors evaluate technical controls such as encryption, access management, and vulnerability assessments to ensure they are effective and in compliance with the relevant framework. This includes verifying that security controls are consistently applied across systems.

Verifying Evidence

Auditors verify evidence such as logs, training records, and incident reports to confirm compliance. They ensure that all necessary documentation is in place and that staff members are adequately trained to handle security and compliance requirements.

Challenges in Implementing Compliance Frameworks

While compliance frameworks offer clear benefits, organizations face several challenges when implementing them.

Complexity

Frameworks like ISO/IEC 27001 require extensive documentation, formal processes, and ongoing audits. The complexity of these frameworks can be overwhelming, particularly for smaller organizations with limited resources.

Metaphorically imagine trying to learn all the bones in the human body in one day – that is how complex some security frameworks can feel. Organizations often struggle because

- There is a lot to remember (like memorizing medical terminology).
- Everything needs to be documented (like keeping detailed patient records).
- Processes need to be followed exactly (like surgical procedures).

Costs

Implementing advanced security controls and compliance measures can be costly. Organizations may need to invest in new technologies, training, and personnel to meet compliance requirements, which can strain budgets.

Just as good healthcare is not cheap, good security comes with a price tag:

- New equipment needed (like buying modern medical devices).
- Staff training required (like continuing medical education).
- Expert help is necessary (like hiring specialists).

Think of it like setting up a new hospital wing – you need:

- The right equipment.
- Trained staff.
- Proper procedures.
- Regular maintenance.

Staying Updated

Compliance frameworks and regulatory requirements are constantly evolving. Organizations must stay current with updates to frameworks like GDPR, NIST, etc. to ensure continued compliance.

Integration

Aligning multiple frameworks, particularly for organizations operating across different regions or industries, can be resource intensive. Integrating various frameworks into a cohesive cybersecurity strategy requires careful planning and execution.

Imagine a patient seeing multiple doctors – they all need to work together and share information. Similarly, different security frameworks need to work together:

- Different departments have different needs.
- Various regulations might apply.
- Everything needs to work as one system.

Best Practices for Cybersecurity Auditors

Cybersecurity auditors play a vital role in ensuring that organizations comply with industry standards and frameworks. To conduct effective and efficient audits, auditors should follow these best practices:

Stay Updated

Given the fast-evolving nature of cybersecurity regulations, auditors must stay informed about changes to frameworks and emerging compliance requirements. Continuous learning is key to ensuring audits are current and relevant.

Just as doctors need to keep up with new medical discoveries:

- Stay current with security changes.
- Learn about new threats.
- Understand new protection methods.

Leverage Automation

Using GRC tools can streamline audits by automating manual tasks such as policy reviews, gap analysis, and reporting. Automation improves efficiency and reduces the risk of human error.

Think of automation tools like modern medical equipment:

- They make work faster (like digital X-rays vs. traditional ones).
- They are more accurate (like automated blood tests).
- They help spot problems (like medical scanning equipment).

Tailor Recommendations

Auditors should align their recommendations with the organization's goals, ensuring that actions taken to address compliance gaps also enhance overall security. Tailored recommendations increase the likelihood of successful implementation.

Just as every patient is different, every organization needs personalized recommendations:

- Consider their specific situation.
- Account for their resources.
- Focus on their biggest risks.

Foster a Compliance Culture

Building a strong compliance culture within the organization is essential. Auditors should encourage regular training and employee awareness programs to ensure that everyone understands the importance of security and compliance.

Just as doctors promote healthy living:

- Encourage good security practices.
- Promote awareness.
- Make security part of daily routine.

Making It Work: A Practical Approach

Think of implementing security frameworks like running a healthy hospital:

- *Start with the Basics*:
  - Like washing hands and basic hygiene.
  - Begin with fundamental security practices.
  - Build up gradually.

- *Focus on What Matters Most*:
  - Like treating the most serious conditions first.
  - Prioritize critical security measures.
  - Address high-risk areas immediately.
- *Train Your Team*:
  - Like teaching proper medical procedures.
  - Ensure everyone knows their role.
  - Make security part of the culture.
- *Regular Check-Ups*:
  - Like scheduled health screenings.
  - Monitor security regularly.
  - Catch problems early.

Key Takeaways

Start with what you can manage and gradually build up your security practices over time. Keep learning and improving to stay ahead of emerging threats, and always focus on what matters most: protecting the organization's critical assets. Make compliance and security practices part of the routine, just as health and safety are integral to running a hospital. While it may take extra effort, it's essential for ensuring the protection of what matters most.

In this section, we covered the following points:

- *Compliance Frameworks are Essential for Cybersecurity Audits*:
  - Compliance frameworks help organizations secure systems, protect data, and ensure adherence to legal requirements.
  - By selecting the right framework and following best practices, organizations can strengthen cybersecurity defenses, mitigate risks, and build trust with stakeholders.

- *Frameworks as Health Protocols*:
  - Following security frameworks is like following medical protocols – though initially complicated or costly, it is essential for maintaining the health and safety of systems and data.
  - Just as hospitals need proper procedures to protect patients, organizations need security frameworks to protect data and systems.
- *Key to Effective Audits and Continuous Improvement*:
  - Proficiency in key compliance frameworks empowers auditors to conduct effective assessments and contributes to the continuous improvement of cybersecurity practices across industries.

Cybersecurity Audit vs. Penetration Testing

Cybersecurity audits and penetration testing are two critical components of a comprehensive security strategy. Both play an important role in identifying vulnerabilities, enhancing protection, and ensuring compliance, but they differ significantly in terms of purpose, methodology, and outcomes. Understanding the distinctions between these two practices is essential for organizations seeking to strengthen their overall cybersecurity posture.

Think of cybersecurity as taking health care. Just as both regular check-ups and stress tests are needed to stay healthy, organizations need two key types of security assessments: cybersecurity audits and penetration testing.

The key differences between cybersecurity audits and penetration testing, how they complement each other, and best practices for their effective use are explored in the following.

Cybersecurity Audit: A Comprehensive Evaluation

A cybersecurity audit is an in-depth review of an organization's policies, procedures, and controls to assess how well it adheres to security standards, regulations, and best practices. The audit is focused on governance, compliance, and risk management rather than direct technical vulnerabilities. It examines internal processes, identifies gaps, and evaluates the effectiveness of existing security measures.

CHAPTER 1   INTRODUCTION TO CYBERSECURITY AUDITS

A cybersecurity audit is like the annual physical examination. Just as the doctor reviews medical history, checks vital signs, and ensures that health protocols are followed, auditors examine an organization's security policies and procedures. They are checking if the proper "security hygiene" is followed – like making sure that not only antibiotics are prescribed (security measures) but also that they are taken correctly (implementing them properly).

Key Features of Cybersecurity Audits:

- *Scope*: A cybersecurity audit covers a broad range of organizational aspects, including security policies, governance, access controls, employee behavior, and operational procedures. It ensures that the organization's security measures are aligned with industry standards and regulatory requirements.

- *Objective*: The primary objective of a cybersecurity audit is to verify that an organization's practices and controls are following relevant security frameworks, laws, and regulations (such as ISO 27001, GDPR, or NIST). Auditors also evaluate the effectiveness of security policies in mitigating risks and maintaining security governance.

- *Approach*: Auditors typically conduct document reviews, interviews with staff members, and control validation to assess policies and security frameworks. The audit is often qualitative and examines procedural adherence rather than technical exploitation.

- *Output*: The outcome of a cybersecurity audit is a comprehensive report that highlights findings, identifies any compliance gaps, and provides actionable recommendations for addressing these gaps. The report will also include a review of how well existing policies and procedures protect the organization.

Penetration Testing: Simulating Real-World Attacks

In contrast, penetration testing (or "pen testing") is a hands-on, technical approach to identifying security vulnerabilities by simulating real-world attacks on an organization's systems. The goal of penetration testing is to identify weaknesses in a system that could potentially be exploited by attackers.

Penetration testing is more like a stress test on a treadmill. Instead of just checking if the heart looks healthy on paper, the doctor wants to see how it performs under pressure. Penetration testers push systems to their limits, just like how a cardiologist monitors a heart when it is working its hardest. They are not just asking, "Do you have security?" but rather, "Does your security hold up when someone's actively trying to break it?"

Key Features of Penetration Testing:

- *Scope*: Penetration testing targets specific systems, applications, or networks within an organization. It is focused on the technical side of cybersecurity and aims to expose vulnerabilities that could be exploited by malicious actors.

- *Objective*: The main objective of penetration testing is to evaluate the security of specific systems by simulating attacks that could be launched by an external hacker or malicious insider. Pen testers exploit vulnerabilities to assess their severity and potential impact on the organization's security.

- *Approach*: Ethical hackers, also known as penetration testers, employ both manual and automated tools to simulate attacks. These testers attempt to gain unauthorized access, escalate privileges, or bypass security mechanisms, mimicking how cybercriminals might infiltrate a system.

- *Output*: The result of penetration testing is a detailed report that outlines identified vulnerabilities, ranks their severity, and provides remediation steps. The findings help organizations understand their security gaps and how they can improve their defenses.

Key Differences Between Cybersecurity Audits and Penetration Testing

While both cybersecurity audits and penetration testing are designed to improve an organization's security posture, they differ significantly in their approach, scope, and outcomes.

Table 1-5. Key differences between cybersecurity audit and penetration testing

	Cybersecurity audit	**Penetration testing**
Scope	Broad review of policies, controls, and compliance.	Specific focus on technical vulnerabilities and systems.
Objective	Ensure compliance with regulations and industry standards.	Identify and exploit vulnerabilities in systems or networks.
Approach	Document reviews, interviews, and control validation.	Simulated attacks using manual and automated techniques.
Output	Report on compliance gaps and recommendations.	Detailed list of vulnerabilities, risks, and remediation steps.
Timing	Periodic reviews, typically annual or biannual.	Conducted on demand or after significant changes or incidents.

How Cybersecurity Audits and Penetration Testing Complement Each Other

Although these practices serve different purposes, they are highly complementary and together provide a holistic approach to cybersecurity.

The beautiful synergy between these approaches mirrors modern healthcare. Think about it:

- *Prevention and Detection*:
  - Just as an annual physical helps prevent health issues (audit), the stress test finds hidden problems before they become critical (penetration testing).
  - The doctor checks both health records (policies) and actual physical condition (technical vulnerabilities).
- *Complementary Roles*:
  - A doctor would not just read medical history without also listening to the heart; similarly, organizations should not just review security policies without evaluating their effectiveness.

- Blood tests show what is happening internally (audit findings), while physical stress tests reveal how well the body responds to external challenges (penetration test results).

- *Risk Management*:
  - Just as some patients need more frequent check-ups due to hereditary conditions (high-risk industries), some systems require more rigorous security testing due to their sensitive nature.
  - Both approaches help create a comprehensive "treatment plan" for maintaining optimal health/security.

Compliance and Security

Audits ensure that an organization is following established security frameworks and regulations, which is crucial for maintaining compliance and legal protection.

Penetration testing complements audits by providing a real-world assessment of the organization's technical defenses. It uncovers potential weaknesses that may not be identified during a traditional audit.

Preventing Oversight

Audits focus on governance, controls, and policies but may miss system-specific vulnerabilities that could be exploited by attackers.

Penetration testing fills this gap by targeting the organization's systems, applications, and networks directly, identifying vulnerabilities that could otherwise go unnoticed.

Robust Security Posture

Audits ensure that the organization has the right policies, processes, and controls in place to maintain security and compliance.

Penetration testing provides proactive, actionable insights into how well those policies are implemented in practice and whether the organization's systems are truly secure.

Together, these approaches create a comprehensive security framework that addresses both high-level governance and detailed technical vulnerabilities.

Challenges and Considerations

Each practice has its own challenges, and organizations need to understand the potential limitations of both cybersecurity audits and penetration testing.

Cybersecurity Audits

Limited in Real-Time Vulnerability Identification: Audits focus on compliance and controls, which means they may not always uncover real time, technical vulnerabilities.

Resource Intensive: Audits require extensive documentation and coordination, and conducting thorough reviews can demand significant time and resources.

Penetration Testing

Limited Scope: Penetration tests target specific systems, and while they are effective in identifying technical weaknesses, they may miss broader governance or compliance issues.

Expertise and Tools: Successful penetration testing requires skilled ethical hackers and the use of sophisticated tools. The quality of the test depends on the expertise of the tester and the tools used.

Integration Challenges

When integrating both practices into a security strategy, careful planning is necessary to avoid overlaps and ensure comprehensive coverage. A well-coordinated approach ensures that both audits and penetration tests are addressing different aspects of the organization's security.

Best Practices for Organizations

To maximize the effectiveness of cybersecurity audits and penetration testing, organizations should follow these best practices:

Adopt a Hybrid Approach

Use cybersecurity audits to ensure compliance with frameworks and evaluate the effectiveness of controls.

Use penetration testing to perform targeted, in-depth security assessments of systems and applications.

Schedule Regular Tests

Audits should be conducted periodically (annually or bi-annually) to ensure ongoing compliance and risk management.

Penetration tests should be conducted at least once a year or after major system updates, changes, or incidents.

Leverage Tools Effectively

Utilize compliance software and penetration testing tools to streamline audits and tests. These tools can help improve efficiency, identify vulnerabilities, and track remediation progress.

Collaborate Across Teams

Encourage collaboration between auditors and penetration testers to share insights, understand risks from both a compliance and technical perspective, and create a more comprehensive risk management plan.

Key Takeaways

Just as annual checkups alone cannot maintain health, cybersecurity cannot be assured by merely ticking boxes in an audit. Both careful monitoring (audits) and practical testing (penetration testing) are essential for maintaining a healthy, strong security posture. In both healthcare and cybersecurity, an ounce of prevention is worth a pound of cure!

In this section, we covered the following points:

- *Cybersecurity Audits and Penetration Testing as Complementary Practices*:
  - Cybersecurity audits ensure compliance and evaluate the effectiveness of security policies, while penetration testing targets specific vulnerabilities in systems.

- By understanding these practices and their complementary roles, organizations can address both governance and technical security challenges, creating a stronger, more resilient cybersecurity posture.

- A hybrid approach integrating both audits and penetration tests enhances security, mitigates risks, and ensures compliance with relevant regulations.

- *Security Incidents as Health Emergencies*:
  - Think of security incidents like health emergencies – it's better to prevent them through regular check-ups (audits) and stress tests (penetration testing) rather than wait for a breach (heart attack).
  - Just as blood pressure readings alone don't evaluate cardiovascular fitness, audits alone don't assess defenses under real-world attack conditions.

- *The Prescription for Good Cybersecurity Health*:
  - Regular check-ups (audits) ensure adherence to healthy security practices, while stress tests (penetration testing) verify defenses' ability to handle attacks.
  - This combination creates a holistic approach to security wellness, keeping organizations fit and resilient against cyber threats.

Essential Skills for Cybersecurity Auditors

Just as a skilled physician needs a comprehensive set of abilities to diagnose and treat patients effectively, a cybersecurity auditor requires a diverse toolkit of skills to keep organizations digitally healthy. Let us explore the vital capabilities these "digital doctors" must possess.

The role of a cybersecurity auditor is crucial in today's digital landscape, where organizations face increasing threats to their digital assets, regulatory requirements, and operational continuity. A cybersecurity auditor safeguards these assets, ensures compliance with relevant regulations, and identifies vulnerabilities within systems. However, this role requires more than just an understanding of technology; it demands a

CHAPTER 1   INTRODUCTION TO CYBERSECURITY AUDITS

unique blend of technical expertise, analytical thinking, problem-solving, communication abilities, and knowledge of industry regulations. In the following are explored the essential skills that cybersecurity auditors must possess to be successful in their work.

Technical Expertise in Cybersecurity

A cybersecurity auditor must have a solid foundation in technical concepts to effectively assess and evaluate an organization's security posture. The role requires an understanding of networks, systems, applications, and cyberattack methods, as well as prevention strategies.

Think of technical expertise as the equivalent of a doctor's medical knowledge. Just as physicians must understand human anatomy and physiology, cybersecurity auditors need deep knowledge of digital systems.

Key Areas of Technical Knowledge:

- *Networking*: A deep understanding of networking protocols (e.g., TCP/IP), firewalls, Virtual Private Network (VPNs), and intrusion detection/prevention systems is essential. Auditors should be able to identify weak points in network configurations and potential security holes that could be exploited. Like understanding the circulatory system, auditors must know how data flows through network "veins and arteries" (protocols, firewalls, and VPNs).

- *Systems Security*: Familiarity with operating systems, both Windows and Linux, is crucial, as vulnerabilities can exist in any system. Auditors need to assess the security configurations of these systems and recognize common weaknesses, such as insecure default settings or inadequate patch management. Like knowing different organ systems, auditors must understand various operating systems and their potential ailments.

- *Vulnerability Assessment*: Cybersecurity auditors must be proficient with various tools to identify weaknesses in systems and applications. Understanding how to use vulnerability scanners and interpret their results is a key skill. Comparable to diagnostic tools like X-rays and Magnetic Resonance Imaging (MRIs), these are the tools auditors use to spot digital diseases.

- *Encryption and Data Protection*: Knowledge of encryption standards such as Advanced Encryption Standard (AES), RSA, and Transport Layer Security (TLS) are important. Auditors must verify that sensitive data is properly encrypted and protected, both in transit and at rest. Think of this as understanding how to protect vital organs (sensitive data) with various protective measures.

Knowledge of Compliance Frameworks and Regulations

A significant part of a cybersecurity auditor's role is to ensure that an organization adheres to the required industry regulations and standards. This compliance is vital not only for avoiding legal consequences but also for maintaining trust and safeguarding data.

Cybersecurity auditors need to be well-versed in various frameworks and regulations, including

- *ISO/IEC 27001*: A standard for establishing, implementing, maintaining, and continually improving an ISMS.

- *PCI DSS*: The Payment Card Industry Data Security Standard, which sets requirements for safeguarding payment card data.

- *GDPR*: The General Data Protection Regulation, which focuses on data protection and privacy for individuals in the European Union.

- *CCPA*: The California Consumer Privacy Act, which regulates how businesses collect and use personal information.

- *NIST CSF*: The National Institute of Standards and Technology Cybersecurity Framework, a set of guidelines designed to improve the cybersecurity of critical infrastructure.

Understanding the specific compliance requirements relevant to an organization's industry ensures that auditors can accurately assess whether proper controls are in place and whether the organization is at risk of non-compliance.

CHAPTER 1   INTRODUCTION TO CYBERSECURITY AUDITS

Analytical and Problem-Solving Skills

Auditors must possess strong analytical skills to assess complex systems, identify gaps, and recommend effective security improvements. This ability is essential for understanding the nuances of an organization's security framework and detecting vulnerabilities that could otherwise go unnoticed. Like medical diagnosticians, auditors must piece together complex puzzles. Just as doctors analyze symptoms to identify illnesses, auditors examine system behaviors to detect security issues.

Applications of Analytical Skills:

- *Detecting Anomalies or Breaches*: Auditors often analyze log data to identify unusual patterns that may indicate a breach or a vulnerability. Detecting such anomalies quickly is crucial in preventing or mitigating damage. Like identifying irregular heartbeats or fever spikes.

- *Assessing the Business Impact of Vulnerabilities*: Cybersecurity auditors must evaluate the potential impact of vulnerabilities, not only from a technical standpoint but also in terms of how they might affect the organization's operations, reputation, and financial stability. Like evaluating how an illness might affect a patient's daily life.

- *Recommending Tailored Mitigation Strategies*: Auditors should be able to think critically about the most effective solutions for addressing the specific risks identified during the audit and provide recommendations that are both practical and aligned with the organization's business goals. Comparable to creating personalized treatment plans.

Risk Assessment and Management

A significant part of a cybersecurity auditor's role is to assess the risks that an organization faces and recommend strategies to mitigate these risks. This requires a thorough understanding of risk management principles, including how to identify, assess, and prioritize threats. This mirrors preventive healthcare, where doctors assess patient risk factors for various conditions. Similarly, auditors evaluate an organization's risk factors for security incidents.

Key Components of Risk Management:

- *Identifying Threats, Vulnerabilities, and Exploitation Likelihood*: Auditors must be able to identify potential threats, such as cyberattacks or insider threats, and assess the likelihood of these threats exploiting system vulnerabilities. Like identifying genetic predispositions to certain diseases.

- *Evaluating the Impact of Breaches*: It is crucial to understand the potential business impact of a security breach, which could range from reputational damage to financial losses or legal consequences. Like assessing how severe a condition might become if left untreated.

- *Suggesting Effective Recommendations*: Auditors need to provide actionable recommendations that can effectively mitigate risks. This involves offering both technical and non-technical solutions to address the identified vulnerabilities. Comparable to prescribing preventive measures and lifestyle changes.

Communication Skills

Just as doctors must clearly explain complex medical conditions to patients, auditors must communicate technical findings to various stakeholders. Communication is one of the most important skills for a cybersecurity auditor. The ability to communicate findings clearly and effectively is essential for ensuring that decision-makers understand the risks, the severity of vulnerabilities, and the necessary steps for remediation.

Key Aspects of Communication:

- *Report Writing*: Auditors must produce clear, concise, and actionable audit reports. These reports should detail findings, identify risks, and provide recommendations that can be easily understood by both technical and non-technical stakeholders.

- *Stakeholder Engagement*: Effective auditors can explain technical risks in business terms to executives and other stakeholders. This is particularly important when discussing security issues with those who may not have a technical background.

CHAPTER 1   INTRODUCTION TO CYBERSECURITY AUDITS

- *Collaboration*: Cybersecurity auditors need to work closely with IT and security teams to address vulnerabilities. Their recommendations should be implemented in collaboration with the technical teams, ensuring that the right resources and actions are taken.

Familiarity with Audit Tools and Technologies

Proficiency with various tools and technologies is essential for effective audits. These tools help auditors identify vulnerabilities, streamline audits, and ensure compliance. Familiarity with vulnerability scanners, risk assessment software, and audit management tools is necessary to efficiently conduct cybersecurity audits. Like doctors must master various medical instruments, auditors need proficiency with digital diagnostic tools. Think of vulnerability scanners as the stethoscopes and MRI machines of the cyber world.

Attention to Detail

Attention to detail is a critical skill for cybersecurity auditors. Small errors or overlooked vulnerabilities can have significant consequences, so auditors must be thorough and meticulous in their work.

Applications of Attention to Detail:

- *Checking Firewall Rules and Configurations*: Auditors need to closely examine firewall settings to ensure that there are no misconfigurations that could expose the network to attack.

- *Verifying Encryption Keys and Certificate Validity*: Ensuring that encryption keys are properly managed, and certificates are valid is essential for maintaining data confidentiality and integrity.

- *Reviewing User Access Logs for Unauthorized Activity*: Auditors should scrutinize logs to detect any unusual or unauthorized access patterns that might indicate a security breach or improper access controls.

Key Takeaways

Just as a doctor's oversight can be the difference between health and illness, a cybersecurity auditor's vigilance can mean the difference between security and vulnerability. Cybersecurity is not just about treating symptoms; it's about maintaining wellness through prevention, early detection, and continuous care. The most effective auditors, like the best physicians, combine technical knowledge, communication, and attention to detail. Staying current with the latest developments is essential for success in both fields, because the stakes are too high for anything less than excellence.

In this section, we covered the following points:

- *Cybersecurity Auditors as Digital Guardians*:
  - Cybersecurity auditors play a crucial role in protecting an organization's digital assets by combining technical expertise, analytical skills, communication abilities, and knowledge of compliance frameworks.
  - They must understand risk management principles, pay attention to detail, and be proficient with audit tools and technologies.
  - By continually refining these skills and staying updated on emerging threats and regulations, auditors help organizations mitigate risks, enhance security, and maintain compliance in a complex digital environment.
- *The Medical Parallel*:
  - Just as healthcare requires doctors to be both skilled practitioners and informed advisors, cybersecurity auditors must combine technical expertise with soft skills.
  - They act as the guardians of digital health, guiding organizations through regular check-ups (audits), preventive measures (risk management), and treatment plans (recommendations).

- *Preventing, Diagnosing, and Treating Security Issues*:
  - Auditors prevent, diagnose, and treat security issues before they escalate, ensuring the long-term health of an organization's digital systems and protecting against critical incidents.
  - Their role mirrors that of doctors, where trust and skill are essential for maintaining wellness in both physical and digital ecosystems.

The Audit Lifecycle: From Planning to Reporting

A successful cybersecurity audit is not just a one-off activity; it is a comprehensive process that spans from the initial planning stage to the final follow-up. The audit lifecycle is a structured approach that helps auditors evaluate an organization's security posture, identify vulnerabilities, and recommend improvements to enhance resilience. In the following is explored the cybersecurity audit lifecycle by comparing it to a comprehensive medical examination process. Just as doctors follow a structured approach to patient care, auditors follow a systematic process to assess and improve an organization's digital health.

Figure 1-2 highlights the main steps and the flow, which are described in the following sections.

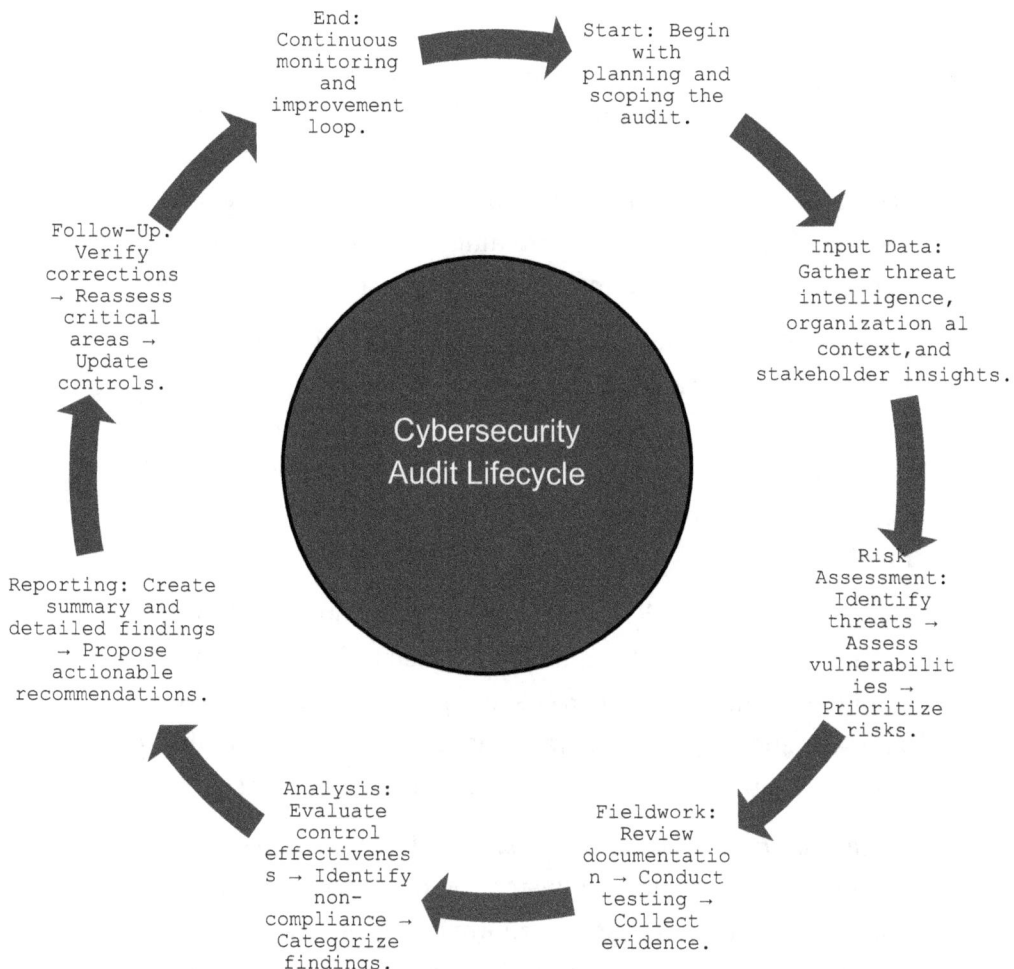

Figure 1-2. *Cybersecurity audit lifecycle*

Planning: Defining the Foundation of the Audit

The planning phase is where auditors define the audit's scope, objectives, and resources. It is the critical first step that sets the tone for the entire audit process. Without a clear and well-structured plan, the audit may lack focus, potentially leading to missed vulnerabilities or inefficient use of resources. Like a doctor reviewing a patient's medical history before an examination, the planning phase sets the foundation for the audit.

CHAPTER 1   INTRODUCTION TO CYBERSECURITY AUDITS

Key Activities in Planning:

- *Defining the Scope*: The first task is identifying which systems, processes, or standards the audit will focus on. Auditors need to determine if the audit will cover a specific area such as network security, compliance with a regulation like ISO 27001, or a broader organizational audit. Like determining which medical tests are needed based on symptoms or concerns.

- *Engaging Stakeholders*: Collaborating with key stakeholders such as IT, security, and compliance teams is essential. These teams can provide insights into the organization's existing controls, security risks, and previous audit results, which will help shape the audit's approach. Like consulting with specialists and gathering family medical history.

- *Developing an Audit Plan*: Once the scope is defined, auditors create a roadmap for the audit, outlining the timeline, key deliverables, and resources required. This plan ensures that the audit process runs smoothly and that all necessary areas are covered. Comparable to creating a patient care plan and scheduling necessary tests.

- *Understanding the Business Context*: Auditors must consider the organization's operations, industry, and the specific risks it faces. For example, an e-commerce platform may have different security priorities compared to a financial institution. Understanding this context will help the audit focus on areas that are critical to the organization's overall security posture. Like considering a patient's lifestyle and risk factors.

Risk Assessment: Identifying and Prioritizing Threats

Just as doctors perform preliminary screenings to identify potential health risks, auditors assess the organization's risk landscape. The risk assessment phase helps auditors identify the most critical risks and prioritize areas that need attention. Since cybersecurity audits often cover large and complex systems, it is important to optimize resources by focusing on high-impact areas.

Key Activities in Risk Assessment:

- *Identifying Threats*: Auditors begin by evaluating potential risks such as outdated software, phishing campaigns, or insider threats. They will gather threat intelligence and leverage frameworks like the NIST CSF to understand the landscape of risks affecting the organization. Like identifying potential health risks based on age, genetics, and lifestyle.

- *Assessing Vulnerabilities*: Next, auditors assess the organization's systems and processes to identify weaknesses that could be exploited by attackers. This includes evaluating software configurations, access controls, network vulnerabilities, and employee behavior. Like checking vital signs and performing basic health screenings.

- *Calculating Risk Impact*: Auditors estimate the potential impact of each risk, considering factors like data sensitivity, business operations, and financial consequences. This helps prioritize the most critical risks that could cause the most harm if exploited. Comparable to evaluating how certain conditions might affect quality of life.

Fieldwork and Testing: Gathering Evidence and Testing Controls

The fieldwork phase is where the bulk of the audit takes place. Auditors evaluate security controls, evaluate systems, and collect evidence to assess vulnerabilities and gaps in the organization's security posture. This phase mirrors the actual medical examination and diagnostic testing process.

Key Activities in Fieldwork:

- *Document Review*: Auditors review internal policies, procedures, and compliance documentation to evaluate whether security controls are adequately documented and aligned with best practices and regulatory requirements. Like reviewing past medical records and test results.

CHAPTER 1   INTRODUCTION TO CYBERSECURITY AUDITS

- *Technical Testing*: Auditors review results of performed technical tests such as vulnerability scans, penetration tests, or configuration reviews to evaluate the effectiveness of security controls. Tools like Nessus or Qualys may be used to scan systems for known vulnerabilities, while manual testing techniques can be used to identify more complex or subtle weaknesses. Like conducting blood tests, X-rays, and other diagnostic procedures.

- *Interviews and Observations*: Auditors engage with staff and observe operational processes to gain a deeper understanding of how security policies are applied in practice. Interviews with key personnel help identify areas where training or awareness might be lacking. Comparable to patient interviews and physical examinations.

Analysis and Evaluation: Identifying Gaps and Assessing Control Effectiveness

Like doctors analyzing test results to form a diagnosis, auditors evaluate their findings. Once the fieldwork is complete, auditors analyze the collected data to identify security gaps and evaluate the effectiveness of existing controls. This phase forms the basis for recommendations and guides the audit's next steps.

Key Activities in Analysis:

- *Identifying Non-Compliance*: Auditors look for areas where the organization is not complying with regulatory standards, internal policies, or industry best practices. This could include missed patches, inadequate access controls, or unencrypted sensitive data.

- *Assessing Control Effectiveness*: Auditors evaluate the effectiveness of security controls to determine if they are meeting their intended goals. For example, they might assess whether a firewall is properly configured to block unauthorized traffic or if encryption keys are managed securely.

- *Prioritizing Findings*: The findings from the analysis are categorized by severity and potential business impact. Critical risks that could result in significant financial loss or reputational damage are given priority for immediate attention, while lower-risk issues are addressed later.

Reporting: Communicating Findings and Recommendations

Just as doctors discuss findings and treatment options with patients, auditors present their results and recommendations. The reporting phase presents the audit's findings, analysis, and recommendations in a clear and structured format. A well-written audit report is essential for ensuring that stakeholders understand the risks and can take appropriate action.

Audit Report Components:

- *Executive Summary*: This section provides a high-level overview of the audit's key findings, emphasizing the most critical vulnerabilities and the recommended actions for remediation. It is designed for decision-makers who may not have technical expertise but need to understand the audit's outcomes.

- *Detailed Findings*: This section provides a comprehensive account of the audit's findings, documenting risks, their impact, and evidence supporting the conclusions. It includes technical details such as configuration weaknesses or unpatched vulnerabilities.

- *Recommendations*: Based on the findings, auditors provide prioritized recommendations to address security gaps. These recommendations should be actionable and tailored to the organization's needs, such as implementing new security controls, improving policies, or conducting training.

- *Compliance Status*: The report also includes an evaluation of the organization's compliance with relevant standards, frameworks, and regulations. This provides stakeholders with a clear understanding of where the organization stands in terms of regulatory adherence.

Effective Reporting Communication:

- *Visuals and Data*: Use visuals like graphs, charts, and heat maps to highlight trends, severity levels, and risk rankings. This helps make the data more accessible and actionable for both technical and non-technical audiences.

- *Tailor the Language*: The report should be written in a way that is accessible to both technical staff and business leaders. Complex technical details can be included in appendices or supporting documents for those who require them.

- *Focus on Actionable Recommendations*: The report should prioritize recommendations based on risk and feasibility. It should also include clear guidance on how to address each issue, ensuring that the organization can act swiftly and effectively.

Follow-Up and Continuous Improvement: Ensuring Actionable Outcomes

The audit process does not end with the delivery of the report. Follow-up is critical to ensure that the recommended actions are implemented and that security controls remain effective over time.

Key Activities in Follow-Up:

- Auditors follow up with the organization to ensure that corrective actions have been taken and that vulnerabilities have been addressed. This may involve reviewing updated configurations or conducting additional testing.

- For high-priority risks or vulnerabilities, auditors may conduct a reassessment to verify that the implemented changes have been effective and that the organization is now more resilient to threats.

- Cybersecurity is a constantly evolving field. Auditors ensure that the organization's controls remain up-to-date and effective in addressing new and emerging threats. This might involve recommending the implementation of new tools or technologies.

Key Takeaways

Just as a doctor would not skip steps in a medical examination, auditors must follow each phase of the audit lifecycle carefully. Skipping or rushing through any phase could leave critical vulnerabilities undetected, just as missing a crucial health indicator could result in an incorrect diagnosis. Success in both cybersecurity auditing and medical care comes from methodically applying expertise, paying attention to detail, and committing to continuous improvement. Both professions aim to protect and improve the health of what they care for, whether human bodies or digital assets.

In this section, we covered the following points:

- *The Cybersecurity Audit Lifecycle*:
  - The lifecycle provides a structured approach for auditors to assess an organization's security posture, covering planning, risk assessment, fieldwork, analysis, and reporting.
  - Each phase is essential for a thorough evaluation, and the follow-up phase ensures that security controls remain effective and continue improving.
  - By adhering to best practices throughout the lifecycle, auditors help organizations build stronger security frameworks and ensure compliance with regulations.

- *The Medical Examination Parallel*:
  - Just like a comprehensive medical exam, the cybersecurity audit lifecycle is a systematic process aimed at maintaining and improving digital health.
  - Each phase builds on the previous one, helping auditors gain a thorough understanding of an organization's security posture and providing clear directions for improvement.

CHAPTER 1   INTRODUCTION TO CYBERSECURITY AUDITS

Key Tools and Technologies Used in Cybersecurity

Just as modern medicine relies on advanced diagnostic tools and equipment, cybersecurity professionals depend on sophisticated technologies to assess and protect digital health.

In the fast-evolving landscape of cybersecurity, auditors rely heavily on a wide range of tools and technologies to assess, validate, and strengthen an organization's security posture. The effectiveness of a cybersecurity audit depends on the proper selection and application of these tools, which can uncover vulnerabilities, assess compliance, monitor threats, and manage risks. Let us explore these tools through the lens of medical equipment and procedures.

Vulnerability Scanners: Detecting and Prioritizing Security Flaws

Vulnerability scanners are crucial for identifying weaknesses in systems, networks, and applications. These tools help auditors quickly assess the security landscape by automating the detection of common vulnerabilities that could be exploited by attackers. Like medical X-rays that reveal hidden bone fractures, vulnerability scanners expose unseen system weaknesses.

Popular Vulnerability Scanners:

- *Nessus*: Nessus is one of the most widely used vulnerability scanners, known for its comprehensive detection capabilities. It provides risk-based prioritization, helping auditors focus on the most critical vulnerabilities that could pose the greatest threat to the organization.

- *Qualys*: Qualys offers continuous monitoring and vulnerability scanning. It helps auditors track vulnerabilities in real time, ensuring that organizations can quickly address emerging threats as they arise.

- *OpenVAS*: OpenVAS is an open-source vulnerability scanner that allows auditors to create customized assessments based on specific organizational needs. Its flexibility and cost-effectiveness make it an excellent choice for smaller organizations or those with budget constraints.

CHAPTER 1   INTRODUCTION TO CYBERSECURITY AUDITS

These tools enable auditors to identify vulnerabilities early in the audit process, streamlining the overall evaluation and ensuring that security gaps are addressed before they can be exploited.

SIEM Systems: Monitoring and Analyzing Security Events

SIEM platforms are essential for detecting, analyzing, and responding to security incidents in real time. SIEM tools collect and analyze log data from various sources, enabling auditors to evaluate the effectiveness of an organization's log management processes and identify signs of potential threats. Like hospital monitoring systems that track patient vital signs, SIEM platforms continuously monitor system health.

Popular SIEM Tools:

- *Splunk*: Known for its real-time log analysis and powerful search capabilities, Splunk helps auditors analyze large volumes of machine data, detect anomalies, and gain insights into potential security threats.

- *IBM QRadar*: QRadar correlates log data from multiple sources, enabling auditors to detect and prioritize incidents more effectively. It provides actionable insights by applying advanced analytics to security events.

- *Graylog*: An open-source log management and monitoring tool, Graylog is designed for collecting, storing, and analyzing logs from various sources. It provides an affordable alternative for smaller organizations looking to implement SIEM capabilities.

SIEM systems are critical for auditing an organization's ability to detect and respond to security incidents, ensuring that logs are properly collected, analyzed, and acted upon in a timely manner.

Compliance Management Tools: Streamlining the Compliance Process

Compliance is a foundation of cybersecurity audits. Compliance management tools streamline the audit process by providing templates, checklists, and workflows that help auditors assess whether an organization meets regulatory and industry standards.

CHAPTER 1   INTRODUCTION TO CYBERSECURITY AUDITS

Popular Compliance Management Tools:

- *LogicGate*: LogicGate is a GRC platform that helps auditors manage workflows, track audit findings, and ensure that compliance activities are completed on time.

- *RSA Archer*: This tool provides comprehensive capabilities for managing audits, policies, and compliance needs. It helps auditors track regulatory requirements, identify gaps, and ensure that corrective actions are taken.

- *Vanta*: Vanta automates the process of achieving compliance with standards like SOC 2, ISO 27001, and GDPR. It simplifies compliance audits by automating documentation and monitoring, reducing the burden on auditors.

These tools are invaluable for cybersecurity auditors working to ensure that organizations comply with industry regulations and standards, reducing the risk of penalties and enhancing overall security posture.

Network Monitoring and Analysis Tools: Detecting Anomalies in Network Traffic

Network monitoring tools are essential for analyzing network traffic, detecting suspicious activity, and identifying potential security breaches. By providing visibility into network performance and traffic patterns, these tools help auditors assess whether the organization's network infrastructure is secure. These tools monitor network traffic like doctors monitor blood flow through the body.

Popular Network Monitoring Tools:

- *Wireshark*: A widely used packet analysis tool, Wireshark helps auditors capture and examine network traffic in real time. It is invaluable for identifying anomalies, such as unauthorized communication or malicious traffic patterns.

- *SolarWinds Network Performance Monitor (NPM)*: SolarWinds Network Performance Monitor provides a comprehensive view of network performance and security metrics, allowing auditors to monitor devices, traffic, and system health to detect potential threats.

CHAPTER 1   INTRODUCTION TO CYBERSECURITY AUDITS

- *PRTG*: PRTG is a real-time monitoring solution that tracks network devices, services, and applications. Its customizable alerting capabilities help auditors quickly identify suspicious activity or performance issues that may indicate a security problem.

Network monitoring tools enable auditors to ensure that the organization's network infrastructure is secure, optimized, and capable of detecting and responding to potential threats.

Data Loss Prevention (DLP) Tools: Protecting Sensitive Data

DLP tools are critical for safeguarding sensitive data from unauthorized access or exfiltration. These tools are especially important during audits that focus on data security and privacy compliance.

Popular DLP Tools:

- *Symantec DLP*: Symantec's DLP solution offers comprehensive protection across endpoints, networks, and cloud environments. It helps auditors evaluate data protection practices and identify potential vulnerabilities in the organization's data security protocols.

- *Forcepoint DLP*: Forcepoint DLP offers advanced data protection capabilities, including the ability to monitor and prevent data exfiltration attempts. It also helps auditors evaluate whether the organization's data security policies are effective.

- *Digital Guardian*: Known for its focus on protecting intellectual property, Digital Guardian helps organizations defend against insider threats and ensures that sensitive data is properly secured throughout the organization.

DLP tools play a crucial role in auditing an organization's data security practices, ensuring that sensitive information is protected from theft or misuse.

Risk Assessment and Management Tools: Prioritizing Risks

Risk assessment and management tools help auditors evaluate and prioritize risks based on their likelihood and potential impact. These tools are crucial for identifying the most critical vulnerabilities and determining the appropriate course of action.

Popular Risk Assessment Tools:

- *FAIR*: FAIR is a quantitative risk management framework that helps auditors assess the financial impact of risks. It enables auditors to make informed decisions based on data-driven insights.

- *Archer Insight*: Archer Insight helps auditors quantify risks and develop mitigation plans. It provides tools for evaluating the likelihood and impact of various risks, helping organizations prioritize their cybersecurity efforts.

- *RiskLens*: RiskLens offers a financial modeling approach to risk assessment, helping organizations understand the potential costs associated with cybersecurity risks and make more informed decisions.

These tools enable auditors to evaluate risks systematically and prioritize actions based on their potential impact, improving the organization's overall risk management strategy.

Automated Audit Platforms: Streamlining the Audit Process

Automation is transforming cybersecurity audits, making them faster, more accurate, and less prone to human error. Automated audit platforms streamline tasks such as risk assessments, reporting, and remediation tracking, improving the efficiency of the audit process.

Popular Automated Audit Platforms:

- *AuditBoard*: AuditBoard automates workflows, risk assessments, and reporting, helping auditors save time and improve the accuracy of their findings.

- *Onspring*: Onspring provides real-time analytics and automated processes, allowing auditors to focus on high-priority issues while automating routine tasks.

- *Resolver*: Resolver's platform helps auditors manage findings and track remediation efforts, ensuring that security issues are addressed in a timely and efficient manner.

Automated audit platforms help auditors enhance productivity, reduce errors, and improve the overall effectiveness of the audit process.

Incident Response and Forensic Tools: Responding to Security Incidents

Incident response and forensic tools help auditors investigate and respond to security incidents. These tools are essential for identifying, containing, and analyzing breaches to understand the root cause and prevent future incidents.

Popular Incident Response and Forensic Tools:

- *EnCase*: EnCase is a digital forensic tool used to analyze digital evidence and investigate security incidents. It is widely used by auditors during post-incident audits to trace the cause and impact of security breaches.

- *TheHive*: TheHive is an open-source platform that helps auditors track and resolve security incidents. It provides a centralized hub for incident management, helping organizations respond quickly and effectively to security events.

- *Cortex XSOAR*: This platform automates and integrates incident response, helping auditors streamline the process of identifying, analyzing, and responding to security threats.

Incident response and forensic tools are essential for auditors investigating security incidents, ensuring that organizations can identify and mitigate the impact of breaches.

CHAPTER 1 INTRODUCTION TO CYBERSECURITY AUDITS

Key Takeaways

Like medical equipment that must be calibrated and operated by trained professionals, cybersecurity tools are only as effective as the experts using them. Sophisticated tools in untrained hands can miss critical issues or provide false readings. Success in both cybersecurity and medicine comes from the combination of cutting-edge technology, expert knowledge, and careful attention to detail. The right tools, wielded by skilled professionals, make all the difference between detecting a critical issue early and missing it until it's too late. Whether protecting human health or digital assets, expertise and technology must work together.

In this section, we covered the following points:

- Tools like vulnerability scanners, SIEM systems, and risk management platforms are essential for identifying vulnerabilities, assessing risks, ensuring compliance, and enhancing security practices.

- Leveraging the right tools enables auditors to improve audit effectiveness and help organizations strengthen their security posture.

- Staying updated on the latest tools ensures auditors can address evolving threats and continuously improve security measures in an increasingly complex landscape.

- Just as modern medicine relies on specialized tools and expert knowledge, effective cybersecurity requires both advanced technologies and skilled practitioners.

- Each cybersecurity tool serves a specific purpose, from preventive care to responding to emergencies, ensuring digital health.

Conclusions

Cybersecurity audits are the basis of a robust digital defense strategy, analogous to regular health check-ups for maintaining physical well-being. They provide a comprehensive evaluation of an organization's security posture, identifying vulnerabilities, ensuring compliance, and improving defenses against evolving cyber threats. A proactive approach to these audits helps organizations safeguard their assets, enhance incident response, and build trust with stakeholders.

Effective cybersecurity audits rely on a balanced combination of internal and external assessments, each offering unique benefits. Internal audits provide familiarity and agility, while external audits bring objectivity and specialized expertise. Together, they create a holistic framework to address governance, risk management, and technical security challenges.

Different types of audits, such as regular, compliance, risk-based, and specialized, serve distinct purposes and contribute to a complete security ecosystem. The adoption of risk-based and compliance frameworks further strengthens defenses, enabling organizations to prioritize high-risk areas and meet regulatory standards effectively.

Cybersecurity auditors play a pivotal role, much like skilled healthcare professionals, blending technical expertise with soft skills to diagnose, prevent, and mitigate security issues. Leveraging advanced tools and technologies enhances the effectiveness of audits, ensuring organizations remain resilient in an increasingly complex threat landscape.

Cybersecurity audits are not just about identifying weaknesses but fostering continuous improvement and resilience. By integrating regular audits, penetration testing, and risk management into a comprehensive strategy, organizations can maintain a secure, compliant, and thriving digital environment.

CHAPTER 2

Planning the Cybersecurity Audit

Just as carefully planning home security to protect family and valuables, a cybersecurity audit requires thoughtful preparation. Think of it as conducting a thorough home inspection, where every lock, window, and security system needs checking to ensure the digital residence remains safe from intruders.

Similar to planning home security, also planning a cybersecurity audit is a critical step in ensuring an organization's IT systems and processes are secure and resilient against potential threats. The process begins with defining the scope of the audit, which involves identifying the systems, applications, and infrastructure to be assessed. A clear scope helps focus the audit on key areas, such as sensitive data storage, network security, and access controls, while aligning with organizational goals and compliance requirements. Additionally, this phase includes understanding the regulatory framework the organization must adhere to, such as GDPR, HIPAA, ISO 27001, DORA, NIS2, etc.

The next step is to establish an audit plan that outlines the methodology, timeline, and resources needed for the assessment. This includes selecting the right tools and techniques for testing, such as vulnerability scans, penetration testing, or reviewing policy documentation. It is equally important to assemble a skilled audit team, which may include internal IT staff, external cybersecurity experts, or both. Communication with stakeholders is also key at this stage to ensure alignment and transparency about the audit's objectives and anticipated outcomes.

Finally, planning involves preparing the organization for the audit by gathering necessary documentation, such as security policies, incident response plans, network diagrams, and other relevant evidence. Employees should be informed about the process and their potential involvement, such as interviews or providing access to specific systems. By thoroughly planning the audit, organizations can ensure a structured, efficient approach to identifying vulnerabilities, mitigating risks, and improving their overall cybersecurity posture.

In this chapter analogically, home security is used.

Setting the Scope for a Cybersecurity Audit

In cybersecurity auditing, defining the scope is a critical step that shapes the success of the entire process. A well-defined scope establishes boundaries, aligns with stakeholder objectives, and ensures the efficient use of resources. Without this clarity, audits risk becoming unfocused, wasting time, or failing to address critical vulnerabilities.

Similarly, before installing security measures in the house, a clear plan is needed. Which rooms contain valuables? Where are the potential entry points? What security systems will work best for the needs? Like this, defining the audit scope also helps identify what digital assets need protection and how to best safeguard them.

In the following sections, the significance of defining the audit scope, the key components involved, practical steps for scoping, challenges, tools to assist in the process, and the benefits of a structured and well-documented scope are explored.

The Importance of Defining Audit Scope

The scope of an audit is the foundation of its effectiveness. It determines the audit's focus, resource allocation, and the value it delivers to the organization. A well-defined scope achieves the following:

- *Optimized Resource Utilization*:
    - A focused audit ensures that resources are directed toward critical systems and processes, avoiding unnecessary expenditures on less relevant areas.
- *Alignment with Stakeholder Expectations*:
    - By clearly defining objectives, the audit scope aligns with the organization's business goals and compliance requirements, fostering trust and accountability.

- *Prioritization of High-Risk Areas*:
  - High-risk systems, applications, and processes receive the attention they require, improving the organization's overall security posture and resilience.
- *Consistency and Clarity*:
  - A defined scope reduces ambiguities and ensures that all participants understand the audit's goals and limitations, minimizing miscommunication and inefficiencies.

Think of audit scope as a home security blueprint. It may be needed to install expensive security cameras while leaving the back door unlocked. A well-defined scope ensures:

- *Smart Resource Allocation*: Like choosing between reinforcing windows or installing motion sensors.
- *Family Agreement*: Everyone understands and supports the security measures, just as stakeholders align with audit objectives.
- *Priority Protection*: Securing the master bedroom safe before worrying about the garden shed.
- *Clear Boundaries*: Knowing exactly which areas of the property need monitoring.

Key Components of an Audit Scope

Just as a home security assessment covers specific elements, audit scope should include:

- *Security Goals*: What is being protected and why? Like deciding between basic door locks or a full security system.
- *Inventory Check*: Which digital "rooms" and "valuables" need protection?
- *Property Lines*: Digital property's boundaries, including remote "guest houses" (cloud systems).
- *Building Codes*: Security regulations that must be followed, like neighborhood guidelines.

CHAPTER 2   PLANNING THE CYBERSECURITY AUDIT

- *Project Timeline*: When to install and test each security measure.
- *Coverage Areas*: Which parts of the digital home are included or excluded.

A comprehensive audit scope serves as a roadmap, detailing what the audit will cover and how it will be conducted. Key components include

- Objectives
- Systems and assets
- Geographical coverage
- Regulations and standards
- Timeframe
- Inclusions and exclusions

The details for each component of the cybersecurity audit scope are presented in Table 2-1.

Table 2-1. Key components of an audit scope

Component	Description	Example/Tool
Objectives	Clear goals of the audit, such as compliance, risk assessment, or evaluating specific controls.	Compliance with ISO 27001, GDPR, DORA, etc., evaluating access controls.
Systems and Assets	Identification of networks, servers, applications, databases, and other critical resources.	Use of tools like AssetExplorer or Qualys Inventory for creating inventories.
Geographical Coverage	Specifies the physical or virtual locations covered, including cloud systems or remote offices.	Regional offices, cloud services (e.g., AWS and Azure).
Regulations and Standards	Frameworks and compliance requirements applicable to the audit.	PCI DSS, NIST CSF, GDPR, etc.
Timeframe	Duration of the audit and specific time periods reviewed.	Auditing Q4 2024 data, 4-week audit timeline.
Inclusions and Exclusions	Defines what is and is not part of the audit scope.	Inclusion: Data centers. Exclusion: Personal devices.

CHAPTER 2 PLANNING THE CYBERSECURITY AUDIT

Steps to Define Audit Scope

Like planning home security, defining audit scope follows logical steps:

- *Assess Your Needs*: Survey digital property like a security consultant.

- *Map Key Areas*: Create a floor plan of critical systems and assets.

- *Identify Risks*: Check for weak spots, like old windows or hidden entrances.

- *Consult the Family*: Get everyone's input on security priorities.

- *Document Everything*: Write detailed plans for security setup.

Figure 2-1 presents the steps for defining the audit scope.

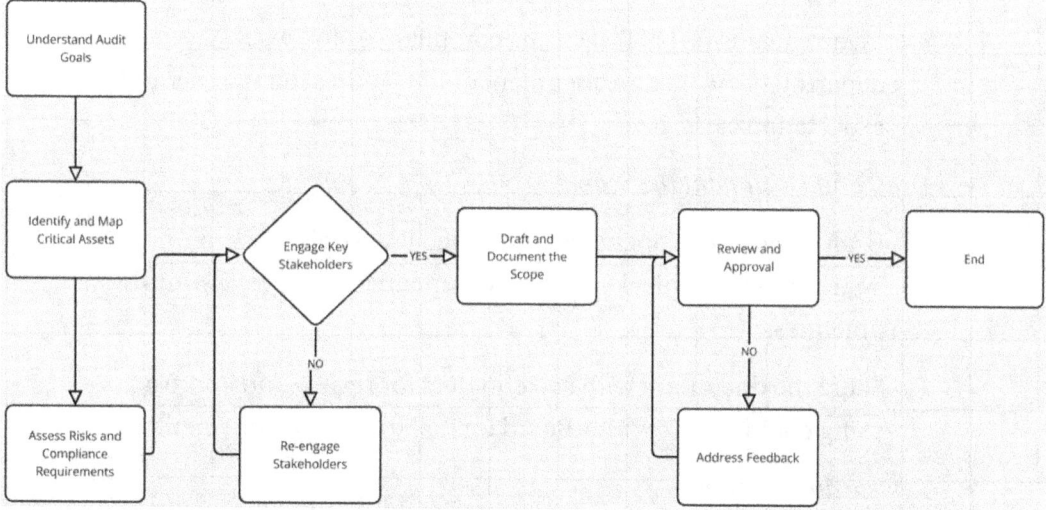

Figure 2-1. *Steps to define audit scope*

Based on the diagram in Figure 2-1, the following steps need to be followed in cybersecurity audits in order to have properly defined the audit scope:

- *Understand Audit Goals*:

  - Begin by consulting with stakeholders to align the scope with business objectives, compliance needs, and risk management priorities.

- Use tools like Lucidchart to visualize workflows, processes, and dependencies that require attention.

- *Identify and Map Critical Assets*:
  - Create an inventory of critical systems and assets that need to be assessed using tools such as AssetExplorer or ServiceNow to ensure comprehensive coverage.

- *Assess Risks and Compliance Requirements*:
  - Conduct a risk analysis using frameworks like FAIR or OCTAVE Allegro to prioritize high-risk areas. Incorporate applicable regulatory requirements and standards into the scope.

- *Engage Key Stakeholders*:
  - Involve teams from IT, security, compliance, and legal departments to ensure alignment on the audit's focus areas and expectations.

- *Draft and Document the Scope*:
  - Draft a detailed scope document, specifying objectives, covered systems, geographical coverage, compliance frameworks, and timelines.
  - Share the document with stakeholders for review and approval, using platforms like AuditBoard for collaborative refinement.

- *Review and Approval*:
  - Approve the audit scope in relevant instances, taking into consideration any feedback received from the line manager or responsible parties for approving the audit scope.

Challenges in Defining Audit Scope

Regarding the audit scope, there may be different challenges; some of the most common challenges faced during the audit scope are as follows:

- *Scope Creep*: Expanding the audit scope beyond initial boundaries can lead to inefficiencies and strained resources. Like starting with a simple alarm system but ending up rebuilding the entire fence.
  - *Solution*: Regularly revisit and align the scope with the original objectives throughout the audit process.
- *Incomplete Coverage*: Failure to identify and include critical systems or assets may result in significant vulnerabilities being overlooked. Forgetting to secure the basement window while focusing on front-door cameras.
  - *Solution*: Leverage automated discovery tools and ensure comprehensive stakeholder input during the planning phase.
- *Balancing Conflicting Objectives*: Organizations often struggle to balance compliance needs with operational priorities. Finding the sweet spot between fortress-level security and comfortable living.
  - *Solution*: Clearly define priorities and address potential conflicts during stakeholder consultations.

Tools for Scoping Audits

Just as home security requires specific tools, audit scoping needs specialized equipment. Effective scoping relies on robust tools to manage assets, align with compliance frameworks, and quantify risks:

- *Asset Inventory Tools*:
  - *SolarWinds IT Asset Management (ITAM)*: Facilitates discovery, categorization, and tracking of IT assets.
  - *Qualys Inventory*: Offers real-time visibility and classification of hardware and software assets.
- *Compliance Platforms*:
  - *Vanta*: Automates the mapping of regulatory requirements to systems and processes.
  - *LogicGate*: Helps align business operations with compliance frameworks through workflows and templates.

- *Risk Management Frameworks*:
  - *FAIR*: Provides quantitative methods for assessing and prioritizing risks.
  - *NIST CSF*: Ensures alignment with best practices and helps refine the scope to address critical areas effectively.

Benefits of a Well-Defined Audit Scope

The advantages of a clear and comprehensive audit scope are numerous; the following are the main advantages:

- *Improved Focus*:
  - Directs efforts toward areas with the greatest impact on security and compliance, ensuring that resources are used efficiently. Like knowing that the most valuable possessions are properly secured.
- *Enhanced Clarity*:
  - Reduces ambiguities and ensures all participants understand the audit's goals, methods, and limitations.
- *Streamlined Processes*:
  - Eliminates redundancy, accelerates the audit process, and simplifies reporting and remediation efforts.
- *Actionable Results*:
  - Delivers clear, practical recommendations that address high-priority risks and vulnerabilities, enabling organizations to take effective action.

Key Takeaways

In both home security and cybersecurity, prevention is always better than cure. A well-planned audit serves as your first line of defense against digital intruders, just as a solid security system protects your physical home. Taking the time to scope your audit properly ensures that you're prepared to defend what matters most in the digital world.

In this section, we covered the following points:

- Defining the scope of a cybersecurity audit is crucial for ensuring alignment with organizational objectives, focusing on critical areas, and conducting efficient audits.

- Properly scoping the audit involves leveraging tools, engaging stakeholders, and documenting the scope meticulously, which provides actionable insights and builds stakeholder confidence.

- A well-scoped audit serves as a strategic tool for managing risks and strengthening resilience against evolving cyber threats.

- The process of defining the scope is like securing your home; careful planning, the right tools, and attention to detail lay the foundation for protecting digital assets.

Stakeholder Engagement in Audit Planning

Just as protecting a home requires cooperation from every family member and trusted neighbor, a cybersecurity audit needs support from all corners of the digital household.

Effective cybersecurity audits are not conducted in isolation. They are deeply intertwined with the organization's operations, culture, and goals. Stakeholder engagement is the keystone of a successful audit process, transforming what might otherwise be a routine compliance exercise into a meaningful effort to bolster security and resilience. When stakeholders are involved from the outset, audits benefit from broader insights, smoother execution, and outcomes that align with organizational priorities.

Cybersecurity audits are not just about technical evaluations or ticking regulatory checkboxes; they are collaborative endeavors that require input and buy-in from across the organization. Stakeholder engagement is the key to this process. By involving key stakeholders early and maintaining clear communication throughout the audit, organizations can ensure that the audit delivers meaningful, actionable results that strengthen security, enhance compliance, and align with business objectives.

But what happens when stakeholders are left out of the process? Critical knowledge can be overlooked, resistance to the audit may grow, and the final findings may fail to address the most pressing risks.

CHAPTER 2   PLANNING THE CYBERSECURITY AUDIT

Think of stakeholder engagement like gathering your family to plan home security. Your teenager might know about that loose window in the basement, while Grandma remembers previous break-in attempts in the neighborhood. Similarly, when planning your digital security:

- The IT team is like your tech-savvy family member who knows all about the latest security gadgets.
- Executives are like homeowners who need to approve security investments.
- Department heads are like family members responsible for different rooms.
- Compliance officers are like building inspectors, ensuring everything meets code.

The Value of Engagement

Cybersecurity audits affect everyone in an organization, from the executive boardroom to the IT helpdesk. When stakeholders are engaged early and effectively, the benefits are immediate and profound.

Firstly, stakeholders provide insights that only they can offer. The IT team might reveal overlooked vulnerabilities in legacy systems, while compliance officers ensure adherence to critical regulatory frameworks. Without their input, audits risk being incomplete or unfocused.

Secondly, involving stakeholders builds trust and minimizes resistance. For instance, department heads who understand how the audit will enhance their operations are far more likely to cooperate than those who see it as an intrusive and unnecessary disruption.

Finally, aligned goals result in better outcomes. An audit that prioritizes areas of shared concern, whether it is securing sensitive customer data or meeting new compliance standards, is not just more efficient; it is more impactful.

Stakeholders play a pivotal role in shaping the scope, execution, and outcomes of a cybersecurity audit. Their involvement ensures that the audit is not only comprehensive but also aligned with the organization's operational realities and strategic goals.

When stakeholders are excluded from the process, several risks emerge:

- *Missed Insights*: Stakeholders often hold critical knowledge about specific systems, processes, or vulnerabilities that auditors might otherwise overlook.

- *Resistance to Audits*: Without engagement, audits can be perceived as intrusive or adversarial, leading to pushback from teams.

- *Misaligned Goals*: A lack of stakeholder input can result in audits that fail to address the most pressing security concerns or compliance needs.

Engaging stakeholders mitigates these risks and transforms the audit into a collaborative effort that benefits the entire organization.

Think like this: just as a home security system fails when family members leave doors unlocked or share alarm codes, cybersecurity weakens without everyone's buy-in. Consider these benefits:

- *Shared Knowledge*: Like how each family member knows different vulnerabilities in your home.

- *United Response*: When everyone knows the emergency plan, responses are faster.

- *Common Goals*: All household members work together to keep the home safe.

Key Stakeholders in Cybersecurity Audits

The success of a cybersecurity audit hinges on the participation of a wide array of stakeholders, each bringing their unique expertise to the table.

- *Executive Leadership*: Guides the audit's strategic direction, allocates resources, and ensures alignment with organizational goals. Like homeowners making final decisions about security investments.

- *IT and Security Teams*: Provide critical insights into technical systems, vulnerabilities, and controls. Like security system installers and maintenance experts.

CHAPTER 2   PLANNING THE CYBERSECURITY AUDIT

- *Compliance Officers*: Offer expertise on regulatory frameworks and assist with audit documentation. Like building inspectors ensuring everything is up to code.

- *Department Heads*: Highlight operational risks and identify areas of potential cybersecurity impact. Like room guardians responsible for specific areas.

- *Third-Party Vendors*: Ensure external systems and services are included in the audit's scope. Like trusted security companies monitoring systems.

Table 2-2 presents key stakeholders and steps on how to engage in planning a cybersecurity audit.

Table 2-2. Key stakeholders and their roles in planning a cybersecurity audit

Stakeholder Group	Role in Cybersecurity Audit	How to Engage	Actionable Steps
Executive Leadership	Guides audit strategy, allocates resources, and ensures alignment with organizational goals.	Schedule concise meetings, provide high-level summaries, and emphasize the strategic importance of the audit.	- Conduct an executive briefing on audit objectives and risks. - Align audit goals with business objectives. - Prepare an ROI-focused summary.
IT and Security Teams	Identify technical vulnerabilities, provide insights into systems, implement controls.	Conduct technical workshops, facilitate open discussions about risks, and involve them in solution development.	- Use threat modelling sessions to identify potential vulnerabilities. - Provide technical audit tools to aid in identifying gaps. - Establish shared KPIs for cybersecurity improvements.
Compliance Officers	Ensure adherence to regulatory frameworks, assist with audit documentation.	Share regulatory updates, provide clear documentation guidelines, and request regular feedback.	- Schedule regular compliance update meetings. - Map regulatory requirements to audit controls. - Share a checklist for documentation readiness.

(*continued*)

Table 2-2. (*continued*)

Stakeholder Group	Role in Cybersecurity Audit	How to Engage	Actionable Steps
Department Heads	Identify operational risks, highlight potential cybersecurity impacts in their domains.	Organize departmental meetings, explain audit benefits for their operations, and address concerns proactively.	- Create a tailored briefing for each department's specific risks. - Provide simple guides on security best practices for non-technical staff. - Involve department heads in post-audit remediation planning.
Third-Party Vendors	Ensure external systems and services are included in the audit scope.	Communicate expectations early, establish clear audit requirements, and schedule regular updates.	- Issue a clear RFI (Request for Information) regarding vendor compliance with cybersecurity standards. - Host vendor workshops to clarify scope and expectations. - Perform risk assessments for vendor services.

Strategies for Engagement

Stakeholder engagement is both an art and a science, requiring structured methods and a flexible, collaborative mindset.

A kickoff meeting is often the first step. This is not just a formality; it is an opportunity to set the tone for the audit, explaining its purpose, scope, and importance. A well-run kickoff meeting establishes trust and provides a forum for stakeholders to voice their expectations.

To gather detailed input, surveys are invaluable. Tools like Microsoft Forms or Google Forms can quickly collect perspectives from a wide range of stakeholders, from executive leaders to individual team members. For more interactive collaboration, workshops are ideal. These sessions bring stakeholders together to align objectives, identify risks, and define success metrics.

Throughout the audit, regular check-ins keep stakeholders informed and engaged. These updates can address emerging challenges, reaffirm the audit's progress, and ensure that any adjustments are made with input from all parties. Documentation platforms such as Confluence or SharePoint further streamline this process, making plans and progress easily accessible to everyone involved.

The engagement of stakeholders needs to go through the following steps:

1. *Start*: The process begins with recognizing the need for stakeholder engagement in cybersecurity audits. This involves setting the foundation to align all parties with a shared understanding of the audit's purpose, scope, and goals.

2. *Initiate Engagement*: Kickoff meetings mark the official start of stakeholder involvement. These meetings are used to set clear goals, explain the audit's purpose, and establish expectations. By aligning stakeholders early, the audit process gains momentum and ensures participation.

3. *Gather Input*: Input is gathered through various methods such as surveys, interviews, and workshops. These tools help collect valuable information from stakeholders, ensuring that the audit captures critical insights, operational risks, and compliance concerns.

4. *Define Roles and Responsibilities*: Tasks and expectations are clearly defined for each stakeholder group. This step ensures that everyone understands their role in the audit, promoting accountability and fostering collaboration across teams.

5. *Regular Communication*: Maintaining regular communication is essential for transparency and alignment. Through periodic check-ins and updates, stakeholders remain engaged, and emerging challenges are addressed proactively.

6. *Document and Review Findings*: Collaboration platforms such as Confluence are used to document findings and share them with stakeholders. This step encourages feedback, ensuring the results are understood and actionable by both technical and non-technical teams.

CHAPTER 2　PLANNING THE CYBERSECURITY AUDIT

7. *Implement and Improve*: The final step focuses on aligning audit results with organizational goals. Stakeholders work together to implement recommendations, enhancing the organization's cybersecurity posture and preparing for future audits.

8. *End*: The process concludes with improved security measures and strengthened stakeholder relationships, ensuring the audit delivers both compliance and strategic value.

The process of stakeholders' engagement is presented graphically in Figure 2-2.

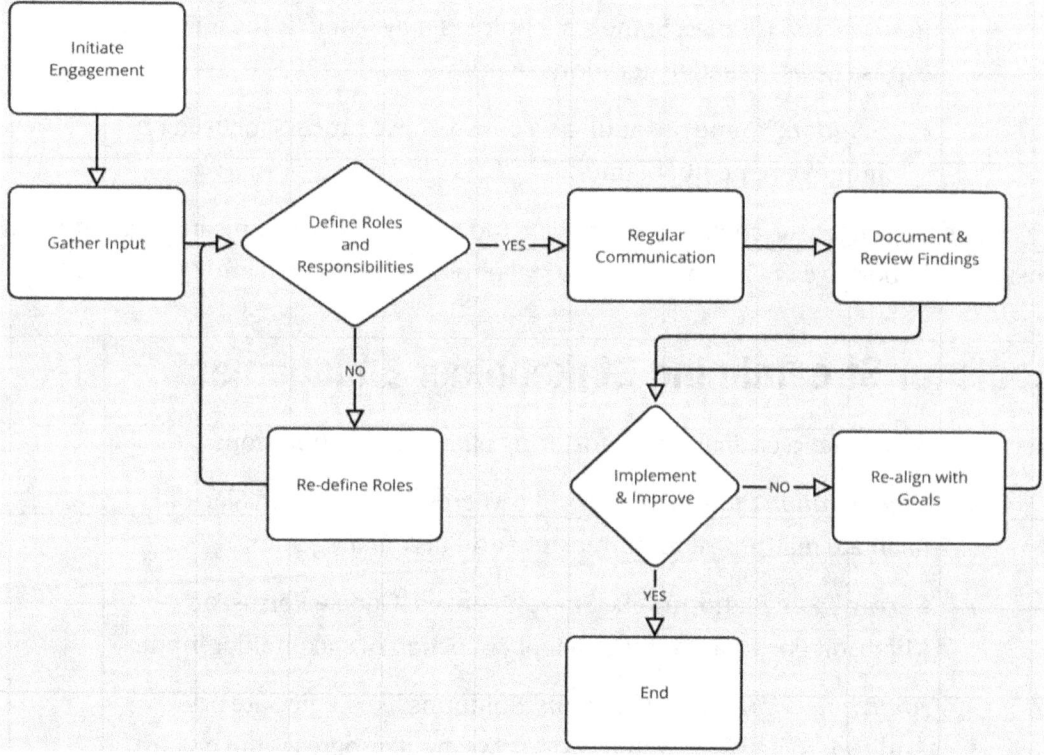

Figure 2-2. *Stakeholder engagement steps*

Overcoming Challenges

Despite its benefits, stakeholder engagement is not without its hurdles. Executives may have limited time to dedicate to the audit, while operational teams may fear that participation will disrupt their workflows.

- *Limited Availability*: Executives and other senior stakeholders may have limited time to dedicate to the audit.
  - *Solution*: Schedule meetings well in advance and provide concise updates to maximize their time.
- *Conflicting Priorities*: Operational teams may view the audit as a distraction from their core responsibilities.
  - *Solution*: Emphasize the long-term benefits of the audit, such as improved security and reduced risk of disruptions.
- *Resistance to Change*: Some stakeholders may fear that the audit will expose flaws or lead to additional work.
  - *Solution*: Frame the audit as a constructive process focused on improvement, not blame.

By addressing these challenges with tact and proactive communication, auditors can foster a collaborative environment where stakeholders feel valued and understood.

Tools for Streamlining Stakeholder Engagement

Technology can play a critical role in fostering effective collaboration:

- *Collaboration Platforms*: Tools like Microsoft Teams and Slack facilitate real-time communication and task management.
- *Survey Tools*: Platforms like SurveyMonkey, Google Forms, or Microsoft Forms allow for efficient collection of stakeholder input.
- *Audit and Compliance Platforms*: Solutions like LogicGate or AuditBoard help streamline workflows, track progress, and ensure alignment with regulatory frameworks.

Best Practices for Stakeholder Engagement

The following principles can help auditors maximize the value of stakeholder participation:

- *Start Early*: Engage stakeholders during the planning phase to align goals and priorities.

- *Define Roles and Responsibilities*: Clearly outline what is expected of each stakeholder group.

- Communicate Regularly: Provide updates and solicit feedback to maintain engagement.

- *Simplify Complex Findings*: Use charts, graphs, and plain language to present audit results to non-technical stakeholders.

- *Recognize Contributions*: Acknowledge and appreciate the efforts of stakeholders to encourage future collaboration.

The Impact of Engagement

When stakeholders are meaningfully engaged, the results are transformative. The audit process becomes more efficient, as resources are focused on the most critical areas. Comprehensive coverage ensures that no major risks are overlooked.

Key benefits of stakeholder engagement include

- *Improved Efficiency*: Streamlined processes save time and resources.

- *Comprehensive Coverage*: Input from diverse stakeholders ensures no critical risks are overlooked.

- *Enhanced Trust*: Transparent communication builds confidence in the audit process.

- *Actionable Results*: Findings and recommendations are aligned with organizational goals, making them more impactful.

Key Takeaways

Just as a home's security depends on everyone's commitment, digital security thrives when all stakeholders work together. It's not just about installing the right locks but ensuring everyone understands how to use them and why they're important.

In this section, we covered the following points:

- Effective stakeholder engagement elevates a cybersecurity audit from a compliance task to a strategic initiative, enhancing the organization's security posture.

- By fostering collaboration and aligning the audit with organizational priorities, stakeholders and auditors work together to create a stronger, more resilient security framework.

- Building trust is key, an audit that reflects the insights and priorities of participants becomes a collaborative effort to secure the organization's future.

- Stakeholder engagement is the foundation for a successful audit, ensuring that the audit process is not just an evaluation but a shared responsibility.

Understanding Business Context Before Auditing

A cybersecurity audit is only as effective as its alignment with the organization's realities. Diving into technical evaluations without first grasping the broader business context can lead to an audit that misses the mark, delivering findings that fail to resonate with stakeholders or address critical vulnerabilities. Understanding the business context ensures audits align with organizational goals, focus on high-priority areas, and offer actionable recommendations that enhance security while supporting business objectives.

Just as every home has its own personality, quirks, and needs, every organization has a unique context that shapes its security requirements. Before installing any security system or implementing protective measures, it is needed to understand what makes a digital home special – from its architectural style to the habits of its residents.

Why Business Context Matters

A strong grasp of the business context provides a roadmap for auditors, allowing them to identify and prioritize what matters most. Without this foundation, audits risk being reduced to checklists that address compliance but fail to strengthen the organization's overall security posture.

Think of walking into a historic Victorian mansion versus a modern smart home. Each requires different security approaches, just as different businesses need tailored cybersecurity measures. A deep understanding of a digital home's character helps identify what truly needs protection and how best to secure it. Think of a family with teenagers who need flexible access for after-school activities versus retirees who maintain regular schedules – their security needs differ dramatically, just as different organizations require unique cybersecurity approaches based on their operations and goals.

Key benefits of understanding the business context include

- *Identifying Critical Assets*: Auditors can pinpoint vital systems and processes, ensuring these areas receive proper attention during evaluations.

- *Focusing the Audit Scope*: Aligning with key priorities like compliance or intellectual property protection prevents resources from being wasted on non-critical areas.

- *Assessing Impact*: Awareness of operational goals allows auditors to evaluate risks in terms of their potential effects on trust, revenue, or strategic initiatives.

- *Securing Stakeholder Buy-In*: Demonstrating alignment with business objectives reassures stakeholders that the audit serves their interests, fostering cooperation.

For example, a retail organization heavily reliant on e-commerce may prioritize protecting customer data and payment systems, while a healthcare provider might focus on patient confidentiality and compliance with HIPAA regulations. Tailoring audits to these priorities ensures outcomes that matter.

Key Elements of Business Context

Understanding the business context involves analyzing multiple interrelated elements that define the organization's risk landscape and operational priorities:

- *Industry and Regulatory Landscape*:
  - Each industry faces unique challenges and operates under specific regulations. Finance, for instance, must comply with PCI DSS to secure cardholder data, while healthcare organizations are subject to HIPAA's stringent privacy rules. Tailoring audits to these requirements ensures relevance and effectiveness.

- *Business Goals*:
  - Strategic objectives, such as expanding into new markets or adopting cloud-based technologies, dictate which areas of cybersecurity are most critical. An audit aligned with these goals can proactively support organizational growth while minimizing associated risks.

- *Organizational Structure*:
  - The internal framework of the organization, including departments, roles, and reporting lines, can highlight potential overlaps or gaps in security responsibilities. Understanding these dynamics enables auditors to recommend more cohesive controls.

- *Critical Processes*:
  - Core workflows, such as supply chain operations, payment processing, or customer service, often house sensitive data or serve as prime attack vectors. Focusing on these processes ensures the audit addresses areas of greatest operational risk.

- *Threat Landscape*:
  - Industry-specific risks, such as ransomware targeting healthcare or phishing attacks prevalent in retail, shape the organization's vulnerability profile. Studying these threats, alongside past incidents, provides a clearer picture of potential weak points.

Like a comprehensive home inspection, understanding business context involves examining multiple crucial aspects. Consider how a home's location in a flood zone influences insurance needs and security measures – similarly, industry and regulatory environment shape cybersecurity requirements. The home's layout, from the number of entrances to the location of valuable items, mirrors an organization's structure and critical assets. Just as a family's daily routines influence security system settings, business processes determine which digital assets need the most protection. This holistic view ensures no vulnerable areas are overlooked, whether they are basement windows in a physical home or remote access points in digital infrastructure.

Steps to Understand the Business Context

Gaining a comprehensive understanding of the business context is a multi-step process that integrates stakeholder collaboration, documentation review, and industry research:

- *Stakeholder Interviews*:
  - Conversations with executives, IT leaders, and department heads yield invaluable insights into organizational goals, risks, and challenges. These discussions help auditors tailor their approach to align with what stakeholders consider critical.

- *Review Documentation*:
  - Existing policies, system diagrams, risk assessments, and prior audit reports provide a baseline understanding of the organization's cybersecurity posture and operational priorities.

- *Map Processes*:
  - Visualizing workflows and data flows using tools like Lucidchart or MS Visio can highlight dependencies, bottlenecks, and vulnerabilities that might otherwise go unnoticed.

- *Study Industry Trends*:
  - Threat intelligence reports and benchmarks, such as those from Recorded Future or ThreatConnect, reveal common risks and emerging threats that could impact the organization.

- *Collaborate Across Departments*:
  - Including departments like Human Resources (HR), legal, and operations ensures a holistic view of risks, capturing perspectives that technical audits might overlook.

CHAPTER 2   PLANNING THE CYBERSECURITY AUDIT

Figure 2-3 presents the process flow of understanding business context, while Figure 2-4 presents a mind map of the understanding business context process.

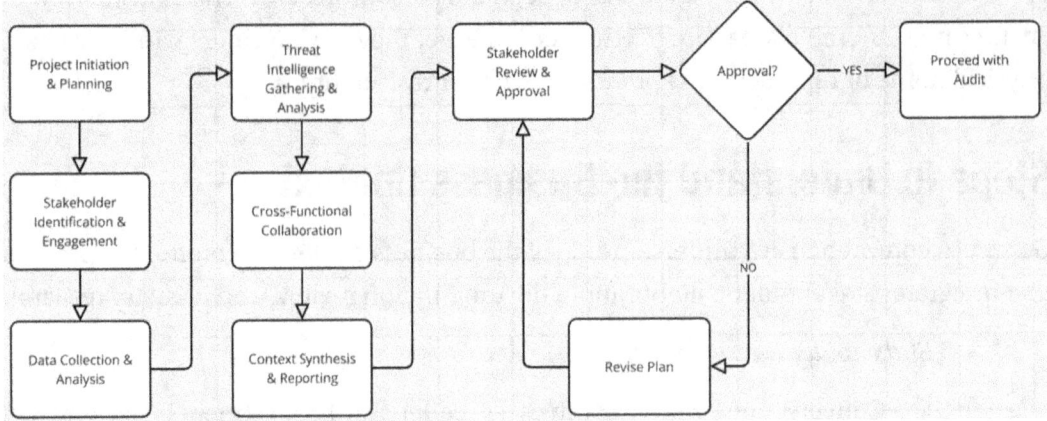

Figure 2-3. *Understanding business context steps*

CHAPTER 2 PLANNING THE CYBERSECURITY AUDIT

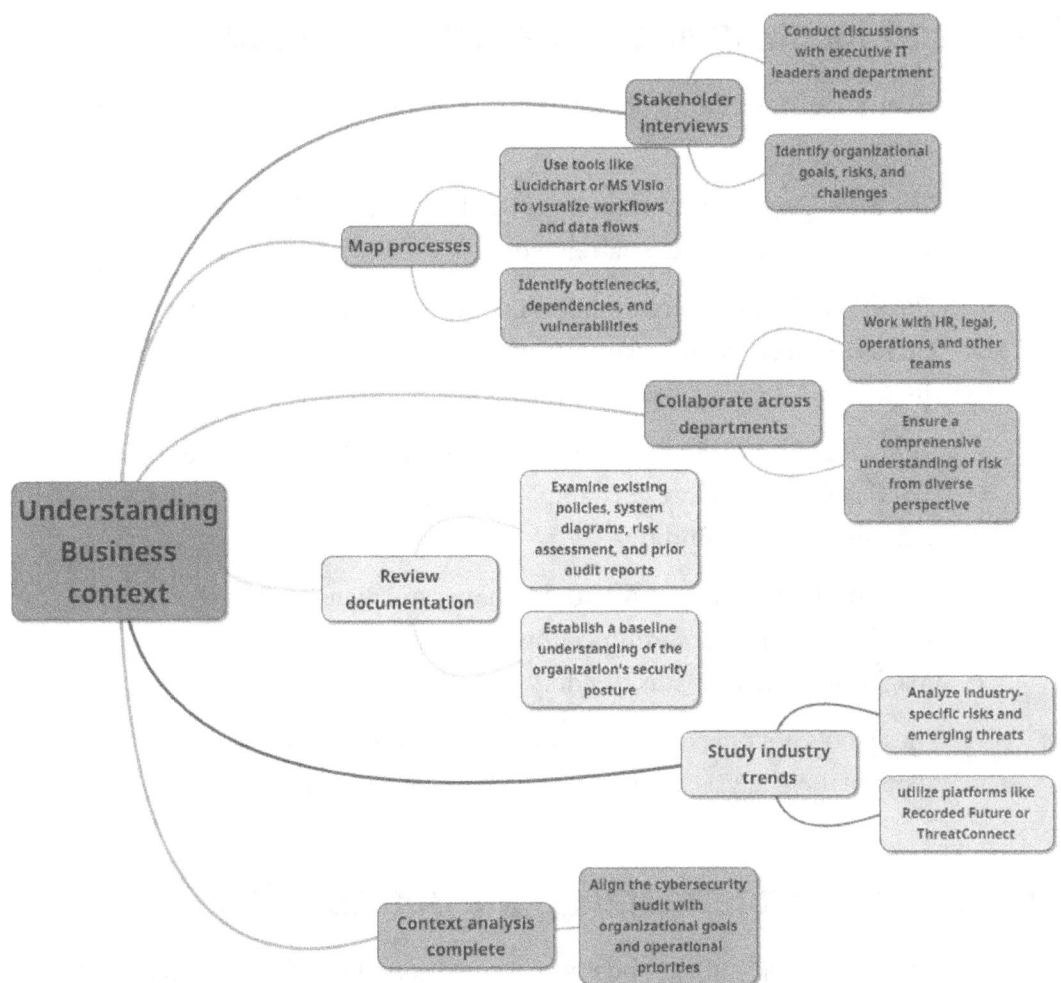

Figure 2-4. *Understanding business context mind map*

Just as a thorough home assessment involves talking to family members, checking building records, and understanding neighborhood patterns, gathering business context requires a multi-layered approach. Walking through each room with residents reveals how spaces are used, just as stakeholder interviews uncover critical workflows and concerns. Reviewing building plans and previous renovation records parallels examining system documentation and past audit reports. Understanding local crime patterns and neighborhood watch programs mirrors studying industry threats and security trends. This comprehensive approach ensures that security measures align perfectly with the home's needs.

Tools and Technologies for Context Gathering

Technology can significantly enhance an auditor's ability to gather and analyze business context efficiently:

- *Risk Management Platforms*: Tools like LogicGate and RiskWatch centralize and organize risk-related data, streamlining assessments.

- *Threat Intelligence Tools*: Platforms such as Recorded Future and ThreatConnect provide real-time insights into industry-specific threats.

- *Data Visualization Tools*: Tableau and Power Business Intelligence (BI) simplify the analysis of complex data, enabling clear communication of findings.

- *Collaboration Platforms*: Microsoft Teams and Slack facilitate interdepartmental communication, making it easier to gather insights from diverse stakeholders.

- These tools not only save time but also improve the accuracy and depth of the analysis, ensuring no critical detail is overlooked.

Challenges in Understanding the Business Context

While essential, understanding the business context can present several challenges:

- Lack of documentation
- Siloed information
- Rapid organizational changes
- Resistance from stakeholders
- Complexity of industry threats

Table 2-3 presents details of the impact, solution, and steps to mitigate the above-mentioned challenges in understanding the business context.

Table 2-3. Challenges in understanding the business context

Challenge	Impact	Solution	Concrete Steps to Mitigate
Lack of Documentation	Gaps in understanding cybersecurity posture and operational priorities.	Conduct interviews and direct observations.	- Meet with key personnel to gather undocumented insights. - Shadow daily operations to identify critical processes.
Siloed Information	Incomplete data due to withheld or fragmented information across teams.	Foster collaboration and shared goals.	- Communicate the audits' purpose and benefits to all departments. - Use collaboration tools like Slack or Teams.
Rapid Organizational Changes	Difficulty in keeping up with shifting priorities or structures.	Maintain flexibility in the audit scope.	- Schedule regular check-ins to gather updates on changes. - Adapt audit plans based on new priorities or goals.
Resistance from Stakeholders	Limited cooperation due to fear of exposure or perceived disruption.	Build trust through transparent communication.	- Highlight the audit's role in improving security. - Address stakeholder concerns early and provide assurance of non-punitive intent.
Complexity of Industry Threats	Inability to focus on the most relevant and emerging threats.	Leverage TIPs.	- Use tools like ThreatConnect for real-time insights. - Incorporate industry benchmarks to align findings with trends.

CHAPTER 2   PLANNING THE CYBERSECURITY AUDIT

The Impact of Business Context on Audit Outcomes

An audit grounded in a thorough understanding of the business context delivers far-reaching benefits:

- *Actionable Recommendations*: Findings are directly applicable to the organization's unique challenges, addressing real risks instead of generic issues.

- *Efficient Use of Resources*: By focusing on high-priority areas, audits maximize their impact without wasting time or effort on irrelevant aspects.

- *Stakeholder Engagement*: When audits align with business goals, stakeholders are more likely to support and implement recommendations.

Ultimately, understanding the business context elevates the audit from a compliance exercise to a strategic initiative that strengthens security, supports operational goals, and enhances organizational resilience in the face of evolving threats.

With the prioritization of business context, auditors can transform their work into a catalyst for meaningful change, delivering not just compliance but true security and operational excellence.

Key Takeaways

A digital home, like the physical one, is a dynamic environment composed of people, processes, and assets. By understanding its unique characteristics, there can be created security measures that not only protect but also enhance the operations of everyone who depends on them.

In this section, we covered the following points:

- Effective audit planning creates a structured roadmap, ensuring clear objectives, scope, and methodologies are defined, leading to focused and impactful audits.

- Understanding the business context is crucial, allowing auditors to align cybersecurity evaluations with organizational goals, industry requirements, and operational needs for relevant and actionable results.

- Cybersecurity audits, like home security systems, must be tailored to the unique characteristics of the organization, considering its operations, culture, and processes.

- Balancing security with business functionality is key; overly restrictive controls can disrupt operations, just as a poorly planned security system can lead to constant false alarms.

- Engaging stakeholders in the audit process ensures that it is not just an external evaluation but a collaborative effort to protect the organization's future and build trust.

- Proper planning ensures that audit outcomes are actionable and that security improvements align with the organization's evolving needs, rather than becoming isolated compliance tasks.

Why Data Flow Diagrams Are Essential for Cybersecurity Audits

In the rapidly evolving landscape of cybersecurity, understanding how data moves within an organization is crucial for effective auditing. Data Flow Diagrams (DFDs) offer a unique advantage by visually mapping the flow of information, highlighting processes, storage locations, and interactions between systems. This clarity enables auditors to pinpoint vulnerabilities, evaluate dependencies, and recommend robust security measures.

DFDs are not merely technical tools; they are strategic assets. By translating complex systems into visual representations, they bridge the gap between technical teams and non-technical stakeholders. They offer a shared language that facilitates collaboration, ensuring everyone from IT staff to executives can understand and contribute to the audit process. This accessibility is vital for audits to not only identify risks but also foster organizational alignment around cybersecurity priorities.

Just as an architect's blueprint reveals the vital pathways of the home – from water pipes to electrical circuits – DFDs expose the critical routes that information takes through a digital household. Understanding these pathways is as essential as knowing where every door and window leads in a physical home.

CHAPTER 2   PLANNING THE CYBERSECURITY AUDIT

The Importance of DFDs in Cybersecurity

Imagine trying to secure a house without knowing where all the entrances are or how utilities flow through the walls. Just as a detailed home blueprint helps identify vulnerable access points and critical systems, DFDs show the paths that sensitive information takes through a digital home. Think of it as having a comprehensive plan that shows not just the obvious front door, but every pet door, mail slot, and utility entrance that could potentially be exploited.

Data Flow Diagrams serve as a foundation in the auditing process for several reasons. First and foremost, they simplify complex systems. Modern organizations often rely on interconnected networks, applications, and databases, making it challenging to understand how data flows. A well-designed DFD breaks these intricate systems into smaller, manageable components, providing a clear picture of how information travels from point A to point B.

Another critical role of DFDs is risk identification. By visually charting data inputs, outputs, storage locations, and processing points, auditors can spot potential vulnerabilities. For instance, they may uncover unencrypted data transfers, unsecured endpoints, or neglected data repositories. These insights enable targeted interventions, ensuring that security measures address the most significant threats.

Benefits of DFDs in Audits:

- *Clarify Complex Systems*: Break down intricate workflows for better understanding.

- *Identify Key Vulnerabilities*: Highlight unprotected data flows and storage.

- *Support Compliance*: Provide clear documentation for regulatory frameworks like GDPR and PCI DSS.

- *Focus Audit Scope*: Target critical processes and data pathways.

DFDs also play a pivotal role in regulatory compliance. Laws like GDPR, HIPAA, and PCI DSS demand organizations document their data handling processes. A comprehensive DFD provides clear evidence of compliance, demonstrating how data is collected, processed, stored, and shared. This transparency is invaluable during regulatory reviews or audits, reducing the risk of penalties and building trust with customers and stakeholders.

Components of a Data Flow Diagram

A standard data flow diagram consists of several key elements. Entities represent external actors that interact with an organization's data, such as customers, users, or third-party vendors. Processes depict the activities that handle or transform data, such as data entry, analysis, or reporting. Data stores, meanwhile, represent repositories like databases or file systems where information is retained. Finally, data flows, represented by arrows, illustrate how information moves between entities, processes, and storage locations.

Like a comprehensive home blueprint that marks load-bearing walls, utilities, and traffic patterns, DFDs consist of crucial components that work together. External entities are like family members and visitors who interact with the house. Processes represent the home's systems – security alarms, heating controls, and communication networks. Data stores are like safe rooms and filing cabinets, while data flows are the hallways and corridors connecting everything together, showing how information moves throughout the digital home.

These components work together to create a holistic view of an organization's data ecosystem. For example, a DFD might show customer information entering through a web form (entity), being processed by an application server (process), and then stored in a database (data store). By labeling the data flows, auditors can also specify the type of information being transferred, such as personal identification numbers or financial details.

Creating an Effective Data Flow Diagram

Building a DFD requires careful planning and collaboration. The first step is defining the scope, identifying which systems, processes, or departments the diagram will cover. This ensures the DFD remains focused and avoids unnecessary complexity.

Building an effective DFD is like working with an architect to design a dream home's security system. It starts by determining which areas need the most protection – perhaps the home office with sensitive documents or the main security control panel. Just as consulting with family members about their daily routines is necessary to design effective security measures, creating a DFD requires collaboration with all stakeholders to understand how information flows through the digital household.

Next, auditors gather information by collaborating with stakeholders from IT, operations, and other relevant teams. These discussions help map the origins, destinations, and pathways of data within the organization. Tools like Lucidchart or Microsoft Visio can be used to design the diagram, providing a professional and accurate representation of data flows.

Once the initial DFD is complete, it is essential to validate it with stakeholders. This review process ensures the diagram reflects the organization's realities and captures all critical data flows. Regular updates to the DFD are also necessary, especially in dynamic environments where systems and workflows evolve rapidly.

The following diagram presents a cyclical process for creating and maintaining an effective DFD. It emphasizes the iterative nature of DFD development and the importance of regular updates to ensure accuracy and relevance. It starts with scope definition and ends with update and re-evaluation.

- *Define Scope*: This is the starting point. Here, can be determined the boundaries of the DFD. This step includes processes as follows:
    - Identification of specific system or process to be modeled.
    - Determination of which departments, teams, or individuals are involved.
    - Decision on the level of detail required.
    - Establishing clear inclusion and exclusion criteria.
- *Gather Information*: This step involves gathering data about the system or process.
    - Conducting stakeholder interviews to understand their roles, responsibilities, and data interactions.
    - Analyzing existing documentation and workflows.
    - Creating a data dictionary to define key terms and data elements.
- *Map Data Flows*:
    - Usage of DFD symbols (processes, data flows, data stores, external entities) to visually represent the movement of data within the system.
    - Creation of a context diagram for a high-level overview.

- Decomposition of complex processes into smaller, more manageable sub-processes.
- Utilization of tools like Lucidchart, Visio, etc.

- *Document Processes*:
  - Providing detailed descriptions of each process in the DFD, including inputs, outputs, logic, and resources.
  - Documenting decision points and the logic used to make decisions.

- *Validate and Update*: This is a crucial step.
  - Presentation of the DFD to stakeholders for review and feedback.
  - Addressing any discrepancies or missing information.
  - Incorporating stakeholder feedback to improve the accuracy and completeness of the diagram.

- *Use Validated DFD*: If the DFD is up-to-date and validated, it can be used for various purposes such as system analysis, process improvement, and risk assessment.

- *Update and Re-evaluate*:
  - Regularly review the DFD to assess its effectiveness.
  - Re-evaluating the scope to ensure it continues to address the organization's needs.
  - Identifying areas for improvement and making necessary adjustments.
  - If the DFD is not up-to-date, return to step 1 (Define Scope) to initiate a new cycle of DFD creation.

CHAPTER 2 PLANNING THE CYBERSECURITY AUDIT

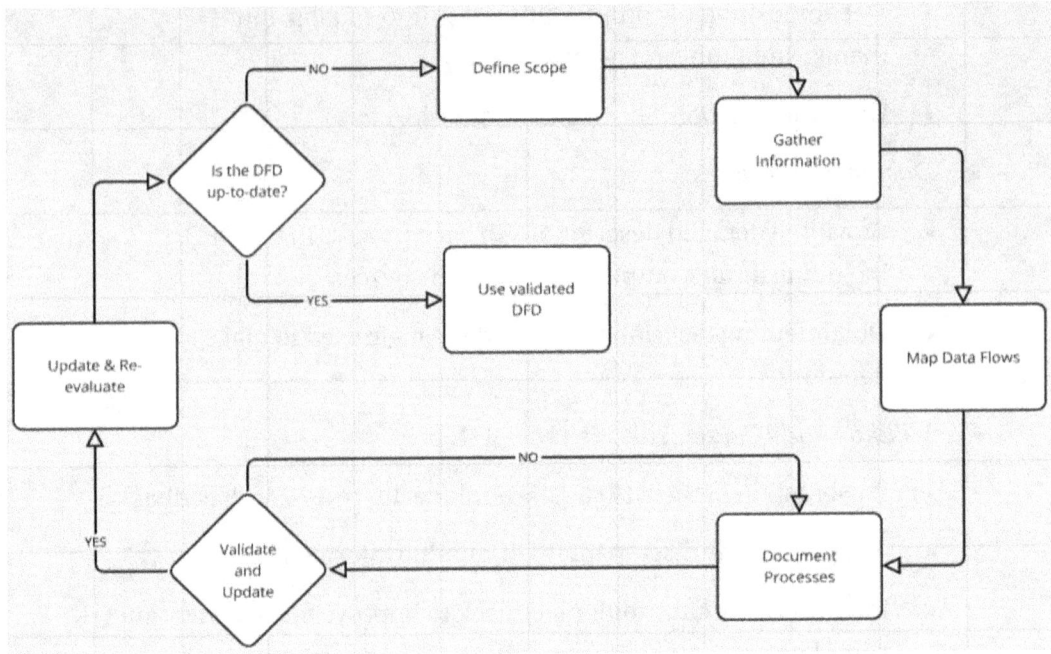

Figure 2-5. *Process flow of DFD creation*

How DFDs Enhance Cybersecurity Audits

The practical benefits of DFDs extend far beyond their creation. They enhance cybersecurity audits by offering actionable insights that drive meaningful improvements. For instance, DFDs help locate sensitive data, such as PIIs or financial records, ensuring these critical assets receive the necessary protections.

Furthermore, DFDs expose unprotected data flows, such as unencrypted transfers or unauthorized access points. These vulnerabilities often go unnoticed in traditional audits but are easily identifiable when data flows are visually mapped. DFDs also assess access points, highlighting areas with weak authentication or excessive permissions that could be exploited by attackers.

Table 2-4 presents key benefits of DFDs.

Table 2-4. Key benefits of DFDs

Key Benefits	Details	Examples	Impact
Locating Sensitive Data	DFDs help identify where critical data, such as PIIs or financial records, is stored or transferred.	- Pinpointing customer data storage for a retail system. - Identifying financial records in Enterprise Resource Planning (ERP) systems.	Ensures that sensitive data is prioritized for security measures and compliance.
Exposing Unprotected Data Flows	Unprotected or vulnerable data transfers (e.g., unencrypted transfers or unauthorized access points) become visible during DFD analysis.	- Detecting unencrypted database connections. - Identifying unsecured APIs in web applications.	Reduces the risk of data breaches by enabling remediation of exposed vulnerabilities.
Assessing Access Points	Highlights areas with weak authentication or excessive user permissions that could serve as entry points for attackers.	- Flagging systems with shared admin credentials. - Identifying unnecessary elevated privileges for users.	Strengthens access control by addressing weak spots and mitigating potential attack vectors.
Improving Audit Coverage	Visual mapping ensures no critical workflows or dependencies are overlooked, resulting in a comprehensive audit.	- Visualizing a payment gateway's integration with customer data. - Mapping IoT device communications.	Enhances the quality and depth of the audit by ensuring all significant areas are analyzed.
Facilitating Risk Prioritization	By clearly showing the most critical data flows and access points, DFDs help focus resources on the highest-risk areas.	- Prioritizing encryption for financial transactions. - Strengthening security for third-party integrations.	Optimizes resource allocation, addressing the most pressing risks first.

CHAPTER 2   PLANNING THE CYBERSECURITY AUDIT

Challenges and Solutions in Using DFDs

While DFDs are invaluable, their creation and maintenance come with challenges. One common issue is dealing with complex systems. Large organizations often have sprawling infrastructures that can be difficult to represent in a single diagram. To address this, auditors can divide the system into smaller sections and create separate DFDs for each component.

Incomplete information is another hurdle, particularly in organizations without robust documentation practices. In such cases, interviews and workshops with key stakeholders can help fill gaps and ensure the DFD is comprehensive. Additionally, dynamic environments where systems and workflows change frequently require regular updates to keep the diagram relevant and accurate.

Common Challenges with DFDs:

- *Complex Systems*: Break down into smaller, manageable components.
- *Incomplete Documentation*: Use interviews to fill gaps.
- *Dynamic Environments*: Regularly review and revise the diagram.

Tools Supporting DFD Creation

Modern technology offers numerous tools to simplify the process of designing and maintaining Data Flow Diagrams. Automated mapping platforms, such as SolarWinds, streamline the creation of network and data flow diagrams, saving time and effort. Tools like the Microsoft Threat Modeling Tool integrate DFDs with risk analysis, offering a comprehensive view of vulnerabilities and potential threats.

Compliance platforms like OneTrust and BigID further enhance DFDs by providing regulatory insights, ensuring alignment with industry standards. These tools not only aid in creating DFDs but also ensure they remain relevant and actionable over time.

The Strategic Importance of DFDs

Incorporating Data Flow Diagrams into cybersecurity audits is not just a best practice; it is a necessity in today's digital landscape. These diagrams provide a visual roadmap for identifying and addressing vulnerabilities, ensuring compliance, and aligning audit efforts with organizational priorities.

By bridging the gap between technical complexity and actionable insights, DFDs empower auditors to deliver results that resonate with both technical teams and business leaders. As technology continues to evolve, the ability to visualize and analyze data flows will remain a foundation of effective cybersecurity audits, enabling organizations to stay ahead of emerging threats and challenges.

Key Takeaways

Cybersecurity audits will increasingly rely on such visual tools to bridge the gap between technical complexity and practical security measures. Organizations that master the creation and utilization of DFDs will be better positioned to protect their assets, maintain compliance, and adapt to evolving threats in the digital landscape.

In this section, we covered the following points:

Data Flow Diagrams represent a critical intersection between technical documentation and strategic security planning. Their importance in modern cybersecurity audits cannot be overstated, as they provide

- *Comprehensive Visibility*:
  - Clear visualization of complex data movements.
  - Identification of critical security checkpoints.
  - Mapping of system interdependencies.
- *Enhanced Risk Management*:
  - Early detection of potential vulnerabilities.
  - Prioritization of security controls.
  - Efficient resource allocation.
- *Improved Compliance*:
  - Documentary evidence for regulatory requirements.
  - Clear tracking of sensitive data handling.
  - Validation of security controls.

- *Stakeholder Alignment*:
    - Common understanding across technical and non-technical teams.
    - Facilitated communication about security priorities.
    - Enhanced collaboration in risk mitigation.

As organizations continue to navigate increasingly complex digital landscapes, DFDs serve as essential tools for

- Identifying and protecting critical data assets.
- Ensuring regulatory compliance.
- Optimizing security investments.
- Supporting informed decision-making.

Developing an Effective Cybersecurity Audit Checklist

The foundation of any successful cybersecurity audit lies in its preparation. Among the tools that ensure a structured, thorough, and efficient audit, the cybersecurity audit checklist is paramount. This checklist is more than a collection of tasks; it is a carefully curated roadmap that aligns the audit process with organizational goals, regulatory requirements, and emerging threats. When developed and executed effectively, it guarantees comprehensive coverage, ensures consistency, and delivers actionable insights.

Just as a thorough home inspection requires a detailed checklist to ensure no vulnerable spots are missed, a cybersecurity audit needs a comprehensive checklist to protect a digital home.

Why an Audit Checklist Is Essential

In the intricate world of cybersecurity, where the smallest oversight can lead to significant vulnerabilities, an audit checklist provides a much-needed safety net. First and foremost, it ensures no critical areas are overlooked. Cybersecurity is vast, encompassing everything from access controls to incident response. A checklist acts as a guide, ensuring auditors examine every crucial aspect of an organization's security landscape.

Moreover, a standardized checklist brings consistency to audits. Whether conducted by different teams or repeated over time, it ensures that the same criteria are applied, yielding reliable and comparable results. Efficiency is another hallmark of a good checklist. By reducing ambiguity and saving time, it allows auditors to focus on analysis and problem-solving rather than figuring out what to assess next.

Think of the cybersecurity audit checklist as the ultimate home inspector's guide. Just as a home inspector methodically checks every foundation crack, loose wire, and squeaky floorboard, a digital security checklist ensures no vulnerability goes unnoticed. Without this systematic approach, it's like trying to secure a home by randomly checking windows and doors – you can easily miss something critical.

Key Benefits of an Audit Checklist:

- *Comprehensive Coverage*: Ensures all critical areas are assessed.
- *Consistency*: Standardizes audits across teams and timelines.
- *Efficiency*: Streamlines processes, saving time and effort.
- *Regulatory Alignment*: Meets standards like PCI DSS, GDPR, HIPAA, etc.
- *Actionable Results*: Identifies gaps and prioritizes remediation.

A robust checklist also supports compliance efforts. Regulatory frameworks like GDPR, HIPAA, and PCI DSS mandate meticulous documentation of security measures. A detailed checklist provides this documentation, offering proof of due diligence during audits or investigations.

Building the Foundation of a Cybersecurity Audit Checklist

The development of a cybersecurity audit checklist begins with understanding its purpose. Is the focus on regulatory compliance, risk mitigation, or improving operational resilience? Defining these objectives lays the groundwork for a checklist that aligns with the organization's needs.

The next step is to align the checklist with established frameworks like NIST CSF, ISO 27001, or specific regulations like GDPR. These standards provide a robust foundation, ensuring the checklist addresses both universal and industry-specific requirements.

Creating an effective security checklist is like designing the perfect home inspection routine. Just as you'd prioritize checking the foundation before worrying about loose doorknobs, your checklist should follow a logical progression through your digital home's critical systems:

- Start with the foundation (core infrastructure).
- Check all entry points (access controls).
- Inspect utility systems (network security).
- Review emergency plans (incident response).
- Verify safety equipment (security tools).

Steps to Develop a Checklist:

- *Define Scope and Objectives*: Establish clear audit goals.
- *Align with Standards*: Reference frameworks like NIST, ISO 27001, GDPR, HIPAA, etc.
- *Organize Audit Areas*: Segment the checklist into focus areas:
    - *Access Controls*: Review authentication, permissions, and privileges.
    - *Data Security*: Examine encryption, backups, and storage.
    - *Network Security*: Assess firewalls, segmentation, and monitoring.
    - *Incident Response*: Test response readiness and recovery plans.
- *Collaborate with Teams*: Work with IT and other stakeholders for accuracy.
- *Leverage Tools*: Use platforms like Tenable or Qualys to streamline checklist creation.
- *Test and Refine*: Pilot the checklist to identify gaps and improve usability.
- *Update Regularly*: Adapt to evolving threats and regulatory changes.

CHAPTER 2　PLANNING THE CYBERSECURITY AUDIT

Each step in this process reinforces the checklist's relevance and effectiveness. Testing and refinement ensure the checklist is not just theoretical but practical, addressing real-world risks and workflows.

The process flow is described in Figure 2-6, where it is presented that audit checklist creation and monitoring is a continuous process.

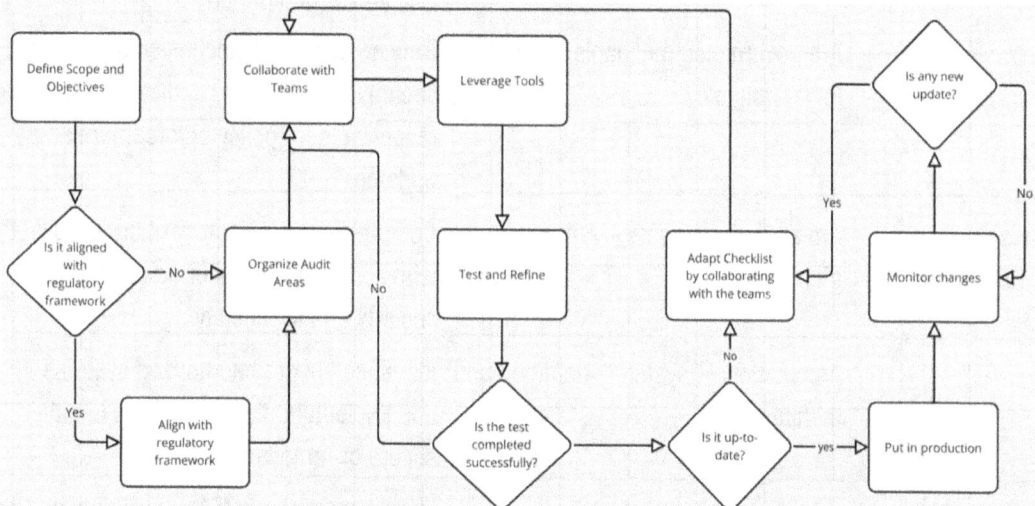

Figure 2-6. *Audit checklist creation and monitoring workflow process*

Key Components of a Cybersecurity Audit Checklist

A well-rounded checklist is divided into sections that cover the critical aspects of cybersecurity. Each section targets specific areas, ensuring a thorough and targeted approach.

Table 2-5 presents key components of the cybersecurity audit checklist. The checklist is presented for seven different areas; for each area, the two most common questions and expected outcomes from each of the questions are presented.

CHAPTER 2   PLANNING THE CYBERSECURITY AUDIT

Table 2-5. *Key components of cybersecurity audit checklist*

Checklist Area	Question	Expected Outcome
Governance and Policies	Are security policies documented and updated?	Documented, up-to-date policies that reflect current cybersecurity practices and regulatory requirements.
	Are governance mechanisms in place for oversight?	Defined oversight mechanisms, such as a security committee or dedicated personnel responsible for policy enforcement and updates.
Asset Management	Are all critical assets inventoried and monitored?	Comprehensive inventory of critical assets with continuous monitoring to ensure security and availability.
	Are shadow IT systems identified and managed?	Identification of unauthorized systems and implementation of controls to either secure or remove them.
Access Control	Is MFA enforced?	Implementation of MFA across critical systems to ensure secure authentication.
	Are the principles of least privilege applied?	User access rights are limited to the minimum necessary for their roles, reducing unnecessary privileges.
Risk Management	Are risks assessed and documented regularly?	Regular risk assessments with detailed documentation of potential threats, vulnerabilities, and associated impacts.
	Are mitigation measures implemented effectively?	Implementation of mitigation controls, tracked and evaluated for effectiveness in reducing identified risks.

(*continued*)

CHAPTER 2 PLANNING THE CYBERSECURITY AUDIT

Table 2-5. (*continued*)

Checklist Area	Question	Expected Outcome
Incident Response	Are response plans tested through simulations?	Conducting regular simulations to evaluate the effectiveness and readiness of incident response plans.
	Are backups secure and accessible?	Implementation of secure, regularly tested backups to ensure data recovery during an incident.
Network Security	Are firewalls, segmentation, and intrusion detection in place?	Deployed and operational firewalls, network segmentation, and intrusion detection systems to safeguard the network.
	Is network traffic monitored for anomalies?	Continuous network traffic monitoring with mechanisms to detect and respond to unusual patterns or unauthorized activities.
Compliance	Are processes and vendors aligned with relevant regulations?	Processes and vendor practices adhere to applicable regulations (e.g., GDPR and HIPAA) to avoid compliance breaches.
	Is documentation maintained for audits?	Accurate and up-to-date documentation of compliance activities, ready for audits or reviews by regulators.

Challenges and Solutions in Checklist Development

Just as home security faces obstacles, developing an audit checklist has its challenges. Use the following strategies to avoid the common pitfalls:

- Don't use a one-size-fits-all approach (like using the same security system for a mansion and an apartment).

- Ensure deep inspection (don't just check if the door is locked; verify the lock's quality).

- Keep it manageable (like breaking down home maintenance into seasonal tasks).

CHAPTER 2   PLANNING THE CYBERSECURITY AUDIT

Creating and using an audit checklist is not without its challenges. One common issue is overgeneralization. Generic checklists often fail to address an organization's unique risks, leaving critical vulnerabilities unexamined. The solution lies in customization, tailoring the checklist to reflect specific systems, workflows, and threats.

Another challenge is the lack of technical depth. Superficial checks may overlook deeper vulnerabilities, such as misconfigurations or hidden exploits. To counter this, auditors can incorporate advanced testing techniques, such as penetration testing, into the checklist.

Finally, there is the issue of checklist fatigue. Long and overly detailed checklists can overwhelm auditors, reducing their effectiveness. A modular approach that prioritizes high-risk areas can make the checklist more manageable and impactful.

Overcoming Common Challenges:

- *Overgeneralization*: Customize checklists to fit specific risks.
- *Lack of Technical Depth*: Include in-depth testing methods.
- *Checklist Fatigue*: Use a modular, prioritized approach.

Tools to Enhance Checklist Development

Modern technology offers a wealth of tools to improve the creation and execution of audit checklists. Automation tools like Qualys and Tenable enable continuous monitoring and automated compliance checks, saving time and reducing errors.

Compliance platforms like LogicGate and OneTrust help align checklists with evolving regulations, ensuring ongoing relevance. Collaboration tools such as Microsoft Teams or Confluence centralize checklist management, facilitating updates and sharing among team members.

Recommended Tools:

- *Automation*: Qualys, Tenable.
- *Compliance Management*: LogicGate, OneTrust.
- *Collaboration*: Microsoft Teams, Confluence.

Automation Tools

Automation tools are essential for improving efficiency and accuracy in audit processes. Tools such as Qualys and Tenable are used for continuous monitoring of IT infrastructure and automated compliance checks, ensuring that the system's security and compliance posture is continuously assessed and up-to-date. These tools also help to automatically update checklists based on the latest data, reducing manual input and the risk of outdated information.

- *Qualys*: Provides vulnerability management, continuous monitoring, and automated compliance checks. It streamlines audit processes by continuously scanning networks for vulnerabilities and aligning them with established security policies.

- *Tenable*: Specializes in risk-based vulnerability management and continuous monitoring. Its automation capabilities ensure real-time updates on security threats, which can then be directly reflected in audit checklists.

Compliance Management Platforms

Compliance is a key part of audit processes, and platforms like LogicGate and OneTrust help manage compliance requirements by providing customizable tools that align with the latest regulations. These platforms allow teams to ensure that checklists are continuously updated and in line with evolving regulations such as GDPR, HIPAA, or ISO standards, providing audit-ready solutions.

- *LogicGate*: Offers risk and compliance management with workflows tailored to specific industries. It ensures that checklists remain up-to-date with regulatory requirements, helping businesses comply with evolving laws.

- *OneTrust*: A comprehensive platform for privacy, security, and data governance. It includes automation for managing compliance processes and integrates with audit tools to update checklists according to the latest privacy regulations and industry standards.

Collaboration Tools

Collaboration is a crucial element for effective checklist development. Tools like Microsoft Teams and Confluence centralize checklist management, enabling team members to collaborate in real time. This ensures that updates are quickly communicated and that checklists reflect the latest input from all stakeholders.

- *Microsoft Teams*: Facilitates communication and real-time collaboration among audit teams. Teams can easily share checklists, track progress, and resolve issues within a central platform, which helps ensure consistency and accuracy across the board.

- *Confluence*: A collaboration and documentation tool that centralizes knowledge sharing. Audit checklists can be stored and shared with all stakeholders, and real-time updates ensure the team is always working from the latest version.

The Strategic Role of an Audit Checklist

An effective cybersecurity audit checklist is more than a guide; it is the foundation of a successful audit. By ensuring comprehensive coverage, driving consistency, and delivering actionable insights, it strengthens organizational defenses and aligns cybersecurity efforts with business goals.

In a world of increasing cyber threats, a well-crafted checklist is a strategic asset, enabling organizations to stay ahead of vulnerabilities, comply with regulations, and build resilience against future challenges. As technology and threats evolve, so must the checklist, adapting to ensure it remains a foundation of effective cybersecurity auditing.

Key Takeaways

A cybersecurity audit checklist is not just a static document; it's a dynamic, living tool. Its value lies in its ability to adapt to emerging threats, incorporate new technologies, and align with evolving regulations. Checklists must continuously evolve to safeguard the organization's digital assets effectively. Treat it as an ongoing security partner, ensuring comprehensive, consistent, and actionable insights to protect and strengthen defenses.

In this section, we covered the following points:

- A cybersecurity audit checklist serves as a structured roadmap, ensuring the audit process is aligned with organizational goals, regulatory requirements, and emerging threats.
- A checklist ensures that all critical aspects of cybersecurity, such as access controls, incident response, and network security, are examined without any oversight.
- Standardized checklists streamline audits, saving time and enabling reliable comparisons across teams and timelines.
- Tailoring the checklist to the organization's unique risks, workflows, and threats ensures its effectiveness and relevance.
- Referencing established frameworks like NIST or ISO 27001 and using tools like Qualys, Tenable, and LogicGate enhances checklist accuracy and usability.
- Address challenges such as overgeneralization, lack of technical depth, and checklist fatigue by incorporating advanced testing, a modular structure, and in-depth risk analysis.
- Beyond task tracking, the checklist serves as a dynamic, evolving tool that strengthens cybersecurity defenses, ensures compliance, and aligns with evolving technologies and threats.

Risk Assessment – Identifying High-Risk Areas in Cybersecurity Audits

In the ever-evolving world of cybersecurity, identifying and mitigating risks is paramount. Risk assessment lies at the heart of effective cybersecurity audits, enabling organizations to focus on the areas that matter most. It is a strategic process that identifies vulnerabilities, evaluates threats, and prioritizes actions to safeguard critical assets and maintain operational resilience.

CHAPTER 2   PLANNING THE CYBERSECURITY AUDIT

Risk assessment in cybersecurity is like inspecting a home for vulnerabilities. Just as with checking for broken locks or unsecured windows, cybersecurity audits focus on identifying weak points in digital environments. By understanding where the risks lie, there can be prioritized efforts to protect most valuable possessions and keep intruders at bay.

The Importance of Risk Assessment in Cybersecurity

A thorough risk assessment is akin to planning a home security system. Before installing cameras or alarms, it is needed to assess which areas, like the front door or backyard, are most vulnerable. Similarly, in cybersecurity, this process helps allocate resources effectively, ensuring critical assets are protected and threats are neutralized before they breach your defenses.

Risk assessment is not just a step in the auditing process; it is the foundation of proactive cybersecurity management. By understanding and quantifying risks, organizations can make informed decisions, optimize their resources, and address the most pressing vulnerabilities.

- *Prioritize Efforts*: Auditors can direct their focus to areas with the highest risk exposure, ensuring that no critical threats are overlooked.

- *Optimize Resources*: By highlighting priority areas, organizations can allocate their tools, personnel, and budgets more efficiently.

- *Inform Decision-Making*: Clear risk insights guide leadership in implementing effective mitigation strategies.

- *Ensure Compliance*: Risk assessments align with frameworks like ISO 27001, NIST, and GDPR, ensuring that regulatory requirements and best practices are met.

Like an experienced guide who knows where predators lurk, risk assessment helps organizations spot digital risks before they strike. This isn't just about spotting tracks; it's about understanding the entire ecosystem of threats and protecting digital expeditions. A well-executed risk assessment provides a foundation for actionable insights, transforming abstract threats into manageable challenges.

Steps in Risk Assessment

Conducting a risk assessment requires a methodical approach to ensure that all critical areas are evaluated. Each step builds upon the last, creating a comprehensive understanding of the organization's risk landscape.

Figure 2-7 presents the process workflow on cybersecurity risk assessment.

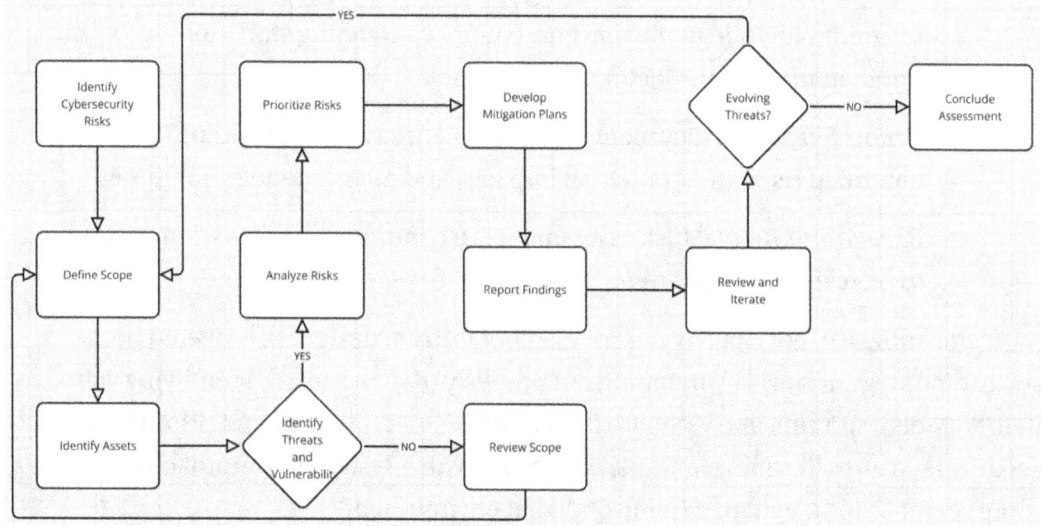

Figure 2-7. *Risk assessment process flow*

- *Define Scope*: Start by clarifying the boundaries of the assessment. Will it cover the entire organization, a specific department, or a particular system? A well-defined scope ensures focus and clarity.

- *Identify Assets*: Create an inventory of all critical assets, including hardware, software, and key business processes. Tools like asset management software can simplify this task.

- *Identify Threats and Vulnerabilities*:
    - *Threats*: Consider potential adversaries, natural disasters, and internal errors.
    - *Vulnerabilities*: Pinpoint weaknesses, such as outdated systems or poor password practices. Tools like Nessus can automate this process.

- *Analyze Risks*: Assess the likelihood of each threat exploiting a vulnerability and evaluate its potential impact on operations, finances, and reputation.

- *Prioritize Risks*: Use frameworks like a risk matrix or the FAIR model to rank risks based on severity and urgency.

- *Mitigation Plans*: Develop strategies to address high-priority risks. Examples include deploying encryption, conducting staff training, or implementing multi-factor authentication.

- *Report Findings*: Document the assessment's results, including identified risks, their potential impacts, and recommended solutions.

- *Review and Iterate*: Risk assessment is a continuous process; it needs to be reviewed regularly.

Performing a cybersecurity risk assessment mirrors designing a layered home security strategy. It starts by mapping out property (define scope), identifying valuable items (assets), spotting entry points (threats and vulnerabilities), and prioritizing security measures like locks, alarms, or patrols. With a systematic approach, it creates a robust defense to safeguard a home or digital environment.

Risk Assessment Frameworks

Frameworks provide standardized methodologies for conducting risk assessments, ensuring consistency and thoroughness.

- *NIST Risk Management Framework (RMF)*: Offers a comprehensive approach to identifying, assessing, and mitigating risks.

- *ISO 31000*: Focuses on integrating risk management into organizational workflows.

- *OCTAVE*: Aligns risk assessment with business objectives, making it ideal for strategic decision-making.

- *FAIR Model*: Provides quantitative risk analysis, offering measurable insights into potential impacts.

Each framework has its strengths, and the choice depends on the organization's needs and regulatory environment.

Technologies for Risk Assessment

Modern tools and technologies enhance the accuracy and efficiency of risk assessments.

- *Vulnerability Scanners*:
  - *Nessus*: Detects system misconfigurations and outdated software.
  - *Qualys*: Provides continuous monitoring and alerts.
- *Threat Intelligence Platforms (TIPs)*:
  - *Recorded Future*: Tracks emerging threats and vulnerabilities.
  - *IBM X-Force*: Identifies industry-specific threat trends.
- *Risk Management Software*:
  - *LogicManager*: Quantifies risks and automates workflows.
  - *RSA Archer*: Offers advanced analytics for risk evaluation.
- *SIEM Tools*:
  - *Splunk*: Analyzes logs and detects anomalies.
  - *LogRhythm*: Provides real-time threat response capabilities.

These tools streamline assessments, ensuring that risks are identified and mitigated promptly.

Overcoming Challenges in Risk Assessment

Risk assessment is not without its obstacles, but understanding common challenges can help organizations navigate them effectively. The following are the three most common challenges in risk assessment:

- *Incomplete Asset Inventory*: Missing assets can lead to overlooked risks.
  - *Solution*: Automate asset tracking with tools like SolarWinds to ensure full visibility.

CHAPTER 2   PLANNING THE CYBERSECURITY AUDIT

- *Evolving Threats*: Static assessments quickly become outdated in a dynamic threat landscape.
  - *Solution*: Leverage real-time TIPs to stay current.
- *Poor Collaboration*: Limited input from stakeholders can hinder accuracy.
  - *Solution*: Use collaboration tools like Microsoft Teams or Jira to engage cross-functional teams.

Addressing challenges in risk assessment is like dealing with unexpected gaps in home security. If a window lock is missing or an alarm battery dies, your safety is compromised. Similarly, missing assets, evolving threats, or poor communication can undermine cybersecurity. Automating processes and staying vigilant ensure your defenses remain intact, just like regular maintenance keeps your home secure.

Best Practices for Effective Risk Assessment

Adopting the best practices ensures that risk assessments are both effective and efficient.

- *Risk-Based Focus*: Prioritize audits based on risk severity rather than treating all areas equally.
- *Automation*: Use automation to streamline repetitive tasks, saving time and improving accuracy.
- *Stay Updated*: Continuously adapt to new threats and changes in the organization's environment.
- *Target High-Impact Risks*: Focus efforts on vulnerabilities that pose the greatest potential harm.
- *Document Thoroughly*: Maintain detailed records of processes, findings, and mitigation plans to ensure accountability and transparency.

These practices not only improve the quality of assessments but also ensure that organizations remain proactive in their cybersecurity efforts.

The Strategic Role of Risk Assessment

Risk assessment is more than a checklist item; it is a strategic tool that empowers organizations to face cybersecurity challenges head-on. By identifying high-risk areas and allocating resources effectively, it strengthens defenses, supports compliance efforts, and enhances decision-making.

A well-executed risk assessment functions like a central command of home security. It helps to coordinate defenses, ensuring every lock, camera, and alarm works together to protect the household. By staying proactive, it not only keeps the home safe today but also prepares it to withstand future challenges, creating peace of mind in an ever-changing world.

In today's fast-paced threat landscape, organizations cannot afford to be reactive. A robust risk assessment process, supported by the right frameworks and technologies, is the foundation for proactive cybersecurity management. It ensures that organizations are not just prepared for today's risks but are resilient enough to face the uncertainties of tomorrow.

Key Takeaways

Risk assessment should be a dynamic, ongoing process. Just like homeowners don't assume their house is always safe, organizations must continuously scan for new threats, adapt, and update their protective measures to ensure a strong cybersecurity posture. A proactive and vigilant risk assessment strategy is crucial for staying ahead of emerging risks.

In this section, we covered the following points:

- Risk assessment is the foundation of cybersecurity audits, helping organizations identify and prioritize vulnerabilities to safeguard critical assets and build resilience against cyber threats.

- The process involves several key steps: defining scope, inventorying assets, identifying threats, analyzing and prioritizing risks, and developing mitigation plans.

- Tools like vulnerability scanners, TIPs, and SIEM tools streamline risk assessments, enhancing accuracy and efficiency.

- Frameworks like FAIR and ISO 31000 provide consistency and guide risk evaluation, improving the overall effectiveness of the process.

- Challenges such as incomplete asset inventories, evolving threats, and collaboration gaps can be overcome through automation, real-time threat intelligence, and cross-functional collaboration tools.

- Adopting best practices like prioritizing high-impact risks, automating repetitive tasks, and maintaining thorough documentation ensures the process remains effective and adaptive.

Aligning Audit Objectives with Business Goals

In the realm of cybersecurity, audits are more than a means of checking compliance or identifying vulnerabilities. When aligned with business goals, they become strategic tools that drive success, mitigate risks, and support organizational growth. Misaligned audits, on the other hand, can overlook critical threats or waste resources on low-impact areas. Tailoring audits to the business's unique needs ensures that cybersecurity efforts reinforce, rather than hinder, overarching objectives.

Aligning cybersecurity audit objectives with business goals is like designing a home security system tailored to lifestyle and priorities. A family with young children might focus on securing windows and doors, while someone with valuable art might prioritize installing advanced surveillance. Similarly, aligning audits ensures cybersecurity efforts protect what matters most, supporting organizational growth and mitigating risks.

Cybersecurity audits are no longer about checking boxes or ensuring compliance with regulations. For organizations to thrive, cybersecurity efforts must be seen as strategic assets that directly contribute to business success. This is where aligning cybersecurity audit objectives with business goals becomes critical. By ensuring that audits are tailored to business needs, organizations can make sure their cybersecurity posture strengthens their overall strategy, reduces risks, and enhances operational resilience.

Why Alignment Matters

Alignment between audit objectives and business goals transforms audits from mere operational exercises into initiatives that deliver real value. It is similar to ensuring home security measures match specific needs. A house near a busy street might require noise-canceling barriers and reinforced gates, while a remote farmhouse might focus on perimeter cameras.

Here are the key reasons why alignment is essential:

- *Supports Strategic Priorities*: Cybersecurity is a critical enabler of modern business initiatives, such as digital transformation, cloud adoption, or customer trust enhancement. Aligned audits help safeguard these priorities by addressing specific vulnerabilities that could derail progress.

- *Improves Risk Awareness*: Each industry faces unique challenges. For example, patient data protection is paramount in healthcare, while payment security is critical in e-commerce. By addressing these risks, audits ensure the organization remains resilient.

- *Enhances Decision-Making*: Meaningful audit insights allow leadership to make informed decisions, whether it is investing in new technologies or refining existing processes.

- *Ensures Compliance*: Regulations like GDPR, HIPAA, and PCI DSS impose stringent requirements. Aligned audits not only help achieve compliance but also avoid costly penalties and reputation damage.

An audit that aligns with business goals is proactive, ensuring the organization stays secure and competitive in an ever-evolving threat landscape.

Steps to Align Audit Objectives with Business Goals

To create an audit that truly supports the organization, auditors must take a structured approach. It is similar to customizing a security system to fit a home's layout. It requires structured steps to cover all vulnerabilities and priorities.

- *Understand Business Objectives*: Begin by engaging with stakeholders across departments to understand strategic priorities. For example, a company focusing on enhancing customer trust might prioritize data privacy, while one undergoing cloud migration might emphasize infrastructure security.

- *Identify Key Risks*: Conduct thorough risk assessments to highlight threats that could jeopardize business goals. A healthcare provider might need to protect patient records, while a retailer could focus on preventing payment fraud.

- *Define Audit Objectives*: Tailor the audit to address the identified risks. For instance, assess compliance with GDPR, validate encryption for sensitive data, or evaluate access control measures.

- *Map Findings to Business Impact*: Technical findings should be translated into business outcomes. For example, identifying an outdated firewall isn't just a technical issue; it is a risk to operational continuity and customer trust.

- *Provide Actionable Recommendations*: Audits should offer clear, implementable solutions. Recommendations like implementing MFA, updating software, or training employees must tie back to reducing specific risks.

- *Communicate Effectively*: Use visuals like dashboards, heat maps, and metrics to present audit results in a way that resonates with non-technical stakeholders. Clear communication bridges the gap between technical insights and business priorities.

Figure 2-8 presents the process flow for aligning audit objectives with business goals.

CHAPTER 2 PLANNING THE CYBERSECURITY AUDIT

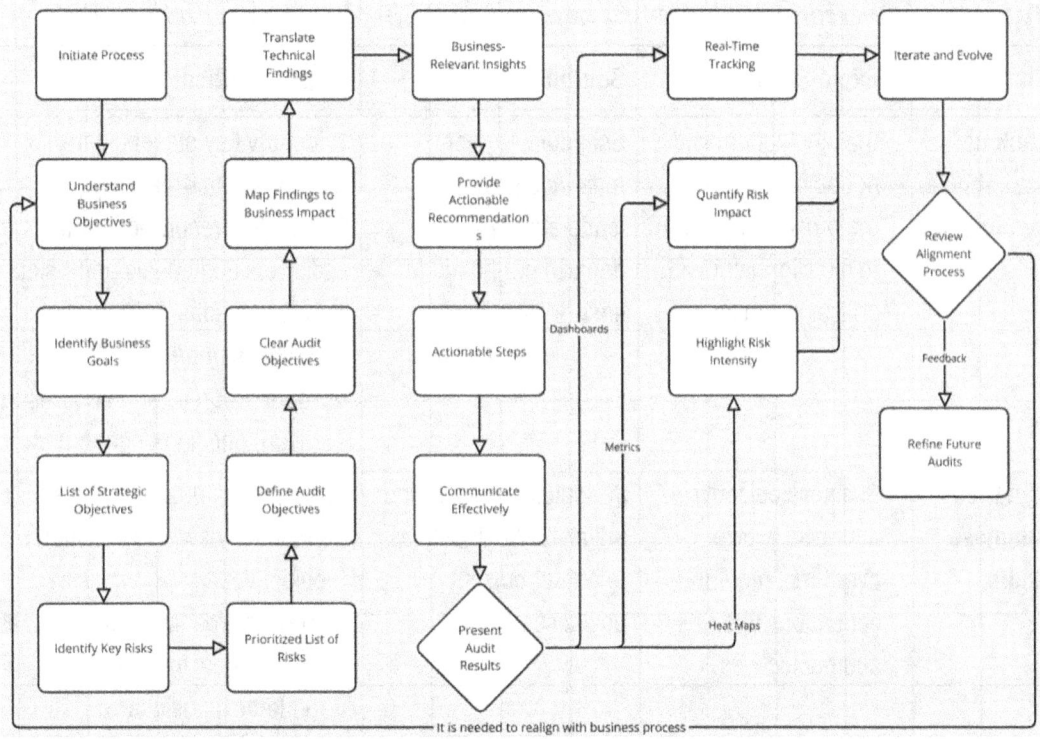

Figure 2-8. *Risk assessment process flow*

Overcoming Challenges

While aligning audit objectives with business goals delivers immense value, it is not without challenges. Addressing these hurdles ensures the process remains effective. Table 2-6 presents some of the most common challenges and their solutions.

Table 2-6. *Overcoming challenges in aligning audit objectives with business goals*

Challenge	Explanation	Solution	Steps to Mitigate
Lack of Stakeholder Involvement	Stakeholders may not be engaged in the process, leading to misalignment with critical priorities.	Schedule regular meetings with leadership and department heads to ensure alignment.	1. Identify key stakeholders across departments. 2. Schedule recurring meetings to discuss audit goals and risks. 3. Gather feedback on critical business priorities. 4. Share progress and updates to ensure ongoing engagement.
Dynamic Business Goals	Business objectives and risks evolve over time, requiring continuous updates to audit objectives.	Periodically review and adjust audit objectives to reflect current business needs.	1. Establish a quarterly or semi-annual review cycle for audit objectives. 2. Monitor organizational changes such as new initiatives or market expansions. 3. Adjust audit frameworks to reflect updated risks and objectives. 4. Communicate changes to all stakeholders and ensure they are factored into the audit plan.

(*continued*)

Table 2-6. (*continued*)

Challenge	Explanation	Solution	Steps to Mitigate
Technical Complexity	Non-technical stakeholders may find it difficult to understand audit findings, resulting in a communication gap.	Use intuitive dashboards, heat maps, or simplified reports to bridge the communication gap.	1. Create simplified visualizations (dashboards, charts) for technical data. 2. Use relatable analogies to explain technical concepts. 3. Conduct training sessions to familiarize non-technical stakeholders with key audit terms and processes. 4. Provide a concise executive summary alongside the technical report to ensure clarity and alignment.
Resistance to Change	Some departments or individuals may resist implementing recommendations due to perceived disruptions or lack of understanding of their benefits.	Communicate the business impact of audit recommendations and engage teams in collaborative implementation.	1. Highlight the potential risks of not implementing the recommendations (e.g., financial loss and reputational damage). 2. Provide data-driven evidence to support the need for change. 3. Engage resistant teams in workshops to co-create solutions. 4. Celebrate quick wins to showcase the benefits of change and build momentum.

(*continued*)

CHAPTER 2   PLANNING THE CYBERSECURITY AUDIT

Table 2-6. (*continued*)

Challenge	Explanation	Solution	Steps to Mitigate
Resource Constraints	Limited time, budget, or personnel can make it challenging to align audits effectively with business goals.	Prioritize high-impact areas and leverage automation tools to optimize resources.	1. Identify critical areas where auditing will have the most significant impact. 2. Use tools like automated risk assessment platforms to streamline processes. 3. Allocate resources to address high-priority risks first. 4. Consider outsourcing certain tasks or hiring consultants to bridge gaps in expertise.
Lack of Updated Data	Audits may rely on outdated or incomplete information, leading to gaps in addressing current risks and priorities.	Implement continuous monitoring and data collection processes to maintain up-to-date information.	1. Deploy automated tools for real-time data collection and monitoring (e.g., vulnerability scanners and asset management tools). 2. Conduct regular data validation exercises to ensure accuracy. 3. Create a feedback loop to collect updated information from all departments. 4. Train teams to report significant changes promptly to ensure accurate audit preparation.

(*continued*)

Table 2-6. (*continued*)

Challenge	Explanation	Solution	Steps to Mitigate
Fragmented Processes	Disconnected systems or siloed departments can create inefficiencies and prevent a holistic view of risks and objectives.	Foster cross-departmental collaboration and integrate tools to unify processes.	1. Identify interdependencies among departments and systems. 2. Use centralized platforms or dashboards to manage audit-related data and workflows. 3. Host cross-functional meetings to ensure a unified approach. 4. Assign a central audit coordinator to oversee alignment and reduce fragmentation.
Overloading Non-Critical Areas	Audits may focus on areas with minimal impact while neglecting high-priority risks due to poor prioritization.	Use a risk-based prioritization model to ensure high-impact areas are addressed first.	1. Develop a risk matrix to rank areas based on severity and likelihood of risks. 2. Review audit plans with stakeholders to validate prioritization. 3. Regularly update priorities based on emerging threats and organizational shifts. 4. Allocate resources proportionally to high-priority areas.

(*continued*)

Table 2-6. (*continued*)

Challenge	Explanation	Solution	Steps to Mitigate
Cultural Misalignment	The organization's culture may not prioritize security or audits, leading to low adoption of recommendations.	Integrate security into the organizational culture through training, awareness programs, and executive sponsorship.	1. Launch a security awareness campaign to educate employees on the importance of audits. 2. Gain leadership buy-in to champion audit initiatives. 3. Incentivize adoption through rewards or recognition programs. 4. Embed security objectives into broader business goals to align cultural practices with audit priorities.

Tools to Facilitate Alignment

Several tools and technologies can simplify the process of aligning audits with business goals:

- *GRC Platforms*: Tools like Archer map audits to risks and organizational objectives, ensuring comprehensive coverage.

- *SIEM Systems*: Platforms like Splunk or LogRhythm provide real-time insights, helping auditors focus on high-impact areas.

- *Risk Frameworks*: Frameworks like NIST and FAIR quantify risks and tie them to business outcomes.

- *Collaboration Tools*: Tools like Microsoft Teams or Confluence facilitate seamless communication between auditors and stakeholders.

These technologies enhance the accuracy, efficiency, and relevance of the audit process.

Best Practices for Alignment

To ensure successful alignment, organizations should adhere to the following best practices:

- *Start with Business Needs*: Let strategic objectives guide the audit's scope and focus, just as home security begins with family requirements.

- *Involve Stakeholders Early*: Collaborate with key stakeholders from the outset to understand priorities and gain buy-in.

- *Quantify Risks with Metrics*: Use measurable indicators to evaluate risks and their potential business impact.

- *Emphasize Value Beyond Compliance*: Position the audit as a tool for enhancing security and supporting growth, not just meeting regulatory requirements.

- *Communicate Findings Effectively*: Present results in terms of business impact, supported by visuals and clear recommendations.

Cybersecurity as a Strategic Asset

Aligning cybersecurity audits with business goals transforms them into strategic assets. These audits do more than check compliance boxes; they safeguard strategic initiatives, strengthen risk management, and foster resilience.

In a world where cybersecurity is intertwined with business success, aligned audits provide clarity, focus, and actionable insights. They enable organizations to view cybersecurity not as an operational task but as a competitive advantage, turning risks into opportunities for growth and innovation.

When aligned with business goals, audits become assets like a state-of-the-art home security system. They protect against risks, support long-term strategies, and foster resilience. Organizations can turn their cybersecurity audits into enablers of innovation, ensuring that threats are managed proactively while creating opportunities for growth.

CHAPTER 2   PLANNING THE CYBERSECURITY AUDIT

Key Takeaways

Cybersecurity audits must remain dynamic, evolving with the organization's changing priorities, just as a home security system adapts to the needs of a family. Aligning audits with business goals transforms cybersecurity from a compliance task into a strategic enabler, creating opportunities for growth and resilience.

In this section, we covered the following points:

- Aligned cybersecurity audits go beyond compliance, transforming them into strategic initiatives that protect business goals, strengthen operational resilience, and mitigate vulnerabilities that impact long-term success.

- By focusing on high-priority risks, audits ensure optimal resource allocation, helping organizations avoid wasting time and budget on less impactful areas.

- Advanced tools such as GRC platforms and SIEM systems enhance the audit process, while frameworks like NIST and FAIR offer actionable insights tied to business outcomes.

- Overcoming challenges in the audit process requires stakeholder engagement and clear communication to ensure alignment with business objectives and effective decision-making.

Defining Audit Metrics for Success

In the complex and ever-evolving world of cybersecurity, the ability to measure success is critical. Without well-defined metrics, audits risk becoming exercises in ineffectiveness, leaving organizations unsure of their strengths, vulnerabilities, or next steps. Audit metrics provide the structure needed to evaluate cybersecurity efforts, track progress, and guide decision-making. They are not merely tools for compliance but are instrumental in strengthening an organization's overall security posture and aligning cybersecurity initiatives with broader business objectives.

Defining effective audit metrics is like setting up home security cameras that capture the right angles and offer a clear picture of the property's safety. Without these well-placed cameras, blind spots could leave the home vulnerable to intrusions. Metrics offer clarity by eliminating ambiguity, much like how motion-activated lights reveal intruders at night. They help stakeholders understand whether cybersecurity goals are being met, evaluate the performance of security controls, and provide actionable insights that guide decision-making.

Metrics are, at their core, about making the intangible measurable. In cybersecurity, where risks often stem from unseen threats or abstract vulnerabilities, metrics offer a way to quantify the effectiveness of controls, identify gaps, and communicate findings in a language that stakeholders can understand. For example, metrics such as the percentage of systems patched on time or the average time taken to respond to incidents transform audit findings into actionable insights that drive meaningful change.

Why Metrics Matter in Cybersecurity Audits

The role of metrics in cybersecurity audits extends far beyond mere evaluation. They provide clarity by defining what success looks like, ensuring that all parties involved have a shared understanding of objectives. Metrics also serve as tools for accountability, enabling organizations to track the performance of their security measures over time and identify areas requiring immediate attention.

- *Clarity*: Metrics eliminate ambiguity, offering a clear framework for measuring success. They help both technical teams and business leaders understand whether the organization is meeting its cybersecurity goals.

- *Evaluation*: By assessing the performance of security controls, metrics reveal strengths and weaknesses, providing a roadmap for improvement.

- *Insights*: Metrics enable data-driven decision-making, highlighting the most critical vulnerabilities and risks to address.

- *Communication*: They translate technical results into a format that is accessible to stakeholders, bridging the gap between cybersecurity teams and organizational leadership.

For instance, an audit focused on improving incident response might include metrics such as the mean time to detect (MTTD) and the mean time to respond (MTTR) to incidents. These metrics provide actionable insights into how quickly the organization can identify and mitigate threats, directly impacting its overall security resilience.

CHAPTER 2   PLANNING THE CYBERSECURITY AUDIT

Key Considerations for Defining Metrics

Defining effective metrics requires a strategic approach. Metrics should not only be relevant to the specific goals of the audit but also practical to implement and measure. To achieve this, organizations must align their metrics with audit objectives, follow established frameworks, and balance quantitative and qualitative measures.

One of the first steps in defining metrics is ensuring they align with the audit's objectives. For example, if the goal of the audit is to enhance data security, relevant metrics might include the percentage of encrypted assets or the adoption rate of MFA. Metrics should also adhere to the specific, measurable, achievable, relevant, and time-bound (SMART) criteria, ensuring they are specific, measurable, achievable, relevant, and time-bound.

In addition to being objective, metrics should also capture qualitative aspects of cybersecurity. While quantitative metrics like the number of vulnerabilities identified are essential, qualitative insights, such as observations on how well employees adhere to security policies, add depth and context to audit findings. A balanced approach ensures a comprehensive evaluation of the organization's security posture.

Examples of Metrics

Metrics can be broadly categorized into technical, compliance, and business-focused measures, much like organizing different types of locks, alarms, and cameras for comprehensive home security. Each category serves a specific purpose, enabling organizations to tailor their audits to address various aspects of cybersecurity.

Technical Metrics

Technical metrics are the backbone of most cybersecurity audits. They provide hard data on the performance of security controls and highlight areas requiring immediate attention. Examples include

- The number and severity of vulnerabilities identified during the audit.
- The percentage of systems patched within a specified timeframe.
- The average time to detect and respond to security incidents.

Compliance Metrics

Compliance metrics measure adherence to regulatory standards and organizational policies. These metrics are particularly critical for industries with stringent compliance requirements, such as healthcare and finance. Examples include

- Scores for meeting standards like GDPR, PCI DSS, or HIPAA.
- Employee compliance rates with mandatory security training.
- The percentage of completed remediation actions post-audit.

Business Metrics

Business metrics focus on the broader impact of cybersecurity efforts, tying technical and compliance findings to organizational goals. Examples include

- The reduction in overall risk levels following the audit.
- Financial savings from avoided penalties and operational disruptions.
- Improved uptime and smoother operations due to enhanced security measures.

Each of these metrics provides unique insights, enabling organizations to address technical vulnerabilities, meet compliance requirements, and achieve business objectives.

Challenges in Defining Metrics

Defining effective metrics is not without its hurdles. It is like configuring a security system to avoid blind spots; it requires careful consideration to address potential gaps and obstacles. Challenges often arise from various factors, including limited data availability, evolving security needs, and difficulties in stakeholder alignment. Table 2-7 presents some of the most common challenges and their solutions related to audit metrics.

Table 2-7. *Challenges in defining metrics and solutions*

Challenge	Explanation	Solution	Steps to Mitigate
Incomplete Data Sets	Missing or inconsistent data (e.g., incomplete logging and fragmented monitoring systems) can lead to unreliable or irrelevant metrics.	Employ robust monitoring tools and establish automated data collection processes.	1. Deploy centralized monitoring tools for consistent data collection (e.g., SIEM solutions). 2. Set up automated logging across all critical systems to reduce manual errors. 3. Regularly audit data sources to identify and resolve inconsistencies.
Evolving Cybersecurity Threats	Metrics that were once effective may become outdated as new threats emerge, leaving blind spots in security strategies.	Continuously review and update metrics to align with emerging cybersecurity threats and business needs.	1. Conduct regular threat intelligence updates to stay informed on the latest trends. 2. Integrate predictive analytics tools to anticipate evolving threat patterns and adjust metrics proactively.
Stakeholder Misalignment	Technical teams may focus on operational data, while business leaders prioritize outcomes, leading to metrics that fail to address key objectives.	Collaborate with both technical teams and business leaders to define metrics that resonate across organizational levels.	1. Organize cross-functional workshops to align on security and business priorities. 2. Develop a balanced scorecard that includes both technical and business-centric metrics.

(continued)

Table 2-7. (*continued*)

Challenge	Explanation	Solution	Steps to Mitigate
Overly Complex Metrics	Metrics that are too technical or detailed can overwhelm stakeholders and hinder their utility in decision-making processes.	Simplify metrics to focus on actionable insights that are easy to understand for all stakeholders.	1. Define metrics using clear language and avoid unnecessary jargon. 2. Categorize metrics into tiers (e.g., operational, tactical, and strategic) based on audience relevance. 3. Test metrics by presenting them to non-technical stakeholders to ensure clarity and usability.
Resource Constraints	Defining and tracking metrics may require significant time, tools, and personnel, which are often limited in smaller organizations.	Prioritize high-impact metrics and leverage automation to streamline metric collection and analysis.	1. Identify key performance indicators (KPIs) that have the greatest impact on security outcomes. 2. Allocate resources toward tracking critical metrics first before expanding coverage. 3. Explore outsourcing or consulting services for initial setup and optimization of metric tracking.

(*continued*)

Table 2-7. (*continued*)

Challenge	Explanation	Solution	Steps to Mitigate
Difficulty in Benchmarking	Without industry benchmarks or internal baselines, it is challenging to determine if metrics indicate good performance or areas for improvement.	Leverage industry reports, standards, and peer comparisons to establish meaningful benchmarks for metrics.	1. Research industry-specific benchmarks from sources like ISACA, NIST, or ISO. 2. Establish internal baselines by analyzing historical data to track improvements over time. 3. Use third-party audits or certifications to validate metric performance against industry standards.
Lack of Real-Time Insights	Metrics that rely on periodic reporting can miss real-time security events, leaving gaps in situational awareness.	Implement real-time monitoring systems to provide immediate insights into security performance and incidents.	1. Deploy real-time monitoring solutions like SIEM platforms to track events as they happen. 2. Integrate alerts for critical metric deviations to ensure timely action. 3. Regularly test the real-time monitoring system to ensure reliability and accuracy.

Best Practices for Audit Metrics

To maximize the impact of audit metrics, organizations should adopt a combination of strategic planning, practical implementation, and continuous improvement.

- *Actionable Focus*: Metrics should drive specific improvements. Avoid measuring for the sake of measurement; focus on areas that offer tangible benefits.

- *Align Metrics with Objectives*: Metrics must tie directly to audit and business goals, ensuring they support the organization's overarching strategies.

- *Adapt to Change*: Regularly update metrics to reflect new threats, technologies, and business needs.

- *Incorporate Quantitative and Qualitative Data*: Balance numerical data with process evaluations to capture a full picture of cybersecurity effectiveness.

- *Automate Where Possible*: Leverage tools like SIEM systems, vulnerability scanners, and GRC platforms to simplify data collection and analysis.

- *Communicate Clearly*: Present findings using visuals such as dashboards or heat maps to make technical data accessible to all stakeholders.

- *Use Historical Data*: Benchmark against past performance to measure progress and identify trends.

- *Prioritize High-Impact Areas*: Focus metrics on areas of greatest risk or potential improvement, ensuring resources are directed effectively.

For example, pairing automated detection tools like Splunk with qualitative assessments of employee adherence to security policies can offer a well-rounded perspective on incident response effectiveness. Additionally, linking metrics to financial outcomes, such as savings from avoided penalties, can strengthen the case for cybersecurity investments. These best practices ensure organizations that their metrics remain relevant, actionable, and impactful, transforming audits into powerful tools for cybersecurity and business success.

Key Takeaways

Cybersecurity metrics must adapt to emerging risks and changing circumstances. Well-defined, dynamic metrics are essential for building a robust security framework, empowering organizations to not only protect against threats but also drive innovation and long-term success.

In this section, we covered the following points:

- Metrics are foundational to effective audits, offering clarity, actionable insights, and alignment with organizational goals, much like surveillance systems are essential for home security.

- They bridge the gap between technical complexities and business priorities, allowing teams to focus resources on high-impact areas and align cybersecurity strategies with the organization's vision.

- Metrics foster continuous improvement, ensuring defenses adapt to evolving cyber threats and maintaining resilience.

- Clear communication of metrics is vital, using visuals like dashboards to make cybersecurity accessible and relevant to stakeholders, guiding informed decision-making.

- Well-defined metrics enhance collaboration across teams, enabling both technical and non-technical stakeholders to understand progress and areas needing attention, strengthening the audit process and overall security posture.

- By incorporating forward-looking metrics, organizations can stay proactive, anticipating emerging threats and addressing vulnerabilities before they escalate into significant issues.

Common Pitfalls in the Audit Planning Phase

The audit planning phase is the key to any successful cybersecurity audit. It establishes the foundation for everything that follows, from identifying critical risks to implementing effective controls. However, despite its importance, this phase is often overlooked or poorly executed, leading to audits that fail to meet their objectives. By addressing common pitfalls in the planning stage, organizations can ensure their audits are comprehensive, efficient, and aligned with both security and business goals.

Planning is more than a preliminary exercise; it is a strategic process that sets the tone for the entire audit. A well-structured plan provides clarity, focuses efforts on high-risk areas, and ensures resources are used effectively. Conversely, poor planning can result in wasted resources, missed vulnerabilities, and findings that lack actionable value.

Why Planning Matters

Audit planning goes beyond assigning tasks and timelines. It involves crafting a strategic blueprint that defines the audit's scope, objectives, and methodologies. Proper planning ensures

- Critical areas are thoroughly covered without overextending resources.
- The audit aligns with business objectives, compliance requirements, and security priorities.
- Risks of overlooking vulnerabilities or misinterpreting findings are minimized.
- Stakeholders remain engaged and informed throughout the process.

Without thoughtful planning, audits can devolve into disorganized, incomplete exercises that fail to deliver meaningful results. For example, an audit that skips a risk assessment may allocate significant resources to low-impact areas while ignoring critical vulnerabilities.

Common Pitfalls in Audit Planning

The planning phase is extensive, with potential missteps that can compromise the audit's success. Recognizing these pitfalls and taking proactive measures to address them is crucial.

CHAPTER 2   PLANNING THE CYBERSECURITY AUDIT

- *Unclear Objectives*: Many audits fail because their objectives are not well-defined. Without clear goals, the audit lacks focus and direction.
  - *Solution*: Collaborate with stakeholders to establish measurable objectives, such as achieving compliance with a specific standard or reducing the number of high-severity vulnerabilities.
- *Unrealistic Scope*: An audit scope that is either too broad or too narrow can lead to inefficiencies. Overly broad scopes strain resources, while narrow scopes risk missing critical issues.
  - *Solution*: Conduct a risk assessment to prioritize high-risk areas and define a manageable scope.
- *Stakeholder Exclusion*: Neglecting to involve key stakeholders can result in misaligned goals and overlooked risks.
  - *Solution*: Engage stakeholders early in the process to clarify expectations and incorporate their insights into the planning phase.
- *Poor Resource Allocation*: Audits often suffer from insufficient time, budget, or expertise, which compromises their quality.
  - *Solution*: Use tools like GRC platforms and engage external experts to optimize resource allocation.
- *Ignoring Context*: Overlooking the organization's regulatory, operational, or technological environment leads to gaps in the audit.
  - *Solution*: Align audit goals with relevant compliance standards, such as GDPR or PCI DSS, and consider the organization's specific operational needs.
- *Technology Blind Spots*: Generic audit plans fail to address unique risks associated with specific technologies, such as cloud platforms or IoT devices.
  - *Solution*: Use specialized tools and frameworks tailored to the organization's technological landscape.

- *No Success Metrics*: Without predefined metrics, it is challenging to evaluate the audit's effectiveness.
  - *Solution*: Establish measurable outcomes, such as vulnerability reduction percentages or compliance scores, to track progress.
- *Neglecting Changes*: Failing to account for recent IT or organizational changes can render the audit outdated.
  - *Solution*: Regularly review and update the audit plan to reflect new systems, processes, and threat landscapes.

Best Practices for Audit Planning

To avoid these pitfalls, organizations can adopt a series of best practices that foster collaboration, streamline processes, and ensure comprehensive coverage.

- *Conduct a Pre-Audit Assessment*: Use tools like vulnerability scanners or SIEM platforms to identify high-risk areas before defining the audit scope.
- *Leverage Standardized Templates*: Create templates for objectives, scope, timelines, and deliverables to ensure consistency and efficiency.
- *Incorporate Automation*: Utilize GRC platforms, such as RSA Archer, to streamline planning and resource allocation.
- *Engage in Regular Communication*: Schedule check-ins with stakeholders to keep everyone aligned and address concerns early.
- *Perform a Dry Run*: Test the audit plan on a smaller scale to identify and resolve gaps before full implementation.
- *Align Metrics with Goals*: Use both quantitative and qualitative measures to track audit success. For example, track the number of vulnerabilities mitigated and the improvement in employee adherence to security policies.
- *Emphasize Documentation*: Maintain detailed records of the planning process, including stakeholder inputs, risk assessments, and scope decisions, to ensure transparency and accountability.

Key Takeaways

The success of a cybersecurity audit begins with thorough planning. A clear, well-structured plan ensures resources are optimized, risks are prioritized, and the audit aligns with business and security objectives. Avoiding pitfalls like unclear goals and poor resource management sets the stage for delivering actionable insights and enhancing organizational security.

In this section, we covered the following points:

- The audit planning phase is vital for the success of any cybersecurity audit, setting the tone for the entire process by defining scope, objectives, and methodologies.

- A strategic approach to planning ensures that all critical areas are addressed, allowing audit teams to focus on high-priority risks while maintaining efficiency and accuracy.

- By avoiding common pitfalls like unclear objectives or insufficient stakeholder involvement, organizations ensure the audit's effectiveness and alignment with business goals.

- Tools like vulnerability scanners and SIEM platforms help identify high-risk areas, streamlining the planning process and improving audit success.

- Regular communication and stakeholder engagement throughout the planning phase enhance alignment and improve the overall outcome.

Best Practices for Effective Planning

The planning phase is the foundation of any successful cybersecurity audit. As explored in earlier discussions, the quality of planning directly determines the effectiveness of the audit, ensuring it aligns with organizational goals, optimizes resources, and mitigates risks. In the following are consolidated the best practices for effective audit planning, providing a comprehensive guide to help organizations navigate this critical phase with confidence.

CHAPTER 2   PLANNING THE CYBERSECURITY AUDIT

Why Effective Planning Matters

Effective planning is more than just setting a timeline or allocating resources; it is about crafting a strategic framework that ensures every aspect of the audit is purposeful and impactful.

Key benefits of meticulous planning include

- *Minimizing Risks*: A well-structured plan identifies and prioritizes high-risk areas, ensuring that critical vulnerabilities are not overlooked. By focusing on areas of greatest concern, audits become targeted and effective.

- *Optimizing Resources*: Time, tools, and personnel are finite resources. A solid plan ensures these resources are allocated wisely, avoiding unnecessary delays and redundant efforts.

- *Aligning with Business Goals*: A successful audit is one that supports the broader organizational strategy. Effective planning bridges the gap between technical assessments and business priorities, ensuring the audit adds measurable value.

- *Ensuring Compliance*: Regulatory standards like ISO 27001, PCI DSS, and GDPR impose strict requirements. Planning helps organizations meet these standards by integrating compliance checks into the audit process.

Best Practices for Cybersecurity Audit Planning

Define Objectives and Scope

Why It Matters: Clear and specific objectives prevent wasted effort and ensure the audit remains focused and comprehensive.

- *How to Do It*:
  - Collaborate with stakeholders to set measurable goals, such as identifying unauthorized access points or assessing encryption practices.

CHAPTER 2   PLANNING THE CYBERSECURITY AUDIT

- Use visual aids like data flow diagrams to map out the scope and boundaries of the audit.
- *Example*: A healthcare organization might define its objective as ensuring compliance with HIPAA by auditing patient data storage and transmission.

Involve Stakeholders Early

Why It Matters: Stakeholders provide diverse perspectives and valuable insights, ensuring the audit plan aligns with organizational priorities.

- *How to Do It*:
  - Schedule planning meetings with representatives from IT, compliance, and management.
  - Clarify roles and expectations, ensuring that technical input, regulatory requirements, and business goals are all considered.
- *Example*: Include IT administrators for system-specific insights, compliance officers for regulatory guidance, and executives to align the audit with strategic objectives.

Conduct a Preliminary Risk Assessment

Why It Matters: Risk assessments focus the audit on areas that pose the greatest threat to security and compliance.

- *How to Do It*:
  - Use established frameworks like OCTAVE or FAIR to evaluate risks.
  - Leverage tools like Nessus for vulnerability scanning or Metasploit for penetration testing to identify and quantify risks.
- *Example*: A financial institution might prioritize securing payment processing systems after identifying them as high-risk during the assessment.

Develop an Audit Checklist

Why It Matters: Checklists ensure no critical steps are overlooked, creating a structured approach to the audit.

- *How to Do It*:
  - Base the checklist on industry frameworks like ISO 27001, NIST CSF, etc.
  - Include tasks like reviewing encryption protocols, assessing physical access controls, and evaluating employee adherence to security policies.
- *Example*: An ISO 27001 checklist might include verifying firewall configurations, auditing backup procedures, and reviewing access logs.

Allocate Resources Effectively

Why It Matters: Thorough audits require the right mix of expertise, tools, and time.

- *How to Do It*:
  - Assign team members with relevant skills to specific tasks, such as cloud security assessments or compliance checks.
  - Use project management tools like Trello or Asana to monitor progress and ensure deadlines are met.
- *Example*: Assign a cloud security expert to assess AWS configurations while a compliance officer reviews GDPR-related processes.

Leverage Automation and Tools

Why It Matters: Automation saves time and enhances accuracy, allowing teams to focus on analysis and remediation.

- *How to Do It*:
  - Utilize tools like Splunk for log analysis, Qualys for vulnerability management, and Wireshark for network monitoring.

CHAPTER 2   PLANNING THE CYBERSECURITY AUDIT

- Automate repetitive tasks such as scanning for misconfigurations or generating compliance reports.
- *Example*: Automated vulnerability scans can detect missing patches in minutes, providing immediate insights for remediation.

Define Success Metrics

Why It Matters: Metrics provide a measurable way to evaluate the audit's effectiveness and highlight areas for improvement.

- *How to Do It*:
  - Set KPIs such as the number of vulnerabilities mitigated, audit completion time, or compliance score improvements.
  - *Example*: A company might track a 20% reduction in high-severity vulnerabilities as a success metric for its audit.

Preparing for Dynamic Environments

Why It Matters: IT landscapes are constantly evolving, and audits must adapt to changes in systems, processes, and threats.

- *How to Do It*:
  - Maintain an up-to-date inventory of systems and track changes or additions.
  - Use configuration management tools to document and monitor updates.
  - *Example*: An organization that recently migrated to a cloud platform would include a detailed review of cloud configurations in its audit plan.

Key Takeaways

A strategic and well-executed audit plan not only meets compliance but also enhances security, builds trust, and creates opportunities for continuous improvement. By aligning audits with organizational goals, you can turn a routine process into a valuable strategic asset.

In this section, we covered the following points:

- Effective planning elevates cybersecurity audits from a routine requirement to a strategic asset, enhancing organizational security and resilience.

- Prioritizing high-risk areas, engaging stakeholders, and leveraging automation are key practices that maximize the value of cybersecurity audits.

- A well-executed audit plan aligns with broader organizational goals, ensuring that findings are actionable, relevant, and supportive of long-term security objectives.

- By focusing on compliance, strengthening security measures, and fostering stakeholder trust, effective planning leads to continuous improvement and proactive threat mitigation.

Conclusions

In the world of cybersecurity audits, careful planning, comprehensive scope definition, effective stakeholder engagement, and dynamic risk assessment are foundational elements that ensure the success of the audit process. Just as the security of a physical home depends on thoughtful planning, detailed risk assessments, and coordinated efforts, a well-executed cybersecurity audit requires the same care and attention to detail to safeguard an organization's digital assets.

The scope of a cybersecurity audit is the foundation of the entire process. By aligning the audit with organizational goals and focusing on critical areas, organizations can ensure their resources are used efficiently and their risks are prioritized appropriately. Properly scoping an audit involves careful documentation, leveraging the right tools, and engaging stakeholders, ensuring that the audit delivers actionable insights

CHAPTER 2 PLANNING THE CYBERSECURITY AUDIT

and strengthens resilience against evolving cyber threats. The planning phase for a cybersecurity audit serves as the first line of defense in mitigating potential vulnerabilities.

Stakeholder engagement further elevates the audit process. It transforms a routine compliance check into a collaborative effort that enhances organizational security posture. When stakeholders are aligned with the audit's goals and priorities, the audit becomes a strategic initiative that not only evaluates existing security measures but also fosters a culture of continuous improvement. The involvement of everyone in the organization ensures that the security system functions optimally and is understood by all.

Moreover, audit planning must be thorough and strategic, addressing the organization's unique operational and security needs. Understanding the business context allows for a tailored approach to cybersecurity that balances robust security measures with operational efficiency. This context-aware planning ensures that audits focus on high-priority risks, optimize resource allocation, and produce results that align with the organization's long-term objectives.

Risk assessment is central to the audit's effectiveness, enabling organizations to identify vulnerabilities, prioritize threats, and allocate resources efficiently. By using advanced tools like vulnerability scanners and SIEM systems, auditors can streamline the risk assessment process, enhancing both accuracy and efficiency. In parallel, metrics provide a dynamic framework for evaluating the audit's success, fostering continuous improvement, and enabling proactive decision-making.

Finally, aligning cybersecurity audits with organizational goals and business outcomes is key. Cybersecurity audits must adapt to changing business priorities and emerging threats. The audit process is not a one-time compliance task but a strategic initiative that supports growth, resilience, and innovation.

A well-planned cybersecurity audit is more than just a checklist; it's a strategic tool that drives an organization's security forward. By integrating comprehensive planning, stakeholder collaboration, risk management, and continuous adaptation, cybersecurity audits become instrumental in safeguarding both digital assets and business objectives. With proactive risk management and dynamic planning, organizations can turn audits into valuable assets that enhance security, build stakeholder trust, and position the organization for success in a constantly evolving digital landscape.

CHAPTER 3

Assessing Security Controls

Assessing security controls is a critical step in safeguarding an organization's digital infrastructure. Security controls are mechanisms such as policies, processes, and technologies designed to mitigate risks, protect assets, and ensure compliance with regulatory requirements. Assessing these controls involves evaluating their design and operational effectiveness to ensure they adequately address identified risks. This assessment can be proactive, such as during implementation, or reactive, such as after a security incident. Key methods include vulnerability assessments, penetration testing, and audits. Each approach provides unique insights into the adequacy of security measures, helping organizations pinpoint weaknesses and areas for improvement.

Picture standing before the Great Pyramid of Giza, its limestone blocks stretching skyward – much like an organization's digital infrastructure reaching into the cloud. Just as ancient Egyptians mastered the art of protecting their Pharaohs' treasures, we must master the protection of our digital assets.

Think of the organization's security controls as the pyramid's elaborate protection systems – from the massive outer blocks to the intricate internal passages and false doors. Each security measure, like each architectural element of the pyramid, serves a specific purpose in the grand design of protection:

- *The Outer Layers*: Just as the pyramid's smooth limestone casing once deflected intruders, the first-line security policies and firewalls ward off basic threats.

- *The Hidden Passages*: Like the pyramid's confusing network of corridors designed to mislead tomb raiders, the security architecture creates complex paths that only authorized users can navigate.

- *The Burial Chamber's Defenses*: Much like the Pharaoh's most precious treasures were protected by multiple layers of security, the most sensitive data requires multiple levels of protection.

In cybersecurity there are different approaches. A structured framework, such as the NIST CSF or ISO/IEC 27001, is often employed to guide the assessment process. These frameworks provide a standardized approach to identifying, analyzing, and documenting security control gaps. For example, NIST's RMF includes steps to categorize information systems, select controls, and assess their effectiveness before authorization. Metrics and benchmarks are essential in this process, as they help measure control performance over time. Regular reassessment ensures that controls evolve in response to emerging threats and changes in the IT environment, maintaining their relevance and effectiveness.

Continuous monitoring plays a pivotal role in the ongoing assessment of security controls. By leveraging automation and tools like SIEM systems, organizations can detect anomalies and assess control performance in real time. This approach allows for quicker identification of ineffective controls or new vulnerabilities, enabling immediate corrective actions. Moreover, assessments should be documented thoroughly to ensure traceability and compliance with regulatory standards. A robust security control assessment process strengthens an organization's overall security posture, reduces the likelihood of breaches, and fosters a culture of accountability and vigilance.

Security controls in ancient Egyptian Pyramids are used analogically in this chapter.

Understanding and Implementing Security Controls

In the ever-evolving landscape of cybersecurity, the importance of security controls cannot be overstated. These controls are the backbone of an organization's defense strategy, protecting systems, data, and networks from a multitude of threats. By understanding their role and implementing them effectively, organizations can safeguard their assets while ensuring compliance with regulatory requirements.

Defining Security Controls

Security controls are essential mechanisms that protect an organization's digital assets, mitigate risks, and ensure that critical data maintains its confidentiality, integrity, and availability. These controls function as strategic safeguards, addressing vulnerabilities and reducing the impact of potential threats. Proactive and evolving by nature, security controls are designed to adapt to the changing cyber threat landscape and organizational needs. They also need to be auditable, providing measurable insights into their effectiveness to align with compliance mandates and business objectives.

Imagine security controls as the ancient Egyptian's sacred protective spells and architectural marvels combined. Like the carefully placed blocks of the pyramids, each control serves as both guardian and guide:

- The outer limestone casing (preventive measures).
- The internal chambers' traps (detection systems).
- The secret escape routes (contingency plans).

Just as the pyramids have stood for millennia, so too must security controls be

- Eternal yet evolving, like the changing sands of the desert.
- Layered like the pyramid's internal chambers.
- Measurable as precisely as the pyramid's perfect angles.
- Adaptable like the Nile's flowing waters.

Key Characteristics of Security Controls:

- *Proactive*: Aim to prevent incidents before they occur.
- *Layered*: Work in harmony to create a defense-in-depth strategy.
- *Evolving*: Adapt to the ever-changing threat landscape and organizational needs.
- *Auditable*: Designed to be assessable and measurable for effectiveness.

A robust cybersecurity framework relies on multiple, layered security controls that work together seamlessly. By adopting a defense-in-depth approach, organizations can create a comprehensive shield against cyberattacks. This involves using a combination of automated tools, well-defined policies, and physical measures to ensure that no single point of failure jeopardizes overall security.

CHAPTER 3   ASSESSING SECURITY CONTROLS

Types of Security Controls

Preventive controls are the first line of defense, aiming to stop threats before they can exploit any vulnerabilities. Firewalls, secure configurations, and MFA are prime examples of preventive measures. They create barriers that block unauthorized access, ensuring that only legitimate users or processes gain entry. For instance, MFA adds an extra layer of protection by requiring multiple authentication factors, making it much harder for attackers to compromise accounts.

Detective controls come into play when preventive measures are bypassed. These controls focus on identifying and responding to security incidents in real time or after they occur. Intrusion Detection Systems (IDS), SIEM tools, and log analysis help organizations detect abnormal behavior, allowing for quick responses to potential breaches.

Corrective controls ensure business continuity by restoring systems and minimizing damage after an incident. Effective corrective controls, such as encrypted backups and robust incident response plans, enable organizations to recover swiftly from disruptions.

Think of security architecture like the layers of a pyramid's defense system:

- *Preventive Controls*: The massive outer blocks and hidden entrances:
    - The digital limestone walls (firewalls).
    - The sacred seals (authentication systems).
    - The guardian statues (access controls).
- *Detective Controls*: The priest's vigilant eyes:
    - The magical scarab beetles (monitoring systems).
    - The sacred scrolls' recordings (log analysis).
    - The temple guards' watchful gaze (intrusion detection).
- *Corrective Controls*: The pyramid's self-healing magic:
    - The restoration rituals (backup systems).
    - The healing hieroglyphs (recovery procedures).
    - The priests' repair ceremonies (incident response).

Categories of Security Controls

Categories of security controls can be described like the three main chambers of the Great Pyramid:

- *Technical Controls*: The mechanical traps and secret mechanisms:
  - The sliding stone blocks (automated systems).
  - The hidden passages (encrypted channels).
  - The sacred geometry (network architecture).
- *Administrative Controls*: The priests' ancient wisdom:
  - The sacred texts (security policies).
  - The scribes' teachings (training programs).
  - The ritual procedures (incident response plans).
- *Physical Controls*: The tangible protections:
  - The temple guards (security personnel).
  - The massive stone blocks (physical barriers).
  - The sacred boundary markers (access points).

Technical controls are automated measures that protect systems and data. Encryption, Endpoint Detection and Response (EDR) tools, and network segmentation are examples of technical controls that address risks directly. These controls are particularly effective in preventing unauthorized access and ensuring data confidentiality. For instance, encrypting sensitive files with AES-256 ensures that even if data is intercepted, it remains unreadable without the decryption key.

Administrative controls are policies, procedures, and training programs that establish how security is managed across the organization. Security awareness training equips employees to recognize phishing attempts and other common threats, reducing the likelihood of human error. Additionally, well-documented incident response plans provide clear steps for addressing security incidents, minimizing confusion and delays during crises.

Physical controls focus on securing tangible assets like servers, storage devices, and workspaces. Biometric access systems, surveillance cameras, and fire suppression systems are examples of physical safeguards. These controls ensure that unauthorized individuals cannot access critical infrastructure and that physical damage is mitigated during disasters.

CHAPTER 3 ASSESSING SECURITY CONTROLS

Why Security Controls Matter

Security controls play a pivotal role in safeguarding sensitive information, mitigating risks, and ensuring compliance with regulations. Effective controls protect data from unauthorized access, modification, or destruction. Encryption and access control mechanisms, for instance, shield sensitive customer or employee information, reducing the likelihood of costly data breaches.

In addition to protection, security controls help organizations meet industry-specific compliance requirements, such as GDPR, HIPAA, PCI DSS, etc. These regulations mandate strict security measures to avoid hefty fines and reputational damage. Furthermore, by mitigating risks and building trust with stakeholders, security controls strengthen an organization's reputation as a secure and reliable partner.

Implementing and maintaining security controls delivers several key benefits:

- *Data Protection*: Security controls like encryption and access management safeguard sensitive information from unauthorized access or breaches.

- *Regulatory Compliance*: Many industries are subject to stringent regulations, such as GDPR, HIPAA, and PCI DSS. Security controls ensure adherence to these standards.

- *Risk Mitigation*: By reducing the likelihood and impact of threats, security controls enhance an organization's resilience against attacks.

- *Building Trust*: Robust security controls foster confidence among stakeholders, including customers, partners, and regulators, demonstrating a commitment to data protection.

Auditing Security Controls

Auditing security controls is essential to ensure they function as intended and provide maximum protection. Audits evaluate the effectiveness of implemented measures, identify gaps, and confirm alignment with organizational goals. This process not only helps uncover vulnerabilities but also fosters continuous improvement in the security framework.

Steps to Audit Security Controls:

- *Define Audit Scope*:
  - Identify critical security controls (e.g., network security, access control, and encryption).
  - Determine audit objectives based on compliance requirements (e.g., ISO 27001, NIST, and GDPR).
  - Engage stakeholders to align expectations and key focus areas.
- *Gather and Evaluate Evidence*:
  - Collect security configurations, logs, and reports from relevant systems.
  - Use automated tools (e.g., Nessus and Qualys) to assess control effectiveness.
  - Interview system administrators and review security policies.
- *Assess Control Effectiveness*:
  - Review results of penetration testing that simulate real-world attack scenarios.
  - Validate security controls against known vulnerabilities and threat intelligence.
  - Measure the performance of preventive, detective, and corrective controls.
- *Identify Gaps and Weaknesses*:
  - Compare actual security posture with expected benchmarks.
  - Document misconfigurations, outdated controls, or non-compliance issues.
  - Classify risks based on severity (e.g., critical, high, medium, and low).

- *Provide Actionable Recommendations*:
  - Prioritize remediation steps based on business impact and risk levels.
  - Suggest improvements such as automation, policy updates, or additional controls.
  - Align recommendations with business goals and regulatory requirements.
- *Communicate Findings to Stakeholders*:
  - Use dashboards, risk heat maps, and clear reports to present findings.
  - Tailor messaging for technical teams (detailed fixes).
  - Conduct review meetings to ensure alignment on next steps.
- *Implement and Monitor Remediation Actions*:
  - Assign responsibilities for addressing audit findings.
  - Automate security monitoring to track ongoing improvements.
  - Conduct follow-up assessments to verify remediation effectiveness.
- *Continuous Improvement and Reassessment*:
  - Schedule regular audits and adapt security controls to evolving threats.
  - Train employees to strengthen security awareness.
  - Update security frameworks to align with industry best practices.

Figure 3-1 presents graphically the process workflow for auditing security controls.

CHAPTER 3 ASSESSING SECURITY CONTROLS

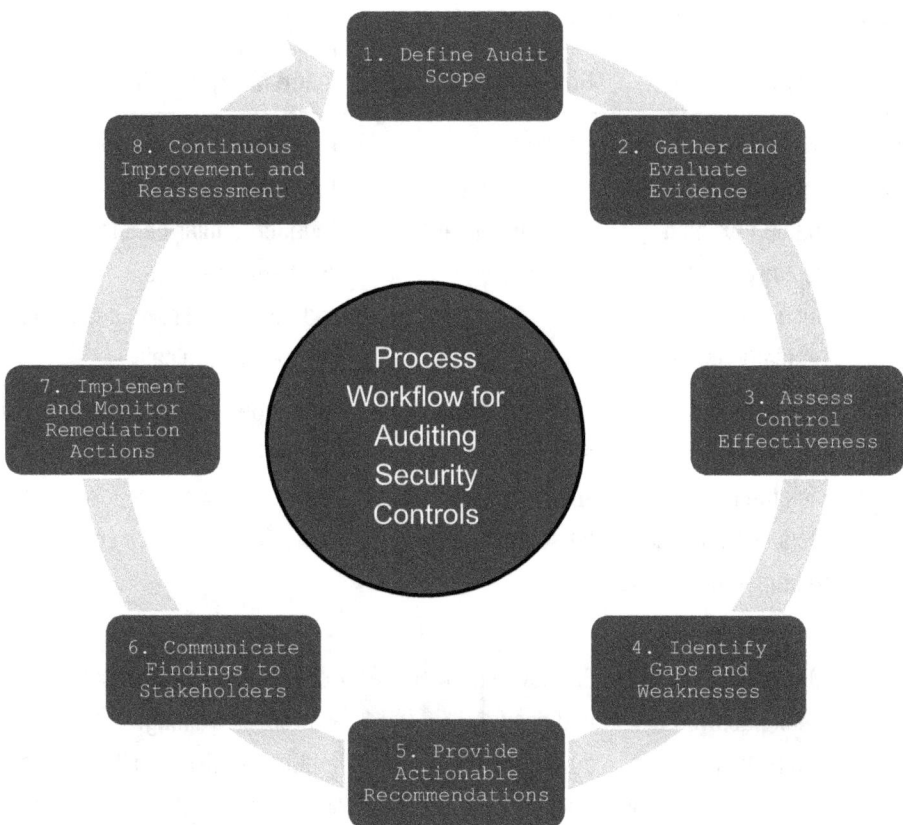

***Figure 3-1.** Process workflow for auditing security controls*

Challenges in Implementing Security Controls

One of the primary challenges in implementing security controls is the rapidly evolving nature of cyber threats. Attackers constantly develop new techniques to exploit vulnerabilities, requiring organizations to update their defenses regularly. Without continuous monitoring and adaptation, even robust controls can become obsolete.

Another challenge is resource constraints, particularly for smaller organizations that may lack the budget or expertise to implement comprehensive controls. Additionally, human error remains a significant risk factor, as misconfigurations or negligence can render even the most advanced security measures ineffective. Addressing these challenges requires leveraging managed security services, conducting regular employee training, and automating repetitive tasks to reduce the margin for error.

Table 3-1 presents some of the most common challenges and their solutions related to implementing security controls.

CHAPTER 3   ASSESSING SECURITY CONTROLS

Table 3-1. *Challenges in implementing security controls and solutions*

Challenge	Description	Solution	Detailed Mitigation Steps
Rapidly Evolving Threats	Cyber threats are constantly evolving, making existing security controls obsolete if not regularly updated.	Continuous monitoring and threat intelligence updates.	1. Implement AI-driven security tools to detect new threats. 2. Conduct regular penetration testing and red team exercises. 3. Update firewall rules and access controls dynamically.
Resource Constraints	Smaller organizations may lack the budget, tools, or expertise to implement strong security controls.	Leverage cost-effective security solutions and outsourcing.	1. Adopt open-source security tools for monitoring and protection. 2. Use cloud-based security solutions to reduce infrastructure costs.
Human Error	Misconfigurations, weak passwords, and lack of awareness increase security risks.	Employee training and security automation.	1. Conduct regular cybersecurity awareness training. 2. Implement MFA for all critical systems. 3. Automate log analysis and alerting to detect configuration errors. 4. Enforce strict access control policies.
Integration Complexity	Security tools and policies may not integrate seamlessly, leading to gaps.	Unified security frameworks and centralized management.	1. Adopt an SIEM system. 2. Standardize security policies across the organization.
Compliance Challenges	Keeping up with evolving regulatory requirements can be difficult.	Regular compliance audits and automated compliance tracking.	1. Implement GRC tools. 2. Automate audit log collection and retention for compliance evidence. 3. Stay updated with industry-specific regulations (e.g., GDPR, HIPAA). 4. Conduct periodic internal audits to identify non-compliance gaps.

A Layered Approach to Security

A layered approach to security, combining preventive, detective, and corrective controls across technical, administrative, and physical domains, provides the most robust defense. Each layer complements the others, creating a holistic strategy that minimizes risks at every level. For example, while a firewall (preventive) blocks unauthorized access, a SIEM system (detective) monitors for suspicious activity, and backups (corrective) ensure quick recovery in case of an attack.

This comprehensive strategy not only protects assets but also ensures business continuity and builds stakeholder confidence. By aligning controls with organizational goals and maintaining them through regular audits and updates, organizations can stay ahead of evolving threats.

Example of a Layered Defense Strategy:

- *Preventive*: Deploy firewalls and enforce MFA.

- *Detective*: Monitor activities with SIEM tools and analyze logs.

- *Corrective*: Maintain encrypted backups and conduct regular patching.

Key Takeaways

Security controls are not static safeguards but dynamic enablers of organizational resilience and success. Like the layers of a pyramid, they must be solid at the base, interconnected, and adaptable to stand the test of time. By fostering a culture of continuous improvement, integrating technology, and empowering people, organizations can transform their security strategies from compliance checklists into enduring pillars of protection and trust.

In this section, we covered the following points:

- Security controls form the backbone of an organization's cybersecurity strategy, mitigating risks, protecting assets, and ensuring regulatory compliance.

- A multi-faceted approach that combines preventive, detective, and corrective controls across technical, administrative, and physical areas is essential for resilience.

- Regular audits, updates, and real-time monitoring ensure controls remain effective against evolving cyber threats and emerging vulnerabilities.

- Employee training and awareness are critical. Even the most advanced controls can fail without proper implementation and informed personnel.

- Security controls should align with organizational goals, balancing strong protection with usability to support operational efficiency.

Evaluating Physical Security Controls

In the ever-evolving landscape of cybersecurity, physical security often receives less attention than its digital counterpart. However, it plays a foundational role in safeguarding an organization's infrastructure, data, and operations. Physical security controls protect tangible assets from unauthorized access, theft, damage, and natural disasters. A strong physical security framework complements digital defenses, ensuring that an organization's overall security posture is robust and reliable.

Imagine the organization as an ancient Egyptian temple complex, where each layer of security guards not just physical treasures but the very essence of the kingdom's power – its data and operations.

In the following are described the importance, types, technologies, challenges, and best practices for evaluating and implementing effective physical security controls.

What Are Physical Security Controls?

Physical security controls are measures designed to prevent unauthorized access to facilities, safeguard critical infrastructure, and protect sensitive data from physical threats. These controls address risks that cannot be mitigated by digital security measures alone, such as theft of hardware, tampering with physical networks, or environmental hazards like fires or floods.

CHAPTER 3 ASSESSING SECURITY CONTROLS

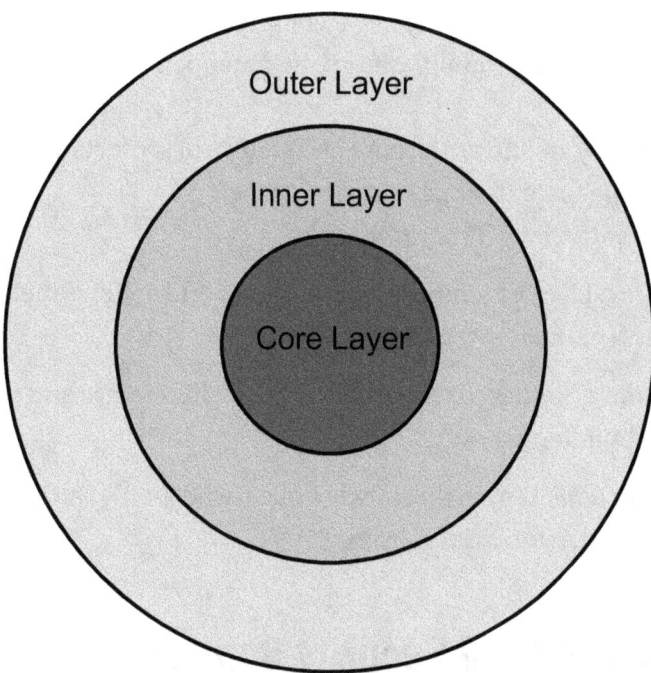

Figure 3-2. *Layers of physical security controls*

At their core, physical security controls are categorized into three interconnected layers:

- *Outer Layer*: This layer establishes the first barrier between the facility and the outside world. It includes fences, security personnel, gates, and surveillance cameras, all of which serve to deter intrusions and monitor potential threats from a distance.

- *Inner Layer*: These controls regulate access to the interior of the facility. Examples include locked doors, Radio-Frequency Identification (RFID)-enabled badges, and mantraps that ensure only authorized personnel gain entry.

- *Core Layer*: This layer is the last line of defense and focuses on protecting the most sensitive areas, such as server rooms, safes, and data centers. Measures like biometric authentication, tamper-proof enclosures, and advanced surveillance systems are commonly deployed here.

These layers work in tandem to create a comprehensive security framework that addresses potential vulnerabilities from the outer perimeter to the innermost critical assets.

Picture the security system as the concentric rings of protection that ancient Egyptians used to safeguard their most sacred spaces:

The Three Sacred Circles of Protection:

- *Outer Ring*: Like the temple's external walls and sphinx-lined pathways (perimeter security).

- *Middle Ring*: Similar to the temple's processional ways and guardian statues (building access).

- *Inner Sanctum*: Akin to the holy of holies, where only the highest priests could enter (critical assets).

Key Types of Physical Security Controls

Perimeter Controls

Perimeter controls serve as the initial line of defense, ensuring that unauthorized individuals cannot approach the facility undetected. Fencing acts as a physical barrier, while security cameras provide constant monitoring. Security guards and vehicle barriers offer additional protection, especially in high-risk facilities like data centers, banks, or government buildings. The presence of these controls not only enhances security but also acts as a psychological deterrent to potential intruders.

For example, a combination of motion-detecting cameras and automated alarms can immediately alert security teams to unauthorized activity at the perimeter, reducing response times and minimizing potential damage.

Access Controls

Access control systems are crucial for regulating who can enter specific areas of a facility. These controls include keypads, RFID-enabled badges, biometric scanners, and turnstiles. MFA adds another layer of security by requiring multiple forms of verification, such as a badge swipe combined with a fingerprint scan.

A robust access control system ensures that only authorized personnel can access sensitive areas. For example, an organization might use different levels of clearance for various departments, restricting entry to server rooms or research and development labs to employees with specific credentials. By logging every access attempt, these systems also create an audit trail that can be analyzed for suspicious activity.

Environmental Controls

Physical security is not just about preventing intrusions; it also involves protecting infrastructure from environmental risks. Environmental controls like Heating, Ventilation, and Air Conditioning (HVAC) systems regulate temperatures in server rooms to prevent overheating, while fire suppression systems safeguard critical equipment from fire damage. Flood barriers and backup generators ensure operational continuity during natural disasters or power outages.

For instance, a healthcare organization that stores Electronic Health Records (EHR) might deploy water sensors in server rooms to detect leaks early, preventing potential data loss or hardware damage.

Technologies in Physical Security

Modern organizations leverage advanced technologies to enhance the effectiveness of their physical security measures. These technologies offer improved monitoring, faster response times, and seamless integration with digital systems.

- *IoT Sensors*: Internet of Things (IoT) devices provide real-time data on environmental conditions and unauthorized access attempts. For example, a smart door sensor might send an alert if a door is left open or tampered with.

- *Centralized Access Management*: Platforms like LenelS2 or Brivo enable organizations to monitor and control access to all entry points from a single dashboard. This streamlines security operations and ensures consistency across multiple facilities.

- *AI-Powered Systems*: Artificial intelligence enhances surveillance by analyzing video feeds for unusual behavior, such as unauthorized entry attempts. These systems can autonomously trigger alerts, freeing security teams to focus on critical tasks.

The integration of these technologies not only strengthens physical security but also bridges the gap between physical and digital defenses, creating a unified security approach.

Real-Life Scenarios

Securing Data Centers

Data centers house critical infrastructure and sensitive information, making them prime targets for physical and cyberattacks. A large multinational corporation might deploy biometric locks, motion-activated cameras, and 24/7 monitoring to protect its data centers. These measures ensure that only authorized personnel can access the facility, reducing the risk of tampering or theft.

Mitigating Insider Threats

Insider threats pose significant risks, especially when employees bypass security protocols. An organization can implement an RFID badge system that tracks employee movements throughout the facility. If someone attempts to access a restricted area without clearance, the system raises an alert, allowing the security team to intervene immediately.

Disaster Preparedness

Disasters such as fires or floods can devastate physical infrastructure. A healthcare provider might install advanced fire suppression systems in its server rooms, ensuring that patient records and operational continuity are protected even during emergencies. Regular testing of these systems ensures their reliability when needed most.

Challenges in Physical Security

Despite its importance, physical security faces several challenges; Table 3-2 presents the most common audit challenges in physical security:

Table 3-2. *Challenges in auditing physical security controls and solutions*

Challenge	Description	Solution
Lack of Standardized Audit Criteria	Organizations may not have clear or consistent guidelines for evaluating physical security measures.	Develop standardized audit checklists based on industry frameworks like NIST, ISO 27001, or PCI DSS.
Integration with Digital Security Audits	Physical security audits are often conducted separately from cybersecurity audits, creating gaps in overall risk assessment.	Align physical security audits with cybersecurity audits to ensure a holistic security review. Implement integrated security monitoring platforms.
Human Error and Non-compliance	Employees may fail to follow security policies, such as propping open doors, sharing credentials, or bypassing security checkpoints.	Implement regular training programs, conduct surprise inspections, and enforce strict access control policies.
Difficulty in Detecting Insider Threats	Insider threats are harder to detect, as employees may have authorized access but misuse it.	Use access logs, video analytics, and AI-driven anomaly detection to identify unusual behavior patterns.
Aging or Inadequate Security Systems	Organizations may rely on outdated physical security technologies, increasing vulnerability.	Regularly update security infrastructure, including surveillance, biometric access controls, and alarm systems.
High Costs of Security Upgrades	Implementing modern physical security measures, such as AI surveillance or biometric authentication, can be expensive.	Conduct a cost-benefit analysis and prioritize upgrades based on risk assessment. Consider phased implementation.
Environmental Risks and Natural Disasters	Fire, flooding, and power failures can compromise physical security.	Implement redundant safety measures such as fire suppression, flood barriers, and backup power sources. Assess these systems regularly.
Inconsistent Log Monitoring and Analysis	Security logs are often not reviewed systematically, leading to missed incidents.	Automate log collection and analysis using SIEM systems and schedule regular audits.

CHAPTER 3   ASSESSING SECURITY CONTROLS

Auditing Physical Security Controls

Auditing is essential to ensure that physical security controls remain effective and aligned with organizational needs. A comprehensive audit involves the following steps:

- *Review Policies and Procedures*: Ensure that all physical security policies are up-to-date and in line with industry standards.

- *Inspect Physical Systems*: Verify that locks, cameras, alarms, and access control mechanisms are functioning properly. Conduct regular maintenance to address wear and tear.

- *Analyze Logs and Records*: Audit access logs for unusual patterns or unauthorized attempts, and ensure they are synchronized with digital security systems.

- *Document Findings and Recommendations*: Identify gaps or vulnerabilities and propose actionable solutions, such as upgrading outdated systems or enhancing employee training.

Regular audits not only improve security but also help organizations adapt to evolving threats and technological advancements.

The physical security controls audit in detail is presented in Figure 3-3.

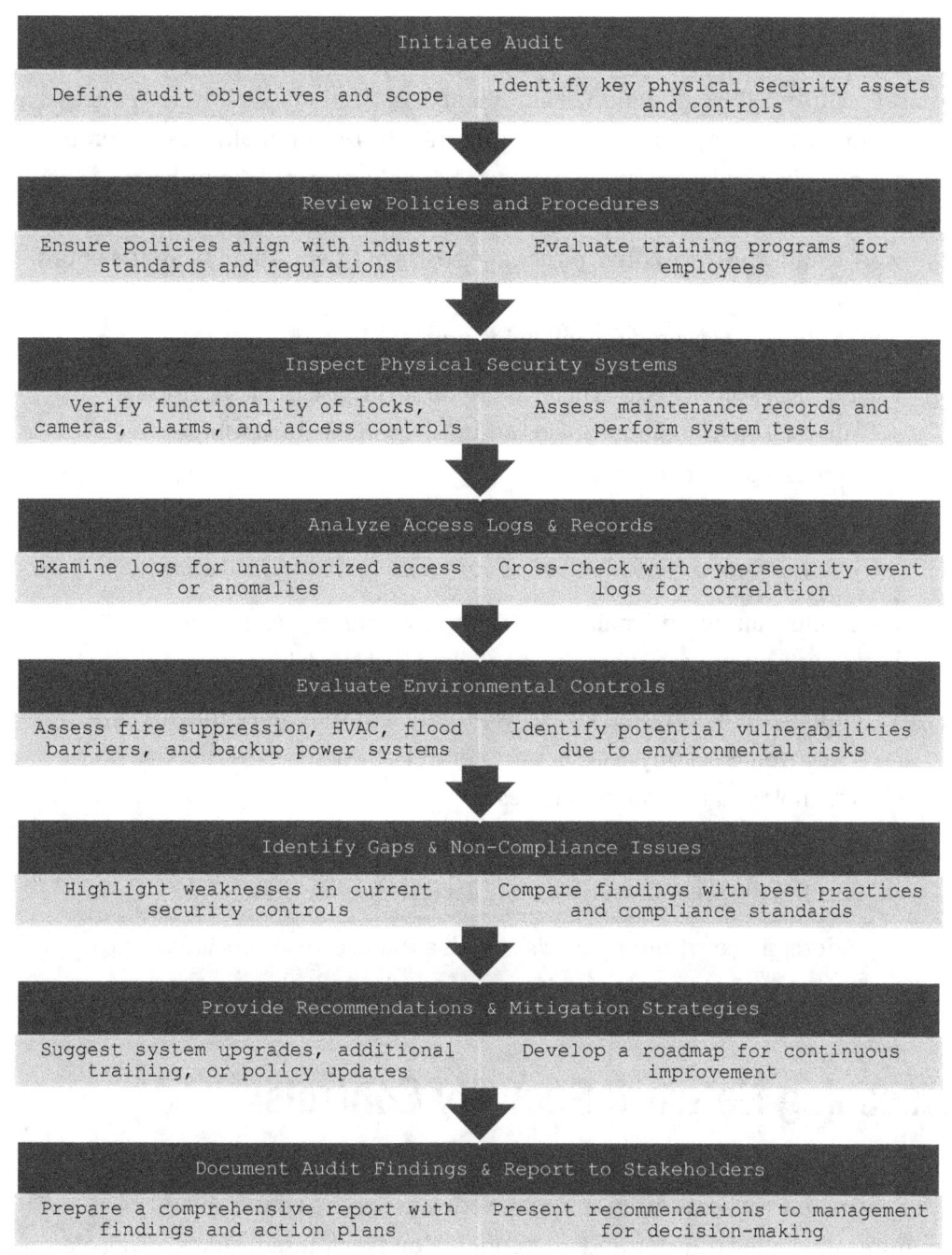

Figure 3-3. *Process of auditing physical security controls*

CHAPTER 3   ASSESSING SECURITY CONTROLS

Key Takeaways

Physical security is the foundation of a resilient organizational defense, as essential as its digital counterpart. A layered approach, supported by regular maintenance, employee training, and advanced integrations, protects both physical and digital assets. Much like the enduring pyramids, built with care and foresight, a strong physical security framework stands the test of time, providing trust, safety, and stability for the entire organization.

In this section, we covered the following points:

- Physical security is as crucial as digital security; a breach in the physical environment can compromise even the most robust cybersecurity measures.

- Implementing a combination of perimeter, access, and environmental controls ensures comprehensive physical security.

- Routine audits and maintenance are essential to keep physical security measures effective and aligned with evolving threats.

- Employee training and awareness significantly enhance the effectiveness of physical security controls, bridging gaps that technology alone cannot address.

- Seamless integration between physical and digital security systems fortifies the organization's overall security framework.

- Addressing environmental risks such as natural disasters is as critical as preventing unauthorized access, ensuring holistic protection.

Assessing Network Security Controls

In today's hyper-connected world, network security forms the backbone of any organization's cybersecurity strategy. Networks serve as the lifeblood of communication, data transfer, and operations. However, these systems are also prime targets for malicious actors seeking to disrupt services, steal sensitive data, or exploit vulnerabilities. Assessing network security controls is vital to ensure that they effectively safeguard data integrity, confidentiality, and availability.

Envision the network as the intricate network of trade routes and waterways that connected the ancient Egyptian empire – vital pathways that needed constant protection from raiders and natural threats. Just as this great waterway carried life-giving resources throughout the kingdom, a network carries vital data across the organization. And just as the Pharaohs protected their precious waterway with elaborate systems of guards, outposts, and watchtowers, we must safeguard our modern digital rivers with sophisticated security controls.

In the following are explored the fundamentals, processes, technologies, and challenges of evaluating network security controls, offering actionable insights to enhance organizational resilience.

What Are Network Security Controls?

Network security controls are mechanisms designed to protect a network from threats, secure communication, and ensure the safe exchange of data across endpoints. These controls defend against unauthorized access, malware, data breaches, and other cyberattacks, forming the first line of defense for an organization's digital assets.

Key Types of Network Security Controls:

- *Preventive Controls (The Watchers)*: These measures aim to stop unauthorized actions before they occur. Examples include firewalls, access control lists (ACLs), and MFA. Preventive controls are proactive, reducing vulnerabilities by implementing robust barriers to entry. Like vigilant sentries posted at strategic points along the Nile, these controls stop threats before they can breach the defenses.

- *Detective Controls (Thee Trackers)*: These tools identify and monitor potential threats in real time. IDS and SIEM platforms fall into this category, providing visibility into network activities. Similar to the scout boats that patrolled the river, constantly searching for signs of trouble

- *Corrective Controls (The Restorers)*: These controls help organizations respond to and recover from attacks. Automated threat response tools, backups, and disaster recovery plans are essential for minimizing the impact of security incidents. Like the repair crews who maintained the dikes and channels, ensuring the river's flow remained uninterrupted

Together, these controls create a layered defense strategy, protecting networks from both external and internal threats.

Steps to Assess Network Security Controls

Just as the Pharaoh's engineers regularly assessed their river defenses, modern organizations must systematically evaluate their network security. This begins with mapping digital territory – understanding every channel, tributary, and port in the network, just as ancient surveyors mapped every bend and branch of the Nile. The security tools are like the ancient fortifications – they must be regularly inspected, tested, and maintained to ensure their effectiveness.

Figure 3-4 presents the process workflow related to the steps for assessing main network security controls.

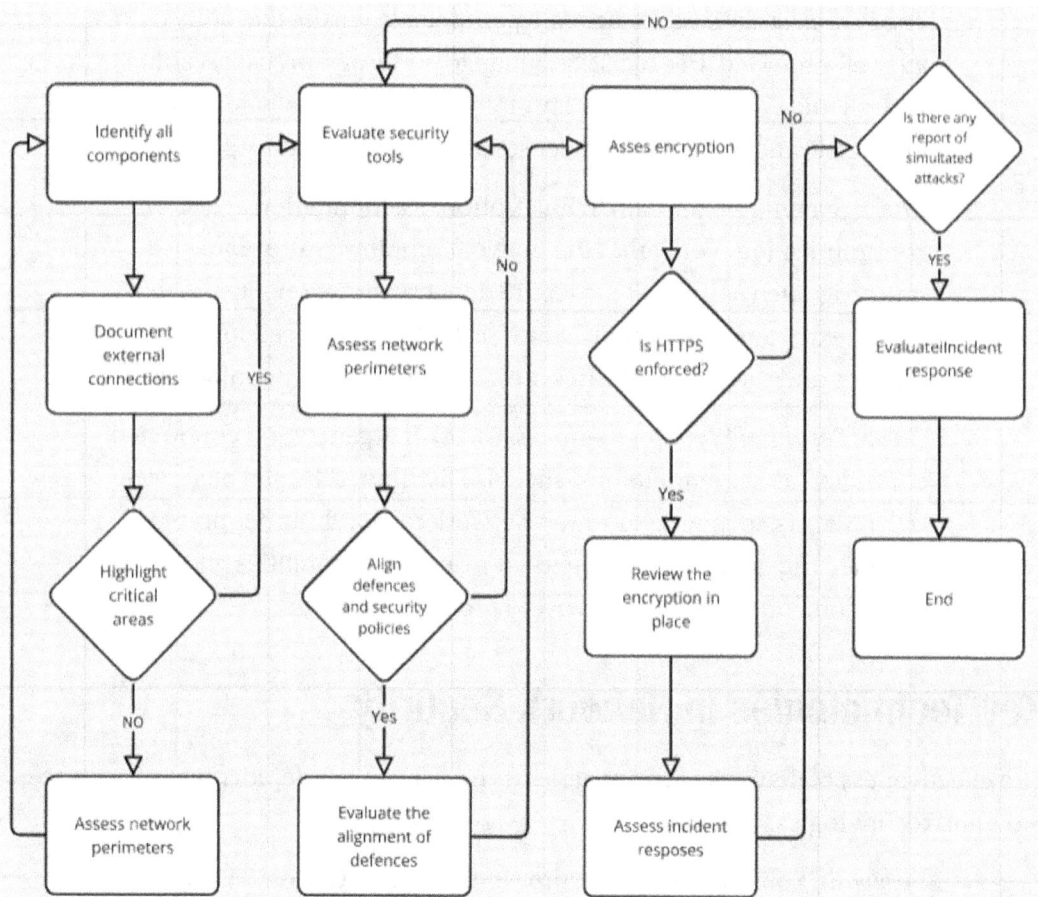

Figure 3-4. *Steps to assess main network security controls*

Evaluating the effectiveness of network security controls involves a structured approach to identify weaknesses, ensure compliance, and enhance resilience.

- *Understand the Network*: Begin by mapping the network topology, including key components such as routers, firewalls, servers, and endpoints. Identify external connections like VPNs or cloud integrations. This provides a comprehensive view of the network's architecture, highlighting critical areas for assessment.

- *Review Security Tools*: Examine the tools used to secure the network, including firewalls, IDS/IPS (Intrusion Prevention Systems), anti-malware software, and Network Access Control (NAC) solutions. Evaluate their configurations, update statuses, and overall effectiveness in detecting and mitigating threats.

CHAPTER 3   ASSESSING SECURITY CONTROLS

- *Test Perimeters*: Assess the network perimeter to ensure that entry points are well-protected. Use tools like Nmap to perform port scans, verify firewall rules, and test the security of VPN gateways. Evaluate whether the organization's perimeter defenses align with its security policies.

- *Check Encryption Standards*: Encryption is a foundation of secure communication. Verify that the network employs up-to-date protocols such as TLS 1.3 for secure data transmission. Ensure that Hypertext Transfer Protocol Secure (HTTPS) is enforced for web services and that all certificates are valid and properly configured.

- *Check Results of Simulated Attacks*: Check if organization conducted controlled attack simulations, such as Distributed Denial of Service (DDoS) tests, to analyze how the network responds under pressure. Evaluate the organization's incident response capabilities, including detection, mitigation, and recovery procedures.

Key Technologies in Network Security

The effectiveness of network security depends heavily on the deployment of advanced tools and technologies.

- *Firewalls*: Solutions like Palo Alto Networks and Cisco ASA protect the network perimeter by filtering incoming and outgoing traffic based on predefined rules.

- *IDS/IPS*: Tools such as Snort and Suricata analyze traffic patterns to detect and block suspicious activities.

- *SIEM Platforms*: Platforms like Splunk or QRadar aggregate and analyze logs from various sources to identify anomalies and generate actionable insights.

- *Zero Trust Architecture*: This model enforces strict access controls, ensuring that no device or user is trusted by default, even within the network.

- *Network Traffic Analysis Tools*: Artificial Intelligence (AI)-based solutions like Darktrace monitor network behavior, identifying potential threats through machine learning algorithms.

These technologies provide robust defenses while offering the visibility and control needed to manage complex network environments. More details related to the tools and techniques are presented in chapter 6.

Challenges in Assessing Network Security

Organizations face several challenges when evaluating network security controls, often stemming from the complexity and dynamic nature of modern networks. Table 3-3 presents the most common audit challenges in assessing network security:

Table 3-3. Challenges in auditing physical security controls and solutions

Challenge	Description	Solution
Evolving Threats	Cyberattacks continuously adapt, leveraging new techniques to exploit vulnerabilities. Organizations must keep up with the latest threats.	- Implement regular updates and patches for network devices. - Subscribe to threat intelligence feeds to stay informed about emerging threats. - Conduct continuous security awareness training for employees.
Complex Architectures	Hybrid networks combining on-premises and cloud systems create intricate environments, making it harder to identify security gaps.	- Use automated security assessment tools to scan for vulnerabilities. - Implement centralized security monitoring with SIEM systems. - Standardize security policies across all network environments.

(continued)

Table 3-3. (*continued*)

Challenge	Description	Solution
Human Error	Misconfigurations, such as open ports or weak passwords, often lead to security breaches.	- Conduct routine penetration testing to detect misconfigurations. - Deploy automated configuration management tools to enforce security baselines. - Provide regular cybersecurity training to IT staff and employees.
Third-Party Risk	External integrations, vendor connections, and third-party applications may introduce vulnerabilities.	- Perform regular security audits on third-party connections. - Enforce strict security policies for vendors, including security questionnaires and compliance checks. - Implement a zero-trust model, requiring verification for all access requests.

Where Network Security Matters

Ransomware Protection

Network security controls play a crucial role in defending against ransomware. Outbound traffic filtering can prevent data exfiltration, while NAC tools restrict unauthorized devices from accessing the network.

Remote Work Security

The shift to remote work has increased reliance on VPNs and cloud services. Enforcing MFA and updating VPN configurations are essential to protect remote connections from cyber threats.

Mitigating Insider Threats

NAC solutions and SIEM platforms can detect and respond to suspicious activities by employees or contractors, reducing the risk of insider threats.

Auditing Network Security Controls

Auditing provides a structured approach to evaluate the effectiveness and compliance of network security measures.

- *Policy Reviews*: Ensure that access controls, firewall rules, and other security policies are well-documented and align with industry standards.

- *Technical Tests*: Leverage tools like Nessus for vulnerability scans and penetration tests to identify gaps in the network's defenses.

- *Log Analysis*: Analyze logs collected by SIEM platforms to detect unusual patterns or suspicious activities. Focus on failed login attempts, unexpected traffic spikes, or unauthorized access attempts.

- *Compliance Checks*: Validate that the organization adheres to relevant regulatory standards, such as ISO 27001, PCI DSS, or GDPR, to avoid penalties and enhance customer trust.

Figure 3-5 presents the detailed network security controls audit.

CHAPTER 3   ASSESSING SECURITY CONTROLS

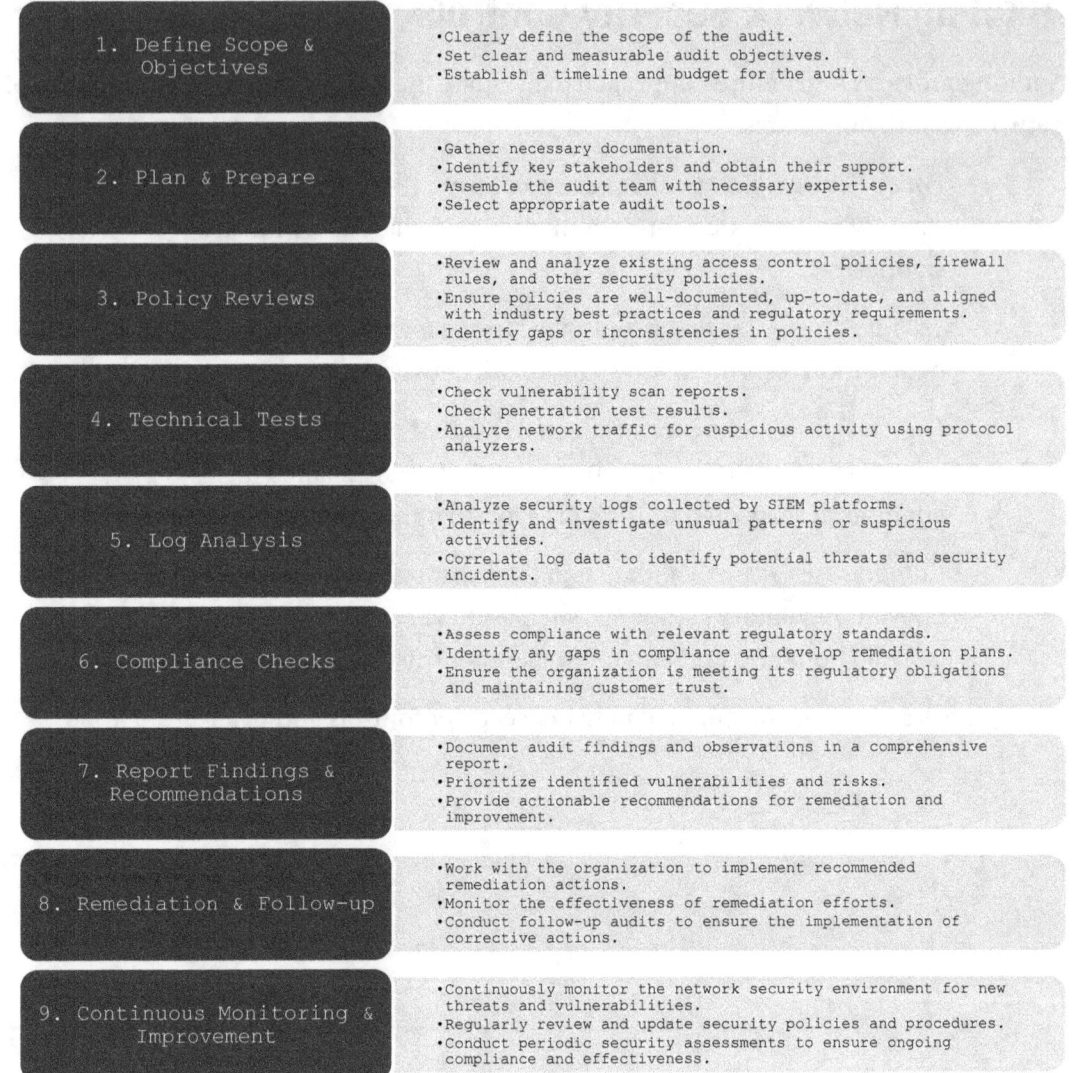

Figure 3-5. Process of auditing physical security controls

Best Practices

To maintain strong network security, organizations should adopt the following practices:

- *Defense-in-Depth*: Implement layered security measures, combining firewalls, IDS/IPS, and endpoint protection for comprehensive coverage.

- *Regular Patching*: Keep all systems and devices up to date to address known vulnerabilities.

- *Continuous Monitoring*: Use SIEM platforms and network traffic analysis tools to monitor activities in real time.

- *Zero Trust Approach*: Treat every device and user as a potential threat, enforcing strict access controls and segmentation.

Key Takeaways

Network security isn't just about deploying firewalls or monitoring systems; it's about creating a dynamic, adaptable framework that protects the lifeblood of your organization. By integrating advanced technologies, performing structured assessments, and learning from the resilience of past civilizations, organizations can build a robust network security posture that safeguards their operations and ensures long-term success.

In this section, we covered the following points:

- Assessing network security controls is an ongoing effort that must adapt to the ever-changing threat landscape.

- Leveraging innovative tools and technologies enhances the ability to detect, prevent, and respond to cyber threats effectively.

- A systematic approach to evaluating network security ensures comprehensive coverage and identification of vulnerabilities.

- Staying ahead of potential threats requires proactive measures such as regular updates, threat intelligence integration, and testing.

- Security measures must be designed to align with an organization's network architecture and business operations without hindering performance.

CHAPTER 3   ASSESSING SECURITY CONTROLS

The Importance of Access Management Controls in Cybersecurity Audits

Access management is a foundational element of any cybersecurity framework, dictating who can access critical systems, applications, and data within an organization. Without robust access management controls, organizations risk exposing themselves to unauthorized access, data breaches, and insider threats. Cybersecurity audits focus extensively on evaluating these controls to ensure that only the right individuals have access to the right resources at the right times.

Imagine an organization's access management system as the sacred temples of ancient Egypt, where different levels of access were carefully controlled – from public courtyards to the most sacred inner sanctums where only the highest priests could enter.

Understanding Access Management Controls

Access management controls encompass the policies, procedures, and technologies used to regulate user access to systems and data. These controls enforce principles like least privilege and RBAC to minimize risks while ensuring compliance with regulatory frameworks.

Like the ancient Egyptian temple complex, modern access management is built on layers of protection. Just as temples had public spaces, priest-only areas, and sacred chambers accessible only to the highest religious authorities, the organization's access controls must create clear boundaries and hierarchies.

Types of Access Management Controls:

- *Physical Access Controls*: Limit physical access to sensitive facilities such as data centers and server rooms, using tools like keycards, biometric scanners, or security guards. Similar to physical barriers, like the temple walls and gates.

- *Logical Access Controls*: Manage digital access to networks, systems, and applications using authentication and authorization mechanisms. Similar to divine authority, like religious hierarchies.

- *Administrative Controls*: Include policies, training, and procedures governing access management to ensure a consistent approach across the organization. Similar to sacred laws, like the temple's rules and traditions

These categories form a cohesive framework that protects both physical and digital assets while aligning with organizational and regulatory requirements.

Why Access Management Controls Are Critical

Just as the Pharaohs understood that protecting their temples' sacred knowledge was crucial to maintaining power and order, modern organizations must safeguard their digital treasures.

Consider This:

The temple analogy continues through each critical aspect:

- *Inner Chamber Protection (Insider Threats)*: Like preventing temple priests from misusing sacred artifacts.

- *Sacred Text Security (Data Protection)*: Similar to guarding holy scrolls.

- *Divine Laws (Regulatory Compliance)*: Following sacred protocols.

- *Guardian Gates (Unauthorized Access Prevention)*: Multiple layers of temple security.

Access management is essential for safeguarding sensitive information and maintaining the integrity of organizational systems. The importance of these controls can be understood through the following lenses:

Minimizing Insider Threats

Poorly managed access rights can lead to misuse by employees, contractors, or malicious insiders. Enforcing the principle of least privilege ensures users only access resources necessary for their roles, reducing the risk of misuse or accidental exposure.

Protecting Sensitive Data

Access controls safeguard sensitive information, such as customer records, financial data, and intellectual property, preventing unauthorized disclosure that could result in reputational or financial damage.

Ensuring Regulatory Compliance

Regulatory frameworks like GDPR, HIPAA, and PCI-DSS mandate strict access management practices to protect PII and other sensitive data. Non-compliance can lead to hefty fines and legal repercussions.

Preventing Unauthorized Access

Strong access controls mitigate risks such as weak credentials, brute force attacks, or compromised accounts, ensuring that only authenticated and authorized users can access critical systems.

Key Components of Access Management Controls

Effective access management comprises several critical components that work together to create a secure and efficient system:

Authentication Mechanisms

Verify user identities using methods such as passwords, biometrics, or MFA. MFA adds an additional layer of security by requiring two or more verification factors. Similar to divine recognition, like priests identifying themselves through sacred symbols.

Authorization Policies

Define which resources users can access and what actions they can perform based on their roles and responsibilities. RBAC simplifies this process by grouping access permissions by job functions. Similar to sacred rights, like different levels of temple access.

Access Provisioning and Deprovisioning

Manage the granting and revocation of access rights, particularly during onboarding, role changes, and offboarding of employees. Automating these processes ensures accuracy and timeliness, similar to rites of passage, like the process of granting or revoking temple privileges.

CHAPTER 3   ASSESSING SECURITY CONTROLS

Auditing and Monitoring

Track and analyze user access activities to detect anomalies, such as access outside normal working hours or failed login attempts. Regular monitoring helps identify and respond to potential security threats. Similar to eternal vigilance, like temple guards recording all movements.

Steps to Audit Access Management Controls

Auditing access management controls ensures their effectiveness and identifies areas for improvement.

Figure 3-6 presents the process workflow related to the steps for assessing main network security controls.

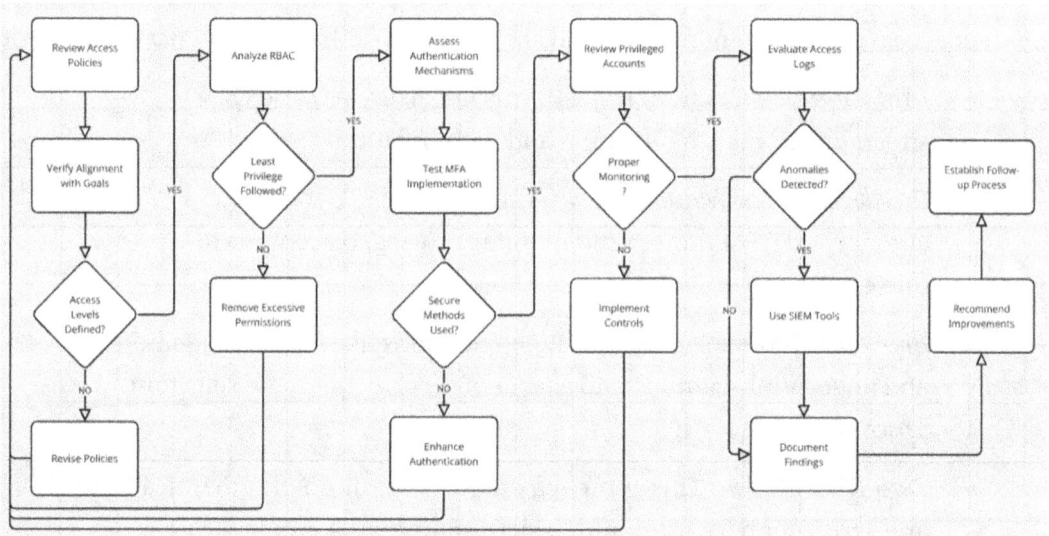

Figure 3-6. *Steps to audit access management controls*

The following steps are key to a comprehensive audit:

- *Reviewing Access Policies*: Examine documented access policies to confirm they align with organizational goals and compliance requirements. Policies should clearly define access levels, responsibilities, and enforcement mechanisms.

- *Analyzing RBAC*: Verify that access rights correspond to user roles and responsibilities, ensuring no unnecessary access permissions are granted.

- *Assessing Authentication Mechanisms*: Test the strength of authentication systems, including MFA implementation and password policy enforcement, to prevent unauthorized access.

- *Reviewing Privileged Accounts*: Pay special attention to privileged accounts, such as system administrators, which often have elevated permissions. Ensure these accounts are appropriately managed, monitored, and secured.

- *Evaluating Access Logs*: Analyze access logs for unusual patterns, such as repeated login failures or access attempts from unfamiliar locations, to identify potential security incidents.

Technologies Supporting Access Management

Modern access management relies on advanced tools to enhance efficiency and security.

- *IAM Solutions*: Centralized platforms like Azure AD and Okta streamline user authentication and authorization.

- *Privileged Access Management (PAM)*: Tools like CyberArk and BeyondTrust protect and monitor privileged accounts to prevent misuse.

- *Biometric Authentication*: Advanced methods like facial recognition and fingerprint scanning add a layer of security to user verification processes.

- *Zero Trust Models*: This approach enforces continuous authentication and verification for users and devices, eliminating implicit trust within the network.

Examples of Audit Insights on Access Management
Securing Financial Data

An audit may reveal that non-financial employees have access to sensitive financial records. Implementing RBAC restricts access to designated finance roles, reducing the risk of data leaks or unauthorized actions.

Strengthening Remote Work Security

Auditors may identify weak passwords among remote workers. Enforcing MFA and conducting secure password training addresses this vulnerability and strengthens remote access controls.

Preventing Unauthorized Privilege Escalation

An audit might uncover active accounts for terminated employees. Automating deprovisioning processes ensures timely revocation of access rights, preventing potential misuse.

Challenges in Access Management Audits

Despite its importance, auditing access management controls comes with challenges. Table 3-4 presents the most common audit challenges in access management audits.

Table 3-4. Challenges in access management audits and solutions

Challenges	Description	Solution
Legacy Systems	Older infrastructure may not support modern access control tools.	- Assess legacy systems for compatibility gaps. - Implement middleware or API gateways for integration. - Develop a phased migration plan to modern IAM solutions.
Excessive Access Rights	Users accumulate unnecessary permissions over time, increasing risks.	- Conduct quarterly access reviews. - Implement automated access request and approval workflows. - Enforce RBAC policies.

(*continued*)

CHAPTER 3   ASSESSING SECURITY CONTROLS

Table 3-4. (*continued*)

Challenges	Description	Solution
Human Error	Misconfigurations and incorrect permission assignments create vulnerabilities.	- Automate provisioning and deprovisioning of user accounts. - Provide regular training on access control policies. - Use policy-based access enforcement to prevent misconfigurations.
Privilege Creep	Employees retain access from previous roles, leading to unauthorized privileges.	- Enforce least privilege access with automatic role reassignment. - Use access recertification processes every 6 months. - Implement time-based access expiration for temporary roles.
Inconsistent Enforcement	Policies may not be uniformly applied across departments or systems.	- Centralize access management under a unified IAM framework. - Standardize policies across all business units. - Automate policy enforcement with compliance monitoring tools.
Audit Complexity	Reviewing access logs and permissions across multiple systems is challenging.	- Use SIEM for centralized logging. - Automate anomaly detection in access logs. - Schedule monthly audits with predefined access control checklists.
Remote Access Risks	Weak remote authentication can lead to unauthorized access.	- Enforce MFA for all remote logins. - Implement geo-restricted and time-based access controls. - Monitor remote login activity with real-time alerts.
Lack of Visibility	Difficulty in tracking privileged account usage and unauthorized changes.	- Deploy PAM solutions. - Maintain detailed logs of all privileged access sessions. - Implement continuous monitoring with alerts for unusual activities.

Key Takeaways

Access management is about more than just control; it represents a sacred trust in safeguarding an organization's most valuable assets. Like the ancient Egyptians who secured their most sacred spaces with complex systems, modern organizations must establish sophisticated and adaptive access management frameworks. By integrating technology, maintaining accountability, and prioritizing regular review, organizations ensure that their digital domains remain secure, resilient, and aligned with their operational needs.

In this section, we covered the following points:

- Effective controls minimize data breaches and insider threats, and ensure regulatory compliance.

- Access must be limited to necessity and authority, ensuring that only those with a legitimate need have access to sensitive resources.

- Implementing multiple layers of authentication and verification strengthens security.

- Regularly auditing and updating access rights ensures alignment with current roles and minimizes risks.

- While technology provides tools for access management, human oversight is crucial to maintain accountability and address unique scenarios.

- Comprehensive logging and tracking of access activities enhance transparency and allow for swift identification of anomalies.

Testing Application Security Controls in Cybersecurity Audits

Application security plays a pivotal role in protecting software systems from vulnerabilities that could potentially lead to severe consequences, such as data breaches, unauthorized access, or system compromise. The evolving landscape of cybersecurity threats makes it increasingly necessary for organizations to ensure their application

CHAPTER 3   ASSESSING SECURITY CONTROLS

security controls are robust, effective, and aligned with industry standards. Cybersecurity audits prioritize the testing of these controls to identify weaknesses, verify compliance with policies, and enhance the overall security posture of an organization.

Why Application Security Controls Matter in Audits

Application security controls are essential for maintaining the integrity and confidentiality of software systems. Their importance in cybersecurity audits stems from their ability to

- *Identify Vulnerabilities*: Audits uncover weaknesses in application design, implementation, or configuration, enabling organizations to address potential risks proactively.

- *Ensure Compliance*: Regulations like GDPR, HIPAA, and PCI DSS mandate stringent security measures for applications that handle sensitive data. Audits confirm adherence to these requirements.

- *Align with Organizational Policies*: Application security controls help enforce internal security policies, fostering a secure operational environment.

By integrating application security controls into the auditing process, organizations can mitigate risks, prevent breaches, and protect their reputations in the digital marketplace.

Understanding Application Security Controls

Application security controls are mechanisms – technical, administrative, and procedural – designed to safeguard software systems from unauthorized access and other cyber threats. These controls encompass a wide range of functions aimed at enhancing the security and resilience of applications. Like the concentric layers of a pyramid, application security controls provide multiple barriers of protection.

Key aspects include

- *Input Validation*: Ensures user inputs are sanitized and validated to prevent injection attacks, such as Structured Query Language (SQL) injection or Cross-Site Scripting (XSS). Acts as the outer limestone casing, deflecting initial attacks.

- *Authentication and Authorization*: Strengthens access security by validating user identities and enforcing role-based permissions. Functions like the grand entrance corridors with their sophisticated locking mechanisms.

- *Encryption*: Protects sensitive data both in transit and at rest, ensuring its confidentiality and integrity. Serves as the hidden chambers protecting the most valuable treasures.

- *Logging and Monitoring*: Captures critical events to enable real-time detection of anomalies or security breaches. Similar to the watchful eyes of guards, recording all activities.

- *Error Handling*: Ensures error messages do not disclose sensitive details, such as database structures or system configurations. Like the false passages designed to mislead tomb robbers.

These controls collectively contribute to a secure application environment, protecting data and functionality from potential threats.

Steps to Audit Application Security Controls

Auditing application security controls involves a combination of manual evaluations and automated testing techniques to ensure a thorough assessment. The key steps include

Define the Scope of the Audit

The first step is to clearly define the audit's scope by identifying the applications to be tested, their functionalities, and the data they handle. This process involves mapping out critical components such as login systems, payment gateways, and Application Programming Interface (API) integrations. By prioritizing high-risk areas, auditors can focus on the most sensitive aspects of the application. Just as Egyptian architects surveyed their construction site, auditors must map their digital territory, identifying critical areas requiring protection.

Conduct Threat Modeling

Threat modeling involves analyzing the application architecture to identify potential vulnerabilities and attack vectors. This process highlights areas prone to exploitation, such as user input fields, data storage mechanisms, and third-party integrations. By understanding the potential threats, auditors can tailor their tests to address these risks effectively. Like designing traps for potential tomb raiders, threat modeling anticipates and prepares for various attack vectors.

Leverage Automated Tools

Automated tools like Burp Suite, the Open Worldwide Application Security Project (OWASP) ZAP, and Netsparker play a crucial role in application security audits. These tools perform static and dynamic analysis to uncover vulnerabilities. Static Application Security Testing (SAST) tools analyze source code for issues, while Dynamic Application Security Testing (DAST) tools evaluate running applications for runtime flaws. The insights gained from these tools form the foundation for further investigation. While ancient builders used plumb lines and levels, modern auditors employ sophisticated tools to measure security effectiveness.

Incorporate Results from Penetration Testing

Penetration testing simulates real-world attacks to evaluate the effectiveness of application security controls. These tests cover various scenarios, including injection attacks, broken authentication, and insecure direct object references (IDOR). The findings provide valuable insights into the application's resilience against cyber threats.

Test Authentication Mechanisms

Authentication mechanisms are a critical component of application security. Auditors validate login processes, including password complexity requirements, multi-factor authentication, and account lockout policies. Additionally, session management is tested to ensure proper session expiration and prevention of token reuse.

Verify Encryption Practices

Encryption is essential for protecting sensitive data. Auditors assess whether data is encrypted using secure protocols such as TLS 1.2 or 1.3 and robust algorithms like AES-256. They also evaluate encryption key management practices to ensure keys are stored and accessed securely.

Review Logging and Monitoring Controls

Logging mechanisms capture vital security events that can indicate potential breaches or malicious activities. Auditors evaluate whether logs are comprehensive and whether monitoring systems can detect and respond to threats in real time. Effective logging and monitoring are critical for maintaining situational awareness in a cybersecurity context.

Analyze Error Handling Mechanisms

Error handling plays a vital role in preventing the exposure of sensitive information. Auditors verify that error messages are generic and do not reveal underlying system details, such as database structures or application logic, which attackers could exploit.

Tools for Testing Application Security

Auditing application security controls relies heavily on specialized tools that detect and mitigate vulnerabilities. These tools fall into several categories:

- *Vulnerability Scanners*:
  - *Nessus*: Scans applications, networks, and systems for known vulnerabilities.
  - *Acunetix*: Focuses on web application security, detecting risks like SQL injection and XSS.
- *Static Application Security Testing (SAST)*:
  - *SonarQube*: Analyzes source code for bugs and vulnerabilities across multiple programming languages.
  - *Checkmarx*: Identifies security issues in source code and third-party libraries.

- *Dynamic Application Security Testing (DAST)*:
  - *AppScan*: Automates detection of vulnerabilities such as XSS, SQL injection, and session management flaws.
  - *WebInspect*: Simulates real-world attacks to uncover runtime vulnerabilities in applications.
- *Manual Testing Tools*:
  - *Burp Suite*: Offers features like traffic interception, vulnerability scanning, and brute force automation.
  - *OWASP ZAP (Zed Attack Proxy)*: Provides intercepting proxies, active scanning, and fuzzing to identify vulnerabilities.
- *API Testing Tools*:
  - *Postman*: Tests API authentication, validation, and response handling.
  - *ReadyAPI*: Facilitates functional, security, and load testing of APIs.

Real-World Audit Examples

Auditing application security controls often reveals actionable insights that lead to significant improvements in application security. Here are some examples:

SQL Injection Prevention

During an audit of a retail application, weak input validation can be discovered, exposing the system to SQL injection attacks. Implementing parameterized queries and stricter validation rules mitigated this risk effectively.

Authentication Flaws

An audit of an e-commerce platform may reveal that session tokens remained active after user logout, creating security vulnerabilities. Enhancing session management controls resolved this issue.

Encryption Protocol Upgrades

A financial services audit may uncover the use of outdated Secure Sockets Layer (SSL) protocols. Upgrading to TLS 1.3 improved encryption and reduced the risk of data breaches.

Challenges and Best Practices in Application Security Audits

Application security audits often face several challenges, including

- *Complex Architectures*: Modern applications frequently use APIs, microservices, and third-party libraries, complicating comprehensive testing.

- *Time Constraints*: Limited audit windows require prioritization of critical components for evaluation.

- *Agile Development Cycles*: Rapid updates in agile environments can introduce untested vulnerabilities, increasing risks.

Organizations can enhance the effectiveness of their application security audits by adhering to the following best practices. Table 3-5 presents the most common audit challenges and their solutions in application security audits.

Table 3-5. Challenges in application security audits and solutions

Challenges	Description	Solution
Complex Architectures	Modern applications rely on APIs, microservices, and third-party libraries, making comprehensive testing difficult.	- Map all components (APIs, microservices, third-party dependencies). - Use automated dependency analysis tools. - Implement API security testing in audit workflows.
Time Constraints	Limited time for audits forces prioritization, potentially leaving critical vulnerabilities undetected.	- Focus on high-risk components using risk-based assessment. - Automate vulnerability scanning to speed up detection. - Conduct continuous security testing rather than relying on periodic audits.
Agile Development Cycles	Rapid application updates introduce untested vulnerabilities, increasing security risks.	- Integrate security testing into the CI/CD pipeline. - Perform static and dynamic analysis on each code deployment. - Conduct frequent threat modeling and security reviews.
Third-Party Dependencies	Applications often rely on external libraries, which may contain undiscovered or unpatched vulnerabilities.	- Continuously monitor third-party libraries for security updates. - Use SCA tools to detect vulnerable dependencies. - Establish a policy for vetting third-party software before integration.

(continued)

Table 3-5. (*continued*)

Challenges	Description	Solution
Insufficient Logging and Monitoring	Weak or missing logging mechanisms make it difficult to detect and investigate security incidents.	- Implement centralized logging solutions like SIEM tools. - Ensure logs capture authentication attempts, privilege escalations, and API calls. - Regularly assess and refine incident response processes.
Inadequate Authentication and Authorization	Weak authentication mechanisms and misconfigured access controls increase the risk of unauthorized access.	- Enforce MFA for all users. - Regularly review RBAC and least privilege principles. - Conduct penetration tests targeting authentication and authorization mechanisms.
Lack of Security Awareness Among Developers	Developers may lack security training, leading to insecure coding practices.	- Conduct regular secure coding training and workshops. - Use security-focused code reviews and pair programming. - Provide developers with automated security testing tools integrated into their workflow.
Regulatory Compliance Challenges	Meeting industry regulations (e.g., GDPR, PCI DSS, HIPAA) can be complex and require continuous adjustments.	- Map application security controls to compliance requirements. - Automate compliance audits where possible. - Keep track of regulatory changes and update security policies accordingly.

CHAPTER 3   ASSESSING SECURITY CONTROLS

Key Takeaways

Just as the ancient pyramids stand as enduring monuments to protective architecture, robust application security controls form the foundation of modern cybersecurity. These digital defenses, built on layers of protection, regular maintenance, and adaptation, safeguard the treasures of our digital age. By combining old wisdom with cutting-edge techniques, organizations can create secure systems that withstand the test of time and emerging threats, ensuring resilience and trust in an ever-evolving cyber landscape.

In this section, we covered the following points:

- Testing application security controls identifies vulnerabilities, ensures regulatory compliance, and strengthens an organization's security posture.

- Effective application security involves multiple layers of protection, mirroring the defensive strategies of ancient architectural marvels.

- A robust strategy incorporates automated tools, manual testing, and adherence to best practices for comprehensive vulnerability detection.

- Continuous evaluation and updates are crucial for maintaining the effectiveness of application security controls in a dynamic threat landscape.

- Just as ancient structures evolved to address new risks, application security must adapt to counter increasingly sophisticated cyber threats.

- Secure applications protect sensitive data and maintain confidence among stakeholders, forming the bedrock of digital trust.

Auditing Data Security Controls for Robust Cybersecurity

In today's digital age, data security is more than just an organizational requirement; it is a foundation of trust, operational stability, and compliance. Organizations handle sensitive information daily, from personal customer details to proprietary business data, making robust security controls non-negotiable. Data security controls play a pivotal role in safeguarding this invaluable resource, ensuring that confidentiality, integrity, and availability are always maintained. With cyber threats continually evolving and regulatory requirements becoming more stringent, auditing these controls has become a critical process to identify weaknesses and reinforce defenses.

As the ancient Egyptians understood that their Pharaohs' treasures required divine protection, modern organizations recognize that their data demands sacred guardianship. Like the carefully chosen pyramid guardians who followed strict protocols and hierarchies, data security controls establish the fundamental rules and structures that protect our digital wealth.

The Role of Data Security Controls in Cybersecurity

Data serves as the lifeblood of modern organizations. Whether it is customer information, financial records, or intellectual property, the value of data cannot be overstated. However, with great value comes great risk. Data breaches, unauthorized access, and data corruption can cause severe financial losses, reputational damage, and legal repercussions. This is where data security controls come into play.

Data security controls are systematic measures designed to protect data from threats. These measures span technical, administrative, and procedural safeguards, ensuring data is accessible only to authorized individuals and remains protected throughout its lifecycle. By implementing these controls, organizations create multiple layers of defense that reduce the likelihood of breaches and ensure compliance with relevant regulations. Cybersecurity audits assess the effectiveness of these measures, helping organizations pinpoint vulnerabilities and ensure their defenses remain robust against emerging threats.

Understanding Data Security Controls

Data security controls encompass a wide range of measures aimed at securing data at every stage: collection, storage, transmission, and disposal. These controls are essential for mitigating risks, maintaining trust, and ensuring compliance with industry standards and regulations. Key categories of data security controls include

CHAPTER 3   ASSESSING SECURITY CONTROLS

Access Controls

Access controls are mechanisms that regulate who can access specific datasets. These controls rely on principles such as least privilege and role-based access to ensure only authorized personnel can interact with sensitive data. Properly implemented access controls help organizations prevent data leaks and unauthorized modifications, fostering a secure environment for data management.

Just as pyramids featured carefully designed entrances with multiple security checkpoints, modern access controls create a hierarchical system of permissions:

- *The Grand Entrance (Primary Authentication)*:
  - Like the main pyramid entrance, requiring specific credentials.
  - Multiple authentication factors (like passing through various chambers).
  - Biometric verification (comparable to ancient physical recognition systems).
- *The Inner Chambers (Privileged Access)*:
  - Reserved for high priests (system administrators).
  - Special ceremonial access (emergency access protocols).
  - Sacred scrolls of access (access logs and documentation).

Encryption

Encryption is a fundamental technique for securing data, ensuring that even if data is intercepted, it remains unreadable without the appropriate decryption key. Encryption protects data both at rest (stored in databases or devices) and in transit (being transmitted across networks), serving as a critical defense against unauthorized access.

As ancient Egyptians used hieroglyphics to protect sacred knowledge, modern encryption safeguards sensitive data:

- *The Hieroglyphic Code (Encryption Algorithms)*:
  - Known only to trained scribes (encryption keys).
  - Multiple layers of meaning (encryption layers).
  - Sacred combinations (key management).

Data Masking

Data masking hides sensitive information by replacing it with fictitious but functional data. This technique is particularly useful in non-production environments, such as testing or development, where access controls may be more relaxed. By masking data, organizations can mitigate risks while maintaining system functionality.

Like the false walls and chambers in pyramids that protected true treasures, data masking creates protective illusions:

- *False Chambers (Test Environments)*:
    - Replica treasures (masked production data).
    - Practice ceremonies (development testing).
    - Training grounds (Quality Assurance (QA) environments).

Backup and Recovery

Backup and recovery controls ensure that data remains accessible even in the event of incidents such as cyberattacks, hardware failures, or natural disasters. Regular backups and efficient recovery mechanisms are essential for minimizing downtime and maintaining business continuity.

Just as pyramids were designed to preserve their contents for eternity, backup systems ensure data immortality:

- *The Preservation Rituals (Backup Procedures)*:
    - Daily offerings (incremental backups).
    - Monthly ceremonies (full backups).
    - Sacred restoration rites (disaster recovery).

Data Loss Prevention (DLP)

DLP solutions monitor and control data transfers across an organization's network. These tools prevent unauthorized data exfiltration by identifying and blocking risky behaviors, such as sending sensitive files over email or copying data to external drives.

Like the ever-vigilant guards protecting pyramid treasures, DLP systems maintain constant surveillance:

- *The Guardian's Watch (Monitoring Systems)*:
  - Perimeter patrols (network monitoring).
  - Internal inspections (endpoint protection).
  - Sacred alarms (alert systems).

Key Areas to Audit

A thorough audit of data security controls evaluates their implementation, effectiveness, and alignment with organizational objectives and regulatory requirements.

Figure 3-7 presents the key areas to audit in detail.

CHAPTER 3 ASSESSING SECURITY CONTROLS

Figure 3-7. *Key areas to audit*

Data Classification

An essential step in securing data is understanding its value and sensitivity. Auditors should assess whether the organization has classified its data into categories such as public, internal, and confidential. They should also verify that controls are tailored to each classification level, ensuring that sensitive data receives the highest level of protection.

Access Control Mechanisms

RBAC ensures that only individuals with a legitimate need can access specific data. Auditors should evaluate the implementation of RBAC policies and test the efficacy of MFA systems. By doing so, they can confirm that access control mechanisms effectively prevent unauthorized access.

Encryption Practices

Encryption is only as effective as its implementation. During audits, assess whether encryption is applied consistently to data at rest and in transit. Review encryption protocols, such as TLS 1.3, and key management practices, ensuring that keys are rotated, securely stored, and promptly revoked when necessary.

Backup and Recovery Plans

Backup and recovery processes are crucial for resilience. Auditors should validate the frequency and comprehensiveness of backups and test recovery procedures to ensure they align with the organization's Recovery Time Objectives (RTOs) and Recovery Point Objectives (RPOs).

DLP Solutions

Data loss prevention tools are essential for safeguarding sensitive information. Auditors should evaluate the configuration and effectiveness of DLP systems, focusing on policies for monitoring data movement through emails, USB drives, and cloud platforms.

Challenges and Best Practices in Auditing Data Security

Auditing data security controls comes with its own set of challenges, driven by the complexity of modern data environments:

- *Data Sprawl*: The rapid proliferation of data across cloud services, personal devices, and third-party platforms makes it difficult to maintain visibility and control over sensitive information.

- *Complex Regulations*: Data protection regulations like GDPR and HIPAA impose stringent requirements that vary by region and industry. Auditors must navigate these complexities to ensure compliance.

- *Evolving Threats*: Cyber threats are constantly evolving, with new tactics such as ransomware attacks and insider threats requiring continuous updates to security measures.

- *Lack of Visibility*: Without a clear understanding of data flows and storage locations, organizations may struggle to implement effective controls or detect potential vulnerabilities.

The following best practices help in reviewing data security controls:

- *Adopt a Data-Centric Security Approach*: Focus on protecting the data itself, rather than relying solely on perimeter defenses. This ensures that security measures remain effective even if other defenses are breached.

- *Leverage Automation*: Automated tools streamline the auditing process, enabling real-time monitoring and reporting while reducing human error.

- *Ensure Regulatory Compliance*: Align data security controls with standards such as GDPR, HIPAA, or ISO/IEC 27001 to meet legal and industry requirements.

- *Collaborate Across Teams*: Effective audits require input from IT, legal, compliance, and business teams. Collaboration fosters a holistic understanding of risks and ensures comprehensive assessments.

- *Perform Regular Testing*: Routine penetration testing and recovery drills validate the effectiveness of security measures and prepare organizations for potential incidents.

CHAPTER 3 ASSESSING SECURITY CONTROLS

Table 3-6 presents the most common challenges and their solutions in auditing data security controls.

Table 3-6. Challenges and solutions in auditing data security controls

Challenges	Description	Solutions
Data Sprawl	Sensitive data is dispersed across multiple environments, including cloud, on-premise, and third-party services, making it hard to track and secure.	- Implement data discovery and classification tools to locate and categorize sensitive data. - Use centralized data management strategies and enforce strict access controls.
Complex Regulations	Compliance requirements (e.g., GDPR, HIPAA, ISO 27001) vary across industries and regions, making audits more complicated.	- Establish a compliance framework that aligns with global regulations. - Automate compliance tracking using GRC (Governance, Risk, and Compliance) tools.
Evolving Threats	Cyber threats such as ransomware, insider threats, and zero-day vulnerabilities continuously change, making security audits a moving target.	- Conduct continuous security assessments and red team exercises. - Stay updated with threat intelligence feeds and implement real-time monitoring solutions.
Lack of Visibility	Organizations may not have a clear understanding of where sensitive data is stored, processed, or transmitted.	- Use data flow mapping, SIEM solutions, and CSPM tools to enhance visibility.
Access Control Gaps	Inadequate RBAC and weak authentication mechanisms can lead to unauthorized access.	- Enforce least privilege access, implement MFA, and regularly review access control policies.
Inefficient Backup and Recovery	Poorly managed backup policies may result in data loss or prolonged downtime during an incident.	- Implement a robust backup and disaster recovery plan. - Test backups regularly to ensure quick and effective restoration.

CHAPTER 3 ASSESSING SECURITY CONTROLS

Key Takeaways

The enduring legacy of the pyramids offers timeless lessons in security: implement multiple layers of protection, classify and prioritize what's most valuable, strictly control access, maintain constant vigilance, and ensure regular testing and updates. By combining these principles with modern tools and practices, organizations can build resilient digital fortresses, safeguarding their data against threats for generations to come.

In this section, we covered the following points:

- Robust data security controls protect sensitive information, ensure regulatory compliance, and build stakeholder trust, making it a strategic imperative.

- Effective data security requires layered defenses, combining firewalls, encryption, access controls, and continuous monitoring to create a comprehensive security framework.

- Just as the most sacred artifacts were placed in secure chambers, organizations must classify data and apply the highest protection to sensitive information.

- Sophisticated authentication and authorization mechanisms ensure only authorized individuals access sensitive data, minimizing risks.

- Encryption, akin to ancient hieroglyphics, transforms sensitive data into unreadable formats, protecting it from unauthorized access while ensuring usability for key holders.

- Ongoing security monitoring allows organizations to detect and respond to potential threats swiftly, maintaining vigilance against evolving cyber risks.

- Detailed documentation, regular audits, and employee training programs ensure the effectiveness of security controls while fostering a culture of security awareness and adaptation.

CHAPTER 3   ASSESSING SECURITY CONTROLS

Evaluating Cloud Security Controls for Enhanced Cybersecurity

The adoption of cloud computing has significantly transformed how organizations operate, providing scalability, cost efficiency, and operational flexibility. This shift has enabled businesses to optimize their resources and adapt to dynamic market demands more effectively. However, alongside these advantages come unique security challenges that require meticulous attention. As organizations migrate their infrastructure, data, and applications to the cloud, ensuring robust security controls becomes a fundamental necessity. Without adequate security measures, cloud environments can expose businesses to a variety of risks, including data breaches, unauthorized access, and operational disruptions. In this context, cybersecurity audits serve as an essential mechanism to assess the effectiveness of cloud security controls, identify vulnerabilities, and ensure compliance with industry regulations.

The Role of Cloud Security Controls

Cloud security controls serve as the foundation for protecting cloud-based systems, data, and applications from breaches, unauthorized access, and disruptions. These controls aim to mitigate risks while maintaining compliance with regulatory frameworks and ensuring operational continuity. Broadly, cloud security controls are classified into three categories:

- *Preventive Controls*: Designed to stop security incidents before they occur, preventive measures include access controls, firewalls, and encryption.

- *Detective Controls*: These controls identify and respond to security incidents, such as IDS and logging mechanisms.

- *Corrective Controls*: Focused on mitigating the impact of security incidents, corrective measures include incident response plans and disaster recovery solutions.

By integrating these controls into their cloud environments, organizations create a layered defense system capable of addressing diverse threats.

Key Areas to Evaluate in Cloud Security Audits

A comprehensive audit of cloud security controls evaluates their design, implementation, and effectiveness. The auditors focus on the below critical areas:

- IAM
- Data Protection Mechanisms
- Network Security Controls
- Compliance and Regulatory Alignment
- Logging and Monitoring
- Tools like AWS CloudTrail or Azure Monitor are used to monitor activities effectively.

Table 3-7 presents a detailed description and auditor focus.

Table 3-7. Key areas to evaluate in cloud security audits

Key Area	Description	Audit Focus Areas
Identity and Access Management (IAM)	Ensures only authorized users access cloud resources.	- Implementation of RBAC. - Use of MFA for privileged accounts. - Identification of inactive or overly permissive accounts.
Data Protection Mechanisms	Secures data at rest and in transit to prevent breaches.	- Encryption implementation (e.g., TLS for data in transit). - Key management (secure storage, rotation, and revocation). - Data masking or tokenization for sensitive information.

(continued)

Table 3-7. (*continued*)

Key Area	Description	Audit Focus Areas
Network Security Controls	Protects cloud environments from unauthorized access and threats.	- Use of VPNs and Virtual Private Clouds (VPCs) for secure communication. - Configuration of firewalls, security groups, and ACLs. - Deployment of IPS and network monitoring tools.
Compliance and Regulatory Alignment	Ensures adherence to industry standards and legal frameworks.	- Compliance with GDPR, HIPAA, and PCI-DSS. - Validation of cloud provider certifications (SOC 2, ISO/IEC 27001, and FedRAMP).
Logging and Monitoring	Provides visibility into security events and potential threats.	- Logging enabled for critical events (e.g., access attempts and config changes). - Secure log storage and periodic review for anomalies. - Use of monitoring tools like AWS CloudTrail and Azure Monitor.

Technologies for Cloud Security Audits

Several advanced tools and technologies enhance the efficiency and accuracy of cloud security audits:

- *Cloud Access Security Brokers (CASBs)*: Solutions like Netskope and McAfee MVISION enforce security policies and provide visibility into cloud usage.

- *Encryption and Key Management*: Tools such as AWS Key Management Service (KMS) and HashiCorp Vault secure encryption keys and sensitive data.

- *Security Posture Management*: Platforms like Prisma Cloud and Azure Security Center identify misconfigurations and compliance gaps.

- *Monitoring and Analytics*: Systems like Splunk and Elastic Stack collect and analyze logs to detect anomalies and potential threats.

- *Penetration Testing Tools*: Tools like Metasploit and OWASP ZAP simulate attacks to identify vulnerabilities in cloud configurations and applications.

Challenges in Evaluating Cloud Security Controls

Cloud environments present unique challenges that can complicate audits:

- *Shared Responsibility Model*: Security responsibilities are divided between the organization and the Cloud Service Provider (CSP), requiring clear understanding and delineation.

- *Dynamic Environment*: The cloud's elasticity and scalability make it difficult to monitor and maintain consistent configurations.

- *Shadow IT*: Unauthorized use of cloud services by employees can bypass established security controls and introduce risks.

- *Vendor Lock-In*: Reliance on a single CSP can limit flexibility and complicate the implementation of additional controls.

- *Lack of Standardization*: Variability in security practices across CSPs creates challenges in multi-cloud environments.

Effective cloud security audits require a strategic approach that addresses the complexities of cloud environments. Key best practices include

- *Understand the Shared Responsibility Model*: Clearly define and audit the respective roles of the organization and CSP in securing cloud resources.

- *Automate Security Assessments*: Leverage tools like AWS Inspector or Azure Security Center to identify vulnerabilities automatically.

- *Prioritize Data Security*: Enforce encryption, access control, and secure key management for sensitive data.

- *Focus on Configuration Management*: Regularly review and update cloud configurations to prevent misconfigurations.

- *Test Continuously*: Conduct periodic penetration testing to evaluate the resilience of cloud security controls.

- *Ensure Compliance with Standards*: Verify adherence to industry regulations such as GDPR, HIPAA, DORA, NIS2, and ISO/IEC 27001.

- *Audit Access Management*: Implement least privilege for all accounts and regularly review permissions.

- *Monitor Cloud Activity*: Enable logging and analyze activity using tools like CloudTrail or Sentinel to detect suspicious behavior.

- *Evaluate Third-Party Risk*: Assess the security posture of CSPs and any third-party integrations to ensure they meet organizational standards.

- *Implement Incident Response Plans*: Develop, test, and refine cloud-specific incident response procedures to ensure preparedness.

Table 3-8 presents the most common challenges and their solutions in evaluating cloud security controls.

Table 3-8. Challenges and solutions in evaluating cloud security controls

Challenge	Description	Impact on Security Audits	Solutions
Shared Responsibility Model	Security responsibilities are divided between the organization and the CSP.	- Requires clear delineation of roles to avoid security gaps. - Misunderstandings can lead to unaddressed vulnerabilities.	- Clearly define security responsibilities in contracts and agreements. - Regularly review CSP security documentation and compliance reports.
Dynamic Environment	Cloud resources scale and change rapidly, making security monitoring difficult.	- Inconsistent configurations can introduce security weaknesses. - Continuous monitoring is required to maintain security baselines.	- Use automated security posture management tools like AWS Security Hub or Azure Security Center. - Implement Infrastructure as Code (IaC) to enforce security policies consistently.

(*continued*)

Table 3-8. (*continued*)

Challenge	Description	Impact on Security Audits	Solutions
Shadow IT	Unauthorized use of cloud services by employees outside IT governance.	- Bypasses security controls, increasing the risk of data breaches. - Creates unknown attack surfaces that are difficult to audit.	- Enforce strict access controls and security awareness training. - Deploy CASB solutions to monitor and control cloud usage.
Vendor Lock-In	Dependence on a single CSP limits flexibility and security customization.	- Reduces ability to implement competitive security solutions. - Increases risk if the CSP has security weaknesses.	- Adopt a multi-cloud or hybrid-cloud strategy to reduce dependency. - Ensure portability by using containerized applications and open standards.
Lack of Standardization	Security practices vary across different CSPs and multi-cloud environments.	- Difficult to maintain a unified security posture. - Compliance challenges arise due to differing security implementations.	- Use cloud-agnostic security frameworks such as the CSA Cloud Controls Matrix (CCM). - Implement centralized security monitoring and logging across cloud environments.

Key Takeaways

Cloud security is a dynamic and ongoing process. By addressing key areas such as IAM, data protection, network security, and compliance while conducting regular audits, organizations can ensure their cloud environments remain secure and resilient. As businesses increasingly rely on the cloud, a proactive approach to cloud security controls is essential to maintaining trust, protecting assets, and navigating the complexities of modern cybersecurity.

In this section, we covered the following points:

- Evaluating cloud security controls is essential to protecting organizational assets and mitigating risks in modern cloud environments.
- Addressing IAM, data protection, network security, and compliance ensures a comprehensive cloud security posture.
- Routine audits provide critical insights into the effectiveness of cloud security controls and help identify vulnerabilities.
- Proactive evaluation and updates to cloud security controls are vital for adapting to the dynamic threat landscape.
- Effective controls must protect data and operations while preserving the scalability and agility that cloud environments offer.
- Adhering to industry standards and regulations safeguards against legal and financial repercussions, strengthening stakeholder trust.
- Continuous assessment and improvement of cloud security controls are integral to building a resilient and secure cloud infrastructure.

Common Control Failures and How to Identify Them

Cybersecurity controls are foundational to safeguarding an organization's digital assets and maintaining its operational integrity. These controls are designed to mitigate risks, protect sensitive data, and ensure compliance with legal and regulatory standards. However, even the most meticulously designed controls can fail, leading to vulnerabilities that threaten the organization's security posture. Control failures often arise due to a combination of human errors, outdated practices, misconfigurations, and insufficient monitoring. Identifying these failures is a critical aspect of cybersecurity audits, enabling organizations to address vulnerabilities proactively and strengthen their defenses.

The following section explores the nature of control failures, their root causes, and the profound impacts they can have on network security, data protection, and compliance. It also explores common failures, effective techniques for detecting them,

Understanding Control Failures

Control failures occur when cybersecurity measures fail to perform their intended function, leaving the organization vulnerable to internal and external threats. These failures can stem from various factors, including poorly designed controls, improper implementation, and inadequate maintenance. For instance, a firewall may lack appropriately defined rules, or a patch management process might not be updated to address new vulnerabilities, exposing the organization to significant risks.

The impact of control failures is far-reaching, affecting critical domains such as network security, data integrity, and compliance with industry regulations. Common contributors to control failures include

- *Human Errors*: Weak passwords, accidental misconfigurations, or a lack of adherence to security protocols.

- *Outdated Controls*: Legacy systems and practices that cannot effectively counter modern threats.

- *Compliance Gaps*: Failure to align controls with regulatory requirements like GDPR, HIPAA, or PCI-DSS.

- *Monitoring Blind Spots*: Limited visibility into critical systems or activities, making anomaly detection challenging.

- *Third-Party Risks*: Unpatched vendor systems or insecure practices that introduce vulnerabilities into the supply chain.

These failures highlight the importance of proactive auditing and continuous improvement to minimize risks and enhance organizational resilience.

Like ancient architects discovering weaknesses in their pyramid defenses, modern security professionals must understand how protective measures can fail. Just as a pyramid's defenses consisted of multiple elements – massive stone blocks, hidden chambers, false passages, and vigilant guards – modern security controls form a complex protective system where each component must function properly.

The parallels are striking:

- A loose stone in the pyramid wall (misconfigured firewall rules).
- Worn-away hieroglyphic passwords (weak authentication systems).
- Abandoned guard posts (unmonitored security controls).
- Damaged seal mechanisms (broken encryption protocols).
- Forgotten secret passages (undocumented access points).

Common Control Failures and Their Detection

Auditors must pay close attention to specific areas where control failures are most likely to occur. Below are some of the most prevalent control failures, their impacts, and effective methods for detection:

Weak Password Policies

Weak or reused passwords remain one of the most significant security vulnerabilities. They make it easier for attackers to compromise accounts through brute force or credential-stuffing attacks. Detection involves using password management tools like LastPass or Dashlane to assess password strength and ensuring that MFA is implemented across critical systems. Like broken seals on a Pharaoh's tomb, weak passwords provide easy entry for intruders. Just as Egyptian priests regularly inspected sacred seals, modern organizations must continuously audit password strength and implement robust authentication mechanisms.

Misconfigured Firewalls

Firewalls with overly permissive rules or incomplete configurations allow unauthorized access to sensitive resources. Detection requires conducting vulnerability scans using tools like Nessus or Qualys and analyzing network traffic patterns through SIEM solutions. As gaps in pyramid walls could allow unauthorized entry, misconfigured firewalls create dangerous openings in digital defenses. Regular inspection of these defensive barriers, using modern tools rather than ancient measuring ropes, remains crucial.

Lack of Patch Management

Unpatched systems expose the organization to exploits targeting known vulnerabilities. Detection involves reviewing patch logs and utilizing tools like Microsoft System Center Configuration Manager (SCCM) or Windows Server Update Services (WSUS) to automate and track patch management processes. Just as pyramid maintenance crews had to replace weathered stones and repair damage, modern systems require constant patching and updates to maintain their defensive integrity.

Over-Permissive Access Controls

Granting excessive privileges to users increases the risk of insider threats and unauthorized access. IAM tools such as Okta and SailPoint help audit access permissions, identifying inactive or overly privileged accounts that need to be reviewed or revoked.

Inadequate Encryption

Failing to encrypt sensitive data at rest or in transit leaves it exposed to interception and unauthorized access. Detection methods include inspecting network traffic for unencrypted transmissions and verifying adherence to encryption protocols.

Weak Endpoint Security

Endpoints are a frequent target for attackers. Poor security measures, such as inadequate anti-malware solutions or lack of device encryption, compromise organizational security. Detection focuses on verifying the deployment of EDR tools and ensuring compliance with encryption policies.

Insufficient Logging and Monitoring

Limited logging and monitoring capabilities reduce the ability to detect and respond to incidents promptly. Detection involves auditing log retention policies, ensuring secure storage of logs, and validating the integration of monitoring tools with SIEM platforms.

CHAPTER 3   ASSESSING SECURITY CONTROLS

Poor Incident Response Plans

Unstructured or outdated incident response plans delay recovery and exacerbate the impact of security incidents. Detection includes evaluating the completeness of response plans and conducting regular tabletop exercises to simulate potential scenarios.

Effective Auditing Techniques

To uncover and address control failures, cybersecurity audits must leverage a combination of automated tools and manual processes. Effective auditing techniques include

- *Vulnerability Scanning*: Identifies system weaknesses and vulnerabilities using tools like OpenVAS and Nessus.

- *Penetration Testing*: Simulates real-world attacks to evaluate security posture, utilizing frameworks such as OWASP ZAP or Metasploit.

- *Configuration Audits*: Reviews system and cloud configurations with tools like Prisma Cloud and Azure Security Center.

- *Log Analysis*: Analyzes log data for anomalies and suspicious activities using platforms like Elastic Stack and Splunk.

- *Policy Reviews*: Examines cybersecurity policies to identify gaps and outdated practices.

- *Access Review Automation*: Streamlines the review process using IAM tools to ensure adherence to the principle of least privilege.

Mitigating Control Failures

Organizations can address control failures effectively through a combination of technology, training, and continuous monitoring. Key mitigation strategies include

- *Employee Training*: Regularly educating employees on cybersecurity best practices reduces the risk of human errors.

- *Automating Processes*: Implementing automated tools for patch management, access reviews, and monitoring minimizes manual errors and improves efficiency.

- *Enhanced Monitoring*: Deploying real-time monitoring solutions ensures visibility into critical systems and enables timely detection of anomalies.

- *Regular Audits*: Conducting frequent audits helps assess the effectiveness of controls and identify areas for improvement.

- *Incident Response Plan Testing*: Periodically testing and updating response plans ensures preparedness for emerging threats and incidents.

Key Takeaways

As the pyramids stood the test of time through meticulous maintenance and vigilance, modern security frameworks demand constant care and evolution. Lessons from ancient builders guide us: regular maintenance and inspections are indispensable, a multi-layered defense offers the best protection, and human vigilance is as vital as technological measures. Thorough documentation preserves essential security knowledge, and regular testing identifies weaknesses before attackers exploit them. By continuously adapting and improving, organizations can build a resilient security posture capable of protecting their digital treasures against evolving threats.

In this section, we covered the following points:

- No security framework is perfect; proactive measures such as regular audits and continuous monitoring are essential to minimize the impact of failures.

- Automating repetitive tasks like patch management and access reviews improves efficiency and reduces human error.

- Training employees to recognize threats like phishing and enforce strong password practices is critical for a resilient cybersecurity culture.

- Developing, maintaining, and regularly testing a robust incident response plan ensures swift action to minimize downtime and mitigate security breaches.

CHAPTER 3 ASSESSING SECURITY CONTROLS

- Like the pyramids, multiple layers of security, combining physical, technical, and administrative controls, create a more resilient defense.

- Continuous monitoring and regular assessments help detect and address vulnerabilities before attackers can exploit them.

- Comprehensive documentation and knowledge sharing ensure organizational continuity and strengthen security preparedness.

Validation of Security Control Effectiveness

In the ever-evolving landscape of cybersecurity, implementing robust security controls is a fundamental necessity for organizations striving to protect sensitive information, systems, and networks. However, implementation alone does not guarantee success. Cybersecurity controls must be validated regularly to ensure they are functioning as intended. This validation process is critical to identifying gaps, verifying compliance with internal policies and regulatory requirements, and addressing the dynamic and ever-changing threat landscape. Without validation, organizations risk relying on a false sense of security, leaving them vulnerable to exploitation.

Validation of security controls is not merely about testing the existing measures but about embedding a culture of continuous improvement in the organization's cybersecurity practices. As attackers become more sophisticated, even the most well-designed controls can become outdated or ineffective. Regular validation ensures these measures evolve alongside the threats they are designed to counter, providing organizations with the assurance they need to operate confidently in the digital realm.

What Does Validating Security Controls Mean?

Validation of security controls is a comprehensive process that involves systematically testing, monitoring, and reviewing the implemented cybersecurity measures to evaluate their performance. It aims to confirm that the controls meet their intended objectives and continue to protect the organization against identified risks. In essence, it is a proactive method to ensure that the controls are not only present but also operating optimally and in alignment with the organization's security goals.

Effective validation entails several key aspects. First, it ensures that the controls are properly configured and operational, functioning as intended without any lapses. Second, it evaluates whether these controls effectively mitigate identified risks, such as unauthorized access, data breaches, or ransomware attacks. Third, it ensures compliance with regulatory frameworks and organizational policies, which is essential for maintaining trust and avoiding penalties. Lastly, validation helps in identifying potential gaps or weaknesses in the controls, enabling organizations to address them before they can be exploited by malicious actors.

Key objectives of validation include

- Ensuring that controls are properly configured and operational.
- Verifying that they effectively mitigate identified risks.
- Aligning controls with compliance frameworks and organizational policies.
- Detecting and addressing potential gaps or weaknesses proactively.

For example, a firewall configured to block unauthorized traffic might be functioning but could have rules that inadvertently allow unnecessary access. Without validation, such misconfigurations might go unnoticed, creating vulnerabilities in the system. Similarly, encryption mechanisms might be in place but fail to use updated protocols, leaving sensitive data exposed to advanced decryption techniques. Through validation, these issues can be identified and rectified in a timely manner.

Steps to Validate Security Control Effectiveness

Validating the effectiveness of security controls involves a structured, multi-step process designed to thoroughly assess their functionality, alignment with best practices, and resilience against potential threats. Below are the detailed steps organizations can follow:

CHAPTER 3   ASSESSING SECURITY CONTROLS

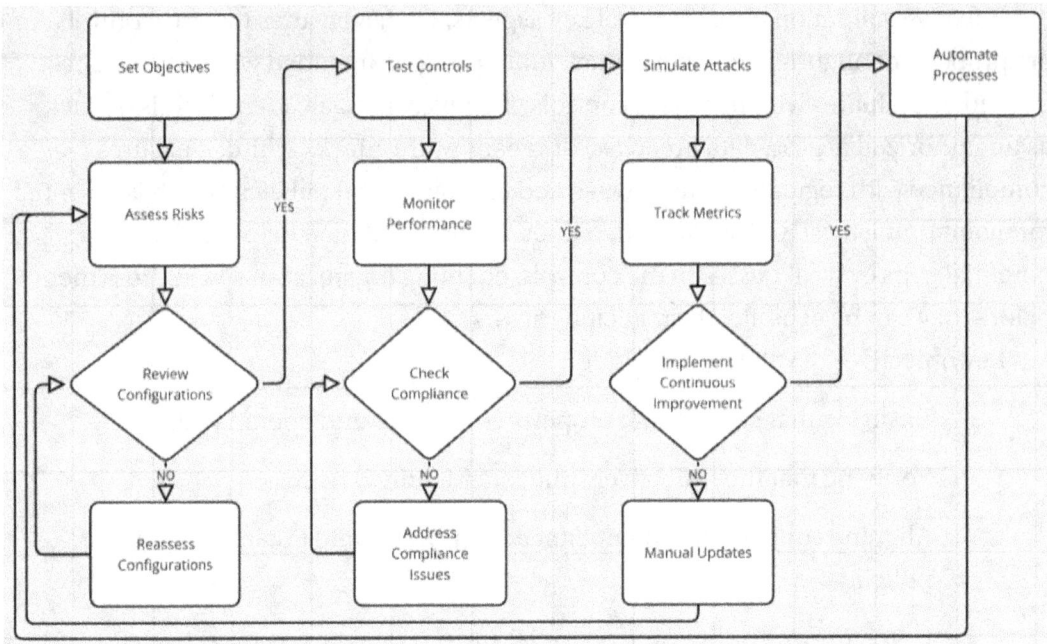

Figure 3-8. *Workflow for validating security control effectiveness*

Set Objectives

Begin by defining the purpose and intended outcomes of each security control. For instance, a control might be designed to prevent unauthorized access, encrypt sensitive data, or detect unusual activity within the network. Clearly understanding the objectives ensures that validation efforts are focused on assessing the critical aspects of the controls.

Assess Risks

Identify and prioritize high-risk areas within the organization, such as systems handling customer data, financial records, or intellectual property. Risk assessment frameworks like the National Institute of Standards and Technology Risk Management Framework (NIST RMF) or the FAIR can provide structured methodologies for evaluating and categorizing risks.

Review Configurations

Examine the configurations of security controls to ensure they align with industry standards and best practices. For example, validate that firewall rules are correctly defined, endpoint security solutions are up-to-date, and communication protocols such as TLS 1.3 are implemented to secure data in transit.

Test Controls

Conduct comprehensive testing to simulate real-world scenarios and uncover vulnerabilities. Some common testing methods include

- *Penetration Testing*: Simulating cyberattacks using tools like Metasploit or Kali Linux to assess the system's resilience against potential breaches.

- *Vulnerability Scanning*: Identifying known vulnerabilities with tools such as Nessus, Qualys, or OpenVAS.

- *Phishing Simulations*: Evaluating email security and employee awareness by conducting mock phishing campaigns.

Monitor Performance

Regularly monitor the performance of security controls using data from IDS such as Snort or Suricata and SIEM solutions like Splunk or QRadar. Analyze logs and alerts to evaluate the accuracy and timeliness of responses to potential threats.

Check Compliance

Validate that the controls align with regulatory requirements such as ISO 27001, GDPR, or PCI-DSS. Compliance validation ensures that the organization is not only secure but also adheres to legal and industry standards, avoiding potential fines or reputational damage.

Simulate Attacks

Conduct incident response simulations to test the organization's preparedness for various cyberattacks, such as ransomware or distributed denial-of-service (DDoS) attacks. These simulations help refine response strategies and improve overall resilience.

Track Metrics

Define and monitor key performance indicators (KPIs) such as incident detection rates, response times, and the success rate of patch deployments. These metrics provide quantifiable insights into the effectiveness of the security controls and help identify areas for improvement.

Implement Continuous Improvement

Security control validation is not a one-time activity but an ongoing process that requires continuous refinement. Organizations should proactively address vulnerabilities identified during validation and implement necessary updates to strengthen defenses. This involves regularly reassessing risk factors, adapting to new threat landscapes, and ensuring security measures remain aligned with evolving regulatory requirements. Automating validation tasks using tools like Ansible, Chef, or AWS Security Hub can improve efficiency and reduce human error. Additionally, organizations should foster a culture of continuous learning by analyzing security incidents, updating policies, and enhancing employee awareness through training programs.

Validation Challenges

While validation is a critical component of a robust cybersecurity strategy, it is not without challenges. The rapidly evolving nature of cyber threats means that security controls that were effective yesterday might be inadequate today. This dynamic environment requires continuous adaptation and vigilance.

Resource limitations can also pose significant obstacles, particularly for smaller organizations with limited budgets and manpower. These constraints can hinder thorough testing and monitoring efforts, leaving gaps in the validation process. Furthermore, overconfidence in existing controls can lead to complacency, resulting in skipped validations and undetected vulnerabilities.

For example, an organization may assume that its legacy systems are secure because they have not been breached yet, neglecting to validate their effectiveness against modern attack techniques. Similarly, the lack of skilled personnel or advanced tools can prevent organizations from conducting the deep and comprehensive assessments needed for effective validation.

To address these challenges and ensure effective validation, organizations should adopt the following best practices:

- *Test Regularly*: Make validation an ongoing activity rather than a one-time effort. Continuous testing ensures that controls remain effective against evolving threats.

- *Diversify Methods*: Combine automated tools and manual testing to capture a broad spectrum of vulnerabilities. Automated tools are efficient for routine checks, while manual testing provides deeper insights into complex issues.

- *Stay Current*: Regularly update security controls to incorporate the latest technologies and address emerging threats.

- *Integrate Governance*: Embed validation activities into the organization's overall security strategy, ensuring alignment with business objectives and risk management goals.

- *Automate Where Possible*: Use automation tools like Chef, Puppet, or Ansible to streamline repetitive tasks, improving efficiency and reducing the likelihood of human error.

Table 3-9 presents the most common challenges and their solutions in security control validation.

Table 3-9. Challenges and solutions in security control validation

Challenges	Description	Solutions
Evolving Threat Landscape	Cyber threats constantly change, making previously effective security controls outdated.	Implement continuous monitoring, threat intelligence, and regular security updates to adapt to new risks.
Resource Limitations	Small organizations may lack the budget, tools, or personnel for thorough validation.	Use automated security tools, outsource security testing, and prioritize critical assets for validation efforts.
Overconfidence in Existing Controls	Organizations may assume their controls are effective without regular testing.	Establish periodic validation processes, conduct penetration testing, and enforce a zero-trust security model.
Legacy Systems and Compatibility Issues	Older systems may not support modern security measures, creating validation gaps.	Develop a migration plan, apply compensating controls, and use segmentation to isolate vulnerable systems.
Lack of Skilled Personnel	Cybersecurity skills shortages can hinder comprehensive validation.	Provide ongoing training, leverage managed security services, and use AI-driven security automation.
Inconsistent Testing and Monitoring	Ad hoc or irregular validation efforts reduce security effectiveness.	Implement a structured validation schedule, integrate validation into governance frameworks, and automate assessments where possible.
Regulatory Compliance Challenges	Keeping up with evolving compliance requirements can be complex.	Regularly update security policies, use compliance automation tools, and engage legal/security teams for guidance.
Foster a Culture of Security	Employees play a crucial role in validation and risk mitigation.	Conduct regular security awareness training, implement phishing simulations, and encourage a proactive security mindset.
Continuous Improvement	Security control validation should be an iterative process.	Regularly analyze incidents, update security controls, and refine response strategies based on lessons learned.

Key Takeaways

Validation of security controls is a continuous process that guarantees the integrity and adaptability of an organization's defense. By regularly assessing, testing, and monitoring controls, organizations can stay ahead of emerging threats while ensuring regulatory compliance and building trust. Like the careful maintenance of ancient structures, ongoing validation is key to protecting digital assets and sustaining a resilient cybersecurity posture.

In this section, we covered the following points:

- *Validation Is Essential for Resilience*: Regular validation ensures security controls are effective in addressing current and emerging risks.

- *Proactive Identification of Vulnerabilities*: Validation processes like risk assessments and configuration reviews help uncover and address gaps before threats materialize.

- *Regulatory Alignment*: Consistent validation ensures controls meet compliance requirements and strengthens the organization's trustworthiness.

- *Integration with Strategy*: Validation should be part of the broader security strategy to create an adaptive, resilient defense posture.

- *Automation Enhances Efficiency*: Automation tools support consistent validation while allowing teams to focus on strategic tasks.

- *Continuous Improvement*: Ongoing validation drives continuous refinement and strengthening of cybersecurity defenses.

- *Comprehensive Protection*: Prioritizing control validation enables organizations to protect assets, ensure operational continuity, and navigate the evolving threat landscape confidently.

Documentation Tips for Control Assessment

In the field of cybersecurity audits, effective documentation is a foundation of success. It provides a structured foundation for understanding, evaluating, and enhancing security controls. Beyond just recording information, documentation fosters transparency, ensures consistency, supports compliance efforts, and serves as a trusted reference for stakeholders. Whether addressing regulatory requirements, simplifying future assessments, or aiding decision-making, well-crafted documentation is indispensable in achieving audit objectives and maintaining a resilient cybersecurity posture.

The importance of documentation cannot be overstated. It acts as a comprehensive record of control assessments, creating a reliable audit trail that can be revisited to understand how evaluations were conducted, what findings emerged, and what actions were taken. This transparency builds trust among stakeholders and ensures that all parties – technical teams, business leaders, and external regulators – can align their understanding of cybersecurity measures. Furthermore, standardized documentation practices eliminate ambiguity and pave the way for consistent, repeatable assessments, which are essential in managing cybersecurity effectively over time.

Why Documentation Is Crucial in Control Assessment

Effective documentation is more than just a formal requirement; it is an operational necessity in cybersecurity audits. Its benefits span across multiple dimensions:

- *Audit Trail*: Comprehensive documentation records every step of the assessment process, creating a detailed trail that is invaluable for tracing decisions, understanding outcomes, and demonstrating accountability.

- *Transparency*: Detailed records provide clarity about evaluation methodologies and findings, ensuring that stakeholders can understand the basis of conclusions and recommendations.

- *Consistency*: By adhering to standardized formats and structures, documentation ensures that assessments are conducted uniformly across time and teams, reducing variability and increasing reliability.

- *Compliance*: Many regulatory frameworks, including PCI-DSS, ISO 27001, and GDPR, mandate robust documentation as part of their requirements. Meeting these standards demonstrates organizational commitment to cybersecurity.

- *Future Audits*: Good documentation simplifies future assessments by providing baseline data, insights into past improvements, and references for continuous enhancement efforts.

When documentation is thorough and methodical, it not only serves the immediate needs of an audit but also becomes a valuable asset in building a strong cybersecurity foundation.

Key Elements of Effective Control Assessment Documentation

Creating robust and effective documentation for control assessment is a multi-faceted process that involves capturing the entire scope of an assessment with clarity and precision. Each element plays a vital role in ensuring that the documentation not only serves immediate audit needs but also acts as a reliable resource for future reference and decision-making. Below are the detailed components that form the foundation of impactful control assessment documentation:

Executive Summary

The executive summary provides a high-level overview of the assessment, summarizing its objectives, scope, methodology, and key findings. This section is particularly useful for non-technical stakeholders, such as executives or board members, who need to understand the results without delving into technical jargon. By highlighting the most critical outcomes, risks, and recommendations, the executive summary sets the tone for the rest of the documentation and ensures that all readers grasp the importance of the findings.

Scope and Methodology

Clearly defining the assessment's scope ensures that all parties understand the boundaries and objectives of the evaluation. This section should outline the systems, applications, processes, and data sets included in the assessment. Additionally, it should detail the methodologies employed, such as risk-based approaches, compliance-based reviews, or technical testing. Mentioning the tools and frameworks used, like the NIST CSF, COBIT, or OCTAVE, demonstrates alignment with industry best practices and adds credibility to the process.

Inventory of Controls

An organized inventory of controls provides a structured view of the cybersecurity measures in place. Controls should be categorized based on their type and function:

- *Preventive Controls*: These measures, like firewalls, MFA, and access controls, are designed to prevent incidents before they occur.

- *Detective Controls*: Tools like SIEM systems, IDS, and monitoring platforms fall under this category. They focus on identifying and alerting teams to potential or active threats.

- *Corrective Controls*: These include incident response plans, disaster recovery mechanisms, and patch management solutions, which aim to mitigate the impact of an incident after it occurs.

This detailed breakdown helps auditors and stakeholders understand how different controls work together to safeguard the organization's assets.

Assessment Findings

Documenting the results of the control assessment in detail is critical. This section should outline the strengths of the existing controls, as well as areas where they fall short. Highlight risks, vulnerabilities, and compliance gaps, providing a balanced view of the organization's cybersecurity posture. Using structured templates or matrices to present findings ensures clarity and helps prioritize areas needing improvement. For example, separating findings into categories such as "High Risk," "Medium Risk," and "Low Risk" can guide remediation efforts effectively.

Evidence Collected

Supporting artifacts form the backbone of credible documentation. These include logs, screenshots, configuration files, and test results from tools like Nessus, Qualys, Metasploit, or Burp Suite. Including this evidence substantiates the findings and provides an audit trail that can be reviewed by internal or external parties. To maintain security, sensitive evidence should be redacted or encrypted where necessary, ensuring compliance with data protection regulations.

Recommendations and Remediation

Providing actionable recommendations is a key deliverable of any control assessment. This section should outline remediation steps for identified gaps, prioritizing them based on their potential impact and likelihood. Frameworks like the FAIR can be used to assign risk levels and guide prioritization. For each recommendation, include estimated timelines, required resources, and potential challenges to implementation. This proactive approach helps stakeholders address issues efficiently and strategically.

Compliance Mapping

Linking controls to relevant regulatory requirements and industry standards is a crucial aspect of documentation. For instance, map data encryption measures to GDPR Article 32 or password management practices to ISO 27001 Annex A.9.4.3. This mapping not only demonstrates the organization's commitment to compliance but also simplifies regulatory audits by providing a clear alignment of controls with legal and industry mandates.

Metrics and KPIs

Quantifiable metrics provide an objective measure of control effectiveness. Include key performance indicators (KPIs) such as the average incident detection time, vulnerability remediation rates, and the frequency of policy violations. Tracking these metrics over time offers valuable insights into trends, helping organizations assess whether their cybersecurity efforts are improving or require additional adjustments.

Sign-Offs and Approvals

Formalizing the documentation process through sign-offs ensures accountability. This section should record the approval of findings and recommendations by key stakeholders, including technical teams, management, and external auditors. By documenting these sign-offs, the organization establishes a clear record of who reviewed and accepted the assessment, reinforcing its validity and ensuring alignment across departments.

Best Practices for Documentation

To create impactful documentation that serves its intended purpose, organizations should follow these best practices:

- *Clarity and Consistency*: Use simple, jargon-free language and maintain a consistent structure throughout the documentation to ensure that it is accessible to both technical and non-technical stakeholders.

- *Leverage Technology*: Use collaborative tools like SharePoint, Confluence, or Splunk to streamline documentation processes, automate version control, and enhance accessibility.

- *Secure Sensitive Information*: Protect sensitive data in documentation by implementing access controls and encryption using tools like BitLocker or VeraCrypt.

- *Regular Updates*: Periodically review and update documentation to reflect changes in the control environment, new regulatory requirements, or emerging threats. Maintain version histories to track modifications.

- *Align with Frameworks*: Ensure that documentation aligns with industry-recognized standards such as NIST SP 800-53, ISO 27001, or COBIT 2019 to enhance credibility and effectiveness.

Key Takeaways

Effective documentation serves as the foundation for successful cybersecurity control assessments. By providing clear, transparent, and up-to-date records of processes, findings, and changes, it not only facilitates compliance but also strengthens long-term cybersecurity resilience. Just as building blueprints guide construction projects, well-organized documentation ensures informed decision-making, proactive risk management, and seamless auditing processes, helping organizations confidently navigate the complexities of cybersecurity.

In this section, we covered the following points:

- Documentation ensures transparency; it provides a structured record of assessments, findings, and recommendations, fostering trust with stakeholders.

- Effective documentation serves as a baseline for future audits and helps track changes in controls, regulatory requirements, and security measures.

- Well-organized documentation enables organizations to address risks more proactively by reflecting the latest threats and controls.

- Continuously updating documentation ensures it stays relevant and reflective of evolving security needs.

- Comprehensive and clear documentation supports long-term cybersecurity resilience and decision-making.

- Following best practices in documentation ensures it meets both immediate and future cybersecurity needs efficiently.

Conclusions

In this chapter, it is explored that various aspects of cybersecurity underscore the intricate, layered, and dynamic nature of building a resilient defense posture in modern organizations. Security controls form the backbone of an organization's cybersecurity strategy, mitigating risks, protecting assets, and ensuring regulatory compliance. By adopting a layered approach, combining preventive, detective, and corrective measures across technical, administrative, and physical dimensions, organizations enhance their resilience against evolving threats.

Continuous monitoring and validation emerge as fundamental pillars in maintaining the effectiveness of security controls, ensuring they adapt to emerging vulnerabilities and threats. Regular audits, updates, and integration with organizational goals align cybersecurity efforts with operational efficiency and strategic objectives.

The human factor remains indispensable; employee training and awareness amplify the effectiveness of even the most advanced controls. Automation of repetitive tasks, such as patch management and access reviews, complements this by reducing human error and improving operational efficiency. Seamless integration of controls, spanning physical, network, application, data, and cloud security, fortifies the organization's overall security posture, ensuring no gaps are left unaddressed.

Documentation and knowledge sharing play pivotal roles, acting as the foundation for successful assessments, audits, and incident response. Comprehensive, clear, and up-to-date documentation not only supports compliance but also enables informed decision-making, proactive risk management, and long-term cybersecurity resilience.

Drawing timeless lessons from the enduring pyramids, cybersecurity strategies must prioritize robust defenses through multiple layers of protection, regular maintenance, and continuous improvement. Much like the ancient builders who evolved their designs to counter new threats, modern organizations must integrate historical wisdom with cutting-edge technology to build secure, adaptive, and enduring digital fortresses.

A holistic cybersecurity approach, encompassing strategic alignment, robust documentation, proactive validation, and a balance between human and technological elements, ensures organizations can confidently navigate the complexities of the cybersecurity landscape. Through vigilance, adaptability, and an unwavering commitment to safeguarding their assets, organizations can achieve a resilient posture capable of withstanding the tests of time and the ever-evolving threat environment.

CHAPTER 4

Compliance and Regulations

In today's digital landscape, organizations are faced with the critical responsibility of safeguarding sensitive information and ensuring that their cybersecurity practices align with legal and regulatory standards. Cybersecurity compliance refers to the adherence to various laws, guidelines, and frameworks that govern how businesses must protect data, infrastructure, and user privacy. These regulations are designed to mitigate risks associated with cyber threats such as data breaches, identity theft, and cyberattacks. Understanding and complying with these regulations is not only a legal obligation but also a key component of building trust with customers and stakeholders.

Much like soldiers in an army are trained to follow orders with precision to maintain the integrity and safety of their unit, organizations must adhere to cybersecurity regulations to ensure the overall security of their digital ecosystem. Just as a lapse in discipline on the battlefield can jeopardize an entire mission, noncompliance in cybersecurity can expose an organization to critical vulnerabilities, putting its operations, reputation, and stakeholders at risk.

One of the most significant sets of regulations is the GDPR, which governs how businesses collect, store, and process personal data of individuals within the European Union. This regulation has set a global benchmark for privacy protection, compelling organizations to reassess their data security measures and develop robust systems to ensure data protection. Similarly, HIPAA in the United States requires healthcare organizations to adopt strict controls over health-related data to ensure confidentiality and prevent unauthorized access. These regulations serve as the rules of engagement in the battle against cyber threats, highlighting the importance of specialized compliance standards for different industries and regions and emphasizing the need for tailored approaches in meeting cybersecurity objectives.

CHAPTER 4   COMPLIANCE AND REGULATIONS

Failure to comply with cybersecurity regulations can result in severe consequences, including hefty fines, legal action, and reputational damage. To mitigate these risks, organizations must implement comprehensive compliance strategies that encompass employee training, routine audits, and the use of advanced security technologies. Regular assessments are necessary to identify vulnerabilities, track compliance status, and ensure that organizations are staying ahead of evolving threats and regulatory updates. Regulatory frameworks such as the PCI DSS and the Federal Information Security Management Act (FISMA) further underscore the need for ongoing diligence in compliance. Just as a disciplined military unit conducts routine drills to stay prepared for unforeseen challenges, organizations must maintain vigilance and adaptability in their compliance efforts.

In addition to established regulations, recent and upcoming legislative measures continue to shape the cybersecurity landscape. DORA is a key regulation set to impact the financial sector, focusing on improving the operational resilience of financial service providers against cyber threats and disruptions. DORA mandates stringent requirements for risk management, incident reporting, and third-party oversight, aiming to ensure that financial institutions can maintain critical operations during times of crisis. Similarly, the NIS2 expands the scope of cybersecurity obligations across sectors, enhancing the resilience of critical infrastructure in the EU. NIS2 introduces more rigorous security requirements for essential services, including energy, transport, and healthcare, and mandates better cooperation and information sharing between member states. The EU Cybersecurity Act, which strengthens the European Union Agency for Cybersecurity (ENISA), also introduces a new EU-wide certification framework for cybersecurity products and services. These evolving regulations emphasize the importance of strict adherence to cybersecurity protocols, much like an army continually adapts its strategies and tools to defend against evolving threats.

In this chapter analogically is used similar to following the rules in army.

Navigating Key Cybersecurity Regulations

In a world where data breaches and cyberattacks are as frequent and relentless as enemy ambushes, cybersecurity regulations serve as the army's tactical manuals and field orders. These regulations establish the rules of engagement, ensuring that sensitive data, the mission-critical intelligence of the digital battlefield, is protected with precision and diligence. For auditors, mastering these frameworks is akin to understanding the chain of command: a prerequisite to organizing effective defenses and fortifying the security perimeter of any organization.

This section explores key cybersecurity regulations, illustrating their significance and the auditor's role in aligning the organization's strategies with these frameworks, much like a commanding officer devising battle plans in harmony with overarching military directives.

The Role of Cybersecurity Regulations

Cybersecurity regulations are the steadfast generals of the digital battleground, issuing orders that dictate the course of action to safeguard sensitive personal, financial, and operational data. Adherence to these frameworks mirrors a soldier's discipline on the field, failing to comply risks penalties as severe as dishonorable discharges:

- Enhancing protection for sensitive data is akin to fortifying a base against infiltration.

- Maintaining compliance ensures operational readiness, preventing vulnerabilities that adversaries could exploit.

- Building trust with stakeholders reflects the camaraderie and mutual respect within a well-disciplined platoon.

Non-compliance can lead to crippling consequences, much like a lapse in following orders can compromise an entire mission. For auditors, these regulations form the battle map, guiding their efforts to uncover vulnerabilities and shore up defenses before the enemy strikes.

Key Cybersecurity Regulations and Their Significance

Each cybersecurity regulation is a distinct theater of war, with its own rules, objectives, and terrains to navigate. Auditors must approach these frameworks as tacticians, tailoring strategies to meet the unique challenges of each operational zone.

CHAPTER 4   COMPLIANCE AND REGULATIONS

General Data Protection Regulation (GDPR)

The GDPR is a landmark regulation designed to protect the personal data of EU citizens. Its global applicability means that any organization handling EU citizens' data, regardless of location, must comply with its stringent requirements. GDPR emphasizes transparency, accountability, and the rights of individuals, requiring organizations to obtain explicit consent for data processing, ensure data portability, and notify authorities of breaches within 72 hours.

The GDPR stands as the field marshal of data privacy, enforcing rigorous standards with the authority of a commanding officer. Its global reach ensures that no soldier, or organization, can ignore its call to arms, compelling compliance with demands for transparency, accountability, and individual rights.

The financial penalties for non-compliance are among the most severe, reaching up to €20 million or 4% of global annual turnover. However, the regulation's true impact extends beyond fines; it compels organizations to embed data privacy into their core operations. For auditors, GDPR assessments focus on data encryption, access controls, breach response readiness, and the effectiveness of Data Protection Impact Assessments (DPIAs).

Key elements include

- *Region*: European Union (Global reach)

- *Objective*: GDPR is a landmark regulation that safeguards the personal data of EU citizens. It applies to any organization that processes such data, regardless of its geographical location.

- *Key Requirements*: Organizations must ensure transparency in data handling, obtain consent for processing, support individuals' data rights (e.g., right to access and erase), notify authorities of data breaches within 72 hours, and use encryption to secure sensitive information.

- *Impact*: Non-compliance can result in fines up to €20 million or 4% of global annual turnover, whichever is higher.

- *Audit Focus*: Auditors evaluate access controls, encryption methods, and compliance with data breach notification policies.

Health Insurance Portability and Accountability Act (HIPAA)

HIPAA is a US-based regulation aimed at protecting the confidentiality, integrity, and availability of electronic Protected Health Information (ePHI). It applies to healthcare providers, insurers, and their business associates, ensuring that patient data is handled securely. HIPAA mandates regular risk assessments, robust access controls, encryption of ePHI, and mandatory employee training to prevent unauthorized disclosures.

HIPAA operates as the medic of the cybersecurity forces, safeguarding the lifeblood of healthcare data with precision protocols and rigorous discipline. Its requirements for risk assessments and employee training parallel the constant drills and exercises that keep soldiers combat-ready.

Fines for non-compliance can be as high as $50,000 per violation, with annual caps of $1.5 million. However, the reputational damage from a breach can far exceed these monetary penalties. Auditors conducting HIPAA assessments must ensure adherence to the Security Rule, evaluate access logs, identify vulnerabilities, and verify employee training programs.

Key elements include

- *Region*: United States

- *Objective*: HIPAA ensures the confidentiality, integrity, and availability of electronic Protected Health Information (ePHI) while facilitating electronic health transactions.

- *Key Requirements*: Risk assessments, access controls, encryption, and mandatory employee training.

- *Impact*: Violations can incur fines of up to $50,000 per violation, with annual caps reaching $1.5 million.

- *Audit Focus*: Auditors examine compliance with the Security Rule, evaluate access logs, and identify potential vulnerabilities in systems handling ePHI.

CHAPTER 4   COMPLIANCE AND REGULATIONS

Payment Card Industry Data Security Standard (PCI-DSS)

PCI-DSS is a global standard developed to protect cardholder data and minimize the risk of credit card fraud. It applies to all entities that store, process, or transmit cardholder information. Key requirements include securing networks through firewalls, encrypting sensitive data, conducting regular vulnerability testing, and restricting access to authorized personnel.

PCI-DSS is the fortress architect of the digital economy, designing impenetrable defenses to protect cardholder data. Its guidelines for securing networks and encrypting sensitive information mirror the blueprints for building a fortified outpost under constant threat.

Non-compliance can result in fines, increased transaction fees, or even the revocation of payment processing privileges. For auditors, PCI-DSS assessments focus on encryption practices, access control mechanisms, and evaluating penetration testing results to identify weaknesses in systems that handle payment data.

Key elements include

- *Region*: Global
- *Objective*: PCI-DSS aims to protect cardholder data and reduce credit card fraud through stringent security practices.
- *Key Requirements*: Secure network configurations, encryption of cardholder data, regular vulnerability testing, and restricted access to sensitive data.
- *Impact*: Non-compliance can lead to hefty fines, increased transaction fees, or the loss of payment processing privileges.
- *Audit Focus*: Auditors analyze encryption practices, review access control mechanisms, and assess penetration testing results on payment systems.

NIST Cybersecurity Framework (CSF) 2.0

The NIST Cybersecurity Framework (CSF) 2.0 is an enhanced version of the original NIST CSF, designed to provide a flexible and adaptable cybersecurity risk management framework for organizations across industries. With expanded guidance on governance, supply chain risk management, and continuous security control validation, CSF 2.0 aligns cybersecurity best practices with business objectives to foster resilience against evolving cyber threats.

NIST CSF 2.0 is the strategic command center of cybersecurity, offering a structured yet adaptable approach that organizations can tailor to their risk environment. Its emphasis on continuous improvement ensures that security programs evolve alongside emerging threats and business needs.

Key updates in CSF 2.0 include a sixth core function, "Govern," which emphasizes executive oversight and cybersecurity risk alignment with business priorities. The framework also expands guidance on supply chain security, zero trust architecture, and performance measurement for cybersecurity programs.

While CSF 2.0 is voluntary, many industries and government agencies use it as a foundational cybersecurity framework. Auditors leveraging CSF 2.0 assess organizations' maturity across the framework's functions and categories, ensuring that cybersecurity controls are effectively integrated into operational and strategic objectives.

Key Elements of NIST CSF 2.0:

- *Region*: United States (widely adopted globally)

- *Objective*: CSF 2.0 provides a structured cybersecurity risk management framework that enhances resilience and aligns security practices with business goals.

- *Key Requirements*: Organizations must assess cybersecurity maturity across six core functions: Identify, Protect, Detect, Respond, Recover, and Govern, and implement risk-based security controls, continuous monitoring, and supply chain risk management.

- *Impact*: Adoption improves risk management capabilities, strengthens cybersecurity governance, and aligns security investments with business objectives.

- *Audit Focus*: Auditors evaluate control effectiveness within the six CSF 2.0 functions, assess risk management processes, review cybersecurity governance maturity, and ensure alignment with organizational goals.

CHAPTER 4   COMPLIANCE AND REGULATIONS

Federal Information Security Management Act (FISMA)

FISMA is a US regulation that ensures the security of federal information systems. It requires federal agencies to implement a risk-based approach to information security, guided by frameworks such as NIST SP 800-53. FISMA mandates regular security assessments, the development of incident response plans, and continuous monitoring of control effectiveness.

FISMA compliance is critical not only for national security but also for the operational integrity of federal agencies. Auditors working on FISMA assessments rely on NIST frameworks to evaluate security controls, monitor compliance, and recommend enhancements that align with federal guidelines.

Key elements include

- *Region*: United States (Federal Agencies)

- *Objective*: FISMA enhances the security of federal information systems through mandatory risk management practices.

- *Key Requirements*: Implementation of NIST frameworks, periodic security assessments, comprehensive response plans, and continuous monitoring.

- *Impact*: Compliance with FISMA is critical for national security and operational integrity within federal agencies.

- *Audit Focus*: Auditors leverage NIST SP 800-53 to assess control effectiveness and monitor compliance across federal systems.

California Consumer Privacy Act (CCPA)

The CCPA grants California residents enhanced rights over their personal data, including the right to access, delete, and opt out of the sale of their information. Organizations subject to the CCPA must be transparent about their data collection practices, provide clear opt-out mechanisms, and respond promptly to consumer requests.

Fines for non-compliance can reach $7,500 per violation, making adherence crucial for organizations operating in or serving California residents. Auditors assess data mapping processes, verify the implementation of consent mechanisms, and ensure that organizations can handle data access and deletion requests efficiently.

Key elements include

- *Region*: California, United States

- *Objective*: CCPA grants California residents enhanced privacy rights, such as the right to access, delete, and opt out of the sale of their personal information.

- *Key Requirements*: Transparency in data collection practices, opt-out mechanisms for data selling, and robust processes to address data access and deletion requests.

- *Impact*: Fines for violations can reach $7,500 per instance.

- *Audit Focus*: Auditors review data mapping efforts, verify consent processes, and assess mechanisms for honoring opt-out requests.

ISO/IEC 27001

ISO/IEC 27001 is an international standard for managing information security risks through an ISMS. The standard emphasizes a risk-based approach, requiring organizations to conduct regular risk assessments, review their ISMS, and provide ongoing employee training to maintain compliance.

Certification under ISO/IEC 27001 not only demonstrates a commitment to security but also builds trust among customers and business partners. Auditors play a key role in evaluating the maturity of an organization's ISMS, assessing control effectiveness, and ensuring compliance with the standard's Annex A requirements.

Key elements include

- *Region*: International

- *Objective*: ISO/IEC 27001 establishes a framework for managing information security risks through an ISMS.

- *Key Requirements*: Conduct risk assessments, regularly review the ISMS, and provide employee training to ensure compliance.

- *Impact*: Certification enhances organizational credibility and trustworthiness in the global market.

- *Audit Focus*: Auditors assess the ISMS's maturity, evaluate control effectiveness, and ensure compliance with Annex A requirements.

CHAPTER 4   COMPLIANCE AND REGULATIONS

Digital Operational Resilience Act (DORA)

DORA, introduced by the European Union, focuses on ensuring the resilience of financial institutions against cyber threats and operational disruptions. It mandates robust ICT risk management, detailed incident reporting, operational continuity planning, and oversight of third-party providers.

Regulation underscores the importance of a proactive approach to managing technology risks, especially in critical sectors. For auditors, DORA assessments involve evaluating ICT risk management strategies, testing incident response readiness, and monitoring the compliance of third-party vendors with resilience standards.

Key elements include

- *Effective Date*: January 17, 2025.
- *Region*: European Union.
- *Objective*: DORA focuses on ensuring the resilience of financial institutions in the face of cyber threats and operational risks.
- *Key Requirements*: DORA mandates the implementation of robust ICT risk management, incident reporting, operational continuity planning, and third-party risk monitoring.
- *Impact*: Financial institutions and their service providers must align with DORA to avoid penalties and ensure uninterrupted service.
- *Audit Focus*: Auditors evaluate ICT risk management policies, incident response readiness, and third-party compliance assessments.

Network and Information Security Directive 2 (NIS2)

NIS2 builds on the original NIS Directive to enhance cybersecurity across critical infrastructure sectors in the European Union. It introduces stricter requirements for risk management, incident response, and governance, while expanding its scope to include additional sectors.

Organizations must conduct comprehensive risk assessments, establish governance frameworks, and report incidents within strict timelines. Non-compliance can result in substantial penalties and reputational harm. Auditors focus on evaluating the completeness of risk assessments, the effectiveness of incident management processes, and alignment with sector-specific guidelines.

CHAPTER 4 COMPLIANCE AND REGULATIONS

Key elements include

- *Effective Date*: October 17, 2024.
- *Region*: European Union.
- *Objective*: NIS2 aims to strengthen cybersecurity across critical infrastructure sectors, ensuring greater preparedness and resilience against cyber incidents.
- *Key Requirements*: NIS2 requires entities to conduct risk assessments, implement incident response plans, report incidents promptly, and establish governance frameworks for cybersecurity.
- *Impact*: Non-compliance can lead to significant financial penalties and reputational harm.
- *Audit Focus*: Auditors focus on incident management processes, risk assessment completeness, and compliance with sector-specific guidelines.

System and Organization Controls 2 (SOC 2)

SOC 2 is a voluntary compliance framework developed by the American Institute of Certified Public Accountants (AICPA) to assess the security, availability, processing integrity, confidentiality, and privacy of information systems. It applies to service organizations that manage customer data, ensuring they implement adequate controls to safeguard information.

SOC 2 emphasizes operational security, requiring organizations to demonstrate the implementation of controls that align with the Trust Services Criteria (TSC). These controls are evaluated through a third-party audit, resulting in a SOC 2 report, which is often essential for building trust with clients and stakeholders.

The framework is particularly significant for cloud providers, SaaS vendors, and managed service providers, as it demonstrates a commitment to security and compliance in handling sensitive data.

Key elements include

- *Region*: Global.

- *Objective*: SOC 2 ensures that service organizations meet specific standards for security, availability, processing integrity, confidentiality, and privacy.

- *Key Requirements*: Organizations must define, implement, and monitor controls related to the TSC, with a focus on risk management, incident response, and system monitoring.

- *Impact*: Achieving SOC 2 compliance builds trust with customers and stakeholders, reduces risk exposure, and enhances organizational credibility in competitive markets.

- *Audit Focus*: Auditors evaluate the design and operational effectiveness of controls, ensuring alignment with TSC. Focus areas include access controls, incident management, risk assessments, and system monitoring.

Sarbanes–Oxley Act (SOX)

The Sarbanes–Oxley Act (SOX) is a US federal law enacted in 2002 to improve corporate governance and enhance the accuracy and reliability of financial reporting. While its primary focus is financial compliance, SOX has significant cybersecurity implications, especially regarding internal controls over information systems that impact financial data.

Section 404 of SOX mandates the establishment and evaluation of internal controls, requiring organizations to assess and document the effectiveness of these controls annually. This includes securing systems that store, process, and transmit financial data, as well as implementing robust access controls, monitoring mechanisms, and incident response capabilities.

Non-compliance with SOX can result in severe penalties, including personal liability for executives. For auditors, SOX assessments focus on identifying risks to financial systems, verifying control effectiveness, and ensuring alignment with the organization's financial compliance objectives.

Key elements include

- *Region*: United States.

- *Objective*: SOX aims to enhance corporate governance and the accuracy of financial reporting by ensuring robust internal controls over financial systems.

- *Key Requirements*: Establishing internal controls, documenting their effectiveness, securing systems handling financial data, and ensuring executive accountability.

- *Impact*: Non-compliance can result in significant fines, reputational harm, and legal consequences for executives and the organization.

- *Audit Focus*: Auditors review internal control frameworks, evaluate system security measures, monitor access logs, and assess compliance with financial reporting requirements.

Cyber Resilience Act (CRA) – Regulation (EU) 2024/2847

The CRA introduces mandatory cybersecurity requirements for digital products and software placed on the EU market. It enforces a security-by-design ethos, demanding that manufacturers build and maintain secure products throughout their lifecycle, from code to post-deployment patching.

CRA is the armorer of the digital economy, equipping every connected device and software package with baseline defenses before it enters the battlefield.

Key elements include

- *Expected Enforcement*: 2027

- *Region*: European Union

- *Objective*: Secure digital products and software from design to decommissioning, reducing vulnerabilities in the EU digital market.

- *Key Requirements*: Built-in security-by-design mechanisms; ongoing vulnerability monitoring and disclosure; maintenance of technical compliance documentation; 24-hour vulnerability and incident reporting.

- *Impact*: Elevates baseline cybersecurity across industries, reduces supply-chain risks, and strengthens consumer trust.

- *Audit Focus*: Examine security-by-design documentation, validate vulnerability management processes, and confirm regulatory compliance readiness.

Summary of Key Cybersecurity Regulations and Their Audit Considerations

Table 4-1 provides a structured comparison of key cybersecurity regulations and frameworks, highlighting their objectives, key functions, audit focus areas, similarities with other regulations, and unique characteristics. These regulations shape the cybersecurity landscape by enforcing data protection, risk management, and governance requirements across industries. Auditors play a critical role in assessing compliance with these frameworks, ensuring that organizations implement effective security controls, minimize risks, and adhere to legal and regulatory mandates. Understanding these regulations collectively helps organizations develop a comprehensive cybersecurity compliance strategy while aligning security initiatives with business objectives.

Table 4-1. Key cybersecurity regulations/frameworks

Name	Short Description	Key Functions	Key Areas to Focus in Audit	What It Has in Common	Unique Feature
General Data Protection Regulation (GDPR)	EU regulation ensuring data privacy and protection for individuals.	Enforces data transparency, accountability, breach notification, and individual data rights.	Data encryption, access controls, breach response readiness, DPIAs.	Strong emphasis on data privacy like CCPA; requires breach notifications like NIS2.	Global reach affecting any organization processing EU citizens' data; highest fines for non-compliance.
Health Insurance Portability and Accountability Act (HIPAA)	US regulation ensuring the security of healthcare data (ePHI).	Mandates risk assessments, access controls, encryption, and employee training.	Security rule compliance, access logs, employee training, and vulnerability management.	Similar to GDPR and CCPA in protecting personal data; requires risk assessments like NIST CSF.	Specific to healthcare data, with fines per violation rather than overall turnover-based fines.
Payment Card Industry Data Security Standard (PCI-DSS)	Global standard protecting cardholder data and preventing fraud.	Enforces secure network configurations, encryption, and access restrictions.	Encryption practices, access control mechanisms, and penetration testing results.	Similar to ISO 27001 in security best practices, it has a risk-based approach like NIST CSF.	Applies specifically to payment card transactions, with penalties affecting business operations.

(*continued*)

Table 4-1. (continued)

Name	Short Description	Key Functions	Key Areas to Focus in Audit	What It Has in Common	Unique Feature
NIST Cybersecurity Framework (CSF) 2.0	Voluntary framework for managing cybersecurity risks.	Provides structured security risk management across six functions (Identify, Protect, Detect, Respond, Recover, and Govern).	Control effectiveness, risk management maturity, and governance oversight.	Shares a risk-based approach with ISO 27001 and FISMA; aligns with SOC 2 for governance.	Newly introduced "Govern" function; widely adopted across industries, not just mandated sectors.
Federal Information Security Management Act (FISMA)	US law ensures federal agencies implement risk-based cybersecurity practices.	Requires security assessments, continuous monitoring, and adherence to NIST SP 800-53.	Control effectiveness, compliance with federal standards, incident response plans.	Similar to NIST CSF in risk-based security, like SOX, it involves compliance monitoring.	Mandatory for US federal agencies; highly dependent on NIST frameworks.
California Consumer Privacy Act (CCPA)	US state law granting California residents data rights.	Enforces transparency, data access and deletion rights, and opt-out mechanisms.	Data mapping, consent mechanisms, handling access/deletion requests.	Similar to GDPR in granting consumer data rights; focuses on individual control like HIPAA.	Specific to California residents; has an opt-out mechanism for data sales.

Framework	Description	Key Requirements	Relation to Other Frameworks	Unique Features
ISO/IEC 27001	International standard for managing information security risks through an ISMS.	Requires risk assessments, ISMS maintenance, and security control effectiveness.	ISMS maturity, Annex A compliance, risk-based security assessment.	Aligns with NIST CSF in security governance; compliance-driven like SOC 2.	Global credibility through certification; structured approach to ISMS.
Digital Operational Resilience Act (DORA)	EU regulation ensuring financial institutions' resilience against cyber threats.	Mandates ICT risk management, incident reporting, and operational continuity planning.	ICT risk policies, incident response readiness, and third-party vendor risk.	Similar to NIS2 in critical infrastructure security; and aligns with ISO 27001 in resilience.	Exclusive to financial institutions; strong focus on third-party vendor risk management.
Network and Information Security Directive 2 (NIS2)	EU directive enhancing cybersecurity across critical sectors.	Enforces risk management, incident response, and governance requirements.	Risk assessments, incident management, sector-specific compliance.	Risk-based like NIST CSF; governance-focused like SOX.	Stricter than the original NIS, with a wider scope covering more sectors.
System and Organization Controls 2 (SOC 2)	Voluntary framework ensuring security, availability, processing integrity, confidentiality, and privacy.	Requires organizations to implement controls aligning with TSC.	Access controls, risk assessments, incident management, and system monitoring.	Like ISO 27001, it assesses security controls, similar to NIST CSF in risk-based evaluation.	Essential for cloud service providers and SaaS vendors; reports focus on operational security.

(continued)

CHAPTER 4   COMPLIANCE AND REGULATIONS

Table 4-1. (*continued*)

Name	Short Description	Key Functions	Key Areas to Focus in Audit	What It Has in Common	Unique Feature
Sarbanes–Oxley Act (SOX)	US federal law enhancing corporate governance and financial reporting accuracy.	Mandates internal controls, financial system security, and executive accountability.	Internal controls, system security, access logs, and compliance with financial reporting.	Governance-focused like NIST CSF and ISO 27001; compliance-driven like PCI-DSS.	Primarily financial compliance but with cybersecurity implications for data integrity.
Cyber Resilience Act (CRA)	EU regulation for digital product cybersecurity throughout the lifecycle.	Security by design, vulnerability management, incident reporting, and compliance documentation.	Product lifecycle security, vulnerability handling, and design documentation audits.	Emphasizes product risk like ISO 27001; lifecycle monitoring like CRA.	Focuses on digital product manufacturers, distributors, and importers.

CHAPTER 4   COMPLIANCE AND REGULATIONS

Auditor's Perspective: Ensuring Regulatory Compliance

Auditors play a pivotal role in bridging the gap between regulatory requirements and an organization's cybersecurity framework. Regulatory compliance extends beyond mere adherence to prescribed standards; it requires a strategic approach to integrating these requirements into the organization's operations and ensuring ongoing vigilance.

Auditors are the drill sergeants of compliance, instilling discipline and rigor into the organization's security practices. Their role extends beyond mere inspections; they act as strategic advisors, enabling organizations to operate with the precision and foresight of an elite military unit.

Auditors must thoroughly understand the specific obligations of each regulation to tailor their assessments. For example, GDPR necessitates a focus on data protection mechanisms such as encryption, breach notification readiness, and DPIAs. In contrast, PCI-DSS emphasizes securing payment card data, requiring auditors to assess encryption practices, vulnerability management, and access control mechanisms.

Figure 4-1 presents key steps in auditing for regulatory compliance.

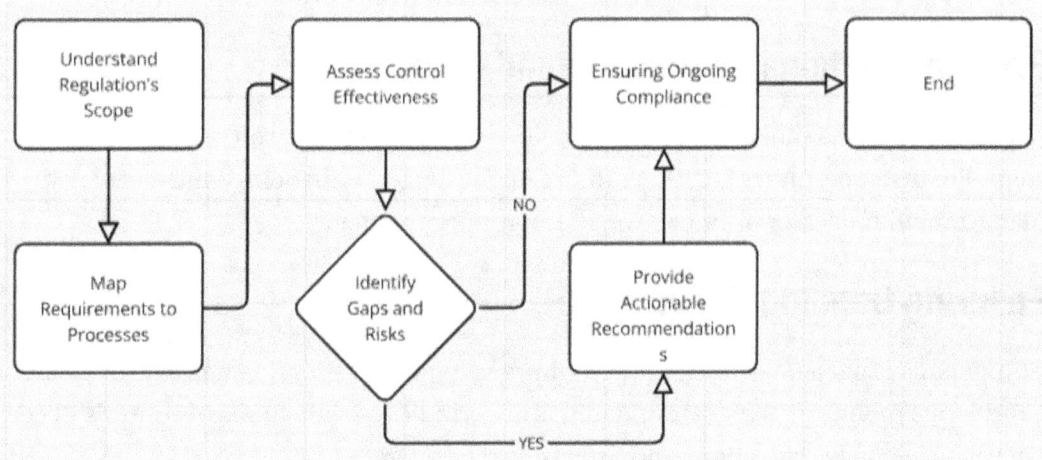

Figure 4-1. *Workflow for auditing for regulatory compliance*

Understanding the Regulation's Scope

Auditors begin by familiarizing themselves with the regulation's objectives, scope, and specific requirements. This understanding helps in defining the audit's scope and identifying key areas for evaluation, such as data protection, incident response, or third-party risk management.

CHAPTER 4   COMPLIANCE AND REGULATIONS

Mapping Requirements to Organizational Processes

Effective audits require mapping regulatory requirements to the organization's existing policies, procedures, and controls. For instance, under HIPAA, auditors may evaluate how risk assessments are conducted and whether encryption is consistently applied to protect electronic Protected Health Information (ePHI).

Assessing Control Effectiveness

Auditors assess the design and operational effectiveness of security controls. This involves reviewing policies, testing technical controls, and interviewing personnel to ensure that controls not only exist but are implemented and functioning as intended.

Identifying Gaps and Risks

Auditors identify areas of non-compliance or weaknesses in control implementation. For example, under NIS2, gaps might include incomplete incident response plans or insufficient governance frameworks.

Providing Actionable Recommendations

Recommendations should prioritize risk, offering clear guidance on remediation steps. For instance, under DORA, auditors might suggest enhancing third-party risk management processes or improving ICT continuity strategies.

Ensuring Ongoing Compliance

Compliance is not a one-time effort. Auditors help organizations establish processes for continuous monitoring, regular updates, and periodic re-evaluations of controls to keep pace with evolving regulations and threats.

Tools and Techniques for Regulatory Audits

Modern regulatory audits rely on a combination of manual expertise and automated tools to achieve accuracy, efficiency, and comprehensiveness. Given the complexity of cybersecurity regulations and the volume of data to evaluate, these tools are indispensable for auditors seeking to streamline their processes and provide actionable insights.

Key Tools for Regulatory Audits

- *Compliance Management Tools*:

    - *Archer*: Offers end-to-end compliance tracking, including policy management, control monitoring, and evidence documentation.

    - *AuditBoard*: Simplifies audit workflows, enhances collaboration, and centralizes compliance data.

    - *OneTrust, BigID*: Facilitate data discovery, regulatory mapping, and privacy management, enabling organizations to align with GDPR, CCPA, and other frameworks.

- *SIEM Tools*:

    - *Splunk, QRadar*: Provide centralized logging and analysis, helping auditors assess control effectiveness by identifying anomalies and generating compliance reports.

- *Vulnerability Assessment Tools*:

    - *Nessus, Qualys, OpenVAS*: Automate the detection of vulnerabilities across systems, enabling auditors to identify risks tied to non-compliance with regulations like PCI-DSS or FISMA.

- *Incident Response and Simulation Tools*:

    - *CrisisSim, Cyberbit*: Simulate attack scenarios to test the effectiveness of incident response plans, as required by frameworks like ISO/IEC 27001 or DORA.

- *Risk Management Frameworks*:

    - *NIST SP 800-53, FAIR*: Provide structured approaches to evaluating and mitigating risks. Tools such as RiskLens can help quantify risks in financial terms, aiding compliance efforts.

- *Policy and Procedure Review Tools*:

    - *Confluence, SharePoint*: Facilitate the centralized management and review of policies and procedures, ensuring they align with regulatory requirements.

CHAPTER 4   COMPLIANCE AND REGULATIONS

Techniques for Conducting Regulatory Audits

- *Data Mapping and Discovery*:
  - Regulations like GDPR and CCPA require organizations to understand how data flows through their systems. Auditors use tools to map data lifecycles, ensuring compliance with data handling and retention requirements.

- *Configuration Reviews*:
  - Auditors evaluate system configurations to ensure they align with regulatory requirements. For instance, under PCI-DSS, they might review firewall configurations, while under FISMA, they might assess adherence to NIST-recommended security baselines.

- *Evidence Collection and Validation*:
  - Supporting evidence such as logs, screenshots, and policy documents must be collected and validated. Automated tools streamline this process by centralizing and organizing evidence for efficient review.

- *Penetration Testing and Vulnerability Scanning*:
  - Testing the organization's defenses against simulated attacks is crucial for regulations like PCI-DSS and ISO/IEC 27001. These techniques reveal gaps in security controls and provide actionable insights for remediation.

- *Continuous Monitoring*:
  - Compliance tools integrate with existing IT systems to provide real-time monitoring of controls. This ensures that organizations remain compliant even as threats evolve or regulatory requirements change.

Emerging Trends in Cybersecurity Compliance

Proactive Compliance

Organizations are moving away from periodic audits toward continuous monitoring and real-time risk assessments. Proactive compliance enables early identification and remediation of vulnerabilities, reducing the likelihood of exploitation. This shift ensures that compliance is maintained consistently rather than sporadically.

Rise of Automation

Automation tools like Tenable and Splunk are revolutionizing compliance processes by automating tasks such as reporting, monitoring, and risk assessments. These platforms enhance efficiency by minimizing human errors, expediting detection of non-compliance, and reducing the administrative burden of manual compliance checks.

Global Standardization

As organizations expand across borders, aligning cybersecurity frameworks becomes crucial to ensure cohesive compliance. Harmonization of regulations simplifies adherence for multinational entities, fostering smoother operations and minimizing conflicts between regional requirements.

Emerging Technologies

- *Artificial Intelligence*: AI-powered platforms like Darktrace are transforming compliance by detecting anomalies, predicting risks, and automating threat responses.

- *Blockchain*: This technology offers transparent and immutable audit trails, ensuring the integrity of compliance documentation.

- *Quantum Computing*: While quantum technologies pose challenges to existing encryption protocols, they also demand innovative solutions to meet evolving compliance standards.

Cyber Resilience

The integration of cybersecurity with business continuity planning is redefining organizational resilience. Cyber resilience focuses not just on preventing attacks but also on ensuring operational continuity during and after incidents, making it an essential aspect of future compliance strategies.

Preparing for the Future of Compliance

To stay ahead of evolving cybersecurity compliance demands, organizations must adopt forward-thinking strategies:

- *Leverage Advanced Tools*: Platforms like AuditBoard streamline compliance workflows, offering centralized management and real-time insights.

- *Invest in Training*: Equip teams with expertise in emerging technologies like AI, blockchain, and advanced analytics to ensure they are prepared for future challenges.

- *Focus on Risk*: Prioritize high-risk areas to maximize the impact of security and compliance initiatives.

- *Collaborate Globally*: Engage with international regulators and industry bodies to shape and influence emerging compliance trends.

- *Utilize Threat Intelligence*: Tools such as Recorded Future provide predictive insights into changes in regulations and risks, helping organizations adapt preventively.

Regulatory Bodies' Approach to the Future

Regulatory bodies worldwide are not only updating existing frameworks but also introducing new strategies to address the challenges posed by emerging technologies and threats. Their evolving approach reflects a commitment to fostering collaboration, innovation, and transparency while maintaining stringent compliance standards.

Modernizing Existing Regulations

Regulators are revising established frameworks such as GDPR, PCI-DSS, and HIPAA to incorporate considerations for advanced technologies like AI, machine learning, and quantum computing. This ensures that compliance standards remain relevant and effective against cutting-edge cyber threats. For instance, updates to GDPR may soon include explicit guidelines on managing AI-driven data processing and the ethical considerations surrounding it.

Promoting Collaborative Audits

Regulators increasingly encourage collaboration between organizations, auditors, and regulatory authorities. Cooperative audits foster a better understanding of compliance requirements, improve communication between stakeholders, and streamline the auditing process. This collaborative approach helps bridge gaps between technical controls and regulatory expectations.

Offering Incentives for Proactive Compliance

Recognizing the challenges of maintaining compliance, some regulators now offer incentives such as reduced penalties, extended deadlines, or tax benefits for organizations that demonstrate proactive and exemplary compliance practices. This motivates organizations to go beyond the minimum requirements and adopt forward-thinking cybersecurity measures.

Benefits of Future-Oriented Compliance Strategies

Future-oriented compliance strategies offer significant advantages for organizations, extending beyond regulatory adherence to enhance security, operational efficiency, and stakeholder confidence.

Enhanced Security Posture

By adopting proactive compliance measures and leveraging advanced technologies, organizations can address vulnerabilities before they are exploited. This minimizes the risk of data breaches, ransomware attacks, and other cyber threats, ensuring robust protection for sensitive data.

CHAPTER 4　COMPLIANCE AND REGULATIONS

Operational Continuity and Resilience

Integrating cybersecurity with business continuity planning ensures that organizations can maintain operations even during adverse events. This resilience reduces downtime, minimizes financial losses, and preserves customer trust.

Global Competitiveness

For multinational organizations, aligning with globally recognized frameworks like NIST CSF 2.0 or harmonized EU regulations simplifies cross-border operations. This streamlined compliance fosters smoother business expansion and enhances competitiveness in international markets.

Stakeholder Trust and Confidence

Demonstrating a commitment to advanced compliance and security practices builds trust with customers, investors, and partners. Stakeholders are more likely to support organizations that prioritize data protection and transparency, enhancing brand reputation and loyalty.

Resource Optimization

Future-oriented compliance strategies often leverage automation and advanced tools, reducing manual workloads and improving efficiency. This enables organizations to allocate resources more effectively, focusing on strategic initiatives rather than administrative tasks.

Key Takeaways

Compliance with cybersecurity regulations is not just a legal obligation but a strategic advantage. By prioritizing trust, operational resilience, and accountability, organizations position themselves for long-term success. Meanwhile, auditors play a pivotal role in bridging regulatory requirements with practical security measures, fostering a safer digital ecosystem.

In this section, we covered the following points:

- The evolving cybersecurity regulatory landscape reflects increasing digital complexity and risks.
- Cybersecurity regulations govern key areas such as
  - *Privacy*: Protecting personal and sensitive data.
  - *Data Protection*: Ensuring secure data storage, processing, and sharing.
  - *Operational Resilience*: Preparing organizations to withstand and recover from cyber incidents.
- Compliance serves multiple purposes for organizations:
  - Avoiding legal and financial penalties.
  - Building stakeholder trust.
  - Promoting operational resilience.
  - Fostering a culture of accountability.
- For auditors, understanding regulatory frameworks is critical:
  - Enables comprehensive assessments of security measures.
  - Aligns organizations with global best practices.
  - Identifies gaps and recommends actionable improvements.
- Effective navigation of cybersecurity regulations requires
  - A proactive and integrated approach.
  - Deployment of robust processes and modern tools.
  - Commitment to continuous improvement and adaptation.
- *Emerging Trends in Cybersecurity Compliance*:
  - *Proactive Compliance*: Organizations are shifting from reactive to proactive compliance, focusing on continuous risk management and improvement.
  - *Automation*: The rise of automation tools streamlines compliance processes and reduces manual effort, improving efficiency.

- *Global Standardization*: International harmonization of standards is making compliance processes more consistent across borders.
- *Integration of Advanced Technologies*: Technologies like AI and blockchain are being integrated into compliance frameworks to improve accuracy, transparency, and security.

- *Modernizing Regulatory Approaches*:
  - Regulatory bodies are moving towards more adaptive and forward-thinking strategies.
  - There is a focus on collaboration among stakeholders, promoting proactive compliance over reactive measures.
  - Incentives are being introduced to encourage organizations to adopt comprehensive, long-term compliance strategies.

- *Benefits of Future-Oriented Compliance Strategies*:
  - Enhanced security through proactive identification and mitigation of risks.
  - Improved operational resilience by ensuring systems are secure and prepared for disruptions.
  - Global competitiveness through alignment with international standards.
  - Increased stakeholder trust by demonstrating commitment to security and compliance.
  - Optimized resource utilization through automation and streamlined processes.

- *Staying Ahead of Compliance Requirements*: By embracing emerging trends and preparing for future regulatory changes, organizations can
  - Stay ahead of compliance requirements and industry best practices.
  - Strengthen their cybersecurity posture and reputation.

The Role of Compliance in Cybersecurity Audits

Compliance is the backbone of any effective cybersecurity audit, akin to the discipline that underpins a well-trained military unit. It establishes a systematic approach for organizations to align their operations with legal, regulatory, and industry standards. More than just ticking boxes, compliance represents an organization's commitment to safeguarding sensitive data, mitigating risks, and maintaining trust among stakeholders. The following explores the multifaceted role of compliance in cybersecurity audits, emphasizing its importance, practical application, and the challenges organizations face in achieving and maintaining compliance.

Why Compliance Matters in Cybersecurity Audits

In the ever-evolving landscape of cyber threats, organizations must navigate a growing array of regulations, including GDPR, HIPAA, PCI-DSS, and ISO 27001. These regulations set the minimum standards for data protection and cybersecurity practices, and their significance cannot be overstated.

First and foremost, compliance reduces legal risks. Non-compliance can result in severe penalties, ranging from monetary fines to reputational damage. For instance, GDPR violations can lead to fines of up to €20 million or 4% of an organization's global turnover, whichever is higher. Beyond financial repercussions, non-compliance erodes trust, potentially driving away customers and investors. This is akin to a military commander's failure to follow the rules of engagement, leading to court-martial and loss of respect among the ranks.

Second, compliance improves an organization's overall security posture. Regulatory frameworks often mandate best practices, such as encryption, access controls, and incident response mechanisms, which collectively reduce the likelihood and impact of data breaches. Like a soldier's training to anticipate and counter enemy maneuvers, compliance ensures readiness against cyber adversaries.

Third, compliance builds stakeholder trust. Demonstrating adherence to stringent data protection laws signals a commitment to safeguarding customer and partner information, a vital competitive advantage in today's digital economy. This mirrors the camaraderie and reliability among soldiers who trust each other to follow orders and uphold the mission's integrity.

Finally, in certain industries, compliance is a prerequisite for market access. For example, HIPAA compliance is mandatory for US healthcare providers, while GDPR compliance is essential for businesses operating in the European Union. Without compliance, an organization's operational scope becomes as restricted as a platoon without a supply line.

Compliance Audits in Practice

Compliance audits are a systematic approach to evaluating whether an organization meets regulatory requirements and industry standards. These audits provide a structured mechanism to assess, document, and improve security practices. The process involves multiple steps, each designed to ensure thoroughness and accountability in achieving compliance.

Figure 4-2 presents a simple workflow diagram on compliance audits.

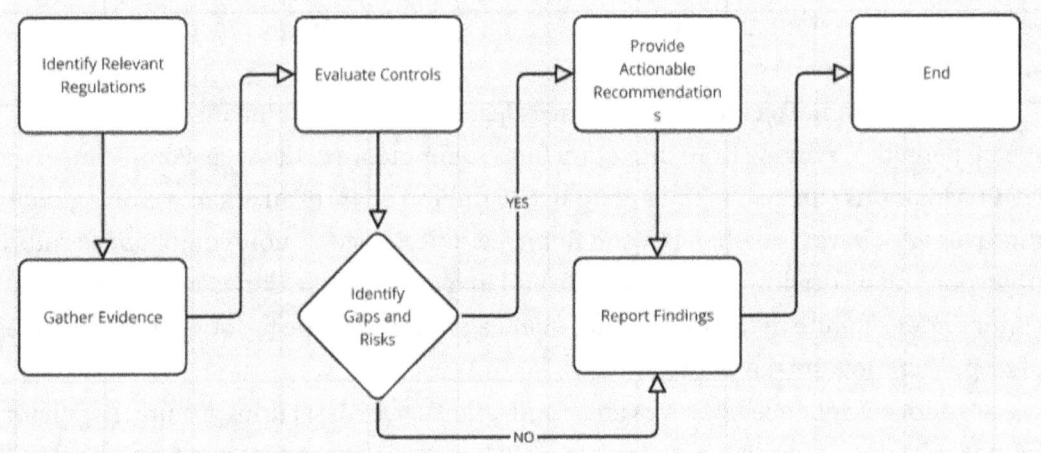

Figure 4-2. Simple workflow diagram on compliance audits

Identifying Relevant Regulations

The first step in a compliance audit is determining which laws, regulations, and standards apply to the organization. This depends on factors such as industry, geographical location, and the nature of data handled.

For example:

- *Healthcare Organizations*: Must comply with HIPAA and HITECH to secure EHRs and other PHI.

- *Financial Institutions*: Follow frameworks like PCI-DSS for payment card data or the Gramm-Leach-Bliley Act (GLBA) to protect customer financial information.

- *Multinational Corporations*: Need to address GDPR for operations in the European Union, as well as regional laws like the CCPA for US customers.

Identifying applicable regulations is critical to setting the scope of the audit and aligning organizational practices with legal requirements.

Gathering Evidence

A key part of compliance audits is evidence collection. Auditors require tangible proof that the organization is implementing the necessary controls and processes.

Common types of evidence include:

- *Policies and Procedures*: Documents outlining how the organization manages access control, incident response, and data encryption.

- *Technical Reports*: Results from penetration testing, vulnerability scans, and firewall configuration reviews.

- *Operational Logs*: Logs from SIEM systems such as Splunk or QRadar to demonstrate monitoring and alerting capabilities.

- *Training Records*: Proof that employees have received training in compliance-related topics such as GDPR principles or HIPAA requirements.

This evidence is essential to verify that security measures are not only implemented but also actively maintained.

CHAPTER 4   COMPLIANCE AND REGULATIONS

Evaluating Controls

Auditors assess the effectiveness of the organization's security controls, focusing on their ability to meet specific regulatory requirements. This involves a detailed review of the following:

- *Access Management*: Evaluating the implementation of MFA, RBAC, and periodic user access reviews to ensure only authorized personnel have access to sensitive information.

- *Data Protection*: Verifying encryption standards for data at rest and in transit, and ensuring secure key management practices are in place.

- *Incident Response*: Assessing the organization's ability to detect, respond to, and recover from security incidents, including the existence of response plans and test results from simulated attacks.

By evaluating these controls, auditors identify gaps or weaknesses that may expose the organization to risks.

Reporting Findings

The final step in the compliance audit process is documenting the findings. This report serves as a roadmap for remediation and a record of the organization's compliance status.

Key components of the report include:

- *Strengths and Achievements*: Areas where the organization meets or exceeds compliance requirements.

- *Gaps and Risks*: Specific deficiencies or vulnerabilities that must be addressed to achieve full compliance.

- *Actionable Recommendations*: Prioritized steps to remediate gaps, often categorized by severity and urgency.

This report is shared with stakeholders to guide decision-making and to provide evidence of compliance during regulatory inspections.

Compliance in Action

The practical application of compliance can vary significantly by industry:

Healthcare Sector

Hospitals and clinics must comply with HIPAA by securing EHRs. This involves implementing robust access controls to limit unauthorized access and encrypting sensitive patient data to protect it during storage and transmission. Regular audits ensure that policies, such as employee training on HIPAA requirements, are up-to-date and effective.

E-commerce Sector

Retailers handling payment card data must comply with PCI-DSS, which requires encryption of cardholder information and securing payment systems against unauthorized access. Tools like Nessus help these organizations regularly scan their networks for vulnerabilities, ensuring continuous compliance.

Challenges in Compliance Audits

While compliance is indispensable, achieving and maintaining it is not without challenges.

Regulatory Changes

Regulations evolve to address new threats and technologies, requiring organizations to constantly update their policies, controls, and documentation. Staying ahead of these changes is a resource-intensive task. Staying ahead of these changes is like adapting battle strategies to counter an agile and evolving enemy.

Complexity in Multinational Organizations

Large organizations operating across multiple jurisdictions must navigate overlapping and sometimes conflicting regulations, adding layers of complexity to compliance efforts. This challenge is akin to coordinating multinational forces in joint operations, where alignment and communication are critical to mission success.

Resource Constraints

Small and medium-sized businesses often lack the financial and human resources needed to conduct thorough compliance audits, leaving them more vulnerable to fines and breaches. It's like sending an under-equipped battalion into a high-stakes conflict; the risk of failure is significantly higher.

Key Takeaways

Compliance audits are more than regulatory checkpoints; they are strategic opportunities to enhance security, protect organizational interests, and build trust. A systematic and adaptive approach ensures not only regulatory alignment but also a resilient and secure foundation for long-term success.

In this section, we covered the following points:

Systematic Approach to Compliance:

- Compliance audits are tailored to specific organizational needs.
- Key steps include
    - Identifying applicable regulations.
    - Collecting and validating evidence.
    - Evaluating controls for effectiveness.
    - Reporting findings in a comprehensive manner.
- Each step interlinks to provide a holistic compliance overview.

Protecting Organizational Interests:

- Reduces the risk of penalties, fines, and reputational harm.
- Aligns practices with legal and regulatory standards.
- Helps avoid costly legal disputes and reinforce stakeholder confidence.

Improving Security Posture:

- Drives the adoption of robust security practices beyond mere compliance.
- Key areas of evaluation include

CHAPTER 4   COMPLIANCE AND REGULATIONS

- Access controls and authorization mechanisms.
- Data encryption practices.
- Incident detection and response capabilities.
- Strengthens the organization's overall security framework.

Building Trust and Accountability:

- Demonstrating compliance shows an organization's dedication to safeguarding sensitive information.
- Promotes transparency, fostering trust with customers, partners, and regulators.
- Strengthens professional and business relationships through accountability.

Adapting to Evolving Requirements:

- Compliance is a dynamic, ongoing process.
- Requires regular updates to policies, controls, and documentation.
- Ensures alignment with regulatory changes and preparedness for emerging cyber threats.

Conducting a GDPR Compliance Audit

GDPR is the sentinel of data privacy laws, a steadfast guard post ensuring personal data is defended against breaches and misuse. Conducting a GDPR compliance audit parallels assembling a disciplined army unit: every soldier (or process) must know their role, follow orders (regulations), and work cohesively to secure the perimeter.

The following section explores the battle-hardened steps, tactical tools, logistical challenges, and critical importance of GDPR audits in fortifying organizational defenses, securing personal data, and maintaining compliance.

Understanding GDPR and Its Importance

The GDPR was introduced by the European Union to provide individuals greater control over their personal data while ensuring transparency and accountability in data processing. It applies to organizations worldwide that collect or process data of EU residents.

The GDPR serves as a general's marching orders, instructing organizations to uphold the principles of lawfulness, fairness, and transparency as if defending their nation's honor. Each principle operates like a different military code.

Key GDPR principles include

- *Lawfulness, Fairness, and Transparency*: Organizations must process data in a manner that is legal and understandable to the individuals involved.

- *Data Minimization*: Only the data necessary for specific purposes should be collected.

- *Accountability*: Organizations must demonstrate compliance through proper documentation and evidence of safeguards in place.

Non-compliance with GDPR carries severe penalties, including fines of up to €20 million or 4% of global turnover, whichever is higher. Beyond fines, failure to comply can erode customer trust and expose organizations to legal and operational risks.

Steps to Conduct a GDPR Compliance Audit

Conducting a GDPR compliance audit is a systematic process that evaluates an organization's adherence to GDPR regulations. Each step ensures that personal data is managed, processed, and protected in line with legal requirements.

Conducting a GDPR compliance audit mirrors preparing for a high-stakes military operation. Every phase is orchestrated to anticipate threats, fortify defenses, and ensure no weak point is overlooked.

Figure 4-3 is a process flow and detailed guide.

Figure 4-3. Process flow: conducting a GDPR compliance audit

Define the Scope

The first step is to clearly outline the audit's boundaries:

- *Identify Data*: Determine all the personal data being collected, processed, or stored by the organization. This includes names, email addresses, IP addresses, and more.

- *Systems and Processes*: Identify all systems, applications, and processes involved in data handling.

- *Geographic Locations*: Map out all locations, including third-party vendors, where data is stored or processed.

- *Stakeholders*: Identify internal and external stakeholders responsible for data handling.

This step ensures that no aspect of data management is overlooked during the audit.

Map Data Flows

A comprehensive data inventory and mapping process is crucial:

- *Collection Points*: Document all sources of data collection, such as websites, applications, and customer interactions.

- *Data Categories*: Identify the types of personal data collected, including sensitive data.

- *Flow Paths*: Trace the journey of data from collection to storage and processing.

- *Automated Tools*: Utilize platforms like OneTrust, BigID, or TrustArc to simplify and automate data mapping.

This provides a clear understanding of how data moves through the organization, highlighting potential risks and areas of concern.

Review of Privacy Policies and Notices

Ensure that privacy policies are transparent and user-friendly:

- *Purpose Statement*: Verify that policies explicitly state the purpose of data collection.

- *User Rights*: Confirm that policies inform users of their rights, such as access, rectification, and deletion.

- *Third-Party Sharing*: Check that data-sharing practices with third parties are disclosed.

This step ensures compliance with GDPR's transparency requirements, fostering trust with data subjects.

Assess Legal Basis for Data Processing

Evaluate the legal justification for data processing:

- *Lawful Basis*: Verify that data processing aligns with one of GDPR's lawful bases, such as consent, contractual necessity, or legitimate interest.

- *Explicit Consent*: Ensure that sensitive data processing requires and records explicit user consent.

- *Audit Trail*: Maintain records of consent to demonstrate compliance during audits.

This step ensures that all data processing activities are legally justified and documented.

Evaluate Data Security Measures

Assess technical and organizational controls to safeguard personal data:

- *Encryption*: Verify the use of robust encryption protocols (e.g., AES-256) for data at rest and in transit.

- *Access Controls*: Ensure that access to personal data is role-based and limited to authorized personnel.

- *Incident Response Plan*: Confirm that an incident response plan exists and complies with GDPR's 72-hour breach notification rule.
- *Penetration Testing*: Conduct regular security testing to identify vulnerabilities.

This step mitigates risks associated with unauthorized access, breaches, or data leaks.

Audit Third-Party Vendors

Third-party vendors play a critical role in data processing:

- *DPAs*: Verify that agreements are in place and align with GDPR requirements.
- *Vendor Assessments*: Evaluate vendors' compliance programs and security measures.
- *Compliance Tools*: Use vendor management platforms like System Applications and Products (SAP) Ariba or Coupa to monitor third-party compliance.

This step ensures that third-party vendors adhere to GDPR standards, minimizing external risks.

Evaluating Data Subject Rights Management

Test the organization's ability to handle data subject requests (Data Subject Access Requests (DSARs)):

- *Access Requests*: Ensure mechanisms are in place for individuals to access their data.
- *Right to Be Forgotten*: Verify processes for data deletion upon request.
- *Data Portability*: Confirm that data can be provided in a portable format.
- *Timeliness*: Validate that DSARs are fulfilled within GDPR's mandated timeline.

This step demonstrates the organization's commitment to respecting individual rights.

Conduct a Gap Analysis

Identify areas of non-compliance:

- *Prioritize Gaps*: Rank non-compliance areas based on risk and impact.
- *Action Plan*: Develop a remediation plan to address weaknesses.
- *Continuous Monitoring*: Establish regular reviews to track progress.

This step helps the organization focus its resources on critical compliance issues.

Document Findings

Compile a detailed report:

- *Compliance Gaps*: Highlight areas of non-compliance.
- *Risks*: Identify potential legal and operational risks.
- *Recommendations*: Provide actionable steps for remediation.
- *Evidence*: Include supporting artifacts such as logs, screenshots, and test results.

This report serves as a reference for management and regulatory authorities, demonstrating due diligence.

Tools and Technologies for GDPR Compliance Audits

Several tools simplify and enhance the GDPR audit process:

- *Data Mapping and Classification*: BigID and TrustArc automate data discovery and classification.
- *Consent Management*: Cookiebot and OneTrust streamline user consent tracking.
- *Security Testing*: Tools like Qualys and Nessus help identify vulnerabilities in systems handling personal data.

- *Incident Response*: Platforms such as Splunk Phantom or Cortex XSOAR support efficient breach detection and response.

- *DSAR Management*: Solutions like DataGrail or WireWheel ensure timely and accurate handling of data subject requests.

Challenges in GDPR Compliance Audits

Despite its importance, GDPR compliance audits present several challenges that organizations must overcome. Table 4-2 presents the main challenges and concrete solution steps.

Table 4-2. *Challenges and concrete solutions in conducting a GDPR compliance audit*

Challenge	Description	Solutions
Complexity of Data Mapping	Organizations store data across multiple systems, including unstructured formats and legacy systems. Identifying, classifying, and tracking personal data can be difficult.	1. Implement automated data discovery tools like BigID or TrustArc to locate and classify personal data. 2. Conduct a full data inventory and mapping exercise, documenting data flow from collection to storage. 3. Establish a centralized database for tracking data sources, processing activities, and retention policies.
Regulatory Changes	GDPR regulations evolve, requiring organizations to adapt policies and procedures. Changes in cross-border data transfer rules add complexity.	1. Subscribe to regulatory updates from EU authorities (e.g., EDPB, national data protection agencies). 2. Assign a GDPR compliance officer or task force to track legal developments and ensure timely updates. 3. Review and update internal policies and third-party agreements quarterly to align with regulatory changes.

(continued)

Table 4-2. (*continued*)

Challenge	Description	Solutions
Third-Party Compliance	Vendors and third-party processors manage personal data, but ensuring their GDPR compliance can be challenging due to a lack of transparency and standardized security practices.	1. Create a vendor compliance checklist and require all third-party vendors to complete GDPR compliance assessments. 2. Implement DPAs that specify GDPR responsibilities and security measures. 3. Use vendor management tools like SAP Ariba or OneTrust to track compliance status and conduct periodic audits.
Resource Constraints	GDPR audits require significant time, budget, and expertise, making it challenging for smaller organizations to conduct thorough assessments.	1. Prioritize high-risk areas by conducting a risk-based audit approach, focusing on data processing activities that involve sensitive information. 2. Automate compliance tasks such as consent management and data mapping using platforms like OneTrust. 3. Outsource specific audit tasks to GDPR compliance consultants or legal experts to reduce internal workload.
Managing Data Subject Rights	Organizations must efficiently process DSARs while ensuring compliance with GDPR's response timeline.	1. Implement automated DSAR management tools like DataGrail or WireWheel to manage requests efficiently. 2. Establish a standardized workflow for DSAR processing, including verification, data retrieval, and response. 3. Train employees on GDPR rights and response timelines to ensure compliance with the one-month deadline.

(*continued*)

Table 4-2. (*continued*)

Challenge	Description	Solutions
Demonstrating Accountability	GDPR requires organizations to document compliance efforts and maintain audit trails, which can be administratively burdensome.	1. Maintain detailed audit logs of all GDPR-related activities, including data processing, risk assessments, and breach responses. 2. Conduct internal compliance audits every six months to assess adherence to GDPR requirements. 3. Use GRC tools to streamline compliance reporting and evidence collection.

Complexity of Data Mapping

Modern organizations handle vast amounts of data across multiple systems:

- *Unstructured Data*: Personal data often resides in unstructured formats, such as emails or documents, making it difficult to locate.

- *Legacy Systems*: Older systems may lack comprehensive documentation or visibility into data flows.

- *Third-Party Data*: Data shared with vendors or partners adds layers of complexity to mapping efforts.

Organizations must invest in advanced tools and expertise to achieve accurate and complete data inventories.

Regulatory Changes

GDPR is a dynamic framework subject to evolving interpretations and updates:

- *New Guidelines*: Regulatory authorities frequently issue new guidelines or clarifications.

- *Cross-Border Data Transfers*: Changing rules for international data transfers (e.g., invalidation of Privacy Shield) add uncertainty.

- *Overlap with Other Laws*: Aligning GDPR with local regulations, such as CCPA or DORA, can complicate compliance efforts.

Organizations must monitor regulatory updates and adapt their practices accordingly.

Third-Party Compliance

Ensuring that third-party vendors meet GDPR standards is challenging:

- *Lack of Visibility*: Organizations may not have direct insight into vendors' data handling practices.
- *DPA Gaps*: Vendors often lack comprehensive data processing agreements.
- *Risk Management*: Assessing vendor risks and ensuring accountability require robust oversight mechanisms.

Organizations must establish clear expectations and conduct regular vendor audits.

Resource Constraints

Compliance audits can be resource-intensive:

- *Cost of Tools*: Investing in GDPR compliance tools and technologies can strain budgets.
- *Expertise*: Smaller organizations may lack the legal or technical expertise needed for effective audits.
- *Time*: Comprehensive audits require significant time and effort from internal teams.

Organizations must allocate sufficient resources and prioritize compliance initiatives to overcome these constraints.

By addressing these challenges proactively, organizations can strengthen their GDPR compliance programs and reduce the risk of non-compliance penalties.

CHAPTER 4   COMPLIANCE AND REGULATIONS

Key Takeaways

GDPR compliance audits are more than regulatory check-ins; they are integral to maintaining trust, protecting personal data, and fostering accountability. A structured, tool-enhanced, and proactive approach ensures not only compliance but also resilience in a continually shifting regulatory environment.

In this section, we covered the following points:

A Structured Approach Is Vital:

- GDPR compliance audits require a well-defined structure.
- Key steps include
    - Defining the audit's scope.
    - Mapping data flows to identify personal data and its lifecycle.
    - Evaluating policies, controls, and third-party vendor practices.
- Ensures comprehensive alignment with GDPR requirements.

Compliance Strengthens Trust:

- Regular audits reaffirm an organization's dedication to protecting personal data.
- Build confidence among customers and stakeholders.
- Reinforces trust with regulators by demonstrating proactive compliance efforts.

Challenges Require Strategic Solutions:

- GDPR audits can be resource-intensive and complex.
- Effective strategies include
    - Automating repetitive processes to reduce manual effort.
    - Collaborating with third-party vendors to ensure shared compliance.
- Proactively addressing challenges improves audit outcomes and efficiency.

GDPR Is an Ongoing Journey:

- Compliance is not a static achievement; it requires continual effort.
- Regular audits, policy updates, and employee training are essential.
- Maintains compliance amid evolving regulatory demands and technological advancements.

Navigating PCI-DSS Requirements in Audits

PCI-DSS is a foundation of secure payment processing and cardholder data protection. As cyber threats evolve, PCI-DSS remains vital in minimizing the risks associated with payment transactions. For cybersecurity auditors, understanding and navigating PCI-DSS requirements is essential for ensuring organizations maintain compliance and safeguard sensitive financial information. Like an army's code of conduct, adherence to these standards minimizes vulnerabilities and fortifies the organization's defenses.

Understanding PCI-DSS

PCI-DSS provides a robust framework for securing payment card transactions and protecting cardholder data. Established by major credit card companies, the standard ensures a unified approach to mitigating risks in payment processing. PCI-DSS is a particularly structured framework, comparable to a military operations manual, dictating precise actions for safeguarding sensitive information. It is structured in six goals, each supported by 12 detailed requirements:

CHAPTER 4   COMPLIANCE AND REGULATIONS

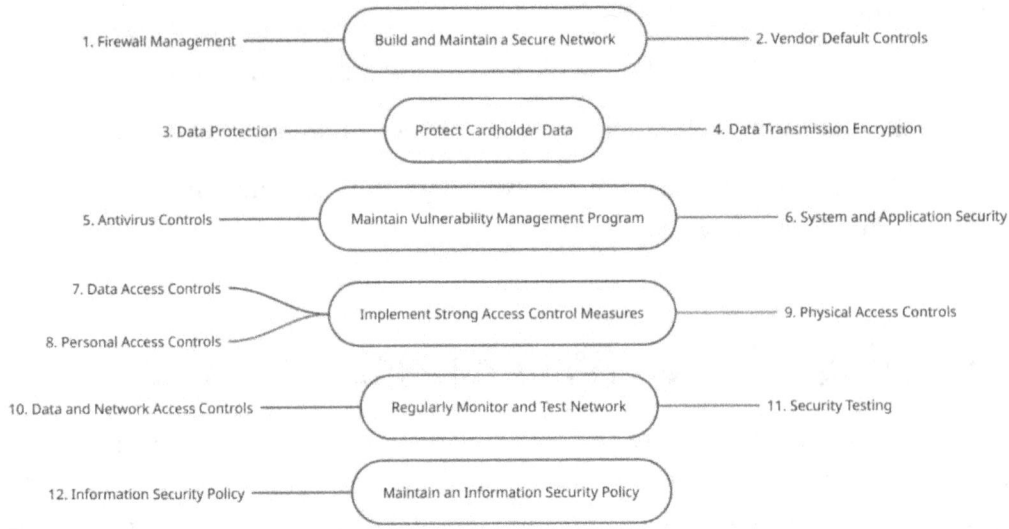

Figure 4-4. PCI DSS Controls

Build and Maintain a Secure Network

Just as an army establishes impenetrable fortifications around its base, organizations must deploy and maintain firewalls to create a secure perimeter around their Cardholder Data Environment (CDE). Organizations must deploy and maintain firewalls to protect cardholder data. These firewalls should be configured with strict rules that segment sensitive environments from general network traffic, minimizing unauthorized access points.

Avoid using vendor-supplied default settings or passwords, as these are common entry points for attackers. Customizing configurations and changing default credentials reduce exposure to cyber threats.

Protect Cardholder Data

All stored cardholder data must be encrypted using strong encryption algorithms, such as AES-256, to ensure that it cannot be accessed in its raw form, even in the event of a breach.

During transmission, sensitive data must be encrypted using secure protocols like TLS 1.2 or higher to protect it from interception or eavesdropping attacks.

Maintain a Vulnerability Management Program

Implement updated antivirus software across all systems. Antivirus solutions must be capable of detecting, preventing, and removing malicious software, including emerging threats.

Ensure all system patches and updates are applied promptly to eliminate vulnerabilities in operating systems, applications, and network devices.

Implement Strong Access Control Measures

Access to cardholder data should be limited to personnel who need it to perform their job responsibilities. Role-based access control ensures users only have permissions aligned with their duties.

Assign unique IDs to each user accessing systems containing cardholder data, enabling detailed activity tracking and accountability. Physical access to systems must also be restricted through measures like keycard systems and secure server rooms.

Regularly Monitor and Test Networks

Implement robust logging and monitoring systems to track all access to cardholder data and detect anomalies. Logs should be reviewed regularly to identify potential security incidents.

Conduct regular security testing, including vulnerability assessments and penetration tests, to identify and address weaknesses before attackers exploit them.

Maintain an Information Security Policy

Develop a comprehensive information security policy that outlines expectations for all employees and contractors. This policy should cover topics such as password hygiene, incident response, and acceptable use of systems.

Ensure the policy is updated regularly to reflect changes in PCI-DSS requirements and emerging threats. Conduct mandatory training sessions to educate employees on their roles in maintaining compliance.

Steps to Conduct a PCI-DSS Audit

Conducting a PCI-DSS audit requires meticulous planning and a structured approach. Figure 4-5 presents the detailed steps to ensure a successful audit.

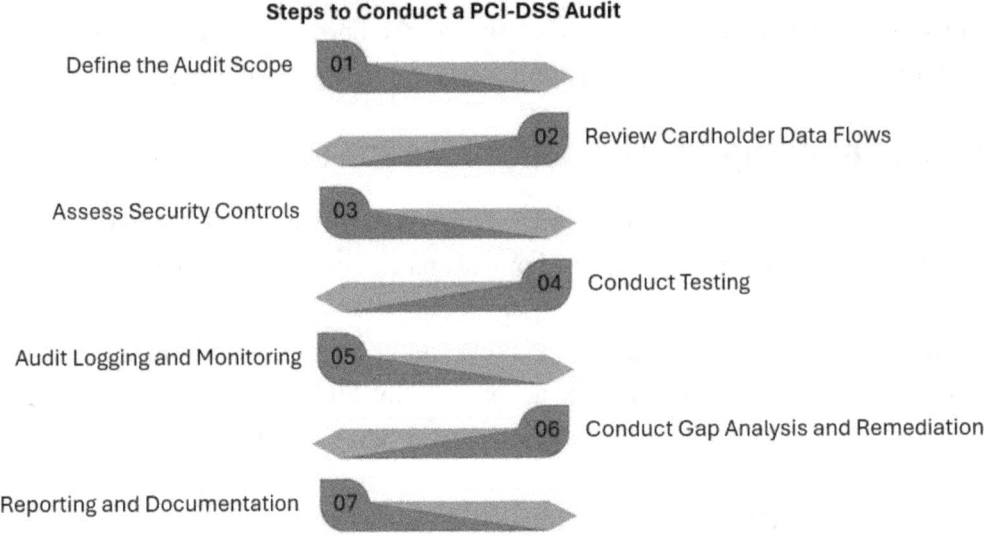

Figure 4-5. *Steps to conduct PCI-DSS audit*

Define the Audit Scope

Defining the scope of a PCI-DSS audit is the foundational step, as it determines the systems, processes, and networks that must adhere to compliance requirements. This involves identifying all components that store, process, or transmit cardholder data, collectively known as the CDE. An organization must map out all interconnected systems, third-party services, and vendors that touch payment card information.

For example, Point-of-Sale (POS) systems, e-commerce platforms, and data storage solutions like cloud services must be included if they interact with cardholder data. Proper network segmentation is crucial to limit the scope. By isolating the CDE from the broader network, organizations can reduce the audit's complexity, improve security, and focus remediation efforts on critical areas. This segmentation should be verified through network diagrams, firewall configurations, and traffic analysis tools to ensure unauthorized access to sensitive systems is blocked effectively.

Review Cardholder Data Flows

Understanding how cardholder data moves through the organization is essential for identifying vulnerabilities and ensuring compliance. Auditors need to map data flows comprehensively, starting from the point of collection, such as online payment forms or card readers, and following the data through transmission, storage, processing, and eventual deletion. Data flow diagrams help visualize these processes, highlighting all systems and applications that interact with sensitive information. Tools like Wireshark or similar network packet analyzers can be employed to monitor traffic and confirm that all data in transit is encrypted using protocols such as TLS 1.2 or higher.

This step is critical for ensuring there are no unencrypted pathways or unauthorized data transfers. Additionally, organizations should identify where data is stored and ensure it is encrypted, masked, or tokenized to reduce exposure risks. The goal is to ensure the organization has a complete and accurate picture of how cardholder data is handled.

Assess Security Controls

Evaluating security controls involves a thorough review of both technical and operational safeguards. Auditors must assess firewalls, which are a foundation of PCI-DSS compliance, to confirm that they are properly configured to block unauthorized traffic and segment the CDE effectively.

Encryption is another critical area, and auditors should ensure that cardholder data is encrypted using robust algorithms such as AES-256 for data at rest and TLS 1.2 or higher for data in transit. The management of encryption keys must also be reviewed, as improper key storage can undermine even the strongest encryption practices.

Access control mechanisms are equally important; auditors must verify that role-based permissions are enforced, ensuring only authorized personnel have access to sensitive data. These permissions should be periodically reviewed and adjusted as roles change.

Antivirus solutions must be updated regularly and deployed across all applicable systems, with mechanisms to detect and address new and emerging threats.

Physical security is another layer that cannot be overlooked. Server rooms and data centers should have secure locks, surveillance systems, and restricted access to ensure the safety of hardware containing cardholder data.

Conduct Testing

Testing is a critical part of the PCI-DSS audit process, as it uncovers vulnerabilities and evaluates the effectiveness of implemented controls. Vulnerability scanning should be performed quarterly and after any significant changes to the network. Tools such as Qualys and Nessus are used to identify misconfigurations, outdated software, and other vulnerabilities in the system.

Penetration testing goes a step further, simulating real-world attacks to exploit weaknesses and assess the organization's ability to detect and respond to threats. Tools like Metasploit and Burp Suite are commonly used for this purpose, enabling auditors to test defenses against sophisticated attack vectors.

Testing also includes examining the organization's incident response capabilities to ensure rapid and effective action in the event of a breach. The results of these tests provide actionable insights that organizations can use to strengthen their security posture.

Audit Logging and Monitoring

Effective logging and monitoring are essential for tracking access to cardholder data and identifying potential security incidents. Auditors must review log settings to ensure that all access to sensitive data is recorded, including user IDs, timestamps, and the nature of the activity.

SIEM tools, such as Splunk or IBM QRadar, are instrumental in collecting and analyzing these logs in real time to detect anomalies or unauthorized access attempts. Logs should be stored securely and retained for at least 12 months, as specified by PCI-DSS, to facilitate forensic analysis in the event of a breach. Regular log reviews and automated alerts further enhance the organization's ability to respond swiftly to threats. The audit also includes verifying the integrity of log data to ensure it has not been tampered with or deleted.

Conduct Gap Analysis and Remediation

A gap analysis identifies areas where the organization falls short of PCI-DSS compliance, allowing auditors to prioritize remediation efforts based on the severity of identified risks.

CHAPTER 4 COMPLIANCE AND REGULATIONS

For example, an organization might discover outdated encryption protocols, inadequate access controls, or missing firewall rules. Once gaps are identified, a remediation plan should be developed, outlining specific actions needed to achieve compliance. This plan might include upgrading encryption standards, implementing two-factor authentication, or enhancing physical security measures. Regular follow-up ensures that remediation efforts stay on track and address all identified vulnerabilities effectively.

Reporting and Documentation

Comprehensive reporting and documentation are critical for demonstrating compliance and guiding future audits. The Report on Compliance (ROC) or Self-Assessment Questionnaire (SAQ) should detail the audit's findings, including evidence of compliance, identified gaps, and steps taken to address them.

Documentation should include network diagrams, data flow maps, and records of testing and remediation activities. This not only fulfills PCI-DSS requirements but also serves as a valuable resource for internal teams to maintain ongoing compliance. Clear and thorough reporting fosters transparency and helps build trust with stakeholders, including customers and regulatory bodies.

Challenges in PCI-DSS Audits

While PCI-DSS audits are essential, they come with their own set of challenges:

- Scope Creep
- Vendor Management
- Legacy Systems
- Resource Constraints
- Continuous Updates

Table 4-3 presents the main challenges and what are concrete solution steps.

Table 4-3. *Challenges and concrete solutions in PCI-DSS audit*

Challenge	Description	Solutions
Scope Creep	Defining the scope of a PCI-DSS audit is complex, especially in large organizations with interconnected systems. Overlooking any system handling cardholder data can lead to security gaps.	1. Conduct a comprehensive asset inventory to identify all systems processing, storing, or transmitting cardholder data. 2. Use network segmentation to isolate the CDE and reduce audit scope. 3. Validate segmentation effectiveness using network scanning tools such as Nmap or Qualys.
Vendor Management	Third-party service providers process cardholder data on behalf of organizations. Ensuring vendor compliance with PCI-DSS is challenging without clear contracts and oversight.	1. Require vendors to sign a DPA outlining PCI-DSS responsibilities. 2. Conduct annual vendor risk assessments and request Attestation of Compliance (AOC) from all third-party providers. 3. Use vendor risk management platforms like OneTrust or Prevalent to track compliance status.
Legacy Systems	Older systems may lack modern security controls required for PCI-DSS compliance. Upgrading them is costly and time-intensive but essential for security.	1. Conduct a gap analysis to identify security weaknesses in legacy systems. 2. Implement compensating controls such as network isolation, additional monitoring, and access restrictions if upgrades are not immediately possible. 3. Plan phased system upgrades to migrate critical applications to compliant infrastructure while minimizing downtime.

(continued)

Table 4-3. (*continued*)

Challenge	Description	Solutions
Resource Constraints	Smaller organizations often lack the personnel, expertise, and tools to conduct a thorough PCI-DSS audit and remediation.	1. Prioritize high-risk areas by focusing audit efforts on systems with the highest exposure to threats. 2. Use automated compliance tools (e.g., Rapid7 InsightVM, Tenable.sc) to streamline vulnerability scanning and reporting. 3. Consider outsourcing PCI-DSS assessments to a Qualified Security Assessor (QSA) if internal resources are insufficient.
Continuous Updates	PCI-DSS standards evolve to address emerging threats, requiring organizations to stay updated and adapt their security practices accordingly.	1. Subscribe to PCI Security Standards Council (PCI SSC) updates and security bulletins to stay informed. 2. Establish a compliance task force responsible for tracking and implementing new PCI-DSS requirements. 3. Conduct quarterly security awareness training for employees to reinforce compliance with the latest security best practices.

Key Takeaways

A successful PCI-DSS audit is not just a regulatory requirement but a commitment to protecting cardholder data and maintaining secure payment systems. By understanding requirements, implementing structured processes, and overcoming challenges with strategic solutions, organizations can build trust, reduce risks, and establish secure environments for their customers.

In this section, we covered the following points:

A successful PCI-DSS audit ensures the protection of cardholder data, strengthens payment security, and builds trust with stakeholders.

- *Understanding PCI-DSS Requirements*: Organizations must adhere to 12 detailed requirements to ensure the secure handling of cardholder data.

- *Comprehensive Audit Steps*: A structured approach, from defining scope to documenting findings, is essential for effective PCI-DSS compliance.

- *Challenges in Implementation*: Organizations face challenges like scope creep, vendor management, and legacy system limitations that require strategic planning and resource allocation.

- *The Role of Testing and Monitoring*: Vulnerability scans, penetration testing, and logging are vital components of the audit process to identify and mitigate risks.

- *Documentation and Reporting*: Clear and detailed reporting ensures transparency and accountability, whether submitting an ROC or completing an SAQ.

How to Handle Non-compliance Findings in Cybersecurity Audits

Non-compliance findings during cybersecurity audits are critical insights into vulnerabilities, inefficiencies, and regulatory gaps that may expose organizations to data breaches, penalties, and reputational harm. These findings, while highlighting weaknesses, offer an opportunity to strengthen security postures and align processes with industry and regulatory standards. This section provides a comprehensive guide to understanding non-compliance findings, addressing them effectively, and overcoming associated challenges. Like an army's code of conduct, adherence to these standards minimizes vulnerabilities and fortifies the organization's defenses.

Understanding Non-compliance Findings

Non-compliance findings are deviations from established security policies, regulations, or best practices discovered during an audit. These findings can range from minor oversights, such as incomplete documentation, to critical lapses, like unencrypted sensitive data or misconfigured firewalls. They often arise in audits for frameworks like GDPR, HIPAA, PCI-DSS, ISO 27001, etc. Recognizing the severity and potential impact of these findings is the first step in addressing them effectively.

Common Examples of Non-compliance Findings:

- *Weak or Default Passwords*: Organizations often overlook the risks of using default or easily guessable passwords, which can be exploited by attackers.

- *Lack of MFA*: Without MFA, systems become vulnerable to unauthorized access if user credentials are compromised.

- *Unpatched or Outdated Software*: Unpatched systems are common attack vectors, allowing exploitation of known vulnerabilities.

- *Unencrypted Data*: Sensitive data left unencrypted, whether at rest or in transit, poses a significant risk of exposure in case of a breach.

- *Incomplete Audit Logs*: Poor monitoring of system activity can hinder the detection of suspicious actions or the ability to conduct forensic analysis.

- *Weak Incident Response Plans*: Inadequate preparation for handling breaches or system failures can amplify the impact of incidents.

Steps to Handle Non-compliance Findings

The process of handling non-compliance findings follows a structured approach. First, issues are prioritized based on risk and regulatory impact. Next, root causes are analyzed to prevent recurrence. A remediation plan is then created, outlining tasks, deadlines, and responsibilities. Corrective actions are implemented and tested to ensure effectiveness. Progress is tracked through monitoring tools and documentation. Finally, follow-up audits verify that fixes are successful and that compliance is maintained.

Figure 4-6 represents a continuous improvement of non-compliance findings.

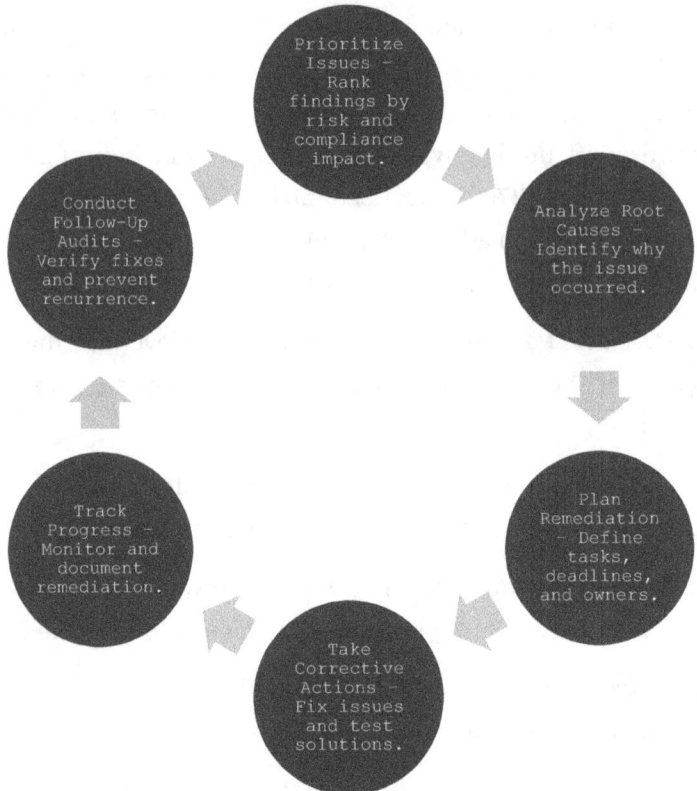

Figure 4-6. *Steps to handle non-compliance*

Prioritize Issues

The first step in addressing non-compliance findings is to assess and prioritize them based on their severity, regulatory implications, and potential impact on operations. High-severity vulnerabilities, such as open ports or unencrypted sensitive data, must be addressed immediately, as they pose the greatest risk. Similarly, regulatory violations that could lead to significant penalties, like GDPR or PCI-DSS breaches, should take precedence. Organizations should use risk assessment frameworks to classify findings and allocate resources effectively.

Analyze Root Causes

Understanding the root cause of each finding is essential for preventing recurrence. For example, human error, outdated policies, or misconfigured systems might be the underlying reasons. Tools like Splunk or Elasticsearch, Logstash, and Kibana (ELK) Stack can be used for log analysis, providing insights into system activities and helping trace the origin of vulnerabilities. This analysis helps identify systemic issues, such as insufficient employee training or gaps in existing controls, enabling organizations to implement long-term fixes.

Plan Remediation

A structured remediation plan should outline tasks, timelines, responsibilities, and required resources. This plan should prioritize high-risk findings while ensuring compliance deadlines are met. For instance, updating encryption protocols or implementing MFA might be immediate tasks, while revising security policies could be part of a broader improvement strategy. A clear and actionable plan ensures that remediation efforts are organized and efficient.

Take Corrective Actions

Corrective actions should directly address identified vulnerabilities. For example, if unencrypted data was flagged, the organization should deploy robust encryption tools like VeraCrypt or OpenSSL. If MFA was missing, solutions like Okta or Duo Security can be implemented. After implementing fixes, organizations should validate their effectiveness through thorough testing using tools like Nessus for vulnerability scanning or Metasploit and Burp Suite for penetration testing. These actions not only resolve immediate issues but also reinforce the organization's overall security posture.

Track Progress

Monitoring the progress of remediation efforts ensures accountability and timely completion. Tools like Jira or Trello can be used to assign tasks, track updates, and document actions. Regular status meetings and progress reports help keep teams aligned and focused on resolving findings. Additionally, maintaining detailed documentation of remediation efforts provides evidence of compliance for future audits.

Conduct Follow-Up Audits

Follow-up audits are essential for verifying that corrective actions have been effective. These audits reassess resolved issues, ensuring that vulnerabilities have been fully addressed and that no new issues have emerged. For example, if a finding involved weak passwords, the follow-up audit should confirm the implementation of stronger password policies and verify compliance across all systems. This step also helps identify and address any overlooked root causes.

Challenges in Addressing Non-compliance Findings

Handling non-compliance findings is not without its challenges.

- *Limited Resources*: Organizations, particularly small and medium-sized enterprises, may face constraints in terms of time, budget, or expertise. For instance, hiring skilled cybersecurity professionals or acquiring advanced tools may be beyond their financial reach.

- *System Complexity*: Large enterprises with integrated or legacy systems often encounter difficulties in implementing fixes. Legacy systems may lack support for modern security features, requiring costly upgrades or replacements.

- *Resistance to Change*: Employees and management may resist adopting new processes or technologies, especially if they perceive compliance initiatives as disruptive or burdensome. Overcoming this resistance requires effective communication and demonstrating the value of compliance for the organization's security and reputation.

Best Practices for Managing Non-compliance

- *Adopt a Risk-Based Approach*: Focus on high-risk vulnerabilities and align remediation efforts with the organization's strategic goals.

- *Promote Continuous Compliance*: Integrate compliance activities into daily operations, conducting regular self-assessments to identify and address issues proactively.

- *Foster a Security-First Culture*: Provide training programs and resources to employees, emphasizing the importance of compliance and security as shared responsibilities.

Key Takeaways

Non-compliance findings should be viewed as opportunities for improvement, not failures. By addressing them proactively, organizations can enhance security, build customer trust, avoid legal consequences, and streamline operations, ultimately creating a more resilient and efficient business environment.

In this section, we covered the following points:

Non-compliance findings are opportunities for improvement rather than mere indicators of failure. Addressing them effectively leads to

- *Stronger Security Posture*: Resolving vulnerabilities reduces the likelihood of breaches and enhances overall resilience.

- *Enhanced Customer Trust*: Demonstrating a commitment to data protection reassures stakeholders and builds brand loyalty.

- *Regulatory Compliance*: Avoiding penalties and legal consequences protects the organization's financial and reputational health.

- *Streamlined Operations*: Implementing the best practices and modern technologies improves efficiency and simplifies compliance processes.

Tips for Communicating Compliance Gaps to Stakeholders

Effective communication of compliance gaps identified during cybersecurity audits is a vital part of ensuring these findings translate into actionable improvements. Whether addressing technical teams, executive leadership, or regulatory bodies, the way you convey these issues significantly impacts the speed and effectiveness of remediation efforts, resource allocation, and organizational alignment. Clear, well-structured communication bridges the gap between technical findings and strategic decisions, enabling organizations to act swiftly and maintain trust with stakeholders.

CHAPTER 4   COMPLIANCE AND REGULATIONS

Why Communicating Compliance Gaps Matters

The importance of effectively communicating compliance gaps cannot be overstated. Poor communication can lead to misunderstood priorities, inadequate resource allocation, and even legal or reputational damage. When stakeholders fail to grasp the urgency of compliance issues, critical actions may be delayed, leaving the organization vulnerable to breaches or penalties.

For example:

- *Misunderstood Priorities*: If executive leaders cannot see how a technical vulnerability impacts the organization's bottom line, they may not allocate sufficient resources for remediation.

- *Regulatory Risks*: Ineffective communication with regulatory bodies can result in non-compliance penalties, reputational harm, or even legal actions.

Proper communication not only mitigates these risks but also aligns compliance efforts with organizational goals, ensuring that all stakeholders understand their roles and responsibilities.

Steps for Communicating Compliance Gaps

Effectively communicating compliance gaps ensures that all stakeholders understand the urgency, impact, and necessary remediation steps. The process begins with identifying and documenting compliance gaps found during cybersecurity audits. Understanding the audience is crucial; executives need business-focused insights, technical teams require detailed remediation plans, and regulatory bodies demand structured compliance reports. A risk-based approach prioritizes gaps based on severity, business impact, and likelihood of exploitation to ensure high-risk issues are addressed first. Using data-driven insights, including dashboards and key performance indicators (KPIs), enhances clarity and decision-making. Structuring communication with executive summaries, detailed technical findings, and actionable roadmaps ensures alignment across teams. Visual aids, plain language, and business-oriented framing improve stakeholder engagement. Leveraging tools like Power BI, Jira, and compliance reporting platforms streamlines communication and tracking. The final steps involve implementing the strategy through meetings, documentation, and continuous updates while monitoring progress and conducting follow-up audits to confirm that compliance

CHAPTER 4 COMPLIANCE AND REGULATIONS

gaps are fully resolved. By following this structured approach, organizations can drive swift remediation, maintain regulatory compliance, and strengthen their security posture.

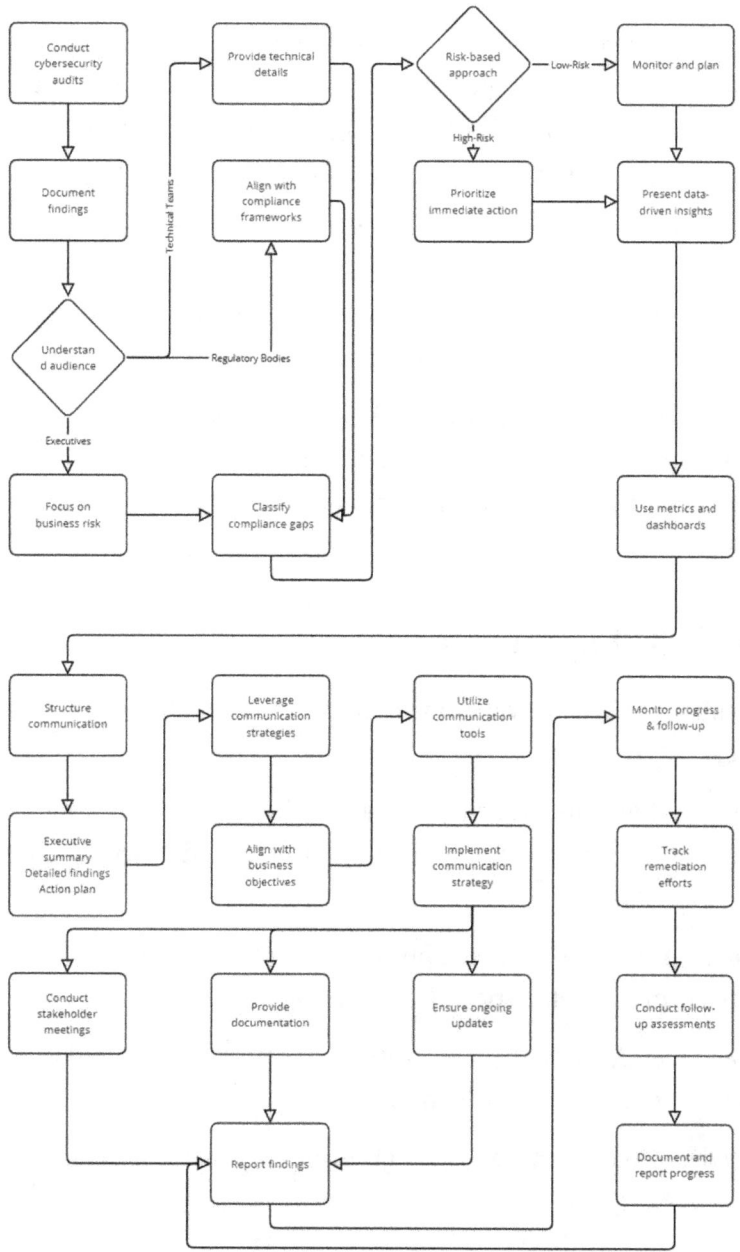

Figure 4-7. *Process workflow for communicating cybersecurity compliance gaps*

Understand Your Audience

Tailoring your message to the audience is essential for ensuring that the communication resonates and drives action. Different stakeholders require different levels of detail and focus:

- *Executive Leadership*: Focus on business risks, potential financial impacts, and the strategic benefits of addressing compliance gaps. For example, highlight how resolving a GDPR non-compliance issue can protect the organization from multimillion-euro fines.

- *Technical Teams*: Provide detailed technical information, such as affected systems, root causes, and specific steps for mitigation. Use precise terms and tools familiar to technical audiences, like system configurations or vulnerability scanning reports.

- *Regulatory Bodies*: Emphasize adherence to compliance standards, detailing specific gaps, remediation steps, and progress timelines. Clear documentation and alignment with regulatory language are critical.

Use a Risk-Based Approach

Prioritize compliance gaps by evaluating their severity, potential impact, and likelihood of exploitation:

- *Severity*: How critical is the gap to overall security? For example, an unpatched critical vulnerability should be addressed before an outdated policy.

- *Impact*: Assess the potential business disruption, reputational damage, or regulatory penalties resulting from the gap.

- *Likelihood*: Consider how easily the gap could be exploited by attackers or result in non-compliance penalties.

A risk-based approach ensures that high-priority issues receive immediate attention.

Present Data-Driven Insights

Supporting communication with data builds credibility and clarity. Use metrics, dashboards, and tools to visualize compliance gaps effectively. For example:

- *Dashboards*: Tools like Tableau or Splunk can create visualizations of compliance gaps, showing affected systems or highlighting trends over time.

- *KPIs*: Include metrics such as the percentage of non-compliant systems, the number of vulnerabilities, or the projected cost of remediation versus non-compliance penalties.

- *Cost Analysis*: Demonstrate potential financial impacts to justify resource allocation. For instance, compare the cost of encrypting sensitive data to potential regulatory fines.

Structure Your Communication Effectively

A clear and logical structure ensures that stakeholders can quickly understand and act on the findings. Consider the following components:

- *Executive Summary*: A high-level overview for leadership, highlighting critical gaps, their impacts, and recommended actions.

- *Detailed Findings*: A technical breakdown for IT teams, including affected assets, root causes, and detailed remediation steps.

- *Action Plan*: A roadmap outlining timelines, resource requirements, and assigned responsibilities. This ensures accountability and progress tracking.

Tips for Effective Communication

Effective communication of compliance gaps requires more than just sharing technical findings. It demands a strategic approach to ensure that every stakeholder, from technical teams to executive leadership, understands the implications and urgency of the issues. Visual aids, plain language, and framing compliance gaps in terms of business objectives are essential tools in the arsenal.

One of the most impactful ways to communicate is by using visual aids. Complex data can be overwhelming, especially for non-technical stakeholders. Tools like Power BI, Tableau, or Lucidchart can turn raw data into easy-to-digest charts, graphs, and heat maps. For example, a heat map showing the severity and location of compliance gaps can help prioritize remediation efforts. By pairing visuals with concise explanations, you make the data more accessible and actionable.

Translating technical jargon into plain language is equally important. This approach ensures that everyone, regardless of technical expertise, can grasp the problem and its potential impact.

Aligning compliance gaps with business objectives is another key strategy. For example, rather than discussing compliance gaps solely in technical terms, explain how these issues could impact revenue, customer trust, or operational efficiency. Leadership teams are more likely to act when they understand how non-compliance affects the organization's bottom line or reputation. Framing compliance in terms of business risk also helps secure resources for remediation.

Lastly, always focus on solutions rather than just highlighting problems. When presenting compliance gaps, emphasize the steps needed to address them. For instance, instead of merely pointing out that sensitive data is unencrypted, propose a specific encryption solution (e.g., AES-256) and outline the steps, costs, and timelines for implementation. Providing actionable solutions not only builds trust but also demonstrates a proactive approach to compliance challenges.

In the following are highlighted key tips for communication:

- *Use Visual Aids*: Charts, graphs, and heat maps make complex data more accessible. Tools like Power BI, Kibana, or Lucidchart can help create intuitive visuals.

- *Translate Technical Jargon*: Use plain language for non-technical stakeholders. Instead of "unpatched CVE-2023-12345," say, "A software vulnerability exists in our payment processing system that could allow unauthorized access."

- *Align with Business Objectives*: Frame gaps in terms of their impact on business goals, like customer trust, operational efficiency, or revenue.

- *Focus on Solutions*: Emphasize actionable steps rather than merely highlighting problems.

- *Anticipate Questions*: Prepare responses on costs, timelines, and resources, using tools like the PCI-DSS Cost Calculator to provide accurate estimates.

- *Benchmarking*: Compare the organization's compliance status with industry standards to contextualize findings.

Tools for Communicating Compliance Gaps

Using the right tools can make a significant difference in how compliance gaps are communicated and addressed. These tools not only help present data clearly but also streamline collaboration, tracking, and reporting.

Visualization tools like Tableau and Power BI allow the creation of tailored dashboards for different stakeholder groups. For instance, an executive dashboard might display high-level metrics, such as the percentage of systems out of compliance or the potential financial impact of non-compliance. On the other hand, a technical dashboard could provide detailed data, such as system vulnerabilities and their root causes. Real-time visualization tools like Kibana are also valuable for tracking live system vulnerabilities, enabling swift action.

Project management platforms like Jira, Asana, or Monday.com are essential for tracking remediation tasks and ensuring accountability. These platforms allow teams to assign tasks, set deadlines, and monitor progress. For example, after identifying a compliance gap, there can be created a task in Jira with a clear description, assigned resources, and a due date. The platform then tracks progress, ensuring that no issue falls through the cracks.

Compliance reporting tools like ServiceNow GRC or OneTrust automate the generation of compliance reports. These tools can pull data directly from your systems, ensuring that reports are accurate and up-to-date. Automated reporting saves time and provides a clear audit trail, which is especially useful for regulatory bodies.

Finally, collaboration platforms like Microsoft Teams or Slack facilitate cross-functional communication. These tools allow teams to share updates, discuss issues, and collaborate on solutions in real time. For instance, a Slack channel dedicated to compliance gaps could include updates on progress, questions from team members, and reminders about upcoming deadlines.

By leveraging these tools, you can enhance the clarity, efficiency, and effectiveness of the communication efforts, ensuring that compliance gaps are addressed promptly and thoroughly.

Practical Example

Scenario

During a GDPR audit, a retailer discovered unencrypted customer data stored in its system. The IT team recognized the risk, but leadership was unaware of the urgency, delaying action.

Communication Strategy

- *To Leadership*: A presentation highlighted the financial implications of non-compliance, including potential fines of up to €20 million or 4% of annual turnover. Visuals demonstrated the cost-effectiveness of encryption solutions.
- *To Technical Teams*: Provided documentation on AES-256 encryption standards and a step-by-step implementation guide.
- *Action Plan*: Presented a timeline with milestones: identify affected systems (7 days), implement encryption (30 days), and test for compliance (45 days).

Outcome

Leadership approved the necessary budget and resources, ensuring timely remediation and enhancing the retailer's security posture.

Benefits of Effective Communication

Effective communication of compliance gaps yields significant benefits, both immediate and long-term. One of the most critical advantages is faster decision-making. When stakeholders receive clear, concise, and actionable information, they can make informed decisions without delay. For example, a well-structured presentation to executive leadership can secure the budget and resources needed for remediation in a single meeting, reducing downtime and minimizing risks.

Another benefit is alignment across teams. Clear communication ensures that all stakeholders, from IT teams to leadership, understand their roles and responsibilities in addressing compliance gaps. This alignment fosters collaboration and prevents misunderstandings or duplication of efforts. For instance, if technical teams know exactly which vulnerabilities to address and leadership understands the resource requirements, the organization can work cohesively toward compliance.

Effective communication also leads to improved compliance. By presenting compliance gaps clearly and prioritizing them based on risk, organizations can address issues more efficiently, reducing the likelihood of penalties or regulatory actions. For example, an organization that promptly resolves a GDPR compliance gap, such as unencrypted customer data, not only avoids fines but also demonstrates a commitment to data protection.

Lastly, clear communication enhances the organization's security posture. Addressing compliance gaps quickly and effectively reduces vulnerabilities, making it harder for attackers to exploit weaknesses. This proactive approach builds trust with customers, partners, and regulators, strengthening the organization's reputation and resilience.

Key Takeaways

Effective communication is key to driving compliance efforts. By tailoring messages for different stakeholders, using visuals to simplify complex data, and focusing on practical solutions, you can ensure that everyone, whether in leadership or technical roles, understands the importance of compliance and is aligned in addressing it.

In this section, we covered the following points:

- *Tailor Communication*: Customize messages for different stakeholder groups, focusing on their specific needs and priorities. Use business language for leadership and technical details for IT teams.

- *Leverage Visual Aids*: Tools like Power BI, Tableau, and Kibana can turn complex data into intuitive visuals, enhancing understanding and engagement.

- *Use Plain Language*: Avoid technical jargon when communicating with non-technical stakeholders. Explain issues in terms of their impact on the business.

- *Focus on Solutions*: Always accompany findings with actionable recommendations, including timelines, costs, and required resources.

- *Utilize Tools*: Incorporate visualization tools, project management platforms, compliance reporting tools, and collaboration platforms to streamline communication and tracking.

- *Highlight Business Impact*: Frame compliance gaps in terms of their impact on customer trust, operational efficiency, and financial performance to secure buy-in from leadership.

Staying Ahead of Regulatory Changes

In an era where data breaches and cyber threats dominate headlines, staying updated on regulatory changes is not just a matter of compliance but a foundation of an organization's risk management strategy. The increasing complexity and dynamism of global regulations, such as GDPR, HIPAA, PCI-DSS, and emerging frameworks like DORA, NIS2, and the EU Cybersecurity Act, present both challenges and opportunities. Organizations that proactively adapt to these changes safeguard their reputation, protect customer trust, and enhance their security posture.

Importance of Staying Updated on Regulations

Keeping pace with evolving regulations is essential for mitigating legal, financial, and operational risks. Non-compliance can result in severe penalties, such as GDPR's €20 million fine or 4% of global turnover. However, the stakes go beyond fines; regulations are designed to address the latest cyber threats, including those posed by artificial intelligence (AI), Internet of Things (IoT) devices, and supply chain vulnerabilities. Organizations that fail to align with updated standards leave themselves exposed to breaches that could undermine their credibility and erode customer trust.

Moreover, staying ahead of regulatory changes can position a business as a leader in cybersecurity. Organizations that prioritize compliance demonstrate a commitment to safeguarding sensitive information, which can differentiate them from competitors. Compliance is not merely a defensive tactic but a proactive investment in building resilience and fostering long-term customer loyalty.

Challenges in Keeping Up with Regulatory Changes

Despite its importance, staying updated on regulatory changes is fraught with challenges.

- *Complexity of Standards*: Regulations like GDPR and HIPAA are nuanced, requiring in-depth understanding and meticulous implementation. For instance, GDPR includes specific requirements for DPIAs and cross-border data transfers, which can be difficult to interpret.

- *Frequent Updates*: Regulatory frameworks are not static. They evolve to address new technologies and emerging threats, demanding constant vigilance. For example, amendments to PCI-DSS now include provisions for cloud environments, adding another layer of complexity.

- *Global Scope*: Multinational organizations face the daunting task of complying with diverse and sometimes conflicting regulations across different jurisdictions. For instance, an organization operating in both the EU and the US must navigate GDPR's stringent requirements alongside sector-specific mandates like CCPA.

- *Resource Constraints*: Smaller organizations often lack the financial and human resources to dedicate to continuous regulatory monitoring and compliance. Without expert guidance or automation tools, they risk falling behind on critical updates.

Adopting a structured and proactive approach can help organizations overcome these challenges.

- *Monitor Regulatory Updates*: Subscribe to official regulatory bodies such as the European Data Protection Board (EDPB) for GDPR updates, the PCI Security Standards Council, and NIST. Regularly review their publications to stay informed about revisions and new standards.

- *Engage in Industry Forums*: Join professional groups like (ISC)², ISACA, or local cybersecurity alliances. These forums provide access to expert discussions, case studies, and insights into regulatory changes and best practices for compliance.

- *Train Your Teams*: Conduct regular training sessions for audit and compliance teams to ensure they are equipped to interpret and implement new requirements effectively. This builds internal expertise and reduces dependency on external consultants.

- *Leverage Automation Tools*: Deploy tools that provide real-time alerts on regulatory changes. Platforms like OneTrust and ServiceNow GRC can streamline compliance management by integrating updates into workflows.

- *Consult Experts*: For complex regulations, partner with legal and cybersecurity specialists who can offer tailored guidance. External consultants can bridge knowledge gaps and help navigate intricate compliance landscapes.

Table 4-4 presents the main challenges, and the solutions for keeping up with regulations are presented.

Table 4-4. Challenges in keeping up with regulatory changes

Challenge	Description	Solutions
Complexity of Standards	Regulations like GDPR and HIPAA have intricate, often ambiguous requirements, making compliance interpretation and implementation difficult.	- Provide in-depth training for compliance teams. - Consult legal and cybersecurity experts. - Use compliance management tools for tracking and interpretation.
Frequent Updates	Regulations evolve frequently to address emerging threats, requiring constant vigilance and adaptation.	- Subscribe to regulatory updates (e.g., NIST, PCI SSC, and EDPB). - Use automation tools like OneTrust for real-time alerts.
Global Scope	Multinational organizations must comply with multiple, sometimes conflicting, regulations across different jurisdictions.	- Develop a unified compliance framework. - Engage legal advisors for region-specific guidance. - Use cross-border compliance management tools.

(*continued*)

CHAPTER 4   COMPLIANCE AND REGULATIONS

Table 4-4. (*continued*)

Challenge	Description	Solutions
Resource Constraints	Smaller organizations often lack the financial and human resources to continuously track and implement compliance updates.	- Prioritize high-risk regulations based on impact. - Use cost-effective compliance automation tools. - Partner with external consultants when needed.
Integration into Audits	Regulatory updates must be incorporated into cybersecurity audits to ensure ongoing compliance.	- Regularly update audit checklists. - Adjust risk assessment frameworks.
Stakeholder Awareness	Leadership and teams need to understand regulatory changes to allocate resources and implement compliance measures effectively.	- Conduct regular training for executives and IT teams. - Provide compliance summaries tailored for different stakeholders. - Highlight business risks and benefits.
Time-Consuming Compliance Efforts	Monitoring, interpreting, and implementing regulatory changes can be time-intensive, leading to potential delays.	- Streamline compliance workflows using GRC platforms (e.g., ServiceNow). - Automate compliance reporting. - Centralize documentation for easy tracking and audits.

Integrating Regulatory Changes into Cybersecurity Audits

Once regulatory updates are identified, incorporating them into the cybersecurity audit process is crucial. This ensures that compliance efforts are aligned with the latest standards.

- *Revise Audit Checklists*: Update compliance checklists to reflect new requirements. For instance, if a regulation mandates encryption for data at rest, ensure this is included in audit evaluations.

- *Reassess Risk Frameworks*: Analyze how regulatory changes impact existing risk assessments. For example, an update to GDPR may require revisiting your DPIA process to address newly identified risks.

- *Adapt Audit Tools*: Configure cybersecurity tools like Qualys, Tenable, or Nessus to evaluate compliance with the updated standards. Automated scans can help identify gaps quickly and accurately.

- *Document Updates in Audit Reports*: Clearly highlight regulatory changes and their implications in audit findings. This ensures that stakeholders understand the rationale for recommended adjustments and their importance to overall compliance.

Benefits of Staying Updated

Organizations that prioritize regulatory updates gain a competitive edge and enhance their overall security posture.

- *Risk Mitigation*: Early identification and resolution of compliance gaps reduce exposure to legal and financial risks.

- *Operational Efficiency*: A streamlined process for integrating updates minimizes disruptions and optimizes resource utilization.

- *Enhanced Security*: Adhering to current standards fortifies defenses against sophisticated cyber threats.

- *Customer Trust*: Demonstrating a commitment to data protection fosters confidence among customers, partners, and stakeholders, strengthening relationships and reputation.

Key Takeaways

Compliance is an ongoing effort that requires continuous adaptation. Proactively monitoring regulatory updates, leveraging the right technology, engaging experts, training teams, and integrating changes into audits are all critical steps to staying ahead of evolving requirements and ensuring robust compliance practices.

In this section, we covered the following points:

- *Proactive Monitoring*: Regularly track updates from regulatory bodies to stay informed about changes and emerging frameworks.

- *Leverage Technology*: Use automation tools like OneTrust and ServiceNow GRC to integrate updates seamlessly into compliance processes.

- *Engage Experts*: Seek external guidance for navigating complex regulations and aligning compliance efforts with organizational goals.

- *Train Teams Continuously*: Equip your workforce with the knowledge and skills needed to interpret and implement evolving requirements.

- *Integrate Updates into Audits*: Ensure that cybersecurity audits reflect the latest standards by revising checklists, tools, and reporting practices.

Building a Robust Compliance Checklist

In the domain of cybersecurity audits, a compliance checklist serves as a foundation for ensuring regulatory adherence and operational excellence. Acting as a structured roadmap, it simplifies the complex task of navigating diverse frameworks such as GDPR, HIPAA, ISO 27001, PCI-DSS, etc. Beyond merely facilitating compliance, a well-crafted checklist empowers organizations to identify gaps, prioritize corrective actions, and strengthen their security posture effectively.

The Importance of a Compliance Checklist

A compliance checklist is more than a document; it's a strategic tool that drives efficiency and ensures thoroughness in cybersecurity audits. By systematically addressing each requirement, organizations can achieve comprehensive coverage, leaving no critical control unchecked.

Firstly, it enhances audit consistency by providing a standardized approach to evaluating regulatory adherence across multiple frameworks. This ensures that even in large or complex organizations, every audit is conducted with precision and uniformity.

Secondly, it improves efficiency by saving valuable time and resources. Instead of scrambling to identify and address gaps during audits, teams can focus on higher-priority areas using the checklist as a guide.

Regulatory alignment is another vital benefit. Frameworks like GDPR or HIPAA often involve intricate requirements, and a checklist simplifies their implementation by breaking them down into actionable tasks. Finally, the checklist serves as a foundation for actionable insights. By identifying gaps and areas needing improvement, it lays the groundwork for targeted remediation strategies, ensuring compliance and strengthening the organization's cybersecurity posture.

Steps to Build an Effective Compliance Checklist

Creating a robust compliance checklist involves strategic planning and collaboration:

- *Understand the Regulatory Landscape*: Start by identifying the regulatory frameworks relevant to your organization. For instance, a healthcare provider may focus on HIPAA, while a global e-commerce platform must comply with GDPR and PCI-DSS.

- *Break Down Requirements*: Translate complex regulatory standards into clear control objectives. For example, GDPR's data minimization principle could be outlined as a checklist item requiring periodic data audits to eliminate unnecessary information.

- *Collaborate with Stakeholders*: Include key teams like IT, legal, and compliance in the checklist creation process. Their collective expertise ensures comprehensive coverage and practical applicability.

- *Categorize Checklist Items*: Organize the checklist into logical sections such as data protection, access management, incident response, and system security. This structure streamlines the audit process.

- *Use Templates or Tools*: Leverage tools like OneTrust, Drata, or Tugboat Logic to accelerate checklist creation and automate compliance tracking.

Key Elements to Include in a Compliance Checklist

Although specific items will vary depending on the regulatory framework, certain elements are universal across most checklists:

- *Data Management*:
    - Is sensitive data encrypted at rest and in transit?
    - Are data retention policies compliant with regulatory requirements?
    - Are data classification and labeling processes in place?
    - Is there a documented process for secure data disposal?
    - Are backups encrypted and stored securely?
    - Are backup restoration tests conducted periodically?
    - Is data anonymization or pseudonymization implemented where applicable?
    - Are mechanisms in place to track and manage data subject requests (e.g., Right to be Forgotten under GDPR)?
- *Access Controls*:
    - Is MFA implemented for critical systems?
    - Are access permissions reviewed and updated regularly?
    - Are RBACs enforced?
    - Is there a process to immediately revoke access for terminated employees?
    - Are privileged access accounts monitored and restricted?
    - Is there an approval process for granting administrative privileges?
    - Are user accounts audited to identify inactive or orphaned accounts?
    - Are Single Sign-On (SSO) and identity federation mechanisms used where appropriate?

CHAPTER 4   COMPLIANCE AND REGULATIONS

- *Incident Response*:
    - Does the organization have a documented incident response plan?
    - Are data breaches reported within the required timeframe (e.g., 72 hours for GDPR)?
    - Are incident response drills and tabletop exercises conducted regularly?
    - Are forensic capabilities available for investigating security incidents?
    - Is a 24/7 security monitoring team or security operations center in place?
    - Are incidents categorized based on severity and impact?
    - Is there a clear escalation process for critical security incidents?
    - Are incident reports documented and used for post-mortem analysis?
- *Risk Management*:
    - Are risk assessments conducted on a regular basis?
    - Are there mitigation plans for identified risks?
    - Is there a risk register to track vulnerabilities and mitigation efforts?
    - Are emerging threats (e.g., AI-driven attacks, supply chain risks) considered in risk assessments?
    - Are third-party risks assessed as part of the overall risk management process?
    - Are risk acceptance and risk transfer (e.g., cyber insurance) strategies documented?
    - Are Business Impact Analyses (BIAs) conducted for critical processes?
    - Are key risk indicators (KRIs) defined and monitored?

- *Employee Training*:
  - Are employees trained in cybersecurity and compliance policies?
  - Are training logs maintained for audit purposes?
  - Are phishing simulations conducted to test employee awareness?
  - Is executive leadership provided with specialized compliance training?
  - Are secure coding practices taught to development teams?
  - Are employees trained in social engineering threats?
  - Are awareness campaigns conducted on a regular basis?
  - Do employees undergo compliance refreshers when regulations change?
- *System Security*:
  - Are firewalls and intrusion detection systems configured and monitored effectively?
  - Is a robust patch management process in place to address vulnerabilities?
  - Are endpoint security measures, such as antivirus and EDR solutions, implemented?
  - Are secure software development practices followed for in-house applications?
  - Are security baselines applied to all IT assets?
  - Are network segmentation and micro-segmentation used to limit attack surfaces?
  - Are logs from critical systems collected and monitored in an SIEM solution?
  - Are security policies enforced on mobile devices and remote endpoints?

CHAPTER 4   COMPLIANCE AND REGULATIONS

- *Third-Party Assessments*:
  - Are vendor contracts reviewed to ensure compliance with obligations?
  - Are regular third-party audits conducted to verify adherence to agreed-upon standards?
  - Are data-sharing agreements aligned with regulatory requirements?
  - Is there a vendor risk management program in place?
  - Are third-party risk assessments conducted before onboarding new vendors?
  - Are vendors required to provide evidence of compliance (e.g., SOC 2 reports and ISO 27001 certification)?
  - Are third-party access controls regularly reviewed and restricted where necessary?
  - Are service-level agreements (SLAs) in place for security incident response from third parties?
- *Audit and Documentation*:
  - Are compliance audit logs maintained and reviewed regularly?
  - Are security policies and procedures documented and accessible?
  - Are previous audit findings tracked to ensure remediation?
  - Are regulatory reporting obligations met in a timely manner?
  - Are audit trails maintained for critical system changes?
  - Are compliance checklists updated to reflect regulatory changes?
  - Are compliance reports generated and reviewed by leadership?
  - Are third-party audit findings integrated into overall compliance reporting?

- *Business Continuity and Disaster Recovery (BC/DR)*:
  - Is there a documented and tested Business Continuity Plan (BCP)?
  - Are disaster recovery (DR) plans in place and regularly tested?
  - Are RTOs and RPOs defined and met?
  - Are backup data centers and failover mechanisms in place?
  - Is cloud disaster recovery incorporated into BC/DR plans?
  - Are crisis communication protocols defined in case of a major incident?
  - Is an alternative workplace strategy in place for critical business functions?
  - Are DR test results documented and used for continuous improvement?
- *Regulatory Compliance Monitoring*:
  - Are regulatory changes tracked and reviewed regularly?
  - Is there a compliance team responsible for interpreting and implementing regulatory updates?
  - Are automated tools used to monitor compliance requirements?
  - Are industry benchmarks and best practices used to measure compliance performance?
  - Are cross-functional teams involved in regulatory compliance discussions?
  - Are compliance gaps identified and remediated proactively?
  - Are external legal and regulatory advisors consulted as needed?
  - Is a framework in place to ensure ongoing compliance across all business units?

CHAPTER 4   COMPLIANCE AND REGULATIONS

- *Data Privacy and Protection*:
  - Is a Data Protection Officer (DPO) appointed if required by regulation?
  - Are Privacy Impact Assessments (PIAs) conducted for new projects?
  - Are consent management processes in place for collecting and processing personal data?
  - Is a mechanism available for individuals to exercise their data rights (e.g., access, rectification, erasure)?
  - Are DPAs established with third-party processors?
  - Is there a documented process for handling and responding to data subject requests?
  - Are privacy policies reviewed and updated regularly?
- *Physical Security*:
  - Are access controls in place for data centers and critical infrastructure?
  - Are visitor logs maintained and reviewed regularly?
  - Are security cameras and surveillance systems deployed in sensitive areas?
  - Are employee ID badges and access credentials regularly reviewed?
  - Is there an environmental monitoring system for detecting physical threats (e.g., fire, flooding)?
  - Are physical security assessments conducted periodically?
  - Are critical IT assets stored in secured, access-controlled locations?
  - Are offsite storage facilities used for backup data secure and compliant?

Technologies for Compliance Checklist Management

Managing a compliance checklist effectively requires more than just manual effort; it demands the integration of advanced technologies that simplify, automate, and streamline the process. These tools not only ensure accuracy but also save valuable time and resources. One of the most impactful categories is GRC platforms, such as RSA Archer, OneTrust, or LogicGate. These platforms provide a centralized hub for compliance activities, allowing organizations to track progress, maintain documentation, and generate real-time compliance reports. With intuitive dashboards, these tools enable stakeholders to visualize compliance status and identify gaps immediately, promoting informed decision-making.

Workflow automation tools like ServiceNow or Asana further enhance efficiency by automating repetitive tasks. For example, they can send reminders for upcoming compliance deadlines, assign tasks to relevant team members, and monitor progress against predefined timelines. By reducing manual oversight, these tools help organizations stay on track without overburdening their teams.

In addition, risk assessment tools such as Qualys and Tenable play a crucial role in compliance checklist management. These tools continuously scan systems for vulnerabilities that could lead to non-compliance, providing detailed insights into risk areas. By integrating these tools with GRC platforms, organizations can create a dynamic compliance checklist that evolves with emerging risks and threats.

Document management systems like SharePoint or Google Workspace ensure that all compliance-related documentation is easily accessible, organized, and secure. These systems provide version control, enabling teams to maintain up-to-date policies, procedures, and evidence needed for audits. Furthermore, collaboration platforms like Microsoft Teams and Slack can be integrated with compliance tools to facilitate cross-functional communication, ensuring all stakeholders are aligned and informed.

By leveraging these technologies, organizations can transform compliance checklist management into a streamlined, proactive process that minimizes errors, enhances accountability, and supports continuous improvement.

Benefits of a Well-Designed Compliance Checklist

The advantages of a carefully crafted compliance checklist extend far beyond regulatory adherence. One of the primary benefits is proactive compliance. By identifying potential gaps and addressing them before an audit, organizations can demonstrate preparedness, reduce the likelihood of penalties, and maintain their reputation with regulators and stakeholders. This forward-thinking approach ensures that compliance becomes an ongoing activity rather than a reactive effort during audits.

Another significant advantage is the enhancement of organizational security. A well-designed checklist focuses on critical control areas, such as encryption, access management, and incident response. By addressing these areas systematically, organizations can mitigate risks effectively, reducing vulnerabilities that could lead to breaches or data loss.

Operational efficiency is also a notable benefit. A checklist standardizes the compliance process, eliminating redundancies and providing a clear roadmap for audits. This saves time and resources, allowing teams to focus on strategic initiatives rather than being bogged down by repetitive tasks. Additionally, a streamlined compliance process reduces audit fatigue, fostering a positive compliance culture within the organization.

Perhaps one of the most impactful benefits is the ability to build confidence among stakeholders. Whether it's customers, partners, or regulatory bodies, a robust compliance checklist demonstrates a commitment to data protection and ethical practices. This transparency strengthens relationships and enhances the organization's reputation in a competitive marketplace.

Moreover, a comprehensive checklist serves as a valuable training and reference tool for employees. By clearly outlining expectations and procedures, it empowers teams to align their efforts with regulatory requirements and organizational goals, fostering a sense of accountability and ownership.

Key Takeaways

A compliance checklist is more than a tool; it's a strategic asset that drives regulatory adherence, strengthens security, and fosters continuous improvement. By integrating technology and focusing on proactive management, organizations can reduce risks, build trust, and set themselves up for long-term success.

CHAPTER 4 COMPLIANCE AND REGULATIONS

In this section, we covered the following points:

- A compliance checklist is a foundational tool for achieving regulatory adherence, improving cybersecurity, and streamlining audit processes.

- Leveraging technologies such as GRC platforms, workflow automation tools, risk assessment solutions, and document management systems enhances checklist management by promoting efficiency, accuracy, and accountability.

- The benefits of a well-designed compliance checklist include proactive compliance, enhanced security, operational efficiency, and increased stakeholder confidence.

- A checklist not only simplifies audits but also fosters a culture of continuous improvement, aligning employees and teams with regulatory and organizational objectives.

- Organizations that prioritize a robust compliance checklist position themselves for long-term success by reducing risks, avoiding penalties, and building trust with their stakeholders.

Audit Reporting for Regulatory Bodies

Audit reporting for regulatory bodies is a foundation of modern cybersecurity practices. These reports provide an essential link between an organization's internal controls and the external authorities tasked with ensuring compliance. When done effectively, they serve as a testament to adherence to regulatory frameworks such as GDPR, HIPAA, or ISO 27001, while also demonstrating a commitment to proactive risk management. Beyond regulatory obligations, audit reports offer an opportunity to showcase an organization's cybersecurity maturity, bolster stakeholder trust, and guide continuous improvement efforts. However, crafting such reports requires a deep understanding of both technical details and the unique expectations of the regulatory bodies involved.

CHAPTER 4   COMPLIANCE AND REGULATIONS

Importance of Audit Reporting for Regulatory Bodies

The significance of regulatory audit reporting cannot be overstated. First and foremost, these reports act as definitive proof of compliance, summarizing an organization's adherence to industry standards and legal requirements. Whether it's demonstrating encryption protocols under GDPR or secure access controls mandated by PCI-DSS, a comprehensive report validates an organization's efforts to maintain compliance.

Another critical function of audit reporting is risk mitigation. By presenting an accurate and transparent picture of compliance status, organizations can proactively address gaps, thus avoiding costly fines, legal repercussions, or reputational damage. For example, an organization that demonstrates its commitment to addressing non-compliance promptly is more likely to gain tolerance from regulators.

Additionally, regulatory audit reports play a vital role in building confidence among stakeholders. Whether it's customers, partners, or investors, these documents serve as a reassurance that the organization prioritizes data protection and cybersecurity. They reflect not only commitment to meeting regulatory standards but also a broader dedication to safeguarding sensitive information.

Finally, audit reports provide actionable insights into ongoing improvements. By analyzing findings and recommendations, organizations can develop targeted strategies to enhance their cybersecurity posture, making future audits smoother and more efficient.

Key Components of a Regulatory Audit Report

An effective audit report is thoroughly structured to address the needs of both technical and non-technical stakeholders while aligning with the specific requirements of the governing body. Below are the essential components.

Executive Summary

The executive summary provides a high-level overview of the audit's scope, objectives, and key findings. It highlights critical risks, compliance gaps, and strengths, making it particularly useful for executives who need to make informed decisions without delving into technical specifics.

Scope

This section outlines the boundaries of the audit, including the systems, processes, and data that were reviewed. It specifies the regulatory standards assessed, ensuring clarity on what the report covers and, equally important, what it does not.

Methodology

Here, the report explains the tools, techniques, and frameworks used during the audit, such as penetration testing, vulnerability scans, or risk assessments. It should also clarify how these methods align with the regulatory standards being assessed, enhancing the report's credibility.

Findings

The findings section is the core of the report, detailing the compliance status for each control. Risks are categorized by severity – critical, high, medium, or low – and accompanied by explanations of their technical details and business implications.

Evidence

Including tangible evidence such as test results, configurations, logs, and screenshots adds credibility and transparency to the findings. This section ensures that the report's conclusions are well supported.

Recommendations

Actionable recommendations address identified gaps, providing prioritized steps for remediation based on risk and impact. This section ensures the report is not just a critique but a roadmap for improvement.

Conclusion

The conclusion summarizes the compliance status and reiterates any urgent issues requiring immediate attention. It may also include a statement of assurance where applicable, reinforcing the organization's commitment to maintaining high cybersecurity standards.

CHAPTER 4   COMPLIANCE AND REGULATIONS

Best Practices for Audit Reporting

To create impactful audit reports for regulatory bodies, adhering to best practices is essential. In the following are described some of the main best practices.

Follow Regulatory Guidelines

Ensure the report aligns with the specific requirements of the governing body, such as GDPR Article 30 or PCI-DSS's ROC. This avoids misinterpretation and ensures that all necessary information is included.

Simplify Technical Language

Present findings in a clear, non-technical manner, especially for non-technical stakeholders. For instance, instead of stating, "TLS 1.0 is deprecated," explain, "Outdated encryption protocols are in use, posing risks to secure communication."

Leverage Automation

Use tools like Splunk, Qualys, or Tenable to generate consistent and accurate data for reports. Automation reduces human error and enhances report reliability.

Maintain Objectivity

Adopt a neutral tone throughout the report, focusing on facts rather than opinions. Objectivity builds trust and credibility with regulators.

Use Visual Aids

Charts, graphs, and heat maps make complex data more accessible. Tools like Tableau or Power BI can help create visuals that clarify findings and highlight priorities.

Secure Report Sharing

Ensure reports are shared securely, using encryption or secure portals to protect sensitive information from unauthorized access.

Example: GDPR Audit Report

In a GDPR audit, a multinational retailer identified the following:

- *Strengths*:
  - Robust AES-256 encryption for sensitive data.
  - Well-documented processes for obtaining and storing customer consent.
- *Weaknesses*:
  - Absence of a documented breach notification process.
  - Weak pseudonymization controls for internal data handling.
- *Recommendations*:
  - Implement a breach response framework, using tools like Cortex XSOAR for automation.
  - Strengthen pseudonymization practices with solutions like TokenEx or Thales CipherTrust.

The report provided clear next steps and reinforced the organization's commitment to privacy and compliance.

Benefits of Effective Audit Reporting

Creating thorough and well-structured audit reports offers numerous advantages. It ensures regulatory compliance, reducing the risk of penalties and legal actions. By clearly documenting controls and remediation efforts, organizations can demonstrate their dedication to maintaining high cybersecurity standards.

Effective reporting also fosters transparency and trust among stakeholders, showcasing an organization's accountability and commitment to safeguarding sensitive data. This is particularly crucial for building long-term customer relationships and maintaining market competitiveness.

Furthermore, audit reports provide actionable insights, guiding organizations toward a more resilient cybersecurity posture. By addressing findings and implementing recommendations, organizations can continuously improve their defenses against evolving threats.

Lastly, comprehensive reporting enhances operational efficiency, streamlining the audit process and ensuring all stakeholders are aligned. It reduces redundancy, minimizes errors, and lays the groundwork for smoother audits in the future.

Key Takeaways

An effective audit report is not just a compliance document; it is a tool for fostering trust, guiding improvements, and ensuring ongoing security and regulatory alignment. By following best practices and leveraging technology, organizations can create impactful reports that drive positive changes and enhance stakeholder confidence.

In this section, we covered the following points:

- Audit reporting for regulatory bodies demonstrates compliance, mitigates risks, and builds stakeholder confidence.
- Effective reports should include an executive summary, scope, methodology, findings, evidence, recommendations, and conclusions.
- Best practices include aligning with regulatory guidelines, simplifying language, leveraging automation, maintaining objectivity, and using visuals.
- Technologies like Splunk, Qualys, and Tableau can enhance report accuracy, clarity, and efficiency.
- A well-crafted audit report not only satisfies regulatory requirements but also fosters trust and guides ongoing cybersecurity improvements.

Conclusions

The dynamic landscape of cybersecurity regulations underscores the growing complexity of digital ecosystems and the increasing prevalence of cyber risks. Regulatory frameworks such as GDPR, PCI-DSS, and emerging mandates like DORA and NIS2 emphasize the importance of privacy, data protection, and operational resilience. Compliance is no longer a mere legal obligation; it has evolved into a strategic enabler for organizations to strengthen their security posture, build stakeholder trust, and foster a culture of accountability and continuous improvement.

A systematic approach to compliance, spanning identification of applicable regulations, evidence collection, evaluation of controls, and comprehensive reporting, ensures holistic alignment with regulatory standards. These efforts reduce legal, financial, and reputational risks while driving the adoption of robust cybersecurity practices. Furthermore, addressing compliance gaps proactively transforms potential vulnerabilities into opportunities for improvement, enhancing operational efficiency and organizational resilience.

Audits play a pivotal role in bridging regulatory requirements with practical implementation. By leveraging structured methodologies, modern tools, and strategic planning, audits provide actionable insights that not only satisfy compliance requirements but also promote transparency, strengthen relationships, and mitigate risks. Tailored communication strategies, which align findings with stakeholder priorities and present actionable solutions, ensure organizational alignment and effective response to compliance gaps.

The future of cybersecurity compliance is marked by adaptability, innovation, and proactive measures. Emerging trends such as automation, global standardization, and the integration of technologies like AI and blockchain are revolutionizing compliance processes. Organizations that embrace these advancements position themselves for long-term success by achieving enhanced security, operational resilience, and global competitiveness.

Ultimately, compliance efforts must be viewed as an ongoing journey rather than a one-time requirement. Regular updates to policies, training programs, and technological tools ensure that organizations remain aligned with evolving regulations and prepared for emerging threats. By prioritizing trust, operational resilience, and proactive compliance, organizations can build a secure and efficient digital environment that supports sustained growth and success in an increasingly interconnected world.

CHAPTER 5

Introduction to Cyber Risk Management

In an era where digital transformation drives business innovation, the accompanying rise in cyber threats makes cyber risk management a foundation of organizational security. As organizations adopt cloud computing, IoT devices, and other advanced technologies, they expose themselves to an evolving array of risks. Cyber risk management provides a structured, proactive approach to identifying, assessing, and mitigating these risks, ensuring operational resilience and regulatory compliance while safeguarding critical assets and data.

In today's interconnected world, cyber risk management is essential for organizational security. As businesses increasingly embrace digital solutions, the prevalence and sophistication of cyber threats grow. Cyber risk management offers a structured approach to identifying, analyzing, and mitigating these risks, safeguarding both data and systems while ensuring business continuity. By integrating this practice into their operations, organizations can achieve a balance between robust security measures and seamless functionality.

What Is Cyber Risk Management?

Cyber risk management involves systematic identification, analysis, and mitigation of risks to an organization's digital ecosystem. It is not a one-time process but a dynamic, continuous cycle aimed at adapting to emerging threats and maintaining a balance between robust security and business functionality.

- *Identifying Risks*: This step entails pinpointing vulnerabilities in systems, data, and infrastructure. Critical assets such as databases, servers, and employee endpoints are cataloged to determine potential exposure.

CHAPTER 5   INTRODUCTION TO CYBER RISK MANAGEMENT

- *Assessing Risks*: Risks are evaluated based on their likelihood and potential impact. This phase uses quantitative or qualitative methods, often guided by established frameworks like FAIR or NIST RMF.

- *Mitigating Risks*: After assessment, appropriate controls, such as firewalls, MFA, and encryption, are implemented to reduce risk exposure.

- *Monitoring Threats*: Continuous monitoring ensures that emerging threats are promptly detected and addressed. Tools like SIEM platforms help automate threat detection.

- *Aligning Security with Organizational Goals*: Effective cyber risk management aligns with broader business objectives, ensuring security measures support operations rather than hinder them.

- The main elements of cyber risk management are presented in Figure 5-1.

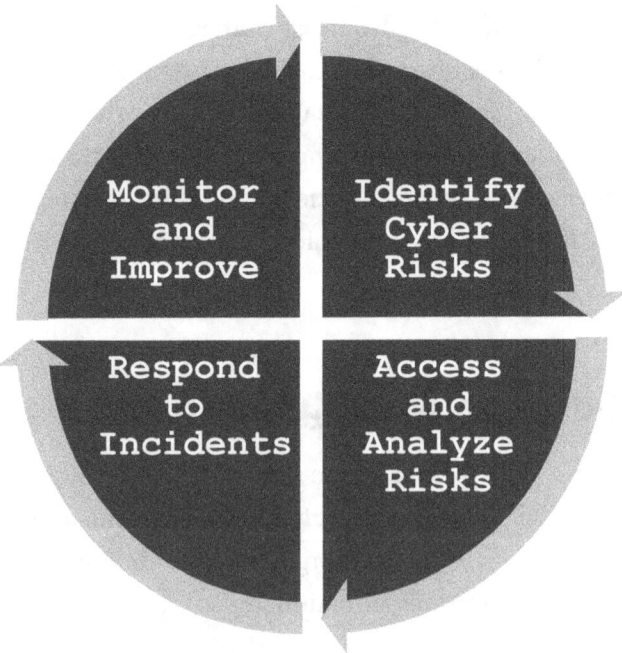

Figure 5-1. Continuous improvement of cyber risk management

This integrated approach not only protects systems but also builds a foundation of trust with stakeholders and regulators, showcasing the organization's commitment to cybersecurity excellence.

Cyber risk management involves

- Identifying risks to systems, data, or infrastructure
- Assessing risk likelihood and impact to prioritize resources effectively
- Implementing controls to reduce identified risks
- Continuous monitoring for emerging threats and vulnerabilities

It aligns cybersecurity initiatives with broader organizational goals, ensuring that security measures do not impede functionality but rather support overall resilience.

Why Cyber Risk Management Matters

Cyber risk management is more than a technical necessity; it is a strategic imperative. By proactively addressing cyber risks, organizations achieve multiple objectives:

- *Protect Critical Assets*: Safeguarding sensitive data, intellectual property, and operational systems ensures the continuity of business operations.

- *Prioritize Investments*: Limited resources can be allocated effectively by focusing on risks that pose the greatest threats.

- *Ensure Compliance*: Adherence to regulations like GDPR, HIPAA, DORA, etc., avoids costly fines and reputational damage.

- *Minimize Disruptions*: A robust risk management framework reduces the likelihood of business interruptions caused by cyber incidents.

- *Build Trust*: Customers, partners, and regulators value proactive risk management as a hallmark of reliability and transparency.

CHAPTER 5   INTRODUCTION TO CYBER RISK MANAGEMENT

Key Components of Cyber Risk Management

Risk Identification

The first step in effective cyber risk management is to understand what needs to be protected. Organizations must identify all critical assets, including networks, databases, and endpoints, that could be targeted. This involves creating a comprehensive asset inventory using tools like SolarWinds, Qualys, or open-source alternatives. Additionally, organizations should identify potential threat vectors, such as insider threats, phishing, or vulnerabilities in third-party vendors, to anticipate potential attack scenarios.

Risk Assessment

Once risks are identified, their likelihood and potential impact must be evaluated. This assessment often employs established frameworks like OCTAVE, FAIR, or NIST RMF. For instance, FAIR quantifies risks in financial terms, aiding in executive-level decision-making, while OCTAVE focuses on operational risks. By categorizing risks as high, medium, or low, organizations can prioritize areas requiring immediate action.

Risk Mitigation

Mitigating risk involves deploying controls to reduce vulnerabilities and protect assets. Common measures include implementing MFA to secure access, encrypting sensitive data both at rest and in transit, and establishing firewalls to monitor and control network traffic. Regular patching of software and systems also plays a crucial role in minimizing exposure to known vulnerabilities. Risk mitigation strategies should be tailored to the organization's specific needs, ensuring efficiency and cost-effectiveness.

Risk Monitoring

Cyber risk management is not a one-time task but a continuous process. Organizations must monitor threats and vulnerabilities in real time using SIEM tools such as Splunk or ArcSight. Regular vulnerability scans and penetration tests further enhance visibility, ensuring that newly discovered weaknesses are promptly addressed. Threat intelligence feeds can also provide actionable insights into emerging risks.

Incident Response

An effective incident response plan is a critical component of cyber risk management. Organizations must create and regularly test these plans to ensure readiness for potential breaches. Automated response tools like IBM Resilient can accelerate containment and remediation, reducing the overall impact of incidents. Additionally, post-incident reviews help organizations refine their response strategies, improving resilience against future attacks.

Technology in Cyber Risk Management

Technology is a foundation of modern cyber risk management, offering tools and platforms to automate and enhance traditional practices.

Automation

Automating repetitive tasks, such as compliance reporting and risk assessments, significantly reduces the burden on cybersecurity teams. Tools like ServiceNow and RSA Archer streamline workflows, enabling organizations to focus on more strategic initiatives. For example, RSA Archer provides dashboards that offer a real-time view of an organization's risk posture, helping leaders make informed decisions.

Artificial Intelligence and Machine Learning

Artificial Intelligence (AI) and Machine Learning (ML) are transforming cyber risk management by enabling proactive threat detection and response. Advanced solutions like Darktrace use machine learning algorithms to analyze network traffic, detect anomalies, and predict potential risks. These technologies allow organizations to identify and address threats before they escalate, improving overall security posture.

Predictive Analytics

Predictive analytics tools, such as Splunk and Azure Sentinel, forecast risks by analyzing historical data and trends. These insights guide decision-makers in implementing preventive measures, reducing the likelihood of future incidents. Predictive models can also help organizations allocate resources more effectively, focusing efforts where they are needed most.

Cloud-Based Solutions

Cloud platforms like Qualys provide scalable, real-time risk management capabilities. These solutions enable organizations to monitor vulnerabilities, track compliance, and manage threats across distributed environments. Cloud-based tools are particularly beneficial for organizations with remote or hybrid workforces, ensuring consistent protection regardless of location.

Preparing for Future Cyber Risks

The ever-evolving cyber threat landscape requires organizations to adopt a forward-thinking approach to risk management.

A proactive stance involves not only addressing current risks but also anticipating future challenges. For instance, emerging technologies like quantum computing could render traditional encryption methods obsolete, necessitating early adoption of quantum-resistant algorithms. Similarly, the rise of AI-powered attacks underscores the need for AI-driven defense mechanisms.

Employee training is another critical element. By fostering a culture of cyber risk awareness, organizations empower their teams to recognize and respond to threats effectively. This includes regular training sessions, simulated phishing campaigns, and workshops on the latest security practices.

Collaboration with cybersecurity experts and third-party vendors can provide additional insights and resources, helping organizations stay ahead of emerging threats. Regularly updating policies and frameworks ensures that they remain aligned with new technologies and evolving regulatory requirements.

Benefits of Cyber Risk Management

The benefits of a robust cyber risk management program extend beyond security, offering significant advantages across various organizational dimensions.

Key benefits of cyber risk management include

- Effective cyber risk management delivers a multitude of benefits, positioning organizations for long-term success in a complex digital landscape.

- *Resilience*: Organizations can withstand and recover from cyberattacks with minimal disruption.

- *Regulatory Confidence*: Proactive compliance fosters trust with regulators, minimizing the risk of fines and penalties.

- *Operational Efficiency*: Automation and streamlined processes reduce manual workloads, allowing teams to focus on critical tasks.

- *Stakeholder Trust*: Demonstrating a commitment to cybersecurity enhances relationships with customers, investors, and partners.

- *Cost Savings*: Avoiding breaches and mitigating risks early reduces the financial impact of cyber incidents.

- *Enhanced Security*: A comprehensive risk management strategy reduces vulnerabilities, strengthens defenses, and minimizes the likelihood of successful attacks. This creates a safer digital environment for both employees and customers.

- *Regulatory Compliance*: Effective risk management ensures adherence to cybersecurity standards and regulations, avoiding costly fines and penalties. Compliance also demonstrates accountability, enhancing the organization's reputation.

- *Business Continuity*: By mitigating risks and preparing for potential disruptions, organizations can maintain operations during incidents, minimizing downtime and financial losses.

- *Cost Efficiency*: Proactively addressing risks reduces the need for costly incident responses and recovery efforts. Allocating resources based on risk prioritization ensures optimal use of budgets.

- *Trust and Reputation*: Demonstrating a commitment to cybersecurity builds trust with stakeholders, including customers, partners, and regulators. This trust translates into stronger business relationships and a competitive edge in the market.

Table 5-1 presents key advantages of benefits of cyber risk management.

CHAPTER 5   INTRODUCTION TO CYBER RISK MANAGEMENT

Table 5-1. Benefits of cyber risk management

Benefit	Description	Key Advantages
Enhanced Security	Strengthens defenses by reducing vulnerabilities and mitigating threats.	- Minimizes risk of data breaches and cyberattacks. - Protects critical assets like databases and networks. - Reduces exposure to insider threats and phishing attacks.
Regulatory Compliance	Ensures adherence to cybersecurity laws, standards, and industry regulations.	- Avoids legal penalties and fines from GDPR, DORA, HIPAA, etc. - Demonstrates accountability to auditors and regulators. - Improves transparency in security governance.
Business Continuity	Helps organizations maintain operations despite cyber incidents.	- Reduces downtime and service disruptions. - Ensures rapid recovery through disaster recovery (DR) plans. - Supports operational resilience against cyber threats.
Cost Efficiency	Reduces financial impact by proactively managing risks.	- Lowers costs associated with data breaches and ransomware. - Optimizes cybersecurity budgets by prioritizing risks. - Avoids reactive spending on emergency incident response.
Stakeholder Trust	Builds confidence among customers, partners, and investors.	- Enhances reputation by demonstrating a strong security posture. - Strengthens customer loyalty through responsible data protection. - Attracts potential business opportunities and investments.

(continued)

Table 5-1. (*continued*)

Benefit	Description	Key Advantages
Operational Efficiency	Streamlines cybersecurity processes through automation and best practices.	- Reduces manual workloads for security teams. - Improves risk visibility and decision-making with AI and analytics. - Enhances collaboration between IT and business units.
Resilience Against Emerging Threats	Enables proactive adaptation to evolving cyber risks.	- Prepares organizations for threats like AI-driven attacks and quantum computing risks. - Encourages continuous improvement in security frameworks. - Ensures long-term adaptability to new regulatory and threat landscapes.

Key Takeaways

Effective cyber risk management is not merely a defensive measure but a strategic enabler. By aligning cybersecurity with organizational goals and proactively adapting to evolving threats, businesses can achieve resilience, build trust, and maintain a competitive edge in today's digital landscape.

In this section, we covered the following points:

- Cyber risk management is a continuous process that involves the ongoing identification, assessment, mitigation, and monitoring of cyber risks to protect an organization's digital ecosystem.

- Organizations must inventory critical assets like databases, networks, and endpoints while recognizing potential threats such as phishing or insider attacks.

- Risk assessment frameworks enhance prioritization; there are established frameworks like FAIR, NIST RMF, and OCTAVE that help evaluate risks based on likelihood and impact, enabling effective resource allocation.

- Mitigation involves implementing controls like MFA, encryption, firewalls, and timely software patching to minimize vulnerabilities.

- Real-time monitoring through tools like SIEM platforms, vulnerability scans, and threat intelligence feeds ensures emerging risks are promptly addressed.

- A well-tested incident response plan, supported by automated tools like IBM Resilient, enables organizations to contain and recover from cyber incidents efficiently.

- Automation, AI, and predictive analytics enhance risk detection and response capabilities, while cloud-based solutions offer scalable, real-time protection.

- Organizations must anticipate emerging threats, such as quantum computing and AI-driven attacks, by updating policies, training employees, and collaborating with experts.

- A robust cyber risk management strategy enhances resilience, compliance, operational efficiency, and stakeholder trust while reducing costs associated with breaches and disruptions.

Identifying Threats and Vulnerabilities

In cybersecurity, the identification of threats and vulnerabilities is foundational to robust risk management. This process enables organizations to uncover the specific risks they face, prioritize mitigation efforts, and protect critical assets. Without a systematic approach to identifying threats and vulnerabilities, organizations may waste resources on low-priority risks while leaving critical areas exposed to potential exploitation.

Understanding Threats and Vulnerabilities

Threats

Threats refer to circumstances, events, or actors capable of exploiting vulnerabilities to compromise organizational assets. Threats can be categorized as intentional, such as cyberattacks by hackers, or unintentional, like human errors or natural disasters. These threats may disrupt operations, compromise sensitive data, or damage an organization's reputation.

Vulnerabilities

Vulnerabilities are weaknesses in systems, applications, or processes that can be exploited by threats. Examples include outdated software, misconfigured servers, weak access controls, or unencrypted data. Identifying vulnerabilities is crucial for implementing effective security measures.

Table 5-2 provides main threats, vulnerabilities, and corrective actions.

Table 5-2. Main threats, vulnerabilities, and corrective actions

Threat Category	Threat Description	Vulnerabilities	Possible Corrective Actions
Cyberattacks	Malicious activities like ransomware, phishing, and DDoS	- Weak authentication mechanisms (e.g., use of weak or reused passwords and lack of multi-factor authentication).	- Enforce MFA to add an extra layer of security for user access.
		- Unpatched software and outdated systems with known vulnerabilities that attackers can exploit.	- Apply regular security patches and updates to eliminate known vulnerabilities.
		- Misconfigured security controls (e.g., overly permissive firewall rules and exposed remote desktop access).	- Conduct frequent security audits and penetration testing to identify and remediate misconfigurations.
		- Insecure endpoints (e.g., unprotected user devices and lack of endpoint detection and response tools).	- Deploy endpoint protection solutions (e.g., EDR, antivirus, and firewalls) to secure user devices.

(continued)

Table 5-2. (*continued*)

Threat Category	Threat Description	Vulnerabilities	Possible Corrective Actions
Insider Threats	Employees or contractors misusing access, intentionally or unintentionally	- Excessive user permissions that grant employees access to unnecessary sensitive data.	- Implement the PoLP to restrict access based on job roles.
		- Lack of user activity monitoring leading to undetected unauthorized actions.	- Deploy UBAs to detect anomalies and potential insider threats.
		- Weak access controls such as shared or default credentials.	- Use PAM solutions to secure and monitor privileged accounts.
Supply Chain Attacks	Compromise through third-party vendors or suppliers	- Lack of vendor security assessment leading to collaboration with insecure suppliers.	- Perform regular third-party risk assessments to evaluate vendor security practices.
		- Unsecured API integrations allowing unauthorized data access.	- Secure API integrations with strong authentication, encryption, and monitoring.
		- No visibility into third-party security controls, making it difficult to assess risk exposure.	- Require vendors to adhere to cybersecurity standards (e.g., ISO 27001 and NIST CSF).
		- Weak third-party authentication mechanisms (e.g., no MFA for vendor access).	- Enforce strict access controls for third-party access, including MFA and time-restricted credentials.

(*continued*)

Table 5-2. (*continued*)

Threat Category	Threat Description	Vulnerabilities	Possible Corrective Actions
Data Breaches	Unauthorized access leading to exposure of sensitive data	- Unencrypted sensitive data, making it easy for attackers to steal or manipulate.	- Encrypt sensitive data at rest and in transit to prevent unauthorized access.
		- Misconfigured databases and cloud storage exposing confidential records.	- Conduct regular security configuration reviews for databases and cloud storage.
		- Weak access control policies allowing unauthorized users to view sensitive files.	- Apply strict access controls (e.g., role-based access control and data classification policies).
		- Lack of real-time monitoring and alerting, failing to detect breaches in time.	- Implement real-time threat detection tools (e.g., SIEM and intrusion detection systems).
Social Engineering	Deception techniques like phishing, pretexting, or baiting	- Lack of employee awareness making staff vulnerable to phishing and deception.	- Conduct regular phishing simulations and security awareness training for employees.
		- No email security filters leading to malicious links and attachments reaching users.	- Deploy advanced email security solutions (e.g., spam filters and anti-phishing protection).
		- Weak verification procedures allowing attackers to impersonate trusted individuals.	- Enforce strict identity verification protocols for sensitive transactions and requests.
		- Over-reliance on trust-based authentication.	- Implement Zero Trust policies requiring verification at every access point.

(*continued*)

Table 5-2. (*continued*)

Threat Category	Threat Description	Vulnerabilities	Possible Corrective Actions
Denial of Service (DoS/DDoS)	Overloading systems to cause service disruptions	- Unprotected network infrastructure making it easy for attackers to overwhelm systems.	- Deploy DDoS protection solutions such as cloud-based mitigation services (e.g., Cloudflare and AWS Shield).
		- Lack of traffic filtering and rate limiting allowing excessive requests to crash servers.	- Implement traffic filtering and rate limiting to control incoming requests.
		- Insecure APIs and applications vulnerable to automated bot attacks.	- Secure APIs and applications with authentication and anomaly detection.
		- No DDoS mitigation solutions in place to absorb and neutralize attack traffic.	- Use Content Delivery Networks (CDNs) to distribute traffic and minimize impact.

(*continued*)

Table 5-2. (*continued*)

Threat Category	Threat Description	Vulnerabilities	Possible Corrective Actions
Zero-Day Exploits	Attacks targeting unknown vulnerabilities before patches are available.	- Delayed patching and software updates leading to prolonged risk exposure.	- Deploy automated patch management systems to quickly address vulnerabilities.
		- Lack of intrusion detection and prevention systems (IDPS) for zero-day threats.	- Use threat intelligence feeds to track emerging zero-day exploits.
		- Insufficient threat intelligence integration to detect new exploits.	- Implement an Intrusion Detection/Prevention System (IDPS) for real-time monitoring.
		- Limited use of application whitelisting, allowing untrusted software execution.	- Apply application whitelisting to prevent execution of unknown programs.
Cloud Security Risks	Misconfigurations, insecure APIs, and lack of visibility in cloud environments	- Poor access controls leading to unauthorized data access.	- Enable CSPM to detect misconfigurations.
		- Insufficient logging and monitoring making incident response harder.	- Log and monitor all cloud activities to detect anomalies.
		- Unsecured cloud storage buckets exposing sensitive information.	- Secure cloud storage with proper encryption and access restrictions.

(*continued*)

Table 5-2. (*continued*)

Threat Category	Threat Description	Vulnerabilities	Possible Corrective Actions
Human Error	Accidental data leaks, misconfigurations, weak security practices	- Lack of security awareness training increasing mistakes.	- Conduct regular cybersecurity training to reduce human errors.
		- Poor policy enforcement leading to security gaps.	- Enforce strong security policies with automated compliance checks.
		- Weak change management processes causing misconfigurations.	- Implement change management processes for IT configurations.
		- Unsecured personal devices increasing risks.	- Adopt Mobile Device Management (MDM) solutions to secure personal devices.

The Importance of Identifying Threats and Vulnerabilities

Identifying threats and vulnerabilities is a proactive step that lays the foundation for a comprehensive cybersecurity strategy. Its benefits include

- *Proactive Risk Management*: Early identification allows organizations to address potential risks before they materialize into incidents, reducing the likelihood of costly breaches.

- *Efficient Resource Allocation*: By focusing on high-risk areas, organizations can optimize their cybersecurity budgets and efforts for maximum impact.

- *Regulatory Compliance*: Frameworks such as GDPR, HIPAA, and ISO 27001 mandate regular assessments of threats and vulnerabilities, ensuring compliance and avoiding penalties.

- *Enhanced Decision-Making*: Identifying risks provides actionable insights that guide the development of effective security policies and controls.

Steps to Identify Threats and Vulnerabilities

Identifying threats and vulnerabilities is a structured process that ensures organizations proactively mitigate cybersecurity risks. Figure 5-2 presents the process of identifying threats and vulnerabilities.

CHAPTER 5 INTRODUCTION TO CYBER RISK MANAGEMENT

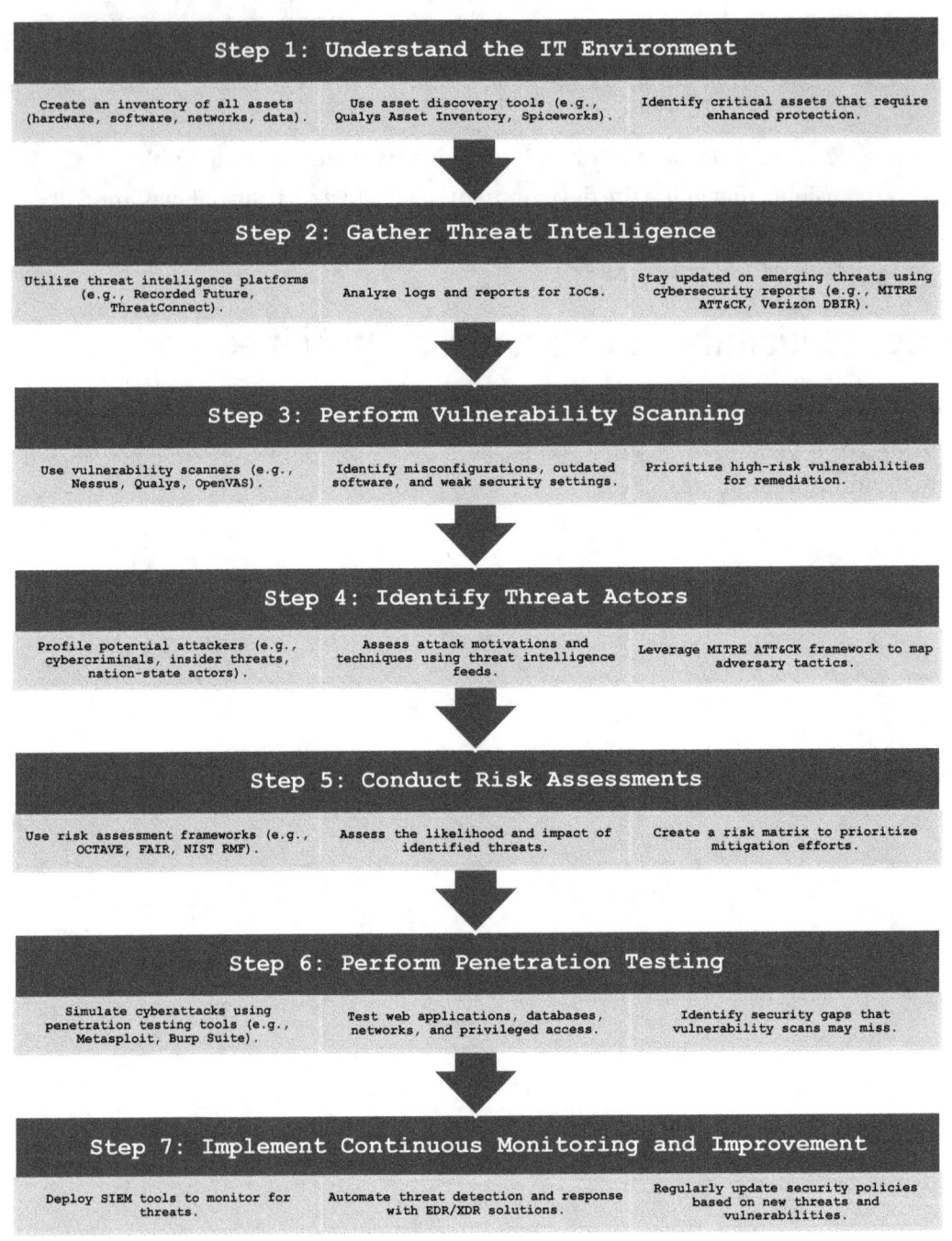

Figure 5-2. *Continuous improvement of cyber risk management*

Understand the Environment

The foundation of an effective threat and vulnerability identification process begins with a comprehensive understanding of the organization's IT environment. This involves mapping out all digital assets, including hardware, software, network infrastructure, cloud services, and data repositories.

Without a clear picture of the IT ecosystem, it becomes nearly impossible to identify potential threats and vulnerabilities. Organizations should maintain an up-to-date asset inventory using automated tools like Qualys Asset Inventory or Spiceworks, ensuring that no critical component is overlooked. Special attention should be given to shadow IT, unauthorized applications, and devices that employees may use, which can introduce security risks.

Additionally, organizations should document data flows, detailing how sensitive information moves between systems, both internally and externally. This step ensures that all potential attack surfaces are identified, providing a strong foundation for the next phases of risk assessment.

Gather Threat Intelligence

Once the IT environment is mapped, the next step is to gather and analyze threat intelligence to stay ahead of emerging cybersecurity risks.

Threat intelligence provides insights into the tactics, techniques, and procedures (TTPs) used by attackers, allowing organizations to anticipate potential threats before they become incidents. Companies can leverage TIPs such as Recorded Future, ThreatConnect, or IBM X-Force Exchange to obtain real-time information about cyber threats. Internally, organizations should analyze security logs, network traffic, and past incidents to identify trends and Indicators of Compromise (IoCs).

Additionally, utilizing frameworks like MITRE Adversarial Tactics, Techniques, and Common Knowledge (ATT&CK) can help security teams understand attacker behaviors and threat actor motivations. Threat intelligence should be continuously updated to ensure that security teams are informed about the latest vulnerabilities and attack trends.

CHAPTER 5   INTRODUCTION TO CYBER RISK MANAGEMENT

Perform Vulnerability Scanning

After gathering intelligence, organizations must conduct regular vulnerability scans to identify security weaknesses across their IT environment. Vulnerabilities can exist in various forms, including unpatched software, weak configurations, outdated operating systems, and insecure network protocols. Using automated vulnerability scanning tools such as Nessus, Qualys Vulnerability Management, OpenVAS, or Rapid7 InsightVM, organizations can systematically detect and assess security gaps in their infrastructure. Scans should be performed on a scheduled basis as well as after significant IT changes, such as new software deployments or system updates.

To ensure effective vulnerability management, organizations should prioritize findings based on severity, exploitability, and potential impact. For example, Common Vulnerability Scoring System (CVSS) ratings can help determine which vulnerabilities pose the highest risk.

Additionally, integrating automated patch management solutions can streamline remediation efforts, reducing the exposure to cyber threats. However, vulnerability scans alone are not sufficient; they must be complemented with manual security reviews to reduce false positives and uncover complex attack vectors.

Identify Threat Actors

Understanding potential adversaries is critical to tailoring security measures and defense strategies. Threat actors vary in motivation, capabilities, and targets, making it essential to categorize them and analyze their attack patterns. Common threat actors include

- *Cybercriminals*: Motivated by financial gain, they use tactics such as ransomware, phishing, and credential theft to extort victims.

- *Insider Threats*: Employees or contractors who misuse their access, either maliciously (e.g., data theft) or unintentionally (e.g., accidental misconfigurations).

- *Hacktivists*: Attackers who target organizations based on ideological or political beliefs, often employing DDoS attacks or data leaks.

- *Nation-State Actors*: Highly sophisticated groups sponsored by governments, aiming to steal sensitive data, disrupt operations, or conduct cyber espionage.

- *Script Kiddies*: Inexperienced attackers using pre-built hacking tools to exploit vulnerabilities without deep technical knowledge.

Organizations should leverage resources such as the MITRE ATT&CK framework and reports like CrowdStrike's Global Threat Report to gain insights into threat actor behaviors, common attack vectors, and targeted industries. Additionally, implementing User and Entity Behavior Analytics (UEBA) solutions can help detect anomalous activities linked to insider threats and Advanced Persistent Threats (APTs).

Conduct Risk Assessments

Once threats and vulnerabilities have been identified, the next step is to conduct a formal risk assessment to quantify and prioritize risks based on their potential impact and likelihood. This step ensures that organizations allocate resources effectively to address the most critical security gaps.

Organizations can use risk assessment frameworks such as

- *OCTAVE*: A structured methodology for evaluating cybersecurity risks based on business impact.

- *FAIR*: A quantitative approach that measures risk in financial terms, helping organizations understand the potential cost of cyber threats.

- *NIST RMF*: A widely adopted framework that integrates security risk management with compliance requirements.

A typical risk assessment process involves

- Identifying critical assets and their associated threats and vulnerabilities.

- Assessing the likelihood of an attack occurring based on historical data and threat intelligence.

- Evaluating the potential impact of successful exploitation, considering financial, reputational, and operational damage.

- Prioritizing risks and recommending appropriate mitigation strategies, such as patching vulnerabilities, enforcing security policies, or investing in advanced threat detection tools.

Risk assessments should be conducted regularly and updated frequently to adapt to evolving threats and changes in the organization's IT landscape.

Engage in Penetration Testing

While vulnerability scanning identifies known weaknesses, penetration testing takes security assessment a step further by simulating real-world cyberattacks to uncover hidden vulnerabilities. Penetration testing involves ethical hackers attempting to exploit weaknesses in an organization's systems, applications, and networks to determine the effectiveness of existing security controls.

There are three main types of penetration testing:

- *Black Box Testing*: The tester has no prior knowledge of the system, simulating an external attack.

- *White Box Testing*: The tester has full access to system architecture and internal information, allowing for a thorough security review.

- *Gray Box Testing*: A combination of both, where the tester has partial knowledge of the system to simulate an insider attack.

Penetration testing is typically conducted in the following phases:

- *Planning and Reconnaissance*: Gathering information about the target, including domain names, IP addresses, and system configurations.

- *Scanning and Exploitation*: Identifying vulnerabilities and attempting to exploit them using tools like Metasploit, Burp Suite, or Cobalt Strike.

- *Post-exploitation Analysis*: Determining the potential impact of successful attacks, such as data theft or system compromise.

- *Reporting and Remediation*: Documenting findings, prioritizing vulnerabilities, and recommending corrective actions.

Continuous Monitoring and Improvement

Cyber threats are constantly evolving, requiring organizations to adopt continuous monitoring to detect and respond to risks in real time.

Implementing SIEM systems enables centralized log analysis and threat correlation, improving detection capabilities. Automated tools like EDR and Extended Detection and Response (XDR) enhance response times to potential threats.

Additionally, organizations should regularly update security policies based on new threat intelligence insights. Cybersecurity awareness training ensures employees remain vigilant against emerging attack techniques. Periodic security audits, compliance reviews, and red team exercises further reinforce an organization's ability to identify and mitigate threats effectively. By continuously refining security strategies, organizations can stay ahead of adversaries and maintain a resilient cybersecurity posture.

Tools and Techniques for Identifying Threats and Vulnerabilities

- *Vulnerability Scanners*: Solutions like Tenable Nessus and Rapid7 InsightVM scan for weaknesses across systems and networks.

- *TIPs*: Platforms such as Anomali and IBM X-Force Exchange offer actionable insights into emerging threats.

- *Network Monitoring Tools*: Tools like Wireshark and SolarWinds Network Performance Monitor detect abnormal network activities that may indicate a threat.

- *Configuration Management Tools*: Tools like Chef or Puppet help ensure systems are configured securely, reducing the likelihood of vulnerabilities.

Challenges in Identifying Threats and Vulnerabilities

One of the most significant challenges in identifying threats and vulnerabilities is the rapidly evolving nature of cyber threats. Attackers continually develop new techniques, exploit novel vulnerabilities, and leverage emerging technologies to bypass existing defenses. Organizations must remain vigilant and update their threat identification processes to keep pace. Additionally, the complexity of modern IT environments, which often include hybrid infrastructures combining on-premises and cloud systems, adds another layer of difficulty. These environments can obscure visibility, making it harder to identify all assets and potential weaknesses.

Automated tools, while essential, often generate false positives, which can overwhelm security teams and divert attention from critical issues. This necessitates manual reviews, which can be time-consuming and resource intensive. Small and medium-sized enterprises (SMEs) face the added challenge of limited resources, both in terms of skilled personnel and budget for advanced tools, hindering their ability to perform thorough threat and vulnerability assessments. Despite these challenges, proactive strategies and collaboration can help organizations overcome these obstacles effectively.

The following are some of the main challenges in identifying threats and vulnerabilities:

- *Evolving Threat Landscape*: Cyber threats are constantly evolving, requiring organizations to stay vigilant and adaptive.

- *Complex IT Environments*: Hybrid environments, combining on-premises and cloud infrastructure, complicate visibility and monitoring efforts.

- *False Positives*: Automated tools often generate false positives, necessitating manual review to validate findings.

- *Resource Constraints*: Smaller organizations may lack the expertise or resources to perform comprehensive assessments.

Best Practices for Success

To successfully identify threats and vulnerabilities, organizations should adopt a proactive and structured approach. Regular assessments are essential to keep up with emerging risks and ensure that existing vulnerabilities are addressed promptly. Automated tools can streamline the process, but they must be complemented by skilled personnel who can analyze findings and make informed decisions. Collaboration with external experts or Managed Security Service Providers (MSSPs) can provide valuable insights and resources, especially for SMEs that lack in-house expertise.

Comprehensive documentation is another critical best practice. Maintaining detailed records of identified threats and vulnerabilities not only aids in compliance with regulatory requirements but also serves as a valuable reference for future audits and risk management initiatives. Additionally, fostering a culture of security awareness across the organization ensures that all employees contribute to identifying and mitigating risks, creating a more resilient security posture.

Benefits of Identifying Threats and Vulnerabilities

Identifying threats and vulnerabilities offers numerous benefits, starting with reduced risk exposure. By addressing risks early, organizations can significantly lower the likelihood of successful attacks, thereby protecting their critical assets and reputation. This proactive approach also enhances compliance with regulatory standards, helping organizations avoid penalties and demonstrate due diligence to stakeholders.

Another key benefit is increased trust. Customers, partners, and regulators are more likely to engage with organizations that prioritize security and take visible steps to safeguard their data. Furthermore, identifying threats and vulnerabilities strengthens an organization's overall resilience. By understanding and addressing risks, organizations can maintain business continuity even in the face of attempted attacks. This resilience not only protects operations but also positions the organization as a leader in cybersecurity best practices.

To summarize, the following are some of the key benefits:

- *Reduced Risk Exposure*: Early detection minimizes the chances of successful attacks.

- *Improved Compliance*: Ensures alignment with regulatory requirements and standards.

- *Increased Trust*: Demonstrates a commitment to protecting data, fostering trust with customers and stakeholders.

- *Enhanced Resilience*: Strengthens the organization's ability to withstand and recover from cyberattacks.

CHAPTER 5   INTRODUCTION TO CYBER RISK MANAGEMENT

Key Takeaways

Identifying threats and vulnerabilities is a foundational, continuous, and strategic process in cybersecurity. It ensures risks are addressed proactively, leverages advanced tools and methods for better accuracy, and fosters trust through compliance and resilience. By making this process a priority, organizations safeguard their digital ecosystem and maintain a competitive edge in the face of evolving cyber threats.

In this section, we covered the following points:

- Threats are potential circumstances or actors capable of exploiting weaknesses, while vulnerabilities are the weaknesses themselves in systems, applications, or processes.

- Early identification of threats and vulnerabilities reduces the likelihood of costly incidents and enhances the overall security posture.

- Identifying and prioritizing high-risk areas ensures optimal use of resources and focuses efforts where they are most needed.

- Regular threat and vulnerability assessments align with frameworks like GDPR, HIPAA, ISO 27001, etc., ensuring compliance and avoiding penalties.

- Steps include understanding the IT environment, gathering threat intelligence, conducting vulnerability scans, and performing penetration tests to uncover weaknesses.

- Evolving threats, complex IT environments, false positives from automated tools, and limited resources for SMEs present ongoing challenges.

- Regular assessments, leveraging automated tools, collaboration with experts, and fostering a culture of security awareness strengthen threat identification efforts.

Risk Scoring and Prioritization

In the ever-evolving landscape of cybersecurity, where threats emerge daily and resources are finite, not all risks can be addressed simultaneously. Risk scoring and prioritization form the foundation of efficient and effective cybersecurity strategies, enabling organizations to focus on the most critical threats and minimize potential damage. These processes are essential for achieving resilience, optimizing resource allocation, and ensuring compliance with regulatory standards.

The Fundamentals of Risk Scoring

Risk scoring is the process of assigning a quantifiable value to risks based on their likelihood and impact. This method enables organizations to move beyond qualitative risk assessments, offering a standardized and objective approach to evaluate and compare risks. By translating qualitative risk data into objective, measurable scores, organizations can

- *Quantify Risks Consistently*: Establish a standardized approach to risk evaluation, ensuring uniformity across teams and systems.

- *Compare Risks Objectively*: Create a basis for ranking and prioritization, aiding in decision-making and resource allocation.

- *Focus on High-Priority Issues*: Allocate resources effectively to mitigate the most critical risks, ensuring optimal security outcomes.

Key Components of Risk Scoring

Likelihood

Likelihood represents the probability of a threat being successfully executed against an organization's systems, data, or operations. It is influenced by multiple factors, including the nature of the threat, existing vulnerabilities, and the effectiveness of current security controls. Organizations should assess likelihood based on

- *Historical Incident Data*: Reviewing past cybersecurity incidents within the organization and across the industry can provide insights into how frequently similar threats have been exploited.

- *Threat Intelligence Feeds*: Leveraging real-time intelligence from platforms such as IBM X-Force Exchange, FireEye Helix, and CrowdStrike Falcon enables organizations to track emerging threats and assess their probability of occurrence.

- *Exploitability of Vulnerabilities*: Evaluating how easily an attacker can exploit a vulnerability using publicly available exploit kits, proof-of-concept (PoC) code, or automated attack tools. The existence of an exploit in the wild significantly increases the likelihood.

- *Attack Surface Exposure*: Determining how exposed an organization is to a particular threat based on factors such as the number of publicly accessible services, remote access mechanisms, and reliance on third-party integrations.

- *Security Control Effectiveness*: Analyzing the robustness of existing security measures, such as firewalls, IDS, MFA, and endpoint protection solutions. Weak or misconfigured controls increase the likelihood of an attack succeeding.

Likelihood is often categorized into scales, such as

- *Rare (1)*: Very low probability of occurrence, requiring sophisticated adversaries or unusual circumstances.

- *Unlikely (2)*: Possible but infrequent, typically requiring specific conditions to be met.

- *Possible (3)*: Could occur under normal circumstances but not frequently.

- *Likely (4)*: Expected to happen based on past trends and industry-wide occurrences.

- *Certain (5)*: Inevitable or already occurring, requiring immediate attention.

Impact

"Impact" refers to the potential consequences of a successful cyberattack or security breach. It extends beyond immediate technical damage and includes financial, operational, legal, and reputational repercussions. Organizations must analyze both direct and indirect impacts to fully understand the severity of a given risk. Key considerations include

- *Financial Losses*: A cyber incident can lead to direct costs such as ransom payments, data recovery expenses, regulatory fines, and legal fees. Indirect financial losses include revenue decline due to customer attrition and decreased market confidence.

- *Operational Disruptions*: Attacks like ransomware or distributed denial-of-service (DDoS) can halt critical business operations, causing downtime that leads to lost productivity, supply chain delays, and missed service-level agreements (SLAs).

- *Reputational Damage*: Customer trust is difficult to rebuild after a security breach. Data leaks, fraud, or operational failures can damage a company's reputation, leading to customer churn, negative media coverage, and loss of business partnerships.

- *Regulatory and Legal Consequences*: Non-compliance with standards such as GDPR, HIPAA, or PCI-DSS can result in significant penalties. A breach involving personal data may trigger lawsuits, government investigations, and mandatory disclosure requirements.

- *Intellectual Property Theft*: APTs often target proprietary research, trade secrets, or confidential designs, which can severely impact competitiveness and long-term business strategy.

- *National Security and Safety Risks*: For critical infrastructure organizations, cyber threats pose risks to public safety and national security. Attacks on power grids, healthcare systems, or transportation networks can have life-threatening consequences.

Impact is usually rated using a standardized scale, such as

- *Negligible (1)*: Minimal or no noticeable effect on operations or finances.
- *Minor (2)*: Some inconvenience but no major damage; operations recover quickly.
- *Moderate (3)*: Noticeable impact on operations, finances, or compliance, but manageable.
- *Severe (4)*: Significant business disruption, financial loss, regulatory penalties, or reputational harm.
- *Catastrophic (5)*: Irreversible damage, long-term financial losses, severe regulatory action, or business failure.

Assessing impact holistically ensures that organizations prioritize risks that could cause the most harm, allowing them to allocate resources efficiently and implement mitigation strategies accordingly.

Scoring Formula

Risk scoring provides a structured and quantifiable approach to evaluating cybersecurity risks by combining likelihood and impact into a single risk score. This helps organizations prioritize threats effectively and allocate resources accordingly.

The most common method is

$$Risk\ Score = Likelihood \times Impact$$

Likelihood and impact are often rated on scales such as 1–5 or classified as low, medium, high, or critical. The resulting score provides a clear picture of risk severity, enabling organizations to make data-driven decisions. Usually, the following scales correspond to the criticality, as presented in Table 5-3.

CHAPTER 5　INTRODUCTION TO CYBER RISK MANAGEMENT

Table 5-3. Risk level categorization

Risk Score Range	Risk Level	Recommended Action
1-4	Low	Accept or monitor risk
5-9	Moderate	Implement mitigation where feasible
10-15	High	Prioritize remediation efforts
16-25	Critical	Immediate action required

Example of Risk Score Calculation:

Likelihood	Impact	Risk Score	Risk Level
1 (Rare)	3 (Moderate)	3	Low
4 (Likely)	5 (Catastrophic)	20	Critical
3 (Possible)	4 (Severe)	12	High

The risk score is used to prioritize risks based on severity, ensuring that high-risk threats receive immediate attention.

Advanced Risk Scoring Models

Organizations often employ enhanced risk assessment methodologies that consider multiple variables beyond likelihood and impact. These models provide a more accurate and context-driven evaluation of cybersecurity risks.

1. Common Vulnerability Scoring System (CVSS)

The CVSS is a widely adopted framework that evaluates vulnerabilities based on multiple metrics, providing a numerical score (0-10) to prioritize threats.

CVSS Components:

- *Base Score*: Reflects the fundamental characteristics of a vulnerability that remain constant over time:
  - *Exploitability Metrics*: How easy it is for an attacker to exploit a vulnerability (e.g., attack vector, complexity, and required privileges).

CHAPTER 5   INTRODUCTION TO CYBER RISK MANAGEMENT

- *Impact Metrics*: The effect on system confidentiality, integrity, and availability.

- *Temporal Score*: Adjusts the Base Score based on real-world conditions, such as

    - *Exploit Code Maturity*: Whether the vulnerability is actively being exploited.

    - *Remediation Level*: Availability of patches or mitigations.

    - *Confidence Level*: The reliability of the reported vulnerability details.

- *Environmental Score*: Adjusts the score based on the organization's specific context, considering

    - *Security Controls*: Existing protections that may reduce risk.

    - *Asset Criticality*: How essential the affected system is to business operations.

Table 5-4 presents the CVSS score.

Table 5-4. CVSS scoring scale

CVSS Score	Severity Level
0.0 - 3.9	Low
4.0 - 6.9	Medium
7.0 - 8.9	High
9.0 - 10.0	Critical

2. FAIR Model (Factor Analysis of Information Risk)

Unlike CVSS, the FAIR model focuses on quantifying risk in financial terms, helping organizations understand the monetary impact of cybersecurity threats.

Key FAIR Risk Factors:

- *Threat Event Frequency (TEF)*: How often a threat is expected to occur.

- *Vulnerability (VULN)*: The probability that the attack will succeed.
- *Loss Magnitude (LM)*: The financial impact if the event occurs.
- *Control Strength (CS)*: How effective security controls are in reducing risk.

FAIR Risk Calculation:

$$Annualized\ Loss\ Expectancy\ (ALE) = TEF \times LM$$

By using FAIR, security teams can

- Justify security budgets with financial data.
- Make cost-benefit decisions on risk mitigation.
- Compare cybersecurity risks with other business risks (e.g., financial fraud).

3. Heat Map Risk Assessment

A heat map is a visual representation of risk severity based on likelihood and impact. Organizations use color-coded matrices to quickly identify and prioritize risks.

4. NIST Risk Scoring Framework

The NIST CSF provides a structured methodology for risk assessment and mitigation. *NIST Risk Scoring Steps*:

- *Identify Assets and Threats*: Inventory critical systems and known cyber threats.
- *Assess Likelihood and Impact*: Determine the probability and consequences of an attack.
- *Calculate Residual Risk*: Measure risk after applying security controls.
- *Prioritize Risks*: Rank based on severity and business impact.
- *Mitigate and Monitor*: Apply controls and continuously reassess.

5. Choosing the Right Risk Scoring Model

By adopting advanced risk scoring methodologies, organizations can strengthen cybersecurity defenses, justify security investments, and ensure compliance with industry standards.

- Risk scoring is essential for prioritizing threats and managing cybersecurity efficiently.

- Advanced models (CVSS, FAIR, Heat Maps, and NIST) provide deeper insights into risk severity.

- Combining quantitative and qualitative risk assessment ensures a well-rounded security strategy.

- Automating risk assessments with AI-driven tools enhances accuracy and efficiency.

Each model has strengths, and organizations often combine multiple frameworks for a more comprehensive risk assessment approach. Table 5-5 presents the best use case of different scoring models.

Table 5-5. Choosing the right risk scoring model

Model	Best Use Case
CVSS	Assessing software vulnerabilities
FAIR	Financial quantification of cyber risk
Heat Maps	Quick visual prioritization of risks
NIST CSF	Comprehensive organizational risk management

The Process of Risk Prioritization

Once risks are scored, they must be prioritized to address the most pressing threats first. Effective prioritization ensures that critical and high-severity risks receive immediate attention, while medium- and low-severity risks are addressed as resources permit. This systematic approach often includes

- *High Priority*: Risks requiring immediate action, such as zero-day vulnerabilities or active exploitation threats. Addressing these promptly prevents catastrophic outcomes.

- *Medium Priority*: Risks that need mitigation within a reasonable timeframe to prevent escalation. These often involve known vulnerabilities with moderate exploit potential.

- *Low Priority*: Risks that can be monitored periodically and addressed as needed, typically involving legacy systems or non-critical assets.

Steps in Risk Scoring and Prioritization

The Risk Scoring and Prioritization Workflow provides a structured approach to identifying, assessing, and addressing cybersecurity risks based on their likelihood and impact. It begins with risk identification, using automated tools and threat intelligence to detect vulnerabilities. Each risk is then evaluated and scored using standardized models like CVSS or FAIR, ensuring objective quantification. Based on the risk score, prioritization ensures that critical threats are addressed first, followed by mitigation strategies such as patching, security controls, or risk transfer. Finally, continuous monitoring and review enable organizations to adapt to evolving threats, ensuring a proactive and resilient security posture. Figure 5-3 presents a high-level workflow process for risk scoring and prioritization.

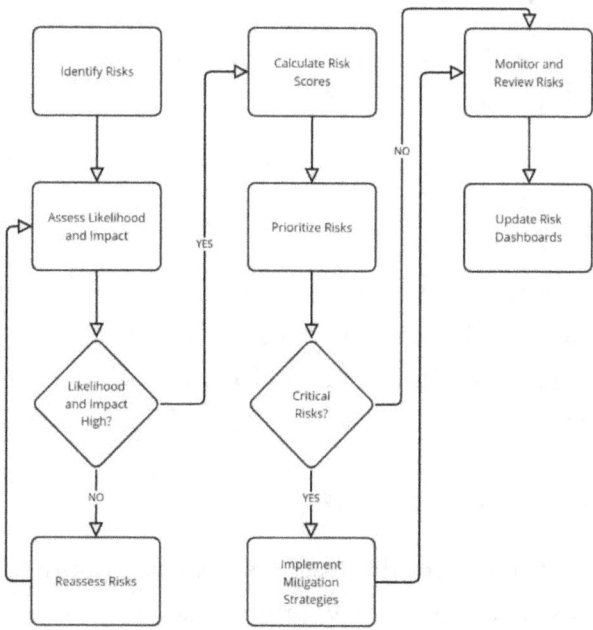

Figure 5-3. *Workflow process for risk scoring and prioritization*

Identify Risks

The process begins with a comprehensive inventory of threats and vulnerabilities. Tools like Qualys, Nessus, and TIPs are invaluable for identifying risks across IT assets, including hardware, software, and networks. This foundational step ensures no critical asset or threat is overlooked.

Assess Likelihood and Impact

Each identified risk is evaluated for its likelihood and potential impact. This step often involves

- Analyzing historical data on similar incidents to gauge likelihood.
- Examining the configuration and security posture of affected systems to identify potential exploit paths.
- Assessing the business and operational consequences of exploitation, including regulatory fines, customer attrition, and operational downtime.

Calculate Risk Scores

Using frameworks like the CVSS or FAIR, risks are assigned numerical scores that reflect their severity. These scores provide a standardized baseline for comparison and prioritization.

Prioritize Risks

Risk scores are used to rank threats, with the highest scores representing the most urgent issues. Visualization tools such as heat maps can aid this process by highlighting critical risk areas. These visual aids facilitate communication between technical and non-technical stakeholders.

Implement Mitigation Strategies

Critical and high-priority risks are addressed first, using appropriate controls, patches, or mitigation strategies. Medium- and low-priority risks are tackled as resources allow, ensuring a balanced approach that optimizes both security and efficiency.

Tools and Technologies for Risk Scoring

Modern tools and platforms streamline the risk scoring and prioritization process, offering automation, integration, and real-time insights. These tools not only enhance accuracy but also reduce the manual effort required, allowing security teams to focus on strategic initiatives.

- *Risk Assessment Platforms*:
- *Archer*: Automates risk assessments and scoring, integrating with existing workflows for seamless operations.
- *RiskLens*: Uses the FAIR model to provide financial quantification of risks, enabling organizations to understand the monetary impact of potential threats.

- *Heat Map Tools*:
- Platforms like Microsoft Power BI or Tableau help visualize risk levels for clear communication. These tools enable stakeholders to quickly identify and prioritize high-risk areas.

- *TIPs*:
- Solutions such as IBM X-Force Exchange provide contextual data on emerging threats, enhancing the accuracy of risk assessments by incorporating real-time intelligence.

Challenges in Risk Scoring and Prioritization

Subjectivity in Scoring

Inconsistent evaluations across teams can lead to discrepancies in risk assessments. This is especially problematic when qualitative judgments influence likelihood or impact ratings, as biases can skew results and undermine decision-making.

Solution:

- *Standardized Scoring*: Adopt consistent methodologies like CVSS or FAIR across all teams, ensuring uniform evaluations.

Dynamic Threat Landscape

The fast-changing nature of cyber threats demands continuous updates to risk scores, which can strain resources. Threat actors frequently adapt their tactics, necessitating real-time adjustments to risk assessments.

Solution:

- *Automation*: Leverage platforms that integrate real-time threat intelligence and automate risk scoring, reducing manual effort.

Limited Visibility

Organizations operating in complex IT environments or lacking comprehensive asset inventories may overlook critical risks. This challenge is compounded by the proliferation of shadow IT and third-party integrations.

Solution:

- *Enhanced Visibility*: Utilize asset discovery tools to maintain an up-to-date inventory, ensuring all assets are accounted for.

Best Practices for Effective Risk Scoring

- *Use Established Frameworks*: Frameworks like FAIR and CVSS provide standardized approaches to scoring and prioritization, ensuring consistency and reliability.

- *Adopt a Holistic Perspective*: Involve IT, operations, and compliance teams to ensure all perspectives are considered. This collaborative approach enhances the comprehensiveness of risk assessments.

- *Update Regularly*: Reassess risks periodically to account for changes in the threat landscape. Regular updates ensure that evolving risks are promptly addressed.

- *Leverage Automation*: Use AI-driven tools to enhance the speed and accuracy of risk assessments, freeing up resources for strategic initiatives.

Benefits of Risk Scoring and Prioritization

Effective risk scoring and prioritization offer numerous advantages, including

- *Efficient Resource Allocation*: Ensures that limited resources are focused on the most critical risks, maximizing their impact and enhancing security outcomes.

- *Improved Decision-Making*: Provides data-driven insights to guide security investments and prioritize remediation efforts, aligning actions with organizational goals.

- *Enhanced Regulatory Compliance*: Aligns with standards and frameworks like ISO 27001, PCI-DSS, and NIST, which mandate risk assessments and mitigation plans. Compliance reduces legal and financial liabilities.

- *Proactive Risk Management*: Enables organizations to address high-risk areas early, preventing incidents before they occur and minimizing potential damage.

Preparing for the Future of Risk Management

As cyber threats evolve, so too must risk scoring and prioritization strategies. Organizations should

- *Invest in Advanced Tools*: Explore platforms with predictive analytics and AI capabilities for enhanced risk analysis. These tools provide foresight into potential risks, enabling proactive measures.

- *Foster a Culture of Security*: Engage employees at all levels in understanding and addressing risks. Building awareness and accountability ensures that security becomes a shared responsibility.

- *Collaborate with Stakeholders*: Work closely with partners, regulators, and industry peers to share insights and strategies. Collaboration fosters a unified approach to tackling cyber threats.

- *Emphasize Continuous Improvement*: Regularly update methodologies and tools to stay ahead of emerging threats. Continuous learning and adaptation are critical for long-term resilience.

CHAPTER 5 INTRODUCTION TO CYBER RISK MANAGEMENT

Key Takeaways

Risk scoring and prioritization are fundamental to modern cybersecurity strategies. They provide a structured, objective framework to identify and address risks effectively. By integrating standardized tools, leveraging advanced technologies, and maintaining a proactive mindset, organizations can enhance their defenses, ensure compliance, and remain resilient in the face of evolving cyber threats.

In this section, we covered the following points:

- Risk scoring and prioritization are critical for effective cybersecurity management, helping organizations focus on the most critical threats while optimizing resource allocation.

- Risk scoring involves quantifying risks based on likelihood and impact, using standardized frameworks like CVSS or FAIR to ensure consistency and reliability.

- The risk prioritization process includes identifying risks, assessing their likelihood and impact, calculating scores, ranking threats, and implementing mitigation strategies.

- Challenges in risk scoring include subjectivity in evaluations, the dynamic nature of cyber threats, and limited visibility of assets and vulnerabilities.

- Leveraging tools like risk assessment platforms, heat maps, and threat intelligence systems enhances accuracy, streamlines processes, and enables real-time updates.

- Adopting best practices such as standardizing methodologies, involving cross-functional teams, leveraging automation, and updating risk assessments regularly improves effectiveness.

- The benefits of risk scoring and prioritization include efficient resource allocation, better decision-making, enhanced regulatory compliance, and proactive risk management.

- Preparing for future challenges requires investing in advanced tools, fostering a culture of security, collaborating with stakeholders, and continuously improving risk management strategies.

How to Perform a Risk Assessment

In the sphere of cybersecurity, one of the most vital practices is performing a thorough risk assessment. This process not only identifies and addresses vulnerabilities but also enables organizations to allocate resources effectively, safeguard critical assets, and ensure regulatory compliance. As cyber threats evolve at an unprecedented pace, a well-executed risk assessment serves as the foundation of a robust security strategy. It lays the foundation for informed decision-making and proactive measures, equipping organizations to face challenges head-on.

What Is a Risk Assessment?

A risk assessment is a systematic approach to identifying security threats, evaluating their potential impact, and prioritizing mitigation efforts. It provides answers to critical questions that help organizations understand and fortify their risk landscape:

- What assets are at risk?
- What are the potential threats to these assets?
- How vulnerable are the systems and processes?
- What are the consequences of a successful attack or failure?

By addressing these fundamental questions, organizations can develop targeted strategies to mitigate vulnerabilities, thereby enhancing their overall security posture and operational integrity. Risk assessments not only help in pinpointing current weaknesses but also guide organizations in anticipating future challenges, ensuring a resilient approach to cybersecurity.

Why Perform a Risk Assessment?

Conducting regular risk assessments is essential for organizations to remain resilient against evolving threats. This practice offers numerous benefits that extend beyond immediate security concerns, influencing operational efficiency and strategic planning:

- *Identify Critical Assets*: Pinpoint the systems, data, and resources most valuable to the organization, ensuring their protection remains a top priority.

- *Mitigate Threats*: Focus efforts on addressing the most significant risks effectively and efficiently, reducing potential damage.

- *Ensure Compliance*: Meet regulatory requirements such as GDPR, HIPAA, or PCI-DSS, avoiding penalties and legal repercussions while fostering trust among stakeholders.

- *Enhance Decision-Making*: Provide data-driven insights to optimize security investments and resource allocation, aligning them with organizational goals.

By understanding and addressing the risks specific to their environment, organizations can build a proactive and adaptive security framework. Regular risk assessments also foster a culture of awareness and accountability, empowering teams to prioritize security at every level.

The Risk Assessment Process

Performing a comprehensive risk assessment involves several key steps. Each step is critical to ensuring a thorough evaluation and effective risk management strategy. The process is iterative and adaptable, allowing organizations to refine their approach as their needs and external conditions evolve.

The Risk Assessment Process Workflow outlines a structured, step-by-step approach to identifying, evaluating, and mitigating cybersecurity risks. It begins with defining the scope and objectives, ensuring clarity on which systems, networks, or assets will be assessed. The next phase involves identifying assets and categorizing them into physical, data, and human components, followed by analyzing threats that could exploit these assets. The process continues with identifying vulnerabilities through vulnerability scans, configuration reviews, and penetration testing. Once threats and vulnerabilities are mapped, the likelihood and impact of risks are assessed using standardized scoring models like CVSS, leading to the calculation of risk levels, classified as high, medium, or low.

Based on the risk classification, a mitigation plan is developed. High-risk issues require immediate mitigation, while medium-risk items follow phased remediation, and low-risk factors are monitored and managed over time. The findings are then documented in detailed reports and communicated to stakeholders for informed decision-making. To ensure long-term security, the process includes continuous monitoring and updates, allowing organizations to adapt to evolving cyber threats. Figure 5-4 presents the workflow, which ensures a proactive and structured approach to cybersecurity, balancing risk mitigation with operational efficiency.

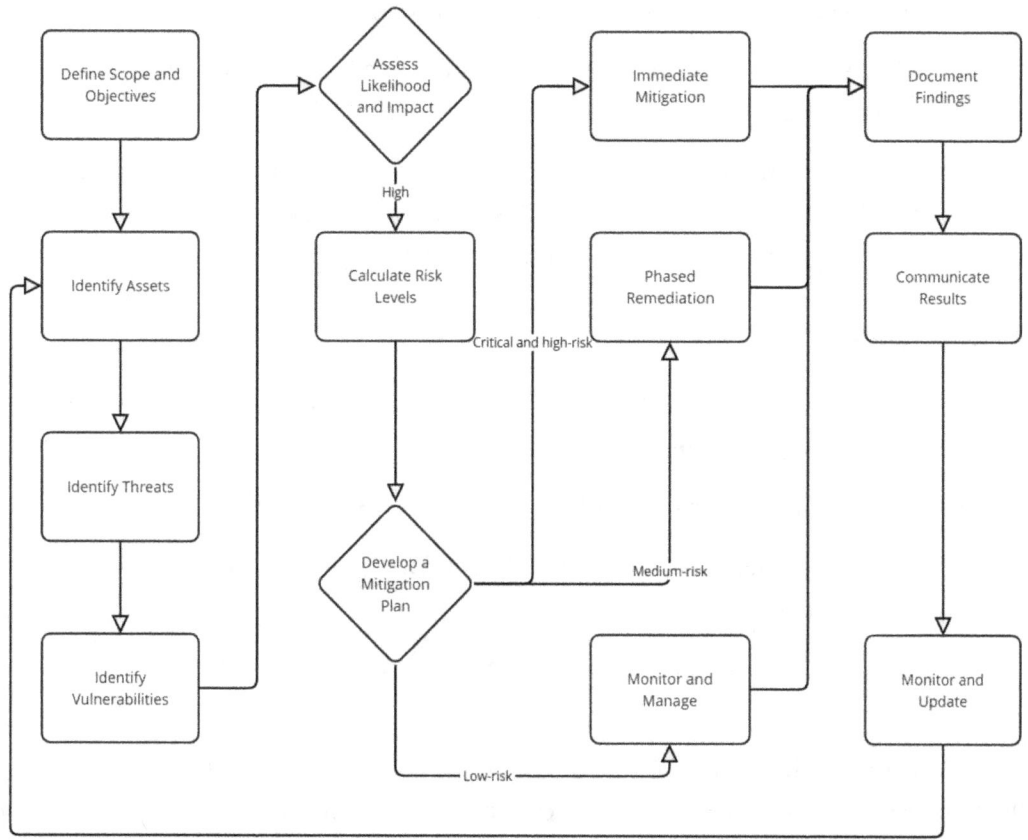

Figure 5-4. Risk assessment process workflow

Define Scope and Objectives

The first step in risk assessment is to clearly define the scope and objectives of the evaluation. This involves identifying which systems, networks, applications, or business processes will be assessed. The scope should be specific to ensure a focused approach, while objectives should align with organizational goals such as compliance with regulatory requirements (e.g., GDPR and HIPAA) or enhancing security posture. By establishing a well-defined scope, organizations can prevent resource wastage and ensure actionable insights. Stakeholders must be aligned to expectations to ensure that the assessment is relevant and provides meaningful outcomes.

This step ensures focus and clarity by addressing

- Which systems, networks, or applications will be evaluated?
- What specific goals should the assessment achieve (e.g., compliance and risk reduction)?

Clearly defined parameters help align the assessment with organizational priorities and ensure actionable outcomes. Establishing a shared understanding among stakeholders ensures that the assessment remains relevant and goal-oriented.

Identify Assets

A detailed inventory of assets within the assessment's scope is fundamental. Assets can be classified into categories such as

- *Physical Assets*: Servers, workstations, and network devices.
- *Data Assets*: Sensitive customer information, intellectual property, and operational data.
- *Human Assets*: Key personnel with privileged access to critical systems.

Understanding the value and role of each asset enables prioritization in protection efforts. It also highlights interdependence among assets, helping organizations identify cascading risks and address them proactively.

Identify Threats

Organizations must identify potential threats to these assets. Common threat categories include

- *External Threats*: Cybercriminals, nation-state actors, ransomware groups, and hacktivists
- *Internal Threats*: Employees with malicious intent, accidental errors, or policy violations
- *Environmental Threats*: Natural disasters, power failures, and hardware malfunctions

Leveraging TIPs, reviewing past incidents, and assessing emerging cyber risks help organizations anticipate and mitigate potential threats before they materialize into real attacks.

Identify Vulnerabilities

Vulnerabilities are weaknesses that can be exploited by threats. These can be identified through

- *Automated Scanning*: Using tools like Nessus, Qualys, or OpenVAS to detect security gaps.
- *Configuration Reviews*: Ensuring secure settings in firewalls, access controls, and encryption protocols.
- *Patch Management Audits*: Assessing whether systems are running outdated software or unpatched applications.

Addressing vulnerabilities proactively minimizes the attack surface and strengthens the organization's overall security posture.

Assess Likelihood and Impact

Once threats and vulnerabilities are identified, the next step is evaluating the likelihood of an attack and the potential impact on business operations. This is done using qualitative and quantitative metrics:

- *Likelihood*: The probability of a threat exploiting a vulnerability, based on historical data and security controls in place.
- *Impact*: The consequences if a risk materializes, financial loss, reputational damage, operational disruption, or regulatory penalties.

Frameworks such as the CVSS provide standardized metrics to assess and rank risks effectively.

Calculate Risk Levels

Risk levels are calculated using the formula:

$$Risk = Likelihood \times Impact$$

This results in categorizing risks into critical, high, medium, or low levels. High-risk threats require immediate attention, while medium and low risks are addressed based on priority. Risk assessment tools like Archer, RiskWatch, or FAIR help automate this process and provide accurate, data-driven insights. Organizations can use risk heatmaps to visualize risk distribution, making it easier to communicate findings to stakeholders.

Developing a Mitigation Plan

After calculating risk levels, organizations must create a detailed mitigation plan that outlines how to address identified risks. Strategies include

- *Critical and High-Risk Threats*: Require immediate remediation, such as patching critical vulnerabilities, implementing stronger access controls, or deploying security monitoring tools.

- *Medium-Risk Threats*: Addressed through phased remediation, such as system upgrades, process improvements, and additional security controls.

- *Low-Risk Threats*: Monitored over time, with periodic reviews to assess whether they escalate into higher risks.

Mitigation plans should be actionable, time-bound, and assigned to specific teams or individuals for accountability.

Document Findings

Comprehensive documentation is essential for tracking risks and ensuring accountability. A well-documented risk assessment report should include

- Asset and threat inventories to provide a clear understanding of risk exposure.

- Risk levels and associated mitigation strategies to support prioritization.

- Timelines for remediation with assigned risk owners for effective follow-up.

Proper documentation helps organizations maintain compliance with regulations, streamline audits, and serve as a reference for future assessments.

Communicate Results

Risk assessment findings must be communicated effectively to stakeholders, including senior management, IT teams, compliance officers, and security personnel. This can be done through

- *Detailed Report*s: Providing in-depth risk insights and recommended actions.

- *Dashboards and Visualizations*: Using heatmaps, graphs, and trend analysis to present data clearly.

- *Executive Briefings*: Summarizing critical risks and required investments for mitigation.

Clear communication ensures alignment of priorities and facilitates informed decision-making. Tailoring reports based on the audience's technical proficiency improves engagement and response.

Monitor and Update

Risk assessments are not one-time exercises; they require continuous monitoring and periodic updates to stay relevant. Organizations must

- *Track Risk Mitigation Progress*: Ensuring that remediation efforts are completed within set timelines.

- *Reassess Risks Regularly*: Conduct periodic evaluations to detect new vulnerabilities.

- *Adapt to Emerging Threats*: Use real-time threat intelligence to address evolving cyber risks.

By maintaining an iterative and adaptive risk management approach, organizations can strengthen resilience and remain prepared for an ever-changing threat landscape.

Challenges and Solutions

Despite its importance, risk assessment is not without challenges. Recognizing and addressing these issues is crucial for success. The main challenges in performing risk assessment are as follows and are presented in detail in Table 5-6:

CHAPTER 5　INTRODUCTION TO CYBER RISK MANAGEMENT

- Lack of Complete Asset Visibility
- Dynamic Threat Landscape
- Limited Resources
- Compliance Complexity
- Stakeholder Misalignment
- Data Overload and False Positives
- Lack of Continuous Monitoring

Table 5-6. Challenges and solutions in risk assessment

Challenge	Description	Solution
Lack of Complete Asset Visibility	Organizations may have blind spots in their IT environment, leading to unidentified risks.	- Implement asset management tools like ServiceNow or Configuration Management Database (CMDB) for real-time inventory tracking.
Dynamic Threat Landscape	Cyber threats evolve rapidly, making it difficult to stay ahead of new attack vectors.	- Utilize AI-driven TIPs. - Conduct regular threat assessments to adjust strategies. - Stay updated with cybersecurity advisories and industry reports.
Limited Resources	Organizations often lack sufficient personnel, budget, or technology to address all identified risks.	- Adopt a risk-based approach to focus on high-impact threats. - Automate security tasks using SOAR tools.

(continued)

Table 5-6. (*continued*)

Challenge	Description	Solution
Compliance Complexity	Meeting regulatory requirements (e.g., GDPR, HIPAA, and PCI-DSS) can be challenging and resource-intensive.	- Leverage automated compliance tools for continuous monitoring. - Conduct regular internal audits to stay ahead of regulatory changes. - Provide staff training on compliance requirements. - Establish a dedicated compliance team to oversee regulatory adherence.
Stakeholder Misalignment	Different departments may have conflicting priorities, delaying risk mitigation efforts.	- Engage cross-functional teams to align security goals. - Establish clear communication channels between business and security teams.
Data Overload and False Positives	Large amounts of security data can lead to analysis paralysis and misprioritization.	- Use SIEM tools to filter and analyze relevant threats.
Lack of Continuous Monitoring	One-time assessments become outdated as new vulnerabilities emerge.	- Establish continuous risk monitoring systems. - Schedule periodic reassessments to update risk profiles. - Implement automated alerting mechanisms to detect new vulnerabilities.

Best Practices for Risk Assessment

A well-structured risk assessment process is essential for organizations to identify vulnerabilities, prioritize risks, and implement effective mitigation strategies. Adopting best practices ensures that risk assessments are not only comprehensive but also aligned with business objectives, regulatory requirements, and evolving cyber threats. Below are the key practices that organizations should follow to enhance the effectiveness of their risk assessment processes.

CHAPTER 5 INTRODUCTION TO CYBER RISK MANAGEMENT

Engage Cross-Functional Teams

A successful risk assessment requires input from multiple departments to ensure a comprehensive evaluation of threats and vulnerabilities. Cybersecurity risks do not exist in isolation; they impact various business functions, including IT, operations, finance, compliance, and human resources. By engaging cross-functional teams, organizations can

- Gain diverse perspectives on risk factors that may otherwise be overlooked.
- Ensure alignment between business objectives and cybersecurity strategies.
- Foster a culture of shared responsibility for security across the organization.
- Improve communication between technical teams and executive leadership to secure necessary resources for risk mitigation.

Collaboration between departments also helps in identifying dependencies among assets, processes, and personnel, which is crucial for assessing cascading risks that may result from a single vulnerability.

Adopt Standardized Frameworks

Using industry-recognized frameworks ensures that risk assessments follow best practices and align with regulatory and compliance requirements. Standardized methodologies provide structured approaches to evaluating threats, vulnerabilities, and risks. Some widely used frameworks include

- *NIST RMF*: A step-by-step approach to managing cybersecurity risks across government and private sector organizations.
- *ISO/IEC 27005*: An internationally recognized standard for managing information security risks.
- *FAIR*: A quantitative risk assessment model that assigns monetary values to risks, helping organizations make data-driven decisions.
- *OCTAVE*: A self-directed assessment approach designed for organizations of various sizes.

Implementing these frameworks enhances consistency, comparability, and repeatability in risk assessment processes, making them more effective and easier to integrate with compliance requirements.

Integrate Threat Intelligence

Threat intelligence provides organizations with real-time data on emerging cyber threats, attack patterns, and vulnerabilities. By integrating external and internal threat intelligence sources into risk assessments, organizations can

- Identify and prioritize threats based on current attack trends.
- Strengthen proactive defense strategies by anticipating potential cyberattacks.
- Improve the accuracy of risk scoring models by incorporating real-world data.
- Reduce the chances of reactive security measures, allowing organizations to stay ahead of adversaries.

TIPs such as IBM X-Force Exchange, Recorded Future, and FireEye Threat Intelligence can provide organizations with actionable insights to enhance their risk assessment processes.

Conduct Regular and Iterative Risk Assessments

Cyber threats evolve constantly, and risk assessments should not be a one-time activity. Instead, they should be conducted regularly and updated based on new findings. Best practices for maintaining ongoing risk assessments include

- Scheduling periodic assessments (e.g., quarterly, biannually, or annually) to ensure risks are consistently evaluated.
- Updating risk assessments following major system changes, mergers, acquisitions, or security incidents.
- Using automation to continuously monitor assets for new vulnerabilities and threats.
- Engaging third-party cybersecurity experts to conduct independent assessments for unbiased evaluations.

Treating risk assessment as a continuous and evolving process, organizations can maintain a proactive security posture and quickly respond to new threats.

Maintain Comprehensive Documentation

Proper documentation of the risk assessment process is crucial for transparency, accountability, and compliance. A well-documented risk assessment should include

- A clear scope and objectives outlining the assets, processes, and systems under evaluation.

- A risk register detailing identified threats, vulnerabilities, likelihood, impact, and mitigation strategies.

- Decision logs capturing key risk management choices, ensuring traceability for audits and compliance.

- Mitigation plans that outline step-by-step actions, responsible parties, and timelines for addressing risks.

- Incident response records to track historical security events and their resolutions for future reference.

Comprehensive documentation not only supports regulatory audits but also serves as a knowledge base for improving future risk assessments.

Leverage Automation for Efficiency

Manual risk assessments can be time-consuming and prone to errors. Automation can enhance the efficiency, accuracy, and consistency of risk assessment processes. Organizations should consider

- Using SIEM tools like Splunk or ArcSight to aggregate and analyze security data.

- Employing risk management platforms such as RSA Archer, RiskLens, or ServiceNow for automated risk scoring and reporting.

- Implementing continuous vulnerability scanning with tools like Qualys, Nessus, or OpenVAS to detect emerging weaknesses.

Automation reduces the burden on security teams, allowing them to focus on high-priority risks and strategic security initiatives.

Establish a Risk Communication Strategy

Clear and effective communication of risk assessment findings is essential for ensuring that key stakeholders understand the security landscape and make informed decisions. Organizations should

- Develop risk dashboards that provide visual representations of risk levels for executives and decision-makers.

- Customize reports based on the audience; technical teams need detailed threat analysis, while executives require high-level risk summaries.

- Conduct regular briefings with leadership and relevant departments to align risk mitigation efforts.

- Provide awareness training to non-technical employees to foster a security-conscious culture.

A well-structured communication strategy ensures that risk assessments lead to actionable outcomes rather than being ignored or misunderstood.

Aligning Risk Assessments with Business Goals

Risk assessments should not be performed in isolation but should align with the organization's broader business objectives. Security teams must

- Understand how cybersecurity risks impact business continuity and revenue generation.

- Prioritize risks based on their financial, reputational, and operational impact.

- Balance security investments with business innovation and growth initiatives.

With the alignment of risk assessments with business goals, organizations can ensure that cybersecurity efforts contribute to overall success rather than becoming a cost center with no clear value.

CHAPTER 5 INTRODUCTION TO CYBER RISK MANAGEMENT

Foster a Security-First Culture

A successful risk assessment strategy extends beyond tools and frameworks; it requires a cultural shift where security becomes a core part of the organization. To build a security-first culture,

- Train employees regularly on security best practices, phishing awareness, and data protection.

- Encourage reporting of security incidents without fear of repercussions to improve early threat detection.

- Involve executives in cybersecurity discussions to secure leadership buy-in and allocate sufficient resources.

An organization-wide commitment to security strengthens resilience and reduces human-related vulnerabilities.

Key Takeaways

A well-executed risk assessment is not just a one-time exercise but a continuous, iterative process. By staying proactive, leveraging modern tools, and fostering collaboration, organizations can build a resilient cybersecurity framework capable of adapting to an ever-changing threat landscape.

In this section, we covered the following points:

- Risk assessments are essential for effective cybersecurity management, enabling organizations to identify, evaluate, and mitigate vulnerabilities to safeguard critical assets and maintain regulatory compliance.

- The process involves defining scope, identifying assets, assessing threats and vulnerabilities, calculating risk levels, and developing mitigation plans tailored to identified risks.

- Challenges such as limited asset visibility, dynamic threats, and resource constraints can be mitigated using asset management tools, real-time threat intelligence, and prioritization strategies.

- Conducting a thorough inventory of physical, data, and human assets is crucial for identifying interdependencies and ensuring comprehensive protection.

- Regular monitoring and updates to risk assessments ensure that organizations remain prepared to address evolving threats and maintain a proactive security posture.

- Adopting standardized frameworks like FAIR, NIST, or ISO 27005 ensures consistency, reliability, and alignment with industry best practices.

- Engaging cross-functional teams and documenting findings thoroughly enhances transparency, accountability, and alignment with organizational goals.

Mitigating Identified Risks: Strategies and Best Practices

Identifying risks is a vital component of any robust cybersecurity strategy. However, recognizing vulnerabilities and threats is only the starting point. The true measure of an organization's preparedness lies in its ability to effectively mitigate these risks. Risk mitigation is an ongoing process that requires strategic planning, the implementation of controls, regular monitoring, and collaboration across departments.

Understanding Risk Mitigation

Risk mitigation involves proactive measures to reduce the likelihood and potential impact of identified threats. It is not merely about addressing vulnerabilities but also ensuring business continuity in the face of evolving risks. Organizations that excel in risk mitigation adopt a structured approach, integrating technical, administrative, and strategic elements into their processes. The objectives of risk mitigation include

- *Reducing Threat Likelihood*: Implementing measures to minimize the probability of threats materializing.

- *Limiting Potential Impact*: Creating safeguards to ensure minimal damage if a threat does occur.

- *Ensuring Business Continuity*: Establishing systems and plans that allow operations to continue uninterrupted during and after incidents.

Effective risk mitigation provides organizations with a competitive advantage, not only by protecting assets but also by building trust among stakeholders, customers, and regulatory bodies.

Core Risk Mitigation Strategies

Risk mitigation strategies help organizations proactively manage cybersecurity threats by reducing the likelihood and impact of potential security incidents. Each organization must tailor its approach based on the type and severity of risks identified. The following core strategies – risk avoidance, risk reduction, risk sharing (or transfer), and risk acceptance – form the foundation of an effective risk management framework.

Risk Avoidance

Risk avoidance involves eliminating or modifying activities, processes, or systems to remove exposure to specific threats. Instead of addressing the impact of a risk, this strategy focuses on preventing it from occurring in the first place.

- *Example*: An organization using outdated, unsupported software may decide to retire these systems entirely and migrate to a secure, cloud-based solution to avoid cybersecurity risks associated with legacy technology.

- *How It Helps*: By eliminating the root cause of a security threat, the organization ensures that the risk is no longer exploitable. This approach is most effective for high-risk scenarios where the cost of mitigation or potential impact outweighs the benefits of continuing the risky activity.

- *Challenges*: Risk avoidance may sometimes lead to operational disruptions or require significant investment in new infrastructure or process changes. Organizations must carefully assess whether avoidance is a practical and cost-effective option.

Risk Reduction

Risk reduction focuses on minimizing the probability or impact of a risk through technical, administrative, and physical controls. This is one of the most applied mitigation strategies, as many risks cannot be entirely avoided but can be controlled.

- *Example*: Regularly updating and patching software to address vulnerabilities prevents attackers from exploiting known security weaknesses.

- *How It Helps*: Strengthening defenses makes it significantly harder for attackers to compromise systems, reducing the organization's exposure to cybersecurity threats.

- *Challenges*: While risk reduction is highly effective, it requires continuous monitoring and investment in security technologies and policies. Organizations must balance security enhancements with operational efficiency.

Risk Sharing or Transfer

Risk sharing (or risk transfer) involves shifting some or all of the financial and operational consequences of a risk to a third party. This is often achieved through insurance policies, outsourcing, or contractual agreements with vendors.

- *Example*: Purchasing cybersecurity insurance to cover financial losses resulting from data breaches, ransomware attacks, or business disruptions.

- *How It Helps*: Transferring risk does not eliminate it but reduces the financial burden and provides additional resources for recovery.

- *Challenges*: While risk transfer helps reduce financial exposure, organizations remain responsible for managing their security posture and ensuring third-party partners meet security expectations.

Risk Acceptance

In some cases, organizations may choose to acknowledge a risk and take no immediate action if its impact is minimal or the cost of mitigation outweighs the potential consequences. Risk acceptance is a strategic decision rather than negligence and is based on thorough risk assessments.

- *Example*: A company may choose not to patch a low-risk vulnerability in a non-critical system if exploitation is unlikely and resources are better allocated to addressing high-priority threats.

- *How It Helps*: Allows organizations to focus their resources on more significant risks while continuously monitoring low-priority threats.

- *Considerations*:
  - Regular risk reviews ensure that accepted risks remain low-impact and do not escalate over time.
  - Contingency planning ensures that if an accepted risk materializes, the organization is prepared to respond effectively.

- *Challenges*: Without proper monitoring, accepted risks may grow in severity, leading to unforeseen consequences. Organizations must continuously reassess their risk landscape and adjust strategies accordingly.

Steps to Mitigate Identified Risks

A systematic approach is essential for effective risk mitigation. Each step builds upon the previous one, ensuring comprehensive coverage of all identified vulnerabilities.

Effective risk mitigation is a dynamic and continuous process, requiring organizations to identify, assess, and address threats methodically. The workflow begins with Step 1: Identify and Assess Risks, where potential vulnerabilities are evaluated based on their likelihood and impact on business operations. At this stage, organizations must adopt a risk assessment framework to classify threats accurately, allowing for informed decision-making. If a risk is determined to be high, it demands Step 2: Implement Immediate Mitigation, a rapid response strategy that neutralizes or significantly reduces the potential damage of critical threats. This step ensures that pressing security issues are swiftly addressed before they escalate into full-blown incidents. Conversely, if the risk is not deemed high, it proceeds directly to Step 3: Develop and Implement a Long-Term Mitigation Plan, which involves a more strategic approach to security. This phase may include applying security patches, refining policies, enhancing employee awareness programs, or deploying additional protective technologies to reinforce the organization's defenses.

Following the implementation of mitigation strategies, organizations must evaluate their effectiveness through a crucial decision point: Was the remediation successful? If the answer is affirmative, the process advances smoothly; however, if vulnerabilities persist or if residual risks remain, organizations must transition into Step 4: Monitor and Manage Low-Risk Issues. This step acknowledges that not all risks can be completely eradicated and emphasizes the importance of ongoing supervision and risk prioritization. Next, organizations engage in Step 5: Continuous Monitoring and Testing, a proactive phase that ensures security measures remain effective over time. Techniques such as vulnerability scans, penetration testing, security audits, and real-time monitoring play a pivotal role in detecting emerging threats before they can cause significant harm. By integrating continuous assessment into their cybersecurity strategy, organizations maintain a strong defense against evolving attack vectors.

As threats are ever-changing, the final stage of the workflow ensures organizations remain adaptable and resilient. A key decision point asks: Have new risks been identified? If new vulnerabilities emerge, the workflow loops back to the beginning, reinforcing the importance of continuous assessment and adaptation. However, if no new risks are detected, organizations proceed to Step 6: Review, Update, and Improve Risk Mitigation Strategies. This concluding step solidifies the organization's security posture by refining policies, incorporating lessons learned, and staying ahead of emerging threats through ongoing education and technological advancements. By following this structured and cyclical approach, organizations can not only mitigate risks effectively but also foster a culture of resilience, ensuring long-term security and compliance. Figure 5-5 presents a high-level process workflow.

CHAPTER 5   INTRODUCTION TO CYBER RISK MANAGEMENT

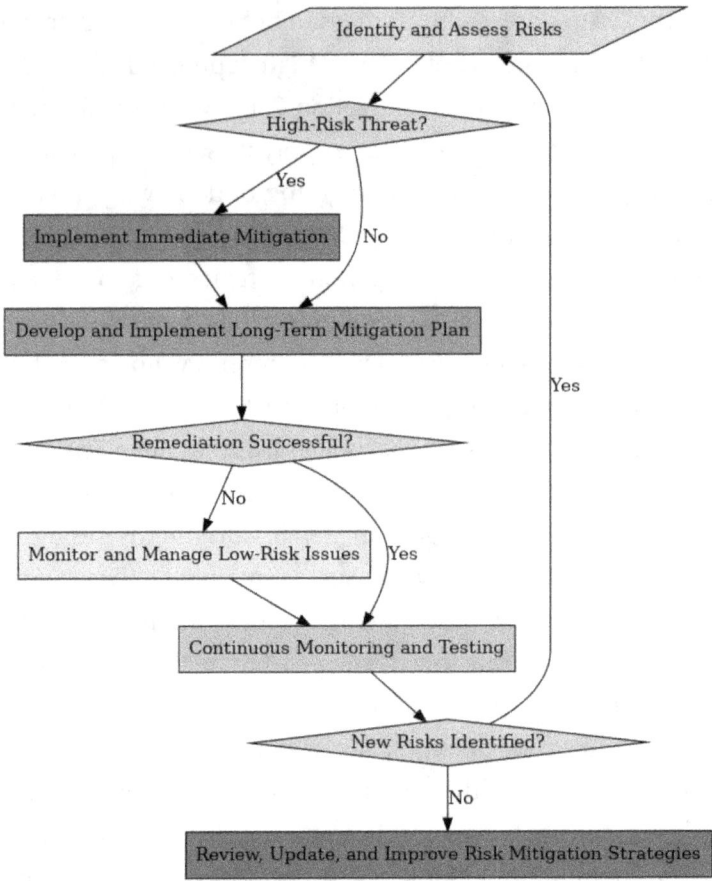

Figure 5-5. Process workflow related to steps to mitigate identified risks

Prioritize Risks Based on Severity

Not all risks are created equal. Using a risk matrix to evaluate the likelihood and potential impact of vulnerabilities allows organizations to focus on the most pressing threats first.

- *Critical and High-Risk Issues*: Require immediate attention, such as unpatched critical vulnerabilities or exposed sensitive data.

- *Medium-Risk Issues*: Can be addressed over time through planned upgrades or process refinements.

- *Low-Risk Issues*: Should be monitored periodically and addressed as needed.

396

Implement Technical Controls

Technology plays a critical role in mitigating risks. Key technical controls include

- *Firewalls*: Restrict unnecessary network traffic and prevent unauthorized access.

- *Encryption*: Protect sensitive data, both in storage and during transmission, from unauthorized access.

- *MFA*: Adds an extra layer of security to critical systems by requiring multiple forms of verification.

Strengthening Administrative Controls

Administrative measures complement technical controls by establishing clear policies, procedures, and training programs.

- Incident Response Plans: Outline the steps to take during and after a security breach.

- Employee Training: Regularly educate staff on recognizing phishing attempts and other common threats.

- Access Control Policies: Implement role-based privileges to ensure that employees only have access to information and systems relevant to their roles.

Monitor and Test Regularly

Risk mitigation is not a one-time activity. Regular monitoring and testing ensure that implemented measures remain effective over time:

- *Vulnerability Scanning*: Identify new weaknesses that may emerge due to changes in the environment.

- *Penetration Testing*: Simulate real-world attacks to uncover potential gaps in defenses.

- *SIEM Solutions*: Provide real-time monitoring and alerts for suspicious activity across the network.

Foster Cross-Department Collaboration

Effective risk mitigation involves stakeholders from various departments working together. This ensures a comprehensive approach:

- *IT Teams*: Focus on technical controls and system integrity.

- *HR Departments*: Play a key role in insider threat management and employee education.

- *Legal Teams*: Ensure compliance with data protection regulations and industry standards.

- *Operations Teams*: Help integrate mitigation efforts without disrupting critical business processes.

Technologies That Drive Risk Mitigation

Modern tools and technologies significantly enhance the efficiency and effectiveness of risk mitigation efforts:

- *EDR*: Tools like CrowdStrike or SentinelOne detect and neutralize endpoint threats in real-time.

- *Network Segmentation*: Isolating networks into smaller zones prevents attackers from moving across within the system.

- *Automated Patch Management*: Platforms like Ivanti ensure timely deployment of patches, reducing exposure windows for known vulnerabilities.

- *Zero Trust Architecture*: Enforces the principle of "never trust, always verify," ensuring that access requests are continually authenticated and authorized.

CHAPTER 5   INTRODUCTION TO CYBER RISK MANAGEMENT

Challenges in Risk Mitigation

Despite its critical importance, risk mitigation often faces several challenges as follows, while details are presented in Table 5-7:

- Resource Constraints
- Evolving Threat Landscape
- Complex Regulatory Requirements
- Difficulties in Measuring Effectiveness

Table 5-7. Challenges and solutions in risk mitigation

Challenge	Description	Solution
Resource Constraints	Organizations often lack the necessary budget, personnel, or time to implement comprehensive risk mitigation strategies.	- Prioritize risks based on severity and potential impact. - Adopt automation tools to reduce manual workload. - Leverage external cybersecurity services for cost-effective solutions.
Evolving Threat Landscape	Cyber threats continuously change, making it difficult for organizations to maintain up-to-date defenses.	- Utilize TIPs to stay informed about emerging risks. - Implement adaptive security frameworks such as Zero Trust. - Conduct regular security audits and update mitigation strategies accordingly.

(continued)

Table 5-7. (*continued*)

Challenge	Description	Solution
Resistance to Change	Employees or departments may be reluctant to adopt new security protocols, technologies, or risk mitigation measures.	- Foster a security-aware culture through ongoing education and training. - Clearly communicate the benefits of risk mitigation to stakeholders. - Implement gradual transitions to new security measures to ease adaptation.
Complex Regulatory Requirements	Compliance with various industry regulations (e.g., GDPR, HIPAA, and NIST) adds complexity to risk mitigation efforts.	- Develop a compliance roadmap aligned with cybersecurity frameworks. - Automate compliance reporting to streamline audits. - Consult legal and regulatory experts to ensure adherence to evolving requirements.
Difficulties in Measuring Effectiveness	Organizations struggle to quantify the success of their risk mitigation strategies, making it hard to justify investments.	- Establish clear Key Performance Indicators (KPIs) for cybersecurity effectiveness. - Regularly test mitigation controls through vulnerability assessments and penetration testing.

Best Practices for Risk Mitigation

To achieve sustained success in risk mitigation, organizations should follow these best practices:

- *Document Actions*: Maintain thorough records of all mitigation efforts to support audits and accountability.

- *Communicate Clearly*: Ensure stakeholders understand the rationale behind mitigation strategies and their importance.

- *Be Proactive*: Regularly update systems and processes to stay ahead of potential threats.

- *Test Continuously*: Use simulations and assessments to verify the effectiveness of implemented controls.

Examples of Risk Mitigation in Action

Example 1: Ransomware Protection

- *Risk*: Vulnerable backups exposed to ransomware.
- *Mitigation*: Deployed immutable backups and isolated backup systems to prevent tampering.

Example 2: Phishing Prevention

- *Risk*: Employees frequently falling victim to phishing attacks.
- *Mitigation*: Introduced an email filtering system and conducted regular phishing simulations.

Example 3: Vendor Risk Management

- *Risk*: Inadequate security measures among third-party vendors.
- *Mitigation*: Required vendors to comply with security standards and conducted periodic assessments.

Key Takeaways

Risk mitigation is not a one-size-fits-all approach but a tailored and evolving process that requires consistent effort, innovation, and collaboration. By integrating technical tools, administrative measures, and strategic planning, organizations can build resilience, ensure business continuity, and confidently face the ever-changing cybersecurity landscape.

In this section, we covered the following points:

- Risk mitigation is a dynamic process that transforms identified vulnerabilities into manageable challenges by applying proactive strategies and ongoing controls.

- Core strategies like avoidance, reduction, sharing, and acceptance allow organizations to customize their risk response based on the severity and nature of identified threats.

- Technical controls such as firewalls, encryption, and MFA enhance security, while administrative controls, like employee training and incident response plans, support effective implementation.

- Prioritization of risks using a risk matrix ensures high-severity vulnerabilities receive immediate attention, while lower-severity issues are monitored or addressed as resources permit.

- Regular monitoring and testing, including vulnerability scans, penetration tests, and the use of SIEM solutions, ensure that mitigation strategies remain effective and adaptive to evolving threats.

- Cross-department collaboration integrates diverse perspectives from IT, HR, legal, and operations teams, ensuring a holistic and efficient approach to risk management.

- Leveraging modern technologies like EDR tools, automated patch management, and zero-trust architecture enhances the efficiency and precision of risk mitigation efforts.

- Challenges such as resource constraints, evolving threats, and resistance to change can be addressed through focused prioritization, TIPs, and fostering a culture of security awareness.

Conducting a Risk-Based Cybersecurity Audit

In the complex world of cybersecurity, where threats evolve faster than ever, a risk-based audit emerges as an indispensable approach. This type of audit focuses on high-risk areas, ensuring that limited resources are allocated effectively to address vulnerabilities with the most significant potential impact. Unlike traditional audits that might treat all risks equally, a risk-based audit allows organizations to prioritize and target the most critical threats, ensuring better security, enhanced compliance, and efficient resource management. By understanding the organization's unique challenges and tailoring the audit process to address its specific risks, risk-based audits become a strategic tool for safeguarding assets and maintaining trust.

Why Risk-Based Audits Are Important

Risk-based audits have become a basis of modern cybersecurity strategies. Their importance stems from several pressing factors that organizations cannot afford to overlook. Firstly, limited resources are a reality for most businesses. Budget constraints, tight schedules, and a shortage of skilled personnel make it essential to focus efforts on areas where they will have the greatest impact. A risk-based approach ensures that these resources are used carefully, targeting the most significant vulnerabilities.

Secondly, the evolving threat landscape necessitates a dynamic and prioritized approach. Cybercriminals continually develop new attack methods, and organizations must remain agile to address these emerging risks. Traditional, one-size-fits-all audits fail to keep pace with such rapid changes, but risk-based audits focus on immediate, high-priority threats to stay ahead of adversaries.

Lastly, regulatory pressure plays a critical role. Compliance with frameworks like ISO 27001, NIST, GDPR, and HIPAA requires organizations to adopt risk-based methodologies. These standards emphasize the identification and management of risks based on their potential impact and likelihood.

CHAPTER 5   INTRODUCTION TO CYBER RISK MANAGEMENT

For instance, a healthcare organization based on HIPAA might prioritize auditing its EHR systems due to the sensitivity of patient data and the severe penalties for non-compliance. Similarly, financial institutions may direct their efforts toward securing payment processing systems to adhere to PCI DSS standards and protect customer transactions.

Steps to Conduct a Risk-Based Audit

Conducting a risk-based audit involves several well-defined steps, each building on the previous one to ensure a comprehensive evaluation of risks and vulnerabilities. These steps provide a roadmap for auditors to identify, assess, and mitigate critical risks effectively.

This workflow diagram illustrates the steps to conduct a risk-based cybersecurity audit. It provides a structured methodology for identifying, assessing, and mitigating risks within an organization's cybersecurity landscape. Each step in the diagram builds upon the previous one, ensuring a comprehensive evaluation of threats while prioritizing high-risk areas.

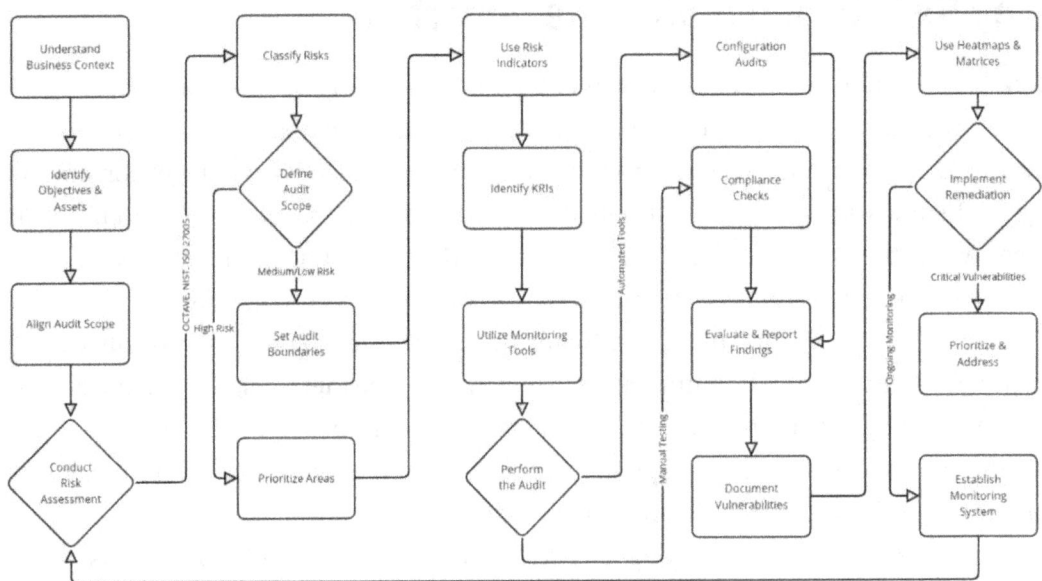

Figure 5-6. Workflow for conducting a risk-based cybersecurity audit

404

Understand Business Context

The foundation of any effective audit lies in understanding the organization's business context. This step involves assessing the company's goals, identifying critical assets, and determining its risk tolerance. By aligning the audit objectives with the broader business strategy, organizations can ensure that the audit addresses the most relevant risks. For example, an e-commerce business focused on customer data security might prioritize its payment gateway and database systems over less critical areas like internal document management.

This phase of the audit involves understanding the business environment to align cybersecurity efforts with organizational goals.

- *Identify Objectives and Assets*: This step ensures that the audit focuses on protecting critical assets, such as customer data, intellectual property, financial systems, and operational technology. Understanding business goals helps auditors determine which areas require the most attention.

- *Align Audit Scope*: The scope is tailored based on the organization's risk tolerance, regulatory requirements (e.g., ISO 27001, NIST, GDPR, and HIPAA), and industry-specific threats. This ensures that resources are allocated efficiently.

Conduct Risk Assessment

A thorough risk assessment is crucial for identifying, categorizing, and prioritizing risks.

- *Classify Risks*: Risks are classified based on their likelihood and potential impact, using risk management frameworks like OCTAVE, NIST, ISO 27005, etc.

- *Define Audit Scope*: This step determines which systems, processes, and assets will be examined. The audit scope differentiates between critical/high-risk (e.g., exposed servers and financial transaction systems) and medium/low-risk (e.g., internal document storage) areas.

- *Set Audit Boundaries*: Clearly defining audit boundaries prevents scope creep and ensures that the audit remains focused. For example, an organization might limit its audit to cloud storage security instead of reviewing all IT assets.

- *Prioritize Areas*: The audit team prioritizes high-risk areas where vulnerabilities could lead to data breaches, financial losses, or regulatory penalties.

Define Audit Scope

With risks prioritized, the next step is to define the scope of the audit. High-risk areas such as sensitive data systems, critical infrastructure, or privileged user accounts should take precedence. Clearly delineating the audit boundaries ensures focus and efficiency. For example, an audit might concentrate on cloud storage configurations rather than a broader review of all IT assets, ensuring that high-impact vulnerabilities are addressed promptly.

Use Risk Indicators

Key Risk Indicators (KRIs) help auditors quantify risks and identify critical weaknesses.

- *Identify KRIs*: Examples of KRIs include high numbers of failed login attempts, frequency of malware infections, number of unpatched systems, or unauthorized data access incidents.

- *Utilize Monitoring Tools*: Automated monitoring tools such as Splunk, IBM QRadar, and Rapid7 InsightVM track these indicators, allowing auditors to detect anomalies in real-time.

Perform the Audit

The audit itself involves using a combination of automated tools and manual techniques. Tools like Nessus can scan for vulnerabilities, while Metasploit facilitates penetration testing to evaluate system defenses. Configuration audits help ensure that policies and procedures align with best practices. During this phase, auditors not only identify vulnerabilities but also assess the effectiveness of existing controls.

Evaluate and Report Findings

The next step involves documenting findings, prioritizing remediation efforts, and presenting results to stakeholders. Visual tools such as heatmaps can be invaluable for highlighting critical risks, making it easier for decision-makers to understand and act upon the audit outcomes. Clear and actionable reporting ensures that the audit results translate into tangible improvements.

The findings from the audit are analyzed, documented, and presented to stakeholders; there are different reporting types, based on the type of audit performed.

- *Configuration Audits*: These ensure that systems and networks are configured according to industry best practices and compliance frameworks (e.g., verifying firewall rules, access controls, and encryption settings).

- *Compliance Checks*: Auditors verify adherence to regulatory and industry standards like PCI DSS, HIPAA, or SOC 2, ensuring that security controls meet legal and business requirements.

- *Evaluate and Report Findings*: Auditors use risk heatmaps and matrices to visually represent vulnerabilities. This makes it easier for executives and security teams to prioritize remediation efforts.

- *Document Vulnerabilities*: Findings are formally recorded, and risk scores are assigned to each vulnerability based on its potential impact.

Implementing Remediation & Continuous Monitoring

The final stage of the audit ensures that identified risks are addressed and that a system for ongoing monitoring is in place.

- *Use Heatmaps and Matrices*: Risk assessment tools like MITRE ATT&CK and FAIR frameworks help categorize vulnerabilities based on their severity and likelihood.

- *Implement Remediation*: This involves applying security patches, updating access controls, implementing additional authentication mechanisms, or reconfiguring firewalls to mitigate risks.

- *Prioritize and Address Critical Vulnerabilities*: The most critical issues (e.g., unsecured APIs, exposed credentials, and misconfigured cloud resources) are addressed first to prevent potential exploits.

- *Establish Monitoring System*: A continuous monitoring system is implemented to track new threats, compliance status, and emerging vulnerabilities. Organizations leverage SIEM tools like Splunk or Microsoft Sentinel for real-time alerts.

Challenges in Risk-Based Audits

Despite their advantages, risk-based audits are not without challenges. Table 5-8 presents the common obstacles.

Table 5-8. Challenges and solutions in conducting a risk-based cybersecurity audit

Challenge	Description	Solution
Identifying Relevant Risks	Organizations struggle to accurately identify and categorize cybersecurity risks due to evolving threats and lack of visibility.	Implement continuous threat intelligence monitoring, leverage frameworks like NIST, ISO 27005, and OCTAVE, and conduct regular risk assessments.
Limited Resources	Budget constraints, staffing shortages, and lack of expertise hinder comprehensive risk-based audits.	Prioritize high-risk areas, use automated security tools (e.g., Qualys and Nessus) for efficiency, and train internal teams on risk assessment.
Resistance from Stakeholders	Business units may resist security audits due to perceived operational disruptions or costs.	Communicate audit benefits in business terms (e.g., cost of breach vs. audit investment) and gain leadership support for risk-based decisions.

(continued)

Table 5-8. (*continued*)

Challenge	Description	Solution
Dynamic and Evolving Threat Landscape	Cyber threats constantly evolve, making static audit assessments ineffective over time.	Use continuous monitoring tools (e.g., Splunk and IBM QRadar) and adopt iterative, adaptive audit cycles to keep pace with emerging risks.
Defining the Scope of the Audit	Unclear scope can lead to audit inefficiencies, missing critical areas, or causing scope creep.	Clearly define the audit scope using risk assessment frameworks and prioritize critical assets based on business impact.
Inadequate Risk Indicators (KRIs)	Lack of well-defined risk indicators can result in misprioritization of risks.	Establish Key Risk Indicators (KRIs), such as failed login attempts, unpatched vulnerabilities, and access anomalies, to focus on measurable risks.
Lack of Effective Reporting	Reports may be overly technical, lacking clarity for decision-makers, or failing to drive action.	Use visual tools like heatmaps, risk matrices, and executive dashboards to clearly present findings and prioritize remediation efforts.
Ensuring Compliance with Regulations	Organizations may struggle to align risk-based audits with multiple regulatory requirements.	Map audit processes to compliance frameworks (ISO 27001, NIST, PCI DSS, and GDPR) and leverage compliance automation tools.
Implementing and Tracking Remediation	Security teams may delay or overlook remediation efforts due to competing priorities.	Establish a structured remediation tracking process, assign risk owners, and use automated tracking systems to ensure timely resolution.
Lack of a Continuous Monitoring System	Without continuous risk monitoring, vulnerabilities may persist undetected between audits.	Deploy SIEM solutions for real-time threat detection and schedule frequent audit updates.

The above table outlines key challenges organizations face when conducting risk-based cybersecurity audits and provides practical solutions to address them. It highlights common obstacles such as identifying relevant risks, limited resources, stakeholder resistance, and the evolving threat landscape. Additionally, it emphasizes the importance of defining audit scope, establishing effective risk indicators, and ensuring compliance with regulatory frameworks. To overcome these challenges, organizations can leverage automation, continuous monitoring, structured reporting, and remediation tracking. By implementing these solutions, businesses can enhance their cybersecurity posture, prioritize high-risk areas, and improve overall audit effectiveness.

Best Practices for Risk-Based Audits

To maximize the effectiveness of risk-based audits, organizations should adopt the following best practices:

- *Align Objectives with Business Goals*: Ensure that audit objectives are directly tied to organizational priorities.

- *Update Risk Profiles Regularly*: Continuously review and update risk profiles to reflect changes in the threat landscape.

- *Leverage Automation*: Use tools like Splunk for efficient log analysis and anomaly detection.

- *Collaborate Across Teams*: Involve IT, legal, and operational teams to ensure comprehensive risk coverage.

- *Communicate Clearly*: Tailor reports and dashboards to meet the needs of both technical and non-technical audiences.

Examples of Risk-Based Audits in Action

Example 1: Financial Institution

- *Finding*: Weak authentication methods for online banking platforms allowed potential unauthorized access.

- *Consequences*: Increased risk of fraudulent transactions, regulatory non-compliance, and reputational damage.

- *Recommendations*: Introduce MFA to strengthen user access security and conduct regular user access reviews to detect anomalies.

Example 2: E-Commerce Business

- *Finding*: Unsecured APIs were exposing customer data to potential interception.

- *Consequences*: Risk of data breaches, loss of customer trust, and potential legal penalties for non-compliance with data protection regulations.

- *Recommendations*: Implement API gateways to monitor and control API traffic, enforce stricter authentication measures, and conduct regular security assessments of APIs.

Example 3: Healthcare Provider

- *Finding*: Outdated medical devices connected to the network lacked critical security patches.

- *Consequences*: Increased risk of ransomware attacks and potential breaches of sensitive patient data, leading to HIPAA violations.

- *Recommendations*: Segment network traffic to isolate vulnerable devices, replace high-risk equipment with updated models, and establish a regular patch management schedule.

Key Takeaways

Risk-based audits are not merely a checkbox exercise but a strategic initiative. By focusing on high-priority threats, employing advanced tools, and fostering collaboration, organizations can enhance their cybersecurity posture, achieve regulatory compliance, and build resilience against evolving cyber risks.

CHAPTER 5   INTRODUCTION TO CYBER RISK MANAGEMENT

In this section, we covered the following points:

- Risk-based audits focus on prioritizing critical vulnerabilities, ensuring resources are allocated effectively to areas with the highest potential impact.

- A structured approach, including steps like understanding business context and conducting risk assessments, ensures the audit process is tailored to the organization's unique challenges.

- Tools such as OCTAVE for risk assessments and Qualys for vulnerability management enhance the precision and efficiency of audits.

- Dynamic threat landscapes require iterative audits and continuous monitoring to keep pace with emerging risks and ensure defenses remain effective.

- Collaboration across departments, including IT, legal, and operations teams, ensures comprehensive coverage of vulnerabilities and alignment with organizational goals.

- Overcoming challenges such as stakeholder resistance or inaccurate risk assessment is possible through clear communication, data-driven methods, and framing risks in business terms.

- Examples from industries like finance, e-commerce, and healthcare demonstrate the tangible benefits of tailored recommendations and targeted risk mitigation.

- Best practices, including leveraging automation and aligning audits with business objectives, drive meaningful improvements in compliance and security.

The Role of Incident Response in Risk Management

In today's rapidly evolving digital landscape, cybersecurity incidents are not a matter of "if" but "when." Incident response (IR) has emerged as a critical component of risk management, enabling organizations to minimize the impact of cyber threats, recover swiftly, and safeguard their data and reputation. Unlike preventive measures that aim to stop attacks from occurring, incident response operates both proactively and reactively. It prepares organizations to deal with unforeseen events and ensures that identified risks are addressed with actionable plans. By integrating incident response into risk management, organizations can not only mitigate immediate threats but also build resilience against future attacks.

Risk management is fundamentally about identifying, assessing, and mitigating potential threats to an organization's operations and assets. Incident response, on the other hand, focuses on handling actual threats as they occur, ensuring swift containment and recovery. Together, these processes create a robust defense mechanism that addresses the full spectrum of cybersecurity challenges. For instance, an effective IRP ensures that an organization can quickly detect and neutralize a phishing attack before it escalates into a larger breach. Simultaneously, the lessons learned from this incident can inform risk management strategies, highlighting vulnerabilities and guiding the allocation of resources to critical areas.

The importance of incident response in risk management cannot be overstated. Its key objectives include limiting damage by containing breaches as quickly as possible, ensuring the efficient recovery of business operations, and fostering continuous improvement through post-incident analysis. These objectives align closely with the goals of risk management, creating a feedback loop where each process enhances the other. By adopting a holistic approach that integrates incident response and risk management, organizations can stay ahead of evolving threats and maintain trust among stakeholders.

Understanding Incident Response in Risk Management

At its core, incident response complements risk management by bridging the gap between theoretical preparedness and practical application. Risk management aims to mitigate potential threats by identifying, assessing, and addressing vulnerabilities. In contrast, incident response handles real-world threats, ensuring that risks materialize into manageable scenarios rather than catastrophic events. Together, they form a continuous cycle where incident response feeds valuable insights back into the risk management process, enhancing its effectiveness over time.

The primary objectives of incident response in the context of risk management are

- *Limiting Damage*: Rapid containment of security breaches to minimize their impact on operations, data, and reputation.

- *Restoring Operations*: Efficiently recovering business functions and reducing downtime to maintain continuity.

- *Learning and Improving*: Analyzing incidents to understand root causes, prevent recurrence, and refine future strategies.

For instance, a ransomware attack on an organization's critical infrastructure requires swift action to isolate affected systems, recover encrypted data, and identify vulnerabilities that enabled the breach. The lessons learned from this process feed directly into the risk management framework, ensuring similar threats are mitigated in the future.

The Incident Response Lifecycle

The incident response process is structured around a lifecycle that ensures incidents are managed effectively from preparation to post-incident review. Each phase plays a crucial role in mitigating risks and enhancing organizational resilience.

Figure 5-7 presents key activities of each phase of the incident response lifecycle.

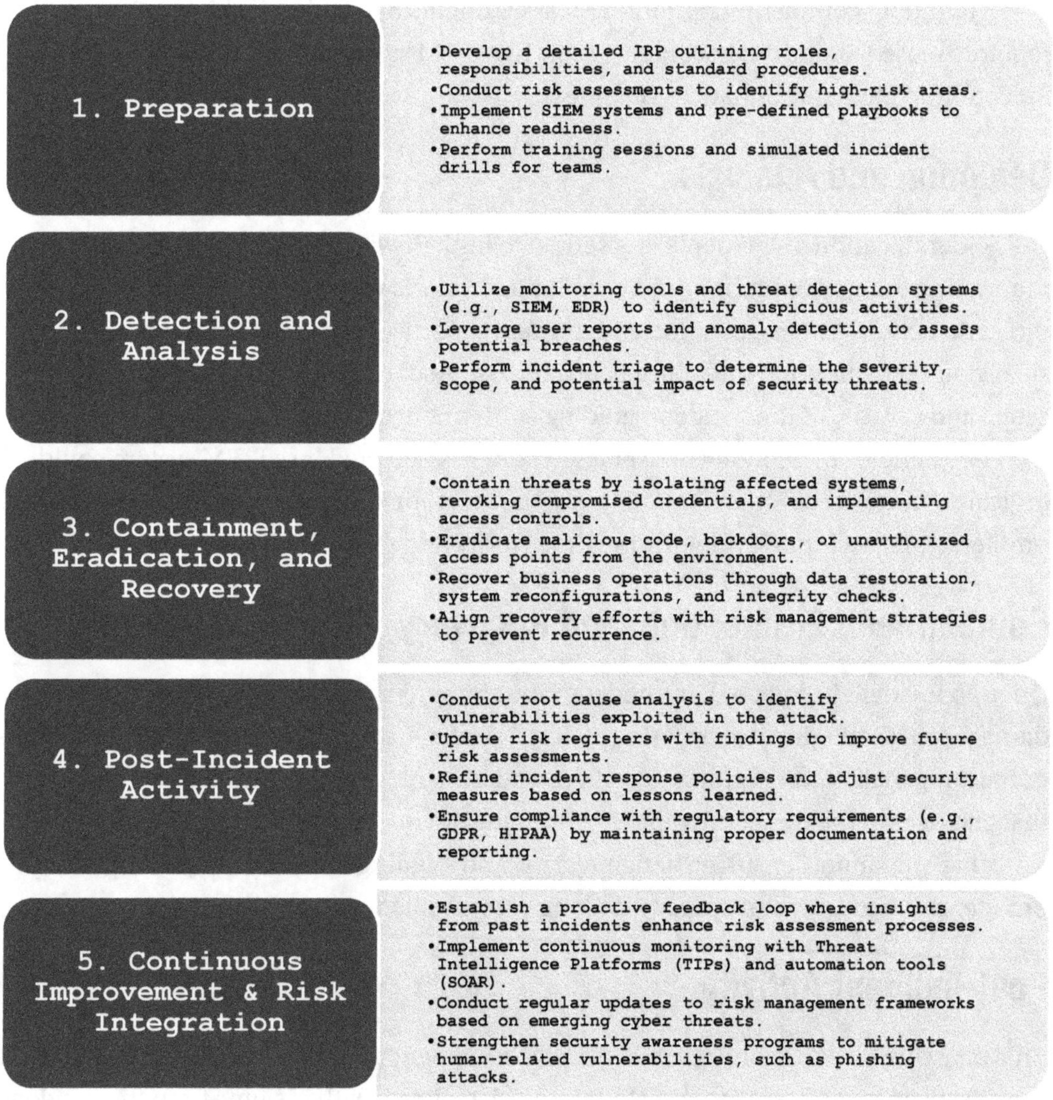

CHAPTER 5 INTRODUCTION TO CYBER RISK MANAGEMENT

1. Preparation
- Develop a detailed IRP outlining roles, responsibilities, and standard procedures.
- Conduct risk assessments to identify high-risk areas.
- Implement SIEM systems and pre-defined playbooks to enhance readiness.
- Perform training sessions and simulated incident drills for teams.

2. Detection and Analysis
- Utilize monitoring tools and threat detection systems (e.g., SIEM, EDR) to identify suspicious activities.
- Leverage user reports and anomaly detection to assess potential breaches.
- Perform incident triage to determine the severity, scope, and potential impact of security threats.

3. Containment, Eradication, and Recovery
- Contain threats by isolating affected systems, revoking compromised credentials, and implementing access controls.
- Eradicate malicious code, backdoors, or unauthorized access points from the environment.
- Recover business operations through data restoration, system reconfigurations, and integrity checks.
- Align recovery efforts with risk management strategies to prevent recurrence.

4. Post-Incident Activity
- Conduct root cause analysis to identify vulnerabilities exploited in the attack.
- Update risk registers with findings to improve future risk assessments.
- Refine incident response policies and adjust security measures based on lessons learned.
- Ensure compliance with regulatory requirements (e.g., GDPR, HIPAA) by maintaining proper documentation and reporting.

5. Continuous Improvement & Risk Integration
- Establish a proactive feedback loop where insights from past incidents enhance risk assessment processes.
- Implement continuous monitoring with Threat Intelligence Platforms (TIPs) and automation tools (SOAR).
- Conduct regular updates to risk management frameworks based on emerging cyber threats.
- Strengthen security awareness programs to mitigate human-related vulnerabilities, such as phishing attacks.

Figure 5-7. Incident response lifecycle in risk management

Preparation

Preparation is the foundation of effective incident response. Organizations must develop a comprehensive IRP that outlines roles, responsibilities, and procedures for handling incidents. Regular training sessions and simulated drills ensure that response teams are well-equipped to act decisively during a crisis.

In addition, conducting periodic risk assessments helps identify high-risk areas that require focused attention. Leveraging tools like SIEM systems and predefined playbooks for common incidents enhances readiness.

Detection and Analysis

Quick identification of incidents is essential to limit their impact. This phase relies on monitoring tools, user reports, and correlation of alerts with known risks. Advanced threat detection systems, coupled with human expertise, can identify anomalies and suspicious activities that might indicate a breach. Accurate analysis determines the scope and severity of the incident, guiding subsequent actions.

For example, an anomaly in user login patterns detected by a SIEM system could indicate a brute-force attack. By analyzing the incident in the context of existing risk profiles, teams can quickly determine the severity and prioritize their response.

Containment, Eradication, and Recovery

Once an incident is detected, immediate containment is necessary to prevent further damage. This could involve isolating affected systems, disabling compromised accounts, or blocking malicious IP addresses. After containment, the eradication phase ensures that all traces of the threat are removed from the environment. Recovery focuses on restoring operations, ensuring data integrity, and aligning recovery efforts with the broader risk management strategy for long-term resilience.

Post-Incident Activity

This phase involves a thorough analysis of the incident to uncover root causes and assess the effectiveness of the response. Updating risk registers with insights from the incident ensures that future risk assessments are more informed. This phase also includes refining the IRP based on lessons learned and addressing any identified gaps.

Continuous Improvement and Risk Integration

Incident response and risk management must operate as a continuous, adaptive process rather than isolated activities. By integrating lessons learned from past incidents into risk management frameworks, organizations can enhance their resilience against future threats. This involves maintaining a proactive feedback loop, where insights from incident response inform risk assessments, allowing security teams to refine their strategies and resource allocations.

Continuous monitoring through TIPs, SIEM systems, and Security Orchestration, Automation, and Response (SOAR) ensures that organizations stay ahead of evolving threats. Additionally, regular updates to risk registers and incident response plans help address new vulnerabilities, improving overall security posture. Employee awareness programs and security training should also evolve based on real-world attack trends, reducing human-related risks such as phishing.

Integrating Incident Response and Risk Management

Incident response and risk management are deeply interconnected. Their integration enhances organizational resilience and ensures a proactive stance against emerging threats. Key aspects of their integration include

- *Proactive Risk Identification*: Incident response teams play a pivotal role in identifying common attack vectors and vulnerabilities, which are then incorporated into risk assessments.

- *Feedback Loop*: Insights gained from incidents inform risk management strategies, enabling better resource prioritization and improved mitigation measures.

- *Continuous Monitoring*: Leveraging SIEM systems for real-time monitoring helps organizations stay ahead of threats by providing actionable intelligence.

- *Regulatory Compliance*: Incident response activities ensure adherence to regulations like GDPR or HIPAA by maintaining proper documentation and demonstrating accountability.

For example, a phishing attack that compromises employee credentials highlights weaknesses in user awareness training. This insight prompts risk management teams to enhance training programs and implement additional email filtering solutions.

CHAPTER 5   INTRODUCTION TO CYBER RISK MANAGEMENT

Technologies for Incident Response in Risk Management

Technologies play an essential role in enhancing the efficiency and effectiveness of incident response. They provide the tools necessary for rapid detection, analysis, and remediation of incidents, while also integrating seamlessly with broader risk management strategies.

- *Threat Intelligence Platforms (TIPs)*: Tools like Recorded Future and ThreatConnect provide real-time insights into emerging threats. By aggregating data from multiple sources, TIPs enable organizations to anticipate attacks and prioritize risks effectively. For example, TIPs can identify phishing campaigns targeting specific industries, allowing organizations to deploy targeted defenses.

- *EDR*: Solutions like CrowdStrike and SentinelOne continuously monitor endpoints for suspicious activities. They provide detailed forensics and automated responses to contain and neutralize threats. EDR tools are particularly effective in detecting APTs that bypass traditional defenses.

- *Automation Tools (SOAR)*: SOAR platforms like Palo Alto Cortex XSOAR automate incident response workflows. They integrate with existing security tools to streamline processes, reduce response times, and eliminate manual errors. For instance, SOAR can automatically quarantine infected devices or block malicious IPs.

- *Backup and Recovery Solutions*: Tools like Veeam and Rubrik ensure that critical data can be restored quickly in the event of ransomware attacks or other data loss incidents. These solutions support risk management by minimizing downtime and data loss, ensuring business continuity.

- *SIEM Systems*: SIEM solutions like Splunk and IBM QRadar provide centralized monitoring and analysis of security events. By correlating logs from multiple sources, SIEM systems help detect anomalies and guide incident response efforts.

CHAPTER 5 INTRODUCTION TO CYBER RISK MANAGEMENT

Challenges and Solutions in Incident Response

Table 5-9 presents main challenges and solutions for incident response:

Table 5-9. Challenges and solutions in incident response & risk integration

Challenge	Description	Solution
Lack of Coordination Between Teams	Security, IT, legal, and business units may operate in silos, leading to delays and misaligned response efforts.	Establish a Cross-functional Incident Response Team (CIRT) with clear roles and responsibilities. Conduct joint training and tabletop exercises.
Delayed Incident Detection	Organizations may struggle to detect threats early due to insufficient monitoring or reliance on manual processes.	Implement SIEM, EDR, and TIPs for real-time monitoring. Automate alerts to quickly identify and respond to anomalies.
Ineffective Post-Incident Learning	Lessons from past incidents are often not documented or incorporated into future risk management strategies.	Create a structured post-incident review process, updating risk registers and response plans based on findings.
Regulatory and Compliance Challenges	Organizations may fail to meet regulatory requirements (e.g., GDPR, HIPAA, and NIST) due to inadequate documentation and incident handling.	Maintain detailed incident logs, conduct regular compliance audits, and automate reporting for regulatory alignment.
Resource Constraints	Limited budgets and staff make it difficult to implement robust incident response and risk integration strategies.	Prioritize response efforts based on risk assessments, leverage automation (SOAR, AI-driven threat detection), and utilize third-party security services.
Resistance to Change	Employees and executives may be reluctant to adopt new processes, tools, or continuous improvement methodologies.	Foster a security-first culture, provide ongoing cybersecurity training, and demonstrate the business value of risk integration.

(continued)

CHAPTER 5   INTRODUCTION TO CYBER RISK MANAGEMENT

Table 5-9. (*continued*)

Challenge	Description	Solution
Inconsistent Response Execution	Variations in how incidents are handled across departments lead to inefficiencies and potential security gaps.	Develop and enforce a standardized IRP with regular simulations to ensure consistency.
Over-Reliance on Technology	While automation enhances efficiency, excessive dependence on tools without skilled analysts can result in missed threats or false positives.	Balance automation with human expertise by investing in skilled cybersecurity professionals and conducting manual threat analysis when necessary.

The above table outlines key challenges organizations face in integrating incident response with risk management and provides practical solutions to address them. Common issues include lack of coordination between teams, delayed incident detection, ineffective post-incident learning, regulatory compliance hurdles, and resource constraints. Solutions emphasize cross-functional collaboration, automation through SIEM and SOAR, structured post-incident reviews, and prioritization of risk-based response efforts. Additionally, fostering a security-first culture and balancing automation with human expertise ensures a proactive and adaptive approach.

Best Practices for Incident Response and Risk Management

Implementing best practices ensures that incident response efforts are aligned with organizational goals and deliver maximum value. Below are detailed steps to achieve this:

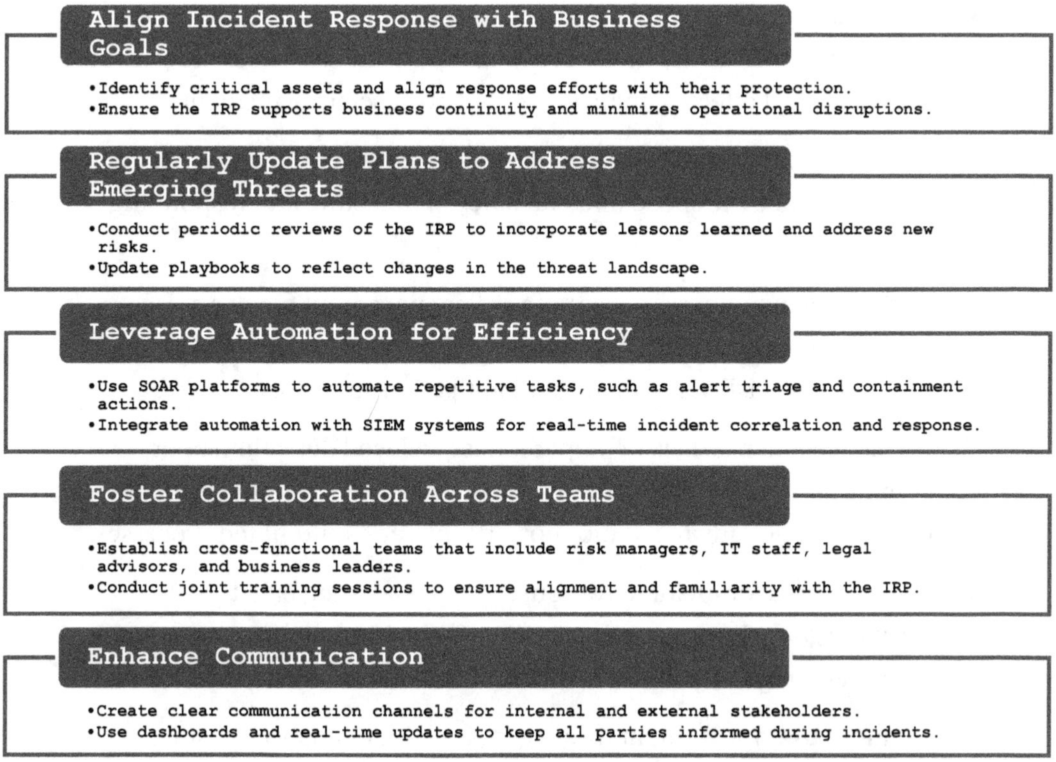

Align Incident Response with Business Goals
- Identify critical assets and align response efforts with their protection.
- Ensure the IRP supports business continuity and minimizes operational disruptions.

Regularly Update Plans to Address Emerging Threats
- Conduct periodic reviews of the IRP to incorporate lessons learned and address new risks.
- Update playbooks to reflect changes in the threat landscape.

Leverage Automation for Efficiency
- Use SOAR platforms to automate repetitive tasks, such as alert triage and containment actions.
- Integrate automation with SIEM systems for real-time incident correlation and response.

Foster Collaboration Across Teams
- Establish cross-functional teams that include risk managers, IT staff, legal advisors, and business leaders.
- Conduct joint training sessions to ensure alignment and familiarity with the IRP.

Enhance Communication
- Create clear communication channels for internal and external stakeholders.
- Use dashboards and real-time updates to keep all parties informed during incidents.

Figure 5-8. Best practices for incident response and risk management

Key Takeaways

Incident response is not just about reacting to incidents as they occur but also about proactively preparing for, learning from, and mitigating risks. By integrating incident response with risk management and employing advanced technologies, organizations can minimize downtime, recover efficiently, and bolster their defense against future threats.

In this section, we covered the following points:

- Incident response is crucial for minimizing the impact of cyber threats, ensuring swift recovery, and safeguarding data and reputation within the broader risk management framework.

- The incident response lifecycle, consisting of preparation, detection, containment, eradication, recovery, and post-incident activities, ensures organized and effective management of cybersecurity incidents.

- Technologies such as Threat Intelligence Platforms (TIPs), EDR, and SOAR enhance the speed and efficiency of detecting and responding to incidents.

- Integrating incident response with risk management creates a proactive feedback loop, where insights from real-world incidents inform future risk assessments and mitigation strategies.

- Challenges such as lack of preparedness, delayed detection, poor communication, and resource constraints can be mitigated through clear protocols, advanced monitoring tools, and automated processes.

- Best practices for incident response include aligning efforts with business goals, leveraging automation, fostering collaboration across teams, and regularly updating plans to address emerging threats.

- Continuous improvement through post-incident analysis ensures that organizations adapt to the evolving threat landscape and enhance resilience against future attacks.

- A holistic approach, integrating incident response with risk management strategies, strengthens organizational security posture, improves business continuity, and ensures regulatory compliance.

Creating a Risk Management Plan

In the ever-evolving cybersecurity landscape, a Risk Management Plan (RMP) is a basis of organizational resilience. It provides a structured approach to identifying, assessing, mitigating, and monitoring risks, ensuring that vulnerabilities are addressed and compliance requirements are met. The creation of an RMP is not merely a checkbox activity but a dynamic process that aligns cybersecurity efforts with business goals, enhances decision-making, and optimizes resource allocation. By anticipating potential threats and preparing actionable strategies, an effective RMP acts as both a shield and a roadmap for the organization's security posture.

A risk management plan serves as a formal document designed to manage risks systematically. It begins with identifying potential threats, both external and internal, and assessing their likelihood and impact. This analysis allows organizations to prioritize risks based on their severity, ensuring that high-risk areas receive immediate attention. The plan outlines strategies to mitigate or eliminate these risks, ranging from technical controls like encryption to procedural changes such as improved access management policies. Moreover, the RMP establishes an ongoing monitoring process to address emerging threats, ensuring the organization remains agile and prepared. In essence, the RMP is a living document that evolves alongside the organization and the threat landscape.

The value of an RMP extends beyond technical safeguards. It fosters a culture of risk awareness, encourages cross-departmental collaboration, and builds stakeholder confidence. For example, aligning the RMP with organizational objectives ensures that cybersecurity initiatives directly support business continuity and growth. The plan also plays a critical role in regulatory compliance, providing a clear framework for meeting standards like GDPR, HIPAA, or ISO 27001. By integrating the RMP into the organization's overall strategy, businesses can navigate risks more effectively, minimize disruptions, and maintain trust among customers and partners.

Steps to Create a Risk Management Plan

Creating a Risk Management Plan (RMP) is a structured process that ensures organizations proactively identify, assess, mitigate, and monitor risks. This process starts with risk identification, where potential threats, both external and internal, are systematically analyzed through frameworks such as ISO 27005. The next phase, risk assessment, prioritizes these risks based on their likelihood and impact using methodologies like FAIR or OCTAVE, ensuring that critical vulnerabilities receive immediate attention. Following assessment, risk mitigation strategies are defined, incorporating technical, procedural, and operational controls to reduce or eliminate identified risks. However, risk management is not a one-time activity; risk monitoring and review ensures continuous evaluation of threats through SIEM tools, audits, and vulnerability scans, keeping the RMP aligned with evolving security challenges. By following these steps, organizations create a dynamic and resilient risk management framework that integrates seamlessly with business operations and compliance requirements. Figure 5-9 presents a continuous process of risk management planning.

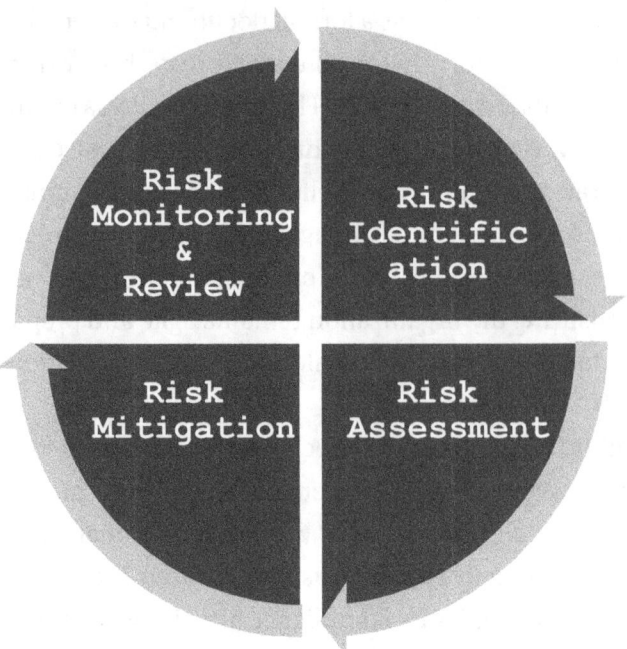

Figure 5-9. *Steps to create a risk management plan*

Risk Identification

The first step in creating an RMP is identifying all potential risks that could impact the organization. This involves a comprehensive review of the threat landscape, including cyber threats, operational vulnerabilities, and regulatory challenges. Tools such as risk assessment checklists or frameworks like ISO 27005 provide structured methodologies for identifying risks. Stakeholder engagement is crucial during this phase; brainstorming sessions with key personnel from IT, legal, operations, and management ensure that all perspectives are considered. Additionally, reviewing historical incidents and audit findings can reveal patterns and previously overlooked vulnerabilities, offering valuable insights for proactive risk identification.

Risk Assessment

Once risks are identified, the next step is to assess their likelihood and potential impact. This prioritization enables organizations to focus on high-risk areas that pose the greatest threat to operations, reputation, or compliance. Methodologies like FAIR or OCTAVE provide frameworks for quantitative and qualitative risk analysis. Heat maps are particularly effective for visualizing risk levels, offering a clear representation of priorities. For instance, a high-likelihood, high-impact risk like an unpatched server exposed to the internet demands immediate attention, while lower-priority risks can be addressed over time.

Risk Mitigation

Risk mitigation involves defining strategies to reduce or eliminate identified risks. These strategies can be technical, procedural, or operational, depending on the nature of the risk. For example, implementing MFA reduces the risk of unauthorized access, while training employees on phishing awareness mitigates the threat of social engineering attacks. Other common mitigation measures include deploying firewalls, encrypting sensitive data, and enforcing strict access controls. Each mitigation action should be accompanied by clear timelines and assigned responsibilities, ensuring accountability and effective execution.

Risk Monitoring and Review

An RMP is not a static document but a dynamic framework that requires continuous monitoring and updates. SIEM solutions like Splunk or QRadar are invaluable tools for real-time monitoring, providing insights into potential threats and anomalous activities. Regular audits and vulnerability scans with tools like Nessus or Qualys help identify new vulnerabilities and assess the effectiveness of existing controls. Periodic reviews of the RMP ensure that it remains aligned with the organization's evolving risk landscape and business objectives.

Key Components of a Risk Management Plan

Risk Register

The risk register serves as the central repository for all identified risks, providing a structured way to document, track, and manage risks over time. Each entry in the risk register typically includes

- *Risk Description*: A brief statement of the identified risk.
- *Likelihood and Impact*: The probability of the risk occurring and its potential effect on business operations, security, or compliance.

- *Risk Owner*: The individual or team responsible for managing the risk.

- *Current Mitigation Measures*: Existing controls in place to reduce the risk.

- *Proposed Actions*: Additional measures to address the risk if current controls are insufficient.

- *Status*: An ongoing update on whether the risk has been mitigated, is being addressed, or remains unresolved.

The risk register is not a static document but an evolving tool that ensures transparency in risk management efforts. It allows stakeholders to understand the organization's risk exposure, prioritize mitigation efforts, and track progress over time. Organizations often use risk management software or GRC platforms to maintain and automate risk register updates.

Mitigation Strategies

Once risks are identified and assessed, organizations must develop mitigation strategies to address them effectively. These strategies typically fall into four categories:

1. *Risk Avoidance*: Eliminating the activity or system that introduces the risk. (e.g., discontinuing the use of outdated software that poses security risks).

2. *Risk Reduction*: Implementing technical, procedural, or operational controls to lower the risk. (e.g., deploying firewalls, conducting regular security training, or enforcing MFA).

3. *Risk Transfer*: Shifting the risk to a third party, such as purchasing cyber insurance or outsourcing security operations to an MSSP.

4. *Risk Acceptance*: Acknowledging the risk and deciding to accept it without mitigation if its impact is minimal or the cost of mitigation is too high compared to the risk's effect.

Each mitigation strategy should include

- Clear implementation plans with specific steps to be taken.

- Timelines for execution to ensure timely risk management.

- Assigned responsibilities to establish accountability for mitigation efforts.
- Performance indicators to measure the effectiveness of mitigation actions.

With the documentation and enforcement of mitigation strategies, organizations can systematically reduce cybersecurity risks and enhance their overall security posture.

Communication Plan

Effective risk management requires seamless communication across various departments, ensuring that all stakeholders remain informed and aligned on risk-related matters. A well-defined communication plan outlines

- Who needs to be informed? (e.g., IT teams, executive management, compliance officers, and legal teams).
- What information needs to be shared? (e.g., risk assessment results, new threats, and mitigation progress).
- How and when will information be communicated? (e.g., regular risk reports, security dashboards, and emergency alerts).

A tiered communication approach is often beneficial:

- *Operational Level*: Technical teams receive real-time alerts and reports from security monitoring tools (e.g., SIEM alerts).
- *Tactical Level*: Mid-level management is updated on risk mitigation progress and operational changes.
- *Strategic Level*: Executive leadership is provided with high-level risk summaries to make informed decisions.

Additionally, automated reporting tools and security dashboards help streamline communication, ensuring timely risk updates across the organization.

Incident Response Integration

An RPM must align closely with the organization's IRP to ensure that identified risks are effectively addressed before and during security incidents. This integration enhances an organization's ability to respond quickly and efficiently to cyber threats.

Key aspects of incident response integration include

1. *Pre-incident Coordination*:

   a. Identifying high-risk scenarios and ensuring that response procedures are in place.

   b. Conducting tabletop exercises to test incident response preparedness.

   c. Ensuring that risk assessments inform the development of incident response playbooks.

2. *Incident Handling and Risk Containment*:

   a. Implementing predefined response procedures based on risk classification.

   b. Enabling automated security controls (e.g., isolating a compromised system upon detection).

   c. Leveraging SIEM and SOAR platforms to detect and respond to threats in real time.

3. *Post-incident Review and Risk Adjustment*:

   a. Conducting post-mortem analysis after incidents to refine risk management strategies.

   b. Updating the Risk Register to reflect newly discovered vulnerabilities.

   c. Strengthening security controls based on incident findings.

Compliance Documentation

Organizations must demonstrate compliance with regulatory and industry-specific standards such as GDPR, HIPAA, ISO 27001, NIST CSF, or PCI DSS. The RMP includes a compliance documentation section to track and document all compliance-related activities.

Key elements of this documentation include

- *Regulatory Requirements Mapping*: Aligning risk management practices with required compliance frameworks.

- *Control Implementation Records*: Documenting security measures deployed to meet compliance requirements.

- *Audit Logs and Evidence Collection*: Maintaining logs of security events, risk assessments, and mitigation actions for audit purposes.
- *Compliance Checklists and Assessments*: Regular self-assessments to ensure ongoing adherence to regulatory mandates.
- *Third-Party Risk Management*: Documenting vendor assessments to ensure supply chain security compliance.

Maintaining detailed compliance documentation helps organizations:

- Reduce legal and financial penalties from non-compliance.
- Demonstrate due diligence to auditors and regulators.
- Enhance trust and credibility with customers, partners, and stakeholders.

Automation tools such as GRC platforms (e.g., Archer and LogicGate) can streamline compliance tracking and documentation, ensuring that organizations remain aligned with evolving regulatory requirements.

Best Practices for Risk Management Planning

Engage Stakeholders

Comprehensive risk management requires input from across the organization. Involve stakeholders from IT, operations, finance, and legal teams to ensure that the RMP addresses diverse perspectives and priorities.

Aligning the Plan with Business Goals

A successful RMP supports the organization's strategic objectives. By aligning risk management efforts with business goals, organizations can ensure that cybersecurity initiatives drive value and enable growth.

Update Regularly for New Risks

The threat landscape is dynamic, and risks evolve rapidly. Regularly reviewing and updating the RMP ensures that it remains relevant and effective in addressing emerging threats.

Using Automation for Efficiency

Automation tools streamline risk management processes, from monitoring and analysis to reporting. Solutions like SOAR platforms and SIEM systems enable faster, more accurate responses to potential risks.

Test with Simulations

Conducting simulations and tabletop exercises tests the effectiveness of the RMP and prepares the organization for real-world scenarios. These exercises reveal gaps and provide opportunities for improvement.

Key Takeaways

A well-crafted and continuously updated Risk Management Plan helps organizations stay ahead of cyber threats, ensuring that risk is systematically managed, incidents are effectively responded to, and business operations remain uninterrupted and compliant with regulatory standards.

In this section, we covered the following points:

- A Risk Management Plan (RMP) is essential for identifying, assessing, and mitigating cybersecurity risks, enabling organizations to proactively address vulnerabilities and meet compliance requirements.

- Key steps in creating an RMP include risk identification, assessment, mitigation, and continuous monitoring to ensure vulnerabilities are addressed and security posture is maintained.

- Critical components of an RMP, such as the risk register, mitigation strategies, communication plan, incident response integration, and compliance documentation, ensure a structured and effective approach to managing risks.

- Best practices for creating a successful RMP include stakeholder engagement, aligning the plan with business goals, regularly updating for new risks, leveraging automation for efficiency, and testing with simulations to identify gaps and improve preparedness.

- Continuous monitoring and updates to the RMP are crucial to address emerging risks and evolving threats, ensuring that the organization remains agile and resilient in the face of cybersecurity challenges.

- The RMP fosters a culture of security awareness within the organization, encourages cross-departmental collaboration, and builds confidence with stakeholders by aligning cybersecurity efforts with business continuity and compliance.

The Link Between Risk Management and Business Continuity

In today's unpredictable cybersecurity landscape, the connection between risk management and business continuity is indispensable. Both disciplines work in tandem to ensure organizational resilience: risk management focuses on identifying and mitigating vulnerabilities, while business continuity ensures that critical operations continue uninterrupted during disruptions. This interdependence creates a robust framework for addressing threats, safeguarding assets, and maintaining trust in a rapidly evolving digital world.

Risk management is the foundation for understanding and mitigating threats. It involves systematically identifying risks, assessing their likelihood and potential impact, and implementing controls to reduce vulnerabilities. Business continuity complements this by ensuring that when disruptions do occur, the organization can recover quickly and maintain critical functions. Together, these two areas form the backbone of organizational resilience, enabling businesses to operate effectively despite adversities.

The integration of risk management and business continuity offers numerous benefits. By proactively addressing vulnerabilities that could disrupt operations, organizations can ensure smoother recovery processes. This synergy improves decision-making by combining insights from both disciplines, helping prioritize the most critical risks and optimize resource allocation. Moreover, aligning these efforts ensures regulatory compliance with standards like GDPR, ISO 22301, and NIST frameworks, which emphasize the importance of integrated approaches. A cohesive strategy also strengthens stakeholder confidence, demonstrating that the organization is prepared to handle potential challenges effectively.

Risk Management and Business Continuity Are Interdependent

Risk management and business continuity are deeply interconnected, each reinforcing the other to create a resilient organizational structure. While risk management identifies, assesses, and mitigates potential threats, business continuity ensures that essential functions can operate during and after an incident. Together, they address the full spectrum of vulnerabilities and operational challenges.

For instance, a risk management process may identify cyberattack as a critical threat to operations, prompting the implementation of enhanced firewall protections and employee training to reduce vulnerabilities. Simultaneously, business continuity planning ensures that even if an attack occurs, data backups are available, and operations can be restored with minimal downtime. This interdependence means that gaps in one area can undermine the effectiveness of the other, highlighting the need for seamless integration.

Key Benefits of Integration

The integration of risk management and business continuity provides organizations with a holistic approach to managing disruptions, safeguarding critical operations, and maintaining trust among stakeholders.

Proactive Mitigation

A reactive approach to risk can leave organizations vulnerable to severe operational disruptions, financial losses, and reputational damage. Integrating risk management with business continuity ensures that risks are identified and mitigated before they escalate into crises.

How Proactive Risk Mitigation Works:

- *Risk Identification and Assessment*: Organizations identify potential risks (cyberattacks, natural disasters, supply chain failures, etc.) and evaluate their impact on operations.

- *Preventive Controls Implementation*: Security measures such as firewalls, intrusion detection systems, data backups, and redundancy planning are implemented to minimize vulnerabilities.

- *Continuous Monitoring and Early Warning Systems*: AI-driven threat detection, automated incident response tools, and real-time monitoring help organizations respond before risks materialize into disruptions.

- *Crisis Preparedness Planning*: Business continuity plans are continuously updated to address newly emerging threats.

Example:
A financial services organization identifies a risk of ransomware attacks through its cybersecurity risk assessment. Instead of waiting for an attack, the organization

- *Implements MFA and endpoint detection solutions.*

- *Sets up secure, offline backups to restore operations quickly in case of an attack.*

- *Trains employees on phishing awareness to prevent social engineering attacks.*

Improved Decision-Making

When risk management and business continuity planning are aligned, organizations gain a comprehensive view of their risk exposure. This enables leaders to make data-driven decisions that prioritize business-critical risks and optimize resource allocation.

How Integration Improves Decision-Making:

- *Risk-Based Prioritization*: Helps identify the most critical threats to operations and allocate resources effectively.

- *Strategic Business Planning*: Provides insights into potential risks, allowing leaders to align continuity strategies with long-term business goals.

- *Optimized Budget Allocation*: Ensures that financial resources are spent efficiently on cybersecurity, IT infrastructure, and redundancy planning.

- *Scenario Planning and Simulation*: Organizations can conduct "what-if" analyses to prepare for different crisis scenarios and refine decision-making processes.

CHAPTER 5   INTRODUCTION TO CYBER RISK MANAGEMENT

Example:

A global logistics company integrates risk management with business continuity planning and discovers that supplier dependency risks could cause major supply chain disruptions. Decision-makers:

- *Identify alternative suppliers in different regions to reduce dependence on a single vendor.*

- *Invest in real-time supply chain tracking technology to monitor risks dynamically.*

- *Develop a business continuity plan to handle supplier disruptions efficiently.*

Regulatory Compliance

Many regulatory frameworks require organizations to demonstrate both risk management and business continuity capabilities. A unified approach ensures compliance with industry-specific regulations while reducing legal risks, fines, and reputational damage.

Key Compliance Standards That Emphasize Integration:

- *ISO 22301 (Business Continuity Management Systems)*: Mandates risk-based business continuity planning.

- *GDPR*: Requires organizations to recover from data breaches while maintaining consumer rights.

- *NIST 800-53*: Emphasizes risk-based security planning and continuity strategies.

- *HIPAA*: Mandates disaster recovery planning for healthcare organizations.

- *SOX*: Requires publicly traded companies to have risk controls for financial reporting continuity.

Example:

A healthcare provider integrates risk management with business continuity to comply with HIPAA regulations. The organization:

- *Implements automated backup solutions to secure patient data.*
- *Conducts annual risk assessments to identify and mitigate vulnerabilities.*
- *Establishes incident response protocols to ensure quick recovery from cyberattacks.*

Increased Stakeholder Confidence

A robust risk and business continuity strategy builds trust among customers, investors, and business partners. When organizations demonstrate preparedness, stakeholders feel more secure about long-term stability and reliability.

How Integration Boosts Stakeholder Confidence:

- *Investor Confidence*: Financial backers see the company as a low-risk, high-resilience investment.
- *Customer Assurance*: Clients trust that their data, services, and transactions remain secure even in crisis situations.
- *Regulator Trust*: Authorities recognize the organization's compliance with risk and continuity regulations.
- *Supply Chain and Partner Trust*: Vendors and business partners prefer working with resilient organizations that have contingency plans in place.

Example:

A cloud service provider integrates risk management with business continuity to reassure enterprise clients. The company

- *Implements redundant data centers across multiple geographic locations.*
- *Publishes an annual risk and resilience report for transparency.*
- *Provides 99.99% uptime guarantees backed by robust continuity plans.*

As a result, the provider attracts high-value clients who require uninterrupted cloud services and trust its resilience capabilities.

Enhanced Organizational Resilience

By aligning risk management and business continuity, organizations create a strong foundation for long-term resilience. This ensures continued operations despite cyberattacks, natural disasters, supply chain failures, or financial crises.

How Integration Strengthens Resilience:

- *Adaptability to Emerging Threats*: Organizations quickly modify continuity plans in response to new risks.

- *Minimal Downtime and Financial Losses*: Quick recovery mechanisms reduce the business impact of disruptions.

- *Crisis-Proof Operations*: Ensures business stability even in high-risk industries like finance, healthcare, and energy.

- *Competitive Advantage*: Resilient organizations outperform competitors by maintaining services during crises.

Example:

A global energy company integrates risk and business continuity efforts to withstand cyber threats and supply chain issues. The company

- *Implements AI-powered fraud detection to mitigate cyber risks.*

- *Sets up alternative warehouse hubs to counter regional supply chain disruptions.*

- *Conducts quarterly risk scenario testing to ensure rapid adaptation to new threats.*

This integration ensures the company remains operational, secure, and profitable despite unexpected challenges.

Practical Integration Steps

Successfully integrating risk management with business continuity requires a structured, methodical approach. Organizations must identify critical risks, prioritize essential functions, develop tailored continuity plans, conduct rigorous testing, and leverage technology for seamless coordination. This section outlines key steps to ensure a smooth and effective integration of these two essential disciplines.

CHAPTER 5   INTRODUCTION TO CYBER RISK MANAGEMENT

Risk Assessment in Business Continuity Planning

The first step in integrating risk management with business continuity is to incorporate risk assessments into the BIA. BIAs identify critical processes and their dependencies, highlighting potential risks that could disrupt these operations. For example, a financial institution might assess risks to its online banking system, considering factors like cybersecurity threats, infrastructure failures, or third-party vendor vulnerabilities.

Steps for Risk Assessment in Business Continuity:

- *Identify Risks*: Assess potential threats such as cyberattacks, supply chain failures, data breaches, natural disasters, and operational disruptions.

- *Analyze Impact*: Determine how each risk affects critical business functions, financial stability, and regulatory compliance.

- *Evaluate Likelihood*: Use qualitative and quantitative methods to assess probability.

- *Assess Current Controls*: Identify gaps in existing risk mitigation strategies and continuity plans.

- *Integrate Findings into BIA*: Ensure that business continuity strategies address the most critical risks identified.

Prioritize Critical Functions

Not all risks are equal, and focusing on the most critical ones is essential. High-priority risks, such as ransomware attacks on customer data systems or disruptions to supply chain logistics, demand immediate attention. By aligning risk management priorities with business continuity objectives, organizations can allocate resources effectively to protect vital functions.

Steps to Prioritize Critical Functions:

- *Classify Business Functions*: Identify core processes that, if disrupted, would cause severe financial, operational, or reputational damage.

- *Define RTO*: Establish maximum acceptable downtime for each function.

- *Set RPO*: Determine how much data loss is acceptable before major consequences arise.

- *Map Dependencies*: Analyze interdependencies between departments, IT systems, vendors, and third-party services.

- *Rank Risks by Impact and Likelihood*: Use a Risk Prioritization Matrix to focus on high-probability, high-impact risks first.

Develop Risk-Based Continuity Plans

Continuity plans should address specific risks identified during the assessment phase. For instance, a healthcare provider might create a continuity plan for managing patient data breaches by including strategies such as secure backups, rapid response protocols, and enhanced employee training. These plans ensure that identified vulnerabilities are mitigated, minimizing downtime and operational impacts.

Steps to Develop Risk-Based BCPs:

- *Design Specific Risk Scenarios*: Prepare for real-world disruptions (e.g., cyberattacks, supply chain failures, and IT system crashes).

- *Establish Response Protocols*: Define step-by-step actions for incident detection, containment, and recovery.

- *Create Alternative Workflows*: Plan for manual processing, backup sites, or cloud-based solutions in case of technology failure.

- *Designate Crisis Management Teams*: Assign roles to incident response teams, IT security staff, and business continuity leads.

- *Document Communication Strategies*: Establish internal & external communication plans for employees, stakeholders, and customers.

Conduct Regular Testing and Training

The effectiveness of continuity plans depends on regular testing and employee preparedness. Tabletop exercises and simulations based on real-world risk scenarios, such as phishing attacks or power outages, help validate the plans and reveal gaps. Training sessions further ensure that all employees understand their roles and responsibilities, enhancing the organization's readiness to respond effectively.

Steps for Regular Testing and Training:

- *Perform Tabletop Exercises*: Simulate real-world scenarios where key teams discuss responses to cyberattacks, data breaches, or natural disasters.

- *Run Disaster Recovery Drills*: Test data recovery, failover systems, and IT incident response procedures.

- *Conduct Phishing and Cybersecurity Awareness Training*: Educate employees on social engineering attacks and security best practices.

- *Update Plans Based on Test Results*: After each drill, document weaknesses and refine continuity plans accordingly.

- *Develop Cross-Departmental Coordination*: Ensure IT, operations, risk management, and business units are aligned in crisis response efforts.

Leverage Technology for Integration

Technology plays a pivotal role in bridging risk management and business continuity. GRC platforms like ServiceNow and RiskWatch enable seamless alignment of risk and continuity efforts. Disaster recovery solutions such as Veeam and Acronis ensure quick data restoration, while incident response platforms like PagerDuty and Splunk automate threat monitoring and response. These tools streamline processes, improve accuracy, and enhance coordination between teams.

Key Technologies for Integration:

- *GRC Platforms*: Automate risk assessments, track compliance, and streamline reporting.

- *Disaster Recovery Solutions*: Ensure quick restoration of critical systems and data.

- *Incident Response and Threat Intelligence Platforms*: Detect threats early and automate responses.

- *Supply Chain Risk Management Tools*: Monitor supplier dependencies and disruptions in real time.

- *Communication and Crisis Management Tools*: Facilitate rapid communication and coordination.

Emerging Trends in Risk Management and Business Continuity

As the cybersecurity landscape evolves, organizations must adapt to emerging trends that shape the future of risk management and business continuity.

Cyber-Resilience

Organizations are increasingly adopting AI and automation to counter advanced cyberattacks. These technologies enable faster threat detection, predictive risk analysis, and automated response strategies, enhancing resilience against sophisticated attacks.

Supply Chain Risks

Third-party vendors and suppliers are critical of business operations, but they also introduce risks. Organizations are focusing on supply chain continuity by assessing vendor vulnerabilities, establishing alternative suppliers, and integrating supply chain risks into overall continuity planning.

Zero Trust Integration

Embedding Zero Trust principles into risk management and business continuity strategies ensures robust security. By verifying every user and device, Zero Trust reduces the likelihood of unauthorized access and improves the organization's ability to maintain operations during incidents.

Key Takeaways

The integration of risk management and business continuity creates a robust framework that strengthens an organization's ability to proactively address risks, minimize disruptions, and ensure long-term success, all while fostering a culture of preparedness and resilience.

In this section, we covered the following points:

- Risk management and business continuity are interdependent disciplines that together enhance organizational resilience. While risk management identifies and mitigates threats, business continuity ensures critical operations continue during disruptions.

- Integration of risk management and business continuity offers significant benefits, including proactive mitigation of risks, improved decision-making, regulatory compliance, and increased stakeholder confidence.

- Practical steps for integrating these disciplines include incorporating risk assessments into BIA, prioritizing critical functions, developing risk-based continuity plans, and conducting regular testing and training.

- Technology plays a vital role in aligning risk management with business continuity. Tools such as GRC platforms, disaster recovery solutions, and incident response platforms help automate, streamline, and coordinate efforts for better preparedness.

- Best practices for alignment include fostering collaboration across teams, conducting regular audits, treating planning as an ongoing process, and training employees to ensure they understand their roles in both areas.

- Emerging trends like cyber-resilience, supply chain risk management, and Zero Trust integration are shaping the future of risk management and business continuity, enabling organizations to better prepare for and respond to evolving threats.

Risk Management Mistakes in Cybersecurity Audits

Effective risk management is a basis of cybersecurity audits, enabling organizations to identify, assess, and mitigate threats to their digital assets. However, even the most experienced teams can fall into common pitfalls that compromise the integrity of the process. Recognizing these mistakes is the first step toward avoiding them, improving audit outcomes, and strengthening the organization's overall security posture. Cybersecurity auditors play a pivotal role in identifying and addressing these issues, ensuring organizations remain resilient in an ever-evolving threat landscape.

Common Mistakes in Risk Management in Cybersecurity Audit

Inadequate Risk Identification

One of the most prevalent mistakes in risk management is failing to comprehensively identify all potential risks. This is particularly concerning when it comes to emerging threats such as ransomware, phishing campaigns, and supply chain vulnerabilities. Organizations that overlook these risks often leave critical gaps in their defenses, exposing themselves to significant financial and reputational damage.

To address this issue, organizations should leverage threat intelligence platforms like Recorded Future or Mandiant to stay updated on evolving risks. Regular threat modeling sessions with cross-functional teams can also uncover vulnerabilities that might otherwise be missed. Historical incident analysis provides additional insights, helping organizations anticipate and prepare for potential threats more effectively.

Example:

- *An organization fails to recognize the threat of ransomware targeting remote desktop protocols.*

- *Consequences: A ransomware attack locks critical systems, halting operations for days and incurring significant financial losses.*

- *Resolution:*

- *Use threat intelligence platforms like Recorded Future or Mandiant to stay updated on evolving risks.*

- *Conduct regular threat modeling sessions with key stakeholders to uncover vulnerabilities.*

Overlooking Low-Probability, High-Impact Risks

Another common mistake is prioritizing only high-probability risks while neglecting low-likelihood events that could have catastrophic consequences. Examples include insider threats or APTs targeting critical infrastructure. Although these events are less likely, their potential impact warrants thorough consideration.

CHAPTER 5   INTRODUCTION TO CYBER RISK MANAGEMENT

Organizations can avoid this pitfall by adopting frameworks like FAIR to evaluate all risks comprehensively. Simulating low-probability events through tabletop exercises provides valuable insights, helping teams understand the implications and refine their preparedness strategies. For example, a tabletop exercise simulating an insider data breach can highlight weaknesses in access control policies and incident response plans.

Example:

- *An organization disregards the possibility of an insider threat involving privileged access misuse.*

- *Consequences: A disgruntled employee leaks sensitive customer data, leading to regulatory fines and reputational damage.*

- *Resolution:*

  - *Leverage frameworks like FAIR to evaluate the potential impact of all risks.*

  - *Simulate low-probability events using tabletop exercises to enhance preparedness.*

Ignoring the Human Element

While technical vulnerabilities often receive significant attention, many organizations neglect the human aspect of cybersecurity. Employees can inadvertently compromise security through weak passwords, unintentional data exposure, or falling victim to phishing scams. Cybercriminals frequently exploit these human weaknesses, bypassing even the most robust technical defenses.

To mitigate this risk, organizations should implement continuous employee training programs that focus on cybersecurity as the best practice. Tools like KnowBe4 and Cofense can simulate phishing attacks, helping employees recognize and respond to real-world threats. Building a culture of security awareness ensures that all employees, from entry-level staff to executives, play an active role in protecting the organization.

Example:

- *Employees frequently fall victim to phishing emails due to inadequate training.*

- *Consequences: Attackers gain access to critical systems through compromised credentials.*

- *Resolution:*
  - *Implement continuous employee training programs on cybersecurity best practices.*
  - *Use phishing simulations with tools like KnowBe4 or Cofense to reinforce awareness.*

Lack of Prioritization

Treating all risks equally is another critical mistake, as it leads to the inefficient allocation of resources. When organizations fail to prioritize risks based on their likelihood and potential impact, they often address minor issues while leaving critical vulnerabilities unaddressed.

A risk-based approach is essential for effective prioritization. Tools like NIST's Risk Management Framework or ISO 31000 provide structured methodologies for assessing and prioritizing risks. Regularly updating risk assessments ensures that organizations remain focused on addressing the most pressing threats.

Example:

- *An organization allocates resources equally to all risks, including minor ones.*
- *Consequences: Critical vulnerabilities like unpatched software are neglected, leading to a data breach.*
- *Resolution:*
  - *Adopt a risk-based approach using tools like NIST's Risk Management Framework or ISO 31000.*
  - *Update risk assessments regularly to reflect the dynamic threat landscape.*

Failing to Involve Stakeholders

Risk assessments conducted in isolation, without input from key stakeholders such as IT, business leaders, and third-party vendors, often result in incomplete evaluations. This disconnect can lead to assessments that fail to address operational realities and organizational objectives.

To overcome this challenge, organizations should establish cross-functional risk management teams that include representatives from various departments. Workshops and collaborative sessions can gather diverse perspectives, ensuring a comprehensive understanding of potential risks and their implications.

Example:

- *IT conducts risk assessments without input from operations or legal teams.*
- *Consequences: The risk management plan fails to address compliance requirements and operational priorities.*
- *Resolution:*
  - *Form cross-functional teams with representatives from various departments.*
  - *Host workshops to gather diverse insights and align on potential risks.*

Overreliance on Technology

While automated tools are invaluable for risk management, relying solely on technology without incorporating human judgment can lead to significant oversights. Automated systems may generate false positives or fail to detect risks unique to the organization's environment.

Organizations should combine automated assessments with manual reviews conducted by skilled cybersecurity professionals. For example, vulnerability scanning tools like Nessus can identify technical weaknesses, but these findings should be validated through penetration testing and expert analysis to ensure accuracy.

Example:

- *An organization uses automated vulnerability scanning tools but ignores manual reviews.*
- *Consequences: False positives overwhelm the team, while unique risks remain undetected.*

CHAPTER 5   INTRODUCTION TO CYBER RISK MANAGEMENT

- *Resolution:*
  - *Combine automated assessments with expert analysis and penetration testing.*
  - *Use different tools for vulnerability scans and validate findings through red team exercises.*

Insufficient Testing and Validation

Implementing risk mitigation measures without thorough testing and validation is a critical mistake. Controls that appear effective on paper may fail under real-world conditions, providing a false sense of security.

Regular testing, such as penetration testing, red team exercises, and disaster recovery simulations, is essential for validating the effectiveness of controls. Tools like Metasploit can be used to conduct controlled exploitation of vulnerabilities, helping organizations identify weaknesses and improve their defenses.

Example:

- *A company implements firewalls but never tests their effectiveness against real threats.*
- *Consequences: Attackers bypass poorly configured firewalls, leading to unauthorized access.*
- *Resolution:*
  - *Test controls regularly through penetration testing and red team exercises.*
  - *Simulate disaster recovery scenarios to validate mitigation strategies.*

Poor Documentation

Incomplete or inconsistent documentation of identified risks and mitigation strategies can hinder tracking, monitoring, and accountability. Without clear records, it becomes challenging to measure progress or demonstrate compliance during audits.

Organizations should utilize risk management software like Archer or LogicGate to maintain comprehensive documentation. Standardizing documentation processes

CHAPTER 5   INTRODUCTION TO CYBER RISK MANAGEMENT

ensures consistency and alignment with audit requirements, making it easier to track and report on risk management activities.

Example:

- *An organization maintains inconsistent records of identified risks and mitigation measures.*
- *Consequences: Teams struggle to track progress or demonstrate compliance during audits.*
- *Resolution:*
  - *Use risk management software like Archer or LogicGate to standardize and maintain comprehensive documentation.*
  - *Aligning documentation practices with audit requirements.*

Neglecting Third-Party Risks

Third-party vendors and partners often introduce significant risks, such as supply chain vulnerabilities or insufficient security controls. Failing to assess these risks can result in data breaches or operational disruptions.

To address third-party risks, organizations should require vendors to comply with established cybersecurity standards and conduct regular audits of their practices. Platforms like CyberGRX or BitSight provide valuable insights into third-party risk profiles, enabling proactive management of these risks.

Example:

- *A supply chain vendor experiences a data breach that impacts the organization.*
- *Consequences: Customer data is exposed, and the company faces regulatory scrutiny.*
- *Resolution:*
  - *Enforce cybersecurity standards for vendors and require regular third-party audits.*
  - *Monitor third-party activities using platforms like CyberGRX or BitSight.*

Treating Risk Management as a One-Time Activity

Viewing risk management as a static process conducted only during audits is a major oversight. Cybersecurity threats are dynamic and constantly evolving, requiring continuous vigilance.

Organizations should implement continuous monitoring solutions using tools like Splunk or QRadar. Regularly updating risk registers and reassessing risks ensures that the risk management process remains relevant and effective in addressing emerging threats.

Example:

- *Risk assessments are conducted annually but not updated for new threats.*
- *Consequences: Emerging threats exploit gaps in outdated risk management plans.*
- *Resolution:*
    - *Implement continuous monitoring with tools like Splunk or QRadar.*
    - *Regularly update risk registers and reassess risks as the threat landscape evolves.*

Best Practices for Effective Risk Management in Cybersecurity Audits

- *Adopt a Holistic Approach*:
    - Address risks across people, processes, and technology to ensure comprehensive coverage.
    - Balance technical measures with human-centric strategies like awareness training.
- *Integrate Risk Management with Business Goals*:
    - Align mitigation strategies with organizational objectives to support growth and resilience.

- Use risk assessments to inform strategic decisions and resource allocation.

- *Leverage Advanced Analytics*:
  - Use AI and machine learning tools to detect emerging risks and analyze trends.
  - Automate routine tasks like vulnerability scanning to focus on critical analysis.

- *Foster a Risk-Aware Culture*:
  - Empower employees to take ownership of cybersecurity risks through continuous training.
  - Establish clear communication channels to report suspicious activities promptly.

- *Enhance Documentation and Reporting*:
  - Standardize documentation practices to ensure consistency and accessibility.
  - Use reporting tools to provide actionable insights to stakeholders.

Key Takeaways

Risk management in cybersecurity audits is an ongoing process that requires vigilance, adaptability, and continuous improvement. Avoiding common pitfalls, such as inadequate risk identification, neglecting human factors, and poor documentation, ensures a stronger security posture. By integrating risk management with business goals, fostering a security-aware culture, and leveraging advanced tools, organizations can stay resilient against evolving threats and maintain effective cybersecurity defenses.

In this section, we covered the following points:

- Recognizing and avoiding common mistakes is essential to effective risk management.
- Examples of pitfalls include inadequate risk identification, overlooking human factors, and poor documentation.

CHAPTER 5   INTRODUCTION TO CYBER RISK MANAGEMENT

- Addressing these challenges involves leveraging advanced tools, stakeholder engagement, and regular testing.

- Holistic strategies and alignment with business goals enhance the effectiveness of cybersecurity audits.

- A risk-aware culture and continuous improvement ensure that organizations remain resilient in a dynamic threat environment.

Conclusions

Effective risk management is the basis of cybersecurity audits, providing organizations with the ability to proactively identify, assess, and mitigate threats that could compromise their digital infrastructure. However, even the most well-intentioned security programs can be undermined by common mistakes, such as inadequate risk identification, overlooking human factors, failing to prioritize threats, and neglecting third-party risks. These oversights create significant vulnerabilities, leaving organizations exposed to cyberattacks, regulatory penalties, operational disruptions, and reputational damage. Recognizing and addressing these pitfalls is essential to strengthening an organization's security posture and ensuring the effectiveness of cybersecurity audits.

One of the most critical aspects of risk management is its dynamic nature. Cyber threats continuously evolve, and new vulnerabilities emerge daily. Organizations that treat risk management as a one-time activity rather than an ongoing process leave themselves vulnerable to sophisticated attacks. Instead, adopting a continuous monitoring approach, leveraging real-time analytics, automated risk assessment tools, and AI-driven threat intelligence, allows for rapid detection and mitigation of risks before they escalate into full-scale security incidents. Technologies such as Splunk, QRadar, and CyberGRX enable organizations to stay ahead of threats by providing deep insights into risk trends, attacker tactics, and potential weaknesses in their security frameworks.

Moreover, risk management should not exist in isolation; it must be integrated with broader business objectives to ensure alignment with organizational goals. A risk-aware culture, where cybersecurity considerations are embedded into decision-making at all levels, is essential for long-term resilience. Business leaders, IT teams, and employees must collaborate to create a security-first mindset, ensuring that risk assessments are not just technical exercises but also strategic tools that support business

CHAPTER 5 INTRODUCTION TO CYBER RISK MANAGEMENT

continuity, regulatory compliance, and financial stability. This integration enhances an organization's ability to allocate resources effectively, prioritize high-impact risks, and develop robust incident response strategies.

A key challenge in cybersecurity audits is the underestimation of the human element in risk management. While organizations often focus on technical controls, many cyber incidents are caused by human errors, such as weak passwords, phishing attacks, or misconfigured security settings. Neglecting employee training and awareness programs significantly increases the likelihood of security breaches. To address this, companies must implement continuous education initiatives, simulated phishing exercises, and behavioral analytics to reinforce secure practices among employees. Platforms like KnowBe4 and Cofense help organizations conduct real-world phishing simulations, training employees to recognize and respond appropriately to cyber threats.

Additionally, third-party risks present a growing challenge, as supply chain vulnerabilities and weak security controls among vendors can introduce significant threats. Organizations must ensure that third-party risk assessments are incorporated into cybersecurity audits, requiring vendors to adhere to strict security standards and conducting regular audits of their practices. Platforms such as BitSight and CyberGRX provide valuable insights into the security posture of external partners, allowing businesses to mitigate risks associated with third-party access to critical systems and sensitive data.

Another crucial element of effective risk management is documentation. Poorly maintained or inconsistent records of risk assessments, mitigation strategies, and audit findings can make it difficult to track progress, demonstrate compliance, and identify areas for improvement. Organizations should leverage risk management software like Archer or LogicGate to ensure standardized documentation practices, making it easier to review risk trends over time and prepare for regulatory audits. Well-documented risk management processes also enhance accountability, ensuring that security teams and leadership have clear visibility into ongoing cybersecurity efforts.

Ultimately, cybersecurity audits should not be viewed as a mere compliance exercise but as a strategic tool to strengthen an organization's resilience against cyber threats. By adopting a holistic, proactive approach, one that combines technology, human awareness, regulatory alignment, and business continuity planning, organizations can create a robust security framework capable of withstanding evolving threats. Regular testing, continuous improvement, and a strong culture of cybersecurity awareness ensure that risk management is not just a defensive measure but a competitive advantage that fosters trust among stakeholders, customers, and regulatory bodies.

Organizations that embrace best practices in risk management, avoiding common mistakes, leveraging advanced tools, involving key stakeholders, and continuously evolving their security strategies, will be better positioned to navigate the complexities of the modern threat landscape. Cybersecurity is no longer just an IT concern but a critical business imperative that requires constant vigilance, adaptation, and collaboration. By prioritizing risk management in cybersecurity audits, organizations not only protect their digital assets but also safeguard their reputation, operational continuity, and long-term success in an increasingly interconnected world.

CHAPTER 6

Tools for Network and Cybersecurity Audits

Effective network and cybersecurity audits rely heavily on specialized tools that provide visibility, analysis, and automation. These tools are designed to identify vulnerabilities, monitor network activity, and assess compliance with security policies. For instance, vulnerability scanners like Nessus, Qualys, and OpenVAS are widely used to detect misconfigurations, missing patches, and outdated software across network devices. These tools provide detailed reports that categorize vulnerabilities by severity, help organizations prioritize remediation efforts, and address critical risks promptly.

Another category of essential tools includes network monitoring and traffic analysis solutions. Tools such as Wireshark, SolarWinds, and PRTG Network Monitor allow auditors to capture and analyze network traffic, identify anomalies, and detect unauthorized activities. Additionally, intrusion detection and prevention systems (IDS/IPS), such as Snort and Suricata, are valuable for real-time threat detection during audits. These tools help organizations understand potential attack vectors, enabling them to reinforce their network defenses against evolving threats.

For cybersecurity audits, compliance management and log analysis tools play a crucial role. Platforms like Splunk, ELK Stack, and AlienVault aggregate and analyze logs from various sources to identify suspicious patterns and ensure adherence to regulatory standards such as GDPR, HIPAA, or PCI DSS. These tools streamline the audit process by automating compliance checks and providing detailed insights into security gaps. By leveraging these advanced solutions, organizations can conduct thorough audits, gain actionable intelligence, and continuously enhance their cybersecurity posture.

CHAPTER 6   TOOLS FOR NETWORK AND CYBERSECURITY AUDITS

Network Security Audits: Tools and Best Practices

In today's rapidly evolving digital landscape, network security audits are indispensable for maintaining a robust cybersecurity posture. These audits aim to identify vulnerabilities, misconfigurations, and potential threats that could compromise an organization's network. The increasing complexity of modern IT environments necessitates the use of specialized tools that streamline the auditing process, enhance accuracy, and provide actionable insights. Leveraging these tools effectively can mean the difference between a secure network and one vulnerable to exploitation.

Network security audits are fundamental to safeguarding organizational assets in an increasingly digitized world. They serve as a vital mechanism for identifying vulnerabilities, detecting misconfigurations, and assessing threats across IT infrastructures. As cyberattacks grow in sophistication, relying on manual methods for audits is impractical. Specialized tools play a pivotal role, automating the audit process, providing actionable insights, and ensuring thorough assessments that align with organizational and regulatory requirements.

Importance of Tools in Network Security Audits

The complexity of modern network environments demands advanced solutions for auditing. Tools streamline the process, enhance accuracy, and reduce the potential for human error. Automated solutions are particularly valuable for identifying hidden vulnerabilities that might be missed during manual reviews. Real-time insights offered by these tools enable quicker responses to potential threats, ensuring proactive mitigation strategies. Additionally, tools provide robust compliance support by generating audit-ready reports tailored to standards like PCI-DSS, NIST, and ISO 27001. By leveraging these tools, organizations can maintain a resilient security posture and protect sensitive data from emerging threats.

Network Security Tools

Selecting the right tools for network security audits is crucial for identifying vulnerabilities, monitoring traffic, and ensuring compliance with industry standards. Each tool serves a specific function, from traffic analysis to real-time threat detection and firewall protection.

CHAPTER 6 TOOLS FOR NETWORK AND CYBERSECURITY AUDITS

Table 6-1 provides a comparative overview of key network security tools, highlighting their advantages, disadvantages, commonalities, and unique features to help organizations make informed decisions when implementing security audits.

Table 6-1. *Comparison of different network security tools*

Name	Advantages	Disadvantages	What It Has in Common	Unique Feature
Wireshark	Free, open-source, supports multiple protocols, granular traffic analysis	Requires expertise to interpret results, not an active security solution	Network traffic analysis tools that help detect unauthorized activity	Packet-level network traffic inspection
SolarWinds Network Performance Monitor	Real-time monitoring, visual dashboards, detects bottlenecks	Expensive, resource-intensive for large-scale networks	Performance monitoring tools that help maintain network efficiency	Advanced bandwidth tracking and alerting
Nmap	Open-source, maps devices and ports, detects unauthorized applications	Can be slow on large networks, requires expertise to use advanced scripting	Network discovery and vulnerability detection tools	Custom scripting for in-depth security assessments
Darktrace	AI-powered anomaly detection, self-learning, autonomous response	Expensive, requires fine-tuning to minimize false positives	Threat detection tools that analyze real-time network behavior	AI-driven autonomous threat response
Palo Alto Networks	Next-gen firewall, automated threat intelligence, granular traffic control	High cost, requires specialized training for full utilization	Firewall and network protection tools	Cloud security integration with automated threat intelligence

Table 6-1 provides more details related to the tools.

CHAPTER 6   TOOLS FOR NETWORK AND CYBERSECURITY AUDITS

Wireshark

Wireshark is a powerful open-source network traffic analysis tool that enables IT teams to capture and inspect data packets for abnormalities or suspicious behavior. By supporting a wide array of protocols, Wireshark allows granular analysis of network communications, making it easier to detect unauthorized data transfers or malicious activities. It also provides detailed graphical representations of traffic flow, which aid in diagnosing network performance issues. For example, using Wireshark, a healthcare provider identified unusual outbound traffic, uncovering an active data exfiltration attempt and promptly mitigating the threat to ensure HIPAA compliance.

- *Purpose*: Network traffic analysis.
- *Features*: Captures and inspects data packets for abnormalities, detects unauthorized data transfers, and supports multiple protocols for granular analysis.
- *Example in Action*: A healthcare provider identified unusual outbound traffic using Wireshark, discovering an active data exfiltration attempt.
- Link to access the tool: https://www.wireshark.org/

SolarWinds Network Performance Monitor

SolarWinds NPM is a comprehensive solution for real-time network performance monitoring. It excels in detecting traffic bottlenecks, monitoring bandwidth usage, and generating intuitive dashboards that visualize the health of a network. Its ability to track performance metrics across distributed systems helps organizations maintain optimal network operations. For instance, a manufacturing organization used SolarWinds NPM to pinpoint underperforming devices in its production network, enhancing both operational efficiency and productivity.

- *Purpose*: Real-time network performance monitoring.
- *Features*: Monitors bandwidth, detects network bottlenecks, and provides visual dashboards for network health.

- *Example in Action*: A manufacturing organization used this tool to identify underperforming devices, enhancing overall productivity.
- Link to access the tool: https://www.solarwinds.com/network-performance-monitor

Nmap (Network Mapper)

Nmap is a versatile tool used for network discovery and security auditing. It identifies devices and open ports within a network, detects unauthorized applications, and provides advanced scripting capabilities for tailored assessments. This makes it ideal for detecting shadow IT and unauthorized devices. For example, an IT team employed Nmap during an audit to locate unapproved IoT devices connected to their corporate network, mitigating risks associated with potential data leaks or unauthorized access.

- *Purpose*: Network discovery and security auditing.
- *Features*: Maps devices and open ports, detects unauthorized applications, and supports scripting for advanced tests.
- *Example in Action*: An IT team used Nmap to locate unauthorized devices, mitigating shadow IT risks.
- Link to access the tool: https://nmap.org/

Darktrace

Darktrace is an advanced AI-powered tool for real-time threat detection and autonomous response. It utilizes machine learning to create a dynamic model of "normal" network behavior, enabling it to identify and respond to anomalies indicative of potential threats. Its self-learning capabilities make it an essential part of modern cybersecurity strategies. A financial institution, for example, used Darktrace to detect and block a zero-day malware attack in progress, preventing data loss and operational disruptions.

- *Purpose*: Threat detection and autonomous response.
- *Features*: Leverages AI to identify and respond to unusual network behaviors in real-time.

- *Example in Action*: A financial institution used Darktrace to block a zero-day attack automatically.

- Link to access the tool: https://www.darktrace.com/

Palo Alto Networks

Palo Alto Networks offers next-generation firewall solutions and advanced threat prevention features. Its automated threat intelligence and granular traffic control capabilities make it invaluable for securing enterprise networks against sophisticated attacks. For example, an e-commerce company leveraged Palo Alto's platform to safeguard its web applications from distributed denial-of-service (DDoS) attacks, ensuring uninterrupted service during peak shopping periods.

- *Purpose*: Firewall and advanced threat prevention.

- *Features*: Provides next-generation firewalls, cloud security, and automated threat intelligence.

- *Example in Action*: An e-commerce company utilized Palo Alto to enhance its defense against DDoS attacks.

- Link to access the tool: https://www.paloaltonetworks.com/

Asset Discovery Tools

Effective asset discovery is essential for maintaining a secure and well-managed IT environment. These tools help organizations track hardware and software assets, ensure compliance, and identify vulnerabilities within their infrastructure.

Table 6-2 provides a comparative overview of key asset discovery tools, outlining their advantages, disadvantages, common features, and unique capabilities.

Table 6-2. Comparison of different asset discovery tools

Name	Advantages	Disadvantages	What They Have in Common	Unique Feature
AssetSonar	Tracks IT assets, ensures license compliance, integrates with other IT tools	May require customization for specific IT environments	IT asset tracking and compliance support	Seamless integration with IT Service Management (ITSM)
SolarWinds IP Address Manager	Automates IP address management, prevents conflicts, simplifies troubleshooting	Can be expensive for smaller organizations	Centralized asset visibility and automation	Reduces IP conflicts in large networks
AssetExplorer	Automates asset discovery, provides lifecycle tracking, enhances resource allocation	May require additional configuration for full automation	Real-time asset discovery and tracking	Identifies underutilized assets to optimize costs
Qualys Inventory	Offers detailed vulnerability insights, helps with compliance, automates asset tracking	Requires integration with other Qualys tools for full functionality	IT asset discovery and vulnerability assessment	Maps IT assets to security risks for proactive mitigation

AssetSonar

AssetSonar provides robust IT asset management capabilities, tracking both hardware and software assets throughout their lifecycle. It ensures license compliance and integrates seamlessly with other IT management tools, helping organizations maintain an accurate inventory. For instance, a tech company streamlined its asset tracking and audit preparation processes using AssetSonar, ensuring regulatory compliance and minimizing the risk of asset misuse.

- *Purpose*: IT asset management.

- *Features*: Tracks software and hardware assets, supports license compliance, and integrates with other IT tools.

- *Example in Action*: A tech company streamlined its inventory processes using AssetSonar, ensuring compliance during audits.

- Link to access the tool: https://www.assetsonar.com/

SolarWinds IP Address Manager

SolarWinds IP Address Manager automates the management of IP addresses, reducing the likelihood of conflicts in large networks. By providing centralized visibility into IP usage, it simplifies troubleshooting and enhances operational efficiency. A retail chain employed this tool to prevent network outages caused by overlapping IP assignments, enabling uninterrupted operations across multiple store locations.

- *Purpose*: IP address tracking and management.

- *Features*: Automates IP address provisioning and reduces conflicts in large networks.

- *Example in Action*: A retail chain avoided network outages by efficiently managing IP assignments.

- Link to access the tool: https://www.solarwinds.com/ip-address-manager

AssetExplorer

AssetExplorer enables IT teams to discover, track, and manage assets effectively. Its automation capabilities for asset discovery and audits provide insights into asset utilization and lifecycle status. For example, a logistics company identified underutilized servers using AssetExplorer, reallocating resources to improve overall system efficiency.

- *Purpose*: IT asset discovery and lifecycle management.

- *Features*: Tracks assets, automates audits, and provides insights into asset utilization.

CHAPTER 6   TOOLS FOR NETWORK AND CYBERSECURITY AUDITS

- *Example in Action*: A logistics company reduced costs by identifying underutilized assets using AssetExplorer.

- Link to access the tool: https://www.manageengine.com/products/asset-explorer/

Qualys Inventory

Qualys Inventory delivers a comprehensive view of an organization's IT assets, identifying associated vulnerabilities and providing actionable insights. It is a valuable tool for maintaining compliance and reducing an organization's attack surface. An enterprise, for example, used Qualys Inventory to uncover outdated software versions across its network, prioritizing remediation efforts and significantly lowering cyber risks.

- *Purpose*: Asset visibility and vulnerability management.

- *Features*: Provides a detailed inventory of IT assets and identifies associated vulnerabilities.

- *Example in Action*: An enterprise uncovered outdated software versions across devices using Qualys.

- Link to access the tool: https://www.qualys.com/apps/global-it-asset-inventory/

IDS/IPS/EDR Tools

IDS, Intrusion Prevention Systems (IPS), and EDR tools play a critical role in identifying, preventing, and responding to security threats. These tools monitor network traffic and endpoints for malicious activity, helping organizations mitigate cyber risks effectively.

Table 6-3 compares key IDS/IPS/EDR solutions, highlighting their advantages, disadvantages, commonalities, and unique features.

Table 6-3. Comparison of different IDS/IPS/EDR tools

Name	Advantages	Disadvantages	What They Have in Common	Unique Feature
Snort	Open-source, customizable rules, real-time traffic monitoring	Requires manual rule configuration, high false positive rate	Detects and prevents intrusions in real-time	Rule-based threat detection with extensive customization
Suricata	High-performance, multi-threaded processing, detailed logging	Higher resource consumption, complex setup	Monitors network traffic for known and unknown threats	Supports deep packet inspection with multi-threading
CrowdStrike	Cloud-native, AI-driven threat hunting, automated response	Subscription-based pricing, dependent on internet connectivity	Provides endpoint protection and automated response	Real-time AI-powered threat detection
SentinelOne	Autonomous endpoint protection, combines EDR and antivirus	Can be resource-intensive for older systems	Prevents, detects, and responds to endpoint threats	Self-healing capabilities with automated rollback

Snort

Snort is a lightweight yet powerful intrusion detection and prevention system (IDS/IPS) capable of monitoring network traffic in real-time. Its rule-based approach allows for precise threat detection and response. For example, an educational institution deployed Snort to identify and block unauthorized access attempts, bolstering its network's security posture.

- *Purpose*: Intrusion detection and prevention.
- *Features:* Detects known attacks, supports custom rules, and monitors network traffic in real time.

CHAPTER 6   TOOLS FOR NETWORK AND CYBERSECURITY AUDITS

- *Example in Action*: An educational institution deployed Snort to detect and block unauthorized network activities.

- Link to access the tool: https://www.snort.org/

Suricata

Suricata is a high-performance IDS/IPS that excels in processing large volumes of traffic. With multi-threading support and detailed event logging, it is well-suited for organizations managing complex and high-speed networks. A research lab utilized Suricata to detect APTs targeting its sensitive data, enabling swift incident response.

- *Purpose*: High-performance intrusion detection.

- *Features*: Processes high volumes of traffic, supports multi-threading, and provides detailed event logging.

- *Example in Action*: A research lab used Suricata to protect sensitive data from targeted attacks.

- Link to access the tool: https://suricata.io/

CrowdStrike

CrowdStrike's EDR platform provides real-time threat hunting and automated remediation capabilities. Its cloud-native design ensures scalability for organizations of all sizes. A global enterprise leveraged CrowdStrike to neutralize ransomware before it could spread, minimizing downtime and data loss.

- *Purpose*: EDR.

- *Features*: Provides real-time threat hunting, malware detection, and automated remediation.

- *Example in Action*: A global enterprise relied on CrowdStrike to neutralize ransomware before it could spread.

- Link to access the tool: https://www.crowdstrike.com/

SentinelOne

SentinelOne combines EDR, antivirus, and incident response capabilities into a single platform. Its autonomous nature allows for rapid identification and resolution of threats without human intervention. A startup used SentinelOne to protect its endpoints against sophisticated phishing attacks, ensuring business continuity.

- *Purpose*: Autonomous endpoint protection.
- *Features*: Combines EDR, antivirus, and incident response in one platform.
- *Example in Action*: A startup used SentinelOne to reduce incident response times, ensuring business continuity.
- Link to access the tool: https://www.sentinelone.com/

Best Practices for Tool Integration in Network Security Audits

Layered Approach

Combining multiple tools ensures comprehensive coverage of vulnerabilities and threats. For instance, use Nmap for network mapping, Wireshark for traffic analysis, and Snort or Suricata for intrusion detection. Implementing a layered approach offers several benefits: it minimizes blind spots, provides cross-validation of findings, and enhances threat visibility. Organizations can integrate tools through centralized dashboards or SIEM solutions to streamline workflows and ensure real-time monitoring.

Regular Updates

Keeping tools updated is critical for identifying the latest vulnerabilities and threats. Regular updates ensure that the tools' threat databases and features remain current. Automating updates through centralized management systems can reduce the manual effort required and ensure consistent protection.

Training and Expertise

Equipping the audit team with in-depth knowledge of the tools enhances their ability to interpret results accurately. Regular training sessions, certifications, and hands-on practice are essential. Vendors often provide workshops and detailed documentation to help teams stay proficient in using advanced features.

Customizable Workflows

Many tools allow users to customize scans, rules, and dashboards to align with organizational needs. Tailoring these settings ensures relevance and reduces unnecessary noise during audits. For example, configuring Snort's rules to focus on critical threats can improve detection accuracy.

Scalability and Automation

Tools like CrowdStrike and Qualys Inventory provide scalable solutions for organizations of varying sizes. Automation features, such as scheduled scans and real-time alerts, enhance efficiency and ensure continuous monitoring without overburdening IT teams.

Key Considerations for Tool Selection

- *Scope of Audit*: Determine whether the primary need is vulnerability scanning (e.g., Nessus) or traffic analysis (e.g., Wireshark).

- *Budget Constraints*: Consider open-source options like Nmap and OpenVAS for cost-effective yet robust solutions.

- *Compliance Needs*: Output of tools like SolarWinds NCM to ensure alignment with regulatory requirements.

- *Integration Capabilities*: Ensure chosen tools can seamlessly integrate with existing systems for streamlined operations.

CHAPTER 6   TOOLS FOR NETWORK AND CYBERSECURITY AUDITS

Key Takeaways

Network security audits are crucial for identifying vulnerabilities and strengthening cybersecurity. Leveraging specialized tools enhances accuracy, streamlines audits, and enables proactive threat mitigation. A layered approach, regular updates, and expert training maximize security resilience in an evolving digital landscape.

In this section, we covered the following points:

- Tools like Wireshark, Nmap, AssetSonar, Snort, and SentinelOne are essential for thorough network security audits, providing capabilities ranging from traffic analysis to automated endpoint protection.

- A layered, multi-tool strategy minimizes risks by uncovering vulnerabilities, detecting intrusions, and managing assets comprehensively.

- Implementing best practices such as regular updates, tool integration, and customization enhances the effectiveness of audits while ensuring regulatory compliance.

- Training IT teams and leveraging automation capabilities maximize tool utility and improve audit outcomes.

- Scalable solutions like CrowdStrike and Darktrace empower organizations to adapt to evolving threat landscapes, ensuring long-term operational resilience.

Advanced Cybersecurity Strategies and Audits with SIEM and DLP Tools

In the modern cybersecurity landscape, organizations are continually seeking robust solutions to safeguard their sensitive data and infrastructure. Two pivotal categories of tools, SIEM and DLP, play a crucial role in achieving comprehensive security. This section delves into the features, applications, and benefits of these tools, along with best practices for integration.

CHAPTER 6 TOOLS FOR NETWORK AND CYBERSECURITY AUDITS

SIEM systems have become indispensable in modern cybersecurity audits. These systems aggregate, analyze, and correlate vast amounts of log data from an organization's IT infrastructure to uncover security events, vulnerabilities, and compliance gaps. By leveraging SIEM systems during audits, organizations can streamline their processes, enhance accuracy, and gain deeper insights into their security posture.

What Is a SIEM System?

A SIEM system is a centralized platform that collects and analyzes log data from various IT components, such as servers, firewalls, endpoints, and cloud environments. Using algorithms and correlation rules, SIEM systems detect threats, identify anomalies, and provide actionable insights. Popular SIEM solutions include Splunk, IBM QRadar, LogRhythm, ArcSight, Elastic Security, etc.. These tools are essential for organizations dealing with complex IT environments, providing a comprehensive view of their security landscape.

SIEM Tools

SIEM tools aggregate, analyze, and manage security events from multiple sources to provide a unified view of an organization's security posture. By correlating log data and detecting anomalies, these tools empower organizations to respond swiftly to potential threats.

Table 6-4 presents comparison of different SIEM tools.

Table 6-4. Comparison of different SIEM tools

Name	Advantages	Disadvantages	What Has in Common	Unique Feature
SolarWinds	Real-time monitoring, automated threat detection, customizable dashboards	May require additional configuration for complex environments	Centralized log management and real-time threat detection	Intuitive interface with compliance reporting features
IBM QRadar	AI-driven analytics, automated workflows, scalable deployment	High resource requirements, complex setup	Correlates network activity for advanced threat intelligence	Pre-built compliance reporting templates
Splunk	Machine learning for anomaly detection, scalable data handling	Expensive for large-scale use, steep learning curve	Collects and analyzes data from multiple sources	Predictive security insights using ML
Microsoft Sentinel	Cloud-native SIEM, AI-powered threat intelligence, seamless Azure integration	Limited outside Azure ecosystem, dependent on cloud infrastructure	AI-driven threat detection and automated response	Customizable workbooks for data visualization
LogRhythm	Security orchestration & automation, advanced analytics for threat detection	Can generate high false positives, requires fine-tuning	Centralized log collection and automated workflows	Built-in SOAR capabilities
Nagios	Cost-effective, extensive plugins for customization	Lacks advanced SIEM features, manual setup needed	Infrastructure monitoring and alerting	Plugin-based extensibility

(continued)

Table 6-4. (*continued*)

Name	Advantages	Disadvantages	What Has in Common	Unique Feature
Ansible	Automates security configurations, integrates with SIEM tools	Not a dedicated SIEM tool, requires scripting knowledge	Automation and orchestration for security tasks	Playbook-driven security response
Graylog	Open-source, real-time log analytics, highly customizable	Requires technical expertise, limited built-in compliance tools	Log management and analysis	Strong extensibility for development teams
AWS CloudTrail	Tracks API activity in AWS, ensures compliance with cloud regulations	Limited to AWS environments, no real-time threat detection	Logs security events for audit and compliance	Granular API activity logging
Azure Monitor	Real-time alerts, integrates with Azure Sentinel for security insights	Best suited for Azure environments, requires cloud expertise	Performance monitoring with security insights	Advanced analytics for troubleshooting
Elastic Stack	Open-source, scalable logging, real-time visualization	Requires significant setup, high storage requirements	Centralized logging and security analytics	ELK stack integration
ArcSight	Advanced threat detection, scalable for large enterprises	High cost, complex deployment	Correlates data from multiple sources for a unified security view	Legacy SIEM with real-time threat hunting capabilities

CHAPTER 6   TOOLS FOR NETWORK AND CYBERSECURITY AUDITS

SolarWinds

SolarWinds SIEM offers powerful log management and real-time monitoring capabilities. It provides automated threat detection through advanced correlation rules and customizable dashboards that simplify complex data visualization. Its intuitive interface ensures accessibility for IT teams, while compliance reporting features streamline adherence to frameworks like HIPAA and PCI-DSS.

- *Purpose*: Centralized log management and threat detection.
- *Features*:
  - Real-time monitoring of network activity.
  - Automated alerts for unusual behavior.
  - Customizable dashboards for analytics and reporting.
- *Example in Action*: A retail company used SolarWinds to detect unauthorized access attempts, preventing a potential data breach by implementing additional access controls.
- Link to access the tool: `https://www.solarwinds.com/`

IBM QRadar

IBM QRadar excels in detecting sophisticated threats by integrating AI-driven analytics. It correlates data across multiple sources to identify patterns indicative of malicious activity. QRadar's automated workflows reduce manual effort, while its scalability supports deployment across diverse environments, from small businesses to large enterprises.

- *Purpose*: Advanced threat intelligence and incident response.
- *Features*:
  - Integration with AI for enhanced threat detection.
  - Correlation of network activity across systems.
  - Pre-built compliance reporting templates.

CHAPTER 6   TOOLS FOR NETWORK AND CYBERSECURITY AUDITS

- *Example in Action*: A financial institution employed QRadar to meet PCI-DSS requirements, successfully identifying and mitigating risks associated with unpatched systems.

- Link to access the tool: https://www.ibm.com/products/qradar-siem

Splunk

Splunk is a versatile SIEM solution known for its data analytics capabilities. It integrates seamlessly with existing IT infrastructure, collecting data from various endpoints. Its machine learning algorithms detect emerging threats and offer predictive insights, enhancing proactive defense measures. Splunk's modular architecture supports customization for specific security needs.

- *Purpose*: Data analytics and security monitoring.
- *Features*:
  - Collects and analyzes data from diverse sources.
  - Provides machine learning capabilities for anomaly detection.
  - Scales to handle large volumes of data.
- *Example in Action*: An e-commerce platform leveraged Splunk to monitor transaction logs, detecting fraudulent activities and protecting customer data.
- Link to access the tool: https://www.splunk.com/

Microsoft Sentinel

Microsoft Sentinel leverages the power of cloud computing to provide scalable SIEM services. Integrated with Microsoft's ecosystem, it enables seamless ingestion of data from Azure and third-party platforms. Its AI-powered threat intelligence and automated response mechanisms enhance threat detection and mitigation.

- *Purpose*: Cloud-native SIEM for proactive threat hunting.
- *Features*:

CHAPTER 6   TOOLS FOR NETWORK AND CYBERSECURITY AUDITS

- AI-driven threat detection and response.
- Integration with Microsoft 365 and Azure services.
- Customizable workbooks for data visualization.
- *Example in Action*: A healthcare provider used Microsoft Sentinel to ensure HIPAA compliance by monitoring patient data access logs and responding to suspicious activities.
- Link to access the tool: `https://azure.microsoft.com/products/microsoft-sentinel/`

LogRhythm

LogRhythm combines SIEM with SOAR capabilities. It provides a centralized platform for monitoring, detecting, and responding to security incidents. LogRhythm's advanced analytics reduce false positives, enabling teams to focus on genuine threats.

- *Purpose*: Streamlined threat lifecycle management.
- *Features:*
    - Centralized log collection and analysis.
    - Automated incident response workflows.
    - Compliance-ready reporting capabilities.
- *Example in Action*: A government agency used LogRhythm to identify and mitigate phishing attempts targeting employee email accounts.
- Link to access the tool: `https://logrhythm.com/`

Nagios

Nagios is a monitoring tool with SIEM capabilities that provides insights into system health and security. Its plugins extend functionality to include log monitoring, vulnerability detection, and alerting for unusual activities. Nagios is well-suited for organizations seeking cost-effective solutions.

- *Purpose*: Infrastructure monitoring and alerting.
- *Features*:

CHAPTER 6 TOOLS FOR NETWORK AND CYBERSECURITY AUDITS

- Tracks system performance and availability.
- Sends alerts for hardware and application failures.
- Integrates with other SIEM tools for enhanced visibility.
- *Example in Action*: A manufacturing company relied on Nagios to monitor production servers, reducing downtime caused by hardware failures.
- Link to access the tool: https://www.nagios.com/

Ansible

Ansible's integration with SIEM workflows automates incident response and threat remediation. By scripting security policies and response actions, it reduces response times and minimizes human error. Ansible's playbooks streamline repetitive security tasks, enhancing overall efficiency.

- *Purpose*: Automation and orchestration for security tasks.
- *Features*:
    - Automates repetitive security configurations.
    - Integrates with SIEM tools for event-triggered workflows.
    - Ensures consistency across multi-cloud environments.
- *Example in Action*: A tech startup automated firewall configurations with Ansible, saving time and reducing human errors during deployments.
- Link to access the tool: https://www.ansible.com/

Graylog

Graylog is an open-source SIEM tool offering log management and real-time analytics. It enables organizations to identify and analyze security incidents through customizable dashboards and alerting mechanisms. Graylog's extensibility makes it a favorite among development-focused teams.

- *Purpose*: Open-source log management and analysis.
- *Features*:
  - Provides real-time log analytics.
  - Offers a highly customizable alerting system.
  - Scalable for large data environments.
- *Example in Action*: A university utilized Graylog to monitor campus-wide IT systems, detecting and resolving network outages promptly.
- Link to access the tool: https://www.graylog.org/

AWS CloudTrail

AWS CloudTrail records and monitors API activity within AWS environments. It supports compliance and security by providing granular insights into access patterns, misconfigurations, and unauthorized activities. CloudTrail integrates seamlessly with AWS's broader security ecosystem.

- *Purpose*: Auditing and monitoring AWS resources.
- *Features*:
  - Logs all API activity within AWS accounts.
  - Provides event history for security analysis.
  - Facilitates compliance with cloud-specific regulations.
- *Example in Action*: An online service provider used CloudTrail to track unauthorized changes in AWS resources, restoring configurations to their original state.
- Link to access the tool: https://aws.amazon.com/cloudtrail/

Azure Monitor

Azure Monitor offers comprehensive observability for Azure-based infrastructures. By integrating with Azure Sentinel, it delivers robust SIEM capabilities, including log correlation, anomaly detection, and compliance monitoring. Azure Monitor's real-time alerts ensure swift incident response.

CHAPTER 6   TOOLS FOR NETWORK AND CYBERSECURITY AUDITS

- *Purpose*: Performance monitoring for Azure-based applications.

- *Features*:

    - Tracks metrics and logs for Azure resources.

    - Integrates with Azure Sentinel for security insights.

    - Provides advanced analytics for troubleshooting.

- *Example in Action*: A SaaS company used Azure Monitor to optimize application performance, reducing downtime and improving user experience.

- Link to access the tool: `https://azure.microsoft.com/products/monitor/`

Elastic Stack

Elastic Stack, or ELK, is a popular open-source solution for log management and security analytics. Its SIEM capabilities include log aggregation, search, and visualization, making it a versatile choice for security operations centers.

- *Purpose*: Data ingestion, analysis, and visualization.

- *Features*:

    - Enables centralized logging with Elasticsearch.

    - Visualizes data through Kibana dashboards.

    - Supports scalability for big data environments.

- *Example in Action*: A logistics company used Elastic Stack to monitor fleet operations, improving efficiency by identifying delays in real time.

- Link to access the tool: `https://www.elastic.co/`

CHAPTER 6   TOOLS FOR NETWORK AND CYBERSECURITY AUDITS

ArcSight

ArcSight is a legacy SIEM platform known for its scalability and advanced threat detection. It provides extensive correlation rules and comprehensive reporting features that support compliance and incident management efforts. ArcSight's robust architecture is ideal for large enterprises with complex networks.

- *Purpose*: Comprehensive threat detection and response.
- *Features*:
  - Correlates data from multiple sources for unified threat views.
  - Offers advanced analytics for detecting unknown threats.
  - Supports real-time threat hunting and mitigation.
- *Example in Action*: A telecommunications organization used ArcSight to identify and respond to DDoS attacks, ensuring uninterrupted services for its customers.
- Link to access the tool: https://www.microfocus.com/en-us/cyberres/arcsight

The Role of SIEM in Cybersecurity Audits

SIEM systems significantly simplify and enhance cybersecurity audits. Their core functionalities contribute to a more efficient and thorough assessment of an organization's defenses.

Centralized Log Data Management

SIEM systems collect logs from across the organization's IT ecosystem, eliminating the need for manual data gathering. This centralized approach ensures no critical data is overlooked.

CHAPTER 6 TOOLS FOR NETWORK AND CYBERSECURITY AUDITS

Correlation of Security Events

By analyzing patterns and correlating events across different systems, SIEM systems identify threats that might go unnoticed in isolated logs. For instance, they can link failed login attempts across multiple devices to detect brute-force attacks.

Streamlining Compliance

Many SIEM systems include pre-built templates and reports tailored to regulatory standards such as GDPR, PCI-DSS, and ISO 27001. These features simplify evidence gathering and documentation for audits.

Real-Time Insights

Unlike traditional auditing methods, SIEM systems provide real-time monitoring and alerts, enabling auditors to assess security incidents as they occur. This dynamic capability helps in evaluating the effectiveness of incident response processes.

Steps to Use SIEM in Audits

Successfully integrating SIEM systems into the audit process involves several key steps. The following process flow outlines the key steps involved in effectively using a SIEM system for auditing purposes. By following these steps, organizations can leverage the power of SIEM data to enhance their security posture, improve incident response, and achieve their audit objectives.

Figure 6-1 presents key activities for key steps of using SIEM in audits.

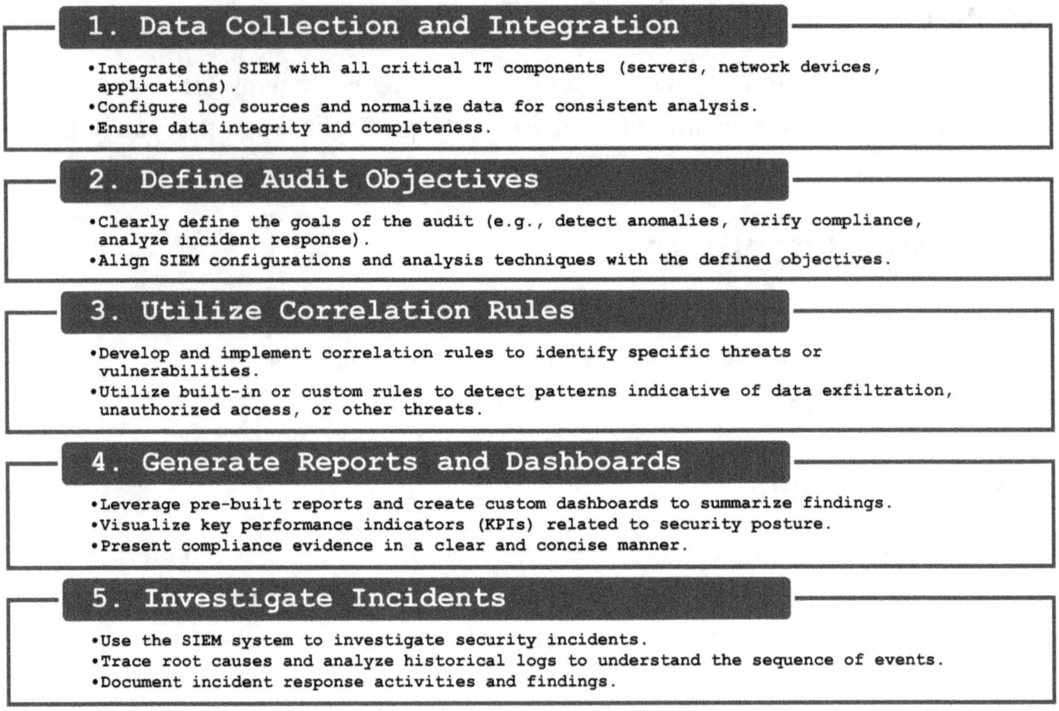

CHAPTER 6   TOOLS FOR NETWORK AND CYBERSECURITY AUDITS

1. Data Collection and Integration
- Integrate the SIEM with all critical IT components (servers, network devices, applications).
- Configure log sources and normalize data for consistent analysis.
- Ensure data integrity and completeness.

2. Define Audit Objectives
- Clearly define the goals of the audit (e.g., detect anomalies, verify compliance, analyze incident response).
- Align SIEM configurations and analysis techniques with the defined objectives.

3. Utilize Correlation Rules
- Develop and implement correlation rules to identify specific threats or vulnerabilities.
- Utilize built-in or custom rules to detect patterns indicative of data exfiltration, unauthorized access, or other threats.

4. Generate Reports and Dashboards
- Leverage pre-built reports and create custom dashboards to summarize findings.
- Visualize key performance indicators (KPIs) related to security posture.
- Present compliance evidence in a clear and concise manner.

5. Investigate Incidents
- Use the SIEM system to investigate security incidents.
- Trace root causes and analyze historical logs to understand the sequence of events.
- Document incident response activities and findings.

Figure 6-1. *Key steps of using SIEM in audits*

DLP Tools

DLP tools are designed to prevent unauthorized access, transfer, or disclosure of sensitive data. By monitoring data movement and applying policies, these tools protect intellectual property and ensure compliance.

Table 6-5 presents a comparison of different DLP tools.

CHAPTER 6　TOOLS FOR NETWORK AND CYBERSECURITY AUDITS

Table 6-5. Comparison of different DLP tools

Name	Advantages	Disadvantages	What It Has in Common	Unique Feature
Symantec DLP	Monitors data in motion, at rest, and in use; detailed audit trails	High cost, requires ongoing policy updates	Prevents unauthorized data access and exfiltration	Comprehensive policy enforcement across endpoints, networks, and storage
Forcepoint DLP	AI-driven threat detection, real-time data monitoring, insider threat protection	Can generate false positives, requires policy fine-tuning	Behavioral analytics-based data protection	Uses AI to detect and mitigate insider threats
Digital Guardian	Endpoint-focused security, real-time alerts, encryption enforcement	Complex deployment, requires integration with SIEM	Tracks data access and usage across endpoints	Deep visibility into endpoint activity with automated encryption

Symantec DLP

Symantec DLP offers granular control over data security with its comprehensive monitoring and policy enforcement capabilities. It identifies sensitive data across endpoints, networks, and storage systems, applying policies to prevent unauthorized access or transfer. Symantec's advanced reporting aids in compliance with regulations like GDPR and CCPA.

- *Purpose*: Prevents unauthorized data access and exfiltration.
- *Features*:
    - Monitors data in motion, at rest, and in use.
    - Identifies and classifies sensitive information.
    - Provides detailed audit trails for compliance.

- *Example in Action*: A law organization implemented Symantec DLP to monitor email communications, preventing the accidental leakage of client data.

- Link to access the tool: https://www.broadcom.com/products/cyber-security/information-protection/data-loss-prevention

Forcepoint DLP

Forcepoint DLP employs behavioral analytics to detect and mitigate risks associated with insider threats and data exfiltration. Its real-time monitoring and automated enforcement of data security policies minimize the risk of data breaches. Integration with cloud services ensures consistent protection across hybrid environments.

- *Purpose*: Data protection through behavioral analytics.

- *Features*:
  - Uses AI to detect insider threats.
  - Blocks unauthorized data transfers in real time.
  - Offers policy-driven data classification.

- *Example in Action*: A financial services provider used Forcepoint DLP to prevent employees from sharing sensitive financial documents over unsecured channels.

- Link to access the tool: https://www.forcepoint.com/

Digital Guardian

Digital Guardian specializes in endpoint-centric DLP, providing visibility and control over data at rest, in motion, and in use. It supports granular policy enforcement, ensuring that sensitive data is accessed and transferred only by authorized users. Its integration with SIEM tools enhances threat detection and response capabilities.

- *Purpose*: Endpoint-focused data loss prevention.

- *Features*:

- Tracks data access and usage at endpoints.
- Enforces encryption for sensitive files.
- Provides real-time alerts for policy violations.
- *Example in Action*: A healthcare organization deployed Digital Guardian to secure patient records, ensuring compliance with HIPAA regulations.
- Link to access the tool: `https://digitalguardian.com/`

Challenges in Using SIEM Systems

While SIEM systems offer numerous benefits, they also present challenges that organizations must address:

- *Cost*: Enterprise-grade SIEM solutions can be prohibitively expensive for small and medium-sized businesses. Open-source alternatives like Elastic Security can be a cost-effective option.
- *Complexity*: Configuring and managing a SIEM system requires skilled personnel. Without proper training, organizations may struggle to extract value from their investment.
- *False Positives*: SIEM systems can generate excessive alerts, overwhelming security teams and potentially masking genuine threats. Fine-tuning correlation rules and implementing AI-based filtering can mitigate this issue. Overly aggressive DLP policies can trigger numerous false positives, overwhelming security teams and causing alert fatigue.
- *Balancing Security and Productivity*: Strict DLP policies can hinder legitimate business operations by blocking access to essential data or delaying workflows.

CHAPTER 6 TOOLS FOR NETWORK AND CYBERSECURITY AUDITS

Best Practices for Tool Integration in Security Strategies

Maximizing the potential of SIEM systems requires adhering to best practices:

- *Regularly Update Correlation Rules*: Keep correlation rules aligned with evolving threats and organizational changes. This ensures the SIEM remains effective against emerging attack vectors.

- *Test Integration Thoroughly*: Regularly validate the integration of all log sources to ensure complete and accurate data collection. Missing logs can result in blind spots during audits.

- *Prioritize High-Risk Areas*: Focus audits on systems and processes that pose the highest risks to the organization. This targeted approach optimizes resource allocation and audit impact.

- *Automate Repetitive Tasks*: Automate log aggregation, analysis, and reporting to reduce manual effort and minimize human error. This approach improves efficiency and allows auditors to focus on more complex tasks.

- *Collaborate with Incident Response Teams*: Share SIEM findings with incident response teams to develop better strategies for mitigating vulnerabilities and responding to security incidents.

Layered Security Approach

Integrating SIEM and DLP tools creates a layered defense system that addresses both proactive threat detection and reactive data protection.

For instance:

- Use SIEM tools like Splunk to detect anomalies in network traffic.

- Combine with DLP solutions such as Symantec to monitor sensitive data transfer.

- Employ automation tools like Ansible to streamline response actions.

Benefits of Integration

- *Enhanced Threat Visibility*: Centralizing logs and data activity provides a holistic view of security.

- *Streamlined Compliance*: Tools generate audit-ready reports, simplifying regulatory adherence.

- *Proactive Defense*: AI-driven analytics in SIEM tools identify threats before they materialize.

- *Data Security*: DLP tools enforce policies that prevent unauthorized access or transfer.

Implementation Strategies

- *Assess Organizational Needs*: Identify specific risks and regulatory requirements to select the right tools.

- *Establish Clear Policies*: Define security and compliance objectives to guide tool configurations.

- *Automate Incident Response*: Integrate tools with automation platforms to expedite threat mitigation.

- *Continuous Training*: Equip teams with knowledge to leverage tool functionalities effectively.

- *Regular Audits*: Use SIEM and DLP tools to conduct ongoing assessments, refining strategies based on evolving threats.

Key Takeaways

Integrating SIEM and DLP tools is essential for a proactive cybersecurity strategy. SIEM solutions provide real-time threat detection, while DLP safeguards sensitive data from unauthorized access and exfiltration. A layered security approach, combined with automation, continuous monitoring, and regular audits, strengthens resilience against evolving threats. By aligning with compliance standards and optimizing security workflows, organizations can enhance visibility, mitigate risks, and protect critical assets in an increasingly complex cyber landscape.

CHAPTER 6   TOOLS FOR NETWORK AND CYBERSECURITY AUDITS

In this section, we covered the following points:

- SIEM tools provide comprehensive threat detection by aggregating and analyzing security events, enabling swift responses to potential incidents.

- *Centralized Analysis*: SIEM systems aggregate log data from diverse sources, enabling holistic analysis of an organization's security posture.

- *Enhanced Threat Detection*: By correlating events and applying predefined rules, SIEM systems identify complex threats that isolated log reviews might miss.

- *Compliance Simplification*: Pre-built templates and reporting tools streamline compliance efforts for standards like PCI-DSS and ISO 27001.

- *Real-Time Insights*: SIEM systems provide dynamic monitoring and alerting, allowing auditors to assess incidents as they occur.

- *Best Practices Matter*: Regular updates, targeted audits, and collaboration with incident response teams maximize the effectiveness of SIEM systems.

- Integrating SIEM systems into cybersecurity audits enhances efficiency, improves accuracy, and provides deeper insights into vulnerabilities and compliance gaps. By addressing challenges like cost and complexity, organizations can leverage SIEM systems to strengthen their overall security framework and ensure successful audit outcomes.

- DLP tools ensure the protection of sensitive data by monitoring and controlling its movement and access.

- Combining SIEM and DLP tools enhances an organization's security posture through layered defense strategies.

CHAPTER 6   TOOLS FOR NETWORK AND CYBERSECURITY AUDITS

- Best practices, such as automation, continuous training, and regular audits, maximize the efficacy of these tools.
- The integration of these tools aligns with regulatory requirements, strengthens operational resilience, and boosts stakeholder confidence.

Advanced Security Tools for Vulnerability Management, SAST, and DAST

In today's fast-evolving digital ecosystem, ensuring robust application and network security is paramount. Organizations rely on specialized tools for vulnerability management, SAST, and DAST to proactively identify, assess, and remediate potential risks. These tools enable teams to maintain compliance, safeguard sensitive information, and build resilient infrastructures.

What Are Vulnerability Scanners?

Vulnerability scanners are software tools designed to automatically scan systems, networks, and applications for known vulnerabilities. They achieve this by leveraging extensive vulnerability databases, such as the National Vulnerability Database (NVD), and adopting standards like the Common Vulnerabilities and Exposures (CVE) system. By identifying weaknesses, these tools offer critical insights that form the backbone of security audits.

The Importance of Vulnerability Scanners in Audits

Vulnerability scanners offer numerous benefits, making them a critical component of cybersecurity audits.

CHAPTER 6   TOOLS FOR NETWORK AND CYBERSECURITY AUDITS

Identifying Security Weaknesses

Vulnerability scanners excel at detecting flaws in network infrastructure, applications, and endpoints. Whether it's outdated software, default configurations, or exposed ports, these scanners provide detailed visibility into an organization's threat landscape.

Prioritizing Risks

By assigning risk scores, such as those based on the CVSS, vulnerability scanners help auditors focus on the most critical issues. This prioritization ensures that limited resources are directed toward resolving vulnerabilities with the greatest potential impact.

Ensuring Compliance

Many regulatory frameworks, including PCI-DSS, HIPAA, and GDPR, mandate regular vulnerability scans. These tools simplify compliance by generating audit-ready reports and demonstrating proactive security practices.

Supporting Continuous Monitoring

Advanced scanners provide ongoing monitoring capabilities, alerting organizations to new vulnerabilities as they emerge. This ensures that security postures remain robust even in dynamic threat environments.

Vulnerability Management Tools

To effectively identify, assess, and mitigate security risks, organizations rely on vulnerability management tools that automate scanning, prioritize risks, and provide actionable remediation insights. These tools play a crucial role in cybersecurity audits by ensuring compliance, reducing exposure to threats, and enhancing overall security posture. Table 6-6 highlights some of the most widely used vulnerability management solutions.

CHAPTER 6   TOOLS FOR NETWORK AND CYBERSECURITY AUDITS

Table 6-6. *Comparison of different vulnerability management tools*

Name	Advantages	Disadvantages	What It Has in Common	Unique Feature
Nessus	Comprehensive scanning, customizable plugin-based architecture, detailed compliance reports	Can generate false positives, requires manual validation	Automates vulnerability detection, supports compliance reporting	Extensive plugin library for detecting emerging threats
Qualys	Cloud-based for easy deployment, real-time vulnerability insights, integrates with patch management tools	Subscription-based pricing, requires internet connectivity for full functionality	Continuous vulnerability assessment, risk-based prioritization	Seamless DevOps integration for early-stage security
QualysGuard	Enterprise-level security analytics, scalable for large infrastructures, advanced executive reporting	High cost for the full feature set, complexity in setup for beginners	Provides detailed vulnerability insights, helps with compliance audits	Granular asset inventory and risk-based prioritization
Rapid7 InsightVM	Dynamic risk scoring, interactive dashboards, integration with IT workflows	Requires skilled personnel for configuration, can be resource-intensive	Risk-based vulnerability assessment, supports continuous monitoring	Threat context integration for prioritizing vulnerabilities

(*continued*)

CHAPTER 6   TOOLS FOR NETWORK AND CYBERSECURITY AUDITS

Table 6-6. (*continued*)

Name	Advantages	Disadvantages	What It Has in Common	Unique Feature
OpenVAS	Open-source and free, regular updates, supports multiple scanning profiles	Can have slower updates compared to commercial tools, requires technical expertise for configuration	Detects and reports vulnerabilities, provides remediation recommendations	Community-driven database with extensive scanning flexibility
Acunetix	Specialized in web application security, automated detection of OWASP Top 10 vulnerabilities, CI/CD integration	Focuses only on web applications, requires additional tools for network security	Helps secure applications, identifies high-risk security flaws	Advanced scanning for SQL injection and XSS vulnerabilities

Nessus

Nessus is a widely recognized vulnerability scanner developed by Tenable, designed to identify security weaknesses across various systems. It supports comprehensive scanning of networks, systems, and applications to uncover misconfigurations, missing patches, and vulnerabilities. Nessus is particularly valued for its ease of use and vast library of plugins, which enable it to detect a wide range of threats. The tool integrates seamlessly with other security systems, making it a versatile choice for organizations of all sizes. Its automated reporting capabilities ensure that security teams have actionable insights to prioritize remediation efforts effectively.

- *Purpose*: Identify vulnerabilities in networks, applications, and devices.

- *Features*:

    - Comprehensive scanning of IT infrastructure.

    - Detailed reports aligned with compliance frameworks like PCI-DSS and ISO 27001.

    - Supports plugin-based architecture for customizable scans.

CHAPTER 6   TOOLS FOR NETWORK AND CYBERSECURITY AUDITS

- *Example in Action*: A healthcare organization utilized Nessus to uncover vulnerabilities in their IoT devices, mitigating potential HIPAA compliance issues.

- Link to access the tool: `https://www.tenable.com/products/nessus`

Qualys

Qualys is a cloud-based vulnerability management tool that provides continuous monitoring and assessment capabilities. Its ability to scan on-premises, cloud, and remote systems ensures a comprehensive view of an organization's security posture. Qualys excels in automation, allowing for seamless integration into DevOps pipelines to enhance security during the software development lifecycle. Additionally, the platform offers a range of modules, including asset inventory and web application scanning, making it a versatile tool for security teams.

- *Purpose*: Perform continuous vulnerability assessment and compliance monitoring.

- *Features*:
    - Cloud-based deployment requiring minimal setup.
    - Real-time visibility into global assets and vulnerabilities.
    - Integration with patch management tools for seamless remediation.

- *Example in Action*: An enterprise reduced its risk exposure by integrating Qualys into its Continuous Integration/Continuous Deployment (CI/CD) pipeline to identify and fix vulnerabilities during development.

- Link to access the tool: `https://www.qualys.com/`

CHAPTER 6   TOOLS FOR NETWORK AND CYBERSECURITY AUDITS

QualysGuard

QualysGuard is an advanced version of the Qualys platform, designed for enterprise-level vulnerability management and compliance. It provides granular insights into vulnerabilities, offering detailed analytics and prioritization based on threat intelligence. With its scalable architecture, QualysGuard can handle large infrastructures and offers advanced reporting capabilities tailored to various stakeholders, from technical teams to executive leadership.

- *Purpose*: Asset discovery and vulnerability assessment with risk-based prioritization.

- *Features*:

  - Combines asset inventory with vulnerability insights.

  - Automated scanning and prioritization based on criticality.

  - Detailed dashboards for executive reporting.

- *Example in Action*: A financial institution used QualysGuard to map its digital footprint, identifying high-risk systems that required immediate patching.

- Link to access the tool: https://www.qualys.com/

Rapid7 InsightVM

Rapid7 InsightVM extends beyond traditional vulnerability management by integrating threat context and providing risk-based insights. Its real-time analytics and dynamic reporting help security teams focus on the most critical vulnerabilities. The platform's live dashboards and integration with IT service management tools enable efficient workflows, ensuring that vulnerabilities are remediated promptly.

- *Purpose*: Deliver continuous vulnerability assessment and risk prioritization.

- *Features*:

- Dynamic risk scoring based on real-world threat data.
- Interactive dashboards and automated reporting.
- Integration with remediation workflows.
- *Example in Action*: A retail company used InsightVM to streamline patch management, reducing vulnerability lifecycle time by 40%.
- Link to access the tool: https://www.rapid7.com/products/insightvm/

OpenVAS

OpenVAS (Open Vulnerability Assessment System) is an open-source tool that provides robust vulnerability scanning and assessment capabilities. It supports scanning of a wide range of devices and applications, making it a cost-effective solution for organizations with limited budgets. OpenVAS offers extensive customization options and integrates with various open-source tools to enhance its functionality.

- *Purpose*: Provide open-source vulnerability scanning for varied infrastructures.
- *Features*:
  - Supports multiple scanning profiles.
  - Regular updates to detect newly discovered vulnerabilities.
  - Detailed remediation recommendations.
- *Example in Action*: A small business utilized OpenVAS to identify security gaps in its web servers, addressing critical issues without additional licensing costs.
- Link to access the tool: https://www.openvas.org/

Acunetix

Acunetix specializes in web application security, offering advanced scanning capabilities to identify vulnerabilities such as SQL injection, cross-site scripting, and misconfigurations. The tool's automated approach ensures that web applications are thoroughly tested for security flaws, providing actionable reports for developers and security teams.

- *Purpose*: Focus on web application vulnerability detection.
- *Features*:
    - Automated scanning of websites and web applications.
    - Detection of SQL injection, XSS, and other web-specific vulnerabilities.
    - Integration with CI/CD pipelines for continuous security testing.
- *Example in Action*: An e-commerce company reduced its attack surface by using Acunetix to identify and mitigate OWASP Top 10 vulnerabilities.
- Link to access the tool: https://www.acunetix.com/

Static Application Security Testing (SAST)

SAST tools analyze source code, bytecode, or binaries for security vulnerabilities without executing the program. These tools help developers identify security flaws early in the Software Development Lifecycle (SDLC), ensuring that issues are addressed before deployment. Below is a comparison of popular SAST tools.

Table 6-7 presents a comparison between SAST tools.

Table 6-7. Comparison of different SAST tools

Name	Advantages	Disadvantages	What It Has in Common	Unique Feature
SonarQube	Open-source with enterprise options, multi-language support, seamless CI/CD integration	Can generate false positives, requires configuration for optimal results	Performs deep code analysis, helps with secure coding practices	Highlights both security and code quality issues
Checkmarx	Supports multiple languages, detailed remediation guidance, DevOps-friendly integration	High licensing costs, can have slow scans for large codebases	Identifies vulnerabilities in source code, integrates into SDLC	Customizable security rules for compliance needs
Veracode	Cloud-based for scalability, comprehensive reporting, automates security in CI/CD pipelines	Limited support for on-premise deployments, requires internet connectivity	Detects security flaws early in development, supports compliance reporting	AI-powered code analysis for better accuracy
Fortify SCA	Strong enterprise support, customizable ruleset, detailed vulnerability explanations	Expensive for small businesses, high learning curve	Helps developers fix security flaws, generates compliance-friendly reports	Granular vulnerability classification for precise risk assessment
Codacy	Lightweight and easy to integrate, supports multiple programming languages, AI-based recommendations	Limited feature set compared to enterprise-grade tools; may require additional tools for deep security checks	Scans code for vulnerabilities, provides developer-focused insights	Code quality and security checks in a single platform

SonarQube

SonarQube is a popular open-source platform for code quality and security analysis. It supports multiple programming languages and integrates seamlessly with CI/CD pipelines to enforce secure coding practices. By providing developers with actionable insights into code vulnerabilities, SonarQube helps enhance software quality and reduce security risks.

- *Purpose*: Perform code analysis to identify vulnerabilities early in the development lifecycle.
- *Features*:
  - Multi-language support with rules tailored for specific programming languages.
  - Integration with IDEs and CI/CD pipelines.
  - Highlighting of code quality issues and security flaws.
- *Example in Action*: A software development team reduced critical bugs by 50% using SonarQube's static analysis capabilities.
- Link to access the tool: https://www.sonarqube.org/

Checkmarx

Checkmarx is a comprehensive SAST tool that identifies vulnerabilities in source code during the development phase. Its support for a wide range of programming languages and frameworks makes it suitable for diverse development environments. Checkmarx offers detailed guidance on resolving vulnerabilities, empowering developers to produce secure code.

- *Purpose*: Identify vulnerabilities in source code and enhance secure coding practices.
- *Features*:
  - Deep scanning of source code for vulnerabilities.
  - Customizable rulesets for industry-specific compliance.
  - Integration with DevOps tools for seamless security integration.

CHAPTER 6 TOOLS FOR NETWORK AND CYBERSECURITY AUDITS

- *Example in Action*: A global enterprise reduced security flaws in its mobile apps by integrating Checkmarx into its agile development workflows.

- Link to access the tool: https://checkmarx.com/

Veracode

Veracode is a cloud-based SAST solution that provides automated security analysis for applications. It is designed to integrate seamlessly into the SDLC and DevSecOps pipelines, helping organizations detect vulnerabilities early in the development process. Veracode's AI-powered scanning technology enhances accuracy and reduces false positives, allowing security and development teams to focus on critical issues.

- *Purpose*: Automate static code analysis and detect security vulnerabilities early in the SDLC.

- *Features*:
  - Cloud-based architecture for scalability and ease of use.
  - AI-driven analysis to reduce false positives and improve detection.
  - Integration with CI/CD pipelines for automated security testing.

- *Example in Action*: A financial services company integrated Veracode into its development workflow, enabling continuous scanning of applications and reducing security flaws by 60%.

- Link to access the tool: https://www.veracode.com/

Fortify SCA (Static Code Analyzer)

Fortify SCA, developed by OpenText Cybersecurity, is a powerful static code analysis tool designed for enterprise security. It provides deep insights into software vulnerabilities by scanning source code, bytecode, or binaries across multiple programming languages. Fortify SCA helps organizations achieve compliance with security standards such as OWASP, PCI-DSS, and NIST.

- *Purpose*: Conduct static analysis to detect security flaws and enforce secure coding standards.

- *Features*:

  - Supports over 25 programming languages and various frameworks.

  - Customizable rulesets to tailor security analysis to organizational needs.

  - Granular risk classification to prioritize vulnerabilities based on severity.

- *Example in Action*: A government agency leveraged Fortify SCA to enhance security in its software development process, ensuring compliance with strict federal cybersecurity standards.

- Link to access the tool: `https://fortifyapp.com/`

Codacy

Codacy is a lightweight, automated code review and static analysis tool designed to help developers maintain high-quality, secure code. It supports multiple programming languages and integrates directly into development workflows, offering security insights alongside code quality checks. Its AI-based recommendations help developers fix vulnerabilities efficiently.

- *Purpose*: Provide automated code review and security analysis within development environments.

- *Features*:

  - Supports multiple programming languages, including Java, Python, JavaScript, and more.

  - AI-driven suggestions to improve code security and maintainability.

  - Seamless integration with GitHub, GitLab, and Bitbucket for automated analysis.

- *Example in Action*: A SaaS company reduced security risks in its web applications by incorporating Codacy into its CI/CD pipeline, catching vulnerabilities before production deployment.

- Link to access the tool: https://www.codacy.com/

Dynamic Application Security Testing (DAST)

DAST tools evaluate running applications by simulating attacks, identifying vulnerabilities such as SQL injection, XSS, and insecure configurations. Unlike SAST tools, DAST does not require source code access and is ideal for testing web applications in real-world conditions. Table 6-8 compares popular DAST tools.

Table 6-8. Comparison of different DAST tools

Name	Advantages	Disadvantages	What It Has in Common	Unique Feature
AppScan	Comprehensive automated scanning, real-time vulnerability detection, supports OWASP compliance	Can produce false positives, requires setup tuning for optimal results	Identifies security flaws in running applications, helps with compliance	Simulates real-world attack scenarios
WebInspect	Advanced API and web service scanning, detailed vulnerability analytics, supports CI/CD integration	Requires expertise for deep customization, can be resource-intensive	Detects web application vulnerabilities, offers automated reporting	Interactive application testing for deeper security insights

AppScan

AppScan, developed by HCL, is a powerful DAST tool designed to identify vulnerabilities in running applications. It simulates real-world attack scenarios to uncover security flaws, providing detailed reports for remediation. AppScan supports automated scanning and integrates with DevOps workflows to enhance application security.

- *Purpose*: Identify vulnerabilities in running web applications.
- *Features*:
  - Automated crawling and testing of web applications.
  - Real-time reporting with remediation guidance.
  - Supports compliance validation against OWASP standards.
- *Example in Action*: A SaaS provider improved its application security posture by detecting and addressing runtime vulnerabilities with AppScan.
- Link to access the tool: https://www.hcltechsw.com/appscan

WebInspect

WebInspect, developed by Micro Focus, is a leading DAST tool for assessing the security of web applications. It performs dynamic testing to detect vulnerabilities such as cross-site scripting, SQL injection, and insecure configurations. The tool's advanced capabilities make it a preferred choice for organizations prioritizing web application security.

- *Purpose*: Assess security vulnerabilities in live applications.
- *Features*:
  - Advanced dynamic testing for web services and APIs.
  - Detailed analysis of application logic vulnerabilities.
  - Integration with CI/CD pipelines for continuous testing.
- *Example in Action*: A logistics company protected its APIs against malicious attacks by incorporating WebInspect into its release pipeline.
- Link to access the tool: https://www.microfocus.com/en-us/cyberres/application-security/webinspect

How Vulnerability Scanners Work in Auditing

Vulnerability scanners follow a systematic process to uncover security gaps and provide actionable insights.

Asset Discovery

Scanners first map the organization's IT assets, creating a comprehensive inventory of devices, systems, and applications. This step ensures that no critical components are overlooked during the audit.

Vulnerability Detection

Once assets are identified, scanners assess them for vulnerabilities using techniques like port scanning, configuration reviews, and software version analysis. They cross-reference findings against vulnerability databases to identify known issues.

Reporting and Analysis

After scanning, the tools generate detailed reports that highlight vulnerabilities, their severity, and recommended remediation steps. These reports also provide systemic insights, helping organizations address root causes and improve overall security.

Challenges in Using Vulnerability Scanners

While vulnerability scanners are invaluable, they are not without challenges:

- *False Positives*: Scanners may flag benign conditions as vulnerabilities, requiring manual verification to avoid unnecessary remediation efforts.
- *Incomplete Coverage*: Some scanners struggle with complex environments, potentially missing vulnerabilities in custom applications, IoT devices, or non-standard configurations.
- *Skill Requirements*: Configuring scanners correctly and interpreting their results demands technical expertise, which may be a barrier for some organizations.

Best Practices for Tool Integration in Security Testing

To maximize the effectiveness of vulnerability scanners, organizations should adopt the following best practices:

- *Regular Scanning*: Schedule scans at regular intervals to ensure vulnerabilities are identified promptly. Frequent scanning reduces the exposure and keeps security measures up-to-date.

- *Targeted Scans*: Focus scanning efforts on critical systems, high-risk areas, and mission-critical applications to optimize resource allocation.

- *Cross-Validation*: Use multiple vulnerability scanners to cross-validate findings, ensuring accuracy and minimizing the risk of overlooking critical issues.

- *Remediation Follow-Up*: After addressing identified vulnerabilities, perform follow-up scans to verify the effectiveness of remediation efforts and ensure no new issues were introduced.

- *SIEM Integration*: Integrate vulnerability scanners with SIEM systems to gain deeper insights and contextualize vulnerabilities within the broader security landscape.

Comprehensive Coverage with Layered Tools

Combining tools from different categories ensures comprehensive coverage of vulnerabilities. For example, using Nessus for vulnerability scanning, SonarQube for static code analysis, and AppScan for dynamic testing creates a robust security framework. This layered approach helps uncover vulnerabilities at various stages of the software lifecycle.

Automation and Integration

Integrating these tools into CI/CD pipelines ensures security is embedded into the development process. Automation minimizes manual effort and enhances efficiency, allowing security teams to focus on critical issues. For instance, integrating SonarQube into a CI/CD pipeline ensures that code vulnerabilities are detected and addressed before deployment.

Regular Updates and Training

Keeping tools updated is crucial to address emerging threats and vulnerabilities. Regular training ensures that security teams can effectively utilize the tools, maximizing their capabilities. For instance, conducting periodic training sessions on AppScan's advanced features helps teams stay proficient in application security testing.

Continuous Monitoring and Reporting

Implementing tools like Rapid7 InsightVM for continuous monitoring provides real-time insights into security posture. Regular reporting helps track progress and ensures accountability, enabling organizations to meet compliance requirements and improve their security frameworks.

Emerging Trends in Vulnerability Scanning

- *AI and Machine Learning*: Modern scanners are increasingly leveraging AI to predict vulnerabilities based on behavioral patterns. This approach moves beyond traditional signature-based detection, enabling more proactive security measures.

- *Cloud-Native Scanning*: With the rise of cloud computing, tools like Qualys and Orca Security specialize in scanning cloud environments for misconfigurations and vulnerabilities unique to these platforms.

- *Continuous Scanning*: Real-time scanning solutions now offer instant alerts for newly discovered vulnerabilities, allowing organizations to address threats as they arise rather than waiting for scheduled scans.

Key Takeaways

Proactive security is key to resilience. Integrating vulnerability management, SAST, and DAST enhances threat detection, automation, and compliance. Prioritizing security at every stage strengthens long-term protection and trust.

In this section, we covered the following points:

- Vulnerability scanners automate the identification of security weaknesses, supporting effective and efficient cybersecurity audits.
- They are crucial for compliance, risk prioritization, and continuous monitoring in dynamic threat landscapes.
- While scanners offer significant benefits, they require careful configuration, cross-validation, and skilled interpretation to overcome challenges like false positives and incomplete coverage.
- Adopting best practices, such as regular scanning and SIEM integration, enhances their value in audits.
- Emerging trends, including AI-driven analysis and cloud-native scanning, are shaping the future of vulnerability management.
- Leveraging tools like Nessus, Qualys, SonarQube, and AppScan provides comprehensive coverage across network vulnerabilities, static code issues, and runtime risks.
- Integrating these tools into workflows reduces security debt, ensures compliance, and enhances overall resilience.
- Continuous monitoring, regular updates, and team training maximize the benefits of these tools, building a proactive security posture for organizations.
- Comprehensive Security Framework: Integrating tools for vulnerability management, SAST, and DAST ensures a holistic approach to identifying and mitigating security risks.
- Efficiency through Automation: Embedding tools into CI/CD pipelines enhances efficiency and reduces manual effort, ensuring secure code delivery.

Automation, Compliance, and Threat Intelligence Tools for Effective Cybersecurity Audit Management

In the rapidly evolving field of cybersecurity, automation is revolutionizing the way audits are conducted. Cyber audits, traditionally a labor-intensive process, now benefit from automation tools that streamline workflows, reduce human error, and provide scalability for increasingly complex IT environments. With cyber threats growing in sophistication and frequency, leveraging automation ensures audits are efficient, accurate, and comprehensive.

The Role of Automation in Cyber Audits

Automation plays a pivotal role in addressing challenges that come with manual auditing processes. Cyber audits involve analyzing large data volumes, checking configurations, identifying vulnerabilities, and ensuring compliance with standards. These tasks, when done manually, can be time-consuming and prone to errors. Automation addresses these issues by:

Accelerating Audit Timelines

Automated tools, such as vulnerability scanners and log analyzers, can process vast amounts of data in minutes, a task that might take humans hours or even days. For instance, tools like Nessus or Qualys can rapidly identify misconfigurations and vulnerabilities across an organization's infrastructure.

Improving Accuracy

Human error is one of the most common pitfalls in manual audits. Automation minimizes this risk by using predefined algorithms and rules to analyze data consistently. This ensures that results are not only reliable but also repeatable.

Enabling Real-Time Auditing

Continuous monitoring tools provide organizations with real-time insights into their security posture. By automating data collection and analysis, auditors can detect and address issues immediately, reducing the window of vulnerability.

CHAPTER 6   TOOLS FOR NETWORK AND CYBERSECURITY AUDITS

Key Benefits of Automation in Cyber Audits

Automation in cyber audits delivers a wide range of advantages that make the process more effective and efficient.

Efficiency

Automated tools perform repetitive tasks like log analysis, vulnerability scanning, and compliance checks at unparalleled speed. This efficiency allows auditors to allocate more time to strategic activities like risk assessment and remediation planning.

Scalability

Modern IT environments often span multiple data centers, cloud platforms, and IoT devices. Automation enables audits to scale across these distributed environments seamlessly, ensuring comprehensive coverage.

Standardization

Automated processes follow consistent methodologies, reducing variability in audit results. This standardization ensures that all systems are evaluated against the same criteria, fostering uniformity in findings and recommendations.

Real-Time Insights

Automation tools equipped with continuous monitoring capabilities, such as Splunk or IBM QRadar, provide immediate alerts for security issues. These real-time insights empower organizations to respond swiftly to emerging threats.

Cost-Effectiveness

While the initial investment in automation tools can be significant, the long-term savings are substantial. By reducing the reliance on manual efforts and minimizing repeated assessments, organizations can lower operational costs while improving audit quality.

Automation and Compliance Tools

Automation tools streamline cybersecurity processes, allowing organizations to maintain compliance, reduce human error, and enhance efficiency. These tools automate routine tasks such as audit preparation, compliance monitoring, and vendor risk assessments, enabling teams to focus on strategic decision-making and threat mitigation. Table 6-9 compares key automation tools used in cybersecurity audit management.

Table 6-9. Automation and compliance tools for effective cybersecurity audit management

Name	Advantages	Disadvantages	What It Has in Common	Unique Feature
AuditBoard	Automates workflows and compliance tracking, reducing manual efforts	High initial cost and requires training	Compliance management and automation	Integrates with third-party platforms and generates audit-ready reports
Onspring	Provides customizable workflows and real-time analytics	Complexity in configuration for first-time users	Risk management and process automation	Enhances incident tracking with risk scoring
Resolver	Supports incident management and compliance with SIEM integration	May require customization for different compliance frameworks	Compliance monitoring and incident tracking	Aligns with NIST and ISO 27001 frameworks
Tenable Compliance Management	Offers continuous compliance monitoring and risk-based prioritization	Can be complex to integrate with all enterprise environments	Vulnerability scanning and compliance monitoring	Provides detailed compliance reports for risk mitigation

(continued)

Table 6-9. (*continued*)

Name	Advantages	Disadvantages	What It Has in Common	Unique Feature
Qualys Compliance	Ensures regulatory adherence through asset discovery and policy compliance checks	Requires strong internet connectivity for cloud-based scanning	Cloud-based security and compliance automation	Automates remediation for faster security enforcement
LogicGate	Automates GRC processes and centralizes risk reporting	Advanced features may require expertise	GRC automation	Offers risk modeling capabilities for decision-making
RSA Archer	Facilitates enterprise risk management and business continuity planning	Can be expensive for small enterprises	Enterprise risk management and compliance	Advanced incident tracking to enhance operational resilience
Vanta	Accelerates SOC 2 compliance with real-time compliance insights	Limited to certain compliance frameworks	Compliance automation and monitoring	Automated evidence collection and cloud platform integration
OneTrust	Streamlines GDPR and privacy compliance with consent tracking	Can be complex for non-technical users	Privacy and compliance automation	Automates privacy assessments and risk management
BigID	Identifies sensitive data and automates risk assessments	Requires integration with existing data management systems	Data discovery and privacy compliance	Maps data flows for regulatory compliance

(*continued*)

Table 6-9. (*continued*)

Name	Advantages	Disadvantages	What It Has in Common	Unique Feature
TrustArc	Enhances privacy management with policy automation	High cost for enterprises with large data sets	Privacy risk assessment and compliance monitoring	Provides regulatory updates and gap analysis
SAP Ariba	Ensures vendor compliance and contract monitoring	Complexity in setting up for procurement processes	Third-party risk management and compliance monitoring	Tracks supplier risks and ensures ESG compliance
Drata	Automates SOC 2 and ISO 27001 compliance	Limited functionality outside of major compliance standards	Continuous compliance monitoring	Integrates real-time monitoring for audit readiness
Tugboat Logic	Reduces audit preparation time with pre-built compliance templates	Focused primarily on security assurance	Security compliance and audit automation	Provides pre-built audit frameworks to simplify certification
AWS Inspector	Automates AWS security assessments with real-time threat insights	Limited to AWS environments	Cloud security and vulnerability assessment	Provides compliance checks for AWS-specific standards
Azure Security Center	Strengthens security posture with workload monitoring	Best suited for Azure-hosted environments	Cloud security and threat intelligence	Provides actionable security recommendations for Azure services

AuditBoard

AuditBoard revolutionizes audit management by automating workflows and compliance tracking, ensuring organizations meet regulatory demands efficiently. With features like integration with third-party platforms and audit-ready report generation, it reduces manual effort.

- *Purpose*: Audit management and compliance tracking.
- *Features*: Automates workflows, integrates with third-party platforms, and generates audit-ready reports.
- *Example in Action*: A multinational company used AuditBoard to streamline its compliance tracking, reducing the time spent on audit preparation by 40%.
- Link to access the tool: `https://www.auditboard.com/`

Onspring

Onspring empowers organizations with customizable workflows and real-time analytics to optimize risk management. Its intuitive interface simplifies incident tracking and risk scoring, enabling proactive responses.

- *Purpose*: Risk management and process automation.
- *Features*: Provides customizable workflows, real-time analytics, and risk scoring.
- *Example in Action*: Onspring enabled a healthcare provider to automate its incident response processes, improving response times by 25%.
- Link to access the tool: `https://onspring.com/`

Resolver

Resolver supports incident management and compliance by integrating seamlessly with SIEM tools and tracking incidents efficiently. It aligns with frameworks like NIST, ensuring robust cybersecurity practices.

CHAPTER 6   TOOLS FOR NETWORK AND CYBERSECURITY AUDITS

- *Purpose*: Incident management and compliance monitoring.
- *Features*: Tracks incidents, integrates with SIEM tools, and supports compliance frameworks like NIST.
- *Example in Action*: Resolver helped an IT organization align its processes with ISO 27001, ensuring seamless compliance during audits.
- Link to access the tool: https://www.resolver.com/

Tenable Compliance Management

Tenable Compliance Management offers a comprehensive view of compliance status through continuous monitoring and risk-based prioritization. By identifying vulnerabilities and providing detailed remediation steps, it minimizes risk.

- *Purpose*: Continuous monitoring of compliance status.
- *Features*: Offers vulnerability scanning, risk-based prioritization, and detailed compliance reports.
- *Example in Action*: A financial institution used Tenable to identify and remediate vulnerabilities, reducing their risk exposure significantly.
- Link to access the tool: https://www.tenable.com/

Qualys Compliance

Qualys Compliance ensures regulatory adherence through cloud-based asset discovery and policy compliance checks. Automated remediation enhances efficiency and security.

- *Purpose*: Cloud-based compliance and vulnerability management.
- *Features*: Provides asset discovery, policy compliance checks, and automated remediation.

- *Example in Action*: Qualys Compliance helped a retail company secure its POS systems, ensuring PCI-DSS compliance.
- Link to access the tool: https://www.qualys.com/

LogicGate

LogicGate simplifies GRC management with automated workflows and centralized reporting. Its risk modeling capabilities provide actionable insights for decision-making.

- *Purpose*: GRC management.
- *Features*: Allows for process automation, centralized reporting, and risk modeling.
- *Example in Action*: LogicGate enabled a telecom provider to manage vendor risks effectively, reducing contractual non-compliance by 30%.
- Link to access the tool: https://www.logicgate.com/

RSA Archer

RSA Archer facilitates enterprise risk management with tools for business continuity planning and regulatory compliance. Its incident tracking capabilities enhance operational resilience.

- *Purpose*: Enterprise risk management and compliance.
- *Features*: Supports business continuity planning, incident tracking, and regulatory compliance.
- *Example in Action*: An insurance company implemented RSA Archer to automate its regulatory reporting, saving 300 hours annually.
- Link to access the tool: https://www.archerirm.com/

CHAPTER 6   TOOLS FOR NETWORK AND CYBERSECURITY AUDITS

Vanta

Vanta accelerates SOC 2 compliance with automated evidence collection and real-time compliance insights. It integrates seamlessly with cloud platforms, ensuring continuous monitoring.

- *Purpose*: SOC 2 compliance and security monitoring.

- *Features*: Automates evidence collection, provides real-time compliance insights, and integrates with cloud platforms.

- *Example in Action*: A SaaS provider achieved SOC 2 certification 50% faster using Vanta's automated processes.

- Link to access the tool: https://vanta.com/

OneTrust

OneTrust offers robust privacy and compliance management, streamlining consent tracking and privacy assessments. Its automation capabilities ensure GDPR adherence.

- *Purpose*: Privacy and compliance management.

- *Features*: Manages consent, automates privacy assessments, and ensures GDPR compliance.

- *Example in Action*: A pharmaceutical company leveraged OneTrust to streamline its data privacy compliance efforts, reducing fines by 20%.

- Link to access the tool: https://www.onetrust.com/

BigID

BigID specializes in data discovery and privacy compliance, identifying sensitive data and automating risk assessments. It enables organizations to map data flows efficiently.

- *Purpose*: Data discovery and privacy compliance.

- *Features*: Identifies sensitive data, maps data flows, and automates risk assessments.

CHAPTER 6   TOOLS FOR NETWORK AND CYBERSECURITY AUDITS

- *Example in Action*: BigID helped an e-commerce organization detect unprotected customer data, ensuring swift remediation.
- Link to access the tool: `https://bigid.com/`

TrustArc

TrustArc enhances privacy management with gap analysis and regulatory updates, ensuring businesses stay compliant. It simplifies policy management to align with evolving laws.

- *Purpose*: Privacy management and risk assessment.
- *Features*: Provides gap analysis, policy management, and regulatory updates.
- *Example in Action*: TrustArc enabled a global enterprise to align its policies with CCPA requirements, enhancing customer trust.
- Link to access the tool: `https://trustarc.com/`

SAP Ariba

SAP Ariba excels in third-party compliance monitoring, automating contract reviews and tracking vendor risks. It ensures transparency and environmental, social, and governance (ESG) compliance.

- *Purpose*: Third-party compliance and procurement monitoring.
- *Features*: Tracks vendor performance, monitors risks, and automates contract reviews.
- *Example in Action*: SAP Ariba helped a manufacturing organization ensure supplier compliance with ESG standards.
- Link to access the tool: `https://service.ariba.com/`

Drata

Drata simplifies automated compliance with real-time monitoring and integrations for SOC 2 and ISO 27001. It enables organizations to maintain continuous audit readiness.

CHAPTER 6 TOOLS FOR NETWORK AND CYBERSECURITY AUDITS

- *Purpose*: Automated compliance and security monitoring.
- *Features*: Supports SOC 2, ISO 27001, and GDPR compliance, with integrations for continuous monitoring.
- *Example in Action*: Drata streamlined compliance for a fintech startup, enabling faster investor approvals.
- Link to access the tool: `https://drata.com/`

Tugboat Logic

Tugboat Logic offers security assurance with pre-built templates and automated audits, reducing preparation time. It ensures compliance with frameworks like ISO 27001.

- *Purpose*: Compliance and security assurance.
- *Features*: Automates audits, provides pre-built templates, and tracks progress.
- *Example in Action*: Tugboat Logic enabled a software company to prepare for SOC 2 audits in record time, reducing stress and effort.
- Link to access the tool: `https://tugboatlogic.com/`

AWS Inspector

AWS Inspector enhances AWS environment security by automating vulnerability assessments and providing actionable insights. It ensures compliance with industry standards.

- *Purpose*: Automated vulnerability assessment in AWS environments.
- *Features*: Identifies vulnerabilities, assesses compliance, and provides actionable insights.
- *Example in Action*: AWS Inspector identified misconfigurations in an AWS-hosted application, preventing potential breaches.
- Link to access the tool: `https://aws.amazon.com/inspector/`

Azure Security Center

Azure Security Center strengthens cloud security posture by monitoring workloads and providing actionable recommendations. It ensures compliance with industry standards.

- *Purpose*: Cloud security posture management for Azure environments.

- *Features*: Monitors workloads, provides security recommendations, and ensures compliance.

- *Example in Action*: Azure Security Center helped a logistics company meet compliance requirements for their Azure-hosted services.

- Link to access the tool: https://azure.microsoft.com/products/security-center/

Threat Intelligence Platforms for Auditing

In the ever-evolving landscape of cybersecurity, staying ahead of adversaries requires proactive measures and deep insights into potential threats. Threat Intelligence Platforms (TIPs) have emerged as a key for robust cybersecurity practices. These platforms play a vital role in cybersecurity audits by providing actionable intelligence on vulnerabilities, attack vectors, and emerging threats. By leveraging TIPs, organizations can fortify their defenses, identify gaps, and align their security measures with evolving risk landscapes.

What Are Threat Intelligence Platforms?

Threat Intelligence Platforms are specialized tools designed to collect, analyze, and disseminate data related to cyber threats. They aggregate information from various sources, including Open-Source Intelligence (OSINT), dark web monitoring, and proprietary threat feeds. TIPs deliver valuable insights, such as

CHAPTER 6   TOOLS FOR NETWORK AND CYBERSECURITY AUDITS

- *Indicators of Compromise (IoCs)*: Information about malicious IP addresses, domains, and file hashes.

- *Threat Actor Profiles*: Detailed data on attackers, including their tactics, techniques, and procedures (TTPs).

- *Vulnerability Exploits*: Insights into how specific vulnerabilities are being targeted in real-world scenarios.

The primary objective of TIPs is to provide cybersecurity teams with actionable intelligence that informs decision-making during audits and enhances overall security. These platforms transform raw data into meaningful insights, enabling organizations to proactively address risks and validate their defenses.

How TIPs Support Cybersecurity Audits

Threat Intelligence Platforms offer multifaceted benefits that elevate the quality and depth of cybersecurity audits. Figure 6-2 presents the main steps for TIPs support to cybersecurity audits:

CHAPTER 6   TOOLS FOR NETWORK AND CYBERSECURITY AUDITS

Step 1: Threat Data Collection
- Input: TIPs gather intelligence from OSINT, dark web sources, proprietary feeds, and security vendors.
- Process: Automated data ingestion and normalization to ensure consistency.
- Output: A centralized database of IoCs, threat actor profiles, and vulnerability exploits.

Step 2: Threat Intelligence Analysis
- Input: Collected threat data.
- Process: AI-driven analytics and machine learning identify attack patterns, emerging threats, and industry-specific risks.
- Output: Actionable insights on active threat campaigns, vulnerability trends, and risk prioritization.

Step 3: Risk Identification for Audits
- Input: Processed threat intelligence reports.
- Process: TIPs map identified threats to an organization's assets, industry, and security posture.
- Output: Auditors receive a prioritized risk assessment highlighting critical security gaps.

Step 4: Proactive Defense Validation
- Input: Identified threats and IoCs.
- Process: TIPs test security controls by simulating real-world attack scenarios against IDS, EDR, and firewall configurations.
- Output: Evaluation of whether security defenses can detect and mitigate known

Step 5: Compliance Mapping & Reporting
- Input: Audit framework requirements (e.g., PCI-DSS, HIPAA, GDPR).
- Process: TIPs correlate identified threats with regulatory controls to ensure compliance alignment.
- Output: Compliance reports with recommendations for closing security gaps.

Step 6: Continuous Monitoring & Incident Response Support
- Input: Ongoing threat intelligence updates.
- Process: TIPs provide real-time alerts for new vulnerabilities, malware strains, and attack techniques.
- Output: Organizations receive early warnings and can proactively update security measures between audits.

Figure 6-2. *Workflow process: How threat intelligence platforms (TIPs) support cybersecurity audits*

Enhanced Risk Identification

TIPs allow auditors to identify threats relevant to the organization's industry, technology stack, and geographical footprint. By analyzing data on active attack campaigns and exploited vulnerabilities, TIPs help highlight areas where an organization might be most at risk. This targeted approach ensures that audits focus on high-priority vulnerabilities and weaknesses.

Proactive Defense Validation

TIPs assess the effectiveness of existing security controls by simulating real-world threats. For example, TIPs can evaluate whether IDS or EDR tools are capable of identifying and mitigating known attack vectors. This validation provides auditors with concrete evidence of an organization's readiness to face current threats.

Regulatory Compliance

Many regulatory frameworks, such as PCI-DSS, HIPAA, and GDPR, emphasize the importance of threat detection and incident response. TIPs simplify compliance audits by mapping identified threats to specific regulatory requirements. This alignment helps organizations demonstrate their adherence to mandated security practices.

Continuous Monitoring

TIPs excel in providing real-time insights into the evolving threat landscape. Between formal audits, TIPs act as an early warning system, ensuring that organizations remain informed of new vulnerabilities, exploits, and attack campaigns. This capability helps maintain a robust security posture even in dynamic environments.

Key Technologies Behind TIPs

Threat Intelligence Platforms are powered by advanced technologies that enable them to process vast amounts of data and deliver precise insights:

- *AI & Machine Learning*: TIPs leverage AI to analyze threat data, identify patterns, and predict potential attack scenarios. Machine learning algorithms reduce false positives and improve the accuracy of threat detection, ensuring auditors focus on genuine risks.

- *Big Data Analytics*: By processing massive datasets from diverse sources, TIPs can extract meaningful insights and identify correlations that might otherwise go unnoticed. This capability is particularly valuable for understanding complex attack campaigns.

CHAPTER 6   TOOLS FOR NETWORK AND CYBERSECURITY AUDITS

- *Automation and Orchestration*: Modern TIPs integrate with SOAR tools to enable automated threat response. This integration ensures that identified threats are promptly addressed, minimizing potential damage.

- *Integration with SIEM and EDR*: TIPs enhance the capabilities of SIEM and EDR systems by providing enriched threat data. This integration improves detection and response times during audits.

- *Threat Feed Aggregation*: TIPs consolidate data from multiple threat intelligence feeds, offering a comprehensive view of the threat landscape. This aggregation ensures that organizations have access to the most relevant and up-to-date information.

Threat Intelligence Tools

Threat intelligence tools empower organizations to stay ahead of emerging cyber threats by providing real-time data, actionable insights, and advanced analytics. These tools enhance situational awareness and enable proactive threat mitigation.

Table 6-10 presents a comparison of main threat intelligence tools.

Table 6-10. Comparison of main threat intelligence tools

Name	Advantages	Disadvantages	What It Has in Common	Unique Feature
Recorded Future	Predictive analytics, real-time threat monitoring, SIEM integration	May generate noise from excessive data	Provides actionable threat intelligence for audits	Uses AI-driven predictive analytics for future threats
ThreatConnect	Collaborative threat sharing, automated analysis, integration with security tools	Requires skilled personnel for optimal use	Aggregates multiple threat sources for intelligence	Strong focus on incident response and automation
IBM X-Force	Global threat intelligence, advanced malware analysis, enterprise-level support	Can be costly for smaller organizations	Offers deep malware analysis and global threat insights	Backed by IBM's extensive research and security expertise
Anomali	Machine learning-based threat detection, cross-platform data correlation	May require additional tuning to reduce false positives	Enhances threat intelligence with automation	Specializes in detecting credential stuffing attacks

Recorded Future

Recorded Future delivers predictive threat intelligence by analyzing vast amounts of data for actionable insights. It integrates seamlessly with SIEM platforms for streamlined incident response.

- *Purpose*: Threat intelligence and risk monitoring.

- *Features*: Offers predictive analytics, integrates with SIEM platforms, and delivers detailed threat reports.

- *Example in Action*: Recorded Future detected a phishing campaign targeting a bank, enabling swift protective measures.
- Link to access the tool: https://www.recordedfuture.com/

ThreatConnect

ThreatConnect combines advanced threat analytics with incident response capabilities, offering a collaborative platform for threat mitigation. It aggregates data from multiple sources for comprehensive intelligence.

- *Purpose*: Threat intelligence platform and incident response.
- *Features*: Aggregates data from multiple sources, enables collaboration, and automates threat analysis.
- *Example in Action*: ThreatConnect streamlined incident response for a tech company, reducing resolution times by 40%.
- Link to access the tool: https://threatconnect.com/

IBM X-Force

IBM X-Force provides global threat insights with advanced malware analysis and incident support. It enables organizations to anticipate and mitigate sophisticated cyberattacks.

- *Purpose*: Advanced threat intelligence and research.
- *Features*: Provides global threat insights, malware analysis, and incident support.
- *Example in Action*: IBM X-Force identified a sophisticated ransomware campaign targeting critical infrastructure, helping mitigate damage.
- Link to access the tool: https://www.ibm.com/security/services/threat-intelligence

Anomali

Anomali enhances threat detection with machine learning, correlating data across platforms for actionable insights. Its automation capabilities streamline threat feeds and incident response.

- *Purpose*: Threat detection and intelligence sharing.

- *Features*: Leverages machine learning, correlates data across platforms, and automates threat feeds.

- *Example in Action*: Anomali enabled a retail chain to detect and prevent credential stuffing attacks, safeguarding customer accounts.

- Link to access the tool: https://www.anomali.com/

Best Practices for Implementing Automation and Using TIPs in Cyber Audits

To maximize the benefits of automation, organizations should follow these best practices:

- *Define Clear Objectives*: Identify areas of the audit process where automation will have the most significant impact, such as log analysis, vulnerability scanning, or compliance reporting. Clear objectives ensure that efforts are focused and resources are used effectively.

- *Select the Right Tools*: Choose automation tools that align with the organization's IT environment and audit goals. For example, a cloud-focused organization might benefit from tools like Orca Security, while an enterprise with legacy systems might prioritize tools that integrate seamlessly with existing infrastructures.

- *Integrate with Existing Workflows*: Ensure that automation tools are compatible with current audit and security workflows. Seamless integration minimizes disruptions and ensures that automation complements, rather than complicates, the process.

- *Keep Tools Updated*: Regular updates are essential to maintain the effectiveness of automation tools. Ensure that the latest patches, vulnerability signatures, and compliance templates are in place to address emerging threats and regulatory changes.

- *Enable Continuous Monitoring*: Implement tools that provide ongoing assessments and real-time insights. Continuous monitoring helps organizations stay ahead of potential vulnerabilities and ensures that audits are not limited to periodic snapshots.

- *Maintain Human Oversight*: While automation enhances efficiency, human expertise remains essential. Combine automated results with expert analysis to derive actionable insights and make informed decisions about remediation strategies.

To maximize the value of Threat Intelligence Platforms in audits, organizations should adhere to these best practices:

- *Select the Right TIP*: Choose a platform that aligns with the organization's size, industry, and threat environment. For example, a financial institution might prioritize a TIP with strong capabilities in detecting phishing campaigns and financial malware.

- *Integrate with Existing Systems*: Ensure that the TIP integrates seamlessly with existing security tools, such as SIEM, EDR, and vulnerability scanners. This integration enhances data sharing and simplifies audit workflows.

- *Focus on Actionable Intelligence*: Use filtering capabilities to focus on threats that are relevant to the organization's infrastructure. Overloading auditors with unnecessary data can hinder their ability to identify critical risks.

- *Train Audit Teams*: Provide training to ensure auditors can effectively interpret threat intelligence reports and integrate them into their assessments. Skilled personnel are crucial for deriving actionable insights from TIPs.

- *Continuous Updates*: Keep the TIP updated with the latest threat feeds and software patches to ensure it remains effective against emerging threats.

Future Trends in Automation and TIPs for Cyber Audits

As automation continues to evolve, several emerging trends are shaping its role in cybersecurity audits:

- *AI-Driven Automation*: Artificial Intelligence (AI) is increasingly being integrated into audit tools to predict vulnerabilities, detect anomalies, and prioritize risks. These advancements enable auditors to focus on the most critical issues, further optimizing the process.

- *Integration with DevSecOps*: Audit tools are becoming part of CI/CD pipelines, ensuring security assessments are conducted at every stage of the software development lifecycle. This integration supports proactive risk management in DevSecOps environments.

- *IoT and Edge Security*: As IoT and edge computing grow, automation tools are being developed to address the unique security challenges posed by these technologies. Automated solutions will play a vital role in auditing devices with limited computing resources and diverse operating conditions.

- *Zero Trust Audits*: Zero Trust architecture is gaining traction, and automation tools are adapting to evaluate compliance with its principles. These tools will assess network segmentation, identity verification, and access controls in hybrid environments, ensuring adherence to Zero Trust policies.

As the cybersecurity landscape evolves, Threat Intelligence Platforms are set to become even more sophisticated:

- *AI-Driven Predictions*: Future TIPs will use AI to predict attacks by analyzing historical and real-time data, enabling organizations to adopt a more proactive approach to threat management.

- *Integration with DevSecOps*: TIPs will become integral to DevSecOps workflows, ensuring that security considerations are embedded throughout the software development lifecycle.

- *IoT and OT Security*: With the rise of IoT and Operational Technology (OT), TIPs will adapt to address the unique challenges posed by these environments, such as device vulnerabilities and insecure communication protocols.

- *Blockchain for Intelligence Sharing*: Blockchain technology may be used to create secure and transparent platforms for sharing threat intelligence between organizations, fostering collaboration in combating cybercrime.

Key Takeaways

Automation, compliance, and threat intelligence are essential for effective cybersecurity audits. Leveraging TIPs, regulatory mapping, and real-time monitoring enhances risk identification, proactive defense, and compliance adherence. Integrating these tools into audit workflows strengthens security resilience, streamlines processes, and ensures continuous protection against evolving threats.

In this section, we covered the following points:

- Automation tools enhance efficiency by streamlining compliance and audit processes, reducing manual efforts.

- Threat intelligence tools empower organizations with actionable insights to preempt and mitigate cyber threats.

- Proper implementation and integration of these tools ensure a cohesive cybersecurity strategy.

- Regular training and updates are crucial for maximizing the effectiveness of both automation and threat intelligence tools.

- *Efficiency and Accuracy*: Automation accelerates audits and reduces human error, ensuring comprehensive and reliable results.

- *Scalability*: Automation supports audits across large and distributed environments, including multi-cloud and IoT setups.

- *Real-Time Insights*: Continuous monitoring provides immediate alerts for emerging security issues.

- *Cost Savings*: Automation reduces the long-term costs associated with manual auditing and repeated assessments.

- *Emerging Trends*: AI-driven automation, DevSecOps integration, and tools tailored for IoT and Zero Trust architectures are reshaping the future of cyber audits.

- *Risk Identification*: TIPs enable targeted identification of vulnerabilities and threats, ensuring audits focus on critical areas.

- *Proactive Validation*: TIPs validate the effectiveness of security measures against known threats, providing actionable insights.

- *Regulatory Alignment*: These platforms simplify compliance audits by mapping threats to relevant standards and frameworks.

- *Future-Ready Technology*: Emerging capabilities like AI-driven predictions and IoT security are set to enhance TIP functionality further.

- *Best Practices*: Organizations must select appropriate TIPs, integrate them seamlessly, and ensure continuous updates for maximum effectiveness.

- By incorporating Threat Intelligence Platforms into cybersecurity audits, organizations gain deeper insights, streamline processes, and bolster their defenses against an increasingly complex threat landscape. TIPs are indispensable for proactive, informed, and comprehensive security assessments.

Penetration Testing Tools for Comprehensive Security Assessments

Penetration testing, or ethical hacking, is a foundation of proactive cybersecurity. By simulating real-world attacks, penetration testing helps organizations identify vulnerabilities before malicious actors can exploit them. These tests mimic the tactics, techniques, and procedures (TTPs) of cyber adversaries to uncover weaknesses in systems, networks, and applications. The insights gained from penetration testing empower organizations to bolster their defenses and prioritize remediation efforts effectively.

CHAPTER 6   TOOLS FOR NETWORK AND CYBERSECURITY AUDITS

The role of penetration testing tools in this process is indispensable. These tools automate and enhance the testing process, offering security professionals the ability to perform comprehensive assessments with precision and efficiency. From network scanning and vulnerability exploitation to web application analysis and phishing simulations, penetration testing tools provide a diverse range of functionalities that cater to varying security needs. Below, we explore some of the most widely used penetration testing tools, detailing their unique capabilities and real-world applications.

These tools, ranging from automated scanners to advanced exploitation frameworks, empower organizations to stay ahead of malicious actors by mimicking their tactics in a controlled and ethical manner. Incorporating penetration testing tools into cybersecurity audits enhances the depth and accuracy of assessments while providing valuable insights into potential attack vectors.

What Are Penetration Testing Tools?

Penetration testing tools are specialized software solutions designed to identify vulnerabilities and exploit them to evaluate the effectiveness of an organization's defenses. They encompass various categories, including

- *Vulnerability Scanners*: Tools like Nessus and OpenVAS identify potential security flaws.

- *Exploitation Frameworks*: Platforms such as Metasploit allow testers to exploit vulnerabilities safely.

- *Password Crackers*: Tools like Hashcat test the strength of authentication mechanisms.

- *Web Application Testing Tools*: Burp Suite and OWASP ZAP specialize in assessing web applications for common vulnerabilities like SQL injection and XSS.

These tools are integral to penetration testing methodologies, enabling auditors to simulate attacks, document findings, and recommend remediation measures effectively.

The Role of Penetration Testing Tools in Cybersecurity Audits

Penetration testing tools offer significant advantages that elevate the quality of cybersecurity audits.

Comprehensive Vulnerability Identification

These tools uncover vulnerabilities that may not be detected through traditional security measures. From unpatched software to weak configurations, penetration testing tools ensure that no critical gap is overlooked.

Realistic Attack Simulation

Penetration testing tools replicate the techniques used by malicious actors, offering a realistic assessment of an organization's ability to withstand cyberattacks. This simulation helps identify weaknesses in a controlled and ethical manner.

Assessment of Security Controls

By exploiting identified vulnerabilities, penetration testing tools validate the effectiveness of security measures, such as firewalls, IDS, and endpoint protection solutions.

Regulatory Compliance

Many frameworks, including PCI-DSS, NIST, and GDPR, mandate regular penetration testing. These tools simplify compliance by providing standardized testing methodologies and detailed reporting capabilities.

Prioritization of Risks

Penetration testing tools classify vulnerabilities based on their severity and exploitability, enabling organizations to prioritize remediation efforts effectively.

CHAPTER 6   TOOLS FOR NETWORK AND CYBERSECURITY AUDITS

Penetration Testing Tools

Penetration testing tools play a crucial role in identifying and mitigating vulnerabilities, enhancing an organization's overall security posture. These tools automate and enhance the testing process, providing security professionals with the ability to perform comprehensive assessments efficiently. From network scanning and vulnerability exploitation to web application analysis and phishing simulations, penetration testing tools cater to various cybersecurity needs. Table 6-11 highlights key penetration testing tools, their advantages, disadvantages, commonalities, and unique features.

Table 6-11. Penetration testing tools comparison

Name	Advantages	Disadvantages	What It Has in Common	Unique Feature
Burp Suite	Comprehensive web application security testing, automated scanning, and manual testing tools.	Can be complex for beginners, requires a paid version for advanced features.	Focuses on web application vulnerabilities.	Provides an intercepting proxy to analyze and manipulate HTTP/S traffic.
Metasploit	Extensive exploit database, supports advanced penetration testing and post-exploitation tasks.	Steep learning curve, potential for misuse if not handled ethically.	Used for exploiting vulnerabilities and validating security controls.	Includes a large collection of exploits, payloads, and auxiliary modules.
OWASP ZAP	Open-source, integrates well with DevSecOps pipelines, supports both automated and manual web application security testing.	Lacks some advanced features found in commercial tools like Burp Suite.	Designed for web application penetration testing.	Provides passive scanning and scripting support for continuous testing.

(continued)

Table 6-11. (*continued*)

Name	Advantages	Disadvantages	What It Has in Common	Unique Feature
Netsparker	Automated scanning with proof-of-exploit to eliminate false positives, detailed remediation guidance.	Expensive compared to open-source alternatives, primarily focused on web applications.	Web application security testing tool.	Proof-based scanning technology ensures vulnerabilities are exploitable.
Kali Linux	Comprehensive penetration testing distribution with 600+ pre-installed tools, supports network, wireless, and social engineering attacks.	Requires deep technical knowledge, can be overwhelming for beginners.	A complete suite for ethical hacking and security assessments.	Pre-installed tools for a full-range penetration testing experience.
KnowBe4	Focuses on security awareness training, phishing simulations, and user behavior analytics.	Not a traditional penetration testing tool, relies on human factors rather than technical vulnerabilities.	Enhances security by addressing human risks.	Simulated phishing campaigns to train employees on recognizing threats.
Cofense	Advanced phishing detection, automated incident response, and threat intelligence capabilities.	Requires integration with existing security infrastructure, focuses on phishing rather than network or application vulnerabilities.	Protects organizations from phishing attacks.	AI-driven phishing detection and automated response capabilities.

Burp Suite

Burp Suite is a powerful and versatile tool specifically designed for web application penetration testing. It enables testers to identify vulnerabilities such as SQL injection, XSS, and broken authentication mechanisms. Burp Suite's intuitive interface, extensive plugin support, and automated scanning capabilities make it a favorite among security professionals. Its features, such as the Intruder and Repeater modules, allow testers to simulate sophisticated attacks and refine payloads for maximum impact.

- *Purpose*: Web application security testing.
- *Features*: Provides tools for scanning, analyzing, and exploiting web application vulnerabilities. Includes a proxy server for intercepting and modifying Hypertext Transfer Protocol / Secure (HTTP / S) traffic.
- *Example in Action*: A security team used Burp Suite to identify an SQL injection vulnerability in an e-commerce platform, enabling timely remediation before it could be exploited by attackers.
- Link to access the tool: https://portswigger.net/burp

Metasploit

Metasploit is one of the most comprehensive penetration testing frameworks available, empowering security experts to assess and exploit vulnerabilities systematically. Its extensive exploit database, coupled with its ability to simulate advanced threat scenarios, makes it a valuable asset in identifying and prioritizing risks. Organizations use Metasploit to validate vulnerabilities, providing actionable insights into the potential impact of an attack.

- *Purpose*: Exploitation and vulnerability validation.
- *Features*: Includes an extensive library of exploits, payloads, and auxiliary modules for penetration testing. Supports post-exploitation tasks like privilege escalation and persistence.
- *Example in Action*: During a penetration test, Metasploit was used to exploit a misconfigured database server, demonstrating the potential for unauthorized data access.
- Link to access the tool: https://www.metasploit.com/

CHAPTER 6   TOOLS FOR NETWORK AND CYBERSECURITY AUDITS

OWASP ZAP

OWASP ZAP is an indispensable tool for web application security testing, especially for organizations committed to DevSecOps practices. Its open-source nature ensures accessibility and continuous improvement, while its comprehensive feature set enables both automated and manual testing. OWASP ZAP is ideal for identifying vulnerabilities like security misconfigurations, sensitive data exposure, and IDOR.

- *Purpose*: Open-source web application security testing.
- *Features*: Provides automated vulnerability scanning, manual testing tools, and integration with CI/CD pipelines.
- *Example in Action*: A development team integrated OWASP ZAP into their CI/CD pipeline, catching critical security flaws in real-time during the development process.
- Link to access the tool: `https://owasp.org/www-project-zap/`

Netsparker

Netsparker is known for its accuracy and ease of use, making it a preferred choice for automated web application security scanning. Its unique proof-based scanning technology ensures that identified vulnerabilities are exploitable, minimizing false positives. Netsparker also integrates seamlessly with issue trackers, enabling streamlined vulnerability management for development teams.

- *Purpose*: Automated web application security scanning.
- *Features*: Detects vulnerabilities such as SQL injection and XSS with proof-of-exploit to eliminate false positives. Provides detailed remediation guidance.
- *Example in Action*: A SaaS company used Netsparker to scan its applications, uncovering critical flaws that were quickly patched before a major release.
- Link to access the tool: `https://www.netsparker.com/`

Kali Linux

Kali Linux is the gold standard for penetration testing, offering a wide array of pre-installed tools designed for both offensive and defensive security purposes. It serves as a one-stop solution for security professionals, providing capabilities for network reconnaissance, vulnerability scanning, social engineering, and more. With its customizable environment and community-driven updates, Kali Linux remains a trusted platform for ethical hackers worldwide.

- *Purpose*: Comprehensive penetration testing and ethical hacking.
- *Features*: Offers a suite of over 600 pre-installed tools for various penetration testing tasks, including network analysis, wireless attacks, and reverse engineering.
- *Example in Action*: A cybersecurity consultant used Kali Linux to conduct a full-scale penetration test, uncovering multiple entry points in a corporate network.
- Link to access the tool: https://www.kali.org/

KnowBe4

KnowBe4 focuses on the human element of cybersecurity, addressing one of the most significant attack vectors: social engineering. Through its engaging training modules and realistic phishing simulations, KnowBe4 empowers employees to recognize and respond to phishing attempts effectively. Its analytics provide organizations with actionable insights into employee performance and areas for improvement.

- *Purpose*: Security awareness training and phishing simulations.
- *Features*: Provides simulated phishing attacks, training modules, and user behavior analytics.
- *Example in Action*: A company reduced phishing susceptibility by 70% after implementing KnowBe4's training program and simulated phishing campaigns.
- Link to access the tool: https://www.knowbe4.com/

Cofense

Cofense is a leading tool in combating phishing threats, providing organizations with end-to-end solutions for detection, reporting, and mitigation. Its advanced threat intelligence capabilities help identify emerging phishing campaigns, while its automation features reduce response times significantly. Cofense also integrates seamlessly with other security tools, enhancing the overall effectiveness of incident response workflows.

- *Purpose*: Phishing defense and incident response.

- *Features*: Includes phishing detection, automated response, and threat intelligence sharing.

- *Example in Action*: Cofense detected a targeted phishing attack against a financial institution, enabling swift containment and prevention of data loss.

- Link to access the tool: `https://cofense.com/`

Best Practices for Leveraging Penetration Testing Tools

To maximize the effectiveness of penetration testing tools during audits, organizations should follow these best practices:

- *Define Clear Objectives*: Establish the scope and goals of penetration testing, such as identifying vulnerabilities, validating controls, or assessing compliance.

- *Select the Right Tools*: Choose tools that align with the organization's IT environment, threat landscape, and audit objectives. For example, Metasploit is ideal for exploitation, while Burp Suite excels in web application testing.

- *Combine Automation and Manual Testing*: Leverage automated tools for efficiency but complement them with manual testing to identify complex vulnerabilities that automation may miss.

- *Integration with Existing Security Measures*: Penetration testing tools should integrate seamlessly with existing systems like SIEMs and firewalls to enhance visibility and streamline workflows.

- *Regular Updates*: Keep penetration testing tools updated with the latest vulnerability signatures and exploits to ensure relevance against evolving threats.

- *Document Findings Thoroughly*: Use detailed reports to document vulnerabilities, their impact, and recommended remediation measures. This documentation is crucial for audit success and stakeholder communication.

- *Collaborate Across Teams*: Share findings with IT, security, and incident response teams to ensure that identified vulnerabilities are remediated promptly and effectively.

Future Trends in Penetration Testing Tools

Penetration testing tools are evolving rapidly to address emerging challenges and technologies:

- *AI-Driven Testing*: AI will enhance penetration testing by identifying vulnerabilities based on behavioral patterns, predicting attack paths, and reducing false positives.

- *Integration with DevSecOps*: Penetration testing tools will become integral to CI/CD pipelines, enabling organizations to identify and address vulnerabilities during development.

- *IoT and OT Testing*: Specialized tools will emerge to address the unique security challenges of IoT devices and operational technology environments.

- *Cloud-Native Testing*: Tools will evolve to assess cloud infrastructures, containerized applications, and serverless environments effectively.

Key Takeaways

Penetration testing tools are vital for identifying vulnerabilities, validating security controls, and strengthening defenses against real-world threats. Leveraging automated scanning, exploitation frameworks, and phishing simulations enhances risk assessment, remediation prioritization, and compliance adherence. Integrating these tools into cybersecurity audits improves security posture, ensures regulatory alignment, and enables organizations to stay ahead of evolving attack tactics.

In this section, we covered the following points:

- Penetration testing tools play a crucial role in identifying and mitigating vulnerabilities, enhancing an organization's overall security posture.

- Tools like Burp Suite, Metasploit, and Kali Linux enable comprehensive assessments, addressing diverse attack surfaces.

- Regular and systematic penetration testing helps organizations stay ahead of emerging threats and maintain compliance with regulatory standards.

- *Enhanced Visibility*: Penetration testing tools uncover vulnerabilities and assess security controls, providing a realistic view of an organization's defenses.

- *Compliance Support*: Many regulatory frameworks mandate penetration testing, and these tools simplify compliance with standardized methodologies and reporting.

- *Tailored Solutions*: Tools like Metasploit, Nmap, and Burp Suite address specific domains, from network security to web applications.

- *Best Practices*: Combining automation with manual expertise ensures comprehensive testing, while regular updates keep tools relevant to evolving threats.

- *Future-Ready*: Emerging trends, including AI integration and cloud-native testing, promise even greater capabilities for penetration testing tools in the years to come.

CHAPTER 6   TOOLS FOR NETWORK AND CYBERSECURITY AUDITS

User Access Management and Encryption Tools for Robust Cybersecurity

Effective user access management and encryption are the foundations of a strong cybersecurity strategy. These tools ensure that only authorized individuals can access sensitive systems while protecting data in transit and at rest. By leveraging advanced technologies in these domains, organizations can prevent unauthorized access, safeguard sensitive data, and comply with stringent regulatory requirements.

User access management tools are critical for controlling and monitoring user access across an organization's IT infrastructure. These tools encompass IAM, PAM, and password management solutions to enforce robust authentication and minimize risks of insider and external threats.

Encryption tools ensure that sensitive data remains protected even if it falls into the wrong hands. Key management solutions further enhance security by securely storing and managing encryption keys.

Role in Cyber Audits

User access management tools are essential in cybersecurity audits, as they provide the foundation for evaluating how access to critical systems and sensitive information is controlled. Each tool plays a distinct role in enhancing the efficiency, accuracy, and depth of these audits:

- *IAM Tools in Audits*: IAM tools help auditors evaluate if the organization implements access controls based on the principle of least privilege. They provide insights into RBAC, lifecycle management for users, and enforcement of MFA. Auditors use these tools to assess compliance with frameworks like GDPR, HIPAA, and NIST 800-53, ensuring that access management policies align with regulatory requirements.

- *PAM Tools in Audits*: Privileged Access Management tools are critical for evaluating how administrative accounts and elevated privileges are monitored and controlled. PAM tools provide auditors with logs of privileged account usage, reports on access anomalies, and evidence of secure credential vaulting. This ensures that the organization mitigates risks associated with insider threats and improper use of administrative privileges.

- *Password Management in Audits*: Password management tools play a vital role in assessing password hygiene across an organization. Auditors evaluate password strength, reuse, and compliance with corporate policies using these tools. By analyzing logs from password managers, auditors can identify weak or compromised passwords and ensure adherence to password complexity requirements.

- *Full-Disk Encryption (FDE) Tools in Audits*: Full Disk Encryption tools demonstrate an organization's commitment to protecting sensitive data at rest. Auditors use these tools to verify that encryption is enabled across all devices and that keys are managed securely. They also assess the organization's capability to meet data protection standards required by laws like GDPR, HIPAA, and CCPA.

Together, these tools provide a holistic view of how access to critical resources is controlled and monitored, ensuring that the organization's cybersecurity posture is aligned with best practices and regulatory standards.

Key Benefits of User Access Management Tools in Cyber Audits

Enhanced Audit Efficiency and Accuracy

User access management tools automate critical auditing processes, such as log analysis, access reviews, and compliance checks. This reduces the time and effort required for audits, allowing auditors to focus on analyzing risks and providing actionable recommendations. Tools like IAM platforms centralize user data, streamlining access control evaluations.

Improved Security Posture

These tools strengthen an organization's defenses against unauthorized access, insider threats, and credential-based attacks. PAM tools protect administrative accounts, while FDE tools ensure that sensitive data remains secure even if devices are lost or stolen. Password managers enhance security by enforcing strong password practices and reducing reliance on manual password creation.

Simplified Regulatory Compliance

Regulatory frameworks like PCI-DSS, SOX, and ISO 27001 require organizations to maintain strict access control measures. Tools like IAM and PAM simplify compliance by providing preconfigured templates and automated reporting capabilities. This ensures that auditors can quickly generate evidence of compliance, reducing audit preparation times.

Real-Time Monitoring and Insights

Many access management tools offer continuous monitoring features, enabling real-time detection of access anomalies, brute-force attacks, and privilege misuse. This allows organizations to address vulnerabilities promptly, improving their overall security posture between scheduled audits.

Scalability for Complex Environments

Modern enterprises often operate in hybrid environments that include on-premises systems, cloud infrastructure, and remote work setups. User access management tools are designed to scale across these environments, ensuring consistent access control policies and simplifying audits regardless of organizational complexity.

Reduced Human Error

By automating processes like password generation, privilege escalation, and role assignment, these tools minimize the risk of human error, which is a leading cause of security breaches. This improves the reliability of audit findings and enhances the organization's cybersecurity maturity.

Identity and Access Management (IAM)

IAM solutions streamline authentication and authorization, ensuring that only legitimate users gain access to critical systems. These tools help enforce access policies, automate user lifecycle management, and enhance security through multi-factor authentication and role-based access control. Table 6-12 highlights key IDM tools, their advantages, disadvantages, commonalities, and unique features.

CHAPTER 6 TOOLS FOR NETWORK AND CYBERSECURITY AUDITS

Table 6-12. IAM tools comparison

Name	Advantages	Disadvantages	What It Has in Common	Unique Feature
Okta	Cloud-native, seamless integrations, adaptive MFA	Limited on-premises capabilities, costly for large deployments	Centralized identity management, SSO, MFA	AI-powered authentication and dynamic access policies
Microsoft Azure AD	Deep integration with the Microsoft ecosystem, strong security analytics	Requires Microsoft infrastructure, complex setup for hybrid environments	RBAC, conditional access	Hybrid identity management for cloud and on-prem
SailPoint	Strong identity governance, automated provisioning	Higher learning curve, expensive for small businesses	Identity lifecycle management, access reviews	AI-driven identity governance and risk analytics

Okta

Okta simplifies identity and access management by providing secure SSO, adaptive MFA, and user lifecycle management. Its cloud-native architecture ensures scalability and seamless integration with various applications. Okta is widely used to centralize user access, enabling consistent policy enforcement and reducing the attack surface.

- *Purpose*: Centralized identity management.

- *Features*: SSO, adaptive MFA, lifecycle management, and detailed analytics.

- *Example in Action*: A multinational retail chain used Okta to enable secure remote access for its employees, significantly reducing unauthorized login attempts.

- Link to access the tool: https://www.okta.com/

Microsoft Azure AD

Microsoft Azure AD offers robust IAM capabilities, including RBAC, conditional access policies, and directory synchronization. Integrated with Microsoft 365 and Azure, it is a natural choice for organizations using these ecosystems, ensuring cohesive access management and enhanced security.

- *Purpose*: Enterprise-level IAM for cloud and on-premises environments.

- *Features*: Conditional access, seamless Office 365 integration, and threat analytics.

- *Example in Action*: A government agency implemented Azure AD to enhance user authentication, achieving compliance with stringent national security standards.

- Link to access the tool: `https://azure.microsoft.com/products/active-directory/`

SailPoint

SailPoint focuses on identity governance, providing automated user provisioning, access reviews, and compliance management. It empowers organizations to manage user identities across hybrid environments effectively, ensuring consistent policy enforcement and reducing compliance risks.

- *Purpose*: Identity governance and administration.

- *Features*: Automated provisioning, RBAC, and risk analytics.

- *Example in Action*: A healthcare provider leveraged SailPoint to automate user access management, reducing manual provisioning errors by 50%.

- Link to access the tool: `https://www.sailpoint.com/`

Privileged Access Management (PAM)

Privileged Access Management (PAM) tools secure and monitor access to critical systems by controlling privileged accounts, reducing the risk of insider threats, and ensuring compliance with security frameworks. Table 6-13 highlights key PAM tools, their advantages, disadvantages, commonalities, and unique features.

Table 6-13. PAM tools comparison

Name	Advantages	Disadvantages	What It Has in Common	Unique Feature
CyberArk	Industry-leading PAM solution, strong credential vaulting	Complex deployment, requires dedicated administration	Privileged account security, session monitoring	Threat analytics for privileged accounts
BeyondTrust	Least-privilege enforcement, secure remote access	Can be expensive for small enterprises	Endpoint privilege management, audit trails	Comprehensive endpoint privilege management

CyberArk

CyberArk is a leader in PAM solutions, offering tools to secure privileged accounts, manage session activity, and enforce least-privilege policies. It minimizes the risks associated with privileged access by isolating and monitoring critical assets, ensuring compliance with industry regulations.

- *Purpose*: Protecting and managing privileged accounts.

- *Features*: Credential vaulting, session monitoring, and threat detection.

- *Example in Action*: CyberArk helped an energy organization to prevent data breaches by securing administrator credentials.

- Link to access the tool: https://www.cyberark.com/

BeyondTrust

BeyondTrust delivers comprehensive PAM solutions, including endpoint privilege management, password vaulting, and session monitoring. Its flexible deployment options cater to diverse organizational needs, providing a holistic approach to securing privileged accounts.

- *Purpose*: Comprehensive PAM and secure remote access.

- *Features*: Endpoint least privilege enforcement, session monitoring, and audit trails.

- *Example in Action*: BeyondTrust enabled an IT services company to implement least-privilege policies, reducing the attack surface significantly.

- Link to access the tool: https://www.beyondtrust.com/

Password Management Tools

Password management tools help enforce strong password policies, securely store credentials, and reduce the risks associated with weak or reused passwords. Table 6-14 presents key password management tools.

Table 6-14. Password management tools comparison

Name	Advantages	Disadvantages	What It Has in Common	Unique Feature
LastPass	Easy-to-use interface, encrypted vault, dark web monitoring	Subscription-based, past security breaches	Secure password storage, autofill	Secure password sharing feature
Dashlane	Password health analysis, cross-device synchronization	Limited free-tier functionality	Password generator, encrypted storage	Built-in VPN for added security

CHAPTER 6   TOOLS FOR NETWORK AND CYBERSECURITY AUDITS

LastPass

LastPass simplifies password management by securely storing credentials, generating strong passwords, and enabling secure sharing. With its intuitive interface and robust encryption, LastPass is a go-to tool for individuals and businesses alike to mitigate risks associated with weak or reused passwords.

- *Purpose*: Centralized password management for individuals and teams.

- *Features*: Encrypted vault, password sharing, and dark web monitoring.

- *Example in Action*: A software development organization used LastPass to centralize password management, reducing security incidents from weak passwords.

- Link to access the tool: https://www.lastpass.com/

Dashlane

Dashlane enhances password security by providing password health reports, dark web monitoring, and encrypted storage. It also offers seamless integration across devices, ensuring consistent access and security for users.

- *Purpose*: Secure password storage and management.

- *Features*: Password health analysis, autofill capabilities, and encrypted storage.

- *Example in Action*: A marketing agency adopted Dashlane to enforce strong password policies, enhancing security across client accounts.

- Link to access the tool: https://www.dashlane.com/

Encryption and Key Management Tools

Encryption and key management tools ensure data confidentiality by securing encryption keys and automating key rotation, access controls, and logging. Table 6-15 highlights key PAM tools, their advantages, disadvantages, commonalities, and unique features.

Table 6-15. Encryption and key management tools comparison

Name	Advantages	Disadvantages	What It Has in Common	Unique Feature
AWS KMS	Seamless AWS integration, automated key rotation	Limited cross-platform usability	Centralized key management, detailed logging	Integration with AWS security services
HashiCorp Vault	Supports dynamic secrets, fine-grained access controls	Requires configuration expertise	Secrets management, access control	Multi-cloud secrets management

AWS Key Management Service (KMS)

AWS KMS simplifies encryption key management by providing a centralized solution for creating, managing, and auditing keys. It integrates seamlessly with other AWS services, making it a natural choice for organizations using the AWS ecosystem.

- *Purpose*: Centralized key management in AWS environments.
- *Features:* Automated key rotation, integration with AWS services, and detailed audit logs.
- *Example in Action*: An e-commerce platform secured customer payment data using AWS KMS, achieving PCI-DSS compliance.
- Link to access the tool: https://aws.amazon.com/kms/

HashiCorp Vault

HashiCorp Vault is a robust tool for managing secrets, encrypting data, and controlling access to sensitive systems. It provides fine-grained access controls, audit logging, and dynamic secrets, ensuring comprehensive security for modern applications.

- *Purpose*: Managing secrets and encryption keys securely.
- *Features*: Dynamic secrets, key rotation, and access control.

CHAPTER 6 TOOLS FOR NETWORK AND CYBERSECURITY AUDITS

- *Example in Action*: A cloud services provider implemented Vault to manage API keys, enhancing the security of its microservices architecture.

- Link to access the tool: `https://www.hashicorp.com/products/vault/`

Full-Disk Encryption Tools

FDE tools protect data at rest, ensuring compliance with data protection regulations and mitigating risks of data breaches in case of device theft. Table 6-16 presents key FDE tools.

Table 6-16. Key FDE tools comparison

Name	Advantages	Disadvantages	What It Has in Common	Unique Feature
BitLocker	Integrated with Windows OS, TPM support, easy deployment	Windows-only, requires TPM for best security	AES encryption, device protection	Native Windows security integration
VeraCrypt	Open-source, supports hidden volumes, cross-platform	Manual configuration required, no centralized management	Encryption for drives, strong security algorithms	Hidden volume feature for extra security

BitLocker

BitLocker, a Microsoft encryption tool, protects data on Windows devices by encrypting entire drives. Its integration with Windows OS and ease of use make it an effective solution for securing endpoints and meeting compliance requirements.

- *Purpose*: Protecting data at rest on Windows devices.

- *Features*: AES encryption, Trusted Platform Module (TPM) integration, and recovery options.

- *Example in Action*: A law company deployed BitLocker across its fleet of laptops, ensuring data confidentiality even in cases of device theft.

- Link to access the tool: `https://learn.microsoft.com/en-us/windows/security/information-protection/bitlocker/bitlocker-overview`

VeraCrypt

VeraCrypt, an open-source encryption tool, offers advanced encryption algorithms and supports hidden volumes for enhanced security. Its flexibility and cost-effectiveness make it a popular choice for individuals and small businesses.

- *Purpose*: Encrypting files, partitions, and drives.

- *Features*: Hidden volumes, strong encryption algorithms, and cross-platform support.

- *Example in Action*: A research organization used VeraCrypt to secure project files, preventing unauthorized access during collaboration.

- Link to access the tool: `https://www.veracrypt.fr/`

Best Practices for User Access Management and Encryption Tools

- *Centralized Identity Management*: Integrate IAM tools like Okta or Azure AD with existing applications to create a unified access management framework. This centralization simplifies monitoring and reduces the risk of unauthorized access.

- *Enforce Least Privilege*: Use PAM tools such as CyberArk or BeyondTrust to ensure that users and applications operate with the minimum necessary permissions. This reduces the attack surface and minimizes potential damage from compromised accounts.

- *Secure Password Practices*: Implement password management solutions like LastPass or Dashlane to enforce strong, unique passwords across all accounts. Encourage frequent password updates and monitor for leaked credentials.

CHAPTER 6   TOOLS FOR NETWORK AND CYBERSECURITY AUDITS

- *Comprehensive Encryption Strategies*: Adopt robust encryption tools like AWS KMS and BitLocker to protect data at rest and in transit. Combine encryption with strict access controls to prevent unauthorized decryption.

- *Regular Training and Audits*: Educate employees about the importance of secure access practices and regularly audit access logs for anomalies. These actions ensure that tools are used effectively and potential risks are identified promptly.

- *Multi-Layered Security Approach*: Combine user access management tools with encryption for end-to-end security. For instance, integrate IAM with encryption solutions to enforce strict access controls over encrypted data.

- *Define Clear Access Policies*: Before implementing any tool, organizations must define comprehensive access policies based on the principle of least privilege. These policies should outline role-based access, data classification levels, and requirements for privileged account management.

- *Integrate Tools with Existing Systems*: To maximize the effectiveness of user access management tools, they should be integrated with existing IT systems, such as SIEM platforms, EDR solutions, and DevSecOps workflows. This ensures seamless data sharing and enhances threat detection capabilities.

- *Regularly Update and Test Tools*: Access management tools must be updated with the latest patches, security fixes, and threat signatures. Regular testing of tools, including simulated attacks and penetration testing, ensures that they function as expected and can withstand evolving cyber threats.

- *Conduct Periodic Access Reviews*: Organizations should schedule regular reviews of user access rights to identify and revoke unnecessary permissions. IAM tools can automate this process, but human oversight is critical to ensure that decisions align with organizational needs.

- *Implement MFA*: MFA adds an additional layer of security to access management, reducing the risk of unauthorized access due to compromised credentials. Organizations should enforce MFA for all critical systems and accounts, including privileged and administrative users.

- *Monitor and Log Access Activities*: User activities should be logged and monitored continuously to detect anomalies, unauthorized access attempts, and policy violations. PAM tools should record privileged sessions, and IAM platforms should log authentication and access events.

- *Educate Employees*: User awareness is a critical component of access management. Regular training sessions should educate employees about the importance of secure access practices, password hygiene, and recognizing phishing attempts.

- *Back Up Encryption Keys*: In the context of FDE, encryption keys should be securely backed up in tamper-proof locations. This ensures that data remains accessible in the event of system failures or device loss.

Future Trends in User Access Management Tools

AI-Driven Access Management

AI and machine learning are revolutionizing access management tools by enabling advanced capabilities such as behavioral analysis, risk-based authentication, and automated policy recommendations. These tools analyze user behavior to detect anomalies in real-time, adjust authentication requirements dynamically, and suggest policies that adapt to evolving security threats, reducing human intervention and improving efficiency.

Zero Trust Security Models

The adoption of zero trust principles is reshaping access management by requiring continuous verification of users and devices. Zero trust models enforce strict identity verification and device compliance, using micro-segmentation and real-time risk assessments. This approach ensures that access is only granted to authorized users, reducing the attack surface and strengthening security.

Biometric and Passwordless Authentication

Traditional passwords are being phased out in favor of more secure methods like biometrics and passwordless authentication. Fingerprints, facial recognition, and cryptographic keys are replacing passwords, offering enhanced security and user convenience. Continuous authentication throughout sessions further bolsters security, ensuring only authorized users maintain access to sensitive systems.

Cloud-Native and SaaS-Based Solutions

As organizations migrate to cloud environments, access management tools are adapting with cloud-native and SaaS-based solutions. These tools offer scalability, seamless integration, and cost-effective management of access across distributed systems. They support hybrid environments, ensuring consistent access control policies for on-premises, cloud, and edge systems in dynamic, remote-first workplaces.

Integration with DevSecOps Pipelines

User access management tools are integrating into DevSecOps pipelines to secure application development. Privileged access is dynamically granted during specific stages of development, while secrets management tools handle API keys and tokens securely. This integration ensures that security remains a priority throughout the software development lifecycle without disrupting workflows.

Enhanced Privileged Access Management (PAM)

PAM tools are evolving to provide advanced features like just-in-time access, which temporarily elevates privileges for specific tasks. Real-time session monitoring captures user activities to enhance accountability. PAM tools are also extending their capabilities to manage access for IoT and OT environments, addressing the unique security challenges of connected devices.

Blockchain for Identity Management

Blockchain is being explored for decentralized identity management, providing users with self-sovereign identities. This technology enables individuals to control their credentials and share them selectively with organizations, enhancing privacy. Immutable blockchain-based audit trails ensure the integrity of access logs, making identity management more secure and audit-ready.

Focus on Privacy-Enhancing Technologies (PETs)

Access management tools are incorporating privacy-enhancing technologies to comply with global regulations. Techniques like data minimization and advanced encryption protect user data and activity logs. PETs also help organizations automate compliance with laws such as GDPR and CCPA, reducing the risk of data breaches and non-compliance penalties.

Full Disk Encryption Advancements

Full disk encryption tools are adapting to modern requirements with capabilities like policy-based encryption and cloud-native support. These advancements ensure that data on physical and virtual devices is protected. Emerging post-quantum encryption methods are also being developed to safeguard data against future quantum computing threats, ensuring long-term security.

Collaborative Security Tools

Access management tools are enhancing collaboration between IT, security, and audit teams with integrated dashboards and shared threat intelligence. Automated reporting simplifies compliance documentation, while unified views of access controls and audit results improve decision-making. These tools foster teamwork and streamline audits, ensuring alignment between security operations and organizational goals.

Key Takeaways

User access management and encryption are fundamental to a strong cybersecurity posture. Implementing IAM, PAM, password management, and encryption tools enhances access control, prevents unauthorized access, and protects sensitive data at rest and in transit. Automating access reviews, enforcing least privilege, and integrating MFA streamline compliance and strengthen security resilience. By leveraging centralized identity management, encryption key security, and continuous monitoring, organizations can proactively mitigate risks, simplify audits, and ensure adherence to regulatory frameworks, creating a robust and adaptive cybersecurity strategy.

In this section, we covered the following points:

- *Centralized Access Control*: Tools like Okta and Azure AD simplify user management while enhancing security through features like MFA and conditional access.

- *Mitigation of Insider Threats*: PAM tools such as CyberArk and BeyondTrust protect privileged accounts, reducing the risk of malicious insider activity.

- *Enhanced Password Security*: Password management tools like LastPass and Dashlane ensure strong, unique passwords across all accounts, reducing vulnerability to attacks.

- *Data Protection*: Encryption tools like AWS KMS and BitLocker safeguard sensitive data, ensuring compliance with regulatory requirements.

- *Comprehensive Security*: Combining user access management and encryption tools creates a multi-layered defense against evolving cyber threats.

- *Operational Efficiency*: Automating access controls and encryption key management streamlines security processes, allowing teams to focus on strategic initiatives.

- *Key Benefits*: These tools enhance audit efficiency, improve security posture, simplify compliance with regulatory frameworks, and reduce human error.

- *Best Practices*: To optimize user access management, organizations should define clear policies, integrate tools with existing systems, enforce MFA, conduct periodic reviews, and educate employees on secure access practices.

- *Future Trends*: Emerging trends include AI-driven access management, zero trust models, and tighter integration of user access tools with cloud environments and DevSecOps pipelines.

Risk Management and GRC Tools: Enhancing Decision-Making and Compliance

In today's complex cybersecurity landscape, risk management and GRC tools are indispensable for organizations aiming to safeguard their assets and ensure regulatory adherence. These tools empower organizations to identify, assess, and mitigate risks while streamlining compliance with regulatory frameworks. They enable a structured approach to risk management, fostering resilience against potential threats and operational disruptions.

Risk management and governance, risk, and compliance tools play a pivotal role in modern cybersecurity audits. They enable organizations to identify, assess, and mitigate risks while ensuring compliance with regulatory standards. These tools streamline audit processes by integrating risk assessments, policy management, and compliance tracking into a single platform, ensuring a robust security posture.

Effective risk management tools go beyond mitigating threats; they drive informed decision-making by providing actionable insights into vulnerabilities and compliance gaps. GRC tools, on the other hand, facilitate alignment with standards such as ISO 27001, GDPR, and HIPAA. By integrating these solutions into their strategies, organizations can maintain operational continuity, build stakeholder trust, and stay ahead of regulatory requirements.

Role of Risk Management and GRC Tools in Cybersecurity Audits

Risk management and GRC tools form the backbone of cybersecurity audits by providing a structured framework for identifying vulnerabilities and aligning risk mitigation efforts with organizational objectives.

Risk Identification and Assessment

These tools facilitate the identification of potential risks across IT systems, networks, and processes. By providing automated assessments, they help auditors prioritize high-impact threats and vulnerabilities, ensuring critical areas are addressed during audits.

Policy and Control Management

GRC tools assist in defining, managing, and auditing security policies and controls. Auditors can use these tools to evaluate whether an organization adheres to predefined security standards and guidelines, ensuring consistent enforcement.

Compliance Tracking and Reporting

With built-in templates for regulatory frameworks such as GDPR, HIPAA, ISO 27001, etc., GRC tools simplify compliance assessments. They generate detailed reports that demonstrate adherence to legal and industry standards, reducing the workload for audit teams.

Centralized Risk and Compliance Oversight

By consolidating risk and compliance data into a unified platform, these tools provide auditors with a holistic view of an organization's risk profile. This centralization enhances decision-making by enabling auditors to track trends, identify gaps, and recommend improvements effectively.

Key Benefits of Risk Management and GRC Tools in Cybersecurity Audits

Enhanced Risk Visibility

GRC tools provide real-time dashboards and analytics, offering a comprehensive view of risks across the organization. This visibility ensures auditors can identify hidden vulnerabilities and assess their potential impact.

Improved Compliance Efficiency

By automating compliance assessments and providing preconfigured frameworks, these tools significantly reduce the time and resources required for audits. This efficiency allows organizations to maintain continuous compliance while focusing on strategic initiatives.

Streamlined Audit Processes

Automation of repetitive tasks such as risk assessments, control mapping, and reporting improves the speed and accuracy of audits. Auditors can spend more time analyzing data and providing actionable recommendations.

Reduced Operational Risk

GRC tools enable proactive risk management by continuously monitoring for new threats and vulnerabilities. This capability minimizes the likelihood of security incidents, ensuring audit findings are focused on improvements rather than remediating crises.

Scalability and Integration

These tools are designed to scale with organizational growth, adapting to new risks and compliance requirements. Their ability to integrate with other systems, such as SIEM and access management tools, provides a unified approach to cybersecurity audits.

Risk Management and GRC Tools

Risk management and GRC tools are essential for modern cybersecurity audits, providing organizations with the ability to identify, assess, and mitigate risks while ensuring compliance with regulatory standards. These tools streamline audit processes by integrating risk assessments, policy management, and compliance tracking into a single platform. Table 6-17 compares key risk management and GRC tools, highlighting their advantages, disadvantages, common features, and unique aspects.

Table 6-17. Key risk management and GRC tools comparison

Name	Advantages	Disadvantages	What It Has in Common	Unique Feature
RSA Archer	Comprehensive risk management, automation of workflows, strong reporting features	High implementation cost, complex setup	Centralized risk management and compliance tracking	Advanced incident response integration
ServiceNow GRC	Real-time dashboards, automated workflows, regulatory compliance checks	Can be resource-intensive, requires customization	Integrated compliance management and risk tracking	Strong workflow automation capabilities
FAIR	Provides quantitative risk analysis, aligns cybersecurity risks with financial impact	Requires expertise in risk quantification, limited to risk analysis	Risk identification and assessment	Standardized framework for evaluating risks in financial terms
Archer Insight	Predictive risk analytics, scenario analysis, real-time risk insights	Requires integration with other GRC systems for full functionality	Advanced risk modeling	Predictive risk analytics with scenario modeling
RiskLens	Enables financial risk quantification, supports decision-making with cost-benefit analysis	Requires FAIR expertise, high data dependency	Quantitative risk analysis	Operationalization of the FAIR framework
OCTAVE Allegro	Structured approach to operational risk assessment, focuses on critical assets	Primarily qualitative, requires manual effort	Operational risk assessment	Step-by-step methodology for asset risk management
RiskWatch	Cloud-based risk assessment, compliance tracking, customizable dashboards	May require additional integrations for full compliance coverage	Compliance tracking and reporting	Cloud-native risk and compliance management

RSA Archer

RSA Archer is a comprehensive GRC platform that integrates risk management, compliance, and incident response capabilities. It enables organizations to track risks, automate workflows, and generate detailed reports.

- *Purpose*: Centralized risk management and GRC automation.
- *Features*: Provides risk assessment, compliance tracking, and incident reporting modules.
- *Example in Action*: A global bank used RSA Archer to streamline its risk assessment process, reducing response times by 30%.
- Link to access the tool: `https://www.archerirm.com/`

ServiceNow GRC

ServiceNow GRC simplifies risk and compliance management by offering integrated workflows and real-time insights. It automates policy management, risk assessments, and compliance monitoring.

- *Purpose*: Integrated GRC management.
- *Features*: Supports real-time dashboards, automated workflows, and regulatory compliance checks.
- *Example in Action*: A healthcare provider leveraged ServiceNow GRC to ensure HIPAA compliance, enhancing audit readiness and reducing manual efforts.
- Link to access the tool: `https://www.servicenow.com/products/governance-risk-and-compliance.html`

FAIR (Factor Analysis of Information Risk)

FAIR is a quantitative risk analysis framework that helps organizations evaluate and prioritize risks based on potential impact and likelihood. It transforms qualitative assessments into actionable data.

CHAPTER 6   TOOLS FOR NETWORK AND CYBERSECURITY AUDITS

- *Purpose*: Quantitative risk analysis.
- *Features*: Provides a standardized framework for evaluating risks and their financial impacts.
- *Example in Action*: An insurance company used FAIR to quantify cybersecurity risks, aligning their mitigation efforts with business objectives.
- Link to access the tool: https://www.fairinstitute.org/

Archer Insight

Archer Insight enhances traditional GRC tools by integrating advanced risk analytics and predictive modeling. It helps organizations identify emerging risks and measure the effectiveness of mitigation strategies.

- *Purpose*: Advanced risk analytics.
- *Features*: Offers predictive modeling, scenario analysis, and real-time risk insights.
- *Example in Action*: A telecom company used Archer Insight to proactively address risks associated with supply chain disruptions, saving millions in potential losses.
- Link to access the tool: https://www.archerirm.com/

RiskLens

RiskLens operationalizes the FAIR framework by providing software solutions for quantitative risk management. It supports decision-making with detailed analysis of risk scenarios and financial impacts.

- *Purpose*: Operationalizing quantitative risk management.
- *Features*: Enables scenario modeling, cost-benefit analysis, and financial impact assessments.
- *Example in Action*: A retail organization utilized RiskLens to justify cybersecurity investments by demonstrating potential savings from mitigated risks.
- Link to access the tool: https://www.risklens.com/

CHAPTER 6   TOOLS FOR NETWORK AND CYBERSECURITY AUDITS

OCTAVE Allegro

OCTAVE Allegro is a qualitative risk management methodology focusing on operational risk assessments. It emphasizes identifying critical assets and their associated risks in a structured manner.

- *Purpose*: Operational risk management.
- *Features*: Provides a step-by-step process for identifying and mitigating risks to critical assets.
- *Example in Action*: A manufacturing corporation applied OCTAVE Allegro to secure its industrial control systems, preventing downtime and enhancing resilience.
- Link to access the tool: `https://insights.sei.cmu.edu/library/introducing-octave-allegro-improving-the-information-security-risk-assessment-process/`

RiskWatch

RiskWatch is a cloud-based risk management platform offering tools for risk assessment, compliance management, and automated reporting. It provides a centralized hub for monitoring and mitigating risks.

- *Purpose*: Cloud-based risk and compliance management.
- *Features*: Includes risk scoring, compliance tracking, and customizable dashboards.
- *Example in Action*: A logistics company utilized RiskWatch to monitor supplier compliance, mitigating risks of regulatory fines.
- Link to access the tool: `https://www.riskwatch.com/`

Best Practices for Implementing Risk Management and GRC Tools

- *Comprehensive Risk Assessment*: Leverage tools like RSA Archer and OCTAVE Allegro to perform detailed risk assessments, identifying vulnerabilities across the organization's infrastructure.
  - *Benefit*: Holistic understanding of risks enhances decision-making.
  - *Implementation* Tip: Use standardized frameworks such as FAIR to quantify risks effectively.
- *Integration Across Functions*: Ensure tools like ServiceNow GRC and RiskLens integrate seamlessly with existing systems to enable centralized monitoring and reporting.
  - *Benefit*: Reduces data silos and improves workflow efficiency.
  - *Implementation* Tip: Conduct a system compatibility check before deployment.
- *Regulatory Alignment*: Use tools that support compliance with multiple regulatory frameworks, such as GDPR and PCI-DSS.
  - *Benefit*: Ensures readiness for audits and minimizes legal risks.
  - *Implementation Tip*: Automates compliance checks using ServiceNow GRC or RiskWatch.
- *Continuous Monitoring and Updates*: Regularly update tools to align with emerging risks and regulatory changes.
  - *Benefit*: Keeps the organization prepared for evolving threats.
  - *Implementation* Tip: Schedules periodic tool reviews and upgrades.
- *Training and Awareness*: Equip staff with the knowledge to utilize tools effectively, ensuring accurate data inputs and interpretation.
  - *Benefit*: Maximizes the value derived from the tools.
  - *Implementation* Tip: Organizes regular training sessions and workshops.

Future Trends in Risk Management and GRC Tools

AI and Machine Learning Integration

AI-powered tools will predict risks and recommend mitigation strategies based on historical and real-time data. Machine learning algorithms will enhance threat detection accuracy and minimize false positives.

Cloud-Native GRC Solutions

As organizations increasingly adopt cloud environments, GRC tools are evolving to manage risks and compliance in hybrid and multi-cloud setups, ensuring seamless coverage across distributed systems.

Blockchain for Compliance Audits

Blockchain technology is being explored for creating immutable audit trails. This innovation ensures transparency and trust in compliance documentation, particularly for regulatory reporting.

Risk Quantification Models

Future tools will focus on quantifying risks in financial terms, helping organizations prioritize mitigation efforts based on potential business impact. This quantification adds a tangible value to audit findings.

Integration with DevSecOps

GRC tools will become an integral part of DevSecOps pipelines, enabling risk and compliance checks during software development. This integration ensures security and compliance are built into applications from the ground up.

IoT and Edge Risk Management

With the rise of IoT and edge computing, GRC tools are evolving to address the unique risks posed by these technologies, ensuring comprehensive risk management and compliance.

Key Takeaways

Risk management and GRC tools are essential for strengthening cybersecurity audits by integrating risk assessment, compliance tracking, and policy enforcement into a unified framework. Leveraging real-time analytics, automated workflows, and quantitative risk models enhances decision-making, streamlines audit processes, and ensures regulatory adherence. Incorporating these tools into audit strategies fosters resilience, mitigates operational risks, and enables proactive threat management in an evolving cybersecurity landscape.

In this section, we covered the following points:

- *Comprehensive Risk Visibility*: Tools like FAIR and RiskLens provide quantifiable insights, enabling informed decisions and prioritization of risk mitigation efforts.

- *Enhanced Compliance*: ServiceNow GRC and RiskWatch simplify adherence to regulatory requirements, ensuring readiness for audits.

- *Cost Efficiency*: Quantitative risk analysis using tools like Archer Insight demonstrates clear Return on Investment (ROI) on cybersecurity investments.

- *Operational Resilience*: OCTAVE Allegro and RSA Archer enable proactive identification and mitigation of risks, ensuring business continuity.

- *Continuous Improvement*: Regular updates, integration, and training enhance the effectiveness of risk management and GRC tools, preparing organizations for evolving challenges.

- Emerging trends such as AI-driven tools, blockchain technology, and DevSecOps integration will further enhance the capabilities of GRC tools in addressing modern cybersecurity challenges.

Visualization and Collaboration Tools

Effective communication and efficient workflows are pivotal in today's fast-paced business environment. Visualization and collaboration tools bridge the gap between complex data, intricate workflows, and team interactions. This section explores a suite of tools that empower organizations to visualize processes, analyze data, and foster collaboration seamlessly.

Visualization and collaboration tools are essential components of modern cybersecurity audits. These tools transform raw data into visual insights, enabling auditors to identify patterns, trends, and anomalies effectively. Simultaneously, collaboration tools enhance team coordination and streamline communication, ensuring a seamless and efficient audit process. By bridging the gap between data analysis and teamwork, these tools elevate the quality and accuracy of cybersecurity audits.

Role of Visualization and Collaboration Tools in Cybersecurity Audits

Simplifying Complex Data Analysis

Visualization tools translate vast amounts of audit data into charts, graphs, and dashboards. These visual formats make it easier for auditors to interpret complex information, identify security gaps, and communicate findings to stakeholders with varying levels of technical expertise.

Facilitating Real-Time Collaboration

Collaboration tools enable audit teams, often spread across locations, to work together in real time. They provide platforms for sharing findings, discussing issues, and jointly developing remediation strategies, ensuring that audits are both comprehensive and coordinated.

Enhancing Stakeholder Communication

Audits often involve multiple stakeholders, including IT teams, executives, and compliance officers. Visualization tools create intuitive reports that non-technical stakeholders can understand, fostering better decision-making and accountability.

Tracking Audit Progress and Tasks

Collaboration platforms allow auditors to assign tasks, monitor progress, and manage timelines. This functionality ensures that audits are completed efficiently and that all critical areas are addressed systematically.

Integrating Data from Diverse Sources

Modern cybersecurity environments rely on multiple systems and tools. Visualization tools consolidate data from various sources, such as SIEM systems, vulnerability scanners, and threat intelligence platforms, into a unified view for more holistic analysis during audits.

Key Benefits of Visualization and Collaboration Tools in Cybersecurity Audits

Improved Clarity and Decision-Making

Visualization tools make audit findings easier to understand by turning technical data into actionable insights. Stakeholders can quickly grasp the state of cybersecurity, enabling informed decisions about risk management and resource allocation.

Enhanced Team Efficiency

Collaboration tools improve productivity by centralizing communication and documentation. Teams can quickly address issues, share updates, and resolve disputes, minimizing delays in the audit process.

Increased Accuracy and Insight

Data visualization highlights trends and anomalies that might be overlooked in raw data formats. By making patterns visible, auditors can uncover hidden vulnerabilities and systemic issues more effectively.

Better Engagement with Stakeholders

Visual and interactive reports foster greater engagement from stakeholders. By providing clear and concise summaries of audit findings, auditors can build trust and ensure that security recommendations are implemented promptly.

Real-Time Monitoring and Updates

Visualization dashboards offer real-time updates on security metrics, enabling auditors to monitor changes and threats dynamically. This capability supports continuous audits and enhances the overall security posture.

Visualizing Workflows

Effective workflow visualization is essential for organizations to understand complex processes, streamline communication, and improve decision-making. The tools in this category enable teams to create visual representations of systems, data flows, and organizational hierarchies, ensuring clarity and collaboration. Table 6-18 presents a comparison of key visualization tools.

Table 6-18. Key visualization tools comparison

Name	Advantages	Disadvantages	What It Has in Common	Unique Feature
Lucidchart	Intuitive interface, real-time collaboration, integrates with Google Workspace and Microsoft 365	Limited data visualization features compared to BI tools	Helps visualize workflows and processes for better communication	Drag-and-drop diagramming for easy workflow creation
Tableau	Advanced data visualization, real-time data integration, AI-driven insights	Requires training for complex visualizations, high cost for enterprise use	Converts raw data into interactive dashboards	Customizable dashboards with advanced analytics
Power BI	Seamless integration with Microsoft tools, AI-driven analytics, customizable reports	Can be complex for beginners, limited offline functionality	Business intelligence and data visualization	Deep integration with the Microsoft ecosystem
MS Visio	Professional diagramming, pre-built templates, Microsoft 365 integration	Not as feature-rich for real-time collaboration, requires licensing	Creates structured workflow diagrams	Specialized for technical and network diagramming
Kibana	Real-time monitoring, interactive dashboards, strong integration with Elasticsearch	Steep learning curve, primarily designed for Elastic Stack users	Data visualization for security monitoring	Geospatial and log analysis visualizations

Lucidchart

Lucidchart is a versatile diagramming tool that enables users to create flowcharts, organizational charts, wireframes, and more. Its intuitive drag-and-drop interface and integration with popular apps like Google Workspace and Microsoft 365 make it ideal for visualizing workflows and processes collaboratively.

- *Purpose*: Collaborative diagramming and flowchart creation.

- *Features*: Intuitive drag-and-drop interface, real-time collaboration, integration with tools like Google Workspace.

- *Example in Action*: A security team used Lucidchart to map their incident response plan, improving team coordination and reducing response times.

- Link to access the tool: `https://www.lucidchart.com`

Tableau

Tableau excels in visual analytics, turning raw data into interactive dashboards. Its user-friendly interface supports real-time data connections and advanced visualizations, making it an essential tool for business intelligence and workflow optimization.

- *Purpose*: Advanced data visualization and analytics.

- *Features*: Drag-and-drop data integration, customizable dashboards, and AI-driven insights.

- *Example in Action*: A company leveraged Tableau to monitor cybersecurity metrics, identifying trends in attempted breaches.

- Link to access the tool: `https://www.tableau.com`

Power BI

Microsoft Power BI is a robust business analytics platform that creates interactive reports and dashboards. Its ability to integrate with a wide range of data sources allows teams to uncover insights and streamline decision-making processes effectively.

- *Purpose*: Business intelligence and data visualization.

- *Features*: Robust integration with Microsoft tools, AI-driven analytics, and customizable reports.

- *Example in Action*: A healthcare organization used Power BI to track compliance data, ensuring adherence to regulatory standards.

- Link to access the tool: `https://powerbi.microsoft.com`

CHAPTER 6 TOOLS FOR NETWORK AND CYBERSECURITY AUDITS

MS Visio

Microsoft Visio is renowned for its professional-grade diagramming capabilities. It offers templates and shapes for creating flowcharts, network diagrams, and more. Visio's seamless integration with Microsoft 365 enhances productivity and team collaboration.

- *Purpose*: Professional diagramming for complex workflows.

- *Features*: Pre-built templates, integration with Microsoft Office Suite, and real-time collaboration.

- *Example in Action*: An IT department visualized their network architecture with MS Visio, streamlining upgrade planning.

- Link to access the tool: `https://www.microsoft.com/en-us/microsoft-365/visio/`

Kibana

Kibana, part of the Elastic Stack, is a powerful visualization tool for exploring and analyzing large datasets. Its rich set of features includes dashboards, graphs, and geospatial visualizations, making it invaluable for IT operations and security teams.

- *Purpose*: Data visualization for Elasticsearch datasets.

- *Features*: Interactive dashboards, real-time monitoring, and customizable visualizations.

- *Example in Action*: A security operations center used Kibana to monitor log data, detecting anomalies in real time.

- Link to access the tool: `https://www.elastic.co/kibana`

Collaboration and Survey Tools

Collaboration and survey tools foster communication and data collection across teams and stakeholders. These tools are invaluable for gathering insights, sharing information, and ensuring coordinated efforts in cybersecurity initiatives. Table 6-19 presents a comparison of key collaboration and survey tools.

CHAPTER 6   TOOLS FOR NETWORK AND CYBERSECURITY AUDITS

Table 6-19. Key collaboration and survey tools comparison

Name	Advantages	Disadvantages	What It Has in Common	Unique Feature
Microsoft Forms	Simple survey creation, real-time response tracking, integrates with Microsoft 365	Limited customization, lacks advanced analytics	Facilitates stakeholder feedback and data collection	Seamless integration with Microsoft tools
Slack	Real-time team communication, integrations with third-party tools, file sharing	Can become cluttered with excessive messages, requires proper organization	Enhances team collaboration and coordination	Channel-based messaging for structured discussions
SurveyMonkey	Advanced survey design, analytics, audience targeting	Higher-tier plans can be expensive, limited free version	Gathers insights and feedback from stakeholders	Customizable survey templates with detailed analytics
Google Forms	Free and easy to use, integrates with Google Workspace, real-time response tracking	Limited analytics compared to SurveyMonkey, lacks branding options	Simplifies survey creation and data collection	Seamless integration with Google Sheets for analysis
Confluence	Centralized knowledge management, integration with Jira, customizable workspaces	Requires setup for structured content organization, not ideal for real-time chat	Improves documentation and team collaboration	Wiki-style documentation for team knowledge sharing

(continued)

Table 6-19. (*continued*)

Name	Advantages	Disadvantages	What It Has in Common	Unique Feature
Jira	Strong project tracking, workflow automation, DevOps integration	Steep learning curve, may be overkill for simple projects	Enhances task management and collaboration	Agile project management with issue tracking
SharePoint	Secure file storage, customizable workflows, Microsoft 365 integration	Can be complex to configure, requires user training	Centralized document management and collaboration	Enterprise-level document version control and sharing

Microsoft Forms

Microsoft Forms is a simple yet powerful tool for creating surveys, quizzes, and polls. Its integration with Microsoft 365 enables easy sharing and collaboration, while real-time response tracking simplifies data analysis.

- *Purpose*: Easy survey creation and data collection.
- *Features*: Pre-built templates, integration with Microsoft tools, and real-time analytics.
- *Example in Action*: A company used Microsoft Forms to survey employees on security awareness, tailoring training programs accordingly.
- Link to access the tool: `https://www.microsoft.com/microsoft-forms`

Slack

Slack revolutionizes team communication with its real-time messaging and collaboration features. Channels, file sharing, and integrations with third-party apps streamline project management and foster a productive work environment.

CHAPTER 6   TOOLS FOR NETWORK AND CYBERSECURITY AUDITS

- *Purpose*: Team communication and collaboration.
- *Features*: Channels for topic-specific discussions, integration with third-party tools, and file sharing.
- *Example in Action*: A security operation center used Slack for real-time updates during incident response, ensuring seamless communication.
- Link to access the tool: `https://slack.com`

SurveyMonkey

SurveyMonkey is a popular platform for designing and distributing surveys. Its advanced analytics and reporting features help organizations gather actionable insights from stakeholders, customers, and employees.

- *Purpose*: Advanced survey design and distribution.
- *Features*: Customizable survey templates, analytics, and audience targeting.
- *Example in Action*: An organization used SurveyMonkey to gauge vendor cybersecurity practices, enhancing their risk management process.
- Link to access the tool: `https://www.surveymonkey.com`

Google Forms

Google Forms offers a free and straightforward solution for creating surveys and collecting responses. Its integration with Google Workspace ensures seamless data collection and analysis through Google Sheets.

- *Purpose*: Simplified survey creation and collaboration.
- *Features*: Free templates, real-time response tracking, and seamless integration with Google Workspace.
- *Example in Action*: A nonprofit used Google Forms to collect cybersecurity incident reports from regional offices.
- Link to access the tool: `https://forms.google.com`

Confluence

Atlassian's Confluence is a collaboration platform that centralizes team knowledge and project documentation. Its flexible workspace enables teams to create, share, and manage content effectively, improving overall productivity.

- *Purpose*: Knowledge management and collaboration.
- *Features*: Document sharing, integration with Jira, and customizable workspaces.
- *Example in Action*: A cybersecurity team used Confluence to centralize incident response procedures, reducing onboarding times for new analysts.
- Link to access the tool: https://www.atlassian.com/software/confluence

Jira

Jira, another Atlassian tool, is designed for agile project management. With features like issue tracking, sprint planning, and roadmap visualization, Jira ensures efficient collaboration among development teams.

- *Purpose*: Project tracking and task management.
- *Features*: Workflow automation, integration with DevOps tools, and real-time updates.
- *Example in Action*: A DevSecOps team used Jira to manage vulnerability remediation tasks, ensuring timely resolution.
- Link to access the tool: https://www.atlassian.com/software/jira

SharePoint

Microsoft SharePoint facilitates collaboration by providing a centralized platform for document management and team communication. Its customizable workflows and integrations with Microsoft 365 enhance organizational efficiency.

- *Purpose*: Enterprise-level document management and collaboration.

- *Features*: Secure file storage, customizable workflows, and integration with Microsoft 365.

- *Example in Action*: An enterprise utilized SharePoint to store and share compliance documents, ensuring version control and easy access during audits.

- Link to access the tool: https://www.microsoft.com/en-us/microsoft-365/sharepoint/collaboration

Best Practices for Using Visualization and Collaboration Tools in Cybersecurity Audits

- *Choose Intuitive and Scalable Tools*: Select tools with user-friendly interfaces and the ability to handle large datasets. This ensures that both technical and non-technical users can engage with the findings effectively.

- *Integrate Tools into Existing Ecosystems*: Ensure visualization and collaboration tools integrate seamlessly with other cybersecurity tools like SIEM systems, vulnerability scanners, and GRC platforms. This integration enables a unified view of audit data.

- *Customize Dashboards for Stakeholders*: Create tailored dashboards for different audiences. For example, executives may require high-level summaries, while technical teams need detailed reports with actionable insights.

- *Maintain Data Accuracy and Relevance*: Regularly update tools to ensure they reflect the latest security metrics and audit findings. Accurate data is critical for effective decision-making and remediation efforts.

- *Promote Team Collaboration Culture*: Encourage open communication and documentation within audit teams. Collaboration tools should be used to foster transparency, assign responsibilities, and track progress effectively.

- *Utilize Interactive Features*: Leverage interactive features like drill-downs and filters in visualization tools. These features allow auditors to explore data in depth and identify root causes of security issues.

Future Trends in Visualization and Collaboration Tools for Cybersecurity Audits

- *AI-Driven Insights*: Future visualization tools will leverage AI to identify patterns, predict risks, and suggest remediation strategies. These capabilities will enhance audit precision and efficiency.

- *Immersive Visualizations*: Technologies like Augmented Reality (AR) and Virtual Reality (VR) will create immersive audit experiences, allowing teams to explore cybersecurity metrics in 3D environments for deeper analysis.

- *Cloud-Based Collaboration Platforms*: With the rise of remote work, cloud-based collaboration tools will become increasingly essential. These platforms will offer secure, real-time communication and document sharing for distributed audit teams.

- *Integration with Workflow Automation*: Collaboration tools will integrate with automation platforms to streamline tasks such as assigning responsibilities, generating reports, and sending alerts, reducing manual effort and errors.

- *Advanced Customization Capabilities*: Visualization tools will offer more granular customization options, enabling auditors to create highly specific dashboards that cater to unique organizational needs and risks.

- *Blockchain for Secure Documentation*: Blockchain technology may be used to secure audit documentation and reports, ensuring integrity and preventing tampering during and after the audit process.

CHAPTER 6   TOOLS FOR NETWORK AND CYBERSECURITY AUDITS

Key Takeaways

Visualization and collaboration tools simplify data analysis, enhance teamwork, and improve decision-making in cybersecurity audits. Integrating these tools strengthens risk assessment, streamlines processes, and ensures clearer communication.

In this section, we covered the following points:

- Visualization and collaboration tools play a crucial role in simplifying data analysis, improving team coordination, and enhancing communication during cybersecurity audits.

- These tools provide real-time insights, support task management, and create engaging reports for stakeholders, ensuring comprehensive and efficient audits.

- Visualization tools like Tableau, Power BI, and Lucidchart simplify data analysis and workflow mapping.

- Collaboration platforms such as Slack, Confluence, and SharePoint enhance team communication and project coordination.

- Survey tools like SurveyMonkey and Microsoft Forms provide insights into stakeholder feedback.

- Integrating these tools into your organization's processes can significantly improve efficiency, transparency, and decision-making.

- Best practices include choosing scalable tools, integrating with existing systems, and tailoring dashboards for different audiences.

- Future trends like AI-driven insights, immersive visualizations, and blockchain integration will further enhance the effectiveness of these tools in cybersecurity audits.

Other Relevant Tools for Cybersecurity Audits

Cybersecurity audits require a diverse set of tools to enhance efficiency, strengthen security, and ensure compliance. Beyond traditional audit techniques, specialized tools for configuration management, incident response, API testing, security posture management, and pseudonymization play a critical role in safeguarding IT

CHAPTER 6   TOOLS FOR NETWORK AND CYBERSECURITY AUDITS

environments. These tools automate key processes, minimize human error, and provide real-time insights, enabling organizations to proactively manage risks and improve their overall security posture.

From configuration management tools like Ansible and Puppet to forensic analysis platforms like EnCase and TheHive, each tool serves a unique function in enhancing cybersecurity audits. Whether automating system configurations, investigating security incidents, or securing sensitive data, leveraging these solutions ensures a structured and effective audit process. This section explores various essential tools, their key features, and how organizations can integrate them to strengthen cybersecurity resilience and compliance.

Configuration Management Tools

Configuration management tools play a vital role in ensuring consistency, scalability, and security across IT environments. These tools automate the deployment, configuration, and management of systems, reducing errors and streamlining operations.

Ansible

Ansible is an open-source automation tool that simplifies IT tasks such as configuration management and application deployment. Its agentless architecture reduces overhead, making it a lightweight yet powerful solution for managing complex infrastructures.

- *Purpose*: Automate configuration management and IT orchestration.
- *Features*: Agentless operation, playbooks for task automation, and support for multiple platforms.
- *Example in Action*: An enterprise used Ansible to configure hundreds of servers simultaneously, reducing setup time by 70%.
- Link to access the tool: https://www.ansible.com/

Puppet

Puppet provides an enterprise-grade solution for configuration management by automating repetitive tasks and enforcing desired states across systems. Its declarative language ensures precise and consistent configurations.

- *Purpose*: Automate system configurations and enforce compliance.
- *Features*: Scalable architecture, integration with CI/CD pipelines, and detailed reporting.
- *Example in Action*: A financial institution utilized Puppet to ensure compliance with security policies across all endpoints, reducing audit failures significantly.
- Link to access the tool: https://puppet.com/

Chef

Chef enables organizations to define infrastructure as code, providing flexibility and version control in managing IT environments. Its robust ecosystem supports a wide range of integrations for seamless operations.

- *Purpose*: Manage infrastructure as code for flexibility and scalability.
- *Features*: Comprehensive automation capabilities, customizable cookbooks, and strong integration support.
- *Example in Action*: A cloud service provider optimized its deployment pipeline by automating server provisioning with Chef.
- Link to access the tool: https://www.chef.io/

CIS-CAT

CIS-CAT offers comprehensive benchmarks to evaluate system configurations against industry standards, ensuring enhanced security and compliance.

- *Purpose*: Assess and improve configuration security.
- *Features*: Benchmark assessments, detailed reports, and remediation guidance.

CHAPTER 6 TOOLS FOR NETWORK AND CYBERSECURITY AUDITS

- *Example in Action*: A healthcare organization used CIS-CAT to align its systems with HIPAA compliance requirements, reducing vulnerabilities.

- Link to access the tool: https://www.cisecurity.org/cis-cat-pro

OpenSCAP

OpenSCAP is an open-source framework for assessing security compliance and managing configurations. It provides tools for vulnerability scanning and hardening systems against potential threats.

- *Purpose*: Enhance security through compliance and configuration assessments.

- *Features*: Security benchmarks, automated scanning, and integration with other tools.

- *Example in Action*: An e-commerce company used OpenSCAP to audit its Linux servers, identifying and remediating critical vulnerabilities.

- Link to access the tool: https://www.open-scap.org/

Incident Response and Forensic Tools

Incident response and forensic tools are critical for detecting, analyzing, and mitigating cyber threats. These tools provide insights into security incidents, helping organizations respond effectively and prevent future breaches.

EnCase

EnCase is a digital forensic tool that facilitates the collection, preservation, and analysis of electronic evidence. Its versatility makes it a go-to solution for legal investigations and incident response.

- *Purpose*: Conduct digital forensic investigations and preserve evidence.

- *Features*: Comprehensive data acquisition, chain-of-custody tracking, and advanced analytics.

- *Example in Action*: A law enforcement agency used EnCase to uncover evidence in a cybercrime investigation, leading to a successful prosecution.

- Link to access the tool: `https://www.opentext.com/en-gb/products/forensic`

TheHive

TheHive is an open-source platform for collaborative incident response, enabling teams to coordinate effectively during cybersecurity incidents.

- *Purpose*: Facilitate collaborative incident response.

- *Features*: Case management, integration with threat intelligence feeds, and real-time collaboration.

- *Example in Action*: A cybersecurity organization used TheHive to streamline its response to a ransomware attack, reducing downtime by 50%.

- Link to access the tool: `https://thehive-project.org/`

Cortex XSOAR

Cortex XSOAR by Palo Alto Networks automates incident response processes, integrating with various tools to provide a centralized platform for managing security operations.

- *Purpose*: Automate and orchestrate incident response workflows.

- *Features*: Playbooks, integrations with SIEM and threat intelligence platforms, and case management.

- *Example in Action*: A retail company used Cortex XSOAR to automate phishing incident responses, saving hundreds of analyst hours.

- Link to access the tool: `https://www.paloaltonetworks.com/cortex/xsoar`

Splunk Phantom

Splunk Phantom is a SOAR platform that streamlines incident management by automating repetitive tasks.

- *Purpose*: Enhance efficiency in incident response through automation.
- *Features*: Customizable playbooks, threat intelligence integration, and real-time monitoring.
- *Example in Action*: A global enterprise automated its malware response processes with Splunk Phantom, reducing response times from hours to minutes.
- Link to access the tool: https://www.splunk.com/en_us/software/splunk-security-orchestration-and-automation.html

CrisisSim

CrisisSim provides simulated environments to test incident response strategies, allowing organizations to identify gaps and improve their readiness.

- *Purpose*: Simulate cyber incidents for training and strategy refinement.
- *Features*: Realistic scenarios, team performance metrics, and customizable exercises.
- *Example in Action*: A government agency used CrisisSim to train its cybersecurity team, identifying weaknesses in its response protocols.
- Link to access the tool: https://www.crisissimulation.com/

Cyberbit

Cyberbit offers a comprehensive suite for cyber range training, incident response, and threat detection, focusing on enhancing team readiness and response capabilities.

- *Purpose*: Train teams and improve incident response effectiveness.
- *Features*: Simulated attack scenarios, real-time feedback, and integration with security tools.

- *Example in Action*: A telecom company enhanced its security operations team's efficiency using Cyberbit's simulated attack scenarios.

- Link to access the tool: `https://www.cyberbit.com/`

API Testing Tools

API testing tools ensure the reliability, functionality, and security of APIs, which are integral to modern applications. These tools identify vulnerabilities and performance issues in APIs, safeguarding data integrity.

Postman

Postman is a popular API testing tool that simplifies the process of designing, testing, and monitoring APIs. Its user-friendly interface and robust feature set make it ideal for developers and testers.

- *Purpose*: Design and test APIs efficiently.

- *Features*: Automated testing, mock servers, and detailed analytics.

- *Example in Action*: A startup used Postman to test API performance, ensuring seamless integration with third-party services.

- Link to access the tool: `https://www.postman.com/`

ReadyAPI

ReadyAPI by SmartBear offers a comprehensive suite for API testing, focusing on functional, security, and load testing to ensure high-quality APIs.

- *Purpose*: Conduct end-to-end API testing.

- *Features*: Automated test generation, security scanning, and performance monitoring.

- *Example in Action*: A fintech company used ReadyAPI to identify security vulnerabilities in its payment gateway, preventing potential breaches.

- Link to access the tool: `https://smartbear.com/product/ready-api/overview/`

CHAPTER 6   TOOLS FOR NETWORK AND CYBERSECURITY AUDITS

Security Posture Management

Security posture management tools provide visibility into an organization's security environment, enabling proactive identification and mitigation of risks.

Prisma Cloud

Prisma Cloud offers comprehensive cloud security posture management, covering compliance, vulnerability detection, and runtime protection for cloud environments.

- *Purpose*: Ensure cloud security and compliance.
- *Features*: Unified visibility, automated threat detection, and compliance checks.
- *Example in Action*: A SaaS provider improved its cloud security posture by using Prisma Cloud, meeting regulatory standards effortlessly.
- Link to access the tool: https://www.paloaltonetworks.com/prisma/cloud

Azure Security Center

Azure Security Center helps organizations secure their Azure workloads by providing advanced threat protection and continuous monitoring.

- *Purpose*: Enhance Azure environment security.
- *Features*: Threat detection, compliance recommendations, and workload monitoring.
- *Example in Action*: A logistics company secured its Azure-based applications using Azure Security Center, reducing vulnerabilities significantly.
- Link to access the tool: https://azure.microsoft.com/products/security-center/

CHAPTER 6   TOOLS FOR NETWORK AND CYBERSECURITY AUDITS

Pseudonymization Tools

Pseudonymization tools help organizations protect sensitive data by replacing identifiable information with pseudonyms, ensuring privacy and regulatory compliance.

TokenEx

TokenEx provides data security through tokenization, replacing sensitive data with tokens that retain usability while reducing exposure.

- *Purpose*: Protect sensitive data through tokenization.

- *Features*: Cloud-based implementation, customizable integration, and support for multiple data types.

- *Example in Action*: A healthcare provider used TokenEx to secure patient information, ensuring compliance with HIPAA.

- Link to access the tool: https://www.tokenex.com/

Thales CipherTrust

Thales CipherTrust offers a robust platform for data encryption and pseudonymization, safeguarding data at rest, in motion, and in use.

- *Purpose*: Enhance data security with encryption and pseudonymization.

- *Features*: Centralized key management, data masking, and advanced encryption algorithms.

- *Example in Action*: A multinational corporation utilized Thales CipherTrust to protect customer data across its global operations, achieving compliance with GDPR.

- Link to access the tool: https://cpl.thalesgroup.com/encryption/ciphertrust-data-security-platform

Best Practices for Leveraging These Tools

Effectively utilizing cybersecurity audit tools requires strategic implementation, automation, and integration with existing security frameworks. Configuration management tools should enforce standardized settings, automate updates, and maintain version control to minimize misconfigurations. Incident response and forensic tools must be integrated with SIEM platforms and used in conjunction with predefined playbooks for swift threat detection and mitigation. API testing tools should facilitate automated security assessments and continuous monitoring to prevent vulnerabilities. Pseudonymization tools should align with compliance requirements like GDPR and ensure seamless data protection across workflows. Regular audits, training, and simulation exercises further enhance the effectiveness of these tools, ensuring organizations stay ahead of evolving cyber threats.

Configuration Management Tools

- *Standardized Configurations*: Use configuration management tools like Ansible or Puppet to maintain consistency across systems, minimizing vulnerabilities arising from misconfigurations.

- *Automated Updates*: Automate configuration updates to ensure systems remain compliant with the latest security standards and patches.

- *Version Control*: Maintain a repository for all configurations, enabling rollback in case of unexpected failures.

- *Regular Audits*: Conduct periodic reviews to identify and rectify deviations from baseline configurations.

Incident Response and Forensic Tools

- *Comprehensive Playbooks*: Develop and integrate incident response playbooks to guide the use of tools like Cortex XSOAR or Splunk Phantom during breaches.

- *Timely Analysis*: Use forensic tools like EnCase and Cyberbit to analyze incidents swiftly, ensuring minimal disruption.

- *Integration with SIEM*: Link forensic tools to SIEM platforms for centralized monitoring and streamlined incident handling.
- *Simulation Exercises*: Conduct regular drills with tools like CrisisSim to enhance preparedness and response efficiency.

API Testing Tools

- *Automate Testing*: Use tools like Postman to automate API tests, ensuring faster detection of vulnerabilities.
- *Comprehensive Coverage*: Test APIs for functionality, security, and compliance to ensure robust performance.
- *Monitor API Changes*: Leverage tools to track and test changes in APIs continuously to prevent disruptions.
- *Collaboration Across Teams*: Share test results using ReadyAPI to foster collaboration between developers and security teams.

Pseudonymization Tools

- *Data Minimization*: Use pseudonymization tools like TokenEx to limit the exposure of sensitive data.
- *Compliance Alignment*: Ensure tools align with data protection regulations like GDPR and CCPA.
- *Integration with Existing Systems*: Incorporate pseudonymization tools seamlessly into workflows for real-time data protection.
- *Audit Trails*: Maintain logs to monitor and verify the pseudonymization process, enhancing transparency and accountability.

Key Takeaways

Leveraging the right cybersecurity audit tools enhances security, compliance, and efficiency. Configuration management tools ensure consistency and reduce misconfigurations, while incident response and forensic tools enable swift threat detection and mitigation. API testing tools safeguard application integrity, and pseudonymization tools protect sensitive data in compliance with regulations. Integrating these tools into audit workflows strengthens risk management, automates processes, and ensures a proactive security posture against evolving threats.

In this section, we covered the following points:

- *Enhanced Efficiency Through Automation*: Configuration management tools like Ansible and Chef enable organizations to maintain consistency and reduce manual efforts, enhancing operational efficiency.

- *Robust Incident Handling*: Forensic and incident response tools ensure swift identification, containment, and resolution of cybersecurity incidents, minimizing damage and downtime.

- *Secure APIs*: API testing tools like Postman and ReadyAPI safeguard APIs, ensuring they remain secure against unauthorized access and exploitation.

- *Data Protection with Pseudonymization*: Tools like TokenEx and Thales CipherTrust offer robust methods to protect sensitive data, enabling compliance with global data privacy regulations.

- *Regular Training and Updates*: Continuous training ensures teams are adept at using these tools effectively, while regular updates keep the tools relevant to emerging threats.

- *Integration for Comprehensive Security*: Integrating these tools with existing systems ensures a holistic approach to security, enabling better visibility and streamlined processes.

- *Proactive Risk Management*: By leveraging configuration and forensic tools, organizations can adopt a proactive stance, identifying potential vulnerabilities before they are exploited.

- *Compliance Assurance*: Tools like CIS-CAT and pseudonymization platforms ensure adherence to regulatory frameworks, reducing the risk of non-compliance penalties.

How to Choose the Right Audit Tools

Selecting the right cybersecurity audit tools is a pivotal step in ensuring a comprehensive, efficient, and effective audit. The abundance of tools available, from vulnerability scanners to compliance management systems, offers great potential but can also be overwhelming, particularly for organizations new to the audit process. The decision requires a strategic approach to align tools with specific organizational needs and audit objectives.

Why Choosing the Right Audit Tools Matters

The success of a cybersecurity audit heavily depends on the tools utilized. Accurate data collection, thorough risk identification, and compliance verification are foundations of the audit process, and the right tools serve as enablers of these outcomes. They simplify complex tasks such as data analysis and risk assessment by automating repetitive processes, thereby reducing time and resource requirements.

Moreover, these tools enhance accuracy by mitigating human error and ensuring that all relevant data is evaluated systematically. They provide auditors with actionable insights to identify vulnerabilities, address risks, and strengthen an organization's overall security posture. Additionally, compliance with industry-specific frameworks such as PCI-DSS, HIPAA, or ISO 27001 often mandates the use of specialized tools to streamline the verification process. Without the appropriate tools, audits risk overlooking critical security gaps or producing inaccurate findings that compromise the organization's security efforts.

Factors to Consider When Choosing Audit Tools

When choosing cybersecurity audit tools, organizations must consider several key factors to ensure effectiveness, accuracy, and long-term viability. The selection process should begin with clearly defining audit objectives, as different tools cater to compliance verification, risk assessment, or vulnerability management.

The complexity of the IT environment also plays a crucial role, tools must be compatible with multi-cloud, on-premise, or hybrid infrastructures to provide comprehensive coverage. Seamless integration with existing security solutions, such as SIEM and endpoint detection systems, enhances audit efficiency and prevents data silos. Additionally, ease of use, real-time monitoring capabilities, and scalability ensure that the tools remain accessible, responsive to evolving threats, and adaptable to future growth. Cost considerations, including licensing models and long-term maintenance expenses, should also be balanced against feature sets to maximize return on investment.

By carefully evaluating these factors, organizations can select audit tools that strengthen security posture, streamline compliance, and optimize audit processes.

Audit Objectives

Clearly defined objectives are crucial when selecting tools. For example, organizations focusing on regulatory compliance may require tools like Qualys Compliance, which specializes in mapping security controls to regulatory frameworks. In contrast, tools such as RiskLens are better suited for organizations prioritizing risk assessment by quantifying financial exposure to cybersecurity threats.

Scope of the Audit

The complexity of an organization's IT environment significantly influences tool selection. Modern environments often include multi-cloud setups, legacy systems, and hybrid networks. Tools chosen must be capable of operating effectively within this context to ensure comprehensive coverage.

Integration Capabilities

The ability of audit tools to integrate seamlessly with existing systems is another critical factor. Tools should work in tandem with SIEM systems, endpoint detection solutions, and other cybersecurity platforms to provide a unified view of security data. This integration prevents data silos and enhances the overall efficiency of the audit process.

Ease of Use

User-friendly interfaces, intuitive dashboards, and automated reporting capabilities make audit tools more accessible to both technical and non-technical team members. Tools with steep learning curves may hinder productivity and delay audit timelines.

Real-Time Monitoring

Cybersecurity is a dynamic field where threats evolve rapidly. Audit tools equipped with real-time monitoring capabilities enable organizations to respond proactively to emerging risks, ensuring that the audit reflects the current threat landscape.

Customization and Scalability

The flexibility to customize tools to meet specific organizational needs is invaluable. Additionally, tools should be scalable to accommodate future growth, ensuring they remain relevant as the organization's IT environment evolves.

Cost Considerations

Balancing features and budget is an important aspect of tool selection. Organizations must weigh subscription-based pricing against one-time purchases, considering both immediate needs and long-term financial implications.

Key Features to Look for in Audit Tools

When selecting cybersecurity audit tools, key features play a crucial role in ensuring a thorough and effective audit process. Robust data analysis capabilities help identify security gaps, while integrated vulnerability management prioritizes risks for remediation. Compliance mapping streamlines regulatory adherence, reducing manual effort and errors. Tools with threat intelligence integration enhance contextual risk assessment, allowing auditors to address emerging threats proactively. Additionally, advanced reporting and visualization features ensure that audit findings are clear, actionable, and accessible to both technical and non-technical stakeholders. Prioritizing these features enables organizations to conduct more efficient, accurate, and insightful cybersecurity audits.

Data Analysis Capabilities

Effective cybersecurity audit tools must offer robust data analysis capabilities, enabling the collection and interpretation of data from various sources such as logs, endpoints, network devices, and cloud environments. These tools streamline the process of identifying patterns and anomalies that indicate potential security threats. Advanced data analysis not only uncovers vulnerabilities but also provides a broader context for understanding how these weaknesses might be exploited. This comprehensive approach ensures auditors can make informed recommendations to bolster the organization's security posture.

Vulnerability Management

An essential feature of audit tools is integrated vulnerability management. These tools should not only detect vulnerabilities but also prioritize them based on factors such as severity, exploitability, and potential business impact. By focusing on high-risk vulnerabilities first, organizations can allocate resources effectively to mitigate critical threats. Additionally, some tools provide automated remediation suggestions, enabling faster response times. This capability is particularly valuable in large or complex environments where manually addressing each vulnerability would be impractical.

Compliance Mapping

Audit tools that offer compliance mapping simplify the process of meeting regulatory and industry-specific standards. Pre-built templates for frameworks such as GDPR, HIPAA, and ISO 27001 allow organizations to quickly assess their compliance status. Automated mapping features further enhance this process by aligning identified vulnerabilities with specific regulatory requirements, saving time and reducing the likelihood of errors. This functionality is especially beneficial for organizations operating in highly regulated industries where compliance is critical to avoid penalties and maintain trust.

Threat Intelligence Integration

The ability to integrate with threat intelligence platforms is a valuable feature for audit tools. By incorporating real-time data on known threats, these tools help auditors contextualize vulnerabilities and assess their relevance to the current threat landscape. For instance, linking IoCs to vulnerabilities allows auditors to prioritize risks associated with active threat actors. This integration enhances the overall effectiveness of the audit by providing a clearer understanding of the risks facing the organization.

Reporting and Visualization

Clear and comprehensive reporting is a basis of any successful cybersecurity audit, making it a critical feature in audit tools. Tools with customizable dashboards and reporting capabilities allow auditors to present findings in a way that is accessible to both technical and non-technical stakeholders. Visual elements such as graphs, heat maps, and charts can highlight critical vulnerabilities, trends, and compliance gaps, facilitating better decision-making. Additionally, detailed reports serve as valuable documentation for future audits, compliance verification, and strategic planning.

Best Practices for Selecting Audit Tools

- *Assess Organizational Needs*: Collaborate with stakeholders to identify specific audit requirements, ensuring that selected tools align with organizational objectives and security priorities.

- *Test Tools Before Deployment*: Leverage free trials or pilot programs to evaluate tool performance and usability. Testing ensures compatibility with existing systems and verifies that tools meet expectations.

- *Check Vendor Support*: Reliable customer support is essential for troubleshooting and maintenance. Choose vendors with a proven track record of responsive and effective support.

- *Seek Recommendations and Reviews*: Peer feedback, case studies, and online reviews provide valuable insights into tool performance and real-world applications. Learn from the experiences of other organizations to make informed decisions.

- *Ensure Scalability and Future-Proofing*: Select tools that can grow with your organization. Scalable solutions and regular updates ensure long-term relevance and usability.

Key Takeaways

Choosing the right cybersecurity audit tools is essential for accuracy, efficiency, and comprehensive risk assessment. Align tools with audit objectives, ensure seamless integration, and prioritize features like real-time monitoring, compliance mapping, and threat intelligence. Usability, scalability, and cost-effectiveness also play a crucial role in long-term success. By selecting the right tools, organizations can streamline audits, enhance security resilience, and maintain compliance with evolving regulatory standards.

In this section, we covered the following points:

- Selecting the right audit tools is crucial for ensuring accuracy, efficiency, and comprehensive coverage during cybersecurity audits.

- Tools must align with audit objectives, organizational scope, and integration requirements to deliver optimal results.

- Best practices include assessing needs, testing tools, and seeking reliable vendor support.

- Future trends, such as AI integration and blockchain technology, will further enhance the capabilities and reliability of audit tools.

Tips for Conducting a Tool-Based Assessment

Tool-based assessments are an indispensable component of modern cybersecurity audits, offering speed, accuracy, and insights that manual methods alone cannot achieve. However, their effectiveness hinges on thoughtful execution, careful configuration, and expert interpretation. This section delves into practical tips for conducting successful tool-based assessments, emphasizing the interplay between technology and expertise in cybersecurity audits.

CHAPTER 6   TOOLS FOR NETWORK AND CYBERSECURITY AUDITS

The Role of Tools in Cybersecurity Audits

Tools are a foundation of modern cybersecurity audits, offering automation, accuracy, and scalability. By streamlining labor-intensive tasks, tools allow auditors to focus on identifying risks and implementing strategic solutions. The role of tools in cybersecurity audits can be summarized as follows:

- *Vulnerability Scanning*: Tools like Nessus and QualysGuard scan IT systems for weaknesses, ensuring potential entry points are identified and mitigated.

- *Configuration Checks*: Tools automate the review of system configurations against security baselines, such as CIS benchmarks, identifying deviations.

- *Log Analysis*: SIEM platforms like Splunk and Elastic centralize and analyze logs, uncovering anomalies and potential threats.

- *Compliance Mapping*: Tools simplify adherence to regulations like PCI-DSS, HIPAA, ISO 27001, etc. by mapping organizational policies to compliance frameworks.

- *Risk Prioritization*: With scoring systems like CVSS, tools help prioritize vulnerabilities, focusing remediation efforts on the most critical risks.

Tips for Effective Tool-Based Audits

Effective tool-based audits require clear objectives, proper configuration, and expert analysis. Choose tools that align with audit goals, customize settings to fit your environment, and integrate multiple tools for a comprehensive assessment. Test configurations before full deployment, document findings clearly, and involve stakeholders early for better collaboration. Prioritize high-risk issues, validate results with manual reviews, and regularly update tools to keep audits accurate and relevant.

Define Clear Objectives

Before initiating an audit, clearly define what you aim to achieve with your tool-based assessment. Are you identifying vulnerabilities, evaluating compliance, or prioritizing risks? The tools you select should align with these objectives. For example, use Nessus or QualysGuard for vulnerability detection, while Splunk or Elastic SIEM are better suited for log and event analysis. Clarity in purpose ensures that the tools deployed address your audit goals effectively.

Understand the Tool's Capabilities and Limitations

Every tool has strengths and limitations that affect its utility in specific environments. For instance, OpenVAS excels in general vulnerability scanning but may struggle with application-layer issues. Similarly, AWS Inspector is well-suited for cloud-native environments but may lack the depth required for hybrid systems. Understanding these nuances helps in choosing tools that provide meaningful and reliable results for your specific audit scope.

Customize the Configuration

Default tool settings rarely align with the unique needs of an organization. Adjust the configurations to reflect the scope of the audit, organizational policies, and the specific infrastructure being assessed. Customization ensures that the tool focuses on relevant areas and reduces the likelihood of false positives or irrelevant findings.

Conduct Initial Tests

Before deploying tools organization-wide, run tests on a subset of systems to ensure proper configuration and minimize disruptions. Initial testing also helps identify potential inaccuracies or gaps in the tool's capabilities, enabling corrective actions before the full assessment.

Integrate Multiple Tools

No single tool can address all aspects of a cybersecurity audit. Combining tools like vulnerability scanners, SIEM systems, and compliance platforms offers a holistic view of the security posture. For example, use Nessus for vulnerability scanning, integrate it with Splunk for log analysis, and complement findings with OpenVAS for additional assurance.

Document and Interpret Findings

Accurate documentation of tool outputs is essential for linking technical findings to real-world risks. Use clear language to translate vulnerabilities into actionable insights, demonstrating their potential business impact. Well-documented results also serve as a valuable reference for future audits and strategic decision-making.

Involve Stakeholders Early

Engage IT and compliance teams from the outset to share interim findings and address issues as they arise. Early collaboration ensures timely remediation of critical vulnerabilities and alignment with organizational goals.

Prioritize Issues Based on Risk

Most tools provide risk-scoring mechanisms to rank vulnerabilities by their potential impact. Focus remediation efforts on high-risk issues first, addressing threats that pose immediate dangers to critical systems. This risk-based approach ensures that resources are allocated efficiently.

Correlate with Manual Assessments

While tools excel in automation, they are not a substitute for human expertise. Combine tool outputs with manual testing methods, such as penetration testing and configuration reviews, to validate findings and uncover gaps that automated systems might miss.

Review and Update Regularly

Cybersecurity is dynamic, with threats and systems evolving constantly. Regularly update tool configurations, vulnerability databases, and system patches to ensure that assessments remain accurate and relevant. This proactive approach guards against outdated tools missing emerging vulnerabilities.

Common Pitfalls in Tool-Based Audits

While tools are indispensable, their misuse can lead to suboptimal results. Understanding these pitfalls and their solutions is essential for effective audits.

- *Common Pitfalls*: Overreliance on Tools: Solely depending on tools without expert analysis can lead to missed vulnerabilities or misinterpreted data.
    - *Solution*: Combine tool outputs with manual testing and expert review to validate findings and uncover gaps.
- *Ignoring Updates*: Outdated tools may fail to detect new vulnerabilities or produce inaccurate results.
    - *Solution*: Regularly update tools, including vulnerability databases, patches, and configurations, to stay current with emerging threats.
- *Failing to Customize Settings*: Default configurations often result in incomplete or irrelevant findings that do not align with organizational needs.
    - *Solution*: Tailor tool settings to reflect the scope, policies, and infrastructure of the organization being audited.
- *Generating Excessive False Positives*: Tools may flag benign issues, overwhelming audit teams and masking real threats.
    - *Solution*: Fine-tune detection thresholds and use filters to focus on high-priority vulnerabilities.
- *Lack of Integration Between Tools*: Using unconnected tools can create silos, leaving critical security gaps.
    - *Solution*: Integrate tools with complementary functionalities, such as combining SIEM and vulnerability scanners for a comprehensive view.

Key Takeaways

Tool-based assessments enhance cybersecurity audits through automation, accuracy, and efficiency, but their effectiveness depends on proper configuration and expert interpretation. Define clear objectives, integrate multiple tools, and validate findings with manual reviews. Regular updates, stakeholder collaboration, and risk-based prioritization ensure audits remain accurate and relevant in an evolving threat landscape.

In this section, we covered the following points:

- *Role of Tools*: Cybersecurity tools streamline tasks like scanning, analysis, and compliance checks but require proper configuration and expert interpretation to deliver value.

- *Tips for Success*: Define objectives, understand tool capabilities, customize configurations, and integrate multiple tools for comprehensive assessments.

- *Manual Validation*: Tools enhance audits but must be complemented with manual reviews for complete accuracy.

- *Pitfalls to Avoid*: Overreliance, outdated tools, and uncustomized settings can undermine audit results.

- *Continuous Improvement*: Regularly update tools, configurations, and audit strategies to adapt to evolving threats and technologies.

Common Tool Misconfigurations in Audits

Cybersecurity audit tools are essential for identifying vulnerabilities, ensuring compliance, and strengthening an organization's security posture. However, their effectiveness is often compromised by misconfigurations, which can lead to inaccurate results, blind spots in coverage, or even new security risks. Common issues such as incomplete scoping, reliance on default settings, and improper credential management can significantly weaken the audit process. Without careful configuration, organizations may miss critical threats or generate misleading findings, undermining the integrity of their security assessments.

To maximize the value of audit tools, organizations must adopt a proactive approach to configuration and maintenance. This includes tailoring tool settings to align with specific security needs, regularly updating tools with the latest patches, ensuring proper integration with other cybersecurity platforms, and training audit teams on best practices. By addressing these challenges, organizations can enhance audit accuracy, improve risk visibility, and strengthen overall security resilience.

The Importance of Proper Tool Configuration

Misconfigurations in cybersecurity tools are a pervasive yet often overlooked vulnerability in audits. These tools are vital for detecting threats, assessing vulnerabilities, and ensuring compliance. However, their effectiveness relies heavily on accurate and context-aware configuration. Improper setups can lead to incomplete coverage, inaccurate results, or even new security risks, undermining the entire audit process.

Proper configuration ensures that cybersecurity tools provide:

- Comprehensive asset coverage for full visibility of potential vulnerabilities.

- Accurate threat detection, reducing the risk of false positives or negatives.

- Efficient utilization of resources, avoiding unnecessary overhead or alert fatigue.

- Enhanced audit integrity, ensuring findings align with real-world risks.

Without careful configuration, organizations risk missing critical gaps or producing unreliable audit results, which can lead to significant security breaches or compliance failures.

Common Tool Misconfigurations in Audits

Common misconfigurations in cybersecurity audit tools can lead to inaccurate assessments, missed threats, and compliance gaps. Issues such as incomplete scoping, reliance on default settings, improper credential management, and outdated tool databases weaken the audit process. Additionally, poor integration with other security systems and misconfigured alerting mechanisms can result in fragmented insights and delayed responses to threats. Addressing these misconfigurations is critical to ensuring that audit tools provide accurate, actionable, and comprehensive security assessments.

Incomplete Scoping

One of the most frequent misconfigurations occurs when tools fail to scan all organizational assets. This often stems from oversight during scoping or neglecting hybrid and cloud environments. For example, a vulnerability scanner like Nessus may bypass cloud-hosted assets, such as misconfigured S3 buckets. The result is a blind spot in security coverage, leaving critical vulnerabilities undetected.

Default Settings

Many tools come with default settings that fail to align with an organization's unique environment. While convenient for initial deployment, relying on these defaults can lead to either excessive false positives or overlooked threats. For instance, an SIEM tool like Splunk might ignore critical logs from niche applications, leaving security gaps.

Improper Credential Management

A lack of proper credentials for security tools often limits their ability to assess systems fully. Without admin-level access, tools may fail to detect misconfigurations, such as weak directory permissions. This is a common issue with vulnerability scanners that require elevated privileges to perform thorough assessments.

Overlooking Updates

Tools that are not regularly updated with patches or threat intelligence become outdated, failing to recognize emerging vulnerabilities. For example, Metasploit may miss critical zero-day threats if its exploit database isn't current, rendering it ineffective in audits.

Poor Integration

Cybersecurity tools often work in silos when not integrated with complementary systems. A lack of integration with platforms like SIEMs or cloud security solutions can result in fragmented insights. For instance, QRadar may fail to correlate events without proper integration with cloud services.

Excessive Sensitivity or Leniency

Misconfigured thresholds can either overwhelm analysts with false positives or leave actual threats unnoticed. A DLP tool set too strict might flag harmless file transfers, while lenient configurations might allow sensitive data exfiltration to go undetected.

Misconfigured Alerts

Alerting mechanisms that aren't properly set up can cause delays or missed responses to critical incidents. For example, a firewall may log intrusions but fail to notify the security team in real time, hindering swift action.

Strategies to Avoid Tool Misconfigurations

Avoiding misconfigurations requires a proactive and systematic approach:

- *Customize Tool Settings*: Tailor configurations to align with the organization's unique infrastructure and audit objectives.
- *Regular Updates*: Keep tools updated with the latest patches and threat intelligence feeds to address evolving risks.
- *Ensure Proper Access*: Grant tools the necessary credentials to access systems and perform comprehensive assessments.
- *Integrate with Other Systems*: Connect tools with platforms like SIEMs to enhance correlation and visibility across environments.
- *Perform Test Runs*: Conduct preliminary scans or assessments to validate tool configurations and refine settings.
- *Review Settings Continuously*: Regularly review and adjust configurations based on audit findings and changing threats.
- *Train the Team*: Provide ongoing training to ensure audit teams understand how to configure and use tools effectively.

CHAPTER 6   TOOLS FOR NETWORK AND CYBERSECURITY AUDITS

Key Takeaways

Proper tool configuration is essential for accurate cybersecurity audits. Common misconfigurations, such as incomplete scoping, default settings, outdated databases, and poor integration, can create blind spots and weaken security assessments. Regular updates, tailored settings, and seamless integration with other security systems help ensure comprehensive and reliable audit results.

In this section, we covered the following points:

- *Configuration Matters*: Proper configuration is critical to ensure tools deliver accurate and actionable results.

- *Common Pitfalls*: Misconfigurations include incomplete scoping, reliance on default settings, lack of updates, and poor integration.

- *Strategic Customization*: Custom settings aligned with organizational needs significantly improve the effectiveness of tools.

- *Update Regularly*: Keeping tools current with patches and threat intelligence is essential to detect emerging risks.

- *Integration Is Key*: Tools should be integrated with complementary platforms to provide a unified view of security risks.

- *Continuous Improvement*: Periodic reviews and updates ensure configurations remain aligned with evolving threats and environments.

Conclusions

Effective cybersecurity auditing is impossible without the right tools, as they provide automation, accuracy, and scalability for assessing risks, detecting vulnerabilities, and ensuring compliance. Throughout this chapter, we have explored various essential tools, including vulnerability scanners, SIEM systems, compliance management platforms, threat intelligence solutions, and penetration testing frameworks. Each of these plays a critical role in modern cybersecurity audits, enhancing the efficiency and depth of assessments. However, their effectiveness is determined not just by their capabilities but also by how well they are selected, configured, and integrated within an organization's security ecosystem.

Choosing the right audit tools requires a strategic approach, aligning capabilities with specific audit objectives, IT infrastructure, and compliance requirements. Factors such as integration with existing systems, ease of use, real-time monitoring, scalability, and cost considerations must be carefully evaluated to ensure optimal performance. Additionally, leveraging key features like advanced data analysis, vulnerability management, compliance mapping, and threat intelligence integration allows organizations to gain deeper insights into their security posture.

However, simply deploying tools is not enough; proper configuration is crucial. Misconfigurations, such as incomplete scoping, reliance on default settings, improper credential management, or outdated databases, can lead to inaccurate findings and security gaps. Organizations must proactively address these issues by customizing settings, performing regular updates, ensuring proper access control, integrating tools effectively, and continuously reviewing configurations.

A successful cybersecurity audit strategy also involves a balanced approach between automated tools and human expertise. While audit tools streamline detection and assessment, they should be supplemented with manual reviews, penetration testing, and expert analysis to validate findings and uncover nuanced security risks. Organizations should also emphasize continuous improvement by periodically reassessing their audit methodologies, updating tools in response to evolving threats, and training audit teams to maximize tool effectiveness.

Cybersecurity audits are a dynamic and ongoing process, requiring adaptability to keep pace with emerging threats, regulatory changes, and technological advancements. By selecting, configuring, and utilizing tools effectively, while integrating them within a comprehensive audit strategy, organizations can strengthen their security posture, enhance compliance, and proactively mitigate cyber risks.

CHAPTER 7

How to Write an Effective Cybersecurity Audit Report

An effective cybersecurity audit report serves as a critical tool for communicating the findings of an audit, ensuring stakeholders understand the security posture of the organization and any vulnerabilities that require remediation. The first step in crafting such a report is to establish a clear and logical structure. This typically includes an executive summary, detailed findings, and actionable recommendations. The executive summary provides a high-level overview tailored for senior management, highlighting the key risks, compliance status, and overall assessment of the organization's cybersecurity framework. By ensuring that this section is concise and easy to understand, decision-makers can quickly grasp the urgency and significance of the findings without delving into technical complexities.

The detailed findings section forms the backbone of the report and should include a comprehensive analysis of the cybersecurity audit's scope, methodology, and results. Each identified issue should be described with its severity level, potential impact, and evidence to support the assessment. Visual aids, such as graphs or charts, can enhance understanding, especially when illustrating trends or risk patterns. Furthermore, mapping the findings to established frameworks like ISO 27001, NIST CSF, or relevant regulatory standards helps contextualize the gaps within a recognized structure. This not only enhances the report's credibility but also provides a clear benchmark for stakeholders to evaluate the organization's compliance.

Actionable recommendations are the foundation of an impactful audit report. For each finding, the report should propose practical and prioritized steps for mitigation or improvement. Recommendations should balance technical feasibility with business considerations, offering solutions that align with the organization's resources and operational goals. To ensure accountability, the report should assign responsibility for each action and include timelines for implementation. A well-crafted cybersecurity audit report is not merely a diagnostic document but a roadmap for strengthening the organization's defenses, fostering proactive risk management, and building a culture of continuous improvement in cybersecurity.

The Purpose of an Audit Report

A cybersecurity audit report is one of the most critical deliverables of an audit, encapsulating the findings, observations, and actionable recommendations to stakeholders. The primary aim of this document is to inform stakeholders about the organization's current security posture, identifying vulnerabilities, compliance gaps, and emerging risks. It serves as a bridge between audit findings and the actionable steps needed to enhance security and achieve compliance.

The report plays an essential role in decision-making processes, particularly for senior management and board members who rely on clear, concise, and actionable insights to allocate resources, secure funding, and set priorities. At the same time, it is a technical roadmap for IT and security teams, outlining specific areas requiring immediate attention. A well-structured report not only ensures accountability by tracking progress against recommendations but also serves as a foundation for follow-up audits, ensuring ongoing security improvements. Without such a report, even the most thorough audit can fail to achieve meaningful results, as its findings may remain buried in technical jargon or lack the clarity needed to drive action.

Key Components of an Audit Report

A properly structured audit report ensures clarity, engagement, and actionability. Figure 7-1 shows the essential components that every effective cybersecurity audit report should include.

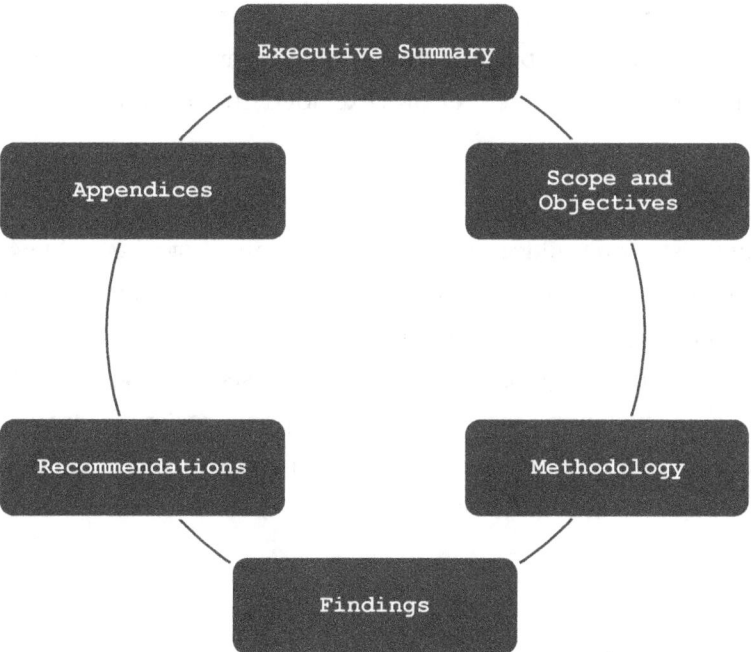

Figure 7-1. Key components of an audit report

Executive Summary

The executive summary is arguably the most important section of the audit report. It provides a high-level overview of the audit findings, summarizing key risks, compliance gaps, and prioritized recommendations. This section is specifically tailored for senior executives and non-technical stakeholders who need to understand the audit's outcomes without delving into technical details. For instance, instead of describing individual vulnerabilities, this section would highlight overarching risks, such as insufficient access controls or outdated encryption protocols, along with recommendations for mitigation.

Scope and Objectives

Clearly defining the scope and objectives ensures that the report aligns with stakeholder expectations. The scope outlines the areas covered during the audit, such as specific networks, applications, cloud environments, or compliance frameworks. The objectives define the audit's purpose, whether it is to assess compliance with standards like

PCI-DSS, identify vulnerabilities in a hybrid infrastructure, or evaluate the effectiveness of security controls. By setting boundaries, this section avoids ambiguity and helps readers understand what was included and excluded from the audit.

Methodology

The methodology section builds credibility by explaining how the audit was conducted. It should detail the tools, techniques, and frameworks used, ensuring transparency in the findings. For example, if Nessus was used for vulnerability scanning or Splunk for log analysis, this should be explicitly mentioned. This section also highlights whether manual techniques, such as penetration testing or policy reviews, were employed to complement automated assessments. Such details reassure stakeholders that the findings are robust and comprehensive.

Findings

The findings section is the heart of the audit report. Each issue identified during the audit should be based on supporting evidence, such as screenshots, logs, configuration details, etc. Findings should be categorized by severity, high, medium, or low, based on their potential impact and likelihood of exploitation. This section should also detail the affected assets and explain the potential business implications of each vulnerability or compliance gap. For instance, a misconfigured firewall may allow unauthorized access, posing a risk of data breaches or regulatory penalties.

Recommendations

Actionable recommendations transform an audit report from a diagnostic tool into a roadmap for improvement. Each recommendation should be specific, measurable, and aligned with the organization's priorities. For example, instead of stating, "Improve access controls," the report should recommend, "Implement multi-factor authentication for all privileged accounts within the reasonable period of time." Each recommendation should include a timeline for implementation and assign responsibilities to ensure accountability.

Appendices

To keep the main body of the report focused and readable, supplementary information such as detailed logs, compliance mappings, or raw data should be included in the appendices. This ensures that technical teams have access to all the necessary details without overwhelming non-technical readers.

Writing Best Practices

A well-crafted audit report follows established best practices to ensure clarity, engagement, and effectiveness. It should be structured logically, use standardized terminology, and avoid excessive complexity. Maintaining a neutral and fact-based tone enhances credibility, while clearly distinguishing between findings, implications, and recommendations ensures that readers can act on the insights provided.

Tailor to the Audience

Understanding the audience is crucial for an effective report. Senior management requires concise summaries that highlight business risks and strategic recommendations, while IT teams need detailed technical insights and actionable steps. A good report balances these needs by using clear headings, summaries, and supplementary appendices.

Be Clear and Concise

Clarity is essential for conveying complex findings effectively. Avoid technical jargon where possible and use visuals such as charts, graphs, and tables to present data. Bullet points, risk matrices, and prioritized lists can help break down complex information into digestible pieces, ensuring readers can quickly understand the most critical points.

Ensure Accuracy

Accuracy is paramount in an audit report. All findings should be validated against tools like Nessus for vulnerabilities or Splunk for log analysis. Cross-referencing findings with compliance frameworks ensures that recommendations are actionable and aligned with industry standards. Mistakes or inconsistencies can undermine the report's credibility and effectiveness.

Focus on Actionability

Every finding in the report should be accompanied by clear, actionable recommendations. Recommendations should be prioritized by risk level and include specific steps, responsible teams, and timelines. For instance, instead of vaguely suggesting "improve patch management," the report could recommend "deploy patches for all critical vulnerabilities identified within 15 days, starting with high-risk servers."

Maintain Objectivity

The tone of the report should remain neutral and solution-focused. Avoid assigning blame for discovered vulnerabilities or compliance gaps, and instead, emphasize the steps needed to address them. Back up all findings with evidence to ensure the report remains credible and professional.

Tools for Report Creation

Selecting the right tools can significantly enhance the efficiency and accuracy of audit reporting. Automated reporting tools can help streamline data collection and formatting, reducing manual errors and ensuring consistency across multiple audits. Additionally, using standardized templates and predefined risk assessment frameworks improves report quality and readability. Organizations should also consider cloud-based collaboration tools that allow multiple auditors and stakeholders to contribute seamlessly, ensuring a well-rounded and comprehensive audit report. The following tools improve audit reporting.

- *Report Automation Tools*: Tools like Dradis and SecurityScorecard streamline the reporting process by automating data aggregation and formatting. These tools save time while ensuring consistency and accuracy in the final report.

- *Visualization Tools*: Platforms like Tableau or Power BI are invaluable for creating dashboards, graphs, and charts that make complex findings more accessible to non-technical stakeholders.

- *Compliance Management Platforms*: Tools like AuditBoard help map audit findings to compliance frameworks, ensuring the report is aligned with regulatory requirements and standards.

Common Mistakes to Avoid

One of the biggest pitfalls in cybersecurity audit reporting is failing to align the report with the intended audience. Technical jargon or overly detailed findings may overwhelm executives, while a lack of depth may leave security teams without sufficient guidance. Another common mistake is overlooking regulatory and compliance requirements, which can lead to missed opportunities for security improvements. By ensuring reports are well-structured, actionable, and reviewed by relevant stakeholders, organizations can maximize the effectiveness of their cybersecurity audit reports. In the following sections, the most common mistakes in report writing are presented.

- *Overloading with Details*: Reports that include excessive technical information can overwhelm non-technical stakeholders, weakening the impact of key findings. Focus on relevance and provide supplementary details in appendices.

- *Lack of Prioritization*: Failing to prioritize risks based on severity and impact can delay addressing critical vulnerabilities. Ensure that high-risk issues are clearly identified and prioritized for immediate action.

- *Inconsistent Formatting*: Disorganized content or inconsistent formatting can make the report difficult to read and reduce its professionalism. Use templates or predefined styles to maintain consistency.

- *Neglecting Follow-Up*: An audit report without a clear action plan risks being shelved without implementation. Ensure that the report includes a follow-up mechanism to track progress against recommendations.

- *Ignoring Stakeholder Input*: Reports that fail to engage key stakeholders during the drafting phase risk overlooking critical perspectives. Collaborate with relevant teams to ensure all priorities are addressed.

CHAPTER 7   HOW TO WRITE AN EFFECTIVE CYBERSECURITY AUDIT REPORT

Key Takeaways

An effective cybersecurity audit report is more than a summary of findings; it's a powerful tool for actionable change, helping organizations strengthen their defenses and meet compliance goals.

In this section, we covered the following points:

- The audit report communicates findings, risks, and recommendations, serving as a roadmap for improving security and compliance.

- A well-structured report includes an executive summary, scope, methodology, findings, recommendations, and appendices.

- Use clear, concise language and visuals to ensure the report is understandable for all stakeholders.

- Recommendations should be specific, prioritized, and include timelines and responsibilities.

- Common mistakes such as overloading with details, inconsistent formatting, or neglecting follow-up can undermine the report's effectiveness.

Tips for Communicating Technical Findings to Non-technical Stakeholders

One of the most critical skills for cybersecurity professionals is the ability to communicate technical findings effectively to non-technical stakeholders. Whether reporting to executives, operational managers, or legal teams, the challenge lies in bridging the gap between highly technical data and the actionable insights needed for informed decision-making. Miscommunication, overly complex explanations, or failing to address stakeholders' specific concerns can lead to delayed responses, underestimation of risks, and missed opportunities to strengthen security. This section delves into actionable strategies for presenting technical audit findings in a clear, engaging, and impactful manner.

Understand Your Audience

Effective communication begins with understanding the audience and their priorities. Different groups within an organization have varying levels of technical knowledge and unique concerns that influence how they interpret cybersecurity risks.

- *Executives and Board Members*: For this audience, emphasize the business implications of findings. Highlight potential costs of inaction, reputational risks, and regulatory consequences. They are less interested in technical details and more focused on strategic outcomes like business continuity and shareholder confidence.

- *Operational Managers*: Managers need to understand how technical issues will impact their teams and day-to-day operations. Discuss the implications for workflow efficiency, resource allocation, and any disruptions they might encounter.

- *Legal and Compliance Teams*: This group focuses on regulatory obligations, contractual requirements, and potential legal liabilities. Frame findings in terms of adherence to standards such as GDPR, PCI-DSS, ISO 27001, etc., making the connection between technical issues and legal consequences clear.

- *Risk Management Teams*: These teams focus on enterprise-wide risk exposure and mitigation strategies. Present findings in the context of overall risk appetite, aligning with risk management frameworks such as Committee of Sponsoring Organizations of the Treadway Commission Enterprise Risk Management (COSO ERM) or FAIR. Show how cybersecurity risks integrate with financial, operational, and reputational risks.

- *IT and Security Teams*: This audience requires detailed technical insights, root causes, and remediation steps. Providing in-depth analysis, including logs, configuration issues, and security control gaps, ensures they can effectively implement corrective actions.

- *Finance Teams*: Cost considerations often drive decision-making. Explaining potential financial impacts, such as cost savings from preventive measures versus post-breach recovery expenses, helps finance teams allocate budgets effectively.

- *HR Teams*: HR teams play a role in security awareness training and insider threat management. Explaining how security vulnerabilities relate to employee behavior, training needs, and access control policies helps them contribute to risk reduction.

- *Customer Service and Operations*: Security issues can directly impact service delivery, customer satisfaction, and business continuity. For these teams, highlighting risks related to data privacy, system availability, and customer trust ensures alignment with business objectives.

- *Third-Party Vendors and Supply Chain Managers*: Many cybersecurity risks stem from third-party integrations. Findings should be presented in the context of supply chain security, vendor risk assessments, and contractual obligations to ensure compliance and risk mitigation.

Use Simplified Language

Complex jargon can alienate non-technical audiences, reducing their ability to comprehend and act on critical findings. Simplified language is essential for bridging the gap between technical and non-technical stakeholders.

- Replace technical terms with relatable explanations: For instance, instead of stating, "A high-severity SQL injection vulnerability exists," say, "Our website has a weakness that could allow hackers to steal customer data." This shifts the focus from the technical term to the real-world implication.

- Answer three key questions for every finding:
  - What happened? Provide a brief description of the issue.
  - Why does it matter? Explain the potential business, legal, or operational impact.
  - How can it be fixed? Present a high-level overview of the solution.
  - By making your language accessible and direct, you ensure your findings resonate across all levels of the organization.

Focus on Business Impact

The key to securing buy-in from non-technical stakeholders is to frame technical findings in terms of their impact on the organization. Stakeholders are more likely to prioritize risks when they understand their broader implications:

- *Reputation*: Highlight how vulnerabilities could erode customer trust or damage the organization's public image. For example, "This weakness could lead to a data breach, which might cause customers to lose confidence in our ability to protect their information."

- *Compliance*: Connect technical gaps to regulatory violations, such as, "Failure to address this issue puts us out of compliance with GDPR, which could result in fines of up to 4% of annual global turnover."

- *Financial*: Quantify the potential costs of inaction, such as revenue losses from downtime or increased spending to recover from a cyberattack.

Use Visual Aids

Visual aids are a powerful tool for simplifying complex data and making findings more digestible. Tools like Tableau, Excel, Power BI, or PowerPoint can help you create visuals that resonate with your audience:

- *Graphs*: Use trend graphs to illustrate the growth of vulnerabilities over time or the frequency of specific attack types.

- *Charts*: Pie charts or bar graphs can be used to break down compliance gaps, highlighting areas that need the most attention.

- *Heatmaps*: Risk heatmaps are particularly effective for showing high-risk areas in systems, processes, or geographic locations.

Visuals not only make data more accessible but also provide a clear focus for discussions, ensuring stakeholders can quickly grasp key points.

Prioritize Findings

Not all risks require immediate action, and stakeholders often rely on cybersecurity professionals to help them prioritize. Use a structured framework to rank findings based on:

- *Severity*: Emphasize vulnerabilities with the highest potential impact on the organization.

- *Compliance Requirements*: Highlight gaps that could lead to regulatory penalties or non-compliance with industry standards.

- *Feasibility*: Point out issues that can be addressed quickly with minimal resources while delivering significant improvements.

A risk matrix categorizing issues by their likelihood and impact is an effective way to guide stakeholders toward the most critical areas. By prioritizing effectively, you help ensure that resources are allocated where they will have the most significant impact.

Provide Clear Action Steps

Non-technical stakeholders are more likely to take action when given clear, concise next steps. For each finding, outline

- What needs to be done? Provide a high-level overview of the required actions.

- Who is responsible? Assign accountability to specific teams or individuals.

- What is the timeline? Set realistic deadlines based on risk severity and organizational capacity.

- What resources are required? Identify tools, budgets, or external support needed to implement the solution.

Providing a detailed roadmap ensures that stakeholders understand their roles in addressing the issues and have the confidence to act promptly.

Anticipate Questions and Concerns

Stakeholders will likely have questions about the implications of your findings and the proposed solutions. Common concerns include:

- *Costs*: "What will it cost to fix this issue, and how does it compare to the potential losses?"

- *Disruptions*: "Will addressing this issue affect day-to-day operations or customer service?"

- *Alternatives*: "Are there other, less resource-intensive ways to mitigate this risk?"

Anticipating these questions and preparing thorough, realistic answers demonstrates professionalism and builds trust. It also helps stakeholders make informed decisions without unnecessary delays.

Leverage Storytelling

Storytelling is an underutilized yet highly effective tool for making technical issues relatable and memorable. Use real-world examples to illustrate risks and their potential consequences:

- "A similar vulnerability was exploited at a competitor last year, leading to a $5 million loss and widespread customer dissatisfaction."

- "If unaddressed, this issue could lead to unauthorized access to sensitive customer data, similar to the 2020 breach that impacted millions of users."

Stories add context and emotional weight to technical findings, encouraging stakeholders to take action.

CHAPTER 7   HOW TO WRITE AN EFFECTIVE CYBERSECURITY AUDIT REPORT

Follow Up with Documentation

After presenting findings, provide stakeholders with a comprehensive written summary. This document should include

- A recap of the key risks and their implications.
- Prioritized recommendations for addressing the risks.
- Any visual aids used during the presentation.

Clear, concise documentation ensures that stakeholders have a reliable reference for planning and implementation, even after the meeting.

Key Takeaways

Effectively communicating technical findings to non-technical stakeholders is essential for driving informed decision-making and ensuring timely risk mitigation. By tailoring the message to the audience, simplifying complex concepts, and focusing on business impact, cybersecurity professionals can bridge the gap between technical data and actionable insights. Clear visuals, prioritized recommendations, and proactive engagement foster collaboration, ensuring that security risks are understood, addressed, and integrated into the organization's broader strategic goals.

In this section, we covered the following points:

- *Understand Audience*: Tailor communication to the concerns and priorities of different stakeholder groups.
- *Simplify Language*: Replace technical jargon with clear, relatable explanations that focus on the what, why, and how.
- *Focus on Business Impact*: Frame risks in terms of reputation, compliance, and financial consequences to drive urgency.
- *Use Visual Aids*: Leverage graphs, charts, and heatmaps to simplify complex data and improve understanding.
- *Prioritize and Act*: Use frameworks like risk matrices to help stakeholders focus on the most critical issues.

- *Prepare for Questions*: Anticipate common concerns about costs, disruptions, and alternatives to ensure smooth discussions.
- *Follow Up*: Provide written documentation summarizing the findings, recommendations, and visual aids for ongoing reference.

The Role of Visuals in Audit Reporting

In the modern era of cybersecurity, where data is abundant and often overwhelming, visuals have become an indispensable tool for communicating audit findings effectively. Cybersecurity audits produce highly technical and data-heavy reports, which, when left in raw textual or numerical forms, can alienate non-technical stakeholders. Without clear communication, critical risks might be misunderstood, overlooked, or underestimated.

Visuals play a pivotal role in simplifying complex information, enhancing comprehension, and driving actionable decisions. By turning data into easy-to-understand graphs, heatmaps, or infographics, auditors ensure their findings resonate across diverse audiences, from executives to IT teams. This section delves into the importance of visuals in audit reporting, the various types of visuals to consider, the tools for creating them, and best practices to ensure their effective use.

Why Visuals Are Crucial in Audit Reporting

Cybersecurity audit reports are often burdened with details, technical jargon, and extensive datasets. For stakeholders outside the technical sphere, such reports can be daunting and difficult to interpret. This is where visuals excel; they translate complexity into clarity.

- *Simplify Complex Data*: Large datasets and intricate concepts can overwhelm stakeholders. Visuals, such as a bar chart showing vulnerability distribution, transform raw data into easily digestible insights.

- *Enhance Decision-Making*: Visuals enable stakeholders to quickly identify critical trends and risks, facilitating more informed and timely decisions. For instance, a heatmap highlighting high-risk areas allows leaders to prioritize actions effectively.

- *Increase Engagement*: Static blocks of text often fail to capture attention. Visuals, on the other hand, are more engaging and hold the reader's interest longer, ensuring that key points are absorbed.

- *Bridge the Gap Between Departments*: Not all stakeholders are well-versed in cybersecurity. Visuals provide a common language that makes technical findings accessible to executives, legal teams, and other non-technical audiences.

Incorporating visuals into audit reporting is not merely about aesthetics; it is about improving the accessibility and utility of critical findings to enhance an organization's security posture.

Types of Visuals to Include

Visuals come in various forms, each tailored to specific types of data and stakeholder needs. To maximize their impact, it's crucial to understand the benefits of each visual type and when to use them.

Table 7-1 presents advantages and disadvantages of main types of visuals.

Table 7-1. Advantages and disadvantages of main types of visuals

Name	Advantages	Disadvantages	Use case
Bar Graphs	Clearly compare data across categories, making it easy to identify high-risk areas.	Can become cluttered if too many categories are included.	Use when comparing metrics like vulnerabilities by department or system.
Pie Charts	Show proportions effectively, making it easy to understand data distribution.	Not ideal for showing trends or comparing multiple data points.	Use when presenting the percentage of vulnerabilities by severity level.
Line Graphs	Excellent for visualizing trends and changes over time.	Can be misleading if the scale or intervals are not chosen carefully.	Use for tracking vulnerabilities, incidents, or security improvements over time.
Heatmaps	Provide a quick visual representation of risk levels using color coding.	Can oversimplify complex data if not paired with additional context.	Use when prioritizing high-risk systems, locations, or processes.
Infographics	Engaging and easy to digest, combining visuals and concise text.	May lack the depth needed for highly technical audiences.	Use for executive summaries or presenting audit highlights to non-technical stakeholders.
Dashboards	Interactive and real-time, allowing stakeholders to explore data dynamically.	Requires specialized tools and ongoing maintenance.	Use for continuous monitoring of compliance, vulnerabilities, and security trends.
Diagrams	Help illustrate complex systems, processes, or network architectures.	Can be challenging to interpret if overly detailed or not well-structured.	Use when explaining system architecture, data flows, or potential attack paths.

Graphs and Charts

Graphs and charts are among the most versatile and commonly used visuals in audit reports. They present data in a structured, easy-to-interpret format, allowing stakeholders to identify trends and patterns quickly.

Bar Graphs

- *Benefits*: Ideal for comparing quantitative data across categories, such as the number of vulnerabilities per department, system, or region.
- *When to Use*: Use bar graphs when you need to emphasize differences between groups or highlight which entities have the highest or lowest metrics.
- *Example*: A bar graph showing vulnerabilities across 10 departments, with bars of varying lengths corresponding to the severity of findings.

Pie Charts

- *Benefits*: Show proportions and percentages, making them perfect for illustrating how data is distributed among categories.
- *When to Use*: Use pie charts to emphasize the composition of a whole, such as compliance versus non-compliance rates.
- *Example*: A pie chart that shows the percentage of critical, high, medium, and low vulnerabilities detected during an audit.

Line Graphs

- *Benefits*: Highlight trends and changes over time, such as increases or decreases in threats, risks, or system health.
- *When to Use*: Use line graphs for time-series data to emphasize progress, deterioration, or the impact of implemented security measures.
- *Example*: A line graph tracking the number of vulnerabilities detected quarterly for the past three years.

Heatmaps

Heatmaps use color coding to visually represent data density, severity, or frequency, making them an excellent choice for risk assessment.

- *Benefits*: Heatmaps allow stakeholders to quickly identify high-risk areas with intuitive color gradients, such as red for critical risks and green for low risks.
- *When to Use*: Use heatmaps when you need to prioritize attention and resources toward the most vulnerable systems or processes.
- *Example*: A heatmap of an organization's network highlighting high-risk servers in red and low-risk systems in green.

Heatmaps are especially useful for presenting findings to stakeholders who need to understand risk distribution across an organization quickly.

Infographics

Infographics combine visuals and concise text to deliver a summary of findings in a highly engaging format.

- *Benefits*: Infographics make complex information relatable and visually appealing, ensuring higher retention of key insights. They are excellent for presenting an overview of audit results to executives or non-technical stakeholders.
- *When to Use*: Use infographics for executive summaries, marketing communications, or when presenting audit highlights to a broader audience.
- *Example*: An infographic summarizing key findings, such as the number of vulnerabilities detected, the top three risks, and the percentage of systems audited.

Dashboards

Dashboards provide an interactive, real-time view of audit findings, often integrating multiple data sources for comprehensive insights.

- *Benefits*: Dashboards allow stakeholders to drill down into details, compare metrics, and monitor changes dynamically. They are particularly useful for ongoing monitoring or follow-up audits.
- *When to Use*: Use dashboards when presenting large datasets or when stakeholders require access to live or regularly updated information.
- *Example*: A cybersecurity dashboard showing current compliance rates, open vulnerabilities by category, and risk trends over time.

Diagrams

Diagrams visually map out processes, architectures, or systems, helping stakeholders understand structural issues and interdependencies.

- *Benefits*: Diagrams provide clarity in understanding complex systems, such as network architectures, data flows, or points of failure. They are particularly helpful in illustrating how a breach might propagate or where vulnerabilities exist.
- *When to Use*: Use diagrams when the report needs to address structural or systemic risks and demonstrate how various elements interact.
- *Example*: A network diagram illustrating critical systems, firewalls, and vulnerable endpoints in an organization's IT infrastructure.

Tools for Creating Visuals

To produce impactful visuals, auditors have access to a wide array of tools. Choosing the right tool depends on the complexity of the data and the level of detail required:

- *Excel*: A reliable option for creating basic charts, graphs, and tables.
- *Power BI*: Provides advanced data visualization capabilities, including customizable dashboards.

- *Tableau*: Excels at handling large datasets and creating detailed, interactive visualizations.
- *Lucidchart or Visio*: Perfect for drawing network diagrams, data flow charts, and process maps.
- *Canva*: Offers templates for infographics and presentation slides, making it ideal for non-technical summaries.

Leveraging these tools enables auditors to transform raw data into polished, professional visuals that enhance the overall impact of their reports.

Best Practices for Using Visuals in Audit Reports

While visuals can elevate a report's effectiveness, they must be used thoughtfully. Poorly designed or irrelevant visuals can confuse stakeholders and detract from the report's credibility. Here are some best practices:

- *Align with Key Messages*: Each visual should support a significant point in the report. Avoid cluttering the report with unnecessary or decorative visuals.
- *Keep It Simple*: Clarity is key. Use clean designs, straightforward labels, and clear legends. Overly complex visuals can overwhelm rather than clarify.
- *Ensure Accuracy and Context*: Misinterpreted visuals can lead to misguided decisions. Always accompany visuals with explanations that highlight their relevance and context.
- *Use Consistent Formatting*: Uniform styles, fonts, and color schemes across all visuals create a professional and cohesive look.
- *Test for Clarity*: Before finalizing the report, test the visuals on a diverse audience to ensure they are easy to understand and interpret.

Well-crafted visuals should not only complement the narrative but also stand on their own as informative elements.

Example Scenario: Visuals in Action

Imagine a cybersecurity audit reveals 500 vulnerabilities spread across 10 departments. Here's how the inclusion of visuals transforms the reporting:

- *Without Visuals*: A table listing department names and their respective vulnerability counts. While detailed, the table is overwhelming and difficult to analyze at a glance.

- *With Visuals*:
  - A bar chart displays vulnerabilities by department, allowing stakeholders to quickly identify high-risk areas.
  - A pie chart breaks down vulnerabilities by severity levels (e.g., critical, high, medium, low), helping prioritize responses.
  - A heatmap visually highlights departments or systems with the highest risk, guiding immediate actions.

These visuals help stakeholders grasp the scale and urgency of the findings in seconds, enabling them to focus on addressing critical vulnerabilities.

Key Takeaways

Incorporating visuals into cybersecurity audit reports is not a luxury but a necessity in today's data-driven world. By presenting findings in a visually compelling manner, auditors can ensure their work drives meaningful action, improves security, and strengthens organizational resilience.

In this section, we covered the following points:

- *The Power of Visuals*: Visuals simplify complex data, enhance decision-making, and engage diverse stakeholders, making them essential for effective audit reporting.

- *Effective Types of Visuals*: Bar graphs, pie charts, heatmaps, infographics, dashboards, and diagrams each serve specific purposes in presenting data.

- *Choosing the Right Tools*: Tools like Excel, Power BI, Tableau, Lucidchart, and Canva provide the resources needed to create impactful visuals.

- *Best Practices*: Ensure visuals align with the report's key messages, maintain simplicity, and provide context for every visual included.

- *Impactful Communication*: Incorporating visuals helps bridge the gap between technical experts and non-technical stakeholders, facilitating quicker and more informed decisions.

Creating an Executive Summary for Audit Reports

The executive summary is the basis of any cybersecurity audit report. It distills complex technical findings into a concise, high-level narrative that senior executives and decision-makers can understand and act upon. By focusing on critical insights and actionable recommendations, the executive summary ensures that key stakeholders remain engaged and informed about an organization's cybersecurity posture.

The Importance of an Executive Summary

Senior executives, including board members and C-suite leaders, often lack the time or technical expertise to dive into the granular details of an audit report. An executive summary serves as their primary window into the audit's findings, ensuring they grasp the urgency and significance of the issues uncovered.

Key benefits of a well-crafted executive summary include

- *Streamlining Information*: It simplifies complex technical data into a narrative that aligns with business priorities.

- *Driving Action*: Clear recommendations encourage prompt and decisive responses to critical risks.

- *Building Engagement*: It fosters collaboration between technical teams and leadership by presenting findings in a business-oriented context.

An executive summary is not just an overview; it's a tool to secure buy-in for cybersecurity initiatives and resources.

CHAPTER 7   HOW TO WRITE AN EFFECTIVE CYBERSECURITY AUDIT REPORT

Essential Elements of a Strong Executive Summary

A strong executive summary is not just an introduction to the audit report; it's a standalone section designed to inform, persuade, and motivate action. Each component plays a distinct role in ensuring the summary is impactful and aligned with the needs of senior decision-makers. Figure 7-2 presents key steps and elements for preparing an executive summary.

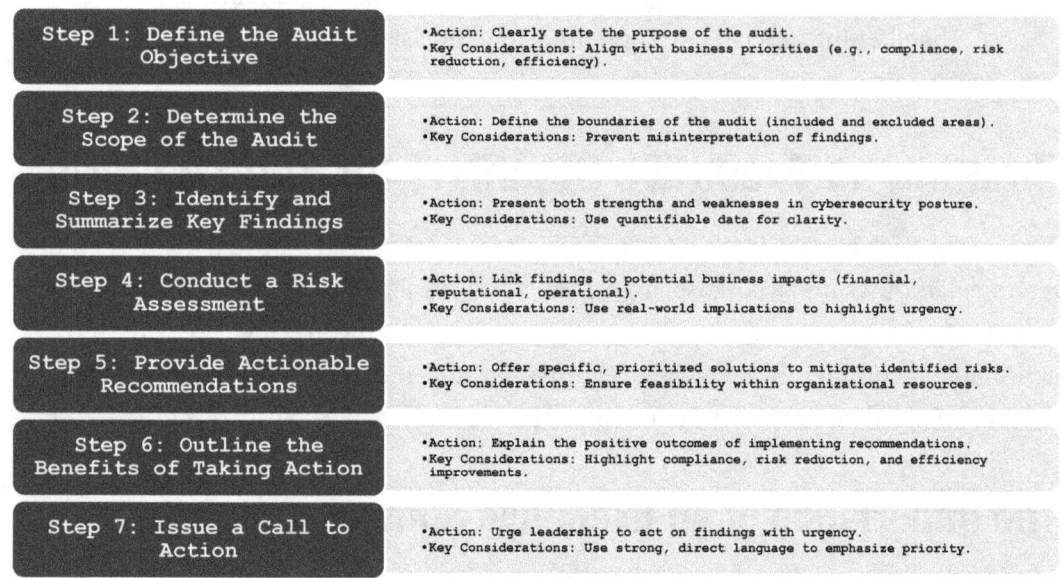

Figure 7-2. Key elements of a strong executive summary

Audit Objective

The objective sets the stage for the entire report, clearly stating why the audit was conducted. It should align with organizational priorities, whether it's to address a specific compliance requirement, evaluate the effectiveness of controls, or uncover potential vulnerabilities.

For example, if the purpose of the audit is regulatory compliance, explicitly mention the specific frameworks, such as NIST CSF, GDPR, or HIPAA. If the focus is on risk reduction, emphasize this to demonstrate alignment with the organization's risk management goals.

Scope of the Audit

The scope outlines the boundaries of the audit, defining what was included and excluded in the assessment. This section helps stakeholders understand the audit's breadth and focus areas, ensuring there are no misconceptions about the extent of the review. For instance, if the audit covers only cloud infrastructure, clarify that on-premises systems or IoT devices were not within scope. A well-defined scope also prevents stakeholders from overestimating or underestimating the report's findings.

Key Findings

This is the heart of the executive summary. Key findings should be presented in a balanced manner, highlighting both strengths and weaknesses to provide a comprehensive view of the cybersecurity posture. Positive findings reassure stakeholders about what is working well, while weaknesses underline critical areas requiring immediate attention.

For example, strengths might include robust IAM with MFA implemented organization-wide. Weaknesses, on the other hand, could point to gaps such as unencrypted sensitive data or outdated systems.

Quantify findings whenever possible. Instead of saying "some vulnerabilities were found," specify, "20% of critical systems are running outdated software, exposing them to potential exploitation."

Risk Assessment

The risk assessment ties the findings to their potential impact on the organization. This section should convey the severity and likelihood of risks in a way that resonates with business leaders. Highlight the consequences of unaddressed issues, such as regulatory fines, data breaches, operational downtime, or reputational damage.

For instance, you might explain, "The lack of encryption for sensitive customer data increases the likelihood of a breach, potentially resulting in GDPR penalties and loss of customer trust."

Recommendations

The recommendations should be actionable, prioritized, and specific. They must provide a clear roadmap for addressing the issues identified in the findings. Highlight quick wins and longer-term strategies, ensuring they align with the organization's capabilities and resources.

For example, "To address encryption gaps, we recommend implementing AES-256 encryption for all sensitive cloud-stored data within the next 30 days. Additionally, automate patch management processes for virtual machines to reduce vulnerabilities by 60% over the next quarter."

Summary of Benefits

This section explains how acting on the recommendations will positively impact the organization. Benefits could include enhanced compliance, reduced risk exposure, improved operational efficiency, or strengthened customer trust. Framing recommendations in terms of their ROI or strategic value increases the likelihood of leadership buy-in.

For instance, "Implementing the suggested improvements will significantly reduce the risk of a data breach, enhance compliance with GDPR, and improve the organization's overall security posture, fostering greater confidence among customers and partners."

Call to Action

End the summary with a direct and compelling call to action. This reinforces the urgency and importance of addressing the findings. Use strong, action-oriented language to motivate leadership to prioritize resources and efforts.

For example, "It is imperative to address encryption gaps and patch management deficiencies immediately to safeguard sensitive data and maintain compliance. Delaying action could expose the organization to significant financial and reputational risks."

Best Practices for Writing an Executive Summary

To maximize its effectiveness, the executive summary must be both professional and engaging. Follow these best practices:

- *Keep It Concise*: Avoid excessive detail while ensuring key points are covered.
- *Use Simple Language*: Avoid technical jargon or overly complex terms; write for a broad audience.
- *Prioritize Findings*: Place the most critical issues at the beginning of the summary to grab attention.
- *Align with Business Goals*: Frame findings in terms of how they support organizational objectives, such as revenue protection or regulatory compliance.

Example Executive Summary

- *Objective*: To assess the organization's cloud security posture and ensure compliance with NIST CSF standards.
- *Scope*: The audit covered three key areas:
  - Cloud data storage and encryption
  - IAM practices
  - Patch management for virtual machines
- *Key Findings*:
  - *Strengths*:
    - Robust IAM with MFA deployed across all critical systems.
    - Regular access reviews reduce insider threat risks.
  - *Weaknesses*:
    - 20% of cloud-stored sensitive data remains unencrypted.

- Infrequent patching of virtual machines leaves vulnerabilities exploitable.
- *Risk Assessment*: Unaddressed vulnerabilities in cloud environments could result in data breaches, non-compliance with GDPR, and reputational harm.
- *Recommendations*:
    - Encrypt all sensitive data stored in the cloud using industry-standard algorithms.
    - Implement automated patch management systems for virtual machines.
- *Benefits*: Taking these actions will enhance security, maintain compliance, and strengthen customer trust.
- *Call to Action*: Leadership is urged to prioritize encryption and patch management initiatives immediately to mitigate critical risks and safeguard organizational data.

From the above details, an executive summary may look like the following.

Executive Summary

This cybersecurity audit evaluated the organization's cloud security posture and its alignment with the NIST Cybersecurity Framework (NIST CSF). The assessment focused on cloud data storage, identity and access management (IAM), and patch management for virtual machines, while on-premises and IoT systems were excluded to maintain a targeted approach.

The audit identified both strengths and areas for improvement. The organization has strong IAM protocols, including multi-factor authentication (MFA) across critical systems and regular access reviews to mitigate insider threats. However, significant vulnerabilities were also uncovered. Approximately 20% of sensitive cloud data remains unencrypted, exposing it to potential unauthorized access. Additionally, virtual machines are patched infrequently, increasing the risk of exploitation by cyber threats.

These security gaps pose serious risks. The lack of encryption raises the possibility of data breaches, which could lead to regulatory fines, reputational damage, and loss of customer trust. Similarly, inadequate patch manage-

ment leaves critical systems vulnerable to known exploits, increasing the likelihood of operational disruptions and data exfiltration.

To mitigate these risks, we recommend implementing AES-256 encryption for all sensitive cloud data and automating patch management for virtual machines to ensure timely updates. These actions are critical and should be prioritized immediately.

Addressing these vulnerabilities will reduce risk exposure, strengthen compliance with GDPR and other regulations, and enhance overall cybersecurity. Delays in implementing these measures could lead to financial, operational, and reputational consequences.

Key Takeaways

A well-crafted executive summary highlights key risks, actionable recommendations, and the business impact of cybersecurity issues. Clarity, urgency, and alignment with organizational goals ensure leadership buy-in and timely action.

In this section, we covered the following points:

- An executive summary is a vital communication tool that connects technical findings to business priorities.

- Including audit objectives, key findings, risk assessments, and actionable recommendations ensures clarity and focus.

- Visuals, concise language, and alignment with organizational goals enhance the effectiveness of the summary.

- A strong call to action drives urgency, ensuring leadership commits to addressing risks promptly.

Common Cybersecurity Audit Reporting Mistakes and How to Avoid Them

Cybersecurity audit reports are the basis of effective communication between auditors and stakeholders. They provide a clear snapshot of an organization's security posture, identifying vulnerabilities and recommending actions for improvement. However, even well-intentioned reports can fall short if they fail to deliver findings clearly, concisely, or with the appropriate context. Avoiding common pitfalls is critical to ensure audit reports drive action, improve security, and support business objectives.

Importance of Reporting in Cybersecurity Audits

A well-crafted cybersecurity audit report is more than just a document; it's a tool for decision-making. Its purpose is to communicate the audit's objectives, scope, findings, and actionable recommendations to stakeholders who may have varying levels of technical expertise. When done right, it bridges the gap between technical assessments and business priorities.

Without clear reporting, even the most thorough audits can fail to produce meaningful change. Poorly written reports leave stakeholders unsure of risks, unclear on next steps, and disengaged from the urgency of the findings. Effective reporting ensures that technical issues are not only identified but also understood and addressed by decision-makers.

Common Reporting Mistakes

Even the most thorough cybersecurity audit can lose its impact if the findings are not communicated effectively. Common reporting mistakes, such as overly technical language, lack of prioritization, and missing business context, can make it difficult for stakeholders to understand and act on key issues. Reports that overload readers with data, provide vague recommendations, or lack visual elements may fail to engage decision-makers and delay critical security improvements. By recognizing and addressing these pitfalls, auditors can ensure that their reports drive meaningful action and strengthen the organization's overall security posture.

Lack of Clarity

One of the most frequent mistakes is writing reports that are overly technical, dense, or riddled with jargon. While technical terms might resonate with IT teams, they can alienate non-technical stakeholders like executives or board members. For example, stating, "A CVSS score of 9.0 indicates critical vulnerabilities," may not convey the real-world implications of a security gap.

- *Solution*: Simplify language and explain technical terms in relatable business terms. For example, clarify that "A critical vulnerability could allow hackers to exploit our systems, potentially leading to data breaches and regulatory fines."

Failure to Prioritize Findings

Not all findings are equally urgent. Presenting all vulnerabilities in a single list without prioritization can overwhelm stakeholders and delay action on critical issues.

- *Solution*: Categorize findings based on severity (critical, high, medium, and low) and provide actionable insights for addressing them. For instance, highlight vulnerabilities in customer-facing systems as top priorities while assigning a lower priority to those affecting less critical systems.

Missing Business Context

Focusing solely on technical findings without connecting them to business risks is another common oversight. Stakeholders outside IT often struggle to see why specific vulnerabilities matter.

- *Solution*: Link vulnerabilities to potential business impacts. For example, explain how "outdated encryption protocols could lead to a data breach, resulting in reputational damage and GDPR non-compliance fines."

Overloading with Data

Data-heavy reports filled with dense tables, logs, or excessive technical details can obscure the key message. Stakeholders may lose interest or struggle to identify what matters most.

- *Solution*: Summarize the most critical points in the main body of the report and include detailed data in appendices for those who need further analysis.

Vague Recommendations

Generic advice such as "Improve encryption standards" or "Enhance patch management" lacks specificity, leaving stakeholders unclear on how to act.

- *Solution*: Offer precise, actionable steps. For example, recommend: "Implement AES-256 encryption for sensitive cloud data within 30 days and schedule weekly patch updates for critical systems."

Overlooking Visuals

A text-heavy report can be difficult to digest and fail to engage readers. Visual elements like charts, graphs, and heatmaps can significantly enhance comprehension and focus attention on key findings.

- *Solution*: Use visuals strategically. For instance, include a heatmap to highlight high-risk areas or a bar graph to show trends in vulnerability severity over time.

Formatting Issues

Inconsistent formatting, disorganized content, or poor design can reduce the report's professionalism and make it harder to read.

- *Solution*: Use standardized templates and maintain consistent formatting throughout the document. Ensure headings, font sizes, and spacing are uniform.

Best Practices to Avoid Reporting Mistakes

Avoiding common cybersecurity audit reporting mistakes requires a blend of technical expertise, audience awareness, and communication skills. Here are detailed best practices to ensure your reports are impactful and actionable:

Tailor to the Audience

One size does not fit all in audit reporting. The way of presenting findings should reflect the needs and knowledge level of the audience:

- *For Leadership (C-Suite, Board Members)*: Present findings in terms of business risks, such as financial losses, regulatory penalties, or reputational damage. Avoid technical jargon and focus on high-level summaries. For example:

- *Instead of*: "The organization is using TLS 1.0, which is outdated."
- *Say*: "Using outdated encryption protocols could lead to regulatory fines and customer trust issues."

- *For IT Teams*: Provide detailed, technical findings with precise steps for remediation. Include references to relevant tools, frameworks, or methodologies, ensuring that the IT team can act efficiently.

- *For Regulators and Compliance Teams*: Emphasize compliance gaps and corrective actions. Highlight areas where the organization meets regulatory requirements and where improvements are needed.

Tailoring ensures that each audience can quickly understand and act on the information relevant to their role.

Structure Logically

A clear structure ensures the report flows smoothly and stakeholders can locate critical information easily. Follow this proven format:

- *Executive Summary*: Up to a one-page overview highlighting the purpose, findings, and recommendations.
- *Introduction*: Define the audit's objectives, scope, and methodology. Explain what was evaluated and why.
- *Findings*: Categorize findings by severity, using tables or charts for clarity. Provide context for each finding, explaining its impact.
- *Recommendations*: Include specific, actionable steps prioritized by risk level.
- *Conclusion*: Recap the key takeaways, outline next steps, and provide contact details for follow-ups.

A logical structure makes the report more digestible and ensures critical information is not overlooked.

Use Visuals Effectively

Visuals are a powerful tool to enhance comprehension and engagement:

CHAPTER 7   HOW TO WRITE AN EFFECTIVE CYBERSECURITY AUDIT REPORT

- *Bar Graphs*: Highlight vulnerabilities per department to identify areas of concern.

- *Pie Charts*: Show the ratio of compliant vs. non-compliant systems.

- *Heatmaps*: Use color-coding to emphasize high-risk areas.

- *Dashboards*: Provide real-time insights into vulnerability trends or risk levels.

When using visuals:

- Ensure they align with the report's key points.

- Use clear labels and concise explanations.

- Avoid clutter by focusing on one key message per visual.

- Good visuals make data intuitive and actionable, especially for non-technical stakeholders.

Prioritize Findings

Not all vulnerabilities are created equal. Present findings in a prioritized manner to help stakeholders focus on the most critical issues:

- Categorize vulnerabilities into critical, high, medium, and low risk.

- Use a risk matrix to visually represent the likelihood and impact of each finding.

- Provide a timeline for addressing each issue, emphasizing immediate action for high-risk items.

- Prioritization ensures that resources are allocated efficiently, addressing the most pressing issues first.

Simplify Language and Provide Context

Audit reports often fail to resonate with non-technical readers because of dense technical language. Simplify terminology and explain findings in terms of their real-world implications:

- *Instead of*: "The system is vulnerable to a buffer overflow."

- *Say*: "This vulnerability could allow attackers to gain unauthorized access, potentially exposing customer data."
- Adding context helps stakeholders understand the urgency and importance of addressing specific issues.

Provide Specific Recommendations

Generic recommendations undermine the credibility of the report and leave stakeholders unclear on next steps. Be precise in your advice:

- *Generic*: "Improve access controls."
- *Specific*: "Implement role-based access controls for database systems to ensure only authorized personnel can access sensitive data."
- Include timelines, resources required, and responsible parties to turn recommendations into actionable plans.

Use Professional Formatting

Inconsistent formatting or sloppy design can detract from the report's professionalism. Use these tips to enhance presentation:

- Stick to a uniform font and color scheme.
- Use clear headings and subheadings for easy navigation.
- Add page numbers and a table of contents for longer reports.
- Professional formatting builds trust and ensures the report is taken seriously by stakeholders.

Review the Report

Before finalizing the report, review it thoroughly for:

- *Accuracy*: Ensure data is validated and findings are correct.
- *Clarity*: Test the report with someone unfamiliar with the audit to confirm understanding.
- *Grammar and Formatting*: Correct any errors or inconsistencies.

- A well-reviewed report demonstrates attention to detail and instills confidence in its conclusions.

Impact of Well-Written Reports

A well-crafted audit report can significantly influence an organization's cybersecurity posture, fostering a culture of awareness and action. Here are the key impacts:

- *Drives Prompt Decision-Making*: A clear and concise report helps stakeholders quickly identify risks, prioritize actions, and allocate resources. For example, presenting high-risk vulnerabilities alongside actionable steps ensures that critical issues are addressed immediately.

- *Engages Stakeholders Across Departments*: By tailoring content and using visuals, the report resonates with diverse audiences. Decision-makers, IT teams, and compliance officers can align on objectives, fostering collaboration and accountability.

- *Strengthens Business Resilience*: By linking findings to business impacts, a strong report underscores the importance of proactive cybersecurity measures. This approach secures buy-in from leadership for necessary investments, such as enhanced security tools or additional personnel.

- *Enhances Credibility and Trust*: A professionally written, well-structured report builds the auditor's credibility. Stakeholders are more likely to trust and act on findings when they perceive the report as reliable and comprehensive.

- *Supports Compliance and Avoids Penalties*: A detailed report that highlights compliance gaps and corrective actions ensures the organization stays aligned with regulatory requirements.

This proactive approach reduces the risk of fines and reputational damage.

Key Takeaways

Keep reports clear, concise, and actionable. Avoid jargon, vague recommendations, and data overload. Prioritize risks, link findings to business impact, and use visuals. Tailor content to your audience to drive action and strengthen security.

In this section, we covered the following points:

- Avoid common mistakes such as unclear language, vague recommendations, and data overload to ensure your report is effective.

- Prioritize findings based on severity, providing actionable steps and timelines for remediation.

- Leverage visuals to present complex data in a digestible and engaging format.

- Tailor content to resonate with leadership, IT teams, and regulators, ensuring all stakeholders can act on the findings.

- Professional formatting and thorough reviews enhance the report's credibility and ensure its conclusions are trusted.

- Effective reporting bridges the gap between technical findings and business priorities, ensuring audit outcomes drive action.

- Common pitfalls, such as lack of clarity, vague recommendations, or excessive data, undermine the report's effectiveness.

- Best practices, including prioritizing findings, linking to business impacts, and using visuals, ensure reports are clear, engaging, and actionable.

- Structured and professional reports enhance stakeholder trust, support prompt decision-making, and improve the organization's cybersecurity posture.

How to Present Cybersecurity Audit Findings to the Board

Presenting cybersecurity audit findings to the board of directors is not just about conveying technical information. It's about delivering insights that align with the organization's strategic objectives and enabling informed decision-making. A well-prepared presentation can bridge the gap between technical complexities and business priorities, ensuring that cybersecurity remains a top priority at the leadership level.

Understanding the Board's Perspective

Before crafting your presentation, it's essential to understand the board's priorities and concerns. Unlike technical teams, board members focus on the broader business implications of cybersecurity risks. Their interest lies in understanding:

- *Financial Impact*: How will vulnerabilities or breaches affect the organization's bottom line?
- *Reputational Risks*: Could these findings damage the company's brand and customer trust?
- *Compliance and Regulatory Consequences*: What penalties or legal challenges might arise from unresolved issues?
- *Strategic Alignment*: How do the findings and recommendations align with the company's business objectives and risk tolerance?

Structuring Your Presentation

A clear and logical structure ensures that the message resonates with the board and facilitates informed decision-making. Here is a recommended structure for presenting audit findings:

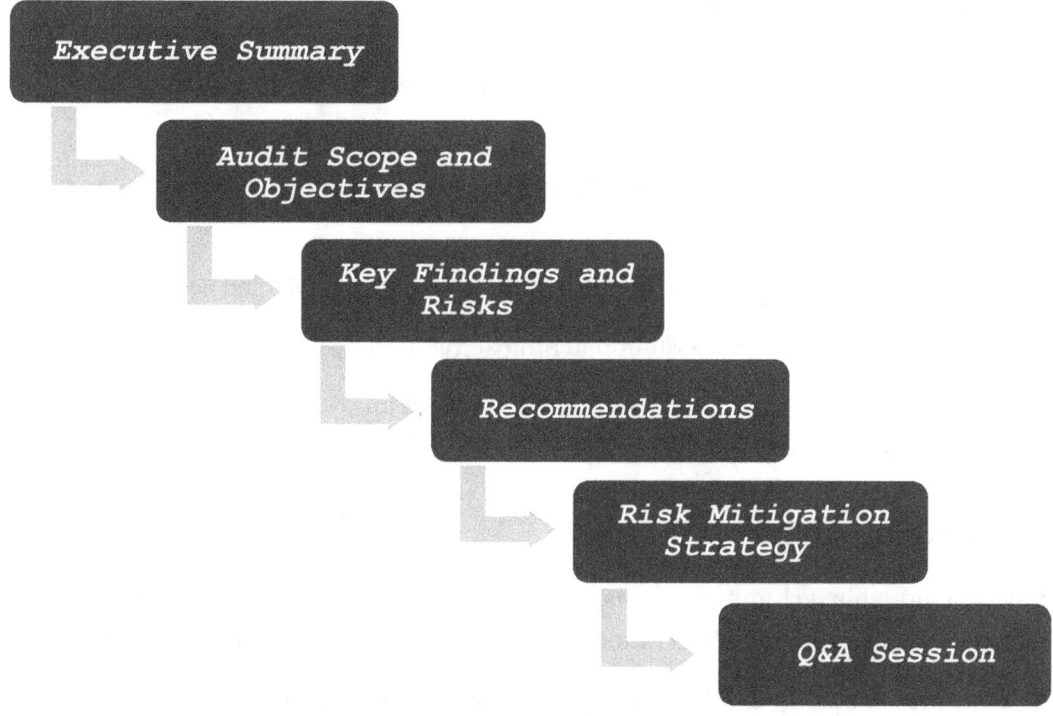

Figure 7-3. *Key steps of audit presentation*

Executive Summary

Start with a high-level overview that outlines the key findings, risks, and recommended actions. Use bullet points or a single slide to capture the main points briefly.

Audit Scope and Objectives

Explain the purpose and scope of the audit. Provide context on what systems, processes, or frameworks were evaluated, and define the objectives clearly. For instance:

- *Scope*: Evaluated cloud infrastructure, endpoint security, and compliance with GDPR.
- *Objective*: Identify vulnerabilities, assess compliance gaps, and recommend risk mitigation strategies.

Key Findings and Risks

Present the audit findings in order of priority, categorizing them as critical, high, medium, or low risk. For example:

- *Critical Finding*: Outdated encryption protocols expose sensitive customer data.
- *High Risk*: Lack of multi-factor authentication for privileged accounts.
- *Medium Risk*: Inconsistent patching across non-critical systems.

Use visuals such as bar graphs, pie charts, or heatmaps to make the data accessible and emphasize the severity of issues.

Recommendations

Provide actionable recommendations, prioritized based on risk levels and potential impact. Include estimated costs, timelines, and expected outcomes for each action:

- *Recommendation*: Implement advanced encryption protocols across all systems.
- *Timeline*: 3 months.
- *Expected Outcome*: Enhanced data security and compliance with GDPR.

Risk Mitigation Strategy

Explain how the proposed recommendations align with the organization's risk tolerance and long-term goals. Show how addressing these issues will reduce risks, improve operational efficiency, and protect the organization from financial or reputational damage.

Q&A Session

Conclude with a dedicated time for questions and discussion. Encourage board members to seek clarifications, offer input, and discuss next steps.

Communicating Effectively

Clear and effective communication is vital when presenting cybersecurity audit findings to the board. The board often comprises individuals with diverse expertise but limited technical knowledge. Therefore, the ability to convey complex issues in an accessible, relevant, and engaging way is critical.

Simplify Concepts

Avoid technical jargon or acronyms that might confuse non-technical board members. Instead, explain findings in plain language, focusing on what they mean for the business. For example:

- *Before*: "*The audit revealed outdated SSL/TLS protocols, leaving the system vulnerable to Man-in-the-Middle Attack (MITM) attacks.*"

- *After*: "*We discovered outdated encryption methods that could allow hackers to intercept sensitive communications.*"

Frame technical issues in terms of real-world consequences, such as financial loss, reputational damage, or regulatory penalties. Use analogies when appropriate to make abstract concepts tangible.

Focus on Business Impact

Board members are interested in how cybersecurity risks and recommendations affect the organization's financial health, reputation, and operational continuity. For each finding, emphasize

- The potential cost of inaction (e.g., regulatory fines and breach-related costs)

- Opportunities for improvement (e.g., cost savings, enhanced efficiency, and competitive advantage)

- Alignment with strategic objectives (e.g., customer trust and market positioning)

Use Stories and Real-World Examples

Stories can make risks and recommendations more relatable. For instance,

> *"A similar vulnerability led to a breach at a competitor, costing them $5 million in fines and lost revenue. Addressing this now could prevent us from facing the same consequences."*

This approach not only clarifies the risks but also underscores the urgency of addressing them.

Be Concise and Organized

Board meetings are time-sensitive, so it's important to deliver your presentation efficiently. Stick to key points and avoid overwhelming the board with excessive detail.

- Use bullet points or concise slides for clarity.
- Structure your discussion logically to ensure seamless flow.

Leveraging Technology for Presentations

Technology can significantly enhance the quality, clarity, and impact of the presentation. The right tools help to create professional visuals, organize data effectively, and deliver key messages in an engaging manner.

Presentation Tools

- *Microsoft PowerPoint*: A staple for structured presentations, allowing you to combine text, visuals, and transitions. Use templates for professionalism and consistency.
- *Google Slides*: A collaborative alternative for creating and sharing presentations in real time.

Data Visualization Tools

Data visualization tools help you convert raw data into meaningful visuals, such as graphs, charts, and heatmaps. Examples include:

- *Tableau/Power BI*: Ideal for creating interactive dashboards and detailed charts to illustrate audit findings and trends.
- *Excel*: Simple but effective for basic charts and graphs to show numerical data clearly.
- *Infogram/Chart.js*: Lightweight options for creating infographics or charts.

Design Tools

For creating professional and visually appealing elements:

- *Canva*: Use to design custom infographics, diagrams, and slides with ease.
- *Lucidchart/Visio*: Perfect for network diagrams and process flows to explain system vulnerabilities.

Remote Presentation Tools

For virtual board meetings, leverage platforms that support screen sharing and real-time collaboration:

- *Zoom*: Allows screen sharing, polls, and Q&A features to engage board members during remote meetings.
- *Microsoft Teams*: Ideal for seamless integration with Office tools and team collaboration.

Multimedia Enhancements

Integrate videos, animations, or interactive elements to engage the board further. For instance,

- Demonstrate how vulnerability could be exploited with a short animated video.
- Show the impact of the recommendations using before-and-after visualizations.

Engaging the Board

Engaging the board goes beyond delivering information. It involves creating dialogue, fostering trust, and inspiring action. Here's how to ensure the board is actively involved in your presentation:

Anticipate Questions and Concerns

Board members often ask questions related to costs, risks, and industry benchmarks. Prepare answers in advance to address

- *Costs*: Provide detailed estimates for remediation efforts, including ROI calculations.
- *Disruption*: Explain how implementing solutions might affect operations and how you plan to minimize downtime.
- *Industry Comparisons*: Use benchmarks to show how the organization compares to peers in terms of cybersecurity posture.

Emphasize Accountability and Ownership

Clearly outline who will be responsible for implementing the recommendations and within what timeline. Use a RACI (Responsible, Accountable, Consulted, Informed) matrix or similar framework to

- Define roles for each action item.
- Assign accountability to specific individuals or teams.
- Clarify reporting structures and deadlines.

When the board sees a well-organized plan, they are more likely to approve and support recommendations.

Inspire Action Through Urgency and Benefits

Highlight the urgency of addressing critical findings. For example:

> "If we do not implement multi-factor authentication within three months, we risk non-compliance with industry regulations, which could lead to fines of up to $500,000."

Simultaneously, emphasize the benefits of acting promptly:

- Reduced risk of data breaches.
- Enhanced customer trust and market reputation.
- Long-term cost savings through improved efficiency.

Foster Two-Way Communication

Encourage questions and feedback throughout the presentation. This not only keeps board members engaged but also ensures they feel invested in the outcomes. Use strategies like

- Pausing after key sections to invite questions.
- Offering specific prompts, such as "Does this align with your view of the company's risk tolerance?"

Follow Up with Documentation

After the meeting, provide board members with a summarized report that includes

- Key findings and recommendations
- Visuals and infographics used in the presentation
- A clear action plan with timelines and assigned responsibilities

This ensures they have a reference document for future discussions and decisions.

Impact of Well-Written Reports and Engaging Presentations

A well-delivered and engaging presentation has far-reaching effects:

- *Informed Decision-Making*: Clear, actionable insights empower the board to make confident decisions.
- *Stronger Commitment*: A professional and compelling presentation fosters trust and secures buy-in for necessary changes.

- *Proactive Risk Management*: Highlighting urgent risks ensures timely remediation, reducing the likelihood of breaches or penalties.

- *Enhanced Credibility*: Demonstrating expertise through clear communication and actionable recommendations builds trust in the audit process.

When combined, effective communication, technological enhancements, and active engagement ensure that cybersecurity remains a strategic priority at the board level, driving meaningful improvements across the organization.

Key Takeaways

Present cybersecurity audit findings clearly and concisely, focusing on key risks, business impact, and compliance gaps. Use visuals, prioritize critical issues, and align recommendations with business objectives. A well-structured presentation ensures leadership understands cybersecurity risks and supports necessary actions.

In this section, we covered the following points:

- Understand the board's perspective by focusing on business impact and aligning findings with strategic goals.

- Structure the presentation to include an executive summary, findings, recommendations, and a risk mitigation strategy.

- Communicate effectively by simplifying language, using visuals, and emphasizing the business implications of cybersecurity risks.

- Leverage technology to enhance the professionalism and clarity of the presentation.

- Engage the board through anticipatory answers, clear accountability, and an emphasis on the urgency and benefits of acting on audit findings.

Action Plans Based on Cybersecurity Audit Recommendations

Cybersecurity audits are essential for identifying vulnerabilities, assessing compliance, and highlighting risks within an organization. However, the true value of these audits lies not in the findings themselves but in how effectively they are addressed. This is where action plans come into play, structured frameworks that translate audit recommendations into actionable steps. A well-crafted action plan doesn't just patch gaps; it strengthens the organization's defenses, aligns resources, and ensures accountability.

Importance of an Action Plan

An action plan serves as the roadmap for addressing audit findings. Without one, even the most insightful recommendations may stagnate, leaving the organization exposed to potential threats.

Why Action Plans Are Crucial:

- *Systematic Issue Resolution*: They ensure vulnerabilities are addressed in a logical sequence, reducing confusion and inefficiency.

- *Resource Alignment*: They help allocate budget, tools, and personnel effectively, ensuring tasks are executed without bottlenecks.

- *Stakeholder Accountability*: By assigning specific responsibilities, action plans ensure no critical steps are overlooked.

- *Enhanced Organizational Focus*: Clear timelines and priorities maintain momentum, preventing delays and fostering a proactive security culture.

- A strong action plan transforms recommendations into measurable improvements, bridging the gap between audit findings and organizational security goals.

Developing an Effective Action Plan

Creating an effective action plan requires a deliberate approach that balances urgency, resources, and long-term strategy.

Categorizing Recommendations

Begin by grouping audit findings based on their nature:

- *Compliance Issues*: Address gaps related to regulatory frameworks, such as GDPR, PCI DSS, DORA, etc.
- *Operational Improvements*: Focus on enhancing processes, such as incident response protocols or data access policies.
- *Risk Mitigation*: Target vulnerabilities that pose the greatest threat to the organization, such as unpatched systems or misconfigured firewalls.

This categorization helps stakeholders understand the scope and focus of the plan while simplifying resource allocation.

Prioritizing Actions

Use a risk-based approach to determine the order in which tasks should be tackled:

- *Critical Risks*: Immediate attention to high-severity vulnerabilities, such as exposed sensitive data or insecure remote access points.
- *Quick Wins*: Simple, low-cost actions with immediate impact, like disabling inactive accounts or updating passwords.
- *Long-Term Projects*: Resource-intensive efforts, such as replacing legacy systems or overhauling identity management frameworks.

Prioritization ensures that high-impact vulnerabilities are mitigated quickly while laying the groundwork for sustained improvements.

Setting Clear Objectives

For every action, define specific and measurable goals. Clear objectives provide focus and enable progress tracking. For example:

- *Objective*: Reduce phishing susceptibility by 70%.
- *Action*: Deploy advanced email filtering tools and conduct quarterly staff training sessions.

Assigning Ownership

Assign each action to specific individuals or teams to establish accountability. Examples include

- *IT Teams*: Responsible for technical tasks, such as implementing firewall updates or installing patches.
- *HR Departments*: Overseeing employee cybersecurity training programs.
- *Compliance Officers*: Ensuring that remediation efforts align with regulatory requirements.

Allocating Resources

Ensure adequate resources are available to implement the plan effectively. This includes

- Budget for tools or services, such as purchasing advanced endpoint protection solutions.
- Personnel with the necessary expertise to execute tasks.
- Access to third-party consultants or vendors for specialized requirements.

Establishing Timelines

Set realistic but firm deadlines for each action item, considering dependencies and resource availability. Use milestones to track progress and ensure accountability.

Implementing the Action Plan

Turning a well-drafted action plan into tangible results requires proper implementation and monitoring mechanisms.

Tools to Support Implementation

Use technology to streamline implementation and track progress:

- *Project Management Tools*: Jira, Trello, or Asana to assign tasks, set deadlines, and track milestones.

- *Vulnerability Scanners*: Tools like Nessus or Qualys to validate remediation actions and confirm vulnerabilities have been resolved.

- *Documentation Platforms*: Centralized systems like SharePoint or Confluence for storing and sharing updates, reports, and timelines.

Monitoring Progress

- *Monthly Review Meetings*: Regularly convene stakeholders to assess progress, discuss roadblocks, and recalibrate priorities if necessary.

- *Key Performance Indicators (KPIs)*: Use metrics like reduced vulnerability count or improved compliance scores to measure the effectiveness of the action plan.

Handling Challenges

- *Resource Limitations*: Reassess priorities to focus on the most critical actions if constraints arise.

- *Technological Bar*riers: Consult external experts or vendors for complex technical issues that the internal team cannot resolve.

- *Stakeholder Resistance*: Foster buy-in by clearly communicating the business benefits of the action plan.

Impact of a Well-Executed Action Plan

When an action plan is effectively implemented, the benefits extend far beyond addressing audit findings:

- *Improved Security Posture*: Reduced risks of data breaches, ransomware attacks, and insider threats.

- *Enhanced Compliance*: Avoidance of regulatory penalties and strengthened alignment with industry standards.

- *Resource Optimization*: Efficient use of time, personnel, and budget to achieve maximum impact.

- *Stakeholder Confidence*: Demonstrates a proactive approach to cybersecurity, building trust with leadership, customers, and regulators.

Key Takeaways

An effective action plan turns cybersecurity audit findings into real improvements. Categorize and prioritize issues, assign clear ownership, allocate resources, and set deadlines to ensure timely resolution. Regular monitoring and tracking of key metrics keep progress on track. A well-executed action plan strengthens security, enhances compliance, and builds stakeholder confidence.

In this section, we covered the following points:

- A well-designed action plan ensures that audit findings translate into tangible improvements, mitigating risks and enhancing security.

- Organize recommendations by type and severity to focus resources on the most critical issues first.

- Assign clear ownership and track progress to maintain momentum and prevent delays.

- Use tools, metrics, and regular reviews to keep implementation on track.

- A robust action plan boosts compliance, optimizes resources, and instills confidence among stakeholders.

CHAPTER 7   HOW TO WRITE AN EFFECTIVE CYBERSECURITY AUDIT REPORT

Follow-Up Audits: Ensuring Compliance

Follow-up audits are a critical but often overlooked component of the cybersecurity audit lifecycle. While an initial audit highlights vulnerabilities and recommends corrective actions, follow-up audits validate whether those actions have been implemented effectively. They ensure that compliance is achieved and risks are mitigated, serving as a foundation for continuous improvement and a robust security posture.

The Purpose of Follow-Up Audits

Follow-up audits fulfill several essential objectives, bridging the gap between initial findings and long-term organizational resilience.

Key Objectives of Follow-Up Audits:

- *Validate Corrective Actions*: Ensure that vulnerabilities identified in the initial audit have been properly addressed.

- *Assess Compliance Progress*: Verify that the organization is on track to meet regulatory or industry-specific compliance requirements.

- *Ensure Accountability*: Hold teams responsible for implementing the recommendations outlined in the initial audit.

- *Identify Residual Risks*: Detect new or lingering vulnerabilities that may have emerged since the original audit.

The Follow-Up Audit Process

Conducting a follow-up audit involves structured phases to ensure thorough evaluation and actionable outcomes.

Figure 7-4 presents key phases of the follow-up audit process.

CHAPTER 7   HOW TO WRITE AN EFFECTIVE CYBERSECURITY AUDIT REPORT

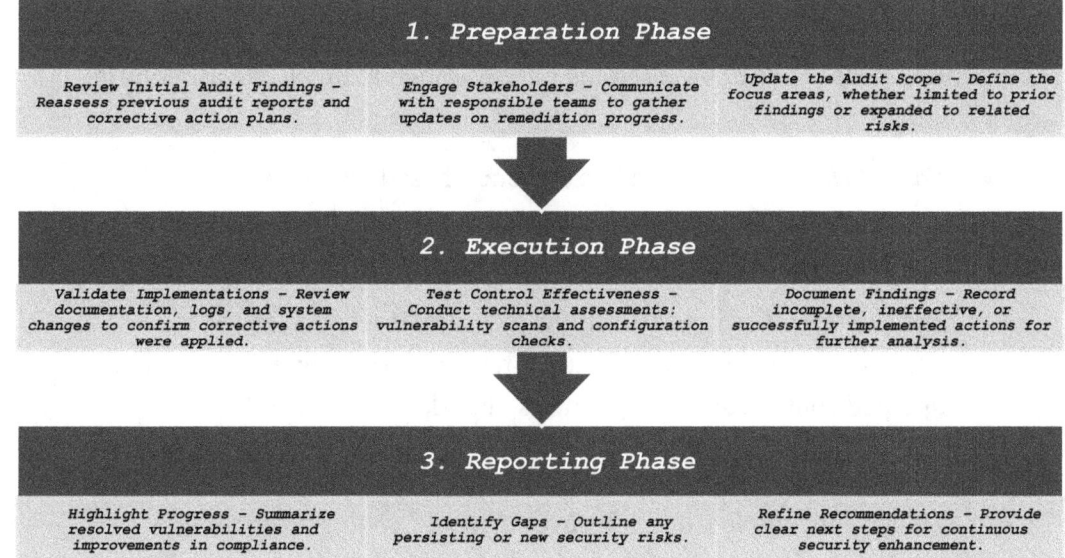

Figure 7-4. Key phases of the follow-up audit process

Preparation Phase

The groundwork for a follow-up audit is critical to its success:

- *Review Initial Audit Findings*: Begin by revisiting the initial audit report to understand the issues identified and the corrective actions recommended.

- *Engage Stakeholders*: Communicate with the teams responsible for implementing the recommended changes to gather updates on their progress.

- *Update the Audit Scope*: Depending on organizational needs, the follow-up audit may focus solely on previously flagged issues or expand to encompass related areas to ensure holistic improvement.

Execution Phase

The execution phase focuses on assessing progress and identifying areas requiring further action:

- *Validate Implementations*: Use evidence-based methods to verify that corrective actions have been executed as planned. This might include reviewing logs, change tickets, or policies.

- *Test Control Effectiveness*: Conduct technical tests, such as vulnerability scans or configuration reviews, to ensure that the new or updated controls are functioning as intended.

- *Document Findings*:
  - Note incomplete or ineffective corrective actions to provide clarity on unresolved issues.
  - Highlight areas where progress has exceeded expectations, celebrating successes to encourage further improvement.

Reporting Phase

The reporting phase communicates results and provides a roadmap for further enhancements:

- *Highlight Progress*: Summarize the resolved issues, showing improvements in compliance metrics or reductions in risk exposure.

- *Identify Gaps*: Offer an updated list of unresolved vulnerabilities or newly identified risks.

- *Refine Recommendations*: Provide actionable, prioritized steps for continuous improvement based on the findings of the follow-up audit.

Benefits of Follow-Up Audits

Organizations that prioritize follow-up audits gain multiple advantages, both immediate and long-term:

- *Continuous Improvement*: By regularly validating corrective actions, follow-up audits help refine security controls and reduce recurring vulnerabilities.

- *Enhanced Compliance Confidence*: Demonstrating proactive follow-ups underscores a commitment to regulatory standards and industry best practices.

- *Stronger Relationships*: Engaging in follow-ups builds trust with clients, partners, and regulators by showing that the organization takes cybersecurity and compliance seriously.

- *Proactive Risk Management*: Identifying residual risks early allows the organization to address them before they escalate, fostering a proactive rather than reactive approach to risk management.

Best Practices for Follow-Up Audits

Effective follow-up audits require careful planning and execution. Adopting the best practices ensures maximum impact and efficiency:

- *Set Clear Timelines*: Define realistic deadlines for implementing and reviewing corrective actions to maintain momentum and accountability.

- *Communicate Expectations*: Ensure all stakeholders understand the scope, goals, and timelines of the follow-up audit to align efforts and avoid surprises.

- *Adopt a Collaborative Approach*: Work closely with teams to address challenges, leveraging their insights to refine the audit process.

- *Focus on Continuous Learning*: Treat follow-ups as opportunities to enhance organizational processes, raise security awareness, and identify training needs.

- *Embedding Follow-Up Audits into Organizational Culture*

- Follow-up audits should not be seen as a one-time event but as an ongoing commitment to security and compliance. By making them a routine part of the audit lifecycle, organizations can foster a culture of continuous improvement and proactive risk management.

Key Takeaways

Follow-up audits ensure that cybersecurity gaps identified in previous assessments have been effectively addressed. They validate corrective actions, confirm compliance, and detect lingering or emerging risks. A structured follow-up process, preparation, execution, and reporting enhance accountability and drive continuous security improvements.

In this section, we covered the following points:

- *Follow-Up Audits Validate Progress*: They ensure that vulnerabilities identified during initial audits have been resolved and that controls are functioning as intended.

- *Residual Risks Must Be Addressed*: Follow-ups detect lingering or new vulnerabilities, preventing potential security breaches.

- *Reporting Drives Accountability*: Clear and actionable follow-up reports highlight progress while refining recommendations for unresolved gaps.

- *Best Practices Ensure Success*: Establishing timelines, clear communication, and collaboration create an efficient and impactful follow-up process.

- *Embedding Follow-Ups Builds Trust*: Regular follow-ups demonstrate to stakeholders that cybersecurity and compliance are ongoing priorities.

How to Handle Disputes Over Cybersecurity Audit Findings

Disputes over cybersecurity audit findings are a common yet challenging aspect of the auditing process. They often arise from misunderstandings, conflicting priorities, or resistance to change. Effectively addressing these disagreements is essential for ensuring the audit achieves its primary goal: enhancing the organization's security posture and compliance. Handling disputes constructively can lead to improved trust, actionable insights, and better long-term outcomes for all stakeholders involved.

Understanding the Causes of Audit Disputes

Disputes over cybersecurity audit findings often stem from various root causes, ranging from technical misunderstandings to resource constraints. Recognizing these causes is the first step in resolving disagreements and ensuring audit findings lead to meaningful action.

Technical Misunderstandings

Stakeholders outside the technical realm may struggle to understand the complexities of cybersecurity findings. For example, the significance of a "high-severity vulnerability" might not resonate with someone unfamiliar with risk scoring frameworks like CVSS. Misinterpretations can lead to resistance or undervaluation of critical risks.

- *Resolution*: Auditors should translate technical terms into business-friendly language and provide analogies or real-world examples to clarify the potential impact of the findings.

Conflicting Priorities

Departments often have varying goals. While IT prioritizes risk mitigation, business units may focus on efficiency, customer experience, or profitability. These differing priorities can result in disputes over whether certain audit recommendations align with organizational objectives.

- *Resolution*: Demonstrate how addressing security gaps contributes to long-term business continuity, aligns with company goals, and protects core operations.

Resource Constraints

Implementing cybersecurity recommendations can require significant investments in time, personnel, or finances, which may not always be immediately available. Resistance often arises when resources are already stretched thin.

- *Resolution*: Propose phased implementations, prioritize critical actions, and explore cost-effective solutions that provide immediate risk reduction while planning for long-term improvements.

Accuracy Concerns

Stakeholders may question the validity of findings, especially if audit methodologies, tools, or sample data seem insufficient or flawed. Doubts about the audit's accuracy can disrupt remediation efforts.

- *Resolution*: Clearly document and communicate the methodology, tools used, and scope of the audit. Offer to revalidate findings if concerns persist.

Resistance to Change

Organizational inertia or fear of disrupting established workflows can lead to pushback on audit recommendations. Teams may perceive changes as overly complex or unnecessary.

- *Resolution*: Emphasize the benefits of proposed changes, showing how they enhance productivity, reduce risk, and contribute to compliance efforts without causing excessive disruption.

Strategies for Addressing Audit Disputes

Resolving disputes requires a combination of technical expertise, communication skills, and a collaborative mindset.

Maintain Objectivity

Objectivity is key to defusing emotionally charged disputes. Audit findings should be presented as impartial facts, supported by evidence such as logs, scans, or penetration test results. Avoid subjective language or appearing defensive. Demonstrating that conclusions are based on data fosters credibility and professionalism, making stakeholders more receptive to recommendations.

Presenting findings with neutrality ensures that the focus remains on the issue at hand rather than personal biases.

- Base all discussions on factual, evidence-based data rather than subjective opinions.
- Provide clear, detailed explanations of methodologies, results, and recommendations to reinforce credibility.

Engage in Active Listening

Listening actively to stakeholders' concerns builds trust and collaboration. Allow stakeholders to express their frustrations or viewpoints fully without interruption. Respond by acknowledging their valid concerns, showing empathy, and reiterating your willingness to find a resolution. This approach turns confrontations into constructive conversations.

Actively listening to stakeholders helps uncover the core of their concerns and builds a foundation of trust.

- Allow stakeholders to voice their perspectives without interruption.
- Acknowledge valid points to demonstrate empathy and collaboration.

Use a Risk-Based Approach

A risk-based approach prioritizes actions that align with the organization's risk tolerance and goals. Demonstrating the business impact of high-risk vulnerabilities, such as potential financial losses or regulatory penalties, helps stakeholders see the urgency of remediation. Prioritizing critical findings while planning lower-risk items for later reassures stakeholders that the audit process is balanced and fair.

A risk-based approach can help prioritize actions and reduce resistance.

- Categorize findings based on their potential impact on the organization, focusing on high-risk vulnerabilities first.
- Clearly articulate how addressing specific risks aligns with business goals, such as preventing fines or protecting customer trust.

Leverage Clear Communication

Clear communication is essential when bridging the gap between technical and non-technical stakeholders. Use simple language to explain findings and their implications. Visual aids, such as bar charts, risk heat maps, or before-and-after scenarios, make the findings relatable and easier to grasp. Tailoring your message to the audience ensures alignment and reduces resistance.

Effective communication bridges the gap between technical and non-technical stakeholders.

- Avoid technical jargon and explain complex issues in plain, accessible language.
- Use visuals, such as heat maps, graphs, and flowcharts, to make findings easier to understand.

Conduct Joint Reviews

Collaboration strengthens trust and resolves disputes effectively. Jointly reviewing disputed findings with the concerned teams creates transparency and allows auditors to clarify their methodologies. This collaborative process helps address misunderstandings and fosters shared ownership of solutions, increasing the likelihood of successful implementation.

Collaboration can help resolve disputes by ensuring all parties feel heard and involved.

- Organize sessions to review disputed findings together, re-examining data or re-running tests if necessary.
- Use these opportunities to clarify misunderstandings and build consensus.

Escalate When Necessary

If a dispute cannot be resolved through discussion, escalation to senior management may be necessary. Present a well-documented case that includes the original findings, stakeholder feedback, and potential risks of inaction. Senior management can provide arbitration, ensuring alignment between technical and business priorities while reinforcing the importance of addressing critical issues.

If disputes remain unresolved, escalate them to senior leadership or an independent arbitration body.

- Provide detailed documentation, including evidence, methodologies, and stakeholder feedback.
- Frame the escalation as an opportunity to align organizational priorities and resolve conflicts professionally.

Best Practices for Resolving Audit Disputes

Adopting best practices ensures disputes are addressed efficiently and constructively.

- *Prepare Evidence Thoroughly*: Collect logs, test results, and detailed documentation in advance to support findings. Ensure your data is clear, verifiable, and specific to reduce ambiguity.
- *Foster Open Communication*: Create a safe environment where stakeholders feel comfortable expressing concerns. This reduces defensiveness and encourages collaboration.
- *Promote Transparency*: Share your methodologies and frameworks upfront to reduce skepticism. Clearly articulate how findings were identified and validated.
- *Document Discussions and Outcomes*: Keep detailed records of disputes, resolutions, and agreed-upon next steps for accountability and future reference.
- *Follow Up on Resolutions*: Ensure that agreed-upon changes are implemented as planned. Regularly check progress to maintain momentum and address any residual concerns.

Benefits of Resolving Disputes Constructively

Handling disputes over audit findings effectively can significantly enhance organizational security and culture.

- *Enhanced Security Posture*: Constructive resolution ensures that critical vulnerabilities are addressed, reducing the organization's exposure to cyber threats.

- *Improved Stakeholder Relationships*: Transparent communication and collaboration build trust between auditors and stakeholders, fostering a sense of shared responsibility.

- *Actionable Outcomes*: Resolved disputes allow findings to translate into concrete actions, driving meaningful improvements in the organization's security framework.

- *Stronger Compliance*: Addressing disagreements ensures alignment with regulatory requirements, reducing the risk of penalties or reputational damage.

- *Cultural Growth*: Demonstrating professionalism and empathy during disputes encourages a culture of accountability, continuous improvement, and open dialogue.

- By resolving disputes constructively, organizations can strengthen their defenses while building a more cohesive and proactive workplace environment.

Turning Disputes into Opportunities

Disputes over audit findings should not be viewed as roadblocks but as opportunities for growth. They provide a chance to engage stakeholders in meaningful discussions about risk management, resource allocation, and process improvement. By addressing disagreements with clarity, empathy, and evidence-based reasoning, auditors can ensure that their findings drive positive change, helping the organization achieve its security and compliance goals while fostering resilience.

CHAPTER 7   HOW TO WRITE AN EFFECTIVE CYBERSECURITY AUDIT REPORT

Disputes over audit findings are often seen as obstacles, but they present valuable opportunities for organizational growth. By addressing disagreements thoughtfully, auditors can transform resistance into engagement and action.

How to Turn Disputes into Opportunities

Disputes are not merely challenges to overcome; they are pivotal moments to strengthen relationships, foster transparency, and drive actionable change. By viewing disputes as opportunities, organizations can improve not only their cybersecurity but also their overall approach to risk and governance.

Disputes over audit findings should not be seen as roadblocks but as opportunities to strengthen security, collaboration, and innovation. By engaging stakeholders early, framing disputes within broader organizational goals, fostering cross-departmental dialogue, and leveraging resistance for process improvements, organizations can turn conflicts into catalysts for growth. This cyclic approach not only resolves disagreements but also enhances risk awareness and continuous security improvement, ensuring that every audit drives meaningful progress.

Figure 7-5 presents a cyclic process of turning disputes into opportunities.

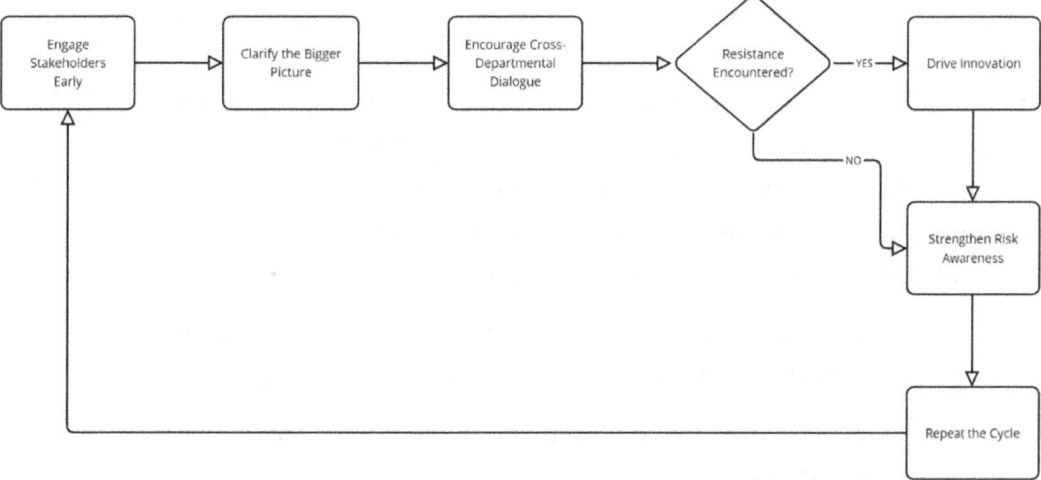

Figure 7-5. Cyclic workflow for turning disputes into opportunities

- *Engage Stakeholders Early*: Early involvement in the audit process reduces misunderstandings and encourages collaboration.

- *Clarify the Bigger Picture*: Frame disputed findings as part of the organization's larger goals, such as enhancing resilience or maintaining customer trust.

- *Encourage Cross-Departmental Dialogue*: Use disputes to open discussions about overlapping responsibilities, creating stronger interdepartmental cooperation.

- *Drive Innovation*: Resistance to change can reveal areas where workflows or processes can be streamlined or improved.

- *Strengthen Risk Awareness*: Addressing disputes educates stakeholders about risks, fostering a culture of proactive risk management.

Key Takeaways

Disputes over cybersecurity audit findings are natural but should be seen as opportunities for engagement and improvement. By addressing disagreements objectively, using clear communication, and adopting a risk-based approach, auditors can transform resistance into constructive dialogue. Active listening, collaboration, and transparency help build trust, ensuring that findings lead to meaningful security enhancements. Viewing disputes as moments for organizational growth fosters a culture of accountability, proactive risk management, and continuous improvement.

In this section, we covered the following points:

- Audit disputes often stem from misunderstandings or conflicting priorities. Addressing them constructively ensures progress.

- Neutral, evidence-based presentations and clear explanations help resolve misunderstandings and build trust.

- Engaging stakeholders in joint reviews fosters cooperation and minimizes resistance.

- Preparation, documentation, and a risk-based approach are essential for effective dispute resolution.
- Successfully addressing disputes strengthens security, enhances trust, and promotes accountability within the organization.

Best Practices for Continuous Communication in Cybersecurity Audits

Effective communication is the backbone of successful cybersecurity audits. It ensures alignment among auditors, stakeholders, and technical teams, paving the way for smooth collaboration, timely decision-making, and effective remediation. Without continuous communication, even the most thorough audit findings may face resistance, delays, or misinterpretation. In the following is explored how to embed communication into every stage of the cybersecurity audit process for optimal results.

Importance of Continuous Communication

Continuous communication is the basis of a successful cybersecurity audit, ensuring that all stakeholders remain aligned throughout the process. It fosters transparency, trust, and collaboration, enabling organizations to effectively address vulnerabilities and improve their security posture. Here's why it matters:

Ensures Transparency

Transparency is vital to keep stakeholders informed about the audit's purpose, progress, and expected outcomes. Continuous communication eliminates surprises during the reporting phase by providing regular updates. When stakeholders understand the "why" and "how" behind the audit, they are more likely to support its findings and recommendations.

Facilitates Timely Decision-Making

Cybersecurity threats evolve rapidly, and addressing vulnerabilities quickly is essential. Regular updates provide decision-makers with the information they need to prioritize and act promptly, minimizing potential risks. For example, if a critical vulnerability is identified during the audit, timely communication can ensure immediate mitigation efforts are initiated.

Reduces Resistance to Change

Resistance often stems from a lack of understanding or fear of disruption. Engaging stakeholders early and maintaining an open dialogue helps alleviate these concerns. When individuals feel included in the process and see their feedback valued, they are more likely to embrace changes.

Promotes Collaboration Across Teams

Cybersecurity audits often involve multiple departments, such as IT, compliance, and finance. Continuous communication fosters a collaborative environment where teams can share insights and coordinate efforts. This synergy ensures smoother implementation of recommendations and prevents siloed decision-making.

Supports Regulatory Compliance

Many industries face strict regulatory deadlines and expectations. Continuous communication ensures that all parties understand compliance requirements, timelines, and their roles in achieving them. Clear communication can help avoid penalties and demonstrate a proactive commitment to regulatory standards.

Best Practices for Continuous Communication

Effective cybersecurity audits require structured and ongoing communication to keep stakeholders aligned. Establishing clear channels, assigning communication roles, and providing regular updates ensure transparency and engagement. Using visuals simplifies complex findings, while two-way feedback fosters collaboration. Proper documentation maintains accountability, supporting both compliance and long-term security improvements.

Define Communication Channels Early

Establishing clear communication channels at the beginning of the audit ensures that information flows seamlessly. Email updates, virtual meetings, and project management tools such as Jira, Trello, or Slack can be leveraged to keep everyone aligned. For example, regular emails can summarize key findings, while virtual meetings provide a platform for in-depth discussions. Clearly defining these channels prevents confusion and streamlines interactions.

Assign Communication Roles

Appoint specific individuals to oversee communication for both the audit team and the stakeholders. For instance, designate a lead auditor as the primary point of contact and assign department representatives to handle approvals and escalations. This structure minimizes miscommunication and ensures accountability. Clearly defining these roles also helps in managing the flow of information efficiently.

Conduct Regular Updates

Schedule weekly or bi-weekly updates to share audit progress, milestones, and unresolved issues. These updates should include progress reports that summarize findings, challenges, and upcoming steps. Regular updates not only keep stakeholders informed but also reinforce a sense of urgency and accountability.

Use Visuals to Simplify Technical Details

Cybersecurity audits often involve complex technical data that may overwhelm non-technical stakeholders. Tools like Tableau or Power BI can create dashboards, charts, and graphs to translate technical findings into easily digestible visuals. For example, a heat map can visually represent risk levels across different systems, making it easier to prioritize remediation efforts.

Encourage Two-Way Feedback

Continuous communication is not a one-way street. Encouraging stakeholders to ask questions and provide feedback fosters collaboration and trust. Surveys, feedback forms, or open Q&A sessions can help clarify misunderstandings and align expectations. Active engagement ensures that everyone feels heard and invested in the process.

Document Communication

Maintaining detailed records of meetings, emails, and progress reports ensures accountability and provides a reference point for future audits. For instance, summarizing action items and decisions made during meetings helps track progress and prevents miscommunication. Proper documentation also supports compliance efforts by demonstrating a clear audit trail.

Challenges in Continuous Communication and Solutions

Despite its importance, continuous communication in cybersecurity audits can face significant challenges. Addressing these effectively requires thoughtful strategies and practical steps.

Technical Barriers

Challenge: Non-technical stakeholders may struggle to understand audit findings, leading to confusion or disengagement.

   Solution:

- Use plain language to explain technical issues, avoiding jargon.
- Create visual aids such as heat maps, dashboards, or graphs to simplify complex findings.

Stakeholder Disengagement

Challenge: Stakeholders may lose interest or fail to prioritize the audit due to competing demands.

   Solution:

- Schedule regular check-ins, such as biweekly progress meetings, to keep stakeholders engaged.
- Emphasize the business value of audit findings, linking them to financial, reputational, or operational impacts.
- Assign specific tasks or roles to stakeholders to encourage active participation.

Information Overload

Challenge: Sharing excessive information can overwhelm stakeholders, making it difficult to identify priorities.

Solution:

- Focus on high-priority findings and actionable insights during updates.
- Use summaries or executive dashboards to condense information.
- Provide detailed reports as supplemental material for those who want a deeper dive.

Inconsistent Updates

Challenge: Irregular communication can lead to misaligned expectations and delays.

Solution:

- Establish a fixed schedule for updates, such as weekly reports or monthly review meetings.
- Use project management tools to provide real-time visibility into audit progress.
- Appoint a communication coordinator to ensure consistency and accountability.

Long-Term Communication Practices

Building sustainable communication practices ensures the benefits of continuous dialogue extend beyond a single audit. Here's how organizations can implement long-term strategies:

Develop a Post-Audit Communication Plan

After the audit, create a plan to monitor and report on the implementation of findings. For example, schedule monthly updates on remediation progress or recurring reviews for unresolved issues. A structured plan ensures accountability and maintains momentum.

Maintain a Knowledge Base

Establish a centralized repository of past audit reports, recommendations, and communication records. Use tools like SharePoint or Confluence to store this information. A well-maintained knowledge base allows teams to learn from previous audits, improving efficiency and consistency in future efforts.

Foster Ongoing Dialogue Between Teams

Encourage continuous communication between IT, compliance, and audit teams, even outside formal audit cycles. Regular cross-departmental meetings or shared dashboards can keep all teams aligned on cybersecurity goals and emerging risks.

Build a Culture of Transparency

Cultivate a culture where open dialogue about cybersecurity risks is encouraged. For instance, conduct risk awareness sessions or town hall meetings to update the organization on security initiatives. Transparency builds trust and reinforces the importance of collective responsibility for cybersecurity.

Benefits of Continuous Communication

Embedding continuous communication into the audit process delivers numerous benefits that extend across the organization:

- *Builds Trust and Confidence*: Transparent and consistent updates foster trust among stakeholders, demonstrating that the audit is conducted with integrity and professionalism. This confidence encourages greater collaboration and buy-in.
- *Enhances Collaboration*: By facilitating open dialogue, continuous communication breaks down silos and promotes teamwork. Different departments can share insights, align priorities, and work together effectively to address vulnerabilities.
- *Enables Proactive Decision-Making*: Timely communication equips decision-makers with the context and insights they need to act decisively. This reduces delays in addressing critical vulnerabilities and improves the organization's overall security posture.

- *Supports Compliance and Accountability*: Clear communication ensures that everyone understands their roles and responsibilities in meeting compliance requirements. Documented updates provide a reliable audit trail, demonstrating diligence to regulators and stakeholders.

- *Prevents Miscommunication*: Regular updates and consistent messaging minimize misunderstandings, ensuring that everyone is on the same page. This reduces the risk of errors, delays, or redundant efforts.

- *Drives Continuous Improvement*: By keeping stakeholders informed and engaged, organizations can use feedback to refine processes, enhance controls, and improve the audit experience over time.

Key Takeaways

Continuous communication is key to successful cybersecurity audits, ensuring transparency, collaboration, and timely action. Best practices include clear channels, regular updates, visual aids, and two-way feedback. Overcoming challenges like technical barriers and disengagement fosters trust and accountability. Strong communication turns audits into proactive security initiatives, driving long-term improvements.

In this section, we covered the following points:

- Continuous communication ensures alignment among stakeholders, auditors, and technical teams.

- Defined roles, regular updates, and visual aids simplify complex findings and keep stakeholders engaged.

- Addressing challenges like disengagement and technical barriers builds trust and strengthens collaboration.

- Transparent communication fosters a culture of accountability, ensuring audit findings drive actionable improvements.

- Through continuous communication, cybersecurity audits become more than a compliance exercise; they evolve into collaborative efforts that enhance resilience, drive change, and embed security into organizational culture.

Conclusions

A well-executed cybersecurity audit is not just about identifying security gaps; it is a strategic process that drives continuous improvement, enhances compliance, and strengthens an organization's resilience against cyber threats. Throughout this guide, we have explored the key elements that make cybersecurity audits more effective, from crafting clear and actionable audit reports to handling disputes and fostering continuous communication.

How to write an effective cybersecurity audit report is explored in this chapter, emphasizing the importance of clarity, structure, and audience-focused reporting. An audit report should not only document findings but also provide meaningful insights and practical recommendations that help stakeholders make informed decisions. Without a well-structured report, even the most thorough audit can fail to deliver value, as stakeholders may struggle to understand or act upon the findings.

Handling disputes over audit findings was examined, recognizing that disagreements are a natural part of the auditing process. Differences in technical understanding, conflicting business priorities, and resource constraints can lead to resistance. However, by approaching disputes with objectivity, active listening, and a risk-based mindset, auditors can turn challenges into opportunities. Collaboration, clear communication, and a focus on shared organizational goals help resolve conflicts and ensure that audit recommendations are implemented effectively.

The importance of continuous communication in cybersecurity audits is highlighted. A lack of transparency and engagement can lead to misinterpretation, delays, or outright resistance to audit findings. By establishing clear communication channels, using visuals to simplify technical concepts, and encouraging stakeholder feedback, auditors can create an open dialogue that strengthens trust and cooperation. Ongoing communication ensures that cybersecurity audits are not just a one-time compliance exercise but an integral part of the organization's security strategy.

By integrating these principles, cybersecurity audits become more than a compliance requirement; they evolve into a proactive and strategic tool for enhancing security. A structured approach to audit reporting ensures findings are actionable, effective dispute resolution fosters collaboration, and continuous communication keeps stakeholders aligned and engaged. Organizations that embrace these best practices can strengthen their security posture, improve compliance efforts, and build a culture of cybersecurity resilience that extends beyond the audit process.

A cybersecurity audit is only as effective as the actions it drives. By prioritizing clear reporting, constructive dispute resolution, and transparent communication, organizations can ensure that audit efforts translate into real-world security improvements. As cyber threats continue to evolve, a proactive, well-communicated, and collaborative approach to cybersecurity auditing will be key to staying ahead and protecting critical assets.

CHAPTER 8

Real-Life Scenarios and Case Studies

Learning from Breaches – A Case Study

Data breaches are among the most significant cybersecurity challenges organizations face today. They result in financial losses, reputational damage, and legal consequences. However, they also present opportunities to learn, improve, and reinforce cybersecurity strategies. This section examines a real-world case study involving an e-commerce company, "SecureShop," highlighting how a cybersecurity audit exposed vulnerability, guided remediation efforts, and helped rebuild trust and resilience.

Background

SecureShop, a mid-sized e-commerce business, fell victim to a data breach that compromised sensitive customer information, including payment card details and personal addresses. The breach led to financial losses, reputational harm, and intense regulatory scrutiny under PCI-DSS. To address the fallout, SecureShop initiated a comprehensive post-breach cybersecurity audit to uncover the root causes, evaluate weaknesses, and prevent future incidents.

CHAPTER 8   REAL-LIFE SCENARIOS AND CASE STUDIES

Audit Scope and Objectives

The cybersecurity audit focused on four critical areas:

- *Incident Analysis*: Understanding the breach's entry point, timeline, and attacker methodologies.

- *Security Control Assessment*: Evaluating the effectiveness and gaps in existing cybersecurity controls.

- *Compliance Review*: Assessing adherence to PCI-DSS and other regulatory standards.

- *Remediation Plan*: Crafting actionable recommendations to address vulnerabilities and bolster defenses.

Findings from the Audit

The cybersecurity audit of SecureShop uncovered several critical vulnerabilities that contributed to the data breach. An unpatched third-party payment processing software allowed attackers to exploit an SQL injection flaw, while weak access controls, including the lack of multi-factor authentication (MFA), made it easier for them to gain entry. Additionally, inadequate network segmentation enabled lateral movement within the system, exacerbating the breach's impact. The audit also revealed ineffective monitoring and logging, where warning signs were ignored due to misconfigured intrusion detection systems (IDS). Lastly, non-compliance with PCI-DSS standards, such as outdated encryption protocols, left sensitive payment data exposed. These findings highlighted the urgent need for improved security practices to prevent future incidents.

Unpatched Software

The breach exploited an unpatched vulnerability in third-party payment processing software. This vulnerability, susceptible to SQL injection attacks, allowed attackers to extract sensitive customer data. Regular software updates and vulnerability management could have prevented this exploitation.

Weak Access Controls

Critical systems lacked MFA, and employee credentials, exposed in previous breaches, provided attackers with access to internal systems. Poor password hygiene and a lack of robust authentication measures significantly increased the attack surface.

Inadequate Network Segmentation

The audit revealed that sensitive customer data was not adequately isolated from the broader network. Once attackers gained access, they moved laterally to the database storing payment card information. Proper segmentation would have limited their movement and mitigated the breach's impact.

Inefficient Monitoring and Logging

Logs showed signs of suspicious activity three weeks before the breach, but alerts were ignored due to false positives and misconfigurations in IDS. These deficiencies underscored the need for enhanced monitoring capabilities and streamlined alert prioritization.

Non-compliance with PCI-DSS

The audit revealed outdated encryption protocols and instances where payment data was not encrypted during transmission and storage. These compliance failures exposed critical customer information to unauthorized access.

Steps Taken to Remediate the Breach

- *Immediate Actions*:
  - SecureShop quickly isolated affected systems to contain the breach, notified customers and regulatory authorities, and followed breach notification laws to minimize further damage.
- *System Upgrades*:
  - Deployed patches to resolve vulnerabilities in third-party software.
  - Upgraded encryption protocols to comply with PCI-DSS standards, ensuring robust data protection.

- *Enhanced Access Controls*:
  - Implemented MFA for all employees and privileged accounts.
  - Enforced strong password policies using tools like LastPass for credential management.
- *Improved Network Security*:
  - Established strict network segmentation to isolate sensitive systems.
  - Leveraged tools like Cisco Identity Services Engine (ISE) to enforce access control policies.
- *Advanced Monitoring*:
  - Deployed a SIEM system, such as Splunk, to enhance threat detection and analysis.
  - Configured IDS to minimize false positives and streamline incident response.
- *Staff Training*:
  - Conducted comprehensive security awareness training to educate employees about phishing attacks, credential management, and secure practices.

Lessons Learned

- *Proactive Vulnerability Management*: Regular patching and vulnerability scanning with tools like Nessus can prevent exploitation of known weaknesses.
- *Continuous Monitoring*: Implementing robust SIEM solutions enables organizations to detect and respond to anomalies in real-time.
- *Regulatory Compliance*: Adherence to standards like PCI-DSS ensures strong encryption and consistent data protection practices.

- *Network Segmentation and Access Control*: Isolating sensitive systems and enforcing strict access controls limit an attacker's ability to move laterally within the network.

- *Incident Response Preparedness*: A well-defined incident response plan reduces recovery time and minimizes the impact of breaches.

How Audits Help Prevent Breaches

Cybersecurity audits serve as a proactive measure to identify and address vulnerabilities before they are exploited. Regular audits:

- Simulate attack scenarios to uncover security gaps through penetration testing results.

- Ensure adherence to regulatory frameworks like PCI-DSS, GDPR, or HIPAA, minimizing legal risks.

- Prioritize critical vulnerabilities to protect high-value assets.

Benefits of Post-breach Audits

- Enhanced Security Posture: Addressing vulnerabilities uncovered during the audit strengthens defenses.

- *Regained Stakeholder Trust*: Transparent communication and swift remediation demonstrate accountability, rebuilding customer and partner confidence.

- *Regulatory Compliance*: Ensures alignment with standards, avoiding fines and legal consequences.

- *Resilience Against Future Threats*: Proactive improvements prepare the organization to withstand emerging cyber risks.

CHAPTER 8   REAL-LIFE SCENARIOS AND CASE STUDIES

Key Takeaways

Data breaches can be costly, but they also provide valuable lessons to strengthen cybersecurity defenses. SecureShop's breach revealed critical weaknesses, including unpatched software, weak access controls, and poor network segmentation. A comprehensive cybersecurity audit helped identify these gaps, guiding remediation efforts such as implementing MFA, upgrading encryption, and enhancing monitoring. This case study highlights the importance of proactive audits, regulatory compliance, and continuous security improvements to prevent future breaches and build resilience against evolving cyber threats.

In this section, we covered the following points:

- Regular updates to software prevent exploitation of known vulnerabilities.
- Implementing MFA and strong password policies reduces unauthorized access.
- Isolating critical systems minimizes the impact of breaches.
- SIEM tools and IDS improve detection and response capabilities.
- Cybersecurity audits highlight weaknesses and enable organizations to address them proactively.

Lessons Learned from a Failed Audit

A failed cybersecurity audit often reveals systemic issues in an organization's security infrastructure, compliance strategies, or internal controls. While the immediate reaction to such failure might be frustration or concern, it is essential to recognize the value these findings provide. Failed audits highlight vulnerabilities that might otherwise go unnoticed, offering an opportunity for corrective action and improvement.

Organizations that fail audits often experience negative outcomes such as fines, reputational damage, or operational disruption. These consequences underscore the importance of preparation and adaptability. However, a failed audit is not just a measure of what went wrong but also a starting point for creating a stronger, more resilient organization. Addressing audit deficiencies proactively can lead to improved security, compliance, and operational efficiency.

What Constitutes a Failed Audit?

An audit is considered failed when the organization does not meet the standards outlined in the audit scope. These standards could include regulatory requirements, internal policies, or industry frameworks such as PCI-DSS, GDPR, or NIST. Key indicators of failure include

- *Non-compliance*: Failure to meet regulatory mandates, exposing the organization to penalties and legal risks.

- *Critical Security Gaps*: Unaddressed vulnerabilities or weaknesses in infrastructure and controls.

- *Inadequate Documentation*: Incomplete or inconsistent records that hinder the ability to verify compliance.

- *Repeat Findings*: Recurring issues from prior audits, demonstrating a lack of progress or commitment to remediation.

The consequences of a failed audit extend beyond regulatory penalties. A failed audit can damage stakeholder trust, increase operational costs, and create a target for cyberattacks. Organizations must see these failures as opportunities to rebuild trust and refine processes.

Example Scenario: A Retailer's PCI-DSS Audit Failure

Consider the case of a mid-sized retailer undergoing a PCI-DSS audit:

- *Encryption Issues*: Payment card data was transmitted without encryption, exposing sensitive customer information.

- *Unsecured Network Segmentation*: Payment systems were accessible from non-critical network segments, increasing risk.

- *Ignored Vulnerabilities*: High-severity vulnerabilities identified in prior scans were not addressed.

- *Weak Logging Mechanisms*: Insufficient logging and monitoring failed to provide a reliable audit trail.

This audit failure highlighted systemic gaps and drove the retailer to implement meaningful changes.

CHAPTER 8   REAL-LIFE SCENARIOS AND CASE STUDIES

Key Lessons Learned from Failed Audits

Recovering from a failed cybersecurity audit requires a strategic and structured approach. Organizations must first conduct a root cause analysis to identify weaknesses, then develop a remediation plan with clear priorities and responsibilities. Strengthening internal controls, improving documentation, and engaging stakeholders are key steps to ensuring long-term compliance and security. Regular follow-up audits and continuous monitoring help prevent future failures, turning the experience into an opportunity for growth and resilience.

Understand Compliance Requirements

Misinterpreting or overlooking compliance requirements is a common reason for audit failure. Organizations need a clear understanding of the frameworks relevant to their industry, such as PCI-DSS for payment processing or GDPR for data protection.

How It Helps:

- Use compliance checklists, such as the PCI-DSS SAQ, to clarify requirements.

- Engage compliance experts or third-party consultants to interpret complex regulatory obligations.

- Conduct regular compliance training for teams to ensure alignment with evolving standards.

- Regularly review updates to regulatory frameworks to avoid falling behind.

- Map specific requirements to operational processes to ensure compliance integration.

Prioritize Risk Mitigation

A failure to prioritize high-risk vulnerabilities often results in severe consequences during audits. Organizations must adopt a risk-based approach to focus on critical areas that pose the greatest threats.

How It Helps:

- Implement frameworks like the NIST RMF to identify and prioritize risks.
- Allocate resources strategically to address vulnerabilities with the highest potential impact.
- Perform regular threat modeling exercises to understand emerging risks.
- Engage cross-functional teams to ensure risks are mitigated from both technical and business perspectives.

Invest in Documentation and Reporting

Incomplete or inconsistent documentation is a frequent cause of audit failure. Comprehensive records of policies, procedures, and remediation actions are essential for demonstrating compliance.

How It Helps:

- Use automation tools like Vanta or Drata to centralize and standardize compliance documentation.
- Maintain detailed records of incident responses, vulnerability scans, and risk assessments for future audits.
- Conduct internal audits regularly to validate the accuracy of documentation.
- Establish a documentation review process to ensure consistency across departments.

Conduct Regular Security Assessments

Failing to conduct periodic security assessments leaves organizations unprepared for audits and increases the risk of vulnerabilities being exploited.

How It Helps:

- Schedule regular vulnerability scans with tools like Nessus or OpenVAS to identify gaps proactively.
- Conduct penetration testing to simulate potential attacks and uncover hidden risks.
- Create a calendar of security assessments to align with audit timelines.
- Share assessment results with stakeholders to encourage accountability and collaboration.

Engage Stakeholders Early

Communication breakdowns between IT, compliance, and leadership teams often derail audits. Early involvement of stakeholders ensures alignment and fosters a collaborative approach.

How It Helps:

- Schedule pre-audit meetings to clarify roles, responsibilities, and expectations.
- Use shared platforms like Microsoft Teams or Slack to facilitate ongoing communication.
- Designate a communication lead to centralize updates and manage queries.
- Provide audit awareness sessions to ensure all stakeholders understand their roles.

How Organizations Can Recover from a Failed Audit

The audit remediation workflow follows a structured approach to address failures and strengthen security. It begins with a root cause analysis to identify compliance gaps and vulnerabilities, followed by developing a remediation plan with clear priorities and responsibilities. Next, internal controls are strengthened through measures like MFA, encryption, and network segmentation. A follow-up audit is then conducted to verify

CHAPTER 8 REAL-LIFE SCENARIOS AND CASE STUDIES

improvements and ensure compliance. Finally, continuous monitoring using SIEM tools and regular security assessments helps maintain resilience and prevent future failures. This process ensures organizations turn audit setbacks into opportunities for long-term security and compliance.

Figure 8-1 presents the cyclic workflow process for continuous improvements.

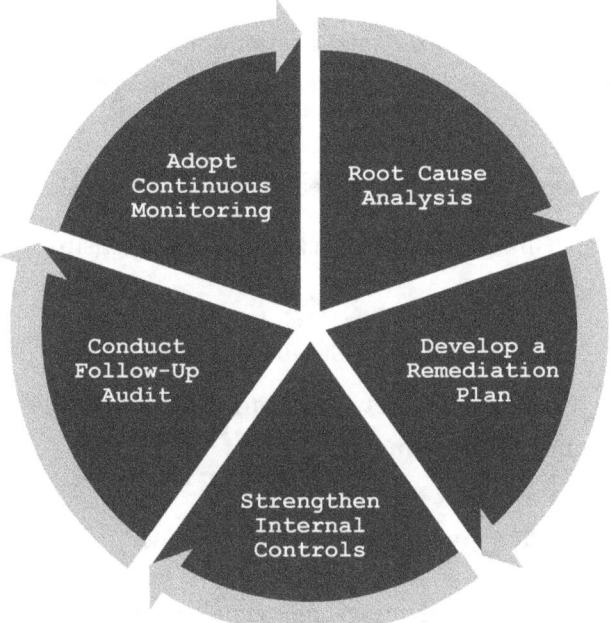

Figure 8-1. *Cyclic workflow process for audit remediation*

Root Cause Analysis

Identifying the underlying reasons for the audit failure is the first step to recovery. This involves a thorough investigation into processes, controls, and compliance gaps.

How to Recover:

- Use tools like Microsoft Defender for Cloud to conduct in-depth analyses of identified gaps.

- Interview relevant stakeholders to gain insights into process failures or misalignments.

- Document the root causes and present findings to leadership.
- Prioritize addressing systemic issues over superficial fixes to prevent recurrence.

Develop a Remediation Plan

Once root causes are identified, a clear and actionable remediation plan is essential. This plan should prioritize high-severity issues while addressing all deficiencies.

How to Recover:

- Assign owners and deadlines to each remediation task.
- Use tools like Jira or Asana to track progress and ensure accountability.
- Incorporate milestones to review and adjust the plan as necessary.
- Share the remediation plan with auditors to demonstrate commitment to improvement.

Strengthen Internal Controls

Audit failures often highlight weaknesses in internal controls, such as inadequate access restrictions or insufficient policy enforcement.

How to Recover:

- Implement MFA and enforce least-privilege access controls.
- Use IAM tools like Okta or Azure AD.
- Regularly review access logs to detect anomalies.
- Train employees in updated security policies and procedures.

Conduct a Follow-Up Audit

Scheduling a follow-up audit demonstrates accountability and validates the effectiveness of remediation efforts.

How to Recover:

- Partner with a trusted third-party auditor to conduct a re-audit.
- Focus the scope on previously identified gaps to ensure closure.
- Prepare a presentation for leadership summarizing the follow-up audit results.
- Use lessons from the re-audit to refine future audit strategies.

Adopt Continuous Monitoring

Continuous monitoring tools help organizations maintain real-time visibility into their compliance and security posture.

How to Recover:

- Deploy SIEM solutions like Splunk or Elastic Security to collect and analyze data.
- Automate alerts for compliance violations or potential threats.
- Integrate monitoring tools with incident response workflows.
- Regularly update monitoring parameters to align with regulatory changes.

Best Practices to Avoid Future Failures

- *Proactive Preparation*: Conduct mock audits and readiness assessments to identify potential issues early.
  - *Example*: Use GRC platforms like LogicGate or RSA Archer to streamline preparations.
- *Update Security Policies Regularly*: Evolve policies to address new threats and changes in regulatory requirements.
  - *Example*: Establish a quarterly review process for all security policies.
- *Train Staff on Compliance*: Ensure employees understand their roles and responsibilities in maintaining security and compliance.

- *Example*: Host annual compliance workshops and training sessions.
- *Leverage Automation*: Automate vulnerability scans, documentation, and compliance tracking to reduce human error.
  - *Example*: Implement tools like Drata or Vanta for real-time compliance monitoring.

Turning Failure into Opportunity

A failed audit can drive transformational change if viewed as a chance to improve. By addressing deficiencies head-on, organizations can

- *Strengthen Defenses*: Resolve vulnerabilities and implement best practices to prevent future risks.
- *Enhance Compliance*: Achieve alignment with regulatory frameworks, reducing penalties and legal exposure.
- *Foster Accountability*: Build a culture where teams proactively address risks and prioritize compliance.
- *Improve Resilience*: Develop processes that allow for quick adaptation to emerging challenges.
- Organizations that learn from failure often emerge stronger, better equipped to navigate the complexities of cybersecurity and compliance.

Benefits of Learning from Failed Audits

- *Improved Risk Management*: Addressing deficiencies reduces exposure to vulnerabilities and strengthens overall security.
  - *Example*: Organizations can reduce attack surfaces by implementing segmentation and access controls.
- *Stronger Regulatory Alignment*: Achieving compliance mitigates the risk of penalties and improves customer confidence.

- *Example*: Compliance with PCI-DSS ensures secure handling of payment data.

- *Cultural Shift*: Embedding lessons learned fosters a culture of continuous improvement and accountability.

  - *Example*: Regular post-audit reviews encourage teams to prioritize compliance.

- *Operational Resilience*: Better-prepared systems and teams can respond effectively to evolving threats.

  - *Example*: Advanced monitoring tools enable real-time threat detection and response.

Key Takeaways

A failed audit is an opportunity to improve security, compliance, and resilience. By addressing root causes, prioritizing risks, and engaging stakeholders, organizations can strengthen defenses and prevent future failures. Continuous monitoring and follow-up audits ensure ongoing security and regulatory alignment.

In this section, we covered the following points:

- *Audit Failure Is a Learning Opportunity*: Addressing gaps strengthens the organization's overall security posture.

- *Understand Requirements*: Clear comprehension of compliance standards reduces the risk of audit failure.

- *Document Everything*: Accurate and consistent records simplify audits and enhance accountability.

- *Engage Stakeholders Early*: Collaboration ensures alignment and smoother audit processes.

- *Adopt Continuous Improvement*: Regular assessments, monitoring, and policy updates keep organizations resilient.

Case Study: Cloud Security Audit Challenges

Cloud computing has become indispensable for modern organizations, offering unparalleled scalability, flexibility, and cost-efficiency. However, these benefits come with their own set of challenges, particularly in ensuring robust security. Conducting a cloud security audit requires a comprehensive evaluation of how well an organization secures its cloud infrastructure, applications, and data against potential threats. In the following is explored the complexities of auditing cloud environments, real-world challenges, and actionable strategies to overcome them, providing a practical roadmap for organizations navigating this critical process.

Cloud environments differ significantly from traditional on-premises systems, introducing new variables that complicate cybersecurity audits. The shared-responsibility model, inherent in cloud platforms, divides security responsibilities between CSPs and their clients, often leading to confusion. Additionally, the dynamic nature of cloud resources, combined with the proliferation of multi-cloud setups and third-party integrations, amplifies the complexity. Without proper visibility, consistent policies, and advanced monitoring capabilities, organizations risk leaving critical vulnerabilities unaddressed.

The Complex Nature of Cloud Environments

Cloud environments present unique challenges due to their fluid and diverse architecture. Unlike static on-premises systems, cloud platforms dynamically allocate resources, making it difficult to track and audit assets. Moreover, the variety of cloud service models, Infrastructure as a Service (IaaS), Platform as a Service (PaaS), and Software as a Service (SaaS), adds further layers of complexity.

In the following sections, key challenges related to the complex nature of the cloud environment are presented.

Shared Responsibility Confusion

The division of security responsibilities between CSPs and clients is often misunderstood. For example, in an IaaS model like AWS, the CSP secures the underlying infrastructure, but clients remain responsible for securing data, applications, and access controls. Misaligned expectations can result in security gaps.

Visibility and Control Issues

Organizations often lack comprehensive visibility in their cloud environments. Limited access to infrastructure-level details restricts their ability to monitor and secure resources effectively.

Dynamic Resource Allocation

The cloud's ability to scale resources dynamically complicates asset tracking. Organizations may struggle to identify which assets are active and which require security measures.

Compliance in Multi-cloud Setups

Using multiple CSPs introduces inconsistent security standards and compliance requirements across platforms, creating additional hurdles in maintaining a unified security posture.

Third-Party Risks

Integrating third-party services into cloud environments can introduce vulnerabilities, especially if these services lack adequate security controls or fail to meet compliance standards.

Example: A Financial Institution's Cloud Audit Challenges

A financial institution migrating critical workloads to AWS and Azure faced several challenges during a cloud security audit.

Misconfigured Identity and Access Management (IAM)

Excessive user privileges were detected, violating the principle of least privilege. For example, developers had admin-level access to production systems, allowing them to bypass security controls.

- *Impact*: This overprovisioning increased the risk of insider threats and unauthorized access to sensitive data.

Unencrypted Data at Rest

Storage buckets containing financial records were left unencrypted, violating data protection laws like GDPR.

- *Impact*: Sensitive customer information was at risk of exposure in case of unauthorized access or data breaches.

Shadow IT

Departments utilized unapproved SaaS solutions to accelerate workflows, bypassing established security policies. For example, a marketing team used an unvetted email automation platform to store client data.

- *Impact*: These shadow IT systems lacked corporate security oversight, increasing the organization's vulnerability to data breaches.

Inadequate Logging and Monitoring

Critical systems lacked sufficient logging, and existing logs were not aggregated or monitored. Suspicious activities, such as multiple failed login attempts, went unnoticed for weeks.

- *Impact*: Delayed detection of unauthorized activities limited the organization's ability to respond promptly to potential threats.

Strategies to Address Cloud Security Audit Challenges

To overcome the complexities of cloud security audits, organizations must adopt proactive strategies that enhance visibility, enforce compliance, and mitigate risks. A well-defined approach involves clarifying security responsibilities, leveraging cloud-native security tools, automating asset management, and enforcing consistent policies across multi-cloud environments. Additionally, strengthening identity and access management, implementing robust encryption, and integrating continuous monitoring are critical steps in securing cloud infrastructure. The following strategies provide practical solutions to address the most common cloud security audit challenges.

Clarify the Shared Responsibility Model

Collaborate with CSPs to define and document the delineation of security responsibilities. This involves leveraging provider-specific guidelines, such as AWS's Shared Responsibility Model documentation.

- *Example*: A retail company using AWS identified a lack of clarity in roles for data encryption during audits. After consulting AWS's guidelines, they implemented explicit encryption practices for all customer data.

- *Impact*: Clear understanding ensured proper implementation of security measures without gaps.

Enhance Visibility with CSP Tools

Deploy CSP-native tools to monitor cloud activity and gain actionable insights into security events. Tools like AWS CloudTrail, Azure Monitor, and Google Cloud Operations Suite provide comprehensive visibility.

- *Example*: An e-commerce company enabled AWS CloudTrail to monitor API calls across its cloud environment, catching suspicious activities before they escalate.

- *Impact*: Improved visibility reduced the likelihood of undetected malicious activity.

Automate Asset Inventory

Use infrastructure-as-code (IaC) tools like Terraform or Ansible to automate the provisioning and tracking of cloud resources.

- *Example*: A healthcare provider used Terraform to maintain an up-to-date inventory of virtual machines, ensuring accurate data for audits.

- *Impact*: Automation minimized the risk of missing or untracked resources during audits.

CHAPTER 8 REAL-LIFE SCENARIOS AND CASE STUDIES

Implement Consistent Security Policies Across Clouds

Adopt a centralized Cloud Security Posture Management (CSPM) solution to enforce uniform security policies across multi-cloud environments.

- *Example*: A logistics company used Prisma Cloud to detect misconfigurations in both AWS and Azure environments, addressing compliance issues proactively.

- *Impact*: Unified security policies ensured consistent protection and simplified compliance reporting.

Focus on Identity and Access Management (IAM)

Regularly review and update IAM policies to enforce the principle of least privilege. Implement MFA and role-based access controls to enhance security.

- *Example*: A tech startup introduced MFA for all privileged accounts, reducing the risk of account compromise through phishing attacks.

- *Impact*: Strengthened IAM reduced unauthorized access and insider threats.

Encrypt Everything

Mandate encryption for data at rest and in transit, leveraging tools like AWS KMS or Azure Key Vault.

- *Example*: A law company transitioned to encrypted Amazon Simple Storage Service (Amazon S3) buckets, ensuring client confidentiality in their cloud environment.

- *Impact*: Encryption safeguarded sensitive data, even in case of unauthorized access.

Adopt Continuous Monitoring

Integrate SIEM solutions for real-time monitoring and incident response. Tools like Splunk and Microsoft Sentinel can provide centralized visibility.

- *Example*: A media company deployed Splunk to monitor real-time anomalies in its cloud environment, mitigating an attempted ransomware attack.

- *Impact*: Real-time monitoring enhanced the organization's ability to respond to threats quickly.

Conduct Regular Cloud Security Training

Human error remains a significant factor in cloud security incidents. Organizations should conduct regular training sessions for IT, security, and DevOps teams to ensure they stay updated on cloud security best practices and compliance requirements.

- *Example*: A fintech company introduced quarterly cloud security workshops covering IAM best practices, encryption techniques, and secure CI/CD pipeline management.

- *Impact*: Enhanced staff awareness reduced misconfigurations and improved overall cloud security hygiene.

Lessons Learned from Cloud Security Audits

Cloud security audits reveal critical gaps in infrastructure and processes, highlighting areas for improvement.

- *Early Adoption of Best Practices*: Misconfigurations like open storage buckets or weak IAM policies are common vulnerabilities.
  - *Mitigation*: Use tools like AWS Config or Azure Policy to detect and fix misconfigurations early.

- *Centralized Logging*: Centralized logging aggregates security data for easier analysis and threat detection.
  - *Mitigation*: Implement logging tools like Elasticsearch or Logstash for real-time visibility.

- *Regular Penetration Testing*: Periodic penetration tests reveal vulnerabilities before attackers can exploit them.
  - *Mitigation*: Engage third-party experts or use automated tools like Metasploit to identify weaknesses.

CHAPTER 8   REAL-LIFE SCENARIOS AND CASE STUDIES

Turning Challenges into Opportunities

Cloud security audits may expose vulnerabilities, but they also create opportunities for improvement:

- *Strengthened Security Posture*: Addressing gaps from audits creates a more resilient security framework. Organizations can better defend against emerging threats by proactively resolving issues.

- *Improved Compliance*: Regular audits ensure adherence to regulations like GDPR, HIPAA, or PCI-DSS. Compliance reduces legal and financial risks while building stakeholder trust.

- *Enhanced Operational Efficiency*: Optimized security controls streamline processes and reduce redundancy. Efficient use of cloud tools and practices leads to cost savings.

- *Cultural Shift Toward Security Awareness*: Frequent audits foster a culture of accountability, encouraging teams to prioritize security.

- *Innovation Through Challenges*: Audit challenges often lead to the adoption of advanced tools and methods, such as AI-driven threat detection or automated compliance solutions.

Key Takeaways

Cloud security audits reveal misconfigurations, access control gaps, and compliance risks. Challenges like shared responsibility confusion, limited visibility, and shadow IT highlight the need for automation, continuous monitoring, and strong security policies. Leveraging CSP tools and proactive measures strengthens security and ensures compliance.

In this section, we covered the following points:

- *Understand the Shared Responsibility Model*: Clearly define security roles between CSPs and clients to avoid gaps.

- *Leverage Native CSP Tools*: Use provider-specific tools to enhance visibility and control.

- *Automate Asset Management*: Automation reduces errors and simplifies resource tracking.

- *Standardized Security Across Platforms*: Consistent policies ensure uniform compliance in multi-cloud setups.

- *Adopt Continuous Monitoring*: Real-time threat detection mitigates potential breaches effectively.

- Cloud security audits, despite their challenges, serve as a critical mechanism for strengthening organizational resilience and ensuring compliance in an increasingly complex digital landscape.

The Impact of Human Error on Cybersecurity Audits

Human error is one of the most pervasive challenges in the cybersecurity landscape, contributing significantly to security vulnerabilities. Despite rapid advancements in technology and automation, humans remain at the core of managing and implementing cybersecurity strategies. This essential involvement introduces the potential for mistakes, which can jeopardize an organization's security posture. Cybersecurity audits, designed to uncover and address such vulnerabilities, often highlight the far-reaching consequences of human errors and provide opportunities to mitigate them effectively.

This section examines the types of human errors encountered during cybersecurity audits, their real-world impacts, and strategies to minimize these risks. Additionally, it highlights the critical role of cybersecurity audits in mitigating the effects of human error and strengthening organizational defenses.

Understanding Human Error in Cybersecurity

Human error manifests at various stages of the cybersecurity lifecycle, from drafting policies to configuring systems and monitoring threats. In cybersecurity audits, errors can take several forms:

- *Policy Misinterpretation*: Misunderstanding or incorrect implementation of security policies.

- *Configuration Errors*: Mistakes in setting up systems, applications, or tools.

CHAPTER 8   REAL-LIFE SCENARIOS AND CASE STUDIES

- *Neglected Updates*: Delays in applying critical patches or updates.
- *Weak Password Practices*: Using weak or reused passwords, exposing systems to attacks.
- *Data Mishandling*: Mishandling sensitive data during storage, sharing, or disposal.
- *Audit Oversights*: Missing critical elements in audit processes due to inadequate attention to detail.

Each of these errors can have severe implications, often leading to vulnerabilities that malicious actors exploit.

Impact of Human Error on Cybersecurity Audits
Case 1: Misconfigured Firewalls

During an audit at an energy institution, misconfigured firewall rules were discovered. Sensitive ports were left open to inbound traffic, exposing the network to potential attacks. The error occurred because the IT administrator misunderstood the policy guidelines provided by the security team.

Potential Impacts:

- Exposed the network to external threats, such as malware or unauthorized access.
- Required immediate corrective action and re-auditing, increasing operational costs.
- Delayed compliance certification, risking regulatory penalties.

Case 2: Unencrypted Backup Files

In a healthcare organization, an audit revealed that backup files containing sensitive patient information were stored unencrypted in a publicly accessible cloud storage bucket. This oversight stemmed from a junior IT staff member's error in configuring storage policies.

Potential Impacts:

- Violated data protection regulations like HIPAA, resulting in hefty fines.
- Damaged the organization's reputation and eroded patient trust.
- Prompted urgent policy reviews and increased oversight to prevent recurrence.

Why Human Error Occurs

Human errors often stem from systemic or individual factors that compromise judgment and efficiency:

- *Insufficient Training*: Staff may lack the necessary skills to handle complex systems and cybersecurity tools.
- *High Workload*: Overburdened teams are prone to skipping critical steps or overlooking vulnerabilities.
- *Complex Systems*: Modern IT environments are intricate, often leading to confusion and mistakes.
- *Poor Communication*: Miscommunication between teams can result in errors during critical processes.
- Over-reliance on automated tools without manual verification can lead to unchecked vulnerabilities.

Mitigating Human Error in Cybersecurity Audits

Building a strong cybersecurity culture is essential in reducing human errors that compromise security. Organizations should foster a mindset of shared responsibility by promoting security awareness, encouraging reporting of potential risks, and integrating security into daily workflows. Leadership plays a crucial role in reinforcing best practices and ensuring that cybersecurity remains a priority at all levels.

Comprehensive Training Programs

Training programs are vital in equipping staff with the necessary knowledge and skills to handle cybersecurity tools and processes effectively. Regular workshops, simulations, and real-world case studies help employees understand emerging threats and how to counter them. These programs ensure that team members are proficient in handling systems, reducing the likelihood of errors.

Benefits:

- Empowers employees to act confidently in managing security tasks.
- Reduces the occurrence of mistakes stemming from ignorance or lack of awareness.
- Enhances the organization's overall security posture by keeping skills up to date.

Example: A manufacturing company reduced phishing incidents by 40% after implementing periodic phishing awareness training for its employees.

Standardized Processes

Establishing clear and detailed procedures ensures consistency in executing tasks like system configurations or data handling. Creating comprehensive checklists for audits reduces the chances of missing critical areas and ensures that processes align with organizational policies.

Benefits:

- Promotes uniformity across teams and reduces variability in outcomes.
- Helps identify gaps and inconsistencies early in the process.
- Simplifies onboarding for new employees by providing structured guidelines.

Example: An insurance company implemented a standardized procedure for firewall configuration, reducing misconfigurations by 35% and ensuring compliance with industry standards.

Automation

Automation minimizes reliance on manual tasks that are prone to human error, such as vulnerability scanning, patch management, and monitoring. Tools like Terraform and Ansible enforce consistent configurations, reducing the chance of oversights.

Benefits:

- Improves efficiency by reducing the time spent on repetitive tasks.
- Ensures consistency in configurations and patch applications.
- Frees up employees to focus on higher-value activities like threat analysis.

Example: A retail company automated its server patching process using Ansible, eliminating delays in updates and reducing the attack surface by 50%.

Peer Reviews

Peer reviews involve cross-checking critical tasks or audit findings to ensure accuracy and completeness. These reviews encourage collaboration and accountability among team members, providing an additional layer of scrutiny.

Benefits:

- Enhances accuracy by leveraging diverse perspectives.
- Builds a culture of shared responsibility and collaboration.
- Identifies gaps or errors that might be overlooked by a single individual.

Example: A tech startup implemented a peer review policy for cloud configurations, reducing security missteps related to permissions by 25%.

Proactive Monitoring

Using advanced tools like SIEM solutions enables real-time monitoring of misconfigurations and unusual activities. SIEM tools provide alerts and detailed analytics, allowing teams to respond swiftly to potential threats.

CHAPTER 8   REAL-LIFE SCENARIOS AND CASE STUDIES

Benefits:

- Identifies vulnerabilities or missteps immediately, minimizing potential impacts.
- Strengthens incident response by providing detailed logs and actionable insights.
- Enhances audit readiness by maintaining up-to-date records of system activity.

Example: A financial institution deployed Splunk to monitor real-time activities, detecting and resolving a potential insider threat before it escalated.

The Role of Cybersecurity Audits in Addressing Human Error

Cybersecurity audits are indispensable for uncovering the vulnerabilities introduced by human errors. They enable organizations to identify:

- *Misconfigurations*: Audits detect issues like open ports, excessive privileges, or unpatched systems.
- *Policy Gaps*: Misalignment between documented policies and actual practices.
- *Training Deficiencies*: Areas where employees require additional guidance or resources.
- Audits also provide actionable recommendations to rectify errors, enhance processes, and mitigate risks effectively.

Examples of How Audits Mitigate Errors:

- *Enhanced Policy Awareness*: Audits often uncover discrepancies in how policies are understood and implemented.
  - *Mitigation*: Clarify policies and conduct focused training sessions.
- *Improved System Hardening*: Regular audits reveal misconfigurations that can be promptly fixed.
  - *Mitigation*: Use automated tools to enforce configurations and reduce errors.

CHAPTER 8 REAL-LIFE SCENARIOS AND CASE STUDIES

- *Better Data Handling Practices*: Audits highlight weak data storage or sharing practices.
  - *Mitigation*: Enforce stricter access controls and encryption protocols.

Turning Human Error into an Opportunity

Human error, while often seen as vulnerability, can become a catalyst for organizational improvement when approached strategically. Figure 8-2 presents concrete steps to leverage these errors constructively:

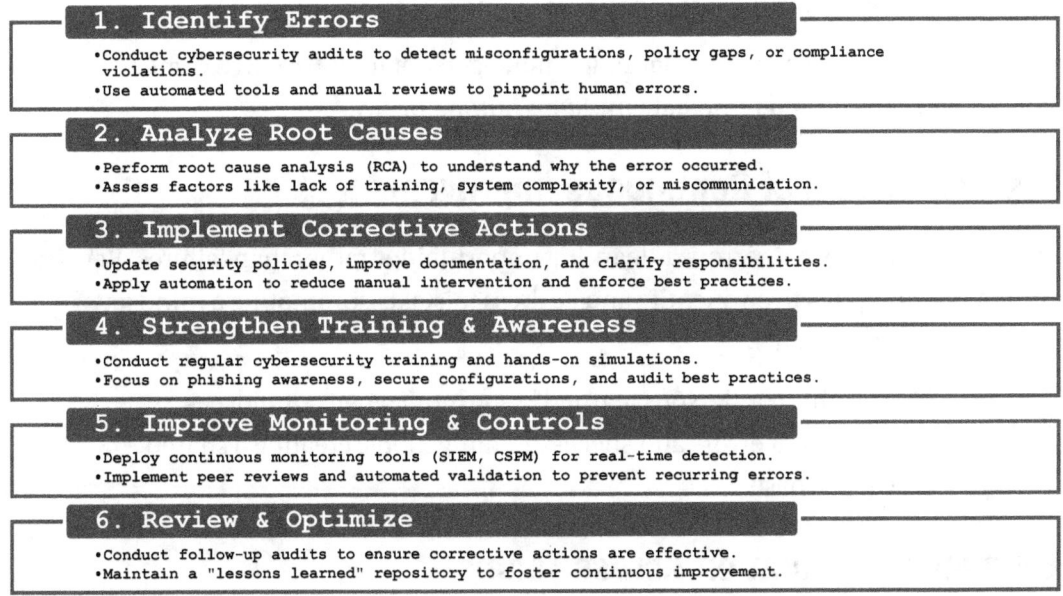

Figure 8-2. Process workflow for addressing human error in cybersecurity audits

Analyze Errors Systematically

When an error is identified, conduct a thorough root cause analysis to understand contributing factors. Use the findings to develop corrective measures that address both the immediate issue and underlying systemic problems.

- *Step*: Implement a feedback loop where teams review errors post-audit to identify patterns and gaps in training or processes.

Refine Training and Onboarding

Use errors to update and enhance training materials, ensuring that employees are better equipped to handle similar scenarios in the future. Tailor onboarding processes to address common mistakes encountered by new hires.

- *Step*: Include real-world case studies and error scenarios in training programs to prepare employees for practical challenges.

Invest in Advanced Tools

Errors often highlight gaps in tools or automation. Invest in solutions that reduce manual interventions and enforce consistency across systems.

- *Step*: Adopt cloud configuration management tools like AWS Config to identify and remediate missteps automatically.

Foster a Culture of Continuous Improvement

Encourage teams to view errors as learning opportunities rather than failures. Reward employees who proactively identify and address mistakes, promoting a mindset of vigilance and adaptability.

- *Step*: Establish a "lessons learned" repository where employees can document errors and successful mitigations, creating a shared knowledge base.

Enhance Collaboration Across Teams

Errors often arise from miscommunication or lack of coordination between teams. Improve collaboration by implementing regular cross-departmental meetings to discuss security strategies and audit findings.

- *Step*: Use collaborative platforms like Slack or Microsoft Teams to facilitate transparent communication and issue resolution.

Benefits of Turning Errors into Opportunities

- Strengthens team resilience by fostering adaptability and learning.
- Builds a proactive security culture where employees are empowered to act.
- Reduces recurrence of similar errors by addressing root causes.
- Enhances organizational credibility by demonstrating a commitment to continuous improvement.

Key Takeaways

Human error in cybersecurity audits leads to misconfigurations, weak controls, and compliance failures. Common mistakes like policy misinterpretation and neglected updates can expose organizations to risks. Mitigation strategies include training, automation, peer reviews, and proactive monitoring. Audits help identify vulnerabilities and drive continuous security improvements.

In this section, we covered the following points:

- *Common Errors*: Misconfigurations, neglected updates, and weak password practices are prevalent issues during audits.
- *Systemic Causes*: Insufficient training, high workload, and poor communication often lead to human errors.
- *Mitigation Strategies*: Comprehensive training, standardized processes, automation, peer reviews, and proactive monitoring are critical to minimizing errors.
- *Audits as Safeguards*: Cybersecurity audits play a vital role in uncovering and addressing vulnerabilities caused by human error.
- *Opportunity for Growth*: Addressing human error helps organizations refine processes, adopt better tools, and build stronger teams.
- By addressing human errors proactively, organizations can significantly enhance their cybersecurity resilience and ensure robust audit outcomes.

CHAPTER 8   REAL-LIFE SCENARIOS AND CASE STUDIES

What Auditors Can Learn from Incident Reports

Incident reports are much more than historical accounts of cybersecurity mishaps; they are treasure troves of real-world insights that provide cybersecurity auditors with the knowledge to refine their methodologies and enhance organizational defenses. These reports, which detail the lifecycle of security incidents, offer a granular view of vulnerabilities, threat vectors, and the effectiveness of existing controls. By studying them, auditors can develop a proactive, informed approach to cybersecurity, turning lessons from the past into strategies for a secure future.

In the following section is delved into the critical role incident reports play in cybersecurity audits, offering practical guidance on integrating these lessons into audit practices while highlighting the value of incident-informed strategies for mitigating future risks.

What Are Incident Reports?

Incident reports are structured documents that outline the details of a cybersecurity incident. These reports serve as a post-mortem analysis of an event, detailing what happened, why it happened, and how it was addressed. Key components of an incident report include

- *Incident Description*: A summary of the event and its nature (e.g., data breach, malware attack, unauthorized access).

- *Timeline of Events*: A chronological account of how the incident unfolded.

- *Affected Systems and Data*: Identification of the compromised systems, applications, and sensitive data.

- *Root Cause Analysis*: A detailed breakdown of the vulnerabilities or actions that enabled the incident.

- *Response Actions*: Measures taken to contain, mitigate, and recover from the incident.

- *Lessons Learned*: Recommendations for preventing similar occurrences in the future.

Why Are Incident Reports Valuable for Auditors?

Incident reports enable auditors to bridge the gap between theoretical risk assessments and real-world cybersecurity challenges. They provide tangible evidence of how threats manifest, offering insights into:

Common Threat Vectors

Incident reports reveal the most frequent attack methods, such as phishing or ransomware. For instance, if several incidents involve email phishing, auditors can prioritize testing email security measures during audits to ensure they're effective at mitigating these prevalent threats.

Weaknesses in Controls

Recurring patterns in incident reports can expose gaps in controls, such as weak encryption or insufficient monitoring. Auditors can focus on validating these areas during audits, ensuring that past failures have been addressed with stronger and more reliable controls.

Response Effectiveness

Incident reports provide a detailed account of how organizations responded to cybersecurity events. Auditors can use this information to evaluate the efficiency of incident response plans, ensuring they are updated and effective for handling future threats in a timely manner.

Future Audit Guidance

By analyzing the details of incidents, auditors can tailor their methodologies to focus on areas of historical weakness. For example, if third-party risks are a recurring issue, auditors might include vendor risk management as a priority in future audits.

CHAPTER 8   REAL-LIFE SCENARIOS AND CASE STUDIES

Examples of Lessons from Incident Reports

Unpatched Vulnerabilities

- *Incident*: A financial institution suffered a breach due to an unpatched vulnerability in its VPN. This emphasizes the importance of timely patch management and proactive vulnerability scanning during audits. Auditors can use this lesson to stress regular updates and review patching schedules.

- *Lesson*: This underscores the importance of regular patch management and proactive vulnerability scans.

Insider Threats

- *Incident*: In one incident, an employee leaked sensitive data after their access wasn't revoked post-termination. This highlights the need for rigorous access controls and monitoring systems, ensuring insider threats are mitigated through periodic reviews and proper offboarding procedures.

- *Lesson*: Highlights the need for robust access controls, user activity monitoring, and policies for revoking access after employee departures.

Supply Chain Attacks

- *Incident*: A company was compromised when malware was introduced through third-party software. This underscores the necessity of conducting vendor risk assessments and verifying the security of software supply chains as a key part of any cybersecurity audit.

- *Lesson*: Emphasizes the need for thorough vendor risk assessments and secure supply chain practices.

How Auditors Can Use Incident Reports

Incident reports are not merely historical records; they are tools for improving future audits. Here's how auditors can leverage them.

Risk Assessment

Incident reports highlight high-risk areas, guiding auditors to focus on vulnerabilities like phishing or ransomware defenses. For instance, auditors can use these reports to assess whether email security tools and training programs effectively minimize phishing risks.

Example: If phishing attacks are frequent, auditors can evaluate the organization's email security protocols, anti-phishing tools, and employee training programs.

Control Validation

Auditors can verify whether past failures, such as weak encryption, have been rectified. By reviewing incident reports, they ensure that corrective actions align with best practices and address the vulnerabilities that were previously exploited.

Example: After a breach caused by weak encryption, auditors can verify whether encryption protocols align with standards like AES-256.

Incident Response Review

Reports offer insight into how incidents were managed, including response times and containment actions. Auditors can analyze these to assess whether incident response plans are effective and suggest improvements where gaps are evident.

Example: Evaluate whether incidents were detected and contained promptly and if all stakeholders were informed appropriately.

Process Improvement Recommendations

Using patterns observed in incident reports, auditors can propose enhancements like automating repetitive tasks. This reduces human error and ensures that the organization is better prepared for future cybersecurity challenges.

Example: If human error is a recurring theme, auditors can suggest automation of high-risk processes to minimize mistakes.

CHAPTER 8   REAL-LIFE SCENARIOS AND CASE STUDIES

Practical Integration of Incident Reports into Audits

Integrating lessons from incident reports into cybersecurity audits strengthens an organization's ability to detect vulnerabilities, validate controls, and refine incident response strategies. By systematically analyzing past incidents, auditors can identify recurring weaknesses, assess the effectiveness of implemented security measures, and recommend proactive improvements. This approach ensures that audits are not only compliance-driven but also strategically aligned with real-world threats, fostering a resilient cybersecurity posture.

Create Incident-Informed Audit Checklists

Auditors can develop checklists based on vulnerabilities highlighted in reports. For example, if incidents reveal a lack of MFA, they can include an MFA verification step in their audit checklists to ensure this critical control is implemented.

Example: Include a checklist item to ensure robust multi-factor authentication across critical systems.

Incorporate Real-World Scenarios

Simulating past incidents, such as phishing attacks, during audits helps assess readiness. For instance, tabletop exercises allow organizations to test their response to simulated breaches, providing valuable insights into their operational resilience.

Example: Conduct a simulated ransomware attack to test the organization's recovery protocols.

Collaborating with Incident Response Teams

Auditors can work closely with incident response teams to understand the tools and processes they use. Reviewing logs from SIEM platforms like Splunk helps auditors evaluate whether real-time monitoring systems are functioning optimally.

Example: Review the use of SIEM tools like Splunk to evaluate the adequacy of real-time monitoring and threat detection.

CHAPTER 8 REAL-LIFE SCENARIOS AND CASE STUDIES

Turning Incident Reports into Opportunities

Incident reports are not just post-event analyses; they are blueprints for building resilience. By leveraging these reports, organizations can:

- *Refine Risk Management*: Use incident data to prioritize high-risk areas and allocate resources effectively.

- *Enhance Training and Awareness*: Tailor training programs to address common errors or oversights identified in incident reports.

- *Strengthening Communication Protocols*: Improve cross-departmental collaboration during incidents by addressing communication gaps noted in reports.

- *Implement Continuous Monitoring*: Deploy advanced tools for real-time threat detection and response, informed by past failures.

Key Takeaways

Incident reports offer auditors real-world insights to refine risk assessments, validate controls, and improve incident response. By leveraging past failures, audits become proactive tools for stronger cybersecurity and resilience.

In this section, we covered the following points:

- *Learn from Real-World Failures*: Incident reports provide concrete examples of how threats materialize and controls fail, offering a roadmap for more effective audits.

- *Focus on High-Risk Areas*: Prioritize areas highlighted by incident reports, such as phishing defenses, access controls, and vendor risk management.

- *Advocate for Proactive Measures*: Use insights from reports to recommend proactive solutions, such as automation and continuous monitoring.

- *Promote a Culture of Resilience*: Encourage organizations to treat incidents as learning opportunities, fostering an adaptable and proactive security culture.

CHAPTER 8   REAL-LIFE SCENARIOS AND CASE STUDIES

A Successful Audit Story: Key Takeaways

Success in cybersecurity audits illustrates how meticulous planning, thorough evaluations, and actionable recommendations can elevate an organization's security posture. These stories are more than just achievements; they serve as roadmaps for auditors and organizations striving to fortify their defenses. This section dives into the journey of a financial services company that transformed its security framework through a comprehensive audit, offering valuable lessons and takeaways for the cybersecurity community.

The Organization: A Financial Services Company

This case focuses on a mid-sized financial services corporation handling millions of daily transactions. Operating in a heavily regulated environment, the organization was subject to compliance with PCI-DSS, ISO 27001, and GDPR. While basic security measures were in place, a breach at a neighboring corporation served as a wake-up call. The company initiated an audit to uncover vulnerabilities and align its security framework with best practices and regulatory requirements.

The Audit Goals

The audit was designed with four clear objectives to ensure a holistic approach to enhancing the organization's security posture:

- *Compliance Assurance*: The organization needed to ensure adherence to PCI-DSS and ISO 27001 standards, with a specific focus on data encryption, secure payment processing, and access control measures. Meeting these standards was critical to avoid regulatory penalties and bolster customer trust.

- *Risk Identification*: The audit aimed to pinpoint vulnerabilities across the organization's network, applications, and processes. This included uncovering misconfigurations, unpatched systems, and insider threats that could expose the company to breaches.

CHAPTER 8   REAL-LIFE SCENARIOS AND CASE STUDIES

- *Incident Readiness Evaluation*: With cyber threats on the rise, the organization sought to evaluate its incident response plan. The goal was to identify gaps in the plan, such as delays in escalation or unclear communication channels, and ensure the company could respond effectively to threats.

- *Data Protection Measures*: Given the sensitivity of customer data, the audit aimed to assess the controls in place to safeguard this information. This included evaluating encryption practices, secure backups, and data access policies to prevent leaks or unauthorized access.

Figure 8-3 presents key audit goals for this case study.

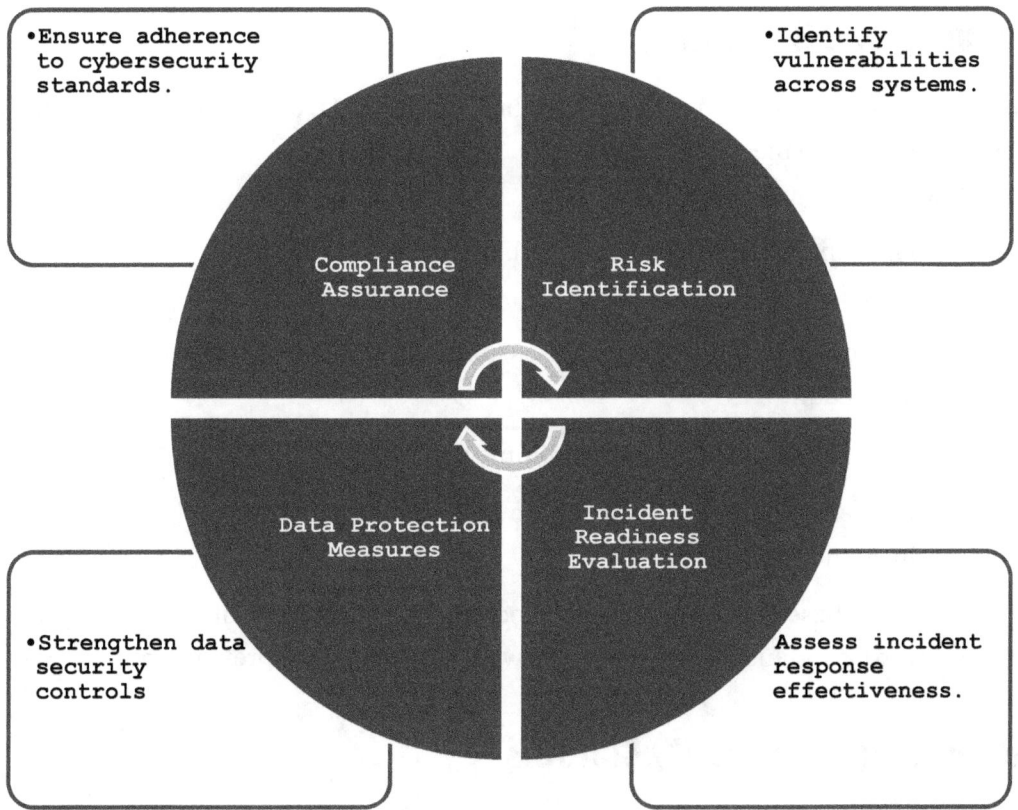

Figure 8-3. *Key audit goals for this case study*

CHAPTER 8   REAL-LIFE SCENARIOS AND CASE STUDIES

The Audit Process

The audit process followed a structured approach, beginning with accurate planning and stakeholder collaboration to define its scope. Key areas such as payment systems, customer data protection, access controls, and incident response readiness were prioritized. The assessment phase combined automated security tools and manual evaluations to identify vulnerabilities in network security, application security, and access management. Compliance validation ensured alignment with PCI-DSS and ISO 27001. A ransomware simulation tested incident response effectiveness, revealing gaps in escalation and communication. This methodical approach ensured that all critical security aspects were thoroughly examined, paving the way for actionable improvements.

Planning and Scoping

The audit team collaborated with key stakeholders across IT, compliance, and executive leadership to define the audit's scope.

The scoping process prioritized

- Payment processing systems, as they were the backbone of the organization's operations.
- Databases containing sensitive customer data to ensure robust protection.
- Employee access controls to minimize risks of insider threats.
- Incident response mechanisms to assess preparedness for cyber incidents.
- This phase also included a detailed timeline and allocation of resources, ensuring all key areas were addressed comprehensively.

Assessment of Security Controls

The audit leveraged both automated tools and manual assessments:

- *Network Security*: Tools like Nessus and Wireshark scanned for open ports and outdated firewalls, which could serve as entry points for attackers.

CHAPTER 8 REAL-LIFE SCENARIOS AND CASE STUDIES

- *Application Security*: Using Burp Suite, static and dynamic testing identified exploitable vulnerabilities in the company's web applications.

- *Access Controls*: A review of IAM practices revealed excessive privileges for 30% of employees, posing a risk of unauthorized access.

- *Incident Response Testing*: A ransomware simulation tested the organization's response effectiveness, highlighting delays in escalation and gaps in communication protocols.

Compliance Validation

Auditors meticulously cross-referenced the organization's controls against PCI-DSS and ISO 27001 checklists. Tools like Qualys confirmed encryption protocols, data security measures, and compliance with regulatory requirements, ensuring no critical areas were overlooked.

Findings and Recommendations

The audit uncovered significant vulnerabilities:

Web Application Vulnerabilities

Finding
The audit revealed that several web application libraries were outdated, leaving the system vulnerable to SQL injection attacks. SQL injection is a common and highly dangerous attack vector, allowing attackers to manipulate backend databases through unsanitized input fields. These vulnerabilities not only exposed sensitive customer data but also posed a significant compliance risk, particularly with GDPR and PCI-DSS requirements.

Recommendation
Implement an automated patch management system to regularly update all software libraries and dependencies. Automated tools such as Dependabot or OWASP Dependency-Check can identify outdated components and streamline patch applications. This approach minimizes downtime, ensures consistent updates, and reduces the attack surface.

CHAPTER 8   REAL-LIFE SCENARIOS AND CASE STUDIES

Added Value

- Enhanced security against exploitation of known vulnerabilities.
- Improved compliance with regulatory standards that require up-to-date software.
- Reduced manual effort for the IT team in tracking updates, allowing them to focus on more strategic tasks.

Excessive Privileges

Finding

A review of access controls found that 30% of employees had unnecessary administrative rights. Excessive privileges increase the risk of insider threats and accidental misuse of sensitive systems. In one instance, an employee with admin-level access inadvertently made changes that disrupted key processes. This lack of adherence to the Principle of Least Privilege (POLP) was a critical gap in the organization's security framework.

Recommendation

Enforce RBAC to ensure employees have only the permissions necessary for their job roles. Review and update user privileges regularly, especially during role changes or terminations. Conduct periodic access audits to maintain adherence to POLP and limit high-level access to essential personnel only.

Added Value

- Significant reduction in the risk of insider threats and accidental changes.
- Streamlined user management and improved audit trails for compliance purposes.
- Strengthened overall security posture by limiting access to critical systems and data.

Weak Incident Response Plan

Finding
The incident response plan lacked clarity in escalation paths and communication protocols. The ransomware simulation conducted during the audit revealed delays in notifying key stakeholders and executing containment measures. These gaps could result in prolonged response times and greater damage during an actual incident.

Recommendation
Refine the incident response plan by

- Establishing clear escalation matrices that define roles, responsibilities, and decision-making authority.
- Conducting quarterly drills, such as tabletop exercises and simulated attacks, to test the plan's effectiveness and familiarize the team with their roles.
- Documenting lessons learned from each drill to continuously improve the plan.

Added Value

- Faster response and containment during actual incidents, reducing potential damages.
- Improved coordination and communication between teams, minimizing confusion under pressure.
- Enhanced organizational resilience through regular preparedness exercises.

Unencrypted Backups

Finding
The audit identified that backup files containing sensitive customer data were stored on external drives without encryption. This posed a critical risk of data theft, especially in cases of physical theft or unauthorized access. Non-compliance with encryption requirements under regulations like GDPR and PCI-DSS further amplified the risk.

CHAPTER 8 REAL-LIFE SCENARIOS AND CASE STUDIES

Recommendation

Encrypt all backup files using robust encryption standards such as AES-256. Migrate backup storage to a secure, cloud-based environment that supports encrypted storage and access controls. Implement backup monitoring to ensure encryption compliance and quick detection of unauthorized access attempts.

Added Value

- Significant reduction in the risk of data breaches through secure storage.
- Compliance with regulatory mandates, avoiding potential fines and reputational damage.
- Enhanced business continuity by ensuring the availability and integrity of encrypted backups during recovery efforts.

Overall Added Value of Addressing These Vulnerabilities

Addressing these vulnerabilities had a profound impact on the organization's cybersecurity framework:

- *Improved Security Posture*: By closing critical gaps, the organization significantly reduced the likelihood of successful cyberattacks.
- *Regulatory Compliance*: Aligning with standards such as PCI-DSS, ISO 27001, and GDPR minimized legal risks and boosted customer confidence.
- *Operational Efficiency*: Automation of updates and role-based access controls reduced manual effort and streamlined processes.
- *Enhanced Resilience*: A robust incident response plan and secure backup practices prepared the organization for potential threats, reducing downtime and financial losses during incidents.

Implementation and Results

Over the next three months, the organization implemented the audit's recommendations:

- *Software Updates*: Automated patch management closed critical security gaps, ensuring all applications were up-to-date.

- *Access Control Enhancements*: Role-based access controls were introduced, reducing unnecessary admin privileges by 50%.

- *Improved Incident Response*: Two incident response drills were conducted, reducing response times by 40% and improving team coordination.

- *Encrypted Backups*: All backups were encrypted and migrated to a secure cloud solution, eliminating risks of data theft.

- These actions not only enhanced security but also improved the organization's compliance standing, increasing customer trust and reducing regulatory risks.

Lessons Learned from Success

Importance of Stakeholder Buy-In

Active participation from stakeholders was crucial for the audit's success. Their involvement ensured that the recommendations were prioritized and resources were allocated efficiently.

Benefits:

- Faster implementation of recommendations.

- Improved communication and collaboration between teams.

- Higher management support for long-term security initiatives.

Continuous Monitoring Matters

Adopting an SIEM system enabled real-time threat detection and proactive responses.
Benefits:

- Reduced time to detect and mitigate incidents
- Enhanced visibility into network activity
- Improved ability to address emerging threats

Training Makes a Difference

Cybersecurity awareness training significantly reduced human error and enhanced the organization's overall security culture.
Benefits:

- 60% reduction in phishing-related incidents.
- Employees became more vigilant against social engineering attacks.
- Increased engagement in reporting suspicious activities.

Regular Audits Are Essential

Committing to annual audits and periodic internal reviews helped the organization maintain its security posture and adapt to evolving threats.
Benefits:

- Consistent compliance with regulatory requirements
- Early identification of potential vulnerabilities
- Continuous improvement in security processes

Key takeaways

Successful cybersecurity audits drive lasting security improvements. By prioritizing compliance, risk mitigation, and incident readiness, organizations can address vulnerabilities, enhance resilience, and strengthen data protection. Implementing proactive measures, such as automation and access controls, ensures long-term security and regulatory alignment.

In this section, we covered the following points:

- *Tailored Scoping*: Ensure the audit scope aligns with the organization's unique needs and risk landscape.

- *Integrated Assessments*: Combine automated tools and manual testing for comprehensive evaluations.

- *Actionable Recommendations*: Provide clear, practical steps for organizations to implement improvements.

- *Emphasize Training*: Advocate for employee awareness programs to address human vulnerabilities.

Case Study: Auditing for Insider Threats

Insider threats pose a unique and complex challenge to organizations, as they originate from individuals who already have authorized access to systems and data. Addressing these risks requires not just technical solutions but also an understanding of human behavior and organizational dynamics. This section delves into a real-world case study of a mid-sized technology company that conducted a comprehensive insider threat audit. The audit revealed critical vulnerabilities, provided actionable insights, and highlighted the importance of a proactive, multi-faceted approach to managing internal risks.

The Organization: A Software Development Company

The subject of this case study is a growing software development company specializing in cloud-based solutions for enterprise clients. With a reputation for innovation, the company manages sensitive client data, proprietary source code, and financial information. The organization employs over 500 people, with its research and development (R&D) and finance departments handling some of the most confidential information. A series of anomalous activities, such as unusual login times and unauthorized data access attempts, triggered concerns about insider threats. These incidents prompted the company to initiate a focused audit to identify vulnerabilities and improve its security posture.

CHAPTER 8   REAL-LIFE SCENARIOS AND CASE STUDIES

The company recognized that its existing cybersecurity measures primarily focused on external threats, leaving internal risks relatively unaddressed. This gap underscored the need for a robust insider threat audit, aimed at uncovering vulnerabilities, strengthening preventive controls, and fostering a culture of accountability.

Audit Objectives

The insider threat audit was structured around the following key objectives:

- *Identify Abnormal Access Patterns*:
    - Examine historical logs to detect patterns of unauthorized or suspicious data access.
    - Assess login records for unusual times, durations, or geolocations that may indicate improper use.
- *Assess Policies and Controls*:
    - Review the organization's access management framework, including RBAC.
    - Evaluate compliance with internal guidelines and regulatory requirements related to data handling.
- *Monitor Employee Activity*:
    - Analyze workstation usage, email communications, and internal messaging platforms for signs of risky or unauthorized actions.
    - Ensure privacy compliance while conducting behavioral monitoring.
- *Strengthen Preventive Measures*:
    - Develop actionable recommendations to reduce insider threat risks, including technical controls, training programs, and improved workflows.
    - Provide a roadmap for continuous monitoring and future audits.

CHAPTER 8   REAL-LIFE SCENARIOS AND CASE STUDIES

The Audit Process

The audit process in this case study consists of the following steps presented in Figure 8-4.

Figure 8-4. *Audit process for case study of auditing insider threats*

Step 1: Planning and Scoping

To achieve the objectives, the audit team engaged in extensive planning with IT, HR, and compliance teams:

- *Identify Key Systems and Departments*: High-risk areas like R&D, finance, and critical data repositories were prioritized.

- *Define Privacy Protocols*: Clear guidelines ensured that employee monitoring respected privacy laws and ethical standards.

- *Set Timeframe*: Six months of logs and communications were selected for detailed analysis.

Step 2: Identifying Abnormal Access Patterns

- *Use Advanced Analytics Tools*: Tools like Splunk and ELK Stack were employed to review login records and detect anomalies in data access patterns.

- *Investigate Flags*: Instances of after-hours access and unauthorized data transfers were isolated for deeper analysis.

Step 3: Assessing Policies and Controls

- *Review RBAC Implementation*: The team checked whether access permissions were aligned with job roles and responsibilities.

- *Audit Compliance Measures*: Policies for onboarding and offboarding were cross-checked against best practices to identify gaps.

CHAPTER 8   REAL-LIFE SCENARIOS AND CASE STUDIES

Step 4: Monitoring Employee Activity

- *Behavioral Analysis*: Tools like ObserveIT were deployed to monitor suspicious workstation activity while maintaining compliance with privacy regulations.
- *Communication Scans*: Filters flagged emails and messages containing sensitive keywords for further inspection.

Step 5: Strengthening Preventive Measures

- *Test Controls*: The audit simulated potential insider threat scenarios to assess the organization's preparedness.
- *Provide Training*: Employees were briefed on the risks of insider threats and the importance of secure data handling practices.

Findings and Recommendations

The audit uncovered several critical vulnerabilities that posed significant risks to the organization:

Excessive Privileges

Finding

Many employees across different departments had access to sensitive systems and data not aligned with their job roles. This not only increased the risk of intentional misuse but also exposed the organization to unintentional data leaks.

Recommendation

The organization should implement a Role-Based Access Control (RBAC) system to ensure employees have access only to the resources necessary for their job functions. Additionally, quarterly access reviews should be conducted to remove unnecessary privileges and align permissions with evolving roles and responsibilities.

Added Value

- Minimizes insider threat risks by restricting unnecessary access.
- Strengthens compliance with access control best practices.
- Enhances data protection and system integrity.
- Builds client and stakeholder confidence in security measures.

CHAPTER 8 REAL-LIFE SCENARIOS AND CASE STUDIES

Lack of Monitoring

Finding
Critical data repositories, including proprietary code repositories and financial databases, were not actively monitored for unusual access or modifications. This made it challenging to detect unauthorized activities.

Recommendation
Deploy DLP tools to monitor, detect, and prevent unauthorized data transfers. Additionally, integrate an SIEM solution to enable real-time detection of anomalous activities, providing proactive threat mitigation.

Added Value

- Enables early detection of suspicious activity.
- Protects intellectual property and sensitive data.
- Reduces the risk of data breaches and regulatory violations.
- Enhances overall cybersecurity resilience and threat response.

Weak Offboarding Processes

Finding
Former employees retained access to non-critical systems for months after leaving the organization due to a lack of coordination between HR and IT departments.

Recommendation
HR and IT workflows should be integrated to automate account deactivation upon employee departure. Regular control checks must be conducted to identify and remove inactive accounts, ensuring that former employees no longer have system access.

Added Value

- Prevents unauthorized access by former employees.
- Strengthens security by reducing outdated accounts.
- Saves time and reduces human error with automation.
- Improves compliance with access control policies.

CHAPTER 8   REAL-LIFE SCENARIOS AND CASE STUDIES

Unintentional Data Sharing

Finding

During a technical support session, an employee inadvertently shared sensitive client data with an external vendor, highlighting the lack of clear data-sharing protocols.

Recommendation

The organization should establish clear data-sharing policies that outline acceptable platforms and encryption requirements for sensitive information. Employees should be trained on secure data transfer practices to prevent inadvertent exposure.

Added Value

- Reduces accidental data leaks and regulatory risks.
- Strengthens security policies around data handling.
- Protects client trust and company reputation.
- Ensures compliance with data protection regulations.

Insufficient Behavioral Monitoring

Finding

There was no mechanism in place to flag risky or suspicious employee behaviors, such as accessing sensitive data outside of working hours or unusual patterns of communication.

Recommendation

Deploy UBA tools to monitor and flag high-risk activities while adhering to privacy regulations. Collaborate with HR and legal teams to develop response protocols for handling flagged behaviors appropriately.

Added Value

- Detects insider threats before they escalate.
- Balances security with employee privacy rights.
- Improves coordination between security, HR, and compliance teams.
- Enhances threat detection without disrupting operations.

Lessons Learned

The insider threat audit provided invaluable insights into the organization's vulnerabilities and offered a roadmap for strengthening internal controls. These lessons emphasize the importance of a balanced approach to managing insider threats.

Proactive Monitoring Is Key

Real-time monitoring of employee activities and system logs is essential for identifying unusual patterns early. By leveraging SIEM and DLP tools, organizations can proactively detect and prevent potential breaches.

Clear Policies Build Strong Foundations

The audit underscored the importance of clear, enforceable policies for access management, data sharing, and insider threat prevention. These policies not only reduce risks but also create a structured framework for employees to follow.

Employee Training Is Non-negotiable

Insider threats often stem from unintentional actions. Training programs focused on data handling, phishing awareness, and secure communication practices empower employees to act as the first line of defense.

Integrated Collaboration Strengthens Defenses

The success of insider threat management depends on the seamless collaboration between IT, HR, and compliance teams. This ensures that technical, procedural, and behavioral controls are aligned and effective.

Regular Reviews Prevent Complacency

Periodic access reviews, audits, and training refreshers are crucial for maintaining a strong security posture. Insider threat management is not a one-time effort but an ongoing process that evolves with organizational needs.

Benefits of Insider Threat Management

- *Reduced Risk of Internal Breaches*: A comprehensive approach minimizes the likelihood of both intentional and accidental insider threats.

- *Improved Compliance*: Aligning policies with regulatory requirements strengthens the organization's legal standing.

- *Enhanced Employee Awareness*: Regular training fosters a culture of vigilance and responsibility.

- *Greater Operational Resilience*: Early detection and mitigation ensure business continuity in the face of potential incidents.

- *Strengthened Client Trust*: Demonstrating robust security measures reinforces client confidence in the organization's ability to protect their sensitive data.

Key Takeaways

Managing insider threats requires a mix of technical controls, behavioral analysis, and strong policies. Proactive monitoring, strict access controls, and regular audits enhance security, ensuring compliance and protecting critical assets.

In this section, we covered the following points:

- Insider threats combine technical and behavioral risks, requiring a multifaceted approach to detection and prevention.

- Tools like SIEM, DLP, and behavioral monitoring systems significantly enhance the organization's ability to detect anomalies.

- Regularly reviewing access controls and refining policies ensures that insider threat management remains effective.

- Employee training and awareness programs are as critical as technical controls in mitigating risks.

- Proactive audits help organizations identify vulnerabilities early, enabling them to take corrective actions before incidents occur.

The Role of Forensics in Cybersecurity Audits

Forensics plays an indispensable role in modern cybersecurity audits, serving as the bridge between uncovering security weaknesses and implementing proactive measures to mitigate future risks. By systematically analyzing digital evidence, forensics enables organizations to gain a deeper understanding of past incidents, assess the effectiveness of their security controls, and identify hidden vulnerabilities. This integration elevates cybersecurity audits from routine checklists to comprehensive evaluations, ensuring that organizations are not only compliant but also resilient against evolving threats.

This section delves into the critical role of forensics in cybersecurity audits, highlighting its methods, tools, and real-world applications to provide a blueprint for leveraging forensic insights to strengthen security postures.

What Is Forensics in Cybersecurity?

Digital forensics in cybersecurity involves structured collection, preservation, and analysis of digital evidence to investigate incidents, determine root causes, and assess the scope of impact. Beyond incident response, forensic techniques play a pivotal role in audits, where they validate system integrity, test the effectiveness of security controls, and identify compliance gaps. Whether analyzing malware behavior, reviewing system logs, or simulating attack scenarios, forensics provides the granular evidence needed to transform audit findings into actionable recommendations.

In an era of increasing cyber threats, forensic capabilities have become essential for organizations aiming to maintain transparency, accountability, and proactive defense mechanisms.

How Forensics Enhances Cybersecurity Audits

Forensic analysis strengthens cybersecurity audits by providing concrete evidence of security gaps, validating controls, and improving incident response. By reconstructing cyber incidents, forensics helps auditors understand attack vectors, assess control effectiveness, and recommend targeted improvements. This data-driven approach enhances security resilience, ensuring organizations remain both compliant and prepared for future threats.

CHAPTER 8   REAL-LIFE SCENARIOS AND CASE STUDIES

Root Cause Analysis of Incidents

Forensic investigations are instrumental in uncovering the specific sequence of events that led to a breach, enabling auditors to pinpoint the vulnerabilities exploited. This involves examining system logs, analyzing malware payloads, and tracing unauthorized access paths. By reconstructing the incident, auditors gain clarity on whether the breach resulted from phishing, misconfigurations, or zero-day exploits. For example, a forensic analysis may reveal that an outdated firewall rule allowed malicious traffic. Understanding these details empowers organizations to implement targeted solutions, such as upgrading firewalls, deploying advanced endpoint protection, or conducting phishing simulations to address the root causes effectively.

Forensic investigations help pinpoint how and why a security incident occurred. By examining digital traces left during breaches, auditors can identify exploited vulnerabilities or misconfigurations.

Example

- In the case of a phishing attack, forensic analysis of email payloads and logs may reveal gaps in email security or employee awareness. These findings can guide recommendations such as improved filtering systems and targeted training.

Added Value

- This approach not only addresses the immediate issue but also strengthens the organization's defenses against similar attacks in the future.

Validation of Security Controls

Forensic techniques provide a robust method for testing the efficiency and reliability of existing security measures. During audits, simulated attacks and real-world data analysis help assess whether controls like IDS and firewalls are functioning as intended. For instance, forensic testing might analyze how quickly an IDS detects unauthorized access attempts or whether it generates actionable alerts. Auditors can identify gaps, such as overly broad detection rules leading to missed threats or excessive false positives that overwhelm response teams. This validation helps organizations fine-tune their controls, ensuring they are optimized to counter evolving cyber threats.

Forensic techniques test the effectiveness of existing security measures by simulating real-world attack scenarios or analyzing historical incidents.

Example

- Reviewing IDS logs using forensic tools can determine whether suspicious activities were appropriately flagged and responded to during a penetration test.

Added Value

- This process ensures that security controls are not only in place but also functioning as intended, reducing the likelihood of undetected breaches.

Identifying Data Exfiltration Patterns

One of the primary goals of forensic analysis is to track unauthorized data transfers that might otherwise go unnoticed. By examining logs, network traffic, and file system metadata, forensic investigators can uncover patterns indicative of exfiltration, such as large outbound data transfers or connections to suspicious IPs. In a GDPR or HIPAA audit, these insights are critical for determining whether sensitive data has been compromised. Forensic techniques can also identify the methods used, such as encrypted payloads or hidden channels, helping organizations address these vulnerabilities through stronger encryption, enhanced network monitoring, and stricter access controls.

Forensic analysis can detect whether sensitive data has been transferred outside the organization, which is critical for compliance with data protection regulations.

Example

- During a GDPR compliance audit, forensic tools can analyze file transfer logs to identify unauthorized exports of personal data.

Added Value

- By uncovering such incidents, auditors can recommend safeguards that protect sensitive information and mitigate regulatory penalties.

Assessing Incident Response and Recovery Efforts

Forensics provides a detailed evaluation of how effectively an organization detects, contains, and mitigates incidents. By analyzing the timeline of events during a breach, forensic investigators can assess whether the response protocols were executed properly. For example, an audit might reveal that delays in isolating infected systems allowed malware to spread. Using this information, auditors can recommend specific improvements, such as automating containment processes, revising escalation procedures, or improving the frequency and realism of incident response drills. This ensures that organizations are better prepared for future incidents, reducing response time and minimizing damage.

Forensics provides insights into how effectively an organization responds to and recovers from incidents, highlighting areas for improvement.

Example

- Following a ransomware attack, forensic investigators might discover delays in isolating infected systems. Auditors can recommend automation and enhanced training for incident response teams.

Added Value

- This ensures faster containment and recovery during future events, reducing downtime and financial losses.

Integrating Forensics into Audit Processes

Integrating forensics into cybersecurity audits requires careful planning, execution, and reporting. Auditors must define forensic objectives, prioritize high-risk assets, and coordinate cross-functional teams for comprehensive analysis. During execution, forensic tools collect and analyze digital evidence while preserving data integrity. In reporting, forensic findings should be mapped to risks and translated into actionable security enhancements. Embedding forensic techniques into regular audit cycles ensures continuous security improvement and proactive risk management.

During Planning

- *Define Objectives*: Clearly outline forensic goals, such as identifying compliance gaps, testing security controls, or analyzing past incidents.

- *Prioritize Critical Systems*: Identify high-value assets, such as sensitive databases, proprietary code repositories, and critical infrastructure, to focus forensic efforts where they matter most.

- *Allocate Resources*: Ensure access to necessary tools, such as forensic analysis software and log management systems, and assign skilled personnel to conduct investigations.

- *Coordinate Teams*: Involve IT, security, and compliance teams to define scope and determine which systems, logs, and artifacts will be analyzed.

During Execution

- *Evidence Collection*: Use tools like EnCase or FTK to collect and preserve digital evidence without altering the original data. Follow strict chain-of-custody protocols to maintain evidence integrity.

- *Log and Traffic Analysis*: Review system logs, network traffic, and endpoint activity using tools like Splunk, Wireshark, and ELK Stack to identify anomalies and potential IoCs.

- *Behavioral Analysis*: Employ UBA to detect unusual activities, such as access outside of working hours or abnormal file transfers.

- *Simulate Attack Scenarios*: Test security controls by simulating attacks, such as phishing attempts or malware injections, to assess detection and response capabilities.

During Reporting

- *Present Forensic Findings*: Include a detailed summary of forensic results, such as identified vulnerabilities, exploited entry points, and data exfiltration evidence, with supporting artifacts like log samples or network diagrams.

- *Map Findings to Risks*: Correlate forensic insights with business risks, compliance gaps, or potential impacts to prioritize remediation efforts.

- *Actionable Recommendations*: Provide specific, evidence-backed recommendations, such as deploying encryption, improving logging mechanisms, or refining incident response plans.

- *Continuous Improvement*: Suggest integrating forensic practices into routine operations, such as regular log reviews and behavioral analysis, to maintain a proactive security posture.

Example of Forensics in Action

A healthcare organization undergoing a HIPAA audit used forensic tools to investigate a breach involving patient data. By analyzing access logs and file transfers, investigators uncovered that an employee's compromised credentials had been used for data exfiltration. The forensic analysis revealed insufficient access controls and inadequate incident response mechanisms. As a result, auditors recommended implementing MFA, deploying behavioral analytics, and refining incident response protocols.

Outcome
These measures significantly reduced the risk of similar incidents, strengthened the organization's compliance posture, and improved stakeholder trust.

Lessons Learned

- *Proactive Incident Analysis*: Forensics enables organizations to investigate past incidents, identify systemic vulnerabilities, and proactively address weaknesses before they are exploited again.

- *Data-Driven Decisions*: Using forensic evidence provides clarity and credibility to audit findings, ensuring that recommended actions are based on concrete insights rather than assumptions.

- *Improved Security Controls*: By validating and testing security measures through forensic methods, organizations can enhance the reliability and resilience of their defenses.

- *Stronger Regulatory Compliance*: Forensic insights help organizations demonstrate due diligence and compliance with frameworks like GDPR, HIPAA, and ISO 27001.

- *Enhanced Incident Response*: By integrating forensic analysis into response planning, organizations can minimize the impact of incidents and improve their recovery strategies.

Benefits of Forensic Integration:

- Enhanced detection of hidden vulnerabilities.

- Better alignment of security controls with industry standards.

- Improved trust with stakeholders through transparent, evidence-based reporting.

- Reduced financial and reputational risks associated with breaches.

Key Takeaways

Forensics enhances cybersecurity audits by uncovering vulnerabilities, validating controls, and strengthening incident response. Its integration ensures proactive defense, compliance, and improved security resilience.

In this section, we covered the following points:

- Forensics in cybersecurity audits elevates audits by uncovering hidden risks and validating controls with factual evidence.

- Employ advanced tools like EnCase, Splunk, and Wireshark to analyze data effectively.

- Forensics transforms cybersecurity audits into comprehensive evaluations, ensuring both preventive and reactive security measures are robust.

- Incorporating forensic practices equips organizations to address current vulnerabilities while preparing for future challenges.

A Day in the Life of a Cybersecurity Auditor

The role of a cybersecurity auditor is multifaceted, demanding a mix of technical prowess, strategic foresight, and interpersonal communication skills. Each day presents unique challenges and opportunities to contribute to an organization's security posture. This section delves into a typical day in the life of a cybersecurity auditor, providing a detailed look at their responsibilities, tools, and methods to address complex cyber threats.

Morning: Planning and Prioritization

The day begins with careful planning, as a well-structured approach sets the tone for an effective audit. Auditors start by revisiting the audit scope and aligning their objectives with organizational priorities. This involves reviewing network logs, prior reports, and system configurations to gauge the organization's security baseline. They also schedule meetings with key stakeholders, such as IT administrators and compliance officers, to outline the audit timeline and discuss any immediate concerns.

Cybersecurity auditors start their day by organizing their tasks and aligning them with the audit's objectives. Key activities include:

- *Revisiting Objectives*: Ensure alignment with organizational goals, regulatory standards, and identified risk areas.

- *Gathering Data*: Collect network logs, system configurations, and previous reports for a security baseline.

- *Scheduling Meetings*: Coordinate with stakeholders to clarify expectations and set timelines.

- *Prioritizing Focus Areas*: Identify high-risk systems or processes that require immediate attention.

For example, before assessing firewall configurations, an auditor may meet with the IT team to understand the network's architecture. This ensures that the audit is both comprehensive and aligned with operational realities. The morning planning phase is crucial, as it allows auditors to focus on high-risk areas and streamline the day's activities.

Mid-Morning: Assessing Security Controls

The heart of an auditor's technical work begins mid-morning, as they evaluate the organization's security controls. This includes reviewing user access privileges to ensure alignment with job roles, scanning systems for vulnerabilities using tools like Nessus or Qualys, and checking server configurations for compliance with industry standards such as CIS or NIST.

Technical assessments are at the core of an auditor's responsibilities. During this phase, they focus on

- *Access Control Reviews*: Examine user privileges to verify the principle of least privilege is applied.

- *Vulnerability Scanning*: Use tools like Nessus or Qualys to identify weaknesses in systems and applications.

- *Configuration Validation*: Check server and endpoint configurations for compliance with standards like CIS Benchmarks.

- *Incident Simulations*: Conduct tests or red team exercises to evaluate the response of security controls.

For example, an auditor might conduct a vulnerability scan on a web application, discovering outdated SSL/TLS protocols that expose sensitive data to potential interception. These findings provide the foundation for actionable recommendations to enhance the organization's defenses. Technical assessments during this phase not only uncover immediate risks but also validate the effectiveness of existing controls, ensuring they align with best practices.

Lunch: Staying Updated

Lunch breaks for cybersecurity auditors are often more than just a pause; they're an opportunity to stay current with the rapidly evolving cybersecurity landscape. Many auditors read industry blogs, participate in forums like OWASP, or attend webinars to learn about the latest threats and countermeasures.

Auditors use their midday break to stay informed and enhance their skills. Common activities include:

- *Reading Blogs and Articles*: Explore sources like Krebs on Security, Dark Reading, or SysAdmin, Audit, Network, and Security (SANS).

- *Engaging in Online Communities*: Participate in discussions on platforms like OWASP or LinkedIn.

- *Attending Webinars*: Learn about new cybersecurity tools, techniques, or regulatory updates.

- *Certification Prep*: Review materials for certifications like Certified Information Systems Auditor (CISA) or Certified Information Systems Security Professional (CISSP).

For instance, while enjoying their meal, an auditor might explore an article on APTs or watch a demonstration of a new threat detection tool. Continuous learning is vital in cybersecurity, as it ensures auditors remain equipped to tackle emerging challenges and refine their methodologies.

Afternoon: Data Analysis and Documentation

The afternoon for a cybersecurity auditor is dedicated to diving deep into the collected data, interpreting findings, and translating technical insights into actionable recommendations. This phase is critical for ensuring that observations are aligned with the organization's objectives and compliance requirements. The process demands thorough attention to detail, analytical thinking, and proficiency with cybersecurity tools to extract meaningful insights.

Key Activities:

- *Log Review*: Examine system, application, and firewall logs to identify anomalies or suspicious activities.

- *Compliance Mapping*: Match findings against industry standards like PCI-DSS or HIPAA to uncover gaps.

- *Data Visualization*: Use tools like Power BI or Tableau to create charts and dashboards for easy communication.

- *Drafting Report*: Start compiling a preliminary audit report with clear, evidence-backed observations.

For example, after analyzing firewall logs, an auditor might uncover multiple failed login attempts from a suspicious IP address, signaling a potential brute-force attack. Such insights are documented in preliminary reports, which outline observations and suggest areas for improvement. This phase requires a balance of technical acumen and attention to detail, as even minor oversights can lead to significant vulnerabilities.

Late Afternoon: Stakeholder Engagement

The late afternoon is often reserved for engaging with key stakeholders to share insights and collaborate on immediate actions. This phase bridges the gap between technical findings and organizational decision-making, ensuring alignment between the audit's outcomes and strategic goals. Effective communication skills are essential here, as auditors must present their findings in a way that resonates with both technical and non-technical audiences.

Key Activities:

- *Interim Reporting*: Present preliminary observations and emphasize critical risks to IT teams and management.

- *Collaborative Discussions*: Work with teams to understand contextual factors behind identified issues.

- *Recommendations*: Propose immediate actions, such as applying patches or strengthening access controls.

- *Feedback Collection*: Gather input from stakeholders to refine final recommendations and foster buy-in.

For example, an auditor might meet with the compliance officer to discuss GDPR-related gaps, suggesting steps like implementing MFA to secure personal data. Effective communication during this phase ensures that all stakeholders understand the audit's findings and are equipped to act on the recommendations.

Evening: Reflection and Continuous Learning

After a busy day, cybersecurity auditors often reflect on their findings and invest time in skill development. This could involve reviewing audit processes for efficiency, experimenting with advanced forensic tools, or studying for certifications like CISSP or CISA.

The evening provides an opportunity for auditors to reflect on their day and invest in professional growth. Activities include

- *Process Review*: Analyze the day's findings to identify gaps or inefficiencies in the audit process.
- *Experimenting with Tools*: Test advanced features of forensic or penetration testing tools like Metasploit.
- *Self-Education*: Study emerging cyber threats or enroll in e-learning courses to stay ahead of trends.
- *Networking*: Connect with peers in the cybersecurity community for knowledge sharing.

For instance, an auditor might explore the advanced features of Metasploit to simulate real-world attack scenarios in future audits. This continuous learning cycle not only sharpens their skills but also enhances the value they bring to their organizations.

Challenges Faced by Cybersecurity Auditors

Cybersecurity auditors navigate complex IT environments, tight deadlines, and evolving threats while ensuring compliance and security. Resistance to change, balancing technical depth with clear communication, and the need for continuous learning add to their challenges. Overcoming these obstacles requires leveraging automation, prioritizing risk-based audits, fostering collaboration, and staying updated on emerging threats. By adopting strategic approaches, auditors can enhance security postures and drive meaningful improvements.

Complex Environments

Modern IT ecosystems often span cloud, hybrid, and on-premises systems, making it difficult to gain a comprehensive view of the security posture. The diverse technologies and configurations in these environments can obscure vulnerabilities and complicate audits.

How to Overcome:

- Leverage automated tools like SIEMs and vulnerability scanners for broad visibility.
- Invest in cross-platform expertise or collaborate with specialists for specific technologies.
- Maintain detailed inventories of assets and configurations for streamlined assessments.

Time Constraints

Audits are often conducted under tight deadlines, which can limit the depth and scope of assessments. Rushing through processes increases the risk of missing critical vulnerabilities.

How to Overcome:

- Use prioritization frameworks like risk-based auditing to focus on high-impact areas.
- Standardize processes with checklists and templates to save time.
- Utilize automation for repetitive tasks, such as log analysis or vulnerability scans.

Resistance to Change

Stakeholders may resist recommendations, citing operational disruption, additional costs, or lack of perceived urgency. This resistance can hinder the implementation of critical security improvements.

CHAPTER 8   REAL-LIFE SCENARIOS AND CASE STUDIES

How to Overcome:

- Present findings with a clear cost-benefit analysis, demonstrating how recommendations mitigate risks.

- Highlight potential consequences of inaction, such as financial penalties or reputational damage.

- Engage stakeholders early in the process to build trust and address concerns collaboratively.

Evolving Threat Landscape

Cyber threats are constantly changing, making it challenging to keep audits relevant and proactive. Static approaches may fail to address emerging risks, leaving organizations vulnerable.

How to Overcome:

- Stay informed about the latest threats through threat intelligence platforms and cybersecurity forums.

- Incorporate dynamic testing methods like red teaming to simulate real-world attack scenarios.

- Regularly update audit frameworks to include new technologies and threats.

Balancing Technical Depth and Communication

Auditors must balance deep technical assessments with the ability to communicate findings effectively to non-technical stakeholders. Miscommunication can result in misaligned priorities or insufficient actions.

How to Overcome:

- Use visual aids like dashboards, charts, and heatmaps to make findings more accessible.

- Tailor communication styles to the audience, simplifying technical jargon for executives.

- Develop strong interpersonal skills to foster collaboration and mutual understanding.

- By addressing these challenges with proactive strategies and a collaborative mindset, cybersecurity auditors can overcome obstacles and deliver value to their organizations.

Key Takeaways

Cybersecurity auditors navigate complex environments, tight deadlines, and evolving threats while ensuring compliance. Overcoming these challenges requires automation, risk prioritization, clear communication, and continuous learning to strengthen security frameworks effectively.

In this section, we covered the following points:

- *Comprehensive Planning*: A well-structured approach in the morning sets the tone for the day, ensuring focus on high-priority areas.

- *Technical Rigor*: Evaluating security controls using advanced tools uncovers vulnerabilities and validates defenses.

- *Continuous Learning*: Staying updated on cybersecurity trends enhances the auditor's effectiveness in addressing emerging threats.

- *Effective Communication*: Collaborating with stakeholders ensures findings are actionable and aligned with organizational goals.

- *Resilience Amid Challenges*: Despite complex environments and resistance to change, auditors play a critical role in strengthening cybersecurity frameworks.

Conclusions

Cybersecurity audits are fundamental in identifying vulnerabilities, ensuring regulatory compliance, and enhancing an organization's security resilience. Throughout this book, we have explored real-life case studies, forensic techniques, and the daily responsibilities of cybersecurity auditors, demonstrating how they contribute to threat detection, risk mitigation, and the continuous improvement of security frameworks. By integrating forensic methods, proactive auditing, and effective stakeholder communication, auditors transform security assessments from routine checklists into comprehensive evaluations that strengthen an organization's defenses.

One of the key insights from this book is the necessity of a proactive, risk-based approach to auditing. Cyber threats evolve rapidly, requiring auditors to stay ahead by continuously updating their knowledge, leveraging cutting-edge tools, and refining audit methodologies. The integration of digital forensics in cybersecurity audits has proven invaluable in uncovering hidden threats, validating security controls, and providing actionable intelligence to prevent future incidents. Additionally, effective communication of audit findings is crucial, as technical insights must be translated into strategic recommendations that drive decision-making and security investments.

Despite challenges such as complex IT environments, time constraints, and resistance to change, cybersecurity auditors can overcome these obstacles through automation, collaboration, and continuous skill development. Organizations that prioritize cybersecurity audits, implement forensic-driven insights, and foster a culture of security awareness will be better prepared to defend against ever-evolving cyber risks.

As cyber threats become more sophisticated, the role of cybersecurity auditors will continue to expand, requiring adaptability and innovation. By applying the principles, techniques, and best practices outlined in this book, auditors can play a pivotal role in securing digital ecosystems, protecting sensitive data, and ensuring compliance with industry standards. The future of cybersecurity auditing lies in its ability to evolve alongside emerging threats, making it an indispensable function in safeguarding organizations against cyberattacks and data breaches.

Bibliography

Accuris. (2023). *IT audit field manual.* Accuris Standards Store. ISBN: 9781835467930

Aditya, B. R., Ferdiana, R., & Santosa, P. I. (2018). *Toward modern IT audit – Current issues and literature review.* 2018 4th International Conference on Science and Technology (ICST). IEEE.

Ahmad, A., Saad, M., & Mohaisen, A. (2019). Secure and transparent audit logs with BlockAudit. *arXiv Preprint.* https://arxiv.org/abs/1907.10484

AICPA. (2022). How effective is your cybersecurity audit? *ISACA Journal*, 3, 12-20. https://www.isaca.org/resources/isaca-journal/issues/2022/volume-3/how-effective-is-your-cybersecurity-audit

Alexander, D., Finch, A., Sutton, D., & Taylor, A. (2013). *Information security management principles* (2nd ed.). BCS Learning & Development. ISBN: 978-1780171753.

Alkhalil, Z., Taib, C., Campbell, P., & McCullagh, A. (2021). The identification of a model victim for social engineering: A qualitative analysis. *Journal of Cybersecurity*, 7(1), 1–13. https://par.nsf.gov/servlets/purl/10249093

Allsopp, W. (2017). *Advanced penetration testing: Hacking the world's most secure networks.* Wiley. ISBN: 978-1119367680.

Al-Matari, O. M. M., Helal, I. M. A., Mazen, S. A., & Elhennawy, S. (2021). Integrated framework for cybersecurity auditing. *Information Security Journal*, 30(4), 189–204. https://doi.org/10.1080/19393555.2020.1834649

Al-Twaijry, A. A. M., Brierley, J. A., & Gwilliam, D. R. (2003). The development of internal audit in Saudi Arabia: An institutional theory perspective. *Critical Perspectives on Accounting*, 14(5), 507–531. https://doi.org/10.1016/S1045-2354(02)00158-2

Alvesson, M., & Spicer, A. (2019). Neo-institutional theory and organization studies: A mid-life crisis? *Organization Studies*, 40(2), 199–218. https://doi.org/10.1177/0170840618772610

BIBLIOGRAPHY

Ammar, J. (2019). Cyber Gremlin: Social networking, machine learning and the global war on Al-Qaida and IS-inspired terrorism. *International Journal of Law and Information Technology*, 27(3), 238–265. https://doi.org/10.1093/ijlit/eaz006

Anderson, R. J. (2008). *Security engineering: A guide to building dependable distributed systems* (2nd ed.). Wiley. ISBN: 978-0470068526.

Arena, M., & Azzone, G. (2009). Identifying organizational drivers of internal audit effectiveness. *International Journal of Auditing*, 13, 43–60. https://doi.org/10.1111/j.1099-1123.2008.00392.x

Association of Healthcare Internal Auditors (AHIA) and Deloitte. (2017). *Cyber assurance: How internal audit, compliance and information technology can fight the good fight together?* Retrieved from https://ahia.org/assets/Uploads/pdfUpload/WhitePapers/CyberAssuranceWhitePaper.pdf

ASX Corporate Governance Council. (2019). *Corporate governance principles and recommendations* (4th ed.). Retrieved from https://www.asx.com.au/documents/asx-compliance/cgc-principles-and-recommendations-fourth-edn.pdf

Banerjee, J., Basu, K., & Sen, A. (2018). On hardening problems in critical infrastructure systems. *International Journal of Critical Infrastructure Protection*, 23, 49–67. https://doi.org/10.1016/j.ijcip.2018.08.001

Bantleon, U., d'Arcy, A., Eulerich, M., Hucke, A., Pedell, B., & Ratzinger-Sakel, N. (2020). *Coordination challenges in implementing the three lines of defense model.* Retrieved from https://ssrn.com/abstract=3663955

Basel Committee on Banking Supervision. (2018). *Cyber-resilience: Range of practices.* Retrieved from https://www.bis.org/bcbs/publ/d454.pdf

Bejtlich, R. (2013). *The practice of network security monitoring: Understanding incident detection and response.* No Starch Press. ISBN: 978-1593275099.

Benaroch, M., & Fink, L. (2021). No rose without a thorn: Board IT competence and market reactions to operational IT failures. *Information & Management*, 58(8), 103546. https://doi.org/10.1016/j.im.2021.103546

Bouraffa, T., & Hui, K.-L. (2025). Regulating information and network security: Review and challenges. *ACM Computing Surveys*, 57(5), Article 126, 38 pages. https://doi.org/10.1145/3711124

Bozkus Kahyaoglu, S., & Caliyurt, K. (2018). Cyber security assurance process from the internal audit perspective. *Managerial Auditing Journal*, 33(4), 360–376. https://doi.org/10.1108/MAJ-02-2018-1804

Calder, A. (2016). *IT governance: Implementing frameworks and standards for the corporate governance of IT* (English edition). IT Governance Publishing. ASIN: B01F5AF5S6.

Cappelli, D., Moore, A., & Trzeciak, R. (2012). *The CERT guide to insider threats: How to prevent, detect, and respond to information technology crimes*. Addison-Wesley Professional. ISBN: 978-0321812575.

Chambers, A. D. (2014). The current state of internal auditing: A personal perspective and assessment. *EDPACS*, 49(1), 1-14. https://doi.org/10.1080/07366981.2014.869962

Chartered Institute of Internal Auditors. (2021). *Mind the gap: Cybersecurity risk in the new normal*. Retrieved from https://www.iia.org.uk/media/1691585/cyber-security-risk-in-the-new-normal-report.pdf

Chen, Y., et al. (2022). *Trauma-informed computing: Towards safer technology experiences*. Proceedings of the CHI Conference on Human Factors in Computing Systems, 1-16. https://emtseng.me/assets/Chen-2022-CHI_Trauma-Informed-Computing.pdf

Christ, M. H., Eulerich, M., Krane, R., & Wood, D. A. (2021). New frontiers for internal audit research. *Accounting Perspectives*, 20(4), 449-475. https://doi.org/10.1111/1911-3838.12272

Coleman, D. D., & Westcott, D. A. (2018). *CWNA Certified Wireless Network Administrator Study Guide: Exam CWNA-107*. Wiley. ISBN: 978-1119425786.

Common Body of Knowledge (CBOK). (2015). *Institute of Internal Auditors Research Foundation*. Retrieved from https://global.theiia.org/iiarf/Public%20Documents/CBOK-2015-Vision-Brochure.pdf

Corten, M., Steijvers, T., & Lybaert, N. (2018). Auditor choice in private firms: A stakeholders' perspective. *Managerial Auditing Journal*, 33(2), 146-170. https://doi.org/10.1108/MAJ-03-2017-1535

Cotteleer, M. J., et al. (2021). *Cybersecurity requirements for AM systems*. In Proceedings of the 2021 Workshop on Additive Manufacturing (3D Printing) Security. ACM. https://doi.org/10.1145/3462223.3485624

Currie, G., & Spyridonidis, D. (2016). Interpretation of multiple institutional logics on the ground: Actors' positions, their agency and situational constraints in professionalized contexts. *Organization Studies*, 37(1), 77-97. https://doi.org/10.1177/0170840615604503

BIBLIOGRAPHY

D'Orazio, C. J., & Choo, K.-K. R. (2017). A technique to circumvent SSL/TLS validations on iOS devices. *Future Generation Computer Systems*, 74, 366–374. https://doi.org/10.1016/j.future.2016.08.019

Dai, J., & Vasarhelyi, M. A. (2017). Toward blockchain-based accounting and assurance. *Journal of Information Systems*, 31(3), 5–21. https://doi.org/10.2308/isys-51804

Deloitte. (2019). *The future of cyber survey 2019*. https://www2.deloitte.com/content/dam/Deloitte/us/Documents/finance/us-the-future-of-cyber-survey.pdf

Donaldson, S. E., Siegel, S. G., Williams, C. K., & Aslam, A. (2018). *Enterprise cybersecurity study guide*. Apress. https://doi.org/10.1007/978-1-4842-3258-3

Dutta, A., Roy, R., & Seetharaman, P. (2022). An assimilation maturity model for IT governance and auditing. *Information & Management*, 59(1), 103569. https://doi.org/10.1016/j.im.2021.103569

Dzuranin, A. C., & Malaescu, I. (2016). The current state and future directions of IT audit: Challenges and opportunities. *Journal of Information Systems*, 30(1), 7–20. https://doi.org/10.2308/isys-51315

Easttom, W. C. (2016). *Computer security fundamentals*. Pearson IT Certification. ISBN: 978-0789757463.

Edwards, G. (2019). *Cybercrime investigators handbook*. Wiley. ISBN: 978-1119596288.

Eilam, E. (2005). *Reversing: Secrets of reverse engineering*. Wiley. ISBN: 978-0764574818.

El-Masry, E. E., & Hansen, K. A. (2008). Factors affecting auditors' utilization of evidential cues: Taxonomy and future research directions. *Managerial Auditing Journal*, 23(1), 26–50. https://doi.org/10.1108/02686900810838155

Erasmus, L., & Coetzee, P. (2018). Drivers of stakeholders' view of internal audit effectiveness: Management versus audit committee. *Managerial Auditing Journal*, 33(1), 90–114. https://doi.org/10.1108/MAJ-05-2017-1558

Erickson, J. (2008). *Hacking: The art of exploitation* (2nd ed.). No Starch Press. ISBN: 978-1593271442.

Etzioni, A. (2015). *Privacy in a cyber age: Policy and practice*. Palgrave Macmillan. ISBN978-1-349-70288-6

Eulerich, A., & Eulerich, M. (2020). What is the value of internal auditing? – A literature review on qualitative and quantitative perspectives. *Maandblad Voor*

Accountancy en Bedrijfseconomie, 94(3/4), 83-92. https://doi.org/10.5117/mab.94.50375

European Confederation of Institutes of Internal Auditors. (2020). *Risk in focus 2021: Hot topics for internal auditors*. https://www.eciia.eu/wp-content/uploads/2020/09/100242-RISK-IN-FOCUS-2021-52PP-ECIIA-Online-V2.pdf

Ezzamouri, N., & Hulstijn, J. (2018). *Continuous monitoring and auditing in municipalities*. In Proceedings of the 19th Annual International Conference on Digital Government Research: Governance in the Data Age (pp. 1-10). ACM. https://doi.org/10.1145/3209281.3209301

Feng, X., & Conrad, M. (2018). *Security audit in mobile apps security design*. In ACM International Conference Proceeding Series. Association for Computing Machinery. https://doi.org/10.1145/3207677.3277925

Gale, M., Bongiovanni, I., & Slapnicar, S. (2022). Governing cybersecurity from the boardroom: Challenges, drivers, and ways ahead. *Computers & Security*, 121, 102840. https://doi.org/10.1016/j.cose.2022.102840

Gale, M., Bongiovanni, I., & Slapničar, S. (2022). Governing cybersecurity from the boardroom: Challenges, drivers, and ways ahead. *Computers & Security*, 121, 102840. https://doi.org/10.1016/j.cose.2022.102840

Gauthier, M. P., & Brender, N. (2021). How do the current auditing standards fit the emergent use of blockchain? *Managerial Auditing Journal*, 36(3), 365-385. https://doi.org/10.1108/MAJ-12-2019-2513

Gosling, M. (2020). Compliance is not a cybersecurity strategy. In *Navigating the digital age. The definitive cybersecurity guide for directors and officers* (pp. 177-186). Palo Alto Networks.

Gray, I., Crawford, L., & Manson, S. (2019). *The audit process: Principles, practice and cases* (7th ed.). Cengage Learning. ISBN: 978-1473760189

Haapamäki, E. (2022). Insights into neo-institutional theory in accounting and auditing regulation research. *Managerial Auditing Journal*, 37(3), 336-357. https://doi.org/10.1108/MAJ-10-2020-2864

Haapamäki, E. and Sihvonen, J. (2019), Cybersecurity in accounting research. *Managerial Auditing Journal*, 34(7), 808-834. https://doi.org/10.1108/MAJ-09-2018-2004

Hadnagy, C. (2018). *Social engineering: The science of human hacking* (2nd ed.). Wiley. ISBN: 978-1119433385.

BIBLIOGRAPHY

Hagen, J., & Toftegaard, O. (2022). Cyber security requirements in the Norwegian energy sector. In *IFIP advances in information and communication technology* (pp. 3-21). Springer. https://doi.org/10.1007/978-3-030-93511-5_1

Hall, J. A. (2015). *Information technology auditing* (4th ed.). Cengage Learning. ISBN: 9781305985384

Harichandran, V. S., Breitinger, F., Baggili, I., & Marrington, A. (2016). A cyber forensics needs analysis survey: Revisiting the domain's needs a decade later. *Computers & Security*, 57, 1-13. https://doi.org/10.1016/j.cose.2015.10.007

Hayes, D. R. (2014). *A practical guide to computer forensics investigations.* Pearson IT Certification. ISBN: 978-0789741158.

Hazaea, S. A., Zhu, J., Khatib, S. F., & Elamer, A. A. (2023). Mapping the literature of internal auditing in Europe: A systematic review and agenda for future research. *Meditari Accountancy Research*, 31(6), 1675-1706. https://doi.org/10.1108/MEDAR-01-2022-1584

Hoag, J. (2013). Evolution of a cybersecurity curriculum. In *Proceedings of the 2013 on InfoSecCD '13 Information Security Curriculum Development Conference – InfoSecCD '13* (pp. 94-99). ACM. https://doi.org/10.1145/2528908.2528925

Hofnagle, C. J., van der Sloot, B., & Borgesius, F. Z. (2019). The European Union General Data Protection Regulation: What it is and what it means. *Information & Communications Technology Law*, 28(1), 65-98. https://doi.org/10.1080/13600834.2019.1573501

Hossain, M. S., Belina, H., Hasan, M. M., & Kim, M. M. (2024). The effects of auditor-level cybersecurity breaches on auditor-client relationships. *European Accounting Review*, 1-28. https://doi.org/10.1080/09638180.2024.2435389

Ibrahim, A., Valli, C., McAteer, I., & Chaudhry, J. (2018). A security review of local government using NIST CSF: A case study. *Journal of Supercomputing*, 74(10), 5171-5186. https://doi.org/10.1007/s11227-018-2479-2

Ignat, G., Şargu, L., Bivol, T., Bivol-Nigel, A., & Şargu, N. (2020). Studies on the importance of internal audit in detection of risks. In *Proceedings of the International Conference Digital Age: Traditions, Modernity and Innovations (ICDATMI 2020)*. Atlantis Press. https://doi.org/10.2991/assehr.k.201212.030

ISACA. (2018). *Cybersecurity audit certificate study guide. Information systems audit and control association.* ISBN 1604207590, 9781604207590.

ISACA. (2021). *Certified Information Systems Auditor (CISA) review manual 2021.* ISACA.

Islam, M. S., Farah, N., & Stafford, T. F. (2018). Factors associated with security/cybersecurity audit by internal audit function. *Managerial Auditing Journal*, 33(4), 377–409. https://doi.org/10.1108/MAJ-07-2017-1595

Islam, M. S., Farah, N., & Stafford, T. F. (2018). Factors associated with security/cybersecurity audit by internal audit function. *Managerial Auditing Journal*, 33(4), 377–409. https://doi.org/10.1108/MAJ-07-2017-1595

Jacobs, J., & Rudis, B. (2014). *Data-driven security: Analysis, visualization and dashboards*. Wiley. ISBN: 978-1118793725.

Jeyraj, A., & Zadeh, A. (2020). Institutional isomorphism in organizational cybersecurity: A text analytics approach. *Journal of Organizational Computing and Electronic Commerce*, 30(4), 361–380. https://doi.org/10.1080/10919392.2020.1776033

Johnson, J. (2019). The AI-cyber nexus: Implications for military escalation, deterrence and strategic stability. *Journal of Cyber Policy*, 4(3), 442–460. https://doi.org/10.1080/23738871.2019.1701693

Johnson, R., & Weiss, M. (2023). *Auditing IT infrastructures for compliance with theory labs* (3rd ed.). Jones & Bartlett Learning. ISBN: 9781284249156.

Kaeo, M. (2003). *Designing network security* (2nd ed.). Macmillan Technical Publishing. ISBN: 978-1587051173.

Kahyaoglu, S., & Çaliyurt, K. (2018). Cyber security assurance process from the internal audit perspective. *Managerial Auditing Journal*, 33(4), 360–376. https://doi.org/10.1108/MAJ-02-2018-1804

Kamiya, S., Kang, J. K., Kim, J., Milidonis, A., & Stulz, R. M. (2021). Risk management, firm reputation, and the impact of successful cyberattacks on target firms. *Journal of Financial Economics*, 139(3), 719–749. https://doi.org/10.1016/j.jfineco.2019.05.019

Khan, S. N., Asad, M., Fatima, A., Anjum, K., & Akhtar, K. (2020). Outsourcing internal audit services: A review. *International Journal of Management*, 11(8), 503–517. https://doi.org/10.34218/IJM.11.8.2020.04

Klarskov Jeppesen, K., & Leder, C. (2016). Auditors' experience with corporate psychopaths. *Journal of Financial Crime*, 23(4), 870–881. https://doi.org/10.1108/JFC-05-2015-0026

Knapp, E. D., & Langill, J. T. (2014). *Industrial network security: Securing critical infrastructure networks for smart grid, SCADA, and other industrial control systems* (2nd ed.). Syngress. ISBN: 978-0124201149

Kotb, A., Elbardan, H., & Halabi, H. (2020). Mapping of internal audit research: A post-Enron structured literature review. *Accounting, Auditing & Accountability Journal*, 33(8), 1969–1996. https://doi.org/10.1108/AAAJ-07-2018-3581

Krutz, R. L., & Vines, R. D. (2010). *Cloud security: A comprehensive guide to secure cloud computing.* Wiley. ISBN: 978-0470589878.

Lankton, N., Price, J. B., & Karim, M. (2021). Cybersecurity breaches and information technology governance roles in audit committee charters. *Journal of Information Systems*, 35(1), 101–119. https://doi.org/10.2308/isys-18-071

Lenz, R., & Hahn, U. (2015). A synthesis of the empirical internal audit effectiveness literature and new research opportunities. *Managerial Auditing Journal*, 30(1), 5–33. https://doi.org/10.1108/MAJ-08-2014-1072

Lenz, R., Sarens, G., & Jeppesen, K. K. (2018). In search of a measure of effectiveness for internal audit functions: An institutional perspective EDPACS – The EDP audit. *EDPACS*, 58(2), 1–36. https://doi.org/10.1080/07366981.2018.1511324

Lin, S., Pizzini, M., Vargus, M., & Bardhan, I. R. (2011). The role of the internal audit function in the disclosure of material weaknesses. *The Accounting Review*, 86(1), 287–323. https://doi.org/10.2308/accr.00000016

Linden, T., Khandelwal, R., Harkous, H., & Fawaz, K. (2020). The privacy policy landscape after the GDPR. *Proceedings on Privacy Enhancing Technologies*, 1, 47–64. https://doi.org/10.2478/popets-2020-0004

Livshitz, I. I., Lontsikh, P. A., Lontsikh, N. P., Golovina, E. Y., & Safonova, O. M. (2020). *The effects of cyber-security risks on added value of consulting services for IT-security management systems in holding companies.* Proceedings of the 2020 IEEE International Conference "Quality Management, Transport and Information Security, Information Technologies" (IT and QM and IS 2020), 119–122. Institute of Electrical and Electronics Engineers Inc. https://doi.org/10.1109/ITQMIS51053.2020.9322883

Maalem Lahcen, R. A., Caulkins, B., Mohapatra, R., & Kumar, M. (2020). Review and insight on the behavioral aspects of cybersecurity. *Cybersecurity*, 3(1), 10. https://doi.org/10.1186/s42400-020-00050-w

Markopoulou, M., & Papakonstantinou, V. (2021). The regulatory framework for the protection of critical infrastructures against cyberthreats: Identifying shortcomings and addressing future challenges: The case of the health sector in particular. *Computer Law and Security Review*, 41, 105502. https://doi.org/10.1016/j.clsr.2020.105502

Melshiyan, M. A., & Dushkin, A. V. (2022). *Information security audit using open source intelligence methods.* Proceedings of the 2022 Conference of Russian Young

Researchers in Electrical and Electronic Engineering (ElConRus 2022), 379–382. Institute of Electrical and Electronics Engineers Inc. https://doi.org/10.1109/ElConRus54750.2022.9755530

Mihret, D. G., & Grant, B. (2017). The role of internal auditing in corporate governance: A Foucauldian analysis. *Accounting, Auditing & Accountability Journal*, 30(3), 699–719. https://doi.org/10.1108/AAAJ-10-2012-1134

Mitnick, K. D., & Simon, W. L. (2011). *Ghost in the wires: My adventures as the world's most wanted hacker.* Little, Brown and Company. ISBN: 978-0316037709.

Moeller, R. (2010). *IT audit, control, and security.* Wiley. https://doi.org/10.1002/9781118269138

No, W. G., & Vasarhelyi, M. A. (2017). Cybersecurity and continuous assurance. *Journal of Emerging Technologies in Accounting*, 14(1), 1–12. https://doi.org/10.2308/jeta-10539

Nokhbeh Zaeem, R., Manoharan, M., Yang, Y., & Barber, K. S. (2017). Modeling and analysis of identity threat behaviors through text mining of identity theft stories. *Computers & Security*, 65, 50–63. https://doi.org/10.1016/j.cose.2016.11.002

Northcutt, S. (2002). *Network intrusion detection.* Sams Publishing. ISBN: 978-0735712652.

O'Hara, B. T., & Malisow, B. (2017). *CCSP (ISC)² certified cloud security professional official study guide.* Wiley. ISBN: 978-1119277415.

Otero, L. D. (2020). *Information technology control and audit* (5th ed.). CRC Press. ISBN 9780367657154

Oussii, A. A., & Boulila Taktak, N. (2018). The impact of internal audit function characteristics on internal control quality. *Managerial Auditing Journal*, 33(5), 450–469. https://doi.org/10.1108/MAJ-06-2017-1579

Polański, P. P. (2017). Cyberspace: A new branch of international customary law? *Computer Law & Security Review*, 33(3), 371–381. https://doi.org/10.1016/j.clsr.2017.03.007

Rae, K. and Subramaniam, N. (2008). Quality of internal control procedures: Antecedents and moderating effect on organisational justice and employee fraud. *Managerial Auditing Journal*, 23(2), 104–124. https://doi.org/10.1108/02686900810839820

Rosati, P., Gogolin, F., & Lynn, T. (2020). Cyber-security incidents and audit quality. *The European Accounting Review*, 31(3), 701–728. https://doi.org/10.1080/09638180.2020.1856162

BIBLIOGRAPHY

Rothrock, R. A., Kaplan, J., & Van Der Oord, F. (2018). The board's role in managing cyber security risks. *MIT Sloan Management Review*, 59(2), 12–15.

Russell, B., & Van Duren, D. (2016). *Practical Internet of Things security*. Packt Publishing. ISBN: 978-1785889639.

Sabillon, R., Serra-Ruiz, J., Cavaller, V., & Cano, J. (2017). *A comprehensive cybersecurity audit model to improve cybersecurity assurance: The cybersecurity audit model (CSAM)*. In 2017 International Conference on Information Systems and Computer Science (INCISCOS), Quito, Ecuador (pp. 253–259). https://doi.org/10.1109/INCISCOS.2017.20

Sabillon, R., Serra-Ruiz, J., Cavaller, V., & Cano, J. (2018). *A comprehensive cybersecurity audit model to improve cybersecurity assurance: The cybersecurity audit model (CSAM)*. In Proceedings – 2017 International Conference on Information Systems and Computer Science (INCISCOS 2017) (pp. 253–259). IEEE. https://doi.org/10.1109/INCISCOS.2017.20

Sanchez-Garcia, I. D., Rea-Guaman, A. M., Gilabert, T. S., & Calvo-Manzano, J. A. (2024). Cybersecurity risk audit: A systematic literature review. In J. Mejía, M. Muñoz, A. Rocha, Y. Hernández Pérez, & H. Avila-George (Eds.), *New perspectives in software engineering* (Vol. 1135, pp. XX–XX). Springer, Cham. https://doi.org/10.1007/978-3-031-50590-4_18

Santos, H. M. D. (2022). *Cybersecurity: A practical engineering approach*. Chapman and Hall/CRC. ISBN: 978-0367252427

Sarens, G., Abdolmohammadi, M. J., & Lenz, R. (2012). Factors associated with the internal audit function's role in corporate governance. *Journal of Applied Accounting Research*, 13(2), 191–204. https://doi.org/10.1108/09675421211254876

Sarens, G., De Beelde, I., & Everaert, P. (2009). Internal audit: A comfort provider to the audit committee. *The British Accounting Review*, 41(2), 90–106. https://doi.org/10.1016/j.bar.2009.02.002

Schneier, B. (2015). *Data and Goliath: The hidden battles to collect your data and control your world*. W. W. Norton & Company. ISBN: 978-0393352177.

Schneier, B. (2020). *Click here to kill everybody: Security and survival in a hyper-connected world*. W. W. Norton & Company. ISBN: 978-0393357448.

Shostack, A. (2014). *Threat modeling: Designing for security*. Wiley. ISBN: 978-1118809990.

Singer, P. W., & Friedman, A. (2014). *Cybersecurity and cyberwar: What everyone needs to know®*. Oxford University Press. ISBN: 978-0199918119.

Slapničar, S., Axelsen, M., Bongiovanni, I., & Stockdale, D. (2023). A pathway model to five lines of accountability in cybersecurity governance. *International Journal of Accounting Information Systems*, 51, 100642. https://doi.org/10.1016/j.accinf.2023.100642

Slapničar, S., Vuko, T., Čular, M., & Draček, M. (2022). Effectiveness of cybersecurity audit. *International Journal of Accounting Information Systems*, 44, 100548. https://doi.org/10.1016/j.accinf.2021.100548

Slapničar, S., Vuko, T., Čular, M., & Draček, M. (2022). Effectiveness of cybersecurity audit. *International Journal of Accounting Information Systems*, 44, 100548. https://doi.org/10.1016/j.accinf.2021.100548

Spears, J. L., Barki, H., & Barton, R. R. (2013). Theorizing the concept and role of assurance in information systems security. *Information & Management*, 50(7), 598-605. https://doi.org/10.1016/j.im.2013.08.004

Stafford, T., Deitz, G., & Li, Y. (2018). The role of internal audit and user training in information security policy compliance. *Managerial Auditing Journal*, 33(4), 410-424. https://doi.org/10.1108/MAJ-07-2017-1596

Steinbart, P. J., Raschke, R. L., Gal, G., & Dilla, W. N. (2012). The relationship between internal audit and information security: An exploratory investigation. *International Journal of Accounting Information Systems*, 13(3), 228-243. https://doi.org/10.1016/j.accinf.2012.06.007

Steinbart, P. J., Raschke, R. L., Gal, G., & Dilla, W. N. (2016). SECURQUAL: An instrument for evaluating the effectiveness of enterprise information security programs. *Journal of Information Systems*, 30(1), 71-92. https://doi.org/10.2308/isys-51257

Steinbart, P. J., Raschke, R. L., Gal, G., & Dilla, W. N. (2018). The influence of a good relationship between the internal audit and information security functions on information security outcomes. *Accounting, Organizations and Society*, 71, 15-29. https://doi.org/10.1016/j.aos.2018.04.005

Steinbart, P. J., Raschke, R., Gal, G., & Dilla, W. (2012). The relationship between internal audit and information security: An exploratory investigation. *International Journal of Accounting Information Systems*, 13(3), 228-243. https://doi.org/10.1016/j.accinf.2012.06.007

Sun, N., Li, C.-T., Chan, H., Islam, M. Z., Islam, M. R., & Armstrong, W. (2022). How do organizations seek cyber assurance? Investigations on the adoption of the Common Criteria and beyond. *IEEE Access*, 10, 71749-71763. https://doi.org/10.1109/ACCESS.2022.3187211

Tazilah, M. D., Majid, M., & Suffari, N. F. (2019). Effects of outsourcing internal audit functions among small & medium enterprises. *International Journal of Business and Technology Management*, 1(1), 28-34.

Timpson, D., & Moradian, E. (2018). A methodology to enhance industrial control system security. *Procedia Computer Science*, 126, 2117-2126. https://doi.org/10.1016/j.procs.2018.07.240

Toapanta, S. M. T., Peralta, N. A., & Gallegos, L. E. M. (2019). Definition of parameters to perform audit in cybersecurity for public one organization of Ecuador. In ACM International Conference Proceeding Series. Association for Computing Machinery. https://doi.org/10.1145/3375900.3375913

Turetken, O., Jethefer, S., & Ozkan, B. (2019). Internal audit effectiveness: Operationalization and influencing factors. *Managerial Auditing Journal*, 35(2), 238-271. https://doi.org/10.1108/MAJ-08-2018-1980

Ultra, J. D., & Pancho-Festin, S. (2017). A simple model of separation of duty for access control models. *Computers & Security*, 68, 69-80. https://doi.org/10.1016/j.cose.2017.03.012

Vadasi, C., Bekiaris, M., & Andrikopoulos, A. (2019). Corporate governance and internal audit: An institutional theory perspective. *Corporate Governance*, 20(1), 175-190. https://doi.org/10.1108/CG-07-2019-0215

Veltrop, D. B., Molleman, E., Hooghiemstra, R., & van Ees, H. (2018). The relationship between tenure and outside director task involvement: A social identity perspective. *Journal of Management*, 44(2), 445-469. https://doi.org/10.1177/0149206315579510

Verma, P. (2017). Unconditional security through quantum uncertainty. *International Journal of Critical Infrastructure Protection*, 16, 36-38. https://doi.org/10.1016/j.ijcip.2016.09.001

Viega, J., & McGraw, G. (2001). *Building secure software: How to avoid security problems the right way*. Addison-Wesley. ISBN: 978-0201721522.

Vuko, T., Slapničar, S., Čular, M., & Drašček, M. (2024). Key drivers of cybersecurity audit effectiveness: A neo-institutional perspective. *International Journal of Auditing*. https://doi.org/10.1111/ijau.12365

Wallace, L., Lin, H., & Cefaratti, M. A. (2011). Information security and Sarbanes-Oxley compliance: An exploratory study. *Journal of Information Systems*, 25(1), 185-211. https://doi.org/10.2308/jis.2011.25.1.185

Weber, P. A., Zhang, N., & Wu, H. (2020). A comparative analysis of personal data protection regulations between the EU and China. *Electronic Commerce Research*, 20(3), 565–587. https://doi.org/10.1007/s10660-020-09422-3

Wilkin, C. L., & Chenhall, R. H. (2020). Information technology governance: Reflections on the past and future directions. *Journal of Information Systems*, 34(2), 257–292. https://doi.org/10.2308/isys-52632

Yoo, C. W., Goo, J., & Rao, H. R. (2020). Is cybersecurity a team sport? A multilevel examination of workgroup information security effectiveness. *MIS Quarterly*, 44(2), 907–931. https://doi.org/10.25300/MISQ/2020/15477

Zhang, X., Yadollahi, M. M., Dadkhah, S., Isah, H., Le, D.-P., & Ghorbani, A. A. (2022). Data breach: Analysis, countermeasures, and challenges. *International Journal of Information and Computer Security*, 19(3/4). https://doi.org/10.1504/IJICS.2023.10050154

Zhou, L., Thieret, R., Watzlaf, V., Dealmeida, D., & Parmanto, B. (2019). A telehealth privacy and security self-assessment questionnaire for telehealth providers: Development and validation. *International Journal of Telerehabilitation*, 11(1), 3–14. https://doi.org/10.5195/ijt.2019.6276

Zrahia, A. (2018). Threat intelligence sharing between cybersecurity vendors: Network, dyadic, and agent views. *Journal of Cybersecurity*, 4(1), tyy008. https://doi.org/10.1093/cybsec/tyy008

Abbreviations

AD	Active Directory
AES	Advanced Encryption Standard
AI	Artificial Intelligence
AICPA	American Institute of Certified Public Accountants
AOC	Attestation of Compliance
API	Application Programming Interface
AR	Augmented Reality
APT	Advanced Persistent Threats
AWS	Amazon Web Services
BC/DR	Business Continuity and Disaster Recovery
BCP	Business Continuity Plan
BI	Business Intelligence
BIA	Business Impact Analysis
CASB	Cloud Access Security Broker
CCM	Cloud Controls Matrix
CCPA	California Consumer Privacy Act
CDE	Cardholder Data Environment
CI/CD	Continuous Integration/Continuous Deployment
CIRT	Cross-functional Incident Response Team
CISA	Certified Information Systems Auditor
CIS-CAT	Center for Internet Security Configuration Assessment Tool
CISSP	Certified Information Systems Security Professional
CMDB	Configuration Management Database

ABBREVIATIONS

COSO ERM	Committee of Sponsoring Organizations of the Treadway Commission Enterprise Risk Management
CRA	Cyber Resilience Act
CSP	Cloud Service Provider
CSPM	Cloud Security Posture Management
CVE	Common Vulnerabilities and Exposures
CVSS	Common Vulnerability Scoring System
DAST	Dynamic Application Security Testing
DFD	Data Flow Diagram
DLP	Data Loss Prevention
DORA	Digital Operational Resilience Act
DPA	Data Processing Agreement
DPIA	Data Protection Impact Assessment
DPO	Data Protection Officer
DSAR	Data Subject Access Request
EDPB	European Data Protection Board
EDR	Endpoint Detection and Response
ELK	Elasticsearch, Logstash, Kibana
ENISA	European Union Agency for Cybersecurity
ERP	Enterprise Resource Planning
ESG	Environmental, Social, and Governance
EU	The European Union
FAIR	Factor Analysis of Information Risk
FDE	Full-Disk Encryption
FISMA	Federal Information Security Management Act
GDPR	General Data Protection Regulation
GRC	Governance, Risk, and Compliance
HER	Electronic Health Record

ABBREVIATIONS

HIPAA	Health Insurance Portability and Accountability Act
HR	Human Resources
HTTP/S	Hypertext Transfer Protocol/Secure
HVAC	Heating, Ventilation, and Air Conditioning
IAM	Identity and Access Management
ICT	Information and Communication Technology
IDOR	Insecure Direct Object References
IDS	Intrusion Detection Systems
IoCs	Indicators of Compromise
IP	Internet Protocol
IPS	Intrusion Prevention Systems
IR	Incident Response
IRP	Incident Response Plan
ISMS	Information Security Management System
ISO/IEC	International Organization for Standardization/International Electrotechnical Commission
IT	information technology
ITAM	IT Asset Management
ITSM	IT Service Management
KMS	Key Management Service
MDM	Mobile Device Management
MFA	Multi-Factor Authentication
MITM	Man-in-the-Middle Attack
MITRE ATT&CK	Adversarial Tactics, Techniques, and Common Knowledge
ML	Machine Learning
MRI	Magnetic Resonance Imaging
MSSP	Managed Security Service Provider

ABBREVIATIONS

MTTD	Mean Time to Detect
MTTR	Mean Time to Respond
NAC	Network Access Control
NIS	Network and Information Systems Directive
NIST CSF	National Institute of Standards and Technology - Cybersecurity Framework
NPM	Network Performance Monitor
NVD	National Vulnerability Database
OCTAVE	Operationally Critical Threat, Asset, and Vulnerability Evaluation
OSINT	Open-Source Intelligence
OT	Operational Technology
OWASP	The Open Worldwide Application Security Project
PAM	Privileged Access Management
PCI DSS	Payment Card Industry Data Security Standard
PHI	Patient Health Information
PIA	Privacy Impact Assessments
PII	Personally Identifiable Information
POLP	Principle of Least Privilege
POS	Point-of-Sale
QA	Quality Assurance
QSA	Qualified Security Assessor
RACI	Responsible, Accountable, Consulted, and Informed
RBAC	Role-Based Access Control
R&D	Research and Development
RFI	Request for Information
RFID	Radio-Frequency Identification
RMF	Risk Management Framework
RMP	Risk Management Plan
ROC	Report on Compliance

ABBREVIATIONS

ROI	Return on Investment
RPO	Recovery Point Objectives
RTO	Recovery Time Objectives
SANS	SysAdmin, Audit, Network, and Security
SAP	System Applications and Products
SAQ	Self-Assessment Questionnaire
SAST	Static Application Security Testing
SCA	Static Code Analyzer
SCCM	System Center Configuration Manager
SDLC	Software Development Lifecycle
SIEM	Security Information and Event Management
SMART	Specific, Measurable, Achievable, Relevant, and Time-bound
SOAR	Security Orchestration, Automation, and Response
SOC	System and Organization Controls
SOX	Sarbanes-Oxley Act
SQL	Structured Query Language
SSL	Secure Sockets Layer
SSO	Single Sign-On
STRIDE	Spoofing, Tampering, Repudiation, Information Disclosure, Denial of Service, and Elevation of Privilege
TIP	Threat Intelligence Platforms
TLS	Transport Layer Security
TPM	Trusted Platform Module
TSC	Trust Services Criteria
UBA	User Behavior Analytics
UEBA	User and Entity Behavior Analytics
VPN	Virtual Private Network

ABBREVIATIONS

VR	Virtual Reality
WSUS	Windows Server Update Services
XDR	Extended Detection and Response
XSS	Cross-Site Scripting

Index

A

Access management controls
  active accounts, 197
  auditing process, 195, 196
  challenges, 197–199
  components, 194
    accuracy/timeliness, 194
    methods, 194
    monitoring, 195
    policies, 194
  comprehensive, 195
  critical aspect, 193
  financial records, 196
  foundational element, 192
  insider threats, 193
  key points, 199
  principles, 192
  regulatory frameworks, 194
  remote workers, 197
  sensitive information, 193
  technologies/tools, 196
  types of, 192
  unauthorized access, 194
Access management/encryption tools
  AI/ML tools, 548
  auditing processes, 537
  biometrics/passwordless
    authentication, 549
  blockchain, 549
  centralization, 546
  cloud-native/SaaS-based
    solutions, 549
  collaboration, 550
  critical systems/sensitive
    information, 536
  DevSecOps pipelines, 549
  enforce least privilege, 546
  FDE tools, 545, 546
  full disk encryption, 550
  human error, 538
  hybrid environments, 538
  IAM solutions, 538–540
  IAM tools, 536
  key points, 551, 552
  PAM tools, 536, 541, 542, 549
  password creation, 537
  password management, 537, 542, 543
  PETs techniques, 550
  real-time detection, 538
  real-world process, 546–548
  regulatory frameworks, 538
  sensitive systems, 536
  zero trust principles, 548
Action plans
  benefits, 653
  development, 650
    assigning ownership, 651
    categorization, 650
    objectives, 651
    prioritization, 650
    resource allocation, 651
    timelines, 651
  implementation, 652
    handling challenges, 652

INDEX

Action plans (*cont.*)
    monitoring progress, 652
    track progress, 652
  key points, 653
  recommendations, 649
Advanced Encryption Standard (AES), 61
American Institute of Certified Public Accountants (AICPA), 255
Application programming interface (API), 201
  automate testing, 584
  Postman, 580
  ReadyAPI, 580
  testing tools, 580
Artificial intelligence (AI), 267, 314
  automation tools, 523
  cyber risk management, 341
  risk management/GRC tools, 560
Assessment process
  asset identification, 380
  automation, 388
  business objectives, 389
  challenges and solutions, 384–386
  communicate results, 383
  comprehensive documentation, 388
  cross-functional teams, 386
  evaluation/effective, 378
  finding documentation, 382
  identification, 377
  key points, 390, 391
  likelihood/impact, 381
  mitigation plan, 378, 382
  monitoring and periodic updates, 383
  qualitative/quantitative metrics, 381
  regular/iterative, 387
  risk levels, 381
  scope/objectives, 379, 380
  security-first culture, 390
  standardized methodologies, 386
  strategic planning, 377, 378
  systematic approach, 377
  threat intelligence, 387
  threats, 380, 381
  vulnerabilities, 381
  well-structured communication, 389
  workflow, 379, 380
Audit lifecycle
  analysis/evaluation, 70
  fieldwork/testing, 69
  flowchart, 66, 67
  follow-up/continuous improvement, 72
  key points, 73
  meaning, 66
  planning phase, 67, 68
  recommendations, 72
  reporting phase, 71
  risk assessment, 68
Auditors, 709
  activities, 740
  analysis/documentation, 740, 741
  analytical/problem-solving skills, 62
  attention to detail, 64
  capabilities/role, 59
  communication skills, 63, 64
  environments, 743
  frameworks/regulations, 61
  key points, 65, 66, 745
  planning/prioritization, 738, 739
  reflection/continuous learning, 742
  resistance, 743
  risk assessment/management, 62, 63
  stakeholders, 741, 742
  technical assessments, 739
  technical concepts, 60, 61
  technical depth/communication, 744

technical/non-technical
audiences, 741
threat landscape, 744
time constraints, 743
tools and technologies, 64
treat security issues, 66
Audit reports, 603
accuracy, 607
actionable recommendations, 603, 608
audiences, 607
clear/concise, 607
common mistakes, 609
continuous communication, 667–674
detailed findings section, 603
essential components, 604
    appendices, 607
    executive summary, 605
    findings section, 606
    methodology section, 606
    recommendations, 606
    scope and objectives, 605
executive summary
    benefits, 628, 630
    call action, 628
    creation, 625
    definition, 630–632
    elements, 626
    findings, 629
    key benefits, 625
    key findings, 627
    key points, 631
    objective, 626, 629
    professional/engaging steps, 629
    recommendations, 628, 630
    risk assessment, 627, 630
    scope outlines, 627
    senior executives, 625
follow-up audits, 654–658
handling disputes, 659–667
    accuracy, 660
    actively listening, 661
    clear communication, 662
    collaboration, 662
    cyclic workflow, 665, 666
    efficient/constructive, 663
    escalation, 663
    findings, 659
    key points, 666, 667
    misinterpretations, 659
    objectivity, 661
    opportunities, 664
    organizational security/culture, 664
    primary goal, 659
    priorities, 659
    resistance, 660
    resource constraints, 660
    risk-based approach, 661
key points, 610
objective, 608
reporting, 632
stakeholders, 604
technical findings, 610
tools, 608
visuals, 617–625
Audit tools
balancing features and budget, 588
capabilities, 588
complex tasks, 586
compliance mapping, 589
customization, 588
data analysis capabilities, 589
factors, 587
integration, 588
key features, 588
key points, 591
misconfigurations

Audit tools (*cont.*)
    alerting mechanisms, 599
    configuration, 597
    credentials, 598
    default settings, 598
    integration, 598
    issues, 596
    key points, 600
    lenient configurations, 599
    patches/threat intelligence, 598
    proactive approach, 596, 599
    scoping, 598
  modern environments, 587
  objectives, 587
  organizational objectives, 590
  real-time monitoring, 588
  recommendations/reviews, 590
  reporting/visualization, 590
  scalable solutions, 591
  strategic approach, 586
  testing, 590
  threat intelligence, 588, 590
  vendors, 590
  vulnerability management, 589
Automation tools
  accuracy, 503
  advantages, 504
  auditing process, 503
  benefits, 521
  compliance monitoring, 505–514
  DevSecOps, 523
  efficiency, 504
  emerging trends, 523
  IoT/edge computing, 523
  key points, 524, 525
  operational costs, 504
  real-time insights, 503, 504
  scalability, 504
  standardization, 504
  TIPs, 521
  vulnerability/log analyzers, 503
  zero trust architecture, 523

B

Blockchain, 267
Business context
  benefits, 108
  challenges, 106–108
  departments, 103
  dynamic environment, 108, 109
  key benefits, 101
  map processes, 103
  objectives, 100
  process flow, 104, 105
  review documentation, 103
  risk landscape/operational priorities, 101–103
  security approaches, 101
  stakeholders, 103
  technologies/tools, 106
  threat intelligence reports, 103
Business continuity
  management, 431
  risk assessment, 437
Business Continuity and Disaster Recovery (BC/DR), 325
Business Continuity Plan (BCP), 325
Business Intelligence (BI), 106

C

California Consumer Privacy Act (CCPA)
  regulatory compliance, 252, 253, 260
Cardholder Data Environment (CDE), 292
Cloud Access Security Brokers (CASBs), 220

INDEX

Cloud computing
  challenges, 692
  environments, 692
    dynamic resources, 693
    multi-cloud setups, 693
    service models, 692
    shared responsibilities, 692
    third-party services, 693
    visibility/control issues, 693
  financial institution, 693
    logging/monitoring, 694
    production systems, 693
    shadow IT, 694
    unencrypted data, 694
  infrastructure/processes, 697
  key points, 698, 699
  opportunities, 698
  proactive strategies
    automation, 695
    challenges, 694
    conduct regular training sessions, 697
    CSPM solution, 696
    CSP-native tools, 695
    encryption, 696
    role-based access controls, 696
    shared responsibilities, 695
    Splunk/Microsoft Sentinel, 696
Cloud security controls
  advantages, 218
  categories, 218
  evaluation, 219, 220
  key points, 224, 225
  strategic approach, 221
  tools and technologies, 220
  unique challenges, 221–223
Cloud Security Posture Management (CSPM), 696

Collaboration tools
  comparison, 568–570
  Confluence, 571
  Google Forms, 570
  Jira, 571
  Microsoft Forms, 569
  real time, 562
  SharePoint, 571
  Slack, 569
  SurveyMonkey, 570
  survey tools, 567
  visual, 562
Common Vulnerabilities and Exposures (CVE), 485
Common Vulnerability Scoring System (CVSS), 356, 367, 368
Communicating compliance gaps
  audience, 308
  benefits, 312, 313
  breaches/penalties, 306
  business objectives, 310
  collaboration platforms, 311
  components, 309
  data-driven insights, 309
  effective, 309
  identification, 305
  key points, 313, 314
  logical structure, 309
  outcome, 312
  presentation, 312
  proactive approach, 310
  process workflow, 307, 308
  project management platforms, 311
  reporting tools, 311
  risk-based approach, 306, 308
  scenario, 312
  tools, 311

INDEX

Compliance
    accountability, 279
    AI platforms, 267
    automation tools, 267
    blockchain, 267
    bodies approach, 268
    business continuity, 270
    challenges/frameworks, 277
    collaboration, 269
    communication, 305–314
    competitiveness, 270
    cyber resilience, 268
    factors, 274
    frameworks, 269
    gathering evidence, 275
    GDPR audits, 279–291
    global standardization, 267
    hospitals and clinics, 277
    legal risks, 273
    multinational forces, 277
    non-compliance findings, 300–305
    offer incentives, 269
    PCI-DSS, 291–300
    prerequisite, 274
    proactive, 267
    quantum technologies, 267
    regulatory, 245
    report findings, 276
    requirements, 279
    resilience, 270
    resources, 270, 278
    retailers, 277
    security controls, 276
    security posture, 273
    stakeholders, 270
    stakeholder trust, 273
    strategies, 268, 269
    systematic approach, 273, 278, 279
    threats/technologies, 277
    vulnerabilities, 269
    workflow diagram, 274
Compliance audits, 17, 18
Compliance frameworks
    auditors, 47
        evidence verification, 47
        gap analyses, 47
        policies/procedures, 47
        technical controls, 47
    automating manual tasks, 49
    benefits
        building trust, 46
        regulatory standards, 46
        risk mitigation, 46
        security controls, 46
        standardization, 46
    challenges
        complexity, 48
        costs, 48
        integration, 49
        updates, 48
    compliance culture, 50
    DORA, 42, 43
    frameworks/regulations, 44–46
    GDPR framework, 42
    HIPAA framework, 42
    ISO/IEC 27001 standard, 41
    key points, 51, 52
    medical guidelines/
        health codes, 40
    NIS2 directive, 43, 44
    NIST CSF, 40
    PCI DSS framework, 41
    REGULATION (EU) 2024/2847, 44
    security frameworks, 50
    stay updated, 49
    structured approach, 40

tailor recommendations, 50
Compliance tools
    AuditBoard, 508
    Azure Security Center, 514
    BigID, 511
    Drata, 512, 513
    Inspector, 513
    LogicGate, 510
    OneTrust, 511
    Onspring, 508
    Qualys, 509
    resolver, 508, 509
    RSA Archer, 510
    SAP Ariba, 512
    strategies, 505–514
    tenable compliance management, 509
    TrustArc, 512
    Tugboat Logic, 513
    Vanta, 511
Configuration Management Database (CMDB), 384
Configuration management tools, 575
    Ansible, 575
    Chef, 576
    CIS-CAT, 576
    OpenSCAP, 577
    Puppet, 576
    standardized configuration, 583
Continuous communication
    assign communication, 669
    benefits, 672
    channels, 669
    collaborative environment, 668
    decision-making, 668
    documentation, 670
    effective communication, 667
    inconsistent updates, 671
    information overload, 671
    key points, 673
    long-term strategies, 671
        development, 671
        knowledge base, 672
        teams, 672
        transparency, 672
    regular updates, 669
    regulatory compliance, 668
    resistance, 668
    stakeholder disengagement, 670
    stakeholders, 667
    strategies, 670
    structured/ongoing communication, 668
    technical data, 669
    technical stakeholders, 670
    transparency, 667
    two-way feedback, 669
Cross-functional Incident Response Team (CIRT), 419
Cross-Site Scripting (XSS), 200
Cyber Resilience Act (CRA)
    regulatory compliance, 257, 258, 262
Cyber risk management
    benefits, 342–345
    challenge, 451
    collaboration, 342
    components
        assessment, 340
        identification, 340
        incident response plan, 341
        mitigation, 340
        monitor threats, 340
    connection, 431
    continuous improvement, 338
    elements of, 338, 451
    emerging technologies, 342

INDEX

Cyber risk management (*cont.*)
    foundation of, 339
    IR, 412
    key points, 345, 346
    mitigation, 391
        acceptance, 394
        administrative controls, 397
        avoidance, 392
        challenges and solutions, 399–401
        decision-making, 395
        department collaboration, 398
        dynamic/continuous process, 394
        key points, 402, 403
        monitoring/testing, 397
        objectives, 391, 392
        organizations, 401
        phishing prevention, 401
        process workflow, 395, 396
        ransomware protection, 401
        reduction, 393
        sharing (transfer), 393
        strategies, 392, 395
        systematic approach, 394
        technical controls, 397
        threats, 396
        tools and technologies, 398
        vendors, 401
    objectives, 339
    organizations, 452
    risk assessment, 377–391
    risk-based audit
        assessment, 405
        automated tools/manual
          techniques, 406
        business context, 405
        challenges and solutions, 408–410
        e-commerce business, 411
        financial institution, 410
        finding reports, 407
        frameworks, 403
        key points, 412, 413
        key risk indicators (KRIs), 406
        medical devices, 411
        organizational goals, 405
        remediation/continuous
          monitoring, 407
        resources, 403
        scope definition, 406
        strategies, 403, 404
        threat landscape, 403
        workflow diagram, 404
    risk scoring/prioritization, 363–376
    RMP, 422
    robust security/business
        functionality, 337
    strategic tool, 451
    structured approach, 337
    technology, 341
        AI/ML solutions, 341
        automation, 341
        cloud platforms, 342
        predictive analytics tools, 341
    third-party risks, 451
    threats, 337
    threats/vulnerabilities, 346–362
Cybersecurity audit
    audit lifecycle, 66–73
    auditor, 59
    compliance, 3
    continuous improvement, 4
    frameworks, 2
    gaps identification, 2
    HIPAA regulations, 4
    holistic review, 5
    incident response, 4
    internal, 6

INDEX

locks/security system, 1
medical check-ups, 5
penetration testing, 52–59
planning, 83
proactive approach, 5
protective approach, 5
risks, 23–31
SIEM tools, 3
software versions, 4
technical/administrative controls, 2
tools/technologies, 74
    automation, 78, 79
    compliance management, 75, 76
    critical issues, 80
    DLP tools, 77
    incident response/forensic tools, 79
    key points, 80
    monitor system, 75
    network monitoring/analysis, 76, 77
    prioritize risks, 78
    risk assessment/management tools, 78
    SIEM platforms, 75
    vulnerability scanners, 74, 75
types of, 13–15
    cloud security, 21
    compliance, 17, 18
    healthcare system, 23
    medical attention, 22
    primary types, 14
    regular, 16–18
    risk, 20, 21
    specialist, 20–22
    structured/systematic approach, 13
    technical approach, 16
vulnerability scanning, 2
weaknesses and gaps, 3

D

Data breaches
    access controls, 679–681
    benefits, 681
    encryption protocols/instances, 679
    findings, 678
    immediate actions, 679
    incident response plan, 681
    key points, 682
    monitoring/logging, 679, 680
    network security, 680
    real-world case, 677
    scope/objectives, 678
    segmentation, 679
    staff training, 680
    system upgrades, 679
    unpatched software, 678
    vulnerabilities, 680, 681
Data Flow Diagrams (DFDs)
    benefits of, 110
    challenges/solutions, 116
    compliance platforms, 116
    components, 111
    creation, 111–114
    document decision, 113
    gathering data, 112
    key benefits, 114–116
    key points, 117, 118
    map data flows, 112
    process flow, 114
    risk identification, 110
    scope definition, 112
    stakeholders, 112
    strategies, 116
    technical/non-technical stakeholders, 109
    tools, 116

Data Flow Diagrams (DFDs) (*cont.*)
    unique advantage, 109
    utilities flow, 110
Data loss prevention (DLP), 77, 212, 214
    comparison, 478, 479
    digital guardian, 480
    Forcepoint, 480
    SIEM system, 466–485
    symantec control, 479, 480
Data Protection Agreements (DPAs), 28
Data Protection Impact Assessments (DPIAs), 248
Data security controls
    access controls, 210
    areas, 212, 213
    backup and recovery control, 211, 214
    categories, 209
    challenges/solutions, 216
    classification level, 214
    data environments, 215–217
    DLP solution, 212, 214
    encryption, 210, 214
    hierarchical system, 210
    key points, 217
    masking, 211
    mechanisms, 214
    organizational requirement, 208
    systematic measurement, 209
Data Subject Access Requests (DSARs), 284
Denial-of-service (DDoS), 233, 350
Digital Operational Resilience Act (DORA), 42, 43
    regulatory compliance, 254, 261
Disaster recovery (DR), 325
Distributed denial-of-service (DDoS), 365, 458
Dynamic Application Security Testing (DAST), 202, 204
    AppScan, 497, 498
    comparison, 497
    WebInspect, 498

E

Elasticsearch, Logstash, and Kibana (ELK), 303, 475
Electronic Health Records (EHR), 177
Electronic Protected Health Information (ePHI), 249, 264
Encryption, key management tools, 543–545
Encryption tools
    access management, 536
    full disk encryption, 537
Endpoint Detection and Response (EDR), 167
    CrowdStrike, 463
    IDS/IPS, 461
Environmental, social, and governance (ESG) compliance, 512
European Union Agency for Cybersecurity (ENISA), 246
Extended Detection and Response (XDR), 359

F

Factor Analysis of Information Risk (FAIR), 368, 556
Failed cybersecurity audit
    addressing deficiencies, 690
    automation, 690
    benefits, 690
    compliance requirements, 684
    conduct security assessment, 685
    consequences, 683

continuous monitoring, 689
follow-up audit, 688
inconsistent documentation, 685
indicators, 683
internal controls, 688
key points, 691
PCI-DSS audit, 683
proactive preparation, 689
regulatory requirements, 689
remediation plan, 688
risk-based approach, 684
roles/responsibilities, 689
root cause analysis, 687
stakeholders, 686
strategic/structured approach, 684
systemic issues, 682
workflow process, 687, 688

Federal Information Security Management Act (FISMA)
regulatory compliance, 252, 260

Financial services company, 714
audit process, 716
    compliance validation, 717
    scoping process, 716
audit process automation/manual assessments, 716
continuous monitoring, 722
data protection, 715
holistic approach, 714
implementation/results, 721
incident readiness evaluation, 715
key audit goals, 715
key points, 723
risk identification, 714
security framework, 714
security posture/adapt, 722
stakeholders buy-in, 721
training process, 722

vulnerabilities, 717
    addressing values, 720
    backup files, 719
    excessive privileges, 718
    incident response plan, 719
    web application libraries, 717, 718

Follow-up audit
advantages, 657
components, 654
failed cybersecurity audit, 688
key points, 658
objectives, 654
planning/execution, 657
structured phases, 654, 655
    execution, 656
    preparation, 655
    reporting phase, 656

Forensic/incident response tools
comprehensive, 583
Cortex XSOAR, 578
CrisisSim, 579
Cyberbit, 579
EnCase, 577
Splunk Phantom, 579
TheHive, 578

Forensic techniques
benefits, 737
concrete evidence, 731
data-driven decisions, 737
digital evidence, 731
exfiltration process, 733
healthcare organization, 736
incident response/recovery efforts, 734
integration, 731, 734
    execution, 735
    planning, 735
    reporting, 736

INDEX

Forensic techniques (*cont.*)
    key points, 737, 738
    proactive incident analysis, 736
    regulatory compliance, 737
    response planning, 737
    root cause analysis, 732
    security controls, 737
    validation, 732
Fortify SCA (Static Code Analyzer), 495
Full-Disk Encryption (FDE), 537

G

General Data Protection Regulation (GDPR), 42
    challenges/solution
        data mapping, 288
        description, 286–288
        interpretations/updates, 288
        resource-intensive, 289
        third-party vendors, 289
    data subject requests, 284
    document findings, 285
    gap analysis, 285
    key points, 290, 291
    legal justification, 283
    mapping process, 282
    principles, 280
    privacy policies, 283
    process flow, 281, 282
    regulatory compliance, 248, 259
    scope definition, 282
    section explores, 279
    structured approach, 290
    systematic process, 280
    technical/organizational controls, 283
    third-party vendors, 284
    tools/technologies, 285

Governance, risk, and compliance (GRC)
    Archer Insight, 557
    comparison, 555, 556
    FAIR, 556
    OCTAVE Allegro, 558
    RiskLens, 557
    RiskWatch, 558
    role of, 552
    RSA Archer, 556
    ServiceNow GRC, 556
Gramm-Leach-Bliley Act (GLBA), 275

H

Health Insurance Portability and Accountability Act (HIPAA), 42
    regulatory compliance, 249, 259
Human errors
    addressing of, 704
    automation, 703
    backup files, 700
    drafting policies, 699, 700
    misconfigured firewall, 700
    peer reviews, 703
    proactive monitoring, 703
    process workflow
        benefits, 707
        concrete steps, 705
        improve collaboration, 706
        interventions, 706
        key points, 707
        learning opportunities, 706
        onboarding processes, 706
        root cause analysis, 705
        training materials, 706
    standardized processes, 702
    strategies, 699

systemic/individual factors, 701
training programs, 702

I, J

Identity and access management (IAM), 17, 630, 693, 696
   comparison, 539
   Microsoft Azure AD, 540
   Okta, 539
   SailPoint, 540
Incident reports
   assessment, 711
   components, 708
   control validation, 711
   effectiveness, 709
   insider threats, 710
   integration, 712
      checklists, 712
      real-world scenarios, 712
      teams, 712
   key points, 713
   methodologies, 709
   opportunities, 713
   recommendations, 711
   review, 711
   strategies, 708
   supply chain attacks, 710
   threat vectors, 709
   unpatched vulnerability, 710
   weak encryption, 709
Incident response (IR)
   challenges/solutions, 419, 420
   components, 412
   forensic tools, 577
   integration, 428, 429
   key points, 421, 422
   lifecycle
      containment/eradication, 416
      continuous monitoring, 417
      detection systems, 416
      integration, 416
      key activities, 414, 415
      post-incident, 416
      preparation, 415
      recovery, 416
   management, 421, 422
   objectives, 413
   risk management, 413, 417
   technologies, 418
Incident Response Plan (IRP), 27
Indicators of Compromise (IoCs), 355
Information and Communication Technology (ICT), 42
Information Security Management System (ISMS), 41
Infrastructure-as-code (IaC), 695
Insecure direct object references (IDOR), 202
Insider threats
   audit process, 725
   behavioral monitoring, 728
   benefits, 730
   data access patterns, 725
   data sharing, 728
   key points, 730
   monitoring, 727
   monitor suspicious, 726
   objectives, 724
   offboarding processes, 727
   planning and scoping, 725
   policies/controls, 725
   privileges/align permissions, 726
   real-time monitoring, 729
   regular reviews, 729
   seamless collaboration, 729

INDEX

Insider threats (*cont.*)
    software development, 723
    training programs, 729
    unique/complex challenge, 723
Internal vs. external cybersecurity
    comparison, 10, 11
    comprehensive approach, 13
    definition, 10
    effective approach, 12
    external audits, 8, 9
    internal audits, 6–8
        advantages, 8
        fitness level, 6
        key characteristics, 7
    key points, 13, 14
    self-assessments *vs.* independent audits, 6
    self-checks, 12
Internet of Things (IoT), 177, 314
Intrusion detection and prevention system (IDS/IPS)
    comparison, 462–465
    CrowdStrike, 463
    SentinelOne, 464
    Snort, 462
    Suricata, 463
Intrusion detection and prevention systems (IDS/IPS), 166, 453, 678
ISO/IEC 27001
    regulatory compliance, 253, 261

K, L

Key Management Service (KMS), 220, 544
Key performance indicators (KPIs), 234, 241, 306, 652
Key Risk Indicators (KRIs), 409

M

Machine learning (ML)
    access management/encryption tools, 548
    Anomali, 521
    cyber risk management, 341
    risk management/GRC tools, 560
    threat intelligence platforms, 517
Mitigation process
    continuous improvement, 31
    digital diseases, 23
    identification risks, 31
    incident response plan, 27
    insider threat, 24
    misconfiguration, 25
    patch management, 26
    phishing simulations, 29
    privacy risks, 26
    regular check-ups, 30
    social engineering attacks, 28
    third-party vendors/service, 28
    types and cybersecurity risk, 29, 30
    weak access controls, 24
Mobile Device Management (MDM), 352
Multi-factor authentication (MFA), 630, 678

N

National Institute of Standards and Technology (NIST), 40
National Vulnerability Database (NVD), 485
Network and Information Security Directive 2 (NIS2)
    regulatory compliance, 254, 255, 261
Network security audits (tools)
    advantages/disadvantages, 455, 456

asset discovery, 458–461
    AssetExplorer, 460
    AssetSonar, 459, 460
    comparative overview, 458
    Qualys Inventory, 461
    SolarWinds IP Address
        Manager, 460
auditing process, 454
categories, 453
Darktrace, 457
IDS/IPS/EDR solutions, 461–464
key points, 466
Nmap, 457
organizational assets, 454
Palo Alto Networks, 458
real-time insights, 454
SolarWinds, 456, 457
tools, 464
Wireshark, 456
Network security controls
    challenges/solutions, 187, 188
    corrective controls, 184
    detective controls, 183
    insider threats, 188
    key points, 191
    organizations, 190
    preventive controls, 183
    process workflow, 184–186
    ransomware protection, 188
    remote work security, 188
    strategies, 182
    structured approach, 185, 189, 190
    tools and technologies, 186
    types of, 183, 184
    vital pathways, 183
NIST Cybersecurity Framework (CSF), 40
    regulatory compliance, 250, 251, 260
Nmap (Network mapper), 457

Non-compliance findings
    activities, 304
    challenges, 304
    critical lapses, 301
    frameworks, 301
    handling process, 301
        continuous improvement, 302
        corrective actions, 303
        follow-up audits, 304
        plan remediation, 303
        prioritize issues, 302
        root cause, 303
        steps, 302
        track progress, 303
    opportunities, 305
    risk-based approach, 304
    vulnerabilities/fortifies, 300

O

Open-Source Intelligence (OSINT), 514
OpenVAS (Open Vulnerability Assessment
    System), 491

P, Q

Palo Alto Networks, 458
Password management tools
    comparison, 542
    Dashlane, 543
    LastPass, 543
Patient Health Information (PHI), 26
Payment Card Industry Data Security
    Standard (PCI DSS), 41
    cardholder data, 292
    information security policy, 293
    monitoring systems, 293
    payment processing, 291

INDEX

Payment Card Industry Data Security
    Standard (PCI DSS) (*cont.*)
  planning process
    antivirus solutions, 295
    cardholder data, 295
    challenges/solutions, 297–299
    encryption, 295
    gap analysis, 296
    key points, 300, 301
    logging/monitoring, 296
    remediation plan, 297
    reporting and documentation, 297
    scope definition, 294
    security controls, 295
    steps, 294
    structured approach, 294
    testing, 296
    vulnerabilities, 296
  regulatory compliance, 250, 259
  requirements, 291, 292
  role-based access control, 293
  secure network, 292
  vulnerabilities, 293
Penetration testing
  challenges
    audits, 57
    integration, 57
    penetration tests, 57
  components, 52
  comprehensive evaluation, 52, 53
  encourage collaboration, 58
  high-complementation
    approaches, 55, 56
    compliance/security, 56
    security, 56
  hybrid approach, 57
  key differences, 55, 56
  key points, 58, 59

PCI-DSS planning process, 296
real-world attacks, 53, 54
regular tests, 58
security assessments, 52
security hygiene, 53
testing application, 202
threats/vulnerabilities, 358
tool integration
  advantages, 527
  Burp Suite, 530
  categories, 526
  challenges and technologies, 534
  Cofense, 533
  comparison, 528, 529
  ethical hacking, 525
  frameworks, 527
  Kali Linux, 532
  key points, 535
  KnowBe4, 532
  Metasploit, 530
  Netsparker, 531
  organizations, 533, 534
  OWASP ZAP, 531
  prioritization, 527
  realistic assessment, 527
  role of, 526
  security, 527
  vulnerabilities, 527
tools, 58
validation process, 233
Personally Identifiable Information
    (PII), 26
Physical security controls
  access control systems, 176
  categorization, 175
  challenges, 178–180
  comprehensive, 180–182
  data centers, 178

INDEX

disasters, 178
environmental controls, 177
flow process, 181
foundational role, 174
insider threats, 178
key points, 182
layers of, 175–177
perimeter controls, 176
protection, 176
technologies, 177, 178
Planning cybersecurity
    alignment
        best practices, 143
        business goals, 135
        challenges, 137–142
        key points, 144
        objectives, 134
        risk assessment, 137
        strategic assets, 143
        strategic tools, 134
        tools/technologies, 142
        vulnerabilities/priorities, 135–137
    automation/tools, 159
    business context, 108–117
    checklists
        automation tools, 124, 125
        collaboration, 126
        collection, 118
        compliance platforms, 124, 125
        components, 121–123
        creation/monitoring process, 121
        foundation, 120–122
        key benefits, 119, 120
        key points, 127, 128
        strategic asset, 126
        strategies, 123
    comprehensive coverage, 155
    DFDs, 109
    documentation, 83
    dynamic environments, 160
    effectiveness, 160
    effective planning, 157
    key points, 156, 161
    metrics
        business, 147
        category serves, 146
        challenges/solutions, 147–151
        clear framework, 145
        communication, 145
        compliance requirements, 147
        definition, 144
        evaluation, 145
        implementation/continuous improvement, 151
        insights, 145
        key points, 152
        strategic approach, 146
        technical metrics, 146
        threats/abstract vulnerabilities, 145
    objectives/scope, 157
    organizational priorities, 158
    proactive measurement, 153–155
    resource allocation, 159
    risk assessment, 128–135
    scope, 84–91
    security/compliance, 158
    stakeholder engagement, 100–109
    strategic blueprint, 153
    strategic process, 153, 161
    structured approach, 159
Presentation (report)
    board perspective, 640
    effective communication, 643
        business impact, 643
        concepts, 643
        risks/recommendations, 644

INDEX

Presentation (report) (*cont.*)
    stories, 644
    time-sensitive, 644
  far-reaching effects, 647
  findings/risks, 642
  high-level overview, 641
  key points, 648
  logical structure, 640
  mitigation, 642
  objectives, 640
  questions/discussion, 642
  recommendations, 642
  scope/objectives, 641
  technology, 644
    accountability/ownership, 646
    benefits, 646
    board engagement, 646
    costs/risks/industry
      benchmarks, 646
    design, 645
    documentation, 647
    interactive elements, 645
    screen sharing/real-time
      collaboration, 645
    strategies, 647
    tools, 644
    visualization, 645
Principle of Least Privilege (POLP), 718
Privacy-Enhancing Technologies
    (PETs), 550
Privileged Access Management (PAM),
    196, 536
  access management/encryption
    tools, 549
  BeyondTrust, 542
  comparison, 541
  CyberArk, 541
Pseudonymization tools, 582

  data minimization, 584
  Thales CipherTrust, 582
  TokenEx, 582

R

Regular audits, 16–18
REGULATION (EU) 2024/2847, 44
Regulatory compliance
  auditors
    data protection mechanisms, 263
    design/operational
      effectiveness, 264
    mapping requirements, 264
    non-compliance/weaknesses, 264
    ongoing compliance, 264
    recommendations, 264
    requirements, 263
    scope, 263
    techniques, 266
    tools, 264, 265
    workflow, 263
  challenges, 315–317
  checklist
    access controls, 321
    audit and documentation, 324
    audit consistency, 319
    automation tools, 327
    BC/DR plans, 325
    benefits, 328
    data management, 321
    data privacy and protection, 326
    document management
      systems, 327
    employees training, 323
    incident response, 322
    key points, 329
    monitoring, 325

784

INDEX

  physical security, 326
  regulatory alignment, 320
  risk assessments, 322, 327
  strategic planning/collaboration, 320
  structured roadmap, 319
  system security, 323
  technologies, 327
  third-party audits, 324
 complexity/dynamism, 314
 cyber threats, 245
 definition, 246
 emerging trends, 335
 frameworks/regulations, 258–263
 GDPR audits, 279–291
 integration, 317
 key points, 271–273, 319, 320
 non-compliance, 247
 organizations, 318
 penalties, 314
 reporting process, 329
  advantages, 333
  automation, 332
  components, 330
  critical function, 330
  findings section, 331
  key points, 334
  methodology, 331
  non-technical stakeholders, 332
  objectivity, 332
  outlines, 331
  recommendations, 331, 333
  requirements, 332
  sharing report, 332
  strengths, 333
  tangible evidence, 331
  visual aids, 332
  weaknesses, 333
 requirements, 335
 risks penalties, 247
 rules/objectives/terrains, 247–258
 structured/proactive approach, 315
 systematic approach, 335
Reporting process
 action plans, 649–653
 audience, 634
 auditors/stakeholders, 631
 business risks, 633
 comprehension/engagement, 635
 data overloading, 633
 elements, 634
 findings, 633
 formatting issues, 634
 formatting/sloppy design, 637
 generic recommendations, 637
 key points, 639
 language/context, 636
 logical structure, 635
 presentation, 640–648
 prioritize findings, 636
 real-world implications, 632
 review, 637
 technical assessments/business priorities, 632
 vague recommendations, 633
 well-written report, 638
Report on Compliance (ROC), 297
Risk assessment
 challenges, 131, 132
 effective and efficient, 132
 frameworks, 130
 proactive/vigilant risk, 133, 134
 process workflow, 129, 130
 resource allocation, 128
 strategic process, 127
 strategic tool, 133
 tools and technologies, 131

785

INDEX

Risk-based approach
    audit resources, 32
    benefits, 36
        compliance, 36
        resource allocation, 36
        stakeholders, 36
        vulnerabilities, 36
    challenges, 38
    high-risk areas, 39
    implementation, 36
        audit process, 37
        prioritization, 37
        reports, 37
        risk assessment, 37
        scope definition, 37
    key components, 32
        assessment, 32
        effectiveness, 33
        high-risk areas, 34
        identification, 32
        prioritization, 33
        risk management process, 34
    practical application, 38
    prevention, 39
    security guards, 31
    technologies, 38
    threat landscape, 39
Risk-based audits, 20, 21
Risk management/business continuity
    benefits
        data-driven decisions, 433, 434
        integration, 432
        organizational resilience, 436
        proactive mitigation, 432, 433
        regulatory frameworks, 434
        stakeholders, 435
    comprehensive
        documentation, 446
    cyberattack, 432
    documentation/reporting, 449
    emerging trends, 440
        cyber-resilience, 440
        supply chain, 440
        zero trust principles, 440
    high-probability risks, 442
    holistic approach, 448, 449
    human element, 443
    identification, 442
    integration, 431, 436
        continuity plan, 438
        prioritize critical functions, 437
        technologies, 439
        testing/training, 439
    key points, 440, 441, 449, 450
    low-probability events, 443
    organizational resilience, 431
    prioritization, 444
    risk-based approach, 444
    stakeholders, 444
    technologies, 445, 446
    testing/validation, 446
    third-party vendors, 447
    threat intelligence platforms, 442
    treating management process, 448
Risk Management Framework
    (RMF), 130
Risk management/GRC tools, 552–561
    AI-powered tools, 560
    benefits
        compliance assessments, 553
        proactive risk management, 554
        repetitive tasks, 554
        scalability/integration, 554
        visibility, 553
    blockchain, 560
    cloud environments, 560

compliance track/reports, 553
DevSecOps pipelines, 560
identification/assessment, 552
implementation, 559
IoT and edge computing, 560
key points, 561
policies/controls, 553
quantification, 560
risk and compliance data, 553
structured approach, 552
Risk Management Plan (RMP)
    automation tools, 430
    business goals, 429
    components
        communication plan, 427
        compliance documentation, 428, 429
        IR integration, 428, 429
        register serves, 425
        strategies, 426, 427
    continuous monitoring/updates, 425
    continuous process, 423
    external/internal concepts, 423
    identification, 424
    key points, 430, 431
    methodologies, 423, 424
    mitigation, 425
    regular review/updation, 429
    simulations and tabletop, 430
    stakeholders, 429
    step-by-step process, 424
    structured approach, 422
    structured process, 423
    technical safeguards, 423
Role-Based Access Control (RBAC) system, 726
Routine/scheduled audits, 16

S

Sarbanes–Oxley Act (SOX)
    regulatory compliance, 256, 257, 262
Scoping audits
    advantages, 90
    challenges, 88, 89
    components, 84, 86
    comprehensive, 86
    definition, 84, 85
    foundation, 84
    key points, 91
    logical steps, 87, 88
    security assessment, 85
    tools, 89
Scoring risk/prioritization
    advantages, 375
    components
        calculation, 367
        categories, 364
        considerations, 365
        formula, 366, 367
        impact, 365, 366
        level categorization, 367
        likelihood, 363, 364
    context-driven evaluation, 367–370
    dynamic threat landscape, 374
    effective process, 374
    evaluation, 373
    heat map assessment, 369
    key points, 376
    methodologies, 369
    mitigation strategies, 372
    NIST framework, 369
    prioritization, 370
    resources, 363
    standardized/objective approach, 363
    strategies, 375

INDEX

Scoring risk/prioritization (*cont.*)
   systematic approach, 370
   tools/technologies, 373
   visibility, 374
   workflow process, 371
      identification, 372
      likelihood/potential impact, 372
      numerical scores, 372
      standardized models, 371
      visualization tools, 372
Secure Sockets Layer (SSL), 205
Security controls
   access management, 199–206
   cloud computing, 218–224
   continuous monitoring, 164
   control failures, 224–230
      contributors, 225
      detection, 226
      effective auditing techniques, 228
      encrypt sensitive data, 227
      endpoint security, 227
      excessive privileges, 227
      factors, 225
      firewalls, 226
      incident response plans, 228
      key points, 229, 230
      logging and monitoring capabilities, 227
      mitigation strategies, 228
      parallels, 226
      patch logs/utilizing tools, 227
      proactive auditing/continuous, 225
      section explores, 224
      weak/reused passwords, 226
   data security controls, 209–218
   documentation, 238–243
      assessment findings, 240
      benefits, 238
      compliance mapping, 241
      components, 239
      control assessments, 238
      evidence substantiates, 240
      executive summary, 239
      inventory, 240
      key points, 243, 244
      methodologies, 240
      metrics/KPIs, 241
      organization steps, 242
      recommendations/remediation, 241
      sign-offs/approvals, 241
   implementation, 164
      administrative controls, 167
      audits, 168–171
      categories, 167
      corrective controls, 166
      definition, 164, 165
      detective controls, 166
      effective controls, 168
      key benefits, 168
      key characteristics, 165
      key points, 173, 174
      layered approach, 173
      physical controls, 167
      preventive controls, 166
      primary challenges, 171–173
      process workflow, 170, 171
      pyramids defense system, 166
      technical controls, 167
   mechanisms, 163
   network security, 191–200
   physical security, 174–182
   protection systems, 163
   structured framework, 164
   testing application, 199–208
   validation process, 230–237

Security Information and Event
Management (SIEM), 3, 75
  Ansible's integration, 473
  ArcSight, 476
  centralized platform, 467
  challenges, 481
  CloudTrail integration, 474
  comparison, 467–469
  DLP tools, 467–486
  Elastic Stack (ELK), 475
  Graylog, 473
  IBM QRadar, 470, 471
  key activities, 477, 478
  log data management, 476
  LogRhythm, 472
  Microsoft Sentinel leverages, 471
  monitoring, 474
  Nagios, 472
  patterns and correlation, 477
  real-time insights, 477
  regulatory standards, 477
  SolarWinds, 470
  Splunk, 471
  tool integration
    benefits, 483
    implementation, 483
    key points, 484–486
    layered defense system, 482
    security strategies, 482
Security posture management tools, 581
  Prisma Cloud, 581
  Security Center, 581
Self-Assessment Questionnaire
(SAQ), 297
Service-level agreements (SLAs), 28,
324, 365
Small and medium-sized enterprises
(SMEs), 360

Software Development Lifecycle
(SDLC), 492
SolarWinds Network Performance
Monitor, 456, 457
Specialized audits, 21–23
Stakeholder engagement
  benefits, 92, 93, 99
  challenges, 97, 98
  definition, 91
  digital security, 92
  key points, 100
  planning phases, 94–96
  principles, 98
  risks, 93
  steps, 96, 97
  structured methods, 95–97
  tools/technology, 98
Static Application Security Testing (SAST),
202, 203
  Checkmarx, 494
  Codacy, 496
  comparison, 492, 493
  Fortify SCA, 495
  SonarQube, 494
  Veracode, 495
Structured Query Language (SQL), 200
System and Organization Controls
2 (SOC 2)
  regulatory compliance, 255, 256, 261

T, U

Tactics, techniques, and procedures
(TTPs), 355, 525
Technical findings/non-technical
stakeholders
  anticipate questions, 615
  audience/priorities, 611, 612

INDEX

Technical findings/non-technical stakeholders (*cont.*)
   broader implications, 613
   clear action, 614
   communication, 610
   documentation, 616
   key points, 616, 617
   prioritize findings, 614
   simplified language, 612
   stakeholders, 615
   storytelling, 615
   visual aids, 613
Testing application
   authentication mechanisms, 202
   automated tools, 202
   categories, 203, 204
   challenges, 205–208
   components, 201
   definition, 201
   encryption, 203
   error handling, 203
   integrity/confidentiality, 200
   key points, 208
   logging/monitoring controls, 203
   penetration, 202
   real-world audit
      authentication, 204
      financial services, 205
      SQL injection attacks, 204
   severe consequences, 199
   technical/administrative/procedural design, 200, 201
   threat modeling, 202
   time constraints, 206
Threat Intelligence Platforms (TIPs), 32, 418, 422
   aggregate information, 514
   Anomali, 521
   auditing process, 514
   benefits, 515, 522
   comparison, 518
   IBM X-Force, 520
   proactive validation, 517
   real-time insights, 517
   regulatory frameworks, 517
   risk identification, 516
   technologies, 517, 518
   ThreatConnect, 520
   trends, 523
   workflow process, 516
Threats/vulnerabilities
   actors, 356
   benefits, 361
   challenges, 360, 361
   cloud security risks, 351
   comprehensive documentation, 361
   continuous improvement, 354, 355
   continuous monitoring, 359
   corrective actions, 347–352
   cyberattacks, 347
   data breaches, 349
   DDoS protection solutions, 350
   environment, 355
   foundational/continuous/strategic process, 362
   foundational process, 346
   human error, 352
   identification, 352
   insider threats, 348
   key points, 362
   penetration testing, 358
   regular assessments, 360, 361
   risk assessment frameworks, 357
   scanning tools, 356
   social engineering, 349
   structured process, 353

INDEX

supply chain attacks, 348
threat intelligence, 355
threats, 346
tools/techniques, 359
zero-day exploits, 351
Tool integration
    access management and
        encryption, 536–551
    audit tools, 591–596
    automation/compliance/threat
        intelligence, 503–525
    automation features, 465
    considerations, 465
    layered approach, 464
    misconfigurations, 596–600
    penetration testing, 525–535
    regular updates, 464
    risk management and GRC
        tools, 561–570
    scans/rules/dashboards, 465
    SIEM system/DLP tools, 478–497
    tool-based assessments, 591–596
        capabilities/limitations, 593
        customization, 593
        documentation, 594
        initial testing, 593
        integration, 593
        key points, 596
        manual testing methods, 594
        objectives, 593
        regularly update tool, 594
        remediation efforts, 594
        stakeholders, 594
        strategic solutions, 592
        technical findings, 594
    traditional audit
        techniques, 574–586
    training sessions, 465

visualization/collaboration, 562–574
vulnerability management/SAST/
    DAST, 485–502
Transport Layer Security (TLS), 61
Trust Services Criteria (TSC), 255

V, W, X, Y, Z

Validation process
    challenges, 235–238
    compliance, 233
    comprehensive process, 230, 231
    configurations, 233
    continuous improvement, 234
    implementation, 230
    key points, 237
    metrics, 234
    monitor performance, 233
    objectives, 231, 232
    resource limitations, 234
    risk assessment, 232
    simulations, 233
    testing, 233
    workflow, 232
Virtual Private Network (VPNs), 60
Visualization/collaboration tools
    AR/VR technologies, 573
    Blockchain, 573
    comparison, 564, 565
    components, 562
    customization options, 573
    data analysis, 562
    decision-making, 563
    diverse sources, 563
    engagement, 564
    key points, 574
    Kibana, 567
    Lucidchart, 565

INDEX

Power BI, 566
real-time updates, 564
real-world app, 572, 573
stakeholders, 563
Tableau, 566
tasks/monitor progress, 563
team efficiency, 563
trends, 573
Visio, 567
visualization, 564

Visuals
advantages/disadvantages, 619, 620
bar graphs, 620
complexity, 617, 618
dashboards, 622
diagrams, 622
effectiveness, 623
graphs and charts, 620
heatmaps, 621
infographics, 621
key points, 624
line graphs, 620
pie charts, 620
reporting process, 635
technical/data-heavy reports, 617
tools, 622, 623
vulnerabilities, 624

Vulnerabilities, 346
implementation, 347

Vulnerability scanners
Acunetix, 492
asset discovery, 499
challenges, 499
compliance, 486
components, 485
continuous monitoring, 486
definition, 485
identification, 486
key points, 502, 503
management tools, 487–489
Nessus, 488
OpenVAS, 491
prioritization, 486
Qualys, 489
QualysGuard, 490
Rapid7 InsightVM, 490
reporting/analysis, 499
systematic process, 499
techniques, 499
tool integration
automation/integration, 500
comprehensive coverage, 500
continuous monitoring/
reporting, 501
cross-validation, 500
organizations, 500
regular updates/training, 501
trends, 501

GPSR Compliance
The European Union's (EU) General Product Safety Regulation (GPSR) is a set of rules that requires consumer products to be safe and our obligations to ensure this.

If you have any concerns about our products, you can contact us on

ProductSafety@springernature.com

In case Publisher is established outside the EU, the EU authorized representative is:

Springer Nature Customer Service Center GmbH
Europaplatz 3
69115 Heidelberg, Germany

www.ingramcontent.com/pod-product-compliance
Lightning Source LLC
LaVergne TN
LVHW081536070526
838199LV00056B/3680